MW01034970

Dreams in the New Century

UNIVERSITY PRESS OF FLORIDA

Florida A&M University, Tallahassee
Florida Atlantic University, Boca Raton
Florida Gulf Coast University, Ft. Myers
Florida International University, Miami
Florida State University, Tallahassee
New College of Florida, Sarasota
University of Central Florida, Orlando
University of Florida, Gainesville
University of North Florida, Jacksonville
University of South Florida, Tampa
University of West Florida, Pensacola

UNIVERSITY PRESS OF FLORIDA

Gainesville

Tallahassee

Tampa

Boca Raton

Pensacola

Orlando

Miami

Jacksonville

Ft. Myers

Sarasota

DREAMS in the NEW CENTURY

Instant Cities, Shattered Hopes, and Florida's Turning Point

GARY R. MORMINO

The Frank E. Duckwall Foundation is proud to assist with the publication of Dr. Gary Mormino's new book, *Dreams in the New Century: Instant Cities, Shattered Hopes, and Florida's Turning Point,* as he continues his documentation of the social history of Florida that he began with *Land of Sunshine, State of Dreams.*

Published in the United States of America

27 26 25 24 23 22 6 5 4 3 2 1

ISBN 978-0-8130-6934-0
Library of Congress Control Number: 2021947197

The University Press of Florida is the scholarly publishing agency for the State University System of Florida, comprising Florida A&M University, Florida Atlantic University, Florida Gulf Coast University, Florida International University, Florida State University, New College of Florida, University of Central Florida, University of Florida, University of North Florida, University of South Florida, and University of West Florida.

University Press of Florida
2046 NE Waldo Road
Suite 2100
Gainesville, FL 32609
http://upress.ufl.edu

Contents

Introduction

Arise and go toward the south.

Acts 8:26

Any oracle divining the events that whiplashed Florida in the first decade of the twenty-first century would have been pummeled by citrus-greening-infected oranges and foreclosure signs. Neither Carl Hiaasen, Dave Barry, nor Tim Dorsey could have imagined a single decade featuring Y2K silliness, the Elián saga, the melodramatic 2000 election, the heart-stopping, nation-altering events of 9/11, state leaders as interesting and diverse as Jeb Bush, Charlie Crist, Mel Martínez, Marco Rubio, and Rick Scott, a series of technological revolutions that hooked the young and confused the old, the cratering of the printed newspaper business, a searing economic collapse known as the Great Recession, a death spiral of the citrus industry, an opioid crisis, and an environmental reckoning. The Great Rebound in 2010 witnessed a return to normalcy—critics suggest "abnormalcy"—as the rush to Florida renewed and the Sunshine State reclaimed its status as, in Sarah Palin's words, "a hopey-dreamy" state. Meanwhile, the turnstiles in that memorable decade often witnessed 1,000 clicks—many of them immigrants—every single day.

While commercials and bitter winters lured 1,000 newcomers a day during the era 2000–2007, the misfortunes wrought by housing foreclosures, financial shenanigans, and negative publicity turned many Americans sour on Florida. The pipeline bringing newcomers quickly ran dry. The era 2000–2010 was a cautionary tale of two Floridas: the haunting Dickensian ghosts of the Florida Boom and Florida Bust, the Florida Dream and the Florida Nightmare. Postcards and infomercials rarely highlight a once-stunning environment afflicted by red tide and green algae slime, eroding beaches, oil-slicked coastlines, and growing concerns about the future of the fragile environment.

How should one approach such a study? Kevin Starr laid the framework for "dream state studies" in his brilliant but daunting eight-volume series beginning with *Americans and the California Dream* (1973) and ending with *California on the Edge* (1990). In his concluding volume, Starr's reservations surely resonate with many Floridians: "I became fascinated as the 1980s turned into the 1990s by the possibility—sometimes the probability—that California has seriously gone awry." Starr also understood the most salient issue of the era. "There are limits," he pleaded in 1991. "We have a new kind of environmental limit, not so much having to do with damage to the environment but how much population is sustainable in the environmental engineering formula." A proper perspective, indeed![1]

If there is a single quote that serves as a thematic Orange Star, it comes from an unlikely source. As an undergraduate at Millikin University in the late 1960s, I read a book by Will and Ariel Durant, *The Story of Civilization.* They wrote,

> Civilization is a stream with banks. The stream is filled with blood from people killing, stealing, shouting and doing the things historians generally record; while on the banks, unnoticed, people build homes, make love, raise children, sing songs, write poetry and even whittle statues. The story of civilization is the story of what happened on the banks. Historians are pessimists because they ignore the banks for the river.[2]

Millions of persons arrived in Florida during the time frame 2000–2010. New rivers of commerce and travel brought people from around the world on ships, planes, and automobiles. Others arrived on rafts and even by foot. This is a study of Floridians along and around the Withlacoochee and Sopchoppy; Baghdad, Sumatra, and St. Petersburg; Two Egg, Yahoo Junction, and Fort Lonesome; Ozona, Bonita Springs, and Panacea; Naples, Venice, and Genoa; Yankeetown and Dixie County. The book also focuses upon Miami and Hialeah, Tampa and Jacksonville, Orlando and Kissimmee, big cities attracting a more diverse population.

In 2005, journalist David Shribman perfectly captured the era's energy with a spirited essay, "The Future Is Florida": "Florida may have symbolically replaced California as an important cultural indicator. It may be that Florida, rather than California, is the place where the future is best viewed." In almost every significant index of American life—the sheer numbers and influence of the elderly and foreign-born, the old and new nuances of race, the jigsaw patterns of residential life, environmental challenges, the pursuit of happiness and political melodrama—Florida matters. A government official, when asked to offer a glimpse into the future, answered: "the Floridization of the United States." The 2000 Election, 9/11, Terri Schiavo, the escalating tensions over religious politics, the housing collapse, the housing rebound, and sports cannot be understood without the perspective of Florida.[3]

The novelist Wallace Stegner insisted that the geography of the West expressed the "geography of hope." If so, Florida manifested dreams of individual happiness amid tropical splendors. Stegner also believed that California resembles America, only more so. The Sunshine State and Golden State—called "sister Sunbelt giants" by a reporter at the *Ocala Star-Banner*—represent America's two great "dream states." In the half century following World War II, California set the rules and served as a trendsetter for movies and education, music and protest, politics and culture. In the 1960s, comedians joked that all the nuts in America rolled westward. Increasingly, Florida was becoming a weathervane or gyroscope. The murder of Gianni Versace in 1997 on Miami Beach and the earlier rampage of Ted Bundy in Tallahassee spoke to our obsession with the lifestyle of the famous and infamous. Florida and California also shared identities as ethnic-immigrant hothouses, political trendsetters, and economic engines of opportunity.

If the opening years of the new century compressed a single word that explained the juggernaut called Florida, that word would be "more." What does Florida do? Florida grows, adding 1,000 new residents a day. But another word also underscores Florida in the new millennium: "less." Floridians had less confidence in their government and their futures. And still another word clashed with the optimism that was once associated with Florida: "loss." More can be less. Daily, thousands of acres of wetlands, forest, and field were transformed into shopping malls, residential sprawl, and bustling highways. Growth threatened the fragile ecosystem and its beaches, wetlands, and natural springs.

The word "new" also defined millions of residents and their adopted addresses. Some of the fastest-growing and most dynamic communities in Florida did not exist in 1950. Or 1999. Florida brimmed with instant cities: Marco Island, Cape Coral, Lehigh Acres, Golden Gate, East Naples, Port Charlotte, North Port, Spring Hill, Coral Springs, Wellington, Weston, Miami Lakes, Plantation, Davie, Greenacres, Palm Coast, Palm Bay, Viera, and Port St. Lucie. The way Floridians sprawled across the landscape acquired new names distinct from the old suburbs: exurbs and boomburbs, microburbs. The churning and clashing of so many people in new spaces challenges our traditional notions of community.

Writing in 2005, a journalist concluded, "This is a different place than it was; any state that grows by about 800 people a day almost has to be." A year later, Florida was adding 1,000 newcomers every day.[4]

The story of Florida can be understood in myriad ways. Its history involves the movements of people, the mastery of technology, the genius of buying thousands of acres of mosquito-infested cattle ranches and selling the land by the square foot, and the marketing of a place that was for much of its history too isolated, too hot, too humid, too wet, and too disconnected. In spasms of spectacular growth, Florida leaped from a distant destination best known for roadside tourist attractions to a state famous for Cape Canaveral, the world's most modern theme parks, and immigrants from everywhere. In the new century, Florida remained a place where just about everyone came from someplace else. To many outsiders, Florida was also a vast gerentopolis, a place where more seniors were clustered together in what have only recently been called active adult retirement communities. Future historians may select a half-century-old condominium in Surfside to symbolize the state's defining characteristics: migration and immigration, retirement and fantasy, and questions of sustainability and safety on a barrier island.

Florida is everything to everybody, a mirror, but also a house of mirrors. Southern, it is America's "southernmost state" and yet the most unsouthern place in the Deep South. In a Panhandle oyster bar or at a roadside vendor selling smoked fish in Baker County, the taste and smells reflect ancient southern customs and tastes. In Flakowitz's Deli in Boynton Beach, you might swear you are in Brooklyn or Long Island; at Café Versailles on Calle Ocho in Miami, you can fantasize 1958 Havana. Not long ago, midwesterners gathered around horseshoe pits every February at Fort Myers Beach, Sarasota, and Pinellas Park. If Lake Worth in January seems a lot like Finland, Tarpon Springs and Masaryktown radiate Greek and Slavic rhythms.

The study of decades appeals to historians and journalists. However, the practice of writing history through the prism of decades can be fraught with dangers and difficulties. Journalists write the first draft of history. Historians need distance and perspective. The predicament is like that of strangers attempting to understand Italian life: Ten days, just right. Ten years, not enough.[5]

Historians have argued that the 1950s really ended in 1963, while the 1960s extended to 1972. The best argument for the technique may be the 1920s. Called the Roaring Twenties and the Jazz Age, that remarkable decade enjoyed early prosperity but ended in depression and despair. The Roaring Twenties, like the 2000–2010 era, generated spasms of optimism and pessimism, the decade's highest highs and lowest lows. The decade 2000–2010 lacks a catchy nickname. Wikipedia offers "Double Ohs," "the Aughts," "the Aughties." Wise guys prefer an alternative nickname, "The Noughties."[6]

What distinguished this era from others in Florida's history? The 1920s ushered in extraordinary change, the result of a real estate boom that created Coral Gables and Miami Beach, Boca Raton, and Temple Terrace. New highways, manners, and morals accompanied the Age of Speed and Jazz. The 1930s, pockmarked by depression and scarcity, inspired an outpouring of literature and music, still unrivaled. The decades following World War II witnessed the rise of Florida from an underpopulated, marginal state to a Sunbelt power. By the end of the century, Florida had rocketed to become America's fourth-largest state. Increasingly, Florida challenged California to become America's cultural and demographic touchstone. But the era 2000–2010 also seems different: wilder, coarser, scarier, and fractured. The state and world seem simultaneously too distracted and too intense.

The book begins New Year's Eve 2000, at the start of a new century and millennium. Although it would be bruised by the infamous election of 2000 and the tragedy of 9/11, the decade opened with optimism borne of a torrid land boom and record-setting housing sales. In 2000, Al Gore and George W. Bush debated how to spend the billions of peace dollars, the dividends of the Cold War's end. One book captured the mood: in *The End of History*, Francis Fukuyama, confident that fascism and communism had been tossed into the dustbin of history, foretold the spread of liberal democracy and peace. History, instead, took a cruel turn.

"Between 2003 and 2007 was a hell of a time to be a Floridian," observed Adam Weinstein. "It seemed like everyone was a mortgage originator or a house-flipper." Rising home prices seemed to predominate conversations in the first half of the decade. Weekly, it seemed, home sales in general and housing values individually validated reasons for Florida fever. But real estate is boring compared to sports; indeed, baseball, football, and basketball serve as social safety valves. In college football, the era between the 1980s and the early twenty-first century will be nostalgically recalled as a golden age. Never had the University of Miami, Florida State, and the University of Florida all triumphed at such high levels. In a three-year period between 2005 and 2008, the University of Florida pulled off the impossible, winning a total of four national championships in football and basketball. In 1993 and 1999, the Florida State Seminoles won the national football championship, a feat more than matched by the University of Miami in 1983, 1987, 1989, and 2001. In professional football, the Tampa Bay Buccaneers won the 2003 Super Bowl, while the Miami

Marlins won the World Series in 1997 and 2003. The Tampa Bay Lightning—a hockey team playing in the tropics!—brought home the Stanley Cup in 2004.[7]

But Florida increasingly occupied the front page, not merely the sports section. The Elián González saga served as a morality play and political sounding board. The Terri Schiavo case crystallized America's clash of values over the meaning of life and death, the role of the church and state, and the right to live and die. It unfolded in Pinellas Park, Florida, a place where, not long ago, citrus groves flourished. The Elián González melodrama in Miami could have been a made-for-cable movie, except it involved real people caught between freedom and oppression.

In the years between 2007 and 2010, cleaved by the election of the first Black president of the United States and the most serious economic recession since the Great Depression, Floridians experienced a ride wilder than any found at Busch Gardens. "It's fair to say that the Aughts, or whatever we end up calling the first ten years of this century," reflected journalist Howard Troxler, "was not exactly the happiest decade in Florida history." He added, "Actually, it's fair to say that this decade knocked some of the bloom off Florida's orange blossom." Literally and figuratively, the first decade of the new millennium not only knocked the bloom off Florida's official state tree, but a teeny pest also laid waste to the once-vaunted citrus industry, as well as the very enterprise of reporting the story. How bad was it? "By 2008," recollected Troxler, "newspapers were running articles with advice on how to choose a mover to go back north. . . . To recap: tough decade." How bad was it? By the end of the decade, award-winning journalists were searching for new jobs in a collapsing newspaper industry. On 1 January 2012, the *St. Petersburg Times* became the *Tampa Bay Times,* and Howard Troxler took early retirement.[8]

The era 2007–10 will be remembered for a vicious economic downswing, popularly known as the Great Recession. Economists are still debating the precise beginning and causes of the housing and financial collapse (ca. 2007–8), but no one disputes the sheer pain and damage of the recession. Florida's cities and suburbs led the nation in foreclosures. The newest great migration to the Sunshine State halted so dramatically that for the period 2007–9, Florida would have suffered absolute population losses had it not been for immigration (legal and illegal). Scholars are still sorting out the consequences. Unlike the Bourbon monarchy of the French Revolution, Florida's political leaders and financial wizards learned nothing and forgot everything. Leaders might take note that in a 2008 poll of Florida residents, half the respondents confessed that the Sunshine State was losing its luster, that life in Florida was worse than five years earlier.[9]

If America enshrined a national faith, it would be freedom and individualism. From the frontier West and Castle Garden to the Model T and Norman Rockwell posters, Americans worshiped at the altar of individualism. But the stampede to Florida in the late twentieth century redefined the meaning of the protean words "freedom" and "individualism." Huge numbers of elderly Americans decided to leave their families, churches, and social networks behind and become Floridians. Old age and retirement were reinvented or redefined in the process. Elderly Ohioans and young Colombians, Jews and Catholics, Masons and Rotarians migrated to Florida with a respect for communal traditions and belonging. Florida is a state of contrasts. By 2010, seven of America's one hundred largest megachurches were in Florida. But Americans increasingly were "bowling alone," more interested in me than we. Young Americans found new communities online. Florida was a new frontier of individualism. New residents could easily change their names, choose a different church, join a nudist colony or cult. In Minnesota and Rhode Island, voters registered as Republicans or Democrats because of class, ethnic, and familial experiences. But in Florida, they were liberated. And even if their great-grandfathers turned over in their graves, more and more Floridians registered as independents. For increasing numbers of new Floridians, individualism meant gated communities and isolated lifestyles. "In the future," wrote columnist Ross Douthat, "it seems, there will be only one 'ism'—Individualism—and its rule will never end."[10]

If there was an official state metaphor, it might have been the Cincinnati Factor. Governor and U.S. Senator Bob Graham liked to repeat the story to audiences: "John Jones was born in Cincinnati in 1925. He moved to Fort Lauderdale in 1950. He married, built a family and a business, and he became a significant figure in the community of Fort Lauderdale. Funeral services were held at his church. The body is being returned for burial in Cincinnati. His Alma Mater, the Ohio State University, will receive a generous donation." For a time, Tampa International Airport operated a profitable "coffin run," shipping bodies to the "hometowns" of the deceased for burial. Delta was ready when they were! A Florida journalist thought "Mistress State" was a more appropriate metaphor, asking whether a mistress state could become a full partner state?[11]

The eternal quest for regeneration, low taxes, or at least a better February, resulted in a silver-gray wave rinsing Florida. Fittingly for a state whose birth myth was Ponce de León and the search for the Fountain of Youth, Florida was a state of reinvention and second chances. An early Sarasota tourist brochure invited newcomers to migrate to this "healthy country." The brochure promised that the Sarasota climate "invigorates the strong and strengthens the weak." In

2000, almost one in three Sarasota County residents was sixty-five or older. Almost one in five Florida residents was sixty-five years old or older in 2000 and 2010, the highest in America and a demographic aberration in earlier periods of history. One of the dramatic changes in the composition of the "new old" was wealth. For much of Florida history, old people were poor. In many communities, poor farms served as the last refuge for the desperate poor. In the best-selling 1956 book *The Truth about Florida,* a resident testifies that a retired couple in Florida "can live comfortably, have a whale of a good time and save money on an income of about $40 a week." In Pinellas County in the 1950s or early 1960s, a poll was conducted. "Mr. Typical Retiree," the report noted, had a yearly income of $3,400. Affluent retirees reinvented new ways of living: condo towers, gated communities, and active adult communities. In another historical aberration begun in Collier and Sarasota counties, large numbers of retired residents earned a higher percentage of income from investments and entitlements than from wages.[12]

To have lived in Florida between 2000 and 2010 was to be an eyewitness to history. From the presidential election of 2000 to terrorist cells embedded in Hollywood and Pompano Beach, from four hurricanes in 2004 to algae blooms and increasing alarm over the Everglades and water, from Ponzi schemes and the culture of flipping to foreclosure boat tours of Cape Coral and "For Sale" signs in Lehigh Acres, from the *Deepwater Horizon* and Silver Springs to the Zika virus and coral bleaching, from "*Por Salvar a Elián!*" to "Stand Your Ground," from "Tim Tebow for President" bumper stickers to scandals and last-place finishes, Florida seemed to be the center of the universe. Perhaps the most head-slapping moment occurred in 2010, when demographers forecast that very soon Florida would surpass New York as the nation's third-largest state. Almost one in ten Florida residents once called New York home. Florida is the Petri Dish State.

Some fascinating individuals emerged during the dynamic decade. Donald Trump became a Florida celebrity. For decades, he had eluded New York *paparazzi,* journalists, and subpoena servers, but his face (and hair) and corporate brand managed to garner a lot of attention by virtue of his Mar-a-Lago mansion, his hit TV show, and the constant chattering that he might or should run for the presidency (in this era as a Democrat!). From his Palm Beach redoubt, he revealed all the qualities we loved or hated: audacity and boldness, belligerence and hostility. He may also have been the worst neighbor in Florida![13]

Once a marginally important part of the Solid South, Florida leapt into America's political imagination after the 2000 election. Every broadcaster knew the essential vocabulary in understanding Florida politics: the Cuban vote, the

I-4 Corridor, political gurus such as Mac "the Knife" Stipanovich, the emerging Puerto Rican presence, Gold Coast condo commandos, sampling possum at the annual festival in DeLeon Springs, ordering a pastrami sandwich at a Jewish deli in Boynton Beach, asking for a slice of sour orange pie in Sebring, and the mandatory first stop of any Republican running for statewide or national office: The Villages. As the traveling salesmen sang in *The Music Man,* "You got to know your territory!" When presidential candidate Rudy Giuliani campaigned in Florida, pressing the flesh in Boynton Beach and Boca Raton, he called Palm Beach County "New York's sixth borough" and a "firewall."[14]

Geographically, Florida is a massive state, larger than England and Wales. The state boasts 1,350 miles of coastline. Perhaps Florida—the distance between Key West and Pensacola is 832 miles—is too long to be a state? North to south, the Panhandle and peninsula encompass many different ecosystems and climate zones. Florida belongs to the Deep South and the northern Caribbean. Only Alaska boasts more coastline, and lately every new resident wants to live closer to the sand dunes and salt water.

Nature, once a calming force in Florida's past, increasingly became intertwined in dystopian discussions about the environment. A SeaWorld star, Tilikum, the killer whale, attacked and killed his trainer. Killer hurricanes and tropical storms raked the peninsula and Panhandle. The decade's ill-begotten hurricanes—named Michelle, Rita, Dennis, Wilma, Bill, Charley, Frances, Ivan, and Jeanne—left behind heartbreak and misery, including monumental recovery costs. New terms—climate change, global warming, climate deniers—were becoming all too familiar and real. Some Floridians began to discuss a forbidden topic for dream states: limits. Signposts littered the new decade: record numbers of manatees and panthers being killed, the loss of songbird populations, wetlands destruction, and vanishing sea grass.

During the decade, red became the new blue as the Republican Party swept aside Democrats and solidified power and privilege. A biography of Jeb Bush bore the title *Conservative Hurricane: How Jeb Bush Remade Florida.* By 2000, bull-rushing Republicans had finally climbed a mountain few believed possible: for the first time in almost 125 years, the GOP controlled the governor's office and both houses of the Florida Legislature. Florida, like most of the Deep South, abandoned the Democratic Party. Linda Margolis served as president of the Senate in 1991, and Peter Rudy Wallace served as Speaker of the House in the mid-1990s, facts that are now the answer to a trivia question: "Who were the last Democrats to . . ?" Republicans strengthened their positions, even during the recession. Weekly, it seemed, prominent Democrats defected. Called "Dempsey-cats," after longtime Democratic power broker Dempsey Barron (1922–2001), these new enlistees energized the Party of Lincoln. Aging Democratic icons Reubin Askew, Bob Graham, and Bill Nelson offered hope, but the GOP was building corridors across Florida, from the once-blue Panhandle to the Southwest and heart of the peninsula. Only college towns such as Tallahassee and Gainesville, and the Gold Coast counties of Palm Beach, Broward, and Miami-Dade, kept many of the races respectable.[15]

New faces appeared on the Florida political horizon in 2000. In December 1999, political newcomer Marco Rubio was fighting for his political life, facing a runoff for a seat in the Florida House. Forty-two-year-old Katherine Harris had just been elected secretary of state. In 2000, Rick Scott, living in his mansion in Naples, was largely unknown outside a cluster of friends and fellow lawyers. Barack Obama was an obscure Illinois state senator from Chicago. When he announced that he was running for the U.S. Congress in a seat held by a four-time incumbent and former Black Panther, Bobby Rush, friends questioned his political sanity.

The 2000 U.S. Census confirmed the decades of frantic growth. Florida was the fourth-largest state and fast approaching New York. Among the myriad demographic indicators was an extraordinary headline in the *New York Times:* "Florida Has More Hispanics Than Blacks." A century earlier, the African-American population of Florida was 44 percent, with negligible numbers of Hispanics. During the 1990s, 1 million Latins moved to Florida. David Rieff compressed a decade of frantic movement when he wrote, "The great travel story of our time is called migration."[16]

What single individual played the most transactional role in the shaping of modern Florida? Neither a developer nor a governor nor a scientist ignited a series of revolutions that still reverberate today. If Jeb Bush deserved the title "conservative hurricane," Fidel Castro was the "El Huracán Radical." In spasms of political, social, and economic upheaval, the Cuban revolution spread far beyond the island. The word "revolution" is too often employed, but Fidel was a true revolutionary, and his legacy can be seen in Cuba, Venezuela, and South Florida. Hundreds of thousands of Cubans fled Cuba for Florida. Ironically, Fidel loved Florida; indeed, he honeymooned in Miami Beach with his bride, Mirta Diáz-Balart, in 1948.[17]

Violence left deep scars across Florida. The Sunshine State was becoming the Gunshine State. In May 2000, Floridians were rocked by a gun death at Lake Worth Middle School. A thirteen-year-old student shot and killed Barry Grunow, a teacher. Gun sales spiked after 9/11, and a new age of security exhausted and agitated students and citizens across Florida. In 2005, the Florida Legislature passed a bill that Americans soon would know all too well: "Stand Your Ground."[18]

Wordsmiths coined new terms to understand the magical and largely unplanned era of modern Florida, 1945–2000: Sunbelt, space age, jet age, active retirement home, theme park, edge city, sprawl, time-share condominium, snowbird, and climate control. So, too, a new vocabulary defined the succeeding decades, but the words conjured haunting images of terror and fear. The period 2000–2010 shook Florida to its foundations.

The English language absorbed many new words into its lexicon to depict a rapidly changing world and state, and bound and online dictionaries continue to add words and phrases to our vocabulary at a vertiginous rate. New words—Y2K, hanging chad, iPad, smartphone, opioids, transgendered, Latinx, citrus greening, MySpace, Twitter, Wi-Fi, cooking meth, barista art, emoji, online news, 9/11, WMD, Xennials, Homeland Security, Alt-Facts, sexting, LGBTQ, underwater/upside-down/toxic mortgages, short sales, REITs, robo-signings, and flipping—earmark the era 2000–2010.

The new century's lexicon empowered Americans to interpret and traverse both new and old landscapes. Today, glove compartments rarely include gloves or Rand-McNally folded-paper maps. Lest one fear getting lost while navigating Orlando's Colonial Avenue or Tampa's Dale Mabry Highway, GPS and MapQuest make our lives easier, if more complicated. Why bother being disoriented, angry, or wet when one could simply experience a 3D virtual tour?

In modern Florida, Isaiah's prophecies came true: the hot was made cold, the wet was made dry, and the crooked bent straight. A century earlier, progress was measured by human's ability to drain the Everglades, dredge phosphate beds, and spray wetlands for mosquito control. Each new generation brought bolder plans and bigger machines to channelize rivers and tame the environment. The speed of recent technological change has created, stored, and allowed access to vast sums of information, so that everything is now retrievable, but little is understood. Communication is instantaneous, but shallow. If television created a universe of cave dwellers, and the air conditioner spawned generations of couch potatoes, the computer has created a universe of "friends" who lack the social skills to understand friendship.

A computer-driven communications revolution shaped the 1990s, accounting for almost 300 million Internet users by the turn of the decade. Junkyards filled with telephone booths, rotary-dial telephones with cords, and videocassette recorders stand as testament to technological wizardry and obsolescence.

Linguists worked overtime to create new words, such as "dialarhoea," the accidental dialing by a cell phone in a handbag. Old sounds—the noisy clatter of IBM Selectrics, "ring, ring," and "You've got mail"—soon vanished.[19]

In 1999, "Google" was an obscure noun, not yet a very active verb. Mobile phones were riding a consumer wave of demand. But still no iPhones. In one of those extraordinary moments—at the brink of a new century and new decade, a time when Americans thought no society had ever been more "wired" or technologically developed—new revolutions made the old century seem almost quaint.

Lest we become too ecstatic about the impact of "progress," the post-2000 devices and gadgets have also complicated our relationships with other humans and technology. Face-to-face relationships still mattered in the '90s. By 1999, writes journalist Kurt Andersen: "We all had cell phones, but not smartphones; we were not over connected or tyrannized by our devices. Social media had not yet made life both manically nonstop and attenuated."[20]

By 2010, many Floridians had become convinced that something was wrong with Florida, and that any solution must address humans' relationship with nature. The *Deepwater Horizon* Oil Spill in 2010, America's worst, disillusioned many Americans about our ability to harness nature, but it also energized many Floridians, reinforcing the belief that the environmental crisis was America's existential issue of the century. In its natural state, Florida may appear to be poorly designed: meandering rivers, shifting coastlines, and shore-hugging, view-blocking mangroves. Land and water yielded to bulldozers, draglines, dredges, and construction cranes. The new century witnessed constant clashes between environmentalists and developers. The journalist Jon Nordheimer captured Florida's difficulties coming to terms with growth. Still, the state is a marvel, he observed: "Florida seems capable of absorbing blow after blow of development; intruded upon, tacky in wide sweeps, but always producing a subtropical beauty and sense of place unique on this continent." Increasingly, the word of the decade 2000–2010 was "limits." But few listened, and even fewer understood the problem.[21]

To quote Bette Davis in *All about Eve* (1950): "Fasten your seat belt. It's going to be a bumpy ride." And there is no better place to examine the extraordinary events and rhythms of the new century and millennium than Florida.

1

Y2K and Hanging Chads, JEB! and Dubya

Florida and the Election of 2000

2000: The New Millennium and Old Questions

The Oracles at Delphi, Deltona, and DeLand will long ponder the meaning of the year 2000. A centennial and millennial year, 2000 was also an election and census year. While the words "battleground" or "vital" had rarely been affixed to Florida in national elections, Florida really, really mattered in 2000. In the 1950 film *Sunset Boulevard,* Norma Desmond famously proclaims, "Alright Mr. DeMille, I'm ready for my close-up." Florida may have been confident, but it was ready for neither a close-up nor a fadeaway.

World War II and its succeeding decades manifested the "Florida century." On the crossroads of destiny in 1940, Florida lay far from the mainstreams of power and influence, demography and geography. On the eve of Pearl Harbor, Florida had five U.S. congressmen, one fewer than South Carolina and four fewer than Alabama. But the trajectory of modern Florida in the decades after VJ Day was as stunning as it is significant. At the beginning of the century, many of the state's half million inhabitants resided north of Gainesville. Indeed, most residents lived only a wagon's ride from the Alabama and Georgia borders. The 2,981 residents of Tallahassee at the turn of the century could walk to Thomasville, Georgia, in a day. On maps and in people's minds, Florida was the most geographically isolated, sparsely populated, and politically insignificant state east of the Mississippi River.

Amid spasms of promotion and prosperity, bank failures and land busts, ballyhoo and bluster, Florida lurched onto the national stage. Florida has always looked forward rather than backward, its politicians and developers more interested in tomorrow's dreams than today's realities or yesterday's lessons.

Dreams became realities, and the combined forces of peace, prosperity, and progress aligned in the decades after 1945 to create Everyman's Florida. Census takers counted 15,982,378 residents in 2000, representing a stunning 24 percent increase in population since 1990. Miami-Dade County alone accounted for more than 2 million residents, an incredible accomplishment when one considers that in 1900 Dade County (then constituting the future entities of Dade, Broward, Palm Beach, and Martin counties) claimed 4,955 inhabitants. Remarkably, no Florida county registered population losses between 1990 and 2000. Monroe County ranked last in growth, its population increasing only 2 percent, while Flagler County, driven by the explosive growth of the new city of Palm Coast, grew by 70 percent. Perhaps most remarkably, the census revealed fewer than 1 million children aged five years and younger. Historically, societies had always boasted disproportionately more children than elders. However, the number of Floridians aged sixty-five and older had soared to more than 3.5 million. Florida had become the new frontier, a modern twilight zone and gerentopolis for the state's youngest and oldest citizens.[1]

The U.S. Census of 2000 verified Florida's ascent and accent, no trend more astounding than the 2001 headline "Florida Has More Hispanics Than Blacks, Census Shows." Between 1830 and 1910, the territorial and state proportion of Black inhabitants never fell below 40 percent. The term "Hispanic" would not have been recognized until the post–World War II era, and the word "Latinx" was not yet invented. But in 2000, the result of four decades of surging numbers of Cubans, and then Puerto Ricans, Mexicans, Dominicans, and other Spanish-speaking immigrants, the state's Hispanic population topped 16 percent. Those numbers do not reflect the growing numbers of Haitians, Jamaicans, Asians, and other new immigrant groups who are not classified as Hispanic.[2]

Florida's African-American population once inched close to majority status. In 1870, Florida constituted 96,057 whites and 91,691 Blacks. In 2000, only one Florida county boasted a Black majority: Gadsden. In 1870, fully seven counties tilted African-American: Alachua, Gadsden, Jackson, Jefferson, Leon, Madison, and Marion. The Great Migration and the Florida Land Boom of the 1920s and post–World War II changed the racial composition of these counties, bringing in many more whites while losing substantial numbers of African Americans. Once the economic, political, and demographic heart of Florida, the Panhandle and North Florida were fading in importance. But in a sea of red, Gadsden, Leon, and Jefferson counties still glowed blue on election day.[3]

Florida added 834 new inhabitants every day between 1990 and 1999, making the Sunshine State the favorite destination for retirees, snowbirds, and interstate movers. To illustrate this phenomenon, the *New York Times*' Jon Nordheimer chose as his vantage point Interstate 95 near Richmond, Virginia. "All day and through the lonely night the moving vans push southward," he observed, "14-wheeled boxcars of the highway changing the demographic face of America." Strikingly, Florida towns that had been ignored, underdeveloped, or not even developed at all caught the attention of demographers: Naples and North Port, Palm Bay and Palm Coast, and Verona Walk and The Villages.[4]

The 1990s only intensified America's Second Great Migration: the march to the Sunbelt. The once mighty Rust Belt states in the North hemorrhaged residents, political clout, and sports supremacy to the Sunbelt. Coined in 1969 by Republican Party strategist Kevin Phillips, the term "Sunbelt" loosely identified the expanding regions of the South, Southwest, and West into a super-region defined by its moderate to hot weather, reliance upon air-conditioning, support for the military and defense programs, dynamic economy, favorable business climate, modern highways and airports, and drift toward conservatism and, in Phillips's prescient words, an "emerging Republican majority." Columnist Kirkpatrick Sale dubbed this phenomenon the "Southern Rim."[5]

The Sunbelt's buckle sparkled as a diverse contingent of newcomers arrived. "Everyone it seems, is from someplace else." The phrase, quoted so often, might qualify as the state motto, license plate slogan, or football cheer. The *Sun-Sentinel* added a coda to the phrase, "Florida natives have seen so much change they might as well be." Perception nudges reality. In 2000, only one of every three residents qualified as a native Floridian, while two-thirds were transplants. When one calculated the masses of snowbirds and tourists, the imbalance is even more exaggerated. Even Alaska claimed a greater proportion of native-born residents than Florida! In contrast, eight of ten Pennsylvanians and seven of ten Georgians were natives. In Plantation and Sebring, reunions summoned ex–New Jersey residents to reconnect. Comedian and part-time gerontologist Dave Gardner once quipped, "No one ever retires *to* New Jersey!"[6]

Florida census takers, meals on wheels deliverers, and adult active retirement centers heard plenty of New Jersey accents in Florida in 2000. In 1900, about one in twenty-five Floridians had reached the age of sixty-five and older. A New Year's Day 2000 editorial trumpeted a century's progress: "We don't die of as many diseases as we used to: Puerperal fever, pellagra, tuberculosis, polio and malaria aren't the killers they once were." More than 2.8 million residents were sixty-five and over. Floridians born in 1920 had a life expectancy of fifty-four, a dramatic increase from those born in 1900, who were expected to live forty-seven years. In 2000, the Sunshine State boasted 331,000 residents eighty and older! Senior citizens acquired political power, a combination of Claude Pepper's legacy, sheer numbers, and dutiful voting.[7]

On the eve of 2000, *Time* magazine posed a parlor question: "A Second American Century?" The reference was to a 1941 *Time* editorial, in which the magazine's publisher, Henry R. Luce, coined the term "American Century." Luce, the son of missionary parents in China, had then urged the U.S. to serve as the world's peacemaker, a democratic model of God's will, a City on the Hill. Conservative commentator Charles Krauthammer answered the question in emphatic prose: "The world at the turn of the 21st century is not multipolar but unipolar." He quoted British economist Harold Laski, who said of the United States in the aftermath of World War II: "America bestrides the world like a colossus."[8]

In retrospect, the year 1999 seems nostalgic if not idyllic, an American version of Britain or France in 1913, on the eve of the Great War. "If you were born around 1980," argues journalist Ross Douthat, "you grew up in a space happily *between*—between eras of existential threat (Cold War/War on Terror, or Cold War/climate change), between foreign policy debacles (Vietnam/Iraq), between epidemics (crack and AIDS/opioids and suicide), and between two different periods of economic stagnation (the '70s and early Aughts)."[9]

Y2K

Naysayers, fuddy-duddies, and intellectuals grumbled that our obsession with numerical groupings of a thousand years and the decimal system was a frivolous waste of time. Besides, the dawn of the new millennium ought to arrive on 1 January 2001, not 2000! Citizens became aware of an obscure sixth-century Roman monk and scholar, Dionysius the Diminutive. Pope John I had assigned Dionysius the task of developing a Christian chronology. Since the Roman numerical system had no symbol for zero, Dionysius decreed that the modern calendar be aligned with Christ's death, set at AD 1. It also meant that the new century and millennium technically ended 31 December 2000, not 1999. Never mind, the *Tampa Tribune* speculated eerily, "2001 might not be as fun!"[10]

Notwithstanding eggheads' objections, intense curiosity and anxiety surrounded the countdown to the new millennium. Prepare for ruin and wrack, warned millenarians. On the radio, disc jockeys seemed hell-bent to play Jim Morrison and the Doors' 1967 classic "The End." Morrison, who grew up in Florida, rocked and rolled in his Parisian grave. Barry McGuire's 1965 classic "The

Eve of Destruction" also prophesied a violent end. Doomsayers and foes of One World government gleefully predicted that all interdependent technology would crash at midnight, 31 December. Global-gloom narratives predicted nuclear missiles firing aimlessly because of cross-wired launch codes, prison doors swinging open, and computer-flawed ATM machines spewing cash to strangers. Digital dominoes will fall. In one case, on New Year's Eve 2000, Scottish air controllers panicked when their radar screens went blank. Britain had canceled all flights because of fears of the "millennium bug." The worst case seemed to be a consumer who received a bill from his video store for $91,250, the cost of renting *The General's Daughter* for 100 years! *Time* magazine and its corporation's information-technology staff bunkered in a "war room" in the basement of the Time & Life Building, expecting to publish and print the magazine amid the catastrophe.[11]

Floridians prepared to party! "If market baskets are an indicator," reported the *Gainesville Sun*, "the mood Friday in North-Central Florida was more party than Y2K-inspired panic." Journalists noted surging crowds at a Publix on SW 75th Street, where "shoppers were stocking up, but it hardly looked like survival food—corn ships, soda, wine, champagne, cream pies, mixed nuts and party platters were rolling through the checkouts in great numbers."[12]

Whatever! Floridians chose to party. Lakeland hosted a laser light-show countdown. Walt Disney World was so packed that Epcot, the Magic Kingdom, and Disney-MGM closed their doors by midday. In Sunrise, the Bee Gees performed at the National Car Rental Center, while Julio Iglesias and Smokey Robinson crooned to crowds at the Miccosukee Resort and Convention Center, located on the edge of the Everglades. The Spanish singer urged the appreciative crowd to drink California wine and get plenty of exercise, "vertically and horizontally!" A party was held on the fabled launch pad of the Cape Canaveral Air Station. Tickets for the Blondie and Gipsy Kings concert on South Beach sold for $650. Thousands packed the Miami Beach Convention Center for what was advertised as the "largest gay Y2K party on the planet." Key West partied to its own drummers—in this case, the Duval Street masses awaited the dropping of a 6-foot bejeweled high heel carrying Sushi, a Conch drag queen.[13]

How fittingly improbable that the most famous Y2K blowout in Florida occurred at a Seminole Indian Reservation. More than 80,000 Floridians and visitors crowded the Big Cypress Reservation to usher in the New Year with the rock band Phish. Three wars, geographic exile, and physical isolation had forged a sense of identity and identification among the Seminoles and the Everglades. To young Floridians, FSU football and casino gambling defined Seminole culture. To elderly residents, their introduction to the world of the Seminoles probably came through the media, in Walt Disney's *Davy Crockett,* a 1954–55 blockbuster TV series, or as tourists stopping along the Tamiami Trail and gawking at young Seminoles wrestling alligators. But the Seminoles' newfound prosperity meant that saurian opponents were more likely college students or local Hispanics.[14]

New Year's Eve 1999 captured a frozen moment in Florida history. Many celebrations occurred on sites considered unlikely or laughable a decade earlier: trendy urban downtowns. Fifteen thousand celebrants partied across downtown Fort Myers and other urban places. The gaiety also signified other new and old ways of socialization. On the eve of the millennium, however, many Floridians preferred the early-bird special at Top of the World or watching the Dick Clark TV extravaganza to doubling down at the Seminole Hard Rock Casinos in Hollywood and Tampa. Thousands of residents elected to party amid the safety and exclusivity of new gated communities. The Florida Panhandle town of Century—so named because it was founded at the beginning of the last century—hosted a Y2K–5K Last Run of the Century race.[15]

In Palm Beach, a city where lavish parties confirmed wealth, power, and prestige, one celebrity held a $2,000-per-head extravaganza at his vacation home. Donald Trump, described as a "presidential wannabe," promised the New Year's Eve gala held at his Mar-a-Lago mansion would be huge. But it was not the former playboy that attracted the media's glare in 2000; rather it was his glamorous but brief bid for the presidency. Only months earlier, journalists reported that Trump had created an exploratory committee to determine his prospects at winning the 2000 presidential election. Roger Stone, a political gadfly, was rumored to be Trump's only campaign staffer. The Associated Press reported that his first choice for vice president on the Reform Party ticket would be Oprah Winfrey. "The only thing that could interest me is if I could win," he declared. His clarification was pure New York, perfectly understood in South Florida: "I'm not talking about the nomination, I'm talking about the whole megillah." His ex-wife Ivana assured the press that he could not possibly be a candidate because he was too busy running his real estate empire. His Slovenian escort, Melania Knauss, posed on a presidential seal. "Trump was turning himself into a content machine for every outlet," wrote Steve Kornacki. Wildly inconsistent, Trump and his "platform" came across as socially liberal and economically conservative. A quintessential New Yorker, he supported abortion rights and favored a tax on the rich; he singled out Japan for "ripping us off" and opposed illegal immigration. He assured television host Larry King, "The polls have been unbelievable." When pressed for details, Trump pointed to a survey conducted by the *National Enquirer. Saturday Night Live* caricatured a secret plot orchestrated by The Donald, Ross Perot, and Pat Buchanan. By Valentine's Day 2000, candidate Trump became citizen Trump. His political career seemingly over, he teased, "I cannot rule out another bid for the presidency in 2004."[16]

We survived! The state's newspapers chortled over the hubbub. "Y2K," reassured the *Tallahassee Democrat*, turned into "Yawn2K." "Biggest 2000 loser, Y2K furor," smirked the *St. Augustine Record:* "Planes didn't crash, nuclear missiles didn't fire, computers didn't melt. Headlines should have said: OOPS, NOTHING HAPPENED." The *St. Petersburg Times* editorialized, "The Four Horsemen have not gotten loose from their infernal stables . . . and the world has not, in fact, ended." The *Fort Pierce Tribune* reassured readers, "Computers computed, ATMs offered cash . . . and toilets flushed." The *Miami Herald* greeted its readers: "OK! It's over! You can put down your freeze-dried Spam and come out of your bunker!" The *Herald*'s Dave Barry isolated the night's craziest moment: "Four tourists were somehow able to actually get a table at Joe's Stone Crab." The humorist added, "Fortunately, they were quickly apprehended and are now at the Krome Detention Center awaiting deportation to Milwaukee."[17]

Florida's profile can be measured by interstate moves, death rates, and immigration. But babies' names also signify cultural and demographic change as well as tradition. One of the first children born in North America arrived at Pembroke Pines thirty-three seconds after midnight. In Miami, baby Sharieff Hakim Muhammad became Miami-Dade's first newborn, whereas Tampa's Selina Evelyn Rodríguez became Tampa's first twenty-first-century baby. In Fort Pierce, Elida Macedo and Teodoro Pérez's twin boys marked the first babies born in St. Lucie County in the year 2000, while Southwest Florida greeted Julia Rubinelli. Broward County's first wedding couple of the century was Romy Velázquez and Michael Zollo. In Fort Lauderdale, Marjorie Pamblanco and Hicklet Lau endowed their new millennial girl a perfect name: Millie Ann! One Floridian, Miami Beach's Ralph Friedman, was born in the nineteenth century, before there was a Miami Beach![18]

Some communities chose a retro-celebration. On 31 December 1899, Fred Hendry, scion of the powerful Hendry family, rang in the new century with a new church bell at the United Methodist Church in Fort Myers. A century later, Hendry's great-grandchildren rang the same church bell. On New Year's Eve 1900, the local newspaper proudly announced that a telephone line had been strung between Fort Myers and Alva.[19]

For many decades, Florida welcomed streams of immigrants eager to begin their American dream in Florida. In 2000, few places in America heard so many strange accents as Miami-Dade County. Over 1.2 million Miami-Dade residents were foreign-born, including 650,000 Cubans. But on New Year's Day 2000, a strange sight could be seen. Amid fireworks and gaiety, the *Miami Herald* described "a wooden boat treacherously overloaded with 406 Haitian, Dominican and Chinese migrants, chugging unlit toward Key Biscayne." The paper added, "They never made it."[20]

But the novel freshness of welcoming the new millennium soon turned sour. The millennial year proved to be one of the most bizarre and significant milestones in Florida and American history.

Elián

In *The Tempest, A Midsummer Night's Dream,* and *Macbeth,* William Shakespeare entwined politics, culture, and drama along timeless plotlines: innocents plucked from storm-tossed seas; ambitious women plotting personal and political gain; the pain of leaving one homeland and encountering a new, wondrous world; a citizenry furious at feckless leaders in a world turned upside down. The Elián González saga became *The Tempest 2.0,* a tragicomic series of acts that one observer likened to a Fellini movie, "a fable rich in resource and surprise, amazingly durable and divisive, tiresome and riveting at the same time."[21]

On 21 November 1999, Juan Miguel González Quintana arrived to pick up his young son at a schoolhouse in Cardenas, Cuba. There, he was told Elián had already left with his mother, Juan's ex-wife, with whom he shared custody. The Cuban Revolution had severed classes, families, and relationships. Elizabet Brotons Rodríguez and her son set sail for Miami across the Straits of Florida with twelve other Cubans in a tiny aluminum boat with no life preservers. A modern Shakespeare might well have rewritten the opening scene in *Romeo and Juliet:* "Two households, both alike in dignity, In fair Cardenas and Miami, where we lay our scene. . . . Where civil blood makes civil hands unclean."[22]

A beacon of freedom and a graveyard of dreams, Florida beckoned. A malfunctioning gasoline engine complicated what was already a perilous journey. Quickly, the doomed vessel was awash with salt water, and the desperate passengers clung to rubber inner tubes. Scanning the choppy waters off Fort Lauderdale, two fishermen thought someone had concocted "a sick joke," stringing a doll to a float. They soon realized the doll was a five-year-old boy bobbing in the Atlantic Ocean. Tragically, Elián's mother and ten others drowned when their "freedom boat" capsized. A survivor told immigration authorities that "Elizabeth protected her son to the end." To los Cubanos of Little Havana and South Florida, Thanksgiving Day 1999 resonated with deep religious and spiritual meanings.[23]

To Miami's Cubans, there was no question as to how and why Elián survived the passage across the perilous Straits of Florida. A pillar of faith and heritage, La Virgen de la Caridad had guided Elián across troubled waters for a purpose. In Roman Catholicism, dead saints interact daily with the faithful. The disabled prayed to San Rocco; the helpless prayed to Saint Jude; women stricken with breast cancer lighted candles to Saint Agatha. Residents of Little Havana and other Cuban neighborhoods worshiped the patron saint of Cuba, Our Lady of Charity, La Virgen de la Caridad. In 1612, two Native Indians and an African slave child—the "three Juans"—were sailing in a small boat, collecting salt in the Bay of Nipe off the Cuban coast. A violent storm roiled the waters. Desperate, the three began to pray. The African slave wore a medallion with the image of the Virgin Mary. The storm lifted the boat toward an object in the waves. A statue of the Virgin Mary floated atop the waves. She was carrying *la infanta* and a gold cross, annunciating, "I am the Virgin of Charity." In 1916, Pope Benedict XV anointed the Virgin as the patroness of Cuba, the national saint. Clearly, Elián had been blessed by "Cachita," the Virgin's affectionate nickname. Regina Gutiérrez, who fled Cuba for Miami in 1970, explained Cachita's appeal in the simplest of terms: "She is an exile, like us."[24]

Cachita, too, crossed the Straits of Florida. In 1961, 30,000 Cubans squeezed into Bobby Maduro Stadium, a baseball park in Miami. Never had so many Cubans congregated at one place outside the island. No ordinary day, 8 September commemorated the feast day of La Virgen de la Caridad del Cobre. The revolution in Cuba was sweeping away the old, and with it the last vestiges of power belonging to the Catholic Church. But Cachita went underground and overseas, surviving the revolution. A sea of yellow, Cachita's color, was the pigment of the day. Black was not. Relatively few Afro-Cubans had fled Cuba—they first appeared in large numbers with the Mariel exodus in 1980. Cachita, too, remained wildly popular among the island's Afro-Cubans. Rumors had long circulated that the sacred statue of the Virgin had been desecrated and destroyed. In a moment riveted in the memory of Cuban Miami, a handful of men entered the stadium hoisting the statue of La Virgen. Smuggled from Cuba and secreted into the stadium, the Virgin sent the frenzied crowd into raptures. A chant erupted: "*¡Viva La Caridad del Cobre!*" Cuban-born Monsignor Augustín Román described the event as the watershed moment of Hispanic Catholicism in South Florida. "On that day of the Mass," remembered Román, "the Church in Miami realized that the preaching of the Mass should begin to be done in Spanish. . . . The Mass demonstrated the great devotion of people who, in pursuit of freedom, abandoned their country, leaving everything behind except for their Celestial

Mother." A shrine, La Ermitá de la Caridad, was erected on Miami Avenue in Coconut Grove. After all, one of the most popular slogans in Cuba and Miami proclaimed, "The Virgin of Charity unites us."[25]

Cubans in Miami may have credited La Virgen for Elián's good fortune, but he was also afforded advantages not offered to Haitians, Dominicans, or other "boat people" who sought asylum under similar circumstances. A Cuban, Elián was eligible for asylum under America's "wet foot/dry foot" doctrine. Non-Cubans were denied sanctuary. Yet this case was more complicated than most. Juan Miguel González wanted his son returned to Cuba. Quickly, the cause célèbre became a campaign fought on three fronts: the political arena, the courts, and public relations. Fidel Castro led massive rallies, leading the drumbeat that family trumps politics. In Miami, the Cuban community embraced Elián as a symbol of American liberty. Crowds chanted ¡*Viva Cuba Libre!*" In the custody battle, no institution fought more fiercely to keep Elián in Miami than the American Catholic Church. Led by Sister Jeanne O'Laughlin, president of Barry University and a close friend of Janet Reno, the church carried on the Cold War between Communist Cuba and South Florida's exile community.[26]

Elián's plight launched protests, legal maneuverings, and opportunities, shaping 2000 as a year of destiny. It was also the last year of the presidency of Bill Clinton. The president's attorney general, Janet Reno, was a Miami native where she had served as state attorney. The U.S. Immigration Service released Elián, placing him in the home of his father's great-uncle. Amid the pandemonium of news coverage and legal maneuverings, Elián visited Disney World. Finally, the Eleventh Circuit Court of Appeals ruled in April that the child must remain in Miami until relatives filed for an appeal hearing. In response, Attorney General Reno ordered that Elián be returned to his father in Cuba, but the American relatives defied the order. The child became a pawn for competing interests, as Elián's modest home was surrounded by protestors and television crews.

Little Havana also lured bright, young legal luminaries to the struggle. A thirty-two-year-old daughter of Cuban exiles, Barbara Lagoa volunteered as a member of the pro bono legal team to help Elián's relatives keep the young boy in Miami. Born in Hialeah, a Cuban and Republican bastion, she once played the role of the Virgin of Guadalupe in a school play. As a young lawyer, she acquired the nickname Barbara "The Hammer," for her toughness. The first Latina to serve on the Florida Supreme Court, Lagoa was rumored a finalist to replace U.S. Supreme Court Justice Ruth Bader Ginsburg in 2020. Colleagues believe the outcome of the Elián case "seared into her soul" the importance of the rule of law. Lagoa was joined by thirty-five-year-old Brett Kavanaugh in a legal fight to ensure that Elián was not repatriated to Cuba. Kavanaugh acquired the nickname "Forrest Gump" for his uncanny appearance at high-level controversies in Florida. He became a U.S. Supreme Court justice in 2018.[27]

Bruised by her decision to storm the Branch Davidian compound near Waco, Texas, Janet Reno was tormented and aggrieved by the Elián affair. "It wasn't easy for Janet," remembered President Clinton in his autobiography. "She told me that one of her former secretaries would hardly speak to her; the woman's husband had been jailed for fifteen years by Castro."[28]

On 22 April 2000, 130 elite Border Patrol agents stormed 2319 NW Second Street, while photographers snapped pictures of this surreal event. The rescue/abduction lasted three minutes. Miami police pepper-sprayed neighbors who attempted to interfere and arrested 200 protestors; Miami's mayor fired the city's police chief because he refused to foil the raid. The agents abducted/rescued Elián and rushed him to Andrews Air Force Base. The next day was Easter Sunday. The very confused child was exiled/returned to Cuba in May, where he was lionized by leaders. The modest home where Elián briefly lived now resembles a religious shrine. Displayed prominently, a statue of La Virgen de la Caridad comforts pilgrims and refugees. Cuban Americans awaited a miracle. Miami's Archbishop Thomas Wenski explained, "She makes Cubans feel more Cuban." In the parking lot of the popular Cuban sandwich emporium Latin American Cafeteria, an artist painted a mural of Elián rising from the sea[29]

The Elián melodrama combined the passions of a morality play and pilgrimage. It also served as a carnival mirror and Passion play, a loving home and homeless shelter. The narrative amplified and distorted the Cuban American dreams and fears. One version suggests a real-life soap opera about a mother who loved her son so much she embraced martyrdom so he could live in freedom. "We are outraged over the violent kidnapping of 6-year-old Elian Gonzalez in the pre-dawn hours," editorialized the *Baltimore Sun*. "Anyone who thinks that Elian should be returned to his father, who is a pawn of Fidel Castro, should be reminded that in Cuba Elian would be a ward of the state." But when stripped to its veneer, it was also a simple tale about the primacy of family. "To the Miami relatives," writes Martin Dyckman, "it was a struggle between the democracy where they thought he should live and the dictatorship where his sole surviving parent lived." To *Washington Post* journalist Gregory B. Craig, Miami's Cuban American leaders "showed themselves to be single-minded zealots—emotional, unreasonable, even fanatical, driven by wild-eyed anti-Castroism." But Elián was also a tale of immigrants so determined to defy a dictator they were willing to defy American laws that granted their liberties. Elián symbolized freedom for hundreds of thousands of Cubans who had fled a dictatorial island for the American dream. Everyone wanted Elián's story to be their own. Ironically, it was Fidel Castro who won the trophy child. The "loser" turned out to be Miami's Cuban community. In an unusual twist, the media portrayed the embattled exiles in a negative light.[30]

Energized and united, comparing INS agents with jackbooted Nazis or Fidel's secret police, Miami Cubans vowed vengeance in November. Cuban Americans dubbed the retribution, "*el voto castigo*," the punishment vote. Carl Hiaasen mused, imagining the poetic justice if "the presidential election shakes down to a single vote—an overseas ballot from Havana, bearing the child-like signature of one E. González." The timing of the imbroglio could not have been worse for a Democratic Party that had been successfully prying young Cuban Americans from reflexively supporting Republican candidates. Indeed, as many as 35 percent of Florida's Cuban Americans voters supported President Clinton in 1996. Ironically, Vice President Gore supported granting permanent residency to Elián. "It was a pivotal event," insisted Miami businessman Carlos Saladrigas. "It changed the whole dynamic of the Miami community. It changed me." University of Miami law professor David Abraham reflected upon the meaning of the events. "Elián," he explained, "was a trophy in a battle between the Cuban government and the relentless anti-Castro politics of the Miami Cuban community. . . . His case became a venue for group solidarity."[31]

A minor battlefield in 1865, an important battlefront in 1876, Florida emerged as a critical battleground in 2000. Winning Florida was tantamount to victory.

Al Gore and George W. Bush

To Albert Arnold Gore Sr., and his wife, Pauline LaFon Gore, the stories of slavery, the Civil War, and Reconstruction were personal. These native-born Tennesseans had listened to stories as children about their beloved land turned upside down by Union soldiers and freedmen, Democratic scalawags and Republican carpetbaggers. The birth of Albert Arnold Jr. was considered a miracle, and U.S. Senator Gore jawboned the *Nashville Tennessean* to announce the event on page one. Junior spent more time at Suite 809 atop the Fairfax Hotel along Embassy Row in Washington, D.C., than on the family farm in Carthage, Tennessee. He enjoyed the privilege of private schools, gaining admission to Harvard University. His freshman roommate was Tommy Lee Jones. A critic of the war in Vietnam, Gore was uneasy with the campus antiwar movement. A devoted son, he was proud that his father opposed the war. In a letter to his father, he called America's foreign policy a "national madness." In 1969, Al Jr. shocked -classmates when he enlisted in the army. He explained that his motivations were more ethical than political—he did not wish to use his family's influence. Some classmates thought he was also protecting his father, who was facing a tough reelection. His Harvard graduation class numbered more than 1,000, and Al was one of only a dozen Vietnam veterans. In one of the campaign commercials, Senator Gore implores Al Jr., Vietnam-bound and in uniform, "Son, always love your country." Senator Gore lost the election, but Al married Mary "Tipper" Aitcheson, whom he had met at his St. Alban's senior prom and fallen madly in love.[32]

After a brief tour of Vietnam as a journalist, Al returned to Tennessee, where he attended Vanderbilt University Divinity School and worked as an investigative reporter at the *Tennessean*. In 1974, he enrolled at Vanderbilt University Law School. His legal education was interrupted by a successful run for the U.S. Congress two years later. A congressman at age twenty-eight, Gore became a U.S. senator in 1988. That same year, the thirty-nine-year-old campaigned to become the Democratic nominee for president, finishing third overall in the field that saw Michael Dukakis secure the nomination but lose the election to George H. W. Bush. His secure world was shattered when he lost his older sister to cancer and nearly lost his son, hit by an automobile. He described his senatorial career in Washington as that of a "raging moderate." He earned a reputation as an environmentalist and an "Atari Democrat," one passionate about new technologies that were beginning to transform the world. In 1992, he authored his environmental manifesto, *Earth in the Balance*.[33]

In 1992, Bill Clinton and Al Gore Jr. formed a dream team to capture the presidency. Democrats were delirious at the prospects of two young southern liberals with the promise of re-creating a New South, restoring the hopes of a lost golden age of Reubin Askew, Jimmy Carter, and Terry Sanford. "Gore leapt at the vice presidency as his stepping-stone to the Oval Office," argues his biographer, "but by 1998 his partnership with Bill Clinton looked like a Faustian bargain." The Clinton years brought prosperity and optimism, but also excessive drama. The Monica Lewinsky affair tarnished the president's reputation and embarrassed his vice president. Journalist Bill Torque explained Gore's conundrum. "Defending Clinton too vigorously would make him look like First Apologist but stepping too far away would be seen as crass opportunism." Could Gore have it both ways: attaching his identity to a wildly popular if flawed *president and* asserting his independence and brand as the All-American with brains and heart?[34]

It was an era of parallel universes. *Saturday Night Live* and *West Wing* alternately ridiculed and idolized bloviating politicians and principled statesmen. A journalist observed on Election Day 2000: "Imagine being able to walk into the voting booth today and cast your presidential ballot for a man who is brilliant, charming, funny, compassionate, principled, exceedingly well-read and morally upright." Alas, wrote Michael Ollove, we can't. "But, you can watch him on television Wednesday night. . . . His name is Josiah Bartlet. . . . Some NBC executives say he polls better than Gore and Bush. Big surprise." Created by boy genius Aaron Sorkin, *West Wing* portrayed a president devoted to conscience and principle, a man who loved and never cheated on his wife.[35]

In 2000, Al Gore, after a fumbling start and underestimating his principal challenger, U.S. Senator Bill Bradley, raced through the Democratic primaries to become the party's nominee for president. Gore chose U.S. Senator Joe Lieberman of Connecticut as his running mate. In part, the decision was aimed at ensuring the Jewish vote in Florida. Jewish voters checkmate the Cuban vote, each group representing 6 percent of the state electorate. In Broward County, a Democratic linchpin, Jewish voters comprised 20–25 percent of likely voters. The candidates "used their best Yiddish," observed the *New York Times* at a rally in Tamarac, "not just the Jew but the Southern Baptist as well." One aging voter, "a lady with silver hair and red lipstick, told America's first Jewish vice-presidential nominee that kissing his hand was like kissing the Torah." Lieberman introduced Gore as a "*Yiddishe neshoma*" (a Jewish soul). Democrats realized the importance of running up huge margins along the Gold Coast's condominium row.[36]

The politics of religion raised several significant questions. "By choosing Dick Cheney rather than Pennsylvania's Roman Catholic governor, Tom Ridge, or New York's Catholic governor, George Pataki, did George W. Bush compromise his chance to woo the Catholic vote?," asked religious scholar Alan Wolfe. He raised other questions: "Will evangelical Christians find Bush's reference to Jesus Christ, or his proclamation of a 'Jesus Day' in Texas, attractive? Will supporters of the separation of church and state find such talk upsetting?"[37]

Democratic fortunes depended upon the Gold Coast and its huge Jewish vote to stem the Republican tide in Florida. Condominium commandos would have to turn out the votes. But the most famous "condo commando" was Italian, not Jewish. Amadeo Trinchitella, a World War II Marine veteran, a restauranteur, a piano mover who stood up to the mob and New York transplant, served as president of the Century Village retirement complex in Deerfield Beach. "See Trinchi" became sage advice for any candidate running for office in Democratic-rich

Broward County. To win the election, analysts predicted Gore must win Broward by 200,000 votes to carry the state. When "Trinch" died in 2015, Senator Bill Nelson eulogized, "He was the most genuine and influential senior citizen in the United States." "Trinch's" fiancé was Joan Geller, an equally adept political boss and mother to two powerful Broward County figures.[38]

The Republican Party nominated Texas governor George W. Bush to be the standard-bearer. Conveniently, his brother was serving as the popular governor of Florida, having trounced Ocala Democratic congressman Buddy MacKay in 1998. Not since the brothers Rockefeller, Nelson and Winthrop, governed New York and Arkansas, had one family presided over two different states, and not even the Rockefellers had a father who served as president. Employing an authentic Texas aphorism, CBS anchor Dan Rather opined, "You can bet that President Bush will be madder than a rained-on rooster if Jeb fails his big brother."

Jeb Bush

John Ellis Bush—who preferred the acronym "Jeb"—enjoyed a meteoric rise in Florida. Wiseacre journalists preferred "Jeb!" or JEB!" Arriving in the Sunshine State in January 1981, less than two decades later he had made a fortune in business and had become governor of the nation's fourth-largest state. And if he marshalled the resources of the state GOP, he would become kingmaker on 7 November 2000.

Why did Jeb Bush choose Florida to make his fortune? After all, his grandfather Prescott Bush was a U.S. senator from Connecticut. For generations, the Bushes had made their mark at Yale, their fortunes on Wall Street, and their summer homes in Maine. But the son of Prescott Bush, George Herbert Walker Bush, was determined to carve out his own identity. Following World War II and Yale, he moved his family to West Texas, where he gambled successfully in the high-stakes oil industry.

Born in 1953 in Midland, Texas, seven years after his older brother George W., he followed family tradition, enrolling at Phillips Academy in Andover, Massachusetts. The *Boston Globe* summarized Jeb's early years at the prep school as largely "bad grades, marijuana, and apathy." He candidly described his years at Andover: "I was a cynical little turd in a cynical school." Jeb fatefully chose to study abroad in Mexico. There, he acquired a fluency in Spanish and fell in love. Smitten with Columba Gallo, spurning Yale, Jeb attended the University of Texas, where he majored in Latin American studies. Jeb and Columba, a shy, devout Catholic, married in 1974. Jeb's first job was in Houston, Texas, where he worked at a bank founded by a family friend, James A. Baker III. In 1977, Jeb and Columba moved to Caracas, Venezuela, where Jeb became vice president of the bank, drawing upon family relationships and contacts.[39]

Moving to Miami in January 1981, the young couple's timing was auspicious. A city sensationalized by Marielitos and cocaine cowboys, a savage race riot and drugs, Miami in 1981 was also a city on the edge of vast riches and international renown. Arguably, no city or county in America had experienced such profound demographic upheaval in the previous quarter century. Miami, Jeb insisted to friends, "is not a corporate town; it's an entrepreneurial town." Determined to make his own fortune, he found his timing perfect. Between 1981 and 1993, George Herbert Walker Bush held national office. Meanwhile his Florida son was becoming rich as a real estate developer. He was also crafting a network of relationships that forged his future political successes. Shortly after his father was inaugurated president, Jeb spent seven weeks in Nigeria, accompanied by officials of a Florida company manufacturing water pumps. He was part of a team that landed an $80 million deal. *Washington Post* reporters investigated Bush's work, concluding the evidence portrays "a man who, before he was elected governor of Florida in 1998, often benefited from his family connections and repeatedly put himself in situations that raised questions about his judgment and exposed him to reputational risk." When asked to define Jeb's personality during these go-go years, Matthew Corrigan, author of *Conservative Hurricane*, suggested "a little bit of damn the torpedoes, full speed ahead."[40]

Moving to Florida in 1981 also coincided with a Republican revolution, led by President Ronald Reagan. Weekly, prominent state Democrats switched parties. Ronald Reagan, maintained Charles Whitehead, chair of the state Democratic Party in the 1980s, "built the Republican Party of Florida." "From Pensacola to Jacksonville, that's where he really killed us."[41]

South Florida and its Cuban American culture profoundly shaped Jeb Bush. A policy wonk, Jeb also revealed a softer side when he pleaded for compassionate treatment of Cuban exiles. A *Miami Herald* reporter once observed Jeb dining at a tiny Cuban café in Little Havana. A waitress approached him, nervously admitting that she was an illegal immigrant. Jeb promised to plead her case. A Cuban radio host remembered, "The problems of the Cuban community were like part of his own problems." Through his fluency in Spanish and his sincerity for the immigrant cause, Jeb forged close ties to Miami's powerful Cuban communities. His hashtag is revealing: #honorarylatino. "There is no argument that Bush got a leg up in Miami thanks to family connections," concluded the *Miami Herald*, adding, "but he is a product of the city as much as he is of being a Bush."

By the mid-1990s, his net worth had soared over $2 million. Success did not come without baggage. Some of his business associates—Alberto Duque, Hiram Martínez Jr., and Miguel Recarey—were convicted of fraud and spent time in prison or fled the country. Jeb remembers Miami with great affection, telling reporters: "It's a place that is dynamic, aspirational. It looks like the future of the United States. I'll live here the rest of my life."[42]

The Bush name and the rise of the Republican Party in Texas, Florida, and the United States are inseparable. The Bushes are the closest thing to an American dynasty: Consider that between 1981 and 2009, a Bush occupied the White House or vice president's mansion for twenty years. Moreover, Bushes have logged fourteen years in the governorships of the nation's second- and fourth-largest states.

Florida's GOP

Florida became the first modern southern state to develop a competitive two-party system. The 1980s represented a political watershed, the equivalent of a neutron bomb that must have been as miraculous as it was significant to the few surviving Republicans who remembered the lean and barren landscape for most of the late nineteenth and twentieth centuries.

Swiftly, decisively, and, to Yellow Dog Democrats, shockingly, the Grand Old Party (GOP) was becoming the dominant party in Florida. To Floridians four score and ten years old, such developments were as shocking as they were significant. To provide a sense of perspective, consider the year 1942 as a marker midway between Reconstruction-era Florida and the millennial year 2000. In 1942, 604,341 Floridians had registered as Democrats, while 36,530 residents bravely identified themselves as Republicans. Florida's GOP had sunk so low during the Great Depression that it faced elimination from the official ballot. Democratic solons rushed to pass a bill resetting the minimum of voters required in the previous election at 15 percent. When critics questioned why the Party of Jefferson and Jackson should throw a lifeline to a sinking party, state Senator Fred L. Touchton of Dade City (Pasco County) offered a colorful explanation: "We've got Republicans in Florida and we can't shoot 'em. We want to keep them out of the Democratic Party where they might have the balance of power." Not much had changed by the 1950s. The Republican Party was growing, largely the result of the migrations of lifelong Republicans from the North and the Midwest and the "I Like Ike" years. An event in 1951 revealed the challenges Republicans faced. Typically, the appointment of chaplain to the Florida Legislature sparked little controversy. But in 1951, journalists revealed that Rev. Walter R. Faust was a card-carrying member of the GOP![43]

In 1949, William C. Cramer performed the equivalent of Martin Luther's "Here I stand!" defiance at the Imperial Diet of Worms by changing his voter registration card from Democrat to Republican. Fortunately for Cramer, a World War II veteran, he was residing in St. Petersburg. If any city earned the title "Birthplace of Florida's Modern Republican Party," it was St. Petersburg. Florida's growth spurt in the post–World War II years earned Florida two new congressional seats in 1952. In 1954, Cramer broke the glass ceiling, becoming one of the first Republican southerners to be elected to the U.S. Congress in the modern era. Eastern Tennessee and Kentucky had elected Republican congressmen, but not the Deep South. For Cramer's pioneering efforts, his peers called him affectionately "Mr. Republican."[44]

At the dawn of the 1960s, Republican optimism was difficult to muster as the Democratic Party still maintained a five-to-one dominance in registered voters. But the 1960s proved providential, as America veered out of control. The massive exodus of Cubans to Miami became an unexpected Republican bulwark, when the Bay of Pigs fiasco in 1961 veered from military disaster to political opportunity. Democratic voters became disillusioned and then angry as the decade's events boiled over: the civil rights protests, student demonstrations, urban riots, drugs, and Vietnam. In 1966, Floridians elected Claude Kirk governor, the first Republican chief executive in almost a century. A 1968 *St. Petersburg Times* headline confirmed the growing clout of the GOP: "Republicans Show 5,138 Voter Gain, Democrats 432 in Pinellas County." In 1972, a political year remembered as a debacle for the George McGovern–led Democratic Party, registered Democrats in Florida still outnumbered registered Republicans 2.4 million to 975,000 Republicans. Strikingly, only 118,000 Floridians registered as "other."[45]

Republicans learned a painful lesson in 1986, one which they would not forget. In 1986, Florida voters elected Bob Martínez governor. Only five years earlier Martínez had been a registered Democrat, but President Ronald Reagan persuaded the former history teacher, union leader, and mayor to switch parties and register as a Republican. As a businessman, Martínez understood that Florida's tax structure was ill-designed and antiquated, too dependent upon sales tax revenues. If 1,000 newcomers arrived daily, Florida hummed. But the slightest economic chill threw a wrench into the system. A recession meant sinking revenues with few options other than cutting popular programs. But tourists seemed to provide Florida a "Get Out of a State Income Tax" card, supplying as much as 57 percent of state revenue in the 1990s. Florida was one of seven states without a state income tax, putting additional strain upon the sales tax that dated to 1949. Martinez realized that the system was inefficient, since services—dry cleaning, boat rentals, newspapers, etc.—were untaxed. Against the advice of party elders, Martinez convinced the legislature to pass a sales tax bill, one that opponents defined as the largest tax increase in Florida history. In his State of the State address in 1987, the new governor proclaimed, "I am prepared to take on an unpleasant dose of tax medicine this year." Newspapers and media corporations labeled the medicine bitter and unfair and unleashed a bitter counterattack. The legislature rescinded the measure, but not without political damage. The message to Republicans was clear and simple: no new taxes, and never retreat. In 1988, Congressman Connie Mack III was elected to the U.S. Senate from Florida with an ungrammatical but simple message: "Less taxes, less spending, less government, and more Freedom." One of Congressman Mack's close friends who encouraged him to run for the Senate was Georgia congressman Newt Gingrich.[46]

The legendary Speaker of the U.S. House of Representatives Sam Rayburn instructed freshman congressmen with a simple code of conduct: "To get along, go along." Newt Gingrich neither understood nor endorsed that message. If Reagan was wildly popular and gregarious, Newt Gingrich was in-your-face and preached scorched-earth politics. As indispensable as Reagan in the Republican revolution, though having none of Reagan's charm and charisma, Gingrich led an insurgent movement in Congress in the 1980s and '90s, taking no prisoners while seizing control of the U.S. House of Representatives for the first time in four decades. *Time* magazine named Gingrich its "Man of the Year" in 1995. Gingrich once warned a group of College Republicans to avoid Boy Scout slogans "which would be great around the campfire but are lousy in politics." In the post-Watergate era, being a lifer in Congress suddenly became a political liability. Bipartisanship became a toxic label. While Reagan could sit down with Tip O'Neill and share a beer, Gingrich played down-and-dirty and win-at-all costs obstructionism. Reagan could strike a deal to save Social Security while Gingrich gleefully pushed for a government shutdown. Newt understood the role of the 24-hour mass media. "The number-one fact about the news media," preached Newt, "is they love fights." Gingrich, a Georgian, presided over a GOP that shifted its power base from the Midwest to the South and Sunbelt. His Florida counterpart, U.S. Congressman C. W. Bill Young, chaired the powerful House Committee on Appropriations from 1999 to 2005. Few details of his career better document the rise of Florida's modern Republican Party than when Young was first elected to the Florida state Senate in 1960, he also served as the Senate minority leader because he was the *only*

Republican serving in the Upper House! By the 1969–70 session, 16 Republicans comprised a Florida Senate that included 32 Democrats.[47]

Guided by the success of Reagan and Gingrich, the once Solid South was becoming a Republican bulwark. When Louisianan Mary L. Landrieu was defeated in 2015, the *New York Times* observed, "For Democrats, Saturday's outcome was yet another sobering reminder of their party's declining prospects in the South, a region they dominated for much of the 20th century." Florida's U.S. Senator Bill Nelson, a Democrat, had become a rarity and a target.[48]

Saul Alinsky, the legendary community activist, once said a sociologist was someone who needed a research grant to study prostitution when any Chicago cabbie could provide the needed information for a fin. So, too, academics accumulate charts revealing voting trends, changing demographics, and socioeconomic indicators. Sometimes, we should study an individual who never ran for office. If the typical condo commando in Broward County was a Jewish activist who once passed out brochures for Bella Abzug, her counterpart on the Gulf Coast was a Methodist from Wisconsin who liked Ike. Enter Marion Keith. In 1982, a *St. Petersburg Times* reporter introduced his subject, "Marion T. Keith is sitting in her pale green living room, scene of so many conferences with nervous Republican politicians." Ms. Keith was seventy-two, twice widowed, and a resident of an active adult complex in Clearwater. Her passion was the Republican Party. "Backed by a small army of volunteers scattered throughout 60 condominiums," journalist John Harwood wrote, "Marion Keith delivers Republican votes like no one else in Pinellas County. In a political sense, she sits on top of Top of the World. It is the quintessential pocket of the county's Republican strength—a vast retirement village stocked with conservative, elderly, white voters drawn heavily from the nation's Midwestern GOP heartland." Until the early 1980s, Ms. Keith was the condo commando of the largest voter precinct in America, home of 4,800 voters. Ms. Keith is best known in political circles as "Mrs. Republican." A local officeholder explained, "I don't think there's a Republican holding office in Pinellas today that hasn't sat in her living room and answered her questions and asked for her support." Ms. Keith moved to Pinellas County in 1954. That year is considered a milestone among Florida Republicans. William Cramer of St. Petersburg became one of the first Republicans to win a congressional seat in the South in eight decades. Ms. Keith died in 2005 at age ninety-five. Congressman Bill Young described her as "an institution all to herself." Her funeral sermon was sprinkled with several of her favorite political homilies: "You cannot help the poor by destroying the rich. You cannot establish security on borrowed money."[49]

As late as 1980, Democrats held a two-to-one voter registration advantage over Republicans, and both U.S. senators and the governor were Democrats. The death of Governor Lawton Chiles in 1998 symbolized the changing of the guard, the end of a golden age when giants such as LeRoy Collins and Reubin O'D. Askew stalked the Capitol. Only Bob Graham and Bill Nelson stood as symbol and sentinel of Florida's once vaunted and dominant Democratic Party.[50]

In the 1994 race for Florida governor, a brash, youthful Republican challenger, Jeb Bush, was poised to topple an iconic Democrat. Lawton Chiles, who had served as U.S. senator, was now running for reelection as governor. Two other Floridians—Park Trammell and Spessard Holland—had become U.S. senators following their governorships. The triumvirate all hailed from "Imperial" Polk County, the cradle of statesmen. Earning the name "Walkin' Lawton" when he strolled the breadth of Florida in his 1970 race for the U.S. Senate, he shocked the Democratic establishment when he left the Capitol in 1989. Whether he quit the Senate because of his impatience with Washington or health reasons, Chiles played the role of Horatius at the Bridge, the only Democrat capable of holding back the Republican hordes, when he defeated the incumbent, Republican Bob Martínez, in the 1990 gubernatorial race.[51]

A confident incumbent, Governor Chiles announced in 1994 that he would defend the office and party against all challengers. Jeb Bush relished the role of unseating a Democratic pillar and icon. He channeled powerful and personal motivations: "I want to be able to look my father in the eye and say, 'I continued the legacy.'" A self-described "head banging conservative," Jeb berated Chiles for not signing enough death warrants and sympathizing with the "modern victim movements." He surged to a ten-point lead by mid-October. But at times Jeb displayed a careless arrogance. Asked what a Bush governorship might mean for African Americans, the candidate responded flippantly, "Probably nothing." At the final debate, bristling with indignation that this pampered son of a Bush might win, Chiles wagged his finger at Bush, angry that GOP commercials painted him as weak on crime. But the debate's most memorable moment occurred when Chiles stared at his opponent and drawing deep from the wellspring of cracker folk culture, vowed, "The old he-coon walks just before the light of day." Jeb, who was fluent in Spanish but mute in cracker dialect, looked gobsmacked and disoriented. Chiles pulled out the victory, aided by some questionable last-minute telephone calls to senior citizens warning them about Republican budget cuts. Chiles wore his raccoon coat to his inauguration. "It wasn't supposed to have ended that way," wrote journalist Bill Minutaglio. "George W. was 'supposed' to lose to the popular incumbent

Ann Richards; Jeb was 'supposed' to win against Lawton Chiles. And maybe it was supposed to be Jeb Bush being groomed for the presidency." When he speaks about his life after the election, Bush refers to the years of "wandering around." But cautions journalist Karen Tumulty, Jeb "was far from aimless." She argues the humbled Bush "retooled himself from that of a sometimes-cartoonish ideologue" to a more balanced and likeable candidate, "deepening his knowledge of how his state worked, forging relationships that softened his profile."[52]

An afterthought and punching bag in the 1950s, Florida's GOP shattered historic glass ceilings within a half century: the first Republican congressman, governor, and U.S. senator since Reconstruction. But the party had never built upon its individual successes to govern Florida. Republican triumphs came despite seemingly comfortable Democratic Party registration advantage in numbers and Democratic Party–controlled reapportionment. By 1998, red became the new blue. The revolution was complete: the GOP dominated Tallahassee, ruling both houses of the Florida Legislature and the executive branch.

Jeb Bush won the governorship in 1998, defeating Democratic warhorse Buddy MacKay by ten points. He also became the first Florida governor since Reconstruction to work with a Republican-controlled legislature. Whereas Bob Graham was famous for keeping track of daily events by jotting information in tiny notebooks, Jeb was so inseparable from his BlackBerry and his fondness for email that he often called himself the "eGovernor." When a constituent accused the governor of behaving like a Nazi, Jeb responded: "Chill out, John. Do you really believe my rhetoric is fascist and Nazi-like? Take a deep breath and relax." Mel Martínez championed Bush as Florida's "first Cuban-American governor." Finally, the Florida cabinet functioned as a party salon, with an edge to the Republicans. Agricultural Commissioner Bob Crawford was the sole Democrat, and even he supported Jeb Bush for governor in 1998 and endorsed George W. Bush for president in 2000. How confident was the GOP that it would reclaim Florida, following Bill Clinton's resounding victory in the Sunshine State in 1996? "As George W. Bush considers potential running mates, here is an appealing choice," observed *Time* magazine in July 2000. "He is a popular young governor from the fourth largest state, one where Democrats hope to compete ferociously. . . . He is beloved among many Latino voters, a crucial voting bloc. He is Roman Catholic . . . And he has star appeal as a scion of one of the most famous political families." The trouble is his name is Bush." George W. Bush selected Richard Cheney of Wyoming for his running mate in 2000.[53]

Yet Democrats expressed optimism in winning Florida's 25 electoral votes.

After all, the Party of Jefferson and Jackson still benefited from a 380,000 margin in registered voters. Almost 9 million Floridians registered to vote in 2000. In late September, *Time* magazine quoted several Republican leaders who felt "Bush had squandered his summer lead in Florida." One such leader was Governor Jeb Bush, who hedged, "George doesn't have to win Florida to win the election." *Time* commented, Florida "is supposed to be Bush country," adding that perhaps Jeb wished to lower expectations to "avoid blame." The journalist concluded that "Florida was never a sure thing for Bush. . . . It's a moderate state with one Republican and one Democrat in the Senate. . . . It's as diverse as America, and thus, the first battleground state."[54]

If both parties understood that Florida was indispensable to winning the presidency, neither party had taken the Sunshine State seriously in previous elections. Nor had Floridians blazed political trails to leadership positions in either party. Political scientist Darryl Paulson observed in 2017, "Of the 10 most populous states, only Florida . . . never had anyone elected speaker of the House, majority or minority leader of the House of Senate, or never had anyone serve as vice president or president."[55]

The Changing Battlefield and Tools of Political War

Both major parties understood that a new phenomenon threatened the traditional two-party system. In 2000, more than 1.5 million Floridians (17 percent of registered voters) checked the "other" category when registering, meaning they preferred a third party or, most likely, were asserting their independence, expressing their concerns and disillusionment by officially enrolling as independent. As late as 1972, scarcely 100,000 Floridians identified themselves as independents. Such behavior cut across the grain of American history. In the era following the Civil War, one would have been either very foolish or very rebellious *not* to enlist in the Democratic, Republican, Populist, Greenback, or Socialist ranks. Elections had consequences! But more and more Floridians and Americans felt alienated by the major parties in the era following Vietnam, Watergate, and Monicagate. Young persons, who neither liked nor identified with institutions, preferred causes to political parties.[56]

Florida's rootlessness reinforced the independence of voters. Independents and newcomers to Florida neither understood nor cared about the hoary social and political traditions peculiar to the Sunshine State. Once, embracing your family's deep roots to a place meant something to voters, but in Florida, newcomers did not have to join the same church as their parents or vote for candidates endorsed by unions or precinct committeemen. Once, the term "cracker" defined someone, often from the rural poor, who had descended from British or Scottish kin and prided themselves as a staunch democrat and Democrat. By 2000, the word's meaning had been so watered down that a cracker was simply someone who had been born in Florida or resided in Florida. Once an insult, the term "cracker" had become a badge of pride.[57]

The ghosts of Reconstruction politics and the Solid South lingered, evident in Florida election procedures. Most dramatically and disturbingly, large numbers of Floridians were ineligible to vote, despite the fact they were adult citizens. Disenfranchised because they were in prison or had been convicted of a felony, more than half were African American. One aspiring African-American voter, Cuffie Washington, was disfranchised because he had been convicted of stealing three oranges a month before the election. He was not alone.[58]

Not everyone had the freedom to express their political independence by voting for Ross Perot or Ralph Nader. Many Floridians could not even register to vote. Stunning numbers of Floridians, victims of their own actions but also of crass politics, were politically impotent because they had been convicted of a felony crime. In the post-Reconstruction South, Democratic legislatures, fearful of the possible political clout of African-American voters or, worse, a poor white and Black coalition, stripped voting rights from citizens who had been convicted of a felony. The governor and cabinet held the right to restore felons' rights but rarely did so. The racial and political correlation was as obvious in 1880 as 2000. But most states had acted to restore criminals' civil rights once their sentences had been served. Only Iowa, Kentucky, and Florida imposed lifetime bans for citizens released from prison. The numbers are staggering: one-half million Florida men and women—fully one-quarter of Florida's Black adults—are banned from the franchise because of this harsh law. In Florida, former criminals must petition to have their rights restored. The Clemency Board, composed of the governor and the cabinet, has become an especially stern reviewing body. Moreover, the law mandated removing the tainted ex-felons from the voter rolls. Critics charged that the Bush administration was purging the election rolls of African Americans and citizens who had served their penance and now requested atonement.[59]

Consider the cases of Willie Steen and Floredia Walker. Steen had been confused with a convict named Willie O'Steen. A veteran of the Persian Gulf War, Steen took his young son to the polls in Tampa. He was told that he could not vote because he was a convicted felon. Across the bay in St. Petersburg, Ms. Walker was also turned away for the same reason. An employee at the Department of Corrections, her identity had become conflated with that of a thief who had stolen her driver's license years earlier.[60]

Reconstruction-era politics collided with twenty-first-century technology and human foibles. Republican officials in Florida awarded a multimillion-dollar contract to a friendly private technology firm, Accenture, to help "scrub" former inmates from voter rolls, creating inaccurate voter registration lists. Despite warnings from critics and experts that the firm was botching the process by removing eligible voters in its zeal to please Republican officials, the new secretary of state, Katherine Harris, paid little heed and proceeded to disqualify more eligible voters. The *Nation*, a leading liberal magazine, charged that the governor and cabinet cost 50,000 Florida citizens the right to vote in the 2000 election. In 2001, the U.S. Civil Rights Commission released its report on the tainted election, placing the blame on Governor Bush. The Commission found that Black voters were "ten times more likely than white voters to have their ballots rejected." The study also criticized the flawed list of felons and ex-felons that resulted in a purge of legal voters.[61]

Increasingly, the term "I-4 Corridor" became a political trope, an essential talking point in understanding Florida elections. Since the mid-1960s and the construction of the Interstate Highway System, the Corridor became a population magnet. The area, ranging from Volusia County and Daytona Beach in the East to Hillsborough County and Pinellas County on the West Coast, resembled a microcosm of Florida and the United States. The 132-mile stretch of highway included retirees, Hispanics, farmers, soccer moms, and service and high-tech workers amid citrus groves, Disney World, and subdivisions. Moreover, the I-4 Corridor was politically competitive; more than half of the state's most closely divided counties could be found along the busy thoroughfare. "For a generation, American political scientists looked to California for a glimpse of the politics of the future," observed journalist David Shribman. By 2000, political scientists and politicians flocked to Florida to decipher the heavily trafficked runestone. The Republicans held a slight advantage, but every year the influx of new Floridians and voters shifted the balance. For instance, Orange and Osceola counties, once reliably Democratic, had become marginally Republican in the 1990s, until reshaped by Hispanic-leaning Democrats, principally Puerto Ricans. "Hardly a day goes by," opined a *New York Times* correspondent, "when one of the presidential or vice-presidential candidates, or a family member, or a prominent supporter from outside the state is not campaigning somewhere along this narrow corridor."[62]

North Florida had historically been the region most resembling the Solid

South. It was known as the "Black Belt" in the nineteenth century, not for its soil but for its concentration of enslaved Africans imported to harvest cotton. Benefiting from a malapportioned legislature, North Florida sent to Tallahassee and Washington some of Florida's most famous Yellow Dog Democrats, individuals who would sooner vote for a yellow dog before he or she would vote for a Republican. Bob Sikes, Dempsey Barron, and Scott Dilworth Clarke epitomized the cadre. Richard Nixon and Ronald Reagan connected to white North Floridians as much as George McGovern and Michael Dukakis alienated them. Yellow Dog Democrats were becoming Blue Dog Democrats. "Put crudely," writes historian David Colburn, "these dogs claimed they were being choked blue by the leash placed around their necks by the federal government and that they wouldn't necessarily 'go home from the dance with the one who brung 'em.'" How these disenchanted Democrats and independents voted would determine the presidential election. An October poll commissioned by the Democratic Party indicated that North Florida and the Panhandle were leaning Republican by a margin of greater than two to one.[63]

One of the most striking results of the 1998 gubernatorial race was not Jeb Bush's triumph but rather, argues journalist S. V. Dáte, the election's "seismic event" was Jeb's winning 14 percent of the Black vote. "On its face," writes Dáte, "that may not seem like a big deal, but to close observers of American politics, it was extraordinary; not just a Republican, but a *conservative* Republican who four years earlier had offered blacks at best casual indifference had attracted fully 1 out of every 7 black voters, perhaps double what the typical Republican candidate was used to seeing."[64]

But Governor Bush quickly dissipated any goodwill he had garnered with state Black leaders by aggressively tackling hot-button social issues, most notably affirmative action in education. A conservative California firebrand, Ward Connerly, was forcing states to put the question of affirmative action on the ballot. Governor Bush, wishing to avoid the lightning rod brushing his brother, moved decisively to end affirmative action in Florida with his "One Florida" plan. In place of race or gender, universities and colleges would accept all students in the top 20 percent of their class. Some educators praised the new plan, arguing that students from poor districts generally fared poorly when competing against suburban, predominantly white schools. Tellingly, Bush had not communicated with African-American leaders about his bold plan. When the Florida Legislature convened in January 2000, a large, vociferous, predominantly Black crowd estimated at 10,000 protested the new governor's policies. Many brandished signs reading "Jeb Crow." The opposition was led by Florida state Senator Kendrick Meek, who with fellow legislator Tony Hill staged a sit-in demonstration in the governor's office to protest Bush's One Florida initiative. Bush's obstinacy had consequences. "Without Meek," argues Dáte, "George W. would have won Florida easily, just as most Democratic and Republican politicos had been predicting early on in 2000."[65]

The Election of the Century

The election of 2000 occurred during a time of peace, prosperity, and confidence. For all the melodrama of the Clinton presidency, 1993–2001, the economy boomed, and the national debt shrank. Homeownership zoomed to historic rates. With the Cold War over, candidates Gore and Bush debated over how best to use the money America saved through no longer needing to be the world's policeman. Gore elaborated his plan, "I will keep Social Security in a lockbox, that pays down the national debt and the interest savings I would put back into Social Security." Bush proposed the idea of allowing young Americans to opt out of Social Security and invest in their own retirement accounts. Gore's undisguised condescension, his pronounced sighs and gestures may not have endeared him to voters, but comedians loved the theatrics. For those fatigued by the drone of campaign commercials and talking heads, Darrell Hammond and Will Ferrell caricatured the ponderous Gore and the bumbling Bush on *Saturday Night Live*. Analysts and actors debated whether the satire was influencing voters. Ferrell believed that his performance may have humanized the real George W. Bush. Hammond, however, felt that his portrayal of Gore as robotic and lifeless probably hurt the real-life candidate. Ironically, Gore and Bush shared remarkably similar backgrounds: the sons of powerful fathers and impressionable mothers, graduates of elite preparatory schools, and Ivy League educations.[66]

Bush and Gore crisscrossed Florida more than thirty times. But the tickets were crowded, leading to ballot-traffic jams. Ralph Nader ran for president on the Green Party ticket. A brilliant lawyer, always on point and utterly lacking a sense of humor, Nader had gained fame in the 1960s suing General Motors for deadly negligence. His supporters came largely from the liberal ranks who, like their mid-nineteenth-century predecessors, preferred burning down the barn to supporting the lesser of two evils. The Bush camp helped make sure that Nader qualified to be on the November ballot, just as Gore staffers were pleased to see the name of Pat Buchanan there as well. Buchanan, a speechwriter for President Richard Nixon, relished his role as a take-no-prisoners conservative candidate for the Reform Party. "Hoping to boost Ralph Nader in states where he is threatening to hurt Al Gore," the AP reported in late October, "a Republican group is launching TV ads featuring Nader attacking the vice president [Gore]."[67]

Then came the November surprise. Five days before the election, Fox News broke the story that Bush failed to disclose a 1976 arrest in Maine for DUI. Humiliated, he confessed, "I have been straightforward with the people, saying that I used to drink too much in the past." Bush had gone straight and become a teetotaler. "Not disclosing the DUI on my terms may have been the single costliest political mistake I ever made," wrote Bush in his autobiography. Advisor Karl Rove believed that more than 2 million voters either stayed home or changed their votes because of the scandal. "I may have just cost myself the presidency," Bush admitted.[68]

On election eve and Election Day 2000, the Democratic running mates frantically flitted from Miami Beach to Tampa, hoping to nail down victory. In a West Tampa clubhouse, Joe Lieberman asked the largely Hispanic audience, "Do you get the feeling that Florida might be important in this election?" A rim shot seemed more appropriate than a question mark. Al Gore reminded the crowd that Tampa was the team's last campaign stop, "because Florida may well be *the* state that decides the outcome of this election." Whereas Tampa's third-generation Cubans were passionate Democrats, a rally at the Orange Bowl in Miami attracted angry Cuban Republicans. A press conference was held at Elián's home in Little Havana. Activist Armando Gutiérrez exhorted, "It's important to remind people that this is how you get even—at the polls." Meanwhile, "Dubya," chronicled correspondent Jake Tapper, "traveled to Tennessee and Arkansas, 'flipping the political bird to Gore and President Clinton.'"[69]

With computers and polling becoming more sophisticated, election nights were becoming boring. The last nail-biting election cliffhanger had been Ford vs. Carter in 1976 and Nixon vs. Humphry in 1968. Until Bush vs. Gore. The longest day, 7 November 2000, was also the longest night. November 2000 proved to be the most melodramatic, drawn-out election month in American history. It was overtime without a clock, as lawyers assumed the roles of yapping coaches. Computer models crashed. NBC reporter Tim Russert was reduced to writing the name "Florida, Florida, Florida" on a crude chalkboard. "Get out your slates," he announced. CBS's Dan Rather, sprinkling Texas folklore, called the race in Florida "hot enough to peel house paint." Baby boomers smiled when Rather quipped that the election is "closer than Lassie and Timmy." Shifting to New Age speak, he called the race "as tight as a Botox smile."[70]

Rather had inherited his CBS anchor post from Walter Cronkite, the most trusted man in the media, perhaps in America. "Let's get one thing straight from the get-go," he assured viewers, "If we say somebody's carried a state, you can pretty much take it to the bank. Book it!" And then the world cratered around the Bush camp when CBS and then the other networks broke the news that Al Gore had taken Florida. Rather quipped the loss of Florida meant Bush's chances "were shakier than cafeteria Jell-O." At 7:48 p.m. Eastern Standard Time, Senator Bob Graham was being interviewed by Brian Williams on MSNBC when an announcer declared Gore a winner in Florida. The senator who once seemed a likely running mate with Gore, pumped his fist in victory. Later, he paused, thinking, "I was both happy but somewhat mystified, because I thought it was awfully early to be calling the state." Graham's political instincts proved more reliable than malfunctioning machines, the result of human and computer errors. To the consternation and anger of Republicans, the projections came as Floridians in six counties were still voting in the Central Time Zone west of the Apalachicola River. "Oh waiter," CNN's Jeff Greenfield sighed, "One order of crow." A journalist reported that upon hearing the press announce a Gore victory, "Jeb reportedly apologized in tears."[71]

The Four Seasons Hotel in Austin, Texas, may have been the most freaked-out room in America on the evening of 7 November 2000. George Herbert Walker, Barbara Bush, and their sons watched the election results unfold at the presidential suite. The secret service secured the entire floor. The announcement that Gore won Florida was as deflating as it was explosive. The two Bush brothers, reported a journalist, quarreled so much that their father had to intervene. A devastated George and Laura Bush eventually retired for the night. "The car ride back to the Governor's Mansion was quiet. There isn't much to say when you lose," candidate Bush remembered. A frantic phone call came from chief strategist Karl Rove. He was defiant and angry. The kingmaker insisted that the exit polls were wrong; indeed, by 9:55 p.m. Eastern Standard Time, the networks retracted their previous bombshell, announcing that Florida remained in play. Jeb told reporters the next day, "I hope I never have to go through another evening like I did." He added, "It was one of the most amazing and emotionally intense evenings of my life." Journalist S. V. Dáte put it another way: "If election night 1994 was the worst in Jeb's life, election night 2000 was a close second."[72]

After eight years of battling the Clintons, Fox News was energized and determined that conservatism would triumph in 2000. The network was deeply rooted in Florida. In 1990, Roger Ailes purchased WPLS, an AM radio station near his condo in Port St. Lucie. He reorganized the radio station from an oldies format to talk radio. He introduced Rush Limbaugh to Florida's Treasure Coast. In 1996, media mogul Rupert Murdoch tapped Ailes to serve as the CEO of Fox

News. Ailes, who had entered the realm of politics when he worked as a media consultant for presidential candidate Richard Nixon in 1960, learned from the master the political power of resentment against liberal cultural elites. "Individual issues would come and go," wrote historian David Greenberg, "but the attacks on liberals as elite, out of touch and protective of the 'wrong people' came from the same playbook." Ailes also learned from Nixon the value of attacking the mainstream news media. The *New York Times* summarized Ailes's contributions to the 2000 election and American politics. "He was not alone in believing that the mainstream news media was leaving part of America behind—his own part—while abetting a liberal agenda in Washington. Nor was he the only person to come up with the idea of a news network that would have a special appeal to conservative-leaning Americans." The *Times* concluded, "But he was the first to truly pull it off."[73]

On the afternoon of the 2000 election, Fox's conservative brain trust gathered in a conference room. John Prescott Ellis, first cousin of George W. Bush, briefed the luminaries, including Roger Ailes, Brit Hume, Fred Barnes, Bill Kristol, and Michael Barone. Ailes had appointed Ellis chief of Fox's "Decision Desk." In hindsight, Fox might have called it the "Indecision Desk." Ellis brought depressing news for his kinfolk: Al Gore was sweeping the votes of late deciders, and even worse, was winning Florida. Following the briefing, Ellis received a telephone call from candidate Bush, asking his thoughts about the election. "I have no idea," he responded. Later that day, Ellis briefed senior Fox executives about the election. Ailes asked, "What's your gut say?" Playing the roles of oracle and charades pantomime, Ellis pretended to slash a knife across his throat. Critics savaged Fox for using a candidate's relative as a political consultant, one whose thumb tipped the scale to call the race for Bush.[74]

As if the election needed more melodrama, a Voter News Service (VNS) worker mistakenly entered 43,023 Florida votes for Gore into the computer instead of the correct number, 4,301. The Florida numbers game suddenly tilted in favor of the GOP. John Prescott Ellis may well have been the first journalist to call Florida for Bush. Shortly before 2:00 a.m., Wednesday morning, Ellis called his cousin George W. to inform him of the turn of fate: "I think you've got it." Not everyone agreed with Ellis's optimism.[75]

At precisely 2:16 a.m., the television commentator Brit Hume trumpeted: "Fox News now projects George W. Bush the winner in Florida, and thus, it appears, the winner of the presidency of the United States." Less than a minute later, Tom Brokaw and Dan Rather confirmed the news, even though the two candidates were separated by only 1,000 votes in Florida. Graciously, Gore telephoned Bush to concede, remarking, "We sure gave them a cliffhanger." By 3:57 a.m., the networks reversed their earlier calls: the race was too close to call. But Gore's advisors quickly pointed out that key Democratic-heavy precincts in Broward, Palm Beach, and Miami-Dade counties had yet to be counted. Gore then revoked his concession in an awkward exchange with his opponent. Bush recalled the scenario: "I had never heard of a candidate un-conceding. I told him that in Texas, it meant something when a person gave you his word." An indignant Gore famously snapped back, "You don't have to get snippy about it." Bush explained that the networks had made the correct call; indeed, his brother confirmed the numbers. Gore ended the conversation, snapping, "Your little brother is not the ultimate authority on this." Angry, W. told his family that he was going to declare victory, but Jeb cautioned, "George, don't do it. The count is too close."[76]

The networks had not only blown one critical call in the 2000 election drama, but two. "We don't just have egg on our face," admitted NBC's Tom Brokaw, "We have an omelet." Dan Rather had promised viewers that when CBS announced a winner, you could take it to the bank. By early Wednesday morning, a bank panic had begun. Tom Rosensteil, a student of the media, put events in perspective: "I'm not sure television has ever had as bad a night as this." Panic notwithstanding, Americans also tuned in. An astonishing 22 percent of American homes had their televisions on between 2:00 a.m. and 3:00 a.m. CBS anchor Dan Rather, as usual, put the 3:00 a.m. events into perspective: "Florida has just wobbled into Weirdsville."[77]

About this time, Don Evans, chair of the Bush/Cheney 2000 campaign, phoned the suddenly most important person in the Free World: forty-three-year-old Florida secretary of state Katherine Harris. In Florida, the secretary of state also served as the state's chief elections officer. Harris's duties included certifying the election results. She also happened to serve as a co-chair of the Florida Bush Campaign. Evans recalled his testy exchange: "What do you mean you are in bed? Do you understand that the election is in the balance? What's going on?" Ms. Harris immediately called the Bush war room in Austin that evening on her state-paid cell phone. Later, she explained that she had loaned her phone to the state Republican chair, who made the call.[78]

The former Miss Polk Agriculture, granddaughter of citrus magnate Ben Hill Griffin Jr., and a two-term state senator, Harris was more complicated than the "naïve bureaucrat caught in the headlights" media caricature. Her family included citrus barons and bankers but also Christian missionaries who dedicated their lives in Africa and India. She was also well-educated, studying in Spain and Switzerland, and earning a graduate degree in public administration at Harvard.[79]

But Katherine Harris knew a great deal more about Byzantine art than about the byzantine world of election law. For advice, she hired the law firm of Steel, Hector & Davis, a powerful legal team with ties to Governor Bush. Although both Harris and Governor Bush deny the allegations, several reporters claimed that the two participants exchanged emails during the recount. Harris and Jeb Bush were delegates at the Republican National Convention, and she campaigned in New Hampshire for George W. Bush. She and Jeb have never released the emails they exchanged during the recount.[80]

More than a few politicians and lawyers scratched their heads wondering exactly who the ultimate authority might be. Peter Marks of the *New York Times* explained, "It was all part of an extraordinary night of political television." On election night, the *Miami Herald*'s Dave Wilson was assistant managing editor. Around 2:00 a.m., he ordered a press run with the headline "BUSH WINS IT." An hour later, totally confused, he "made a phone call that usually only happens in the movies. 'We have to stop!'" Hours later, Wilson approved the headline "NOT OVER YET." At 3:45 a.m., the election was so close that the word "recount" echoed across America. The media soon dubbed the agonizing process to follow as "The Great Recount."[81]

When Americans awoke the morning after, Bush led Gore by a mere 1,784 votes. He who stood atop the Sunshine State vote count would determine who became president. Considering that more than 5.8 million Floridians voted, the margin was thin and the stakes were monumental. Clay Roberts held the position of director of the Division of Elections. Secretary of State Harris was his supervisor. Roberts, in compliance with the Florida State Constitution, ordered an official recount in all sixty-seven counties. All but three counties quickly retabulated their votes, reducing Bush's lead to 362.[82]

"I was confronted with the most bizarre personnel choice of my public life: Whom to send to Florida to ensure that our lead was protected?" recalled Bush. The choice was obvious: James Addison Baker III. For the Princeton graduate and former Marine, a powerful Houston lawyer and kingmaker, it was not Baker's first rodeo: he had been responsible for running five consecutive Republican presidential campaigns. Al Gore asked the veteran Democratic advisor and warhorse Warren Christopher to head the Florida recount. "Warren Christopher was primarily a lawyer with a sideline in politics," explained historian Jean Edward Smith, whereas "Baker was a politician with a sideline in the law." Planes carrying Baker, Christopher, and an army of lawyers headed to Tallahassee, Florida.[83]

In a chess match, the Gore team moved to order a hand count of 1.8 million presidential ballots in four Democratic strongholds: Volusia, Palm Beach, Broward, and Miami-Dade. On talk shows, election law experts questioned why the Gore camp had not requested a full recount in all sixty-seven counties. On 11 November, the Bush team countered with a federal injunction to halt the hand count, citing the equal protection clause of the U.S. Constitution.[84]

The Great Recount

For thirty-seven days, America watched the Great Recount, as parties "lawyered up," enlisting a who's who of attorneys, advisors, and future luminaries and bores. Perhaps the most grateful beneficiary of the presidential recount was George Koikos. "What a great country this is, God bless America!," the Greek immigrant exclaimed. He was the proprietor of Georgio's, a Tallahassee restaurant that became a favorite hangout of the nation's lawyers in November 2000. Remembered Lucy Morgan, the *St. Petersburg Times* Tallahassee bureau chief: "In one room you might find former Secretary of State Warren Christopher, the chief negotiator for Vice President Al Gore, sitting at a table filled with Democrats. Across the restaurant would be former Secretary of State James Baker dining with Republican legal teams representing Gov. George W. Bush." Laurence Tribe, the Harvard constitutional law professor and head of the Gore defense team, joylessly recalled "a fog of sleepless nights, bad pizza and mediocre wine."[85]

Warren Christopher hoped that he and Baker could at least negotiate and settle the ground rules for the recount. "Baker," wrote legal observer Jeffrey Toobin, "recognized that the race for the Presidency was the ultimate zero-sum game, and he decided not to yield on a single question. Under Christopher, the Gore forces both preached and practiced restraints. . . . The difference between the two sides, and between the two men, was immediately apparent and central to the final result." Political scientist Lance deHaven-Smith concurs with Toobin's assessment. The Bush team "feared that a recount in any form might give sufficient additional votes to Gore for him to be declared the winner. Hence they immediately began to sow doubts about Florida's election laws and the reliability of manual recounts."[86]

Clearly, the award for most valuable player in the Great Recount was Governor Jeb Bush. Focused and on point, he knew what levers to pull and phone calls to make. The governor's communications director, Katie Baur, summarized her boss's role in a July 2001 explanation: "While he [Jeb Bush] recused himself from any involvement in what happened after Nov. 7, he did not recuse himself from his role as brother." He also did not recuse himself from providing Katherine Harris with advice and advisors.[87]

The recount attracted an extraordinary group of young and coming future legal and political luminaries. A future U.S. senator and three U.S. Supreme Court justices rallied to the tocsin of *Bush v. Gore.* For five weeks, twenty-nine-year-old policy advisor Rafael Edward Cruz managed to anger, bore, and alienate almost everyone in Tallahassee he encountered. The *New York Times* profiled Cruz, describing him as infused with "hyper-intelligence, crackling ambition and a laundry list of impeccable insider credentials." Cruz was joined by a young lawyer who worked on Bush's legal team. Brett Kavanaugh arrived as a boy-wonder lawyer already accustomed to the rarefied air of Inside Washington. Raised in Bethesda, Maryland, educated at Georgetown Preparatory School and Yale University, the not-yet thirty-year-old lawyer had already clerked for Supreme Court Justice Anthony Kennedy when he accepted a fateful job offer to join a powerful law firm. Ken Starr persuaded Kavanaugh to join the firm, which then was investigating the Clinton presidency, specifically the accusations of fraud in an Arkansas land deal and the "suicide" of White House deputy counsel Vince Foster. In August 1998, he served as associate independent counsel for the "brain trust" that researched the Monica Lewinsky affair. It was Kavanaugh who wrote the *Starr Report* and proposed confronting the president with a list of X-rated questions regarding the president's intimate relationship with a White House intern. He advised Starr not to give the president "any break." Another future U.S. Supreme Court justice who rallied to the Bush standard was John Roberts. On 6 December 2000, Jeb Bush emailed Roberts: "Thanks you for your time today. I really appreciate your input on my role in this unique and historic situation." In 2020, U.S. Supreme Court Justice Ruth Bader Ginsburg died in late September. Republican President Donald Trump seized upon the opportunity to appoint a conservative justice. He chose Judge Amy Coney Barrett. In 2000, she was working for the powerful law firm of Baker Botts, arriving in Tallahassee to provide the Bush legal "briefing and research" in *Bush v. Gore.*[88]

Jake Tapper, then a correspondent for Salon.com, summarized the immediate postelection scene: "One thing becomes crystal clear very early on in the whole damn mess: Florida election law—especially as it pertains to recounts—is chaos." He followed: "Statutes collide. Provisions are vague. Unlike in other states, those supervising the process are often the harshest of partisans. And, most insanely, the standard by which ballots are assessed is vague, requiring that one assess the 'intent of the voter,' a gauge that can be interpreted differently in different counties. Especially if the counties use punch-card ballots."[89]

Palm Beach County emerged as the poster child of dysfunction. Election canvassing boards resembled Talmudic scholars, as members argued, pleaded, and cried as they attempted to understand voter intentions on ballots tainted by hanging, pregnant, and dimpled chads. Photographs depict the beleaguered officials, some holding the ballots skyward, others using magnifying lens to determine whether chads with one or more corners still attached should count as a completed or incomplete vote. A perfect storm descended upon the sprawling geopolitical unit ranging from Briny Breezes to Belle Glade, from Hypoluxo to Pahokee. Human errors foiled the most earnest intentions. In 1978, the county had installed a state-of-the-art voting machine, dubbed the Votomatic. The machines were also the last punch-card voting device used in Florida or the United States. Votomatic punch cards were first employed in 1963 as an inexpensive, high-tech solution to counting ballots. "In fact," editorialized the *New York Times,* "Votomatic might more appropriately have been called the Countamatic, for what it automated was the counting of ballots. To mark a ballot with the Votomatic, you slide the ballot into the machine, over two tabs to hold the ballot in place, and punch holes with a stylus."[90]

The machine's flaws had long been exposed. In 1988, candidate Buddy MacKay lost a close U.S. Senate race to Republican Connie Mack III, a contest in which one in twelve Miami-Dade County votes were deemed invalid because of machine malfunction. Howard Kleinberg, one of the state's most respected journalists, complained, "Voters should not and cannot be disenfranchised because the current system of vote counting has a built-in glitch, to wit: If the chad is left attached to the ballot, it may cover the hole again in the recount and not count as a vote cast." Broward and Miami-Dade counties also employed Votomatic machines.[91]

The gremlin-like chad also contributed to a problem known as "undervotes." *Time* magazine defined "undervotes" as "ballots that contain votes in some races but not all. Sometimes undervotes are intentional; the voters simply couldn't decide on a candidate, so that part of the ballot was left blank. But sometimes the machine reading a ballot misses a vote that was cast. But sometimes the machine reading the ballot misses a vote that was cast. . . . a chad isn't fully dislodged." Lawyers discovered Florida election law contained no mention of undervotes. Fully 61,000 undervoted ballots became in the words of Phil Beck, a Bush lawyer, "spoilation."[92]

The confusing ballot design aggravated the malfunctioning Votomatics. Ironically, the ballot had been designed to assist elderly voters navigate the ballot. Theresa LePore, the county's veteran supervisor of elections and a registered independent, was confronted with a challenge of how to squeeze the names of ten presidential candidates and their running mates on one page. She decided to enlarge the type, which required the names to be spread across two pages. Despite its designers' good intentions, the "butterfly ballot" flummoxed elderly voters. Twenty-nine thousand ballots were thrown out—fully 4 percent of the votes in Palm Beach County—for reasons ranging from two or more votes for president to faulty punch holes to hanging chads. "Voters confused by Palm Beach County's butterfly ballot cost Al Gore the presidency," concluded the local newspaper. The press ridiculed LePore as "Madame Butterfly." LePore had begun working as a file clerk at the Palm Beach County Elections Office in 1971, when she was a high school student. In 1996 the local newspaper endorsed her for supervisor, applauding her "image of fairness and impartiality" and crediting her for the office's leadership "in terms of technological innovation and voter services."[93]

The unlikely beneficiary was the presidential candidate who had been accused of anti-Semitism and had not even campaigned in Kings Point, Lantana, or Boca Raton. Bush publicist Ari Fleischer played the role of the straight man, explaining the anomaly to reporters, "Palm Beach County is a Pat Buchanan stronghold." There, Patrick Buchanan received 3,704 votes, fully 20 percent of his total vote harvest in Florida. A Palm Beach county commissioner was shocked when he heard 37 residents of Kings Point, a Democratic retiree bulwark, had voted for Buchanan. "You can knock on every door in Kings Point and you wouldn't find 10 votes for Buchanan." Yet the Republican man-of-the-hour also received 950 votes in Century Village, a retirement complex largely populated with Democrat-leaning Jews. When the predominantly Jewish residents of the Lakes of Delray retirement community found out that Pat Buchanan received 47 votes, they exploded. "Impossible," insisted Shirley Datz, a retired systems analyst. "Even one vote for Buchanan would be impossible here." No other Palm Beach County precinct or Florida precinct registered more votes for the gunslinging Buchanan than Precinct 162G.[94]

While no other Florida county copied the butterfly ballot, election chaos was hardly limited to Palm Beach. Altogether, some 50,000 Florida voters went to the polls only to have their votes disqualified because the ballots were "spoiled." While conspiracy theorists point to a vast right-wing conspiracy, most analysts attribute the spoiled ballots to defective technology piled upon human foibles and errors. Miami-Dade County discarded 26,000 overvotes due to the electorate voting for more than one candidate. One must admire the honesty of the Orange County election supervisor explaining Election Day glitches: "Where does their stupidity [poll workers] enter into the picture?" Refreshingly, Orange County voters reelected Bill Cowles, the election supervisor, four years later! Osceola County experienced a voting machine glitch. A faulty computer in Volusia County deleted 16,000 votes from Gore's count. At one point, sheriff's deputies placed yellow tape around the elections' office, reminiscent of a crime scene. In Gadsden County, Florida's last remaining Black-majority county, election officials disqualified 12 percent of Blacks' ballots. Outdated voter registration lists allowed more than 1,200 felons to cast their ballots illegally.[95]

On 22 November 2000, the Miami-Dade County canvassing board began examining almost 11,000 disputed ballots that had never been counted. In the HBO film *Recount*, James Baker, realizing the desperation of the moment, orders his team, "Get me Roger Stone." U.S. Representative John Sweeney, aka "Congressman Kick-Ass," of New York and Roger J. Stone Jr., self-proclaimed agent provocateur and master of the arts of political dirty tricks, rallied fellow Republican partisans to "shut it down." A resident of Florida, a place Stone famously described as "a sunny place for shady people," Sunshine State fate and destiny had brought the political bad boy to put his thumb on the scale of justice. It was Stone who said famously, "One man's dirty trickster is another man's freedom fighter." In "Stone's Rules," his guide to life and politics, he instructs: "Hate is a stronger motivator than love," and "Admit nothing, deny everything, launch counterattack." Stone had paid his dues to the GOP, first volunteering as an undergraduate student in 1972 for Richard Nixon, whom he immortalized in a tattoo on his back! In 2000, Stone had initially worked on Pat Buchanan's Reform Party campaign but joined the Bush forces during the recount. Stone explained that he orchestrated the "riot" from a van, employing a walkie-talkie while snooping on the Democratic recount team.[96]

The protestors, who purportedly wore Hermès ties and khaki slacks, crowded the nineteenth floor of the Stephen Clark Government Center in Miami to make their presence known during the vote recount. "Republicans," observed *Time* magazine, "not usually known for takin' it to the streets," got what they wanted. Elections officials abruptly canceled the hand recount. History remembers the episode as the "Brooks Brothers Riot." Senator Bob Graham remembers the episode differently: "They [Republicans] clearly intended to intimidate the canvassing board and apparently were successful on that."[97]

In an electrifying moment, Katherine Harris became the most famous state secretary of state in American history when she stepped to the microphones on 27 November 2000 and announced, "Accordingly, on behalf of the state Elections Canvassing Commission and in accordance with the laws of the state of Florida, I hereby declare that Gov. George W. Bush the winner of Florida's 25 electoral votes for the president of the United States."[98]

Constitutionally, Secretary of State Harris was responsible for managing state elections. A Republican, she was also co-chair of the George W. Bush election campaign in Florida. The election catapulted Secretary Harris to a tumultuous fifteen minutes of fame. "For her role in the election," observed a reporter, "she was skewered as nakedly partisan and parodied on *Saturday Night Live* as an ambitious harpy caked in enough makeup to embarrass a drag queen." Harris, deeply hurt by the unmerciful caricatures, pleaded, "I don't wear blue eye shadow!" She was later portrayed in an over-the-top performance by Laura Dern in the 2008 HBO film *Recount.* Harris, an intensely religious individual, sought solace in her faith. Even here, the press poked fun when she confessed that she felt like the Old Testament's Esther, the queen of the Jews. "If I perish, I perish," Harris quoted Esther. Harris also channeled her inner Boss Plunkitt of Tammany Hall. The State of Florida paid $4 million to Data Technologies to produce a list of eligible Florida voters. From voter registration rolls, the firm purged 58,000 individuals branded ineligible to vote, largely because they were identified as convicted felons. The new voter roster, accepted by Secretary Harris, was terribly flawed. For example, the new list turned up one such ineligible voter, Linda Howell, who happened to be Madison County's supervisor of elections! When the Monroe County supervisor of elections scanned the purged list, he found the names of his father and an employee![99]

On 8 December 2000, the Florida Supreme Court seemingly handed the Gore camp a timely victory. Florida's sharply divided, liberal-leaning, and largely Democratic-appointed Supreme Court voted 4–3, ordering a statewide manual recount affecting Miami-Dade County and all other counties where undervotes had not been tabulated. The court majority then ordered a total of 283 votes from Palm Beach and Miami-Dade counties to be added to the Gore ticket. Party faithful hailed chief legal counsel for Gore, David Boies, a dragon slayer, a modern Clarence Darrow. Critics argued the recount was flawed because officials focused on the undervotes—hanging and dimpled chads, etc. But the Florida Supreme Court failed to establish clear standards regarding the questionable votes, such as what to do with a dimpled ballot or one with a hanging chad. The Bush camp promptly appealed the Florida Supreme Court ruling to the U.S. Supreme Court. One of the Bush lawyers, Jim Bopp, argued that the Florida recount violated the Constitution's Fourteenth Amendment guarantee of equal protection due to the inconsistent standards as to how to tabulate votes.[100]

Just three days later, the oral arguments began in the U.S. Supreme Court. Ultimately, the U.S. Supreme Court resolved the constitutional crisis in its *per curiam* opinion in *George W. Bush v. Albert Gore Jr. et al.* (2000). The Supreme Court justices delivered six separate opinions, but on the key decision, the five conservative justices ruled on the matter of the Equal Protection Clause. They argued that the Florida Supreme Court, in its decision to order a recount of ballots, had violated Article II of the Constitution, that it is up to the states to set standards for the presidential election. Its holding, however, was based on the Equal Protection Clause of the Fourteenth Amendment of the Constitution, in this case the right to have ballots counted equally and fairly. In other words, the justices rejected the Florida Supreme Court's decision ordering recounts in four counties because the decision did not establish a uniform statewide standard to recount ballots. "Their decision ended the fight," writes historian Robert Patterson. By winning Florida, George H. Bush received 271 votes in the Electoral College and became the forty-third president of the United States.[101]

George W. Bush won Florida by a total of 537 votes. Fully 70.1 percent of registered Floridians—5,963,253 voters—participated in the election. Nationally, Al Gore had received more than a half million more votes than his opponent; indeed, the Tennessean received more votes than any previous Democrat, and more votes than any candidate except Ronald Reagan in 1984. Strikingly, Gore lost nine states that President Clinton carried in 1996.

Forests of trees and warehouses of computer chips have been sacrificed trying to solve the riddle of the 2000 election. Yet so many questions remain. Why did Gore not ask President Clinton to campaign in his behalf? Clinton, despite the Monica Lewinsky episode or because of Congress's ham-fisted efforts to impeach the president, remained a very popular chief executive. Clinton might have helped in Arkansas and Tennessee, states Gore lost. In his autobiography, *My Life*, Bill Clinton repeatedly noted how he traveled the country supporting Democratic candidates who had requested his assistance. While supportive of his vice president, he never addressed why he rarely appeared at Gore rallies. Journalist John F. Harris contends that Gore and many others misunderstood the meaning of the Lewinsky scandal: "He [Clinton] survived because he persuaded a majority that the scandal was not about sex. . . . It was about power. And in power battles, the question that matters most is not 'What is the truth?' It is instead, 'What side are you on?'"[102]

Clio, the muse of history, with one eye on 7 November 2000, and the other eye on 11 September 2001, concluded that George W. Bush was most likely elected president because of Florida's Muslim vote. That conclusion was first announced by GOP strategist Grover Norquist shortly after the November election. One calculation concluded that the Muslim vote in Florida favored Bush by 14,000 votes over Gore. The election was decided by 537 votes. The Bush campaign reached out to Muslims more than Gore's; moreover, Bush had promised in the debates to repeal the Secret Evidence Act, a Clinton-era law that largely targeted Muslims and Arabs.[103]

Many other questions about the election linger. Why did the Gore camp ask for a recount only in the four heavily Democratic counties? A lengthy study commissioned by eight news organizations concluded that George W. Bush would still narrowly have won the race. Some independent investigations turned up serious allegations that democracy was denied to ethnic and racial minorities, as well as individuals refused a ballot because they were incorrectly identified as convicted felons. Cynics question Al Gore's choice of his running mate. Was it because Lieberman had denounced Bill Clinton's moral conduct in the White House, or was it the Connecticut senator's appeal to Jewish voters? Gore, reasoned David Remnick, "felt that Clinton had never publicly owned up to it [the affair]." Had Senator Bob Graham, not Joe Lieberman, been asked to join the ticket, Gore would have won Florida and become president. What if Democratic U.S. Senator Joe Lieberman had not opined that election officials should give the "benefit of the doubt" to military voters? In the six elections contested by the Bush father and sons, the family had averaged 52 percent of Floridians' votes. Bob Graham won five statewide elections averaging 61 percent of the vote. Finally, mistakes botched the election. More than 110,000 overvotes were never counted because of human or machine errors. The *Miami Herald*'s investigative team concluded, "But weeks after the election, actual ballot inspections by *Herald* reporters and some election supervisors found that hundreds or even thousands of valid votes would have been redeemable, if only someone had examined them in time."[104]

A pricklier question asks the impact of Ralph Nader's Green Party. To draw the simplest conclusion, if Bush won Florida by only 537 votes, and if Nader received 97,488 votes, and most of these votes came at the expense of the Democratic candidate, the cantankerous lawyer played the role of spoiler. When asked on the eve of the election how he would feel about George W. Bush as president, a man he ridiculed as "a joke," Nader reasoned, "A bumbling Texas governor would galvanize the environmental community as never before." One could also blame the Socialist Party candidate, David McReynolds, who corralled 622 votes in Florida. For months thereafter, the Socialist Party campaign office voice mail reminded voters, "It's not our fault that Al Gore lost Florida."[105]

But why would Green Party candidate Ralph Nader kneecap Al Gore, described by author Michael Grunwald as "one of the most earth-friendly presidential candidates in history"? George W. Bush was never a champion of Everglades restoration. Grunwald points to "the bizarre swamp politics of the Everglades" as the reason George Bush edged out his rival. A single decision haunted Gore: his refusal to condemn a Clinton initiative to convert the Homestead Air Force Base, badly damaged by Hurricane Andrew, into a commercial airport. Environmentalist Nathaniel Reed believed that single decision cost Gore 10,000 votes. "To some Democrats," writes Grunwald, "the story of Gore and the airport shows how the environmental movement eats its own." Ironically, the Homestead airport was never built.[106]

Florida's attorney general, Bob Butterworth, who also served as state co-chair for the Gore campaign, was an invaluable ally. Butterworth also happened to be an expert in a suddenly valuable field: Florida election law. He had survived a very close election early in his career. It was Butterworth who informed Charles Brunson, Gore's chief of staff, that if an election is decided by a half percent or less, "Florida law requires an automatic recount." The Bush camp criticized Butterworth for his partisan opinions regarding election law.[107]

Florida's enfeebled voting process came under savage fire. "As a result," concluded the *Miami Herald*, "the world's most luminous icon of democracy resembled a banana republic." The U.S. Commission on Civil Rights demanded reforms to guarantee minority voters access to the polls. The *Washington Post*, *New York Times*, and other media demonstrated the power and eloquence of investigative journalism. The words "collusion," and "conspiracy" came up frequently.[108]

Editorial firing squads shot the deserving and innocent. "In the center of these apparent conspiracies was Katherine Harris," writes political scientist Lance deHaven-Smith. "Harris was probably most to blame for election and post-election disorder even if she had not been party to criminal conspiracies, because she had overall responsibility for administering Florida's election process." Her decision to stop the manual recounts was a critical factor in the election aftermath. Critics cite her frequent contact with Republican strategist Mac Stipanovich, who relayed information to the Bush legal team. One of the few nice things said about Secretary Harris came ironically from the *New York Times*. "There is nothing in Mascaragate," noted the paper, "that casts any light whatsoever on the status of the Electoral College or even of the dimpled chad. But in a funny kind of way, it does reveal something surprising about America—and how certain feminist arguments, once extreme, have wound their way into the most unlikely corners of our culture."[109]

For its role in the 2000 presidential election, Florida reinforced its unenviable position as a very strange and scary place. From the dark Michael Moore documentary *Fahrenheit 9/11* to late-night comedians, Americans guffawed, cursed, and hyperventilated. The cartoonist Lloyd Dangle imagined a cluster of Florida motels named "The Recount of Monte Cristo," "Subpoena Sands," and the "Supreme Motor Court." The terms "hanging chads," "pregnant chads," and "dimpled chads" became punch lines pummeling Palm Beach County. Commentators unloaded on the Sunshine State. Diane Roberts, an English professor at Florida State University, observed firsthand the fandango. Her book *Dream State* begins: "It's Tallahassee. It's Friday afternoon. It's November 17, 2000, ten days after the not-election. . . . The Motel 6 still declares NO VACANCY. News anchors still drink Bombay Sapphire martinis in Doubletree. . . . Florida is still the center of the universe." Journalist Craig Pittman reflected, "The 2000 recount also marks the beginning of the modern attitude toward Florida, swinging from 'what a nice place to visit' to 'what a bunch of *weirdos*.'" Gadflies suggested new Palm Beach County license plate slogans: "We Put the 'Duh' in Florida," and "Palm Beach County: So Nice, We Let You Vote Twice." New bumper stickers appeared: "Florida: Relax, Retire, Revote," and "Florida: This Is What You Get for Taking Elian Away from Us," and "Florida: We Just Don't Cheat in Football." A political scientist suggested a new state motto: "Florida—Home of Electile Dysfunction." A Floridian, Tom Bennis, emailed the governor that Florida appeared "even dumber" after the wave of court decisions. Governor Bush responded, "With all due respect, it upsets me more than you will know that Florida is the brunt of the jokes I've seen."[110]

No Floridian occupied the strategic vantage point commanded by Charley Wells. A native Floridian, Wells was born in Orlando in 1939. He attended the University of Florida and was a graduate of its law school. Democratic Governor Lawton Chiles appointed Wells to the Florida Supreme Court in 1994, and in July 2000, he became chief justice of that august body. His memoir, appropriately called *Inside Bush v. Gore*, represents one of many accounts of that memorable election and its aftermath. Wells's book begins, "Like millions of Americans, on the morning of November 7, 2000, I cast my vote for the forty-third president of the United States. As I drove away from the polls, my duty done, I thought my role in the election was over." Wells's summary of the thorny legal questions is masterful:

> Overlaying all of the practical problems was my realization that regardless of how much more counting was done, or what was eventually ordered by our court or by the U.S. Supreme Court, or done by the Florida legislature or Congress, there would not be any more certainty of the correctness of the vote count. At this point I concluded that after all the counting was done, the margin of error was always going to be greater than the margin of victory.[111]

The 2000 election spawned forty-seven lawsuits, but only one really mattered. On 11 December 2000, the U.S. Supreme Court decided *Bush v. Gore:* "The counting of votes that are of questionable legality," the majority of opinion opined, threatens "irreparable harm . . . to the country." In his magisterial book *The Swamp*, Michael Grunwald recounts that historic day that pushed George W. Bush to the presidency. But blocks away, another event unfolded. "At the height of the partisan war over the Florida recount," writes Grunwald, "President Clinton was signing a partisan bill to revive the Florida Everglades, a $7.8 billion rescue for sixty-nine endangered species and twenty national parks and refuges." A nervous but optimistic Governor Jeb Bush arrived at the West Wing for the ceremony. It was the battle over the swamps: Washington vs. Florida. The signing marked "the largest environmental restoration project in the history of the planet." President Clinton handed Governor Bush the first ceremonial pen. As Governor Bush was leaving the historic event, an army of reporters approached him, wishing to discuss the other historic event. "No, no, no, no, you're going the wrong way on that one," Bush implored. "We're here to talk about something that's going to be long-lasting, way past counting votes." Grunwald noted, "It wasn't the slash-and-burn anti-green style some expected from a free-market conservative who was born in a Texas oil patch, became a Miami developer . . . at a time when green Republicans were becoming an endangered species." In Jeb's words, the ceremony represented the culmination of one of his "big hairy audacious goals." The event also provided a cautionary reminder: politicians and elections come and go, but the environment is forever.[112]

The brouhaha generated by the presidential main events shortchanged the Democratic Party's singular statewide triumph. Popular U.S. senator and Republican, fifty-eight-year-old Cornelius Alexander McGillicuddy III, popularly known as Mack III, shocked political insiders by announcing his retirement in March 1999, opening the coveted seat. He had already collected $3 million for his reelection. In 1994, he had defeated Hillary Clinton's brother, winning over 70 percent of the vote. A conservative Republican, Mack displayed genuine camaraderie with fellow U.S. Senator Bob Graham, a relationship that would be rare in the new century of partisan politics. In so many ways, Bill Nelson's election seemed a throwback to an earlier era—twentieth-century Florida! He was not an invisible candidate; after all, the sixty-eight-year-old Florida native had won five straight victories, including two as state insurance commissioner. He had held office since 1972—including a stint in the U.S. Congress—and faced Bill McCollum, a veteran in the U.S. House of Representatives. Elected in an era when Democrats controlled Florida, he quickly became an endangered species in Florida and the South—the sole Democrat elected statewide.[113]

The Mood and Zeitgeist

If there was a feeling that depicted the U.S. and Florida mood in 2000, the word was "optimism": a deep, abiding faith in the future, a time-tested confidence that life was getting better, and that our children would exceed our expectations. The American Dream was alive. Daily, more and more Americans were becoming first-time homeowners; weekly, the economy graduated new classes of dot-com millionaires; monthly, the price of homes was inching upward. The election was merely a formality; for Democrat or Republican, America was on the move. Depression and war were grand illusions, something that happened to our great-grandparents. The Cold War was over. Gallup polled Americans in December 2000, and discovered 60 percent believed the country was headed in the right direction. While that figure had dropped from previous years, the widely shared optimism was striking. Throughout American history, the presidential candidate who projects a more positive, rose-colored vision of America generally wins the election. Consider the elections of John F. Kennedy over Richard Nixon, Ronald Reagan over Jimmy Carter, and Bill Clinton over George H. W. Bush. The campaign slogans of 1960, 1980, and 1992—"A New Frontier," "It's morning in America," "People First," and It's the economy, stupid"—triumphed. In 2000, George W. Bush's campaign slogans were less than inspiring: "Reformer with Results" and "Compassionate Conservatism." Still, for all his less-than-presidential eloquence and stature, he sounded more confident about the future than Gore's jeremiads and his wonky slogan, "Leadership for the New Millennium."[114]

One book perfectly mirrored the nation's mantra. Francis Fukuyama, a conservative intellectual, wrote *The End of History* in 1992, advancing the idea that liberal capitalist democracy, with its ingenious balance between liberty and equality, between tolerance and intolerance, had triumphed. The compass point of liberal democracy perfectly aligned with the new millennium. In its apocalyptic struggle with the Soviet Union, America won. The Cold War was over, won with hardly a whiff of gunshot. Communism and the Soviet Union had been tossed into the dustbin of history. The age of war and totalitarianism were over. The march toward the "universalization of Western liberal democracy as the final form of human government" seemed possible if not inevitable.[115]

A smug sense of certitude reinforced liberalism's spell. Founded in 1923, *Time* had chronicled wars and revolutions, booms and busts. Propelled by the waves of optimism following World War II, the magazine's founder, publishing mogul Henry Booth Luce, coined the term, the "American Century" in recognition of America's combination of international might and domestic power. *Time* magazine, with a nationwide circulation of 4.1 million, ended 1999 with a buoyant headline: "A Second American Century?" The conservative columnist Charles Krauthammer paraphrased Cassius describing Caesar, "America bestrides the world like a colossus." Krauthammer concluded assuredly, "None have the power to challenge America now."[116]

A contracting economy characterized by "jobless recovery" worried economists. On 9 September 2001, House Appropriations Chair C. W. "Bill" Young, a longtime representative who hailed from Pinellas County, warned colleagues of the challenges of a shrinking budget surplus of $127 billion for the fiscal 2001 year. An entire generation would never witness another surplus.[117]

Prologue: 1876

In *Their Eyes Were Watching God,* Zora Neale Hurston writes, "There are years that ask questions and years that answer." The millennial year produced more questions than answers. For many Americans, the 2000 election stigmatized Florida as a loosely knit collection of zany tribes and warring factions; to others, the election merely confirmed Florida's status as the wackiest state in the Union; and to political pundits, Florida emerged as a vital, must-win state. In memorable frames, Americans tuned in daily to witness Cuban protestors, confused senior citizens, angry African Americans, ballot-chasing lawyers, besieged and eye-popping ballot counters, and hanging chads.

History may not repeat itself, but it rhymes. Florida had been involved in another convulsive, transformative year culminating in a head-scratching, chin-rubbing election. The events surrounding 2000 had fascinating overtones—and undertow—to 1876. In both years, accusations of massive political corruption, disputed vote counts, and the legitimacy of a Republican president isolated Florida as a confused but critical state. The 1876 election climaxed a wrenching decade marred by political and racial violence, the rise of the Ku Klux Klan, and social and economic upheaval. The decade also witnessed extraordinary gains by freedmen in the arenas of politics, economy, and urban life.

The arc of one individual illustrates the repression and violence of the 1870s, but also the fluidity. The Civil War's strange trajectory brought Josiah T. Walls to Florida. Born a Virginian in 1842, Walls was impressed into Confederate service and captured at the Battle of Yorktown. Whisked north, he received some schooling in Pennsylvania before enlisting as a private in the Union army. Serving in the U.S. Colored Infantry, he wound up in the Florida Theater, rising to the rank of first sergeant. Walls settled in Alachua County after the war, working in lumber camps along the Suwannee River, but also teaching school at Archer. In Alachua County, where Blacks outnumbered whites two to one, Walls's dignity and eloquence quickly established him as a civic leader. His accomplishments include owning and publishing Florida's first Black newspaper, aptly named the *New Era.* Advancing rapidly in the Republican Party, he was elected the state's first African-American member of the U.S. House of Representatives. More than a century would pass before the next African American represented Florida at the nation's capital. Walls was not alone, as hundreds of African Americans ascended to power at the local and state level between 1867 and the 1920s.[118]

Nationally, Americans felt Reconstruction fatigue and wished to move on from the "southern problem." The Republican Party nominated as its presidential standard-bearer staunch abolitionist, congressman, and Union Civil War general Rutherford B. Hayes. Democrats, optimistic about their chances to win the White House, nominated New York governor Samuel Tilden. Florida may have seemed light-years and miles from Washington, but elections had consequences. In particular, the election of 1876 determined the fate of military Reconstruction, the enforcement of civil rights legislation, and the flood of national patronage that had rewarded Republican postmasters and customs inspectors for a decade. The election would also determine party rule in Tallahassee. Republicans breathed the rarefied air of power, cheering three successive governors. But the Florida GOP was bitterly divided over issues of race, patronage, and national and state affairs.[119]

In 1876 as well as 2000, the Cuban vote was critical. In 1868, a violent insurrection against Spanish rule erupted on the island. Thousands of Cuban émigrés had fled to Key West during the insurrection called the Ten Years' War, 1868–78. In addition, a number of prominent tobacco manufacturers fled to Key West, among them Eduardo Gato and Vicente Martínez Ybor. Gatoville in Key West acknowledged the social and economic influence of the Cuban workforce and the 200 cigar factories that eventually made Cayo Hueso famous for hand-rolled cigars.[120]

Fifty thousand Floridians, white and Black, made their way to polling stations in November 1876. In five of Florida's eight largest cities, Black majorities existed. Election law favored the Democrats. Voters were permitted only five minutes to vote and could not seek help, a measure intended to intimidate illiterate freedmen. In 1876, Key West, along with a dozen other cities, was home to federal troops determined to keep the peace. Democrats expressed optimism at both state and national levels. Republicans quickly recognized that the Democratic surge could be blocked if, and only if, their candidate, a Civil War general, snatched South Carolina, Louisiana, and Florida from the Democratic column. Chaos ensued. Poor communications, vast distances, and geographic isolation delayed ballots from reaching state canvassing boards. Complicating issues, laws dictated no uniform ballot. Dade County became an unlikely dateline when its 14 votes were lost. "Where the hell is Dade?," asked the *New York Herald*.[121]

Twelve companies of U.S. Army troops guarded Tallahassee while votes were tabulated and recounted. Hundreds of journalists and party officials—the latter politely called "visiting statesmen"—attempted to report and influence the fate of the Republic. Wrote one journalist on 14 November 1876, "Tallahassee has been converted into a military camp." An 1876 account of life in Florida insisted that "Tallahassee is a very paradise for bachelors, on account of the number, the beauty, and the charming manners of the ladies." A state canvassing board, composed of one Democrat and two Republicans, disallowed several hundred disputed votes, awarding victory to Republican Rutherford B. Hayes, who lost the popular vote but won the Electoral College. The election ended military Reconstruction in the South, "redeeming" southern Democrats. Southern Republicans and African Americans paid dearly for the "Great Compromise."[122]

Regardless of whether a "Great Compromise" was negotiated at the Wormley Hotel in 1876, Florida experienced a "Great Restoration," popularly called "Redemption." In Florida, George "Millionaire" Drew defeated incumbent Republican Marcellus Stearns for governor. Drew had made a fortune logging oak, cypress, and pine at Ellaville, today a ghost town in Madison County. A Unionist during the war, he voted for Ulysses S. Grant in 1868. Incumbent Republican Governor Marcellus Lovejoy Stearns felt confident about reelection. Born in Maine, Stearns served in the Civil War, losing an arm in combat. He proved that Republicans, too, could wave the bloody shirt. Like many Republicans, he would soon lose confidence in democracy. When electors awarded Florida to the Democrats, Governor Sterns uttered, "The state is gone and forever." Democratic Party officials expressed hope that Drew would appeal to Republicans who found voting for an ex-Confederate abhorrent. Cries of "Redemption!" greeted Drew as he took the oath of office on 2 January 1877. That day, in Tampa, the first families hosted a Ring Tournament. The ancient of lances and horses paid homage to Sir Walter Scott's novel *Ivanhoe*, published a half century earlier. The tournament also celebrated Florida's Restoration. Tampa's *Sunland Tribune* saluted "our deliverance from the rule of mal-administration and robbery by the carpetbaggers and scalawag thieves." In Leon County, Susan Bradford Eppes scribbled in her diary, "If there had been excitement before, it was doubled and trebled now." Federal troops soon departed Florida. State Comptroller Clayton

Cowgill prophesied that Florida's Republican Party "had lost the state for a long, long time." Florida, markedly democratic in the 1870s, had become militantly Democratic in the 1880s. Not until the Second Reconstruction in 1967 would a Florida Republican, Claude Kirk, occupy the governor's mansion. Not until 1968 would Florida elect a Republican to the U.S. Senate, Edward J. Gurney. A young Texan, George W. Bush, received his political baptism working on the Gurney campaign.[123]

Epilogue

Ghosts lingered long past their appointed hours. In November 2016, Fidel Castro and Janet Reno died within a few weeks of one another. Their lives, passions, and personalities could not have been more different, yet they shared a searing moment on the world stage. The Elián affair burnished Fidel's reputation and haunted Reno's. Yet she never regretted her decision to repatriate the young boy to his native land and father. In return, Fidel offered to send election supervisors to Florida in 2000. As she was dying, former president Clinton called, telling Reno that the afternoon he spent with her on the family screen porch was "the best time I've had in fifteen years." Reno's term as attorney general under President Clinton had been turbulent, marked by clashing styles and bracketed by the deaths of seventy-six Branch Davidians in Waco, Texas, the impeachment of her boss, and the Elián crisis. Few remember that Reno was President Clinton's third choice for attorney general. The first two flamed out when reporters sniffed out that the nominees had failed to pay their undocumented immigrant nannies' Social Security taxes. Gene Miller, a legendary *Miami Herald* reporter, volunteered to testify that he was certain that no maid had ever set foot inside the Reno home![124]

Had there been a prize for the most authentic Floridian, Janet Reno was a lock. The daughter of two competing Miami newspaper reporters, she was born and raised in today's Kendall on the edge of the Everglades, in an un-air-conditioned home. Lucy Morgan, a longtime friend and observer described Reno: "She stood 6-foot-2 in her bare feet—and they were often bare when she made it home to the rough-hewn home her mother built." Mother, Jane Wood Reno, dug the foundation, wired the walls, shingled the roof, and laid the bricks in neat rows. The Reno family rule was simple enough: "Tell the truth and don't cheat." Janet always followed the rules. Following Harvard Law School, she became state attorney for Dade County and U.S. attorney general. Wholly lacking glamour, she displayed a sense of humor, appearing on *Saturday Night Live* in 2001 as the host and rock star of the "Janet Reno Dance Party."[125]

When she entered the 2002 race to become the Democratic nominee for governor, a British reporter observed, "If former US attorney general Janet Reno can pull off a stunt as disco queen, then maybe she has a chance of becoming Florida's first female governor." Her biographer described her retro appeal: "Outspoken, outrageous, absolutely indifferent to others' opinions, Janet Reno was truly one of a kind." Consider the reaction of most candidates when citizens ask how they might contact them? Reno handed voters her home phone number! Characteristically, she drove a red 1999 Ford Ranger pickup truck across the state, hoping President Clinton might campaign for her. Instead, Martin Sheen, the actor who played popular President Josiah "Jed" Bartlet on *The West Wing*, headlined a fundraiser. So did Rosie O'Donnell. Reno lost to Tampa lawyer Bill McBride in the Democratic primary by fewer than 5,000 votes. Not even an Elton John fundraiser could deflect rumors that she was battling Parkinson's disease. In November 2016, former President Clinton eulogized his attorney general, remarking, "I don't believe Janet Reno ever cut a corner in her life." Her efforts in the Elián saga were scarcely mentioned that day. A few days after the funeral, Janet's sister Maggy Hurchalla answered the telephone at the Reno homestead in Kendall. "This is the Cuban embassy in Washington, D.C.," the caller said, explaining that they had a message for the family of Janet Reno. The message read: "The family of Elián González would like to convey their love and gratitude for sending their boy home."[126]

Soothsayers divine the future in search of signs and auguries. In 2000, the portents signaled optimism. But as baseball philosopher Yogi Berra once said, "The future ain't what it used to be." Karl Marx, referencing Emperor Napoleon and his star-crossed nephew Louis Napoleon III, said famously, "History repeats itself, first as tragedy, second as farce." If Marx were born a century later, the eighty-one-year-old Jewish retiree in Century Village might well have said, "History repeats itself, first as farce and then as tragedy."

When Americans heard about the deadly USS *Cole* bombing in October 2000, the terrorist act seemed an aberration. Two suicide attackers aboard a small craft detonated explosives that rocked the guided-missile destroyer off the Yemeni port of Aden. The blast killed seventeen American sailors. A search for the mastermind, Jamal-al-Badawi, was launched. He was part of an organization few Americans recognized: al-Qaeda. Badawi belonged to a terrorist cell headed by an elusive figure, Osama bin Laden. Bin Laden and his operatives fled their compound and sought refuge in the Afghan mountains, fearing American reprisals. Neither outgoing President Clinton nor the new Bush administration retaliated. On 10 September 2001, former President Bill Clinton was speaking to a group of Australian businessmen. The subject of Osama bin Laden came up. "He's a very smart guy," Clinton said. "I spent a lot of time thinking about him. And I nearly got him once." Intelligence confirmed that bin Laden was staying in a small town in Afghanistan. "I could have killed him," said Clinton, "but I would have to destroy a little town called Kandahar and kill 300 innocent women and children, and then I would have been no better than him. And so I didn't do it."[127]

2

"Something Wicked This Way Comes"

9/11, the Age of Fear, and the Tropic of Crazy

Witches' mummy, maw and gulf . . .
Scale of dragon, tooth of wolf
By the pricking of my thumbs,
Something wicked this way comes.

The witches in Shakespeare's *Macbeth,* act 4

9/10/2001

Seven months after taking office, President George W. Bush returned to Florida. The past and future of the Republican Party gathered for an illustrious, intimate dinner at the Colony Beach and Tennis Resort on Longboat Key, a barrier island near Sarasota. Former Florida governor and First Lady Bob and Mary Jane Martínez drove from Tampa to join President Bush and Governor Jeb Bush for the celebratory occasion. Ominously, a toxic red tide had recently scoured Sarasota Bay, and the stench of dead fish comingled with the fragrance of frangipani, hibiscus, and bougainvillea.

In Florida, the occasional smell of rotting fish could be confused with prosperity's perfume. Longboat Key perfectly illustrated Florida's fascination and fondness for salt water, sand dunes, and exclusivity. A barrier island stretching nearly 10 miles along Manatee and Sarasota counties, Longboat Key had been so underdeveloped prior to the 1940s that the island served as a bombing range for flight trainees at Sarasota Army Air Field. Prosperity, along with technology in the forms of DDT, bridge building, and modern highways, sped development as Americans transformed the Gulf's barrier islands. A Sarasota County resident recalled his first exposure to Longboat Key. In the mid-1960s, Jim Brown spotted a roadside sign advertising a "tennis resort" on Longboat Key. To reach the resort, Brown traveled "the old humpback bridge" across St. Armand's Key. He then traversed the low, narrow New Pass Bridge. Scrub growth, swamp, and wetlands inundated the island. A few new condominiums had been erected on the beach side. "Finally, we reached the Colony," Brown wrote, "a handful of weather-beaten beach cottages and a few new tennis courts." The decades that followed recast Longboat Key from an idyllic island cluttered with mom-and-pop motels, mobile home parks, and two-bedroom condominiums that cost $30,000 into one of the most exclusive enclaves in Florida. Arthur Vining Davis and his Arvida Corp. invested heavily on Longboat Key.[1]

The original Colony had been the brainchild of Herb Field, who purchased the property in 1952 and cleared 18 acres of palmetto scrub himself. He built 110 wooden cottages in one of the most charming locations anywhere. In 1972, Murray "Murf" Klauber, a Buffalo orthodontist, purchased the property. With a fierce work ethic and attention to detail, Klauber turned the complex into the Colony Beach and Tennis Resort. His friendship with the gregarious tennis impresario Bud Collins popularized the resort. Tennis guru Nick Bollettieri offered lessons to guests. Klauber also respected the island's informal practice that no building could exceed the height of the tallest palm tree. The Colony stood out for its luxury (Frette linens, an imposing wine list, and locally caught stone crabs) and its famous guests. In 1996, Al Gore stayed at the penthouse suite the night before he jousted with Jack Kemp at the vice-presidential debate in St. Petersburg.[2]

While tennis was the sport of choice for the resort's guests, it was baseball that connected the first families of Florida and America. A talented high school player who considered signing a thousand-dollar bonus to catch for the Brooklyn Dodgers minor league system, Bob Martínez wisely married his high school sweetheart and enrolled at the University of Tampa. After surviving harrowing aerial combat in World War II, George Herbert Walker Bush married Barbara Pierce and finally enrolled at Yale, where he became captain of the Elis baseball team. George W. Bush was a managing general partner with the Texas Rangers before he was elected governor of Texas in 1994. "This is as good as it gets," exclaimed George W. on Opening Day 1989. The 2001 baseball season may have been disastrous for the Rangers, Florida Marlins, and the Tampa Bay Devil Rays (two of the three teams finished in last place and the Devil Rays lost one hundred games), but that September evening was as memorable as it was glorious.[3]

Martínez personified the old Democratic Party and the new Republican Party. A grandson of Spanish immigrants and a native of West Tampa, a fiercely Democratic neighborhood comprised of Cubans, Spaniards, and Italians, Martínez taught history at local schools until he became the head of the Hillsborough County Teachers' Union. In 1968, he rallied embattled teachers in a controversial statewide strike directed against an unpopular Republican governor. Martínez left the school system and became a successful restaurateur and in 1979 was elected mayor of Tampa in a nonpartisan race. His wife, Mary Jane Marino, the daughter of Sicilian immigrants, graduated with the charter class at the University of South Florida, becoming a beloved librarian at King High School. In the spring of 1983, Martínez received a fateful call. President Ronald Reagan invited him to the White House. Reagan's Republican revolution was sweeping the land, and Florida was the vortex. Upon arriving at the White House, the governor was escorted into the Oval Office. President Reagan had been well briefed. "Bobby," the president began, "You're a lot like me. We were union leaders. I was once a Democrat. You were head of a teachers' union. . . . We would sure love for you to become a Republican." In July 1983, Bob and Mary Jane Martínez strolled into the office of the Hillsborough County supervisor of elections and formally switched political parties.[4]

The September dinner on Longboat Key embodied individual and collective success. Fortune and timing also brought the guests together. Who could have imagined that someone named Bob Martínez would become the first Hispanic and Roman Catholic governor in modern Florida history? From the vantage point of the Colony's fifth-floor penthouse, costing $1,300 for a night's stay, the guests could see the mansion belonging to Katherine Harris, who helped make this evening as improbable as it was possible. It was an evening to remember. The chef, under the close watch of the Secret Service and knowing the president's fondness for Tex-Mex, had prepared Red Snapper Ranchero as the signature entrée and baked Alaska for dessert. The bill totaled $1,172.72. As the guests were leaving, President Bush signed a menu for Mary Jane Martínez, writing, "With Affection." With a touch of artistry and strategery, Governor Bush drew a heart pierced by an arrow and his name. He also scribbled the date: "9/10/01." The signed menu may be admired as guests enter the Martínez home.[5]

9/11/2001

The next morning began routinely: President Bush jogged on a local golf course and then received the daily intelligence briefing. The schedule seemed more innocent than pressing. The president's Cadillac limousine, followed by a long caravan of press and security, departed at 8:39 a.m. Demonstrators protesting offshore oil drilling and the 2000 election lined the streets.[6]

The first event was a visit to Sarasota's Emma Booker Elementary School. The school was named for a pioneering African-American educator. "Everything was so relaxed," recalled Ann Compton, the ABC White House correspondent. "This was not a big pressure event." Before he entered classroom 301, an aide informed the chief executive that a plane had crashed into one of New York's Twin Towers. The incident was dismissed as an accident. As Bush was reading *The Pet Goat* with sixteen students, White House Chief of Staff Andrew Card relayed the news that "America is under attack." "The minute that I saw Andy Card walk into that classroom, lean over, and whisper to the president, I knew something was direly wrong," reflected Compton. "*Nobody* interrupts the president. Not even in front of a classroom of second-graders." The president, not wishing to alarm the young students, continued to read, nervously. White House Press Secretary Ari Fleischer, standing in the back of the classroom, held up a notepad with a handwritten message: "Don't say anything yet." Noticeably shaken, the president then calmly excused himself and departed. Ten years later, one of the students remembered, "He just looked like he got the worst news in the world." *Time* magazine placed the event in perspective: "There has rarely been a starker juxtaposition of evil and innocence than the moment President George Bush received the news about 9/11 while reading *The Pet Goat* with second-graders in Sarasota, Fla."[7]

The Gates of Hell opened. The fourth sura of the Quran had warned, "Wherever you are, death will find you, even in the looming tower."

President Bush left the classroom and entered a holding room. There he joined millions of Americans watching on television the horrifying replays of airplanes exploding into the World Trade Center, desperate individuals jumping from burning buildings, and crowds of New Yorkers in shock. President Bush also talked and consulted with the vice president and key aides and officials. A shaken president announced, "We're at war." Following a brief meeting with the press, the Bush party left for the Sarasota airport to board *Air Force One.* The Secret Service and media took over the Colony Resort during this tense moment.[8]

On 9/11 Pam Gibson was preparing for work at noon at the Manatee County Central Library in Bradenton. She had lived on Anna Maria Island since 1961, when her parents bought a waterfront home for $17,500. She recalled, "It was a beautiful blue sky and calm blue waters outside Anna Maria Sound." Serenity was interrupted by her eighty-six-year-old father in the front yard shouting, "Turn on the TV, turn on the TV!" She recalled, "When the second plane hit the building," she remembered thinking, "Well that's a different camera angle." Her father gasped, "That's War!"[9]

Curiously, "terrorism" had hardly been discussed in the 2000 presidential debates. Or to recast the point, Americans preferred to forget unsettling events that should have divined 9/11. Scattered and disturbing acts of terror had occurred on American soil in the decade preceding 2001—most notably the 1993 truck bombing in the basement of the World Trade Center that killed six and injured more than 1,000 persons, the Oklahoma City bombing in 1995 that killed 168, and the Unabomber's carnage, 1978–95. At first, everyone concluded simply that a pilot must have made a terrible mistake.

Commandeering a plane was not a new idea. Hijacking—a word formerly associated with bootlegging in the 1920s—became front-page news in 1961, when a gunman demanded that a National Airlines flight from Marathon to Key West be diverted to Havana. Terror in the air had become so commonplace that art imitated life. In 1969, Allen Funt's *Candid Camera* was one of the great success stories on American television. It was a reality show before the term had been invented. *Candid Camera* caught ordinary citizens in awkward moments and secretly recorded their nervous reactions: children walking by talking mailboxes, a waitress serving brawny Teamsters sandwiches with doilies and watercress, and a stevedore asked to move a locked wooden trunk with a man moaning inside. In 1969, Funt and his family were on a vacation flight from Newark to Miami. Midflight, one of the passengers grabbed a stewardess, placed a knife to her neck, entered the cockpit, and ordered the pilot to reroute to Cuba. The pilot announced that the plane would be making an unexpected stop in Havana. The panicked passengers contemplated their uncertain fate—until a woman recognized one of the most familiar faces in America: Allen Funt. "Wait a second!" she exclaimed. "We are not being hijacked. It's a *Candid Camera* stunt." Passengers erupted in laughter, even asking Funt to sign their air-sickness bags. Funt pleaded, "No! Listen, this is a real hijacking!" He even pleaded with a priest to explain the seriousness of the situation. "You can't get me, Allen Funt," the priest howled. The plane landed in Havana, and only when armed Cuban soldiers circled the plane did passengers realize their plight. Eleven hours later, the plane landed in Miami. Funt's daughter, Juliet, reminisced that one of the fatigued passengers yelled at her father, "Smile my ass!"[10]

The decade of the 1970s witnessed a record number of hijackings, but the numbers fell each succeeding decade. But on 9/11, the plotters were not interested in merely taking control of the aircraft. The suicidal crashes resounded with such force that a single day heaved and quaked America's geopolitical tectonic plates. Shockingly and suddenly, Osama bin Laden and al-Qaeda, names few Americans recognized, violently proclaimed their rejection of Western notions of liberalism: progress, religious freedom, and tolerance.

One person who attracted little attention in Florida on 9/11 was Omar Mir Seddique. Born in 1986 on Long Island, New York, he moved with his Afghani parents when he was a young boy to Port St. Lucie, Florida. The family was described as "moderate Muslims." Port St. Lucie was booming, and the Seddique family was living the American dream. The father, a Pashtun immigrant, enjoyed a successful career as an insurance salesman, witnessed by an expensive home and cars. As a student, Omar encountered difficulties. Teachers expressed concern over his violent nature and bullying behavior. School officials assigned fourteen-year-old Omar to Spectrum Junior/High School, an alternative school in Stuart for students with behavioral problems. Spectrum classmates watched the horror unfold on 9/11. Except Omar. One classmate remembered that as the second plane crashed into the Twin Tower, Omar began "jumping-up-and-down cheering on the terrorists." He also boasted that Osama bin Laden was his uncle. The incident resulted in his suspension from school. When Omar's father arrived, he slapped his son across the face. In 2006, the troubled young man petitioned to change his name from Omar Mir Seddique to Omar Mir Seddique Mateen. He soon enrolled at Indian River Community College to become a Florida Department of Corrections officer. In 2016, Mateen killed or wounded more than 100 persons at Orlando's Pulse nightclub in the greatest mass shooting in American history.[11]

In 2001, few Floridians recognized the name Osama bin Laden. But in one of the weirdest factoids to emerge from 9/11, Khalil bin Laden, one of Osama bin Laden's 50-plus siblings, once owned a 1920s mansion in Oakland, 20 miles from Orlando. Khalil bin Laden purchased the stately Mediterranean-style home on the shores of Johns Lake in 1980 for $1.6 million. He and his family fled Florida and America shortly after 9/11. In 2006, Khalil sold the property for $4 million.[12]

The Staging Ground State

Florida served as a staging ground for the tragedy. Eerily, three days before President Bush's visit to Longboat Key, Mohamed el-Atta was spending the night at a Holiday Inn, two miles away. Atta, an Egyptian, was joined at the bar by Marwan al-Shehhi, a United Arab Emirates co-conspirator. Atta tipped the bartender sixteen dollars for a four-dollar rum and Coke. A cohort of Saudis, many of whom had forged camaraderie in a terror cell in Hamburg, Germany, lived and trained in Daytona Beach, Deerfield Beach, Vero Beach, Coral Springs, Hollywood, and Venice. Atta was appointed the leader of this audacious suicide mission. Almost half of the 9/11 plotters called Florida home at some point in 2001. All nineteen hijackers had obtained U.S. visas under their actual names.[13]

As many as a dozen of the nineteen 9/11 terrorists lived and trained in Florida. Their choice of Broward, Palm Beach, Volusia, and Sarasota counties revealed their belief that in a place where almost everyone came from someplace else, they could plot their nefarious scheme undetected. "It's hard to think of a better place to hide if you want to hide in the open," explained a law professor from Nova Southeastern University. "Florida: Terror's Launching Pad," ran one post-9/11 headline, as the paper documented the banality of evil. "South Florida," observed *Miami Herald* columnist Fred Grimm, "with its diverse and transient population, has long been a place where a stranger can disappear in plain sight." Atta, al-Shehhi, and Ziad Jarrah enrolled in flight schools at various cities in Florida and received their FAA pilot's licenses. Jarrah and Al Haznawi shared a sporty Mitsubishi Eclipse. At times, their behavior belied their seriousness. In December 2000, Miami International Airport flight controllers cringed when they saw two men, Atta and al-Shehhi, walking away from a stranded Piper Cherokee on a major runway. Atta called Huffman Aviation in Venice with an unusual question: "How do you restart the plane?" They wound up renting a car and driving back to Venice. In Vero Beach, Abdul Rahman Alomari signed up for classes at Flight Safety Academy. One flight instructor was shocked when a student expressed no interest in learning to land the plane. They also behaved like reckless young tourists, flitting from Key West to Miami to Fort Lauderdale, drinking in excess, frequenting strip bars, and amassing a pile of unpaid traffic tickets.[14]

The conspirators' lifestyles in Florida ranged from prosaic to depraved to spiritual. Only one of the hijackers was over the age of thirty; half were under age twenty-four. Three of the suspects spent their last night cavorting with lap dancers at the Pink Pony Nude Theater in Daytona Beach. One left behind a copy of the Quran at the strip club. Several conspirators went into a Sarasota sound studio and recorded a compact disc, calling themselves the Arab Assassins. Lyrics refer to terrorist acts that "the world will remember." Al-Shehhi purchased two black, four-inch pocketknives at a Sports Authority store in Florida. The Federal Aviation Agency still allowed passengers to carry such knives aboard planes. In Pompano Beach, Waleed Al-Shehri picked up Western clothing at Burdines. He also purchased a one-week gym membership in Lantana. Most of the operatives used public libraries' Internet access. Several became familiar visitors to the Belle Glade and Clewiston airports, where they inquired about crop dusting and spraying chemicals. On the evening of 8 September, Al-Shehhi drank five screwdrivers while Atta preferred cranberry juice with his spicy chicken wings at an oyster bar in Hollywood's fashionable Young Circle.[15]

Around 8:00 a.m. on 11 September 2001, President Bush received his daily intelligence briefing. Thousands of miles away, Atta and four colleagues had boarded a 6:00 a.m. flight from Portland, Maine, to Boston's Logan International Airport. Landing in Boston, Atta and four hijackers were preparing to board American Airlines Flight 11 when Atta took a call at 6:52 from Marwan al Shehhi, a co-conspirator who was also at Logan Airport. At 7:45, American Airlines Flight 11, bound for Los Angeles, departed from Boston's Logan International Airport. Fifteen minutes after the flight departed, Atta had succeeded in entering the cockpit and taking control of the flight, guiding the Boeing 767 into the North Tower of the World Trade Center at 8:46 a.m. His last words to the traffic controllers were, "Don't make any stupid moves." Al-Shehhi and four al-Qaeda operatives left Boston minutes later, waiting thirty minutes before they forced their way into the cockpit and took control. The youngest hijacker-pilot, Al-Shehhi, guided United Airlines Flight 175 into the South Tower at 9:03. The third plane, American Airlines Flight 77, left from Washington's Dulles Airport at 8:20. The fifty-five passengers included five suicidal hijackers. The plane was guided into the Pentagon in Washington, D.C. Delayed, Ziad Jarrah and three fellow hijackers departed from Newark on Flight 93. The Boeing 757, destined for the Capitol or White House, crashed in Shanksville, Pennsylvania. The butchers' bill was steep: 3,000 American deaths. Osama bin Laden had chosen his targets well. The Twin Towers symbolized New York City's financial might, while the Pentagon reflected American power. Commentator George Will observed, "The grim paradox is that terrorism, a primitive act, has a symbiotic relationship with the sophistication of its targets."[16]

Investigations revealed that private security companies conducted shoddy screening at most American airports. Shockingly, the airline hijackers managed to board despite the fact that many carried firearms and bolt cutters and that several lacked proper documentation.

Heroes

Heroes abounded in the air and on the ground. On 4 August 2001, José Meléndez-Pérez worked as an immigration inspector at Orlando International Airport (MCO). A Puerto Rican, a veteran of two tours of Vietnam, and a retired U.S. Army sergeant, he had worked for U.S. Customs and Border Protection since 1992. When twenty-one-year-old Saudi national Mohamed al-Qahtani sought entry into the United States, an official noticed that the visitor had incorrectly filled out his forms. He was sent to a secondary interview, conducted by Meléndez-Pérez. Qahtani received computer clearance—his Saudi passport and U.S. visa were valid—but the immigration inspector noticed that the Saudi possessed $2,800 in cash but no credit cards. He also had not booked a hotel or a return ticket. The inspector asked more questions. His colleagues were perturbed, knowing the influence of the Saudi government in Washington. "My job requires me to know the difference between legitimate travelers to the U.S. and those who are not," he later testified. "He just gave me the creeps," he explained. For ninety minutes, Qahtani answered accusations in perfect English, only to be rejected by the suspicious immigration official. "I'll be back," warned the Saudi. Only later did authorities connect the dots: Qahtani was at MCO to pick up Mohamed Atta. Authorities have speculated that the well-trained Qahtani might have helped his four co-conspirators complete their mission on Flight 93, guiding the plane into the White House or Capitol. Qahtani returned to the Middle East, was captured in Afghanistan, and is currently imprisoned at Guantanamo. His imprisonment has aroused controversy because of accusations that he has been tortured.[17]

On Flight 93, CeeCee Ross Lyles worked as a flight attendant. Raised in Fort Pierce, she had served as a police officer there. The mother to four children, she had only recently switched careers. A reporter noted, "Being a flight attendant was much less dangerous than being a cop," especially a detective who patrolled the crack alleys of Fort Pierce. As the hijackers were being overwhelmed by passengers, she phoned her husband, Loren. Over the screams he could hear in the airplane, Loren said that her last words were: "We've been hijacked. I love you. I love the children." Ms. Ross Lyles defied stereotypes, wrote a journalist. "She was good looking and tough. She loved to dress up, but wasn't afraid to confront a gun-toting perpetrator. . . . Supermom and supercop." A bronze statue of Lyles stands today in Fort Pierce. Adorned with a United Airlines uniform, she gazes across the Intracoastal Waterway. At the statue's dedication, several friends bet that CeeCee was directing the efforts to take back the Boeing 757 from the terrorists.[18]

The Media

Floridians reacted to the unfolding events in myriad ways. New and old technologies defined news and communications. Consider that many Americans did not learn about Pearl Harbor for hours, or even days, whereas 9/11 became a live news-drama, played out on television. Many executives recalled that not since the Kennedy assassination in 1963 had one story demanded so much coverage. An estimated 60.5 million viewers watched the attack coverage on prime-time television. Moreover, consumers viewed the unfolding tragedy commercial-free, as advertisers understandably concluded that tragedy and commercialism was an unseemly fit. Minutes after the first plane hit the North Tower, morning anchors appeared on air, attempting to explain the image of a shattered building belching smoke. When the second plane hit seventeen minutes later, news cameras caught the live event. "Oh my God," gasped Diane Sawyer. Appliance stores and Radio Shack did brisk business selling televisions to customers who had to know what was happening. "It looked eerily like a made-for-TV massacre," remarked media critic Eric Deggans, who added, "This is the utility and horror of 24-hour TV coverage—delivering Technicolor footage of destruction directly to viewers' living rooms in a dizzying array of carnage." It was the age of iconic anchor chairs at ABC, CBS, and NBC. Soon Peter Jennings, Dan Rather, and Tom Brokaw assumed the challenge of making sense of a tragedy unfolding in marathon time. For five days, the networks offered continuous coverage. "We Americans before 9/11 had this feeling of invulnerability and insularity," Rather reflected later. For two decades, the number of viewers watching the evening news on the traditional networks had been in steep decline. The riveting coverage of the 9/11 events brought them back—temporarily.[19]

David Charlebois served as first officer on American Airlines Flight 77 that left Washington, D.C., bound for Los Angeles. The plane crashed into the Pentagon. Charlebois was a 1983 graduate of Embry-Riddle Aeronautical University in Daytona Beach. A Washington, D.C., neighbor of Charlebois told a reporter, "His life was the kind of life I wanted to have someday."[20]

Newspapers rallied to put out special editions and explain the events in passionate and dispassionate prose. Banner headlines screamed, "Today, Nation

Saw Evil," "Evil Acts," "Terrorists Have Ignited American Wrath," and "America under Attack." Although no one realized it, newspapers were experiencing an Indian Summer, an era buoyed by record advertising and handsome profits. The *St. Petersburg Times* and *Miami Herald* earned the highest accolades from media critics, but the *Orlando Sentinel, South Florida Sun-Sentinel*, and *Tampa Tribune* also published impressive papers. It was also a fleeting last moment when readers still preferred the paper copy rather than the relatively novel online version. For its special "Attacked" headline edition, the *Miami Herald* published 50,000 advertising-free copies, while the *St. Petersburg Times* and the Jacksonville *Florida Times-Union* each published 20,000 such editions. The editor of the *Times-Union,* Pat Yack, ordered the papers to be distributed free at grocery stores and meeting spots. The *Tallahassee Democrat,* with a daily press run of only 50,000, rushed to press 15,000 special edition issues. "This incident has shocked people," Yack explained. "There's nothing in people's lifetimes, with the possible exception of Pearl Harbor and President Kennedy's assassination that matches it." And then there were the predictably irreverent headlines published by the *Onion:* "U.S. Vows to Defeat Whoever It Is We're at War With," and "'We Expected Eternal Paradise for This,' Say Suicide Bombers."[21]

Journalists' reactions ranged from unadulterated anger to calls for caution and restraint. A memorable column began: "You monster. You beast. You unspeakable bastard." Following a burst of anger, the *Miami Herald*'s Leonard Pitts Jr. pivoted to write a powerful elegy:

> Let me tell you about my people. We are a vast and quarrelsome family, a family wrent by racial, social, political, and class division, but a family nonetheless. We're wealthy, too, spoiled by the ready availability of trinkets and material goods, and maybe because of that, we walk through life with a certain sense of blithe entitlement. We are fundamentally decent, though, peace-loving and compassionate. . . . Yes, we're in pain now. We are in mourning and we are in shock. . . . You don't know what you just started. But you're about to learn.

Sadly, 9/11 was precisely the type of story that revealed the obsolescence of the printed news. Hereafter, readers and viewers demanded to know what happened five minutes ago, not last night or, in the case of *Time* or *Newsweek*, last week, or with the *Atlantic*, last month. A legislative aide neatly recorded the technological gap between 2001 and its aftermath: "In a time before smartphones and computer tablets, we spent much of the trip flipping around the radio dial to find any bit of news that would help us better understand the attacks." In Southwest Florida, newsstands reported that they could not keep up with the demand for newspapers, as collectors and readers emptied shelves. Few realized it, but 9/11 served as a glorious swan song for newspapers, newsstands, and printed editions.[22]

Floridians React and Respond

Florida shut down. Or so it seemed. Across the state, airports, theme parks, space centers, and schools closed. A rare sight—empty parking lots—resulted from the shut-down shopping malls. International Plaza in Tampa had scheduled its grand opening the week of 9/11. Even the popular Home Shopping Network and QVC went off the air. Civilians were ordered to leave MacDill Air Force Base in Tampa. Soldiers and staff spent three hours in line trying to enter MacDill on 9/11.

"Chaos, it was just chaos," recounted Jack Dees when asked about 9/11. Dees served at MacDill's U.S. Central Command (CENTCOM), the nerve center for America's far-flung military operations between the European and Pacific commands, chiefly the Middle East. Teams of planners tracked the maneuvers of friends and foes halfway around the globe. Commissioned in 1940 on the eve of World War II, MacDill Air Field's role had expanded dramatically. CENTCOM was established in 1983, in the wake of the Soviet invasion of Afghanistan and the Iranian hostage crisis. No aircraft landed at MacDill on 11 September 2001. MacDill was under "lockdown," and spokesmen returned no calls or offered any news briefings. "If multiple terrorist cells were operating on this Tuesday," recollected U.S. Army General Tommy A. Franks, commander of the U.S. Forces Center at MacDill, "the base was an obvious target." To avenge 9/11, CENTCOM launched Operation Enduring Freedom, deploying troops from anywhere in the United States to twenty-five countries from the Red Sea to Central Asia. Dees remembered pre-9/11 MacDill as "the quietest place on the planet." Upon his return, "Getting through the gate was a nightmare . . . a scene of enormous energy."[23]

Over the skies of the Gulf of Mexico, the Blue Angels had been practicing maneuvers for ten minutes when superiors ordered their return to the Pensacola Naval Air Station. Hurlburt Field, headquarters for the Air Force Special Operations Command in the Panhandle, readied for its highest state of alert.[24]

While theme parks and schools closed their doors, one institution had to keep its doors open: Florida's blood banks turned away donors. In Southwest Florida, donors stood in lines, many for as long as sixteen hours. Sam Schwartz appeared at the South Florida Blood Bank collection center in West Palm Beach.

Schwartz survived the Japanese attack at Pearl Harbor, and he was now prepared to help in a new war. "When an American is in trouble, the people come out," he boasted. Americans' admiration for the Red Cross and private charities raising funds for victims' families skyrocketed.[25]

Other businesses also profited. Rental car companies benefited, as passengers bumped from flights scrambled to find transportation. Fleets of cars instantly disappeared. On this unusual occasion, the state turnpikes and toll roads suspended all fees. Hotels around airports also reported brisk traffic.[26]

The question, "Where were you when you heard about the Twin Towers attacks?" will be repeated for many 9/11 anniversaries. Michael Cardello and his family had just been squealing in delight when the announcement came over the speakers: Walt Disney World was closing "due to unforeseen circumstances." The Walt Disney World executives, figuring not illogically that capitalism's "happiest place on earth" was also the most vulnerable place in Florida, cleared the complex in thirty minutes, shuttering its gates. Typically, 200,000 people crowd the Disney complex. Michael Eisner, the CEO of the Walt Disney Company, emailed Governor Jeb Bush asking whether Disney World was in the crosshairs. The governor replied, "I know of no evidence that Disney is a targete [*sic*]." A worker recalled: "We were told not to tell the guests what had happened. . . . Once the guests were forced to the streets of the park because all rides were closed, all the cast members were instructed to hold hands and basically form a human wall and gently (without touching anyone) walk towards the hub of the park and eventually towards Main Street." A cast member recalled that the hardest part was staying "so happy." Busch Gardens in Tampa and SeaWorld in Orlando also closed for the day.[27]

The chaos posed special problems for the hundreds of thousands of teachers and students in Florida. Amid a free fall of fears and tears, administrators scrambled to secure police protection and guidance counselors. Few guidebooks held answers to the questions: "Teacher, what's a terrorist?" "Why are they trying to kill us?" Police scrambled to ensure that one school was not a target: Norman Schwarzkopf Elementary School in Lutz. Nervous parents flooded school parking lots to hug and gather their children. Many parents demanded to know why, when the state colleges and universities closed, the public K–12 schools remained open. William Hartley taught at Lecanto High School in Hernando County. That day, he explained, "I've tried to impress upon them that the country that they will live in after today is going to be different than the world was today when they came to school."[28]

The university, often the subject of criticism and skepticism in the pre-9/11 era, also became a place of contemplation and danger after 9/11. Michael Gannon, a professor of history emeritus at the University of Florida, had spent much of his seventy-four years living in and studying the history of St. Augustine, America's oldest city. He had also been an ordained priest, rising to the rank of monsignor. St. Augustine, more than almost any American city, had witnessed triumph and tragedy. There, the bells of the cathedral tolled to the deaths of kings and governors, pealed news of military victories and royal births. Gannon was asked to speak to students, faculty, and staff at the University Auditorium in the wake of 9/11. He reminded the audience that George Washington and Abraham Lincoln had summoned Americans to national days of prayer and remembrance. He singled out then university president John J. Tigert rallying students in the days after Pearl Harbor, pleading that "the patriotic thing to do is to keep calm." He also confessed: "We are in the presence, my friends, of deep mysteries. And we call upon transcendent powers both within and without us to give that understanding, that solace, and that peace we find so hard to come by with ordinary resources." He ended by asking, "May the Lord of History protect and defend these beloved United States of America."[29]

Azela S. was a senior at the University of Florida in 2001, having just returned from a semester abroad at Aix-en-Provence, France. "9/11 changed everything," she remembered:

> As I was walking on campus to my studio class, it was eerily quiet. As I walked toward the studio, there was a note on the door that stated, "Family Emergency, Class Canceled." So I headed back to the dormitories in the Murphree Area. I was a resident assistant and the Murphree Area did not have A/C except for Fletcher Hall, Sledd Hall, and the Commons Area. . . . As I'm walking into the Murphree Commons, I see all my co-workers huddled around a television set . . . I realized they were watching all the damage after the first tower was hit. . . . It was a time that was etched in all our heads and that would change the course of our lives.[30]

In Tallahassee on the morning of 11 September, Governor Bush was attending a State Board of Administration meeting on Hermitage Boulevard. A security guard handed the governor a note. Bush immediately declared a state of emergency and dispatched the order "Evacuate the Capitol." Mike Fasano refused to leave, reminisced aide Greg Giordano. The majority leader of the Florida House of Representatives "made sure that his entire staff was safely on their way home, and then he stayed behind to offer his assistance" to Speaker Tom Feeney. "When we did finally leave the Capitol," recalled Giordano, "it was a sobering sight, seeing streams of humanity leaving the Capitol Complex, all of us aware that the world had just changed." Only police officers and bomb-sniffing dogs strolled through deserted Capitol hallways.[31]

The business of government halted at the federal, state, and local levels. SWAT teams patrolled the perimeters of many city halls and county commission buildings. In West Palm Beach, county commissioners and staff gathered in front of a bank of televisions to watch the events. Nearby, prospective jurors had just been given instructions when images of the disaster appeared on CNN. Supervisor Arlene Goodman sent the jurors home, explaining that citizens felt very uneasy about being inside a large government building as attacks were occurring.[32]

Small-town Florida and its hinterland also trembled and grieved. A reporter observed how the citizens of LaBelle, in Southwest Florida, expressed their emotions simply: "They prayed. They cried for vengeance. They feared for their children."[33]

Many questions have lingered since 9/11: What role did Florida and Floridians serve in the grand conspiracy to attack America? More precisely, did Saudis living in Florida have knowledge of or help finance the 2001 terrorist attacks?

A Saudi family that had lived in the gated Sarasota neighborhood of Prestancia for six years has been the subject of great scrutiny. The large home was owned by Esam Ghazzawi, a prominent Saudi advisor to the nephew of King Fahd. The home was occupied by Ghazzawi's daughter and son-in-law, who had links to the hijackers training in the Sarasota area. On the eve of the 9/11 attacks, the family simply vanished, vacating a home containing fragments of their lifestyle: clothes, toys, a refrigerator filled with food, and a new Chrysler PT Cruiser. The family left no forwarding address. The fact that most of the 9/11 jihadists were Saudi nationals heightens the mystery. The United Arab Emirates wired $114,000 to Atta and al-Shehhi through Sun Trust banks in Florida. Analysts believe the 9/11 operation required at least a half-million dollars. Investigators confirmed that a car carrying Mohamed Atta and Ziad Jarrah passed through the Prestancia guard gates. An FBI investigation turned up phone records between two of the hijackers and the Saudi family, but officials concluded that the family did not aid the terrorists.[34]

U.S. Senator Bob Graham served as head of the U.S. Senate Intelligence Committee in 2001, and later co-chaired the Congressional Joint Inquiry into 9/11. He has been a persistent critic of the government's secrecy involving this case and the greater investigation. Senator Graham was and remains especially concerned that President Bush redacted twenty-eight pages of the congressional review of the tragedy. President Obama supported President Bush's decision, but in

July 2016, the House Intelligence Committee released the missing documents. The sealed pages pertain to the involvement by Saudis in assisting the jihadists. Saudi Arabia has forcefully denied any connection to the 9/11 conspirators. "We know that Saudi Arabia started al-Qaida," Senator Graham has long maintained. Graham once met secretly with a top FBI agent at Dulles International Airport. Quickly, the senator was whisked away to a secret location, where he was warned to drop the issue of Saudi involvement. Graham remains steadfast in pursuit of answers to 9/11, asserting, "There is a pervasive pattern of covering up the role of Saudi Arabia in 9/11 by all of the agencies of the federal government which have access to information that might illuminate Saudi Arabia's role in 9/11."[35]

Another Floridian garnered attention for his withering criticism of the CIA and intelligence community for their roles in 9/11. Porter Goss filled the role of a secret agent man when he worked as a CIA case officer. The son of patrician New England parents, a student of ancient Greece, Goss was recruited by the CIA while an undergraduate at Yale. He performed clandestine operations for the agency throughout Latin America, the Caribbean, and Europe in the 1960s. In 1970, Goss believed he was poisoned by foreign agents, and he was forced to retire. His retirement was short-lived. He fell in love with his new home on Sanibel Island, founding the *Island Reporter* and, in 1974, successfully running for city council. He became an ardent environmentalist, fighting to preserve Sanibel's charm from being bulldozed by Lee County developers. He won election to the U.S. Congress in 1988, chairing the House Intelligence Committee. Congressman Goss and Senator Graham led and helped establish the Joint Inquiry into Intelligence Community Activities before and after the Terrorist Attacks of September 11, 2001. Goss was critical of President Clinton for his failures to take out bin Laden as well as the report's missing twenty-eight pages implicating Saudi involvement in 9/11. In 2004, President Bush nominated Goss to become the director of the CIA. Goss made few friends at the agency when he characterized it as becoming "a stilted bureaucracy incapable of even the slightest bit of success." Critics charged that Goss's intelligence committee had been missing in action when confronting al-Qaeda and terrorism.[36]

Terrorism once again entangled Saudi Arabia and Florida. Twenty-one-year-old Mohammed Alshamarani was a second lieutenant in the Royal Saudi Air Force. The student naval flight officer was part of a Naval Aviation Schools Command at the Naval Air Station in Pensacola, one of more than 5,000 foreign students assigned to U.S. military bases. In December 2019 Alshamarani shot and killed three U.S. sailors with a Glock 45 9mm pistol that he had purchased legally. Shortly before the attack, the shooter and friends watched videos of mass shootings. He spewed a hate-filled message hours before the attack. The navy grounded 175 Saudi military exchange students assigned to three Florida air bases from flight training, in what was called a "safety stand-down." After an investigation, Attorney General William P. Barr declared that the shooting was an act of terrorism. Federal investigators concluded, after decrypting the Saudi cadet's iPhone, that the gunman had been radicalized as an al-Qaeda operative since 2015. The investigation pitted a fight between the Justice Department and Apple over data privacy.[37]

An unsolved mystery continues to intrigue conspiracy theories and counterfactual "what if" scenarios. On the morning of 11 September 2001, as President Bush prepared to jog at the Colony Beach Resort, a van pulled up to the resort's entrance. The driver announced to the attendant that they had arrived to conduct a "poolside interview" with the president. Confused, the gatekeeper handed the phone to a secret service agent, who had not been informed of any such appointment. The security official told the van's driver to contact the White House, denying the strangers entry into the Colony Beach Resort. The security guard described the driver and occupants as "Middle Eastern." Three years later, the military leader of the Northern Alliance in Afghanistan was assassinated during an interview by a bomb placed in the video camera. The *St. Petersburg Times* asked later, "Were the men on Longboat Key planning to kill Bush in similar fashion?" On Longboat Key, several key witnesses refused to discuss the details of the story or even verify its veracity. Allegedly, secret service agents "suggested we [Shay Sullivan, the journalist who first wrote about the incident, and Carroll Mooneyhan, the Longboat Key fire marshal] back off the story."[38]

Consequences

Understanding 9/11 and its consequences is unnerving and challenging because, unlike conventional wars, the narrative and ending are unconventional. When will the struggle end? How will we even know? By the evening of 7 December 1941, Americans understood the war would end when Imperial Japan surrendered. Strikingly, this new era of warfare began when an old conflict ended in 1991. When the Soviet Union collapsed, imploded by its sheer weight, followed by the tearing down of the Berlin Wall, Americans were wildly optimistic, hoping we could refocus our energies more on domestic tranquility and less on intercontinental ballistic missiles. American leaders erupted in back-slapping praise for Ronald Reagan, John Kennedy, and forgotten Cold Warriors. John J. Mearsheimer, an international relations scholar, asked that we reconsider what we wished for. America, he proposed, will rue the day the Soviet Union fell, arguing that we may well "wake up one day lamenting the loss of the order that the Cold War gave to the anarchy of international relations." The Soviet Union may have been menacing and malignant, but its leaders were neither crazy nor suicidal. They understood the insanity of mutual assured destruction. On 11 September 2001, America and the West were introduced to a stateless enemy without boundaries or treaties, conventions or rules.[39]

The years following 9/11 have numbed, educated, and confused Floridians' attitudes toward the Middle East, the military, and the meaning of war. Anyone who lived through the era acquired a new lexicon of names and terms: Taliban and al-Qaeda, Ayman al-Zawahiri and Ahmad Chalabi, Homeland Security and black sites. President Bush in his 2002 State of the Union address introduced the term "Axis of Evil," branding Iraq, Iran, and North Korea as outlaw states. The president's father, former president George H. W. Bush, disapproved of his son's coarse language and his approach to foreign policy. "Ground zero," which once meant the site of a nuclear explosion, now became identified with the World Trade Center. Americans learned to distinguish the colors of terror alerts: red warning of imminent attack and green indicating tranquility. The War on Terror metastasized into the invasion of Afghanistan, War on al-Qaeda, the Iraqi War, the destruction of Syria, the rise of the Islamic State, and the aftermath spurred the greatest displacement of migrants and refugees since 1945. The War on Terror has broken budgets, dashed dreams, and busted booms. "The war on terrorism has always been less a battle against a specific terror organization than a struggle against a violent, transnational extremist ideology," writes James S. Robbins.[40]

On the eve of 9/11, Gallup polls indicated that President Bush's job approval ratings were sinking, settling at 51 percent. The economy was also beginning to flutter and decline. President Clinton left office in January 2001 with a lofty approval rating of nearly 70 percent. But the public rallied around the new president's efforts to reassure the nation, with his job approval rating soaring to 90 percent in early October, the highest ever recorded. Historically, foreign policy crises—the Korean War, the Cuban Missile Crisis, and the invasion of Granada—initially rallied public support around the chief executive. But history also shows that the public can be impatient and fickle: witness the high disapproval ratings for presidents trapped in the quagmires of Korea and Vietnam.[41]

President Bush was not an eloquent communicator, but he projected the image of a muscular leader in the days following the terrorist attacks. In his moving address to a Joint Session of Congress on 20 September 2001, the president emphatically insisted that America was not at war with Islam. The tragedy united Americans, but Bush failed to harness the desperate energy and creative dynamic of that moment, squandering a rare opportunity. At a time when fewer and fewer Americans had served or were serving in the military, the president never asked or demanded that we had an obligation to pay for the war and not let debts slide to the next generation. He never summoned the American people and discussed the price—human, generational, and economic—of nation building at home and abroad. The president never cast the war as an environmental rallying cry to reconsider the ghastly costs of foreign oil. "Everyone wanted to be of use, and no one knew how," a frustrated George Packer wrote, "as if citizenship were a skilled position for which none of us had the right experience and qualifications." President Bush finally offered advice. "Get down to Disney World in Florida," he implored. "Take your families and enjoy life, the way we want it to be." The administration's policies reflected "an oddly business-as-usual approach," writes historian Andrew J. Bacevich. "Bush told a few of us to go to war," wailed Thomas Friedman, "and the rest of us to go shopping." The national debt between 2001 and 2008 exploded from $6 trillion to $10 trillion. The Manchester *Guardian* calculated the financial cost of 9/11 to the United States at $11 trillion.[42]

"When the twin towers collapsed," wrote a journalist, "Orlando's tourist-dependent economy crumbled with them." Promptly, American authorities imposed a three-day flight ban. Suddenly shattered and exposed, nervous, scared, and with higher priorities, Americans did not feel like taking a vacation to Florida. Harris Rosen, a well-known Orlando hotelier, explained that cancellations began in the wake of 9/11. "The impact was immediate, devastating, and completely understandable," admitted Rosen. Central Florida hotel occupancy rates on the eve of 9/11 were 66 percent, falling quickly to 44 percent. Almost 3 million fewer tourists came to Central Florida in 2001 than in the previous year. Tourism's woes impacted the region's restaurant and service industries. By the end of 2002, the U.S. travel industry had lost 1.8 million jobs. Travel officials call the period 2001–11 "the lost decade."[43]

The 9/11 fallout was not limited to Orlando. In mid-September 2001, five anonymous letters laced with deadly anthrax spores were mailed in Princeton, New Jersey, to Boca Raton. Bob Stevens of American Media died of anthrax poisoning. A week later, health officials found anthrax spores in Lantana, a city previously best known as the headquarters of the *National Inquirer* and vacationing Finns. The biological attack—dubbed "Amerithrax"—killed five persons and injured seventeen. The perpetrator turned out not to be chemical weapons experts in Kabul or Lahore but rather a disgruntled scientist at a government lab. Frightened by images of aircraft missiles slamming into skyscrapers and bioterrorists depositing deadly letters, Americans seemed to be ricocheting from crisis to catastrophe.[44]

A modern Rip Van Winkle, returning from a slumber in Niceville or Seahaven, would be bemused if not unnerved upon arriving at a Florida airport. Airport protocol after 9/11 brought draconian changes in security. Bomb-sniffing dogs, body scanners, and Homeland Security and Transportation Security Administration (TSA) workers suddenly appeared, followed by signs demanding that passengers take off their shoes and belts. The very name "Homeland" conjured up images of the Great Patriotic War and unfurled nationalism. Passengers shook their heads when passing large containers loaded with confiscated vials of shampoo, bottled water, and potential weapons (tweezers, bottles of kombucha and spices, gel shoe inserts, and golf clubs). Welcome to the new normal. "Airport security in America is a sham—'security theater' designed to make travelers feel better and catch stupid terrorists," writes Jeffrey Goldberg. A terrorism expert told Goldberg, "We defend against what the terrorists did last week."[45]

The new fears, followed by discomfort and aggravation, severely wounded the airline industry. New terms greeted customers at airports: alert level, shoe bomb, cell phone lot, and no-fly list. On the eve of 9/11, industry executives were already fretting the bottom line as fares and profits were declining, largely the result of intense competition following deregulation. But the airline industry had managed to make profits in the six years preceding 2001. The nightmare of hijacked aircraft crashing into buildings began a decade-long tailspin: four days of complete shutdowns resulting in $1.4 billion in losses, 26 million fewer passengers the month of September 2001, and $7 billion in losses in 2001. The financial fallout from 9/11 resulted in small and large air carriers filing for bankruptcy. The TSA, a massive new agency created in the wake of 9/11, suddenly took over the role of screening millions of passengers at all U.S. airports. But for six months, National Guard troops were deployed at America's busiest airports until the TSA could train 9,000 federal police officers. The public fumed when they read in July 2011 that a ninety-five-year-old woman was asked to remove her diaper at a Pensacola airport checkpoint. "To the chagrin of the inbound travel industry," an observer wrote, "government programs designed to attract visitors took a back seat to those designed to detail and inspect." But the public demanded security.[46]

The events of 2001 also accelerated a familiar trend: the migration of New Yorkers to Florida. On the day of the attacks, a reporter noted, "All over Port St.

Lucie, former New Yorkers discussed the tragedy . . . [and] waited anxiously on word from loved ones and friends." Many Florida newspapers published special tenth-anniversary issues of 9/11, and one is struck at the number of participants who moved to the Sunshine State. "I am a World Trade center survivor," began a letter written by Christina Guarneri. "I worked in Tower 2, on the 23rd floor. I couldn't handle going to Manhattan every day for work." Ms. Guarneri moved to Hudson, a small community in Pasco County. "I was a firefighter in New York City," began a second letter, from Jim Schuppel. "I have known many of the 343 members who succumbed to the tragedy." Mr. Schuppel relocated to Tarpon Springs. Thomas Paradise sent a moving van to Wesley Chapel after his wife narrowly missed being trapped at a meeting at Windows on the World, a notable restaurant atop one of the Twin Towers. Stephen Cooper was delivering documents in the shadows of the World Trade Center that fateful day in 2001. An AP photographer captured a half dozen men fleeing the scene, with the collapsing South Tower in the background. Running while clutching documents in a manila folder was Stephen Cooper, who was unaware of the iconic photograph. He first saw the images while leafing through a *Time* magazine. Cooper and his wife moved to Delray Beach.[47]

Pam Gibson, a librarian and historian, understood the impact of 9/11 several years after 9/11. Her father, a resident of Anna Maria Island, enjoyed afternoons spent at the Beach House, a restaurant and bar run by former governor and U.S. senator Lawton Chiles's family since the 1930s. Pam and her father befriended a New York City resident who was renting a place in nearby Cortez. "One winter night," reminisced Ms. Gibson, "I pointed out the lights of the Sarasota Airport. She literally freaked when she saw the landing lights. It seems she had been living close to the Towers and lost her apartment to the dust and dirt. Her building was later knocked down as 'uninhabitable. . . . PTSD is real!"[48]

The Security State

Not every industry in Florida suffered because of 9/11; indeed, some sectors boomed *because* of new fears. In the tumultuous aftermath, an economy of fear sprang to life, every bit as powerful as the politics of fear. In times of upheaval and uncertainty, individuals seek shelter. "What was destroyed yesterday," opined columnist Robert Samuelson, "was not just the World Trade Center and part of the Pentagon but Americans' serenity and sense of security." In Florida, professional athletes, along with the rich and famous, sought the protective blanket of bodyguards. Seminars lured the rich, the nervous, and the ambitious with titles such as "Surviving the Kill Zone—Human Factors Are the Key." Florida's Executive Protection Institute offered seminars in the martial arts, evasive driving, and concealed weapons permits. Specialized body shops began installing bulletproof glass and armor-deflecting panels. Miami plays the role of a postmodern Casablanca, the place to meet and watch Colombian drug lords, wealthy Venezuelan refugees, deposed monarchs, and South Beach models and actors. "Unbeknownst to most Miamians," insists the *Miami New Times*, "their city is a central hub in this lucrative but loosely regulated [security] industry." By 2013, more than 1,000 private security companies called South Florida home. CNN News investigated the topic and discovered that many armed security guards "have lax training standards and haphazard oversight." Lukace Shane Kendle was one of 100,000 private security guards working in Florida in 2014. In 2012, he shot two men outside a strip club in Miami. One was killed and the other paralyzed. Kendle suspected they were smoking marijuana. An armed guard, Kendle had been convicted of drunken driving, public drunkenness, and diagnosed with impulse issues. Such past misbehavior did not disqualify Kendle as an armed security guard in Florida.[49]

The USA PATRIOT Act, passed by Congress in the rush to staunch the bleeding, might have been called the Security Relief Act. The act's name is an acronym for "Uniting and Strengthening America by Providing Appropriate Tools Required to Interpret and Obstruct Terrorism." Somewhere, George Orwell is amused, regretful that he had not thought of the acronym for *1984*. President Bush later reflected: "My only regret about the PATRIOT Act is its name. When my administration sent the bill to Capitol Hill, it was initially called the Anti-Terrorism Act of 2001. As a result, there was an implication that people who opposed the law were unpatriotic." "The top-secret world the government created in response to the terrorist attacks of Sept. 11, 2001," observes the *Washington Post*, "has become so large, so unwieldy, and so secretive that no one knows how much money it costs, how many people it employs, how many programs exist within or exactly how many agencies do the same work." Investigators estimated that 1,271 government organizations and 1,931 private companies are funded to combat terrorism and collect intelligence. More than 850,000 persons hold top-secret clearances. Federal dollars have created a vast bureaucracy devoted to counterterrorism and security, and Florida ranks third among all states in organizations devoted to homeland security since 9/11. Florida boasts six Joint Terrorism Task Forces, located in Orlando, Pensacola, West Palm Beach, Jacksonville, Miami, and Tampa. Florida also established an Office of Domestic Security.[50]

Events at the World Trade Center did not create a gun culture in Florida, but the response and backlash weaponized the Right's fear and, for many, intensified their sense of urgency about acquiring firearms. Florida history can be calibrated by the guns we carried: the harquebus, Remington sharpshooter, the .32 caliber pistol, and the Timber Classic Marlin 336C, the favored firearms of conquistadores, crackers, would-be presidential assassins, and hunters.

An economist observed, "It is easier to profit from a big bad thing than a big good thing." As the world seemed to be coming off its axis, Floridians flocked to gun shops and gun shows. As the new century dawned, antigun advocates felt confident in reining in America's gun culture. The Columbine school massacre in April 1999 alarmed many Americans. A 2000 Gallup poll offered encouragement when 51 percent of Americans felt "having a gun in the house makes it more dangerous." Only 35 percent believed a firearm made them feel "safer." That year, fewer than 30,000 Floridians applied or filed for renewal of a permit to carry a gun license. Marion Hammer heard the clarion call for action. The first female to lead the National Rifle Association (NRA), she was well-situated in Tallahassee to thwart any efforts to restrict gun ownership. As the NRA's lobbyist, she skillfully rewarded friends and punished enemies. Republican-dominated legislatures extended the power of gun ownership in Florida. In 2005, the Legislature passed the "Stand Your Ground" law, the right to self-defense. "How overwhelming is Florida's gun culture?" asked the *Huffington Post.* "Florida has 3.2 times as many federally licensed gun dealerships as post offices. In fact . . . 99.3 percent of Sunshine State residents live within 10 miles of a firearms dealer." By 2013, Florida surpassed the one-millionth concealed weapons permit, leading every state in America, including Texas. The Sunshine State had become the Gunshine State. In 2014, when Gallup asked the same question about having a gun in the house, 63 percent believed a firearm made them feel "safer."[51]

The combined wallop of Columbine and 9/11 filtered down to Florida schools and sporting events. Following the school shootings at Columbine in 1999, "lockdown" procedures became part of every principal's responsibility. "After 9/11," writes Dr. Susan Turner, who served as a principal in Tampa during this era, "we went through an extended period of learning how to secure our buildings (duct tape could supposedly be used to keep poisonous gases from entering window and door crevasses!), ordering and storing a sufficient number of water bottles to withstand hours of lock down, locating 'safe havens' close to schools where students could be evacuated."[52]

The schoolhouse, once thought of as a place of innocence and frivolity, responded to 9/11. Parents, teachers, and politicians demanded safe and secure schools. In the years preceding 2001, architects designed schools to be open and airy, more like a modern apartment complex or miniature college quad. Fences, barricades, and bollards immediately appeared to discourage strangers and suicide drivers. "Target-hardened schools" evolved as a new goal: curving walls to frustrate a shooter's line of sight, bulletproof backpacks, and armed teachers. Student cell phones remain a controversial topic. The images of victims aboard doomed aircraft or buildings saying goodbye to loved ones confronts educational policies and the inequities of technology. Most K–12 schools now have a single main entrance. "Today," observed a Central Florida newspaper, "employees have badges, background checks are done on visitors, and school grounds are more secure." The reporter added that "buses have Global Positioning Systems, all because of Sept. 11, school shootings, and stricter predator laws."[53]

The Capitol in Tallahassee was once a place where groups of students on class field trips, lobbyists in search of legislators, and an army of state workers floated freely between government buildings. Motorists dropped off passengers next to state office doors. Shortly after 9/11, Tallahassee resembled a foreign capital under siege, and a siege mentality fraught with fear was much in evidence. Recalled veteran Tallahassee observer Bill Cottrell: "The Capitol got metal detectors at entrances, and everybody now working there now wears photo ID tags. There are also ugly little concrete columns that squat along Monroe Street, lest a car bomber might race up Apalachee Parkway and slam into the building." Cottrell pointed out examples of politicians taking advantage of the climate of suspicion. There was a bill to forbid photographing farm animals without an owner's permission." He added, "It was never known why terrorists might want pictures of horses and cows, but the bill was widely considered a sop to big agriculture, which didn't want animal rights activists documenting inhumane conditions."[54]

If the little red schoolhouse symbolized lost innocence following 9/11, the old rugged cross offered a new generation faith and solace in a troubled time. The Rev. Billy Graham, whose religious fires had been ignited as a student at Florida Bible Institute in Temple Terrace, a Tampa suburb, prayed that Americans "become stronger through all the struggle to rebuild on a solid foundation." *USA Today* editorialized that the sheer magnitude of the returnees to pews and pulpits—estimated as a 25 percent increase—"herald a new religious awakening in the United States after the attacks." Robert Butterworth, a clinical psychologist, explained the phenomenon more simply: "When America gets mad, it turns to the Old Testament. 'An eye for an eye, a tooth for a tooth.'" Many ministers and rabbis explained the delicate tightrope they were walking. Religious leaders, a journalist observed, "counseled worshipers to stay calm, to resist the instinct to hate and to judge. And yet they were careful to speak of the need to respond quickly—and with great force." A decade later, *USA Today* returned to the subject and concluded that the 2001 religious uptick was fleeting, "a mere blip in a long-standing trend away from traditional religious practice." However, scholars have found a lingering "spiritual impact revealed when 9/11 stories are recounted through individual recollections of faith reborn, revitalized, or reshaped."[55]

In a tragedy, religion can serve as buckle and shield, but also as a cudgel and broad axe. A September 2001 televised exchange between evangelists Jerry Falwell and Pat Robertson went viral. Falwell, who served as the chancellor of Liberty University in Virginia, blamed the terrorist attacks on homosexuality, abortion rights, and secular schools and judges. Reverend Falwell railed, "Throwing God out successfully with the help of the federal court system, throwing God out of the public square, out of the school." Throwing kerosene on the fire, he added: "The abortionists have got to bear some burden for this because God will not be mocked. And we destroy 40 million little innocent babies, we make God mad." The remarks were so incendiary that even President Bush denounced the rhetoric. "Among evangelicals," observed the *New York Times,* "the terrorist attacks have unleashed renewed calls for repentance, prayer and spiritual revival."[56]

If one individual exemplified the American dream and its possibilities, but also the pain and suspicion of Islam in America, it was Sami Al-Arian. The son of Palestinian refugees, Al-Arian was born in Kuwait and educated in Egypt. He immigrated to the United States in 1975 and earned his doctorate in engineering in North Carolina. He accepted a teaching position at the University of South Florida (USF) in 1986. He and his family resided in Temple Terrace, a community near Tampa that was attracting large numbers of Muslims and featured a nearby mosque, where he became an imam. Al-Arian passionately fought for Palestinian rights and helped found a charity that raised funds for refugees. In 1990, his efforts led to USF's establishment of the World and Islam Studies Enterprise (WISE). In 1995, a film directed by a well-known critic of Islamic extremism depicted Al-Arian and WISE as a Trojan horse for home-front jihad. Local journalists also investigated WISE's actions. Authorities arrested Al-Arian's brother-in-law for his work with Palestinian terrorists. Ironically, more than 80 percent of Muslim Americans—including Sami Al-Arian, who had a photograph taken with George Bush at a fundraiser—voted for Bush in 2000. A Zogby poll explained that most Muslims identify with the conservative values associated with the Republican Party.[57]

The attack on the Twin Towers transformed the government's case, starkly exposing a Muslim activist in the post-9/11 era. In late September 2001, Al-Arian appeared on the Fox News program *The O'Reilly Factor.* Why Al-Arian agreed to appear on a conservative talk show remains a mystery, but what had been largely a local controversy went viral. Bill O'Reilly, citing a videotape revealing Al-Arian chanting "Death to Israel" at rallies, urged the CIA to monitor the Muslim professor. Judy Genshaft, the new president of USF, found herself in an impossible position, hounded by angry politicians and citizens to purge extremism at "Jihad U" as faculty demanded that she respect academic freedom. Genshaft suspended Al-Arian, placing him on paid leave and banning him from the campus. Local and national teachers' unions and associations pushed back and filed grievances. The fact that Genshaft was Jewish inflamed the Internet chatter. In February 2003, the government indicted Al-Arian, charging him with seventeen counts under the USA PATRIOT Act. The jury acquitted the controversial professor on eight counts and remained deadlocked on nine counts.[58]

Eventually, Al-Arian pleaded guilty to laundering funds to aid the Palestine Islamic Jihad, a charity aiding families of jihadist martyrs. Convicted for violating the USA PATRIOT Act, Al-Arian was sentenced to fifty-seven months in prison. He was tried and retried for criminal contempt and racketeering, but few charges stuck. The *Washington Post* summarized the case: "Was an Islamic professor exercising his freedom or promoting terror?" After one of the Justice Department's most dogged investigations, the United States finally deported Al-Arian to Turkey in 2015. His attorney, Jonathan Turley, Finsisted upon his client's innocence, maintaining that the professor agreed to a plea agreement that allowed him to leave the United States after his prison term. Al-Arian's case, argues Turley, "raised troubling due process, academic freedom, and free speech issues." The case of Sami Al-Arian, and the question of whether he was more sinned against than sinning endures as a much-debated subject.[59]

Muslims throughout Florida and the United States felt the furies of 9/11. Unsubstantiated rumors circulated that crowds of Muslims were seen cheering when the Twin Towers collapsed. Prior to 2001, few American Muslims had experienced hate crimes. In the 2016 presidential race, candidate Donald Trump swore he witnessed televised scenes of Jersey City Muslims erupting deliriously that Satan had been punished. In the year 2000, the FBI recorded only 28 such hate crime incidents. In 2001, that figure spiraled to 481 and never dropped below 100 in the subsequent decade. Minutes following 9/11, callers threatened the Darul Uloom Institute in Pembroke Pines, one of South Florida's largest mosques. On the afternoon of 11 September, a woman steered her car into a school's parking lot. Handwritten signs affixed to the car's windows read, "God Bless USA," and "Death to Terrorists." A sheriff's deputy had been dispatched to the school in anticipation of such incidents. No weapons were found in the car. The woman said she simply "got caught up in everything on the news." Not far away stood the Islamic Academy of Florida. Reporters found Sami Al-Arian, not yet a cause célèbre, announcing that classes had been canceled. On school buses, employees had taped over the word "Islamic." Over the next two years, a Muslim mosque and school were ransacked in Tallahassee, Miami, and Cooper City. In Gainesville, police charged a man with a hate crime for threatening and peppering with bug spray three persons of Indian descent. In Seminole, Pinellas County deputies arrested Dr. Robert Goldstein, charged with possession of destructive devices (including light rockets, a sniper rifle, and 25,000 rounds of ammunition) and a blueprint to attack Islamic centers. In Boca Raton, an individual was sentenced to one month in prison for torching a sign announcing a new Islamic community center and mosque. In 2010, when Rev. Terry Jones of Gainesville announced that he was going to hold a Quran burning on the ninth anniversary of 9/11, the event became a media circus. To ensure that weak-kneed judges did not apply Sharia law in Florida, the legislature enacted a law prohibiting judges from applying foreign legal doctrine in family court cases. In 2016, a study indicated that hate crimes against American Muslims have escalated. An Islamic Center in Fort Pierce was burned by an arsonist in 2016.[60]

But for all the news attention surrounding the individual attacks on Muslims, Florida and America tempered their anger, and the country was not swept away in a wave of xenophobia and nativist violence, as was evident in World War I, when German Americans were branded as "Huns" and immigrants as hyphenated Americans. Others feared the conflict was dividing the world into moral zones of good and evil. Floridians confronted the reality that America was a different place, a place journalist Tom Gjelten argued was "far less white, Christian and European than it used to be."[61]

Howard Troxler, one of Florida's leading journalists, reminded readers that if, indeed, 9/11 was the product of Islamic terrorists, "we should remember that 'Islamic' is not a synonym for 'terrorist,' any more than 'Christian' is a synonym for 'McVeigh.'" Muslim leaders across Florida worked to establish interfaith dialogues. At a 9/11 memorial service at St. Andrew's Episcopal Church in St. Petersburg, Imam Mohammad Sultan Abu Hasaan preached, "God wants us to work together to establish good." Reflected journalist George Packer: "American moralism swings wildly between high-minded idealism and hysterical intolerance. At certain moments—our entry into World War I was one—the transformation happens almost overnight: the muckraker gives way to the night rider, the Progressive city commission to the Red Scare."[62]

To paraphrase Karl Marx, sports is the opiate of the terrified masses. In a nation rattled by suicide bombers, sports offered a comforting return to sanity. "Many believe sports began to weave their way back into our lives on Sept. 21," wrote a columnist. Certainly, sports can comfort us and remind us of more innocent and uncomplicated times—even if there is preciously little innocence in the business of football and baseball. Sports moguls have known for some time that a veneer of patriotism helps keep the glare off the seamier side of the games. Playing the National Anthem, a rarity at sporting events in earlier years, began in earnest during World War I and World War II. Football and baseball games have become recruiting grounds for spectators and viewers, as patriotic spectacles unfold. In 2015, an investigator revealed that the Pentagon paid the National Football League and Major League Baseball $6.8 million to promote patriotic displays and flyovers. NASCAR received $1.6 million. A spokesperson at the Department of Defense defended the expenditures as "integral to its recruiting efforts." Not long ago, fans attending a baseball or football game simply bought a ticket and walked inside the stadium. No more. Attending an athletic event today seems a lot like standing in security lines at the airport, with the now-accustomed body scans, purse inspections, and confiscation drill. Eerily, scenes for the 1976 cult movie *Black Sunday* were filmed at the Orange Bowl in Miami. The movie's plot involves Palestinian terrorists unleashing lethal shrapnel at 80,000 spectators from the Goodyear blimp during a Super Bowl game.[63]

Another casualty of the War on Terror has been political moderation. Consider the meteoric career of Glenn Beck. In 2001, Beck was a largely unknown thirty-seven-year-old radio host, a recovering alcoholic and drug addict. In 2000, he launched the *Glenn Beck Show* in Tampa, replacing a liberal talk slot. He took over a little-listened-to hour at WFLA-AM and found his voice and audience. He once conducted a skit in which Satan pens love letters to Hillary Clinton. His ascendency began the week of 9/11. Radio executives extended his show an extra three hours, offering his program to all stations. Clear Channel, a megamedia empire, recognized Beck's charisma and bet correctly that Beck would connect with a wider audience seeking answers. Within a year, Beck took a hard-right turn out of Tampa and onto the national stage. The following year, Beck had his own national syndicated deal. The *New York Times* explained his appeal, noting that, with his "mix of moral lessons, outrage, and an apocalyptic view of the future . . . [Beck] is capturing the feelings of an alienated class in America." MSNBC and Fox News also rose to prominence during this era. MSNBC, a liberal-leaning network, countered with Keith Olbermann in 2003, while Fox News introduced Sean Hannity on the eve of 9/11. Journalist David

Von Drehle traces the origins of immoderation to the 2000 election: "Partisan Democrats as well as Republicans drew from the Florida's botched election the simple message that the other side can never be trusted. Implacably treacherous, the other side will stop at nothing."[64]

Afghanistan and Iraq

The greatest growth industry since 9/11 may well be governmental overreach. Such developments should not have been a shock. Randolph Bourne, a critic of the Great War, wrote famously, "War is the health of the state." Bourne was not referring to the arms industry or spikes in patriotism; rather, he lamented the aggrandizement of power seized by the federal government during times of crisis. In 1917–18, the state ushered in the Committee of Public Information and the Espionage and Sedition Acts. The Food Administration urged Americans to obey Wheatless Mondays and Meatless Tuesdays. During World War II, the government interned Japanese Americans and rationed food and materiel. In *Schenck v. United States* (1919), the U.S. Supreme Court maintained that dissent in opposition to the draft was equivalent to "yelling fire in a crowded theater."

The USA PATRIOT Act, signed into law by President Bush in October 2001, endures as the most recognized post-9/11 security legislation. But the 107th Congress passed more than 130 security laws, as well as 48 bills and resolutions. Quickly, drone strikes, "sneak and peek warrants," and National Security Administration phone surveillance became accepted practices. Paul Pillar, a veteran CIA analyst and fellow at Georgetown University's Center for Security Studies, offered this brutal assessment of the American response to terror: "In searching for a fix to prevent recurrence of the national trauma of 9/11, Americans reassured themselves with the characteristically American belief that by applying enough ingenuity, resources, and determination, any problem can be solved, and any threat neutralized. The chosen fix focused on intelligence."[65]

Americans are an impatient people. The war dragged on and on. The number of American troops peaked in 2011, with 101,000 troops on the ground. Compared to Vietnam, casualties were light—2,326 as of October 2015—but each death was magnified because of the nature of the new media. Almost 150 Florida service members have been killed in Afghanistan since 2002. President Obama, while admitting that it "was time to turn the page," decided to keep U.S. troops in Afghanistan to 2017. In 2019, President Trump announced plans for a quick withdrawal of the last U.S. troops in Afghanistan by 2020.[66]

In just two years, President Bush's fortunes swiveled from that head-snapping

"America is under attack!" moment at an elementary school to landing a modern jet atop the USS *Abraham Lincoln* and speaking under a banner with a self-satisfied message writ large. From the perspective of 2020, the orchestrated bravado haunts the president's legacy. Tragically, America has been unable to exit without new crises or flashpoints stalling disengagement. But in August 2021, President Biden ordered U.S. troops to evacuate from America's longest war in Afghanistan. "These conflicts will not only define America in the eyes of the world for many decades to come," writes international relations scholar David Rothkopf, "but they will also shape the views of a generation of men and women who will decide where, when and how the United States will flex its muscles internationally." Peter Van Buren, a State Department veteran, wrote a book on the topic with a poignantly tragic title, *We Meant Well*. In late March 2003, 75 percent of Americans approved of the decision to invade Iraq. By May 2015, when asked about the Iraq War, 59 percent of Americans thought the war was a mistake.[67]

The Iraq War accelerated military expenditures to astronomical levels. From a $300 billion military budget in 2001, spending soared to $450 billion in 2004 and to $600 billion in 2007. By 2012 military spending absorbed 37 percent of the budget, as much as health care, poverty programs, and interest on the public debt combined. Adjusted for inflation, the Afghanistan and Iraq Wars have been the most expensive conflicts in American history, except for World War II. The *New York Times* estimated the cost of funding the Gulf Wars at $1.7 billion, and veterans' care costs at $867 billion.[68]

The military's impact upon Florida can be measured in human costs. In 2021, 1.5 million military veterans reside in Florida, a figure representing 8 percent of the state's population. Conspicuously, more than 360,000 veterans of the Gulf Wars make Florida home. Indicative of the new American military, women comprise 8 percent of new veterans. These women and men represent part of the "other 1 percent—the all-volunteer military." Michiko Kakutani, reviewing books on the "Forever Wars," observed, "The emotional distance between Iraq or Afghanistan and the United States cannot be measured in miles, and many soldiers have felt caught somewhere in between, even after leaving the combat zone." Never have so many severely injured soldiers' lives been saved by medical advances. The costs—psychic, medical, rehabilitation—are enormous. Correspondingly, the proportion of Americans who have served in the military is at a historic low, creating a tremendous gap between citizens and soldiers. The U.S. Department of Veterans Affairs has been overwhelmed and underperforming. A series of scandals in 2014 and 2015 damaged the agency's reputation. Some of Florida's veterans' hospitals have received critical reviews.[69]

Perspective: Our Generation's Pearl Harbor

"It was the best of times, it was the worst of times, it was the age of wisdom, it was the age of foolishness." In *The Tale of Two Cities* (1859), Charles Dickens understood that although he was describing life on the eve of the French Revolution, he was also portraying every age. Floridians, like most Americans, tend to be self-absorbed. In a remarkably brief time, from 1 January 2000 to 2003, Florida experienced a wild ride spanning the giddiness of Y2K to the turmoil of the November 2000 elections to the exclamation point of 9/11 to the despair of an unpopular war and national insecurity.

The immediate reaction of many older Americans was to compare 9/11 to Pearl Harbor. Certainly, some similarities mark the two events. Americans employed similar words in reaction to the two events: "treachery" and "sneak attack," "ground zero" and "suicide pilots." Historian John Dower notes that after 9/11, "'Infamy' was the first word many American commentators summoned to convey the enormity of their crimes." The combined shock delivered a psychological blow to citizens and officials. In both cases, the tragedies aroused Americans to a pitch. Massive intelligence failures contributed to the success of the enemies' daring tactics, emboldening critics to suggest vast conspiracies.[70]

But Pearl Harbor and 9/11 were profoundly different events. For all the angry 12/7 denunciations—that the Japanese had stabbed us in the back, had broken the civilized and codified rules of warfare with an unprovoked attack on a Sunday morning against noncombatants in a time of peace, the attacks on Pearl Harbor and the World Trade Center and Pentagon should not be conflated. First, Japan intended to declare war against the United States moments before the Hawaii bombings, but Japanese embassy officials took too long to decode the document. Consequently, Japan declared war on the United States two hours after the military assault.

Second, the Japanese attacked U.S. Navy vessels and installations, that is, military not civilian targets. The World Trade Center and the Pentagon were symbolic targets, resulting in civilian, not military deaths. Pearl Harbor left no doubt as to the enemy; 9/11 left Americans largely confused as to who the enemy was and precisely what the responses should be. Most Americans had no idea of the location of Pearl Harbor. Americans watched live footage of what happened in New York and Washington, D.C. In 1941, officials deliberately filtered the facts, not wanting the Japanese to know its success or citizens to know the full damage.

Third, following the debacles of Pearl Harbor and New York, Americans resolved to destroy the enemy. But Imperial Japan—an island nation composed of a fiercely nationalistic, homogeneous population—profoundly differed from al-Qaeda's crazy-quilt, stateless composition of ethnic and national jihadists. Historian Dower explains that vast differences separated the events of 1941 and 2001. "Unlike Japan and Germany, with their formidable military machines," he writes in *Cultures of War*, "the new antagonists were transnational, crudely armed, loosely organized, and committed to ad hoc 'asymmetric' tactics of confrontation and destruction. They materialized and disappeared like phantoms." The shocking successes of the Japanese and terrorists boosted the confidence of the attackers. In the case of 9/11, the attacks served as a recruiting tool for disaffected Muslims.[71]

Fourth, the war following Pearl Harbor required the patriotism and energies of a united public to mobilize 12 million servicemen and women and marshal the arsenal. World War II galvanized a nation, providing jobs for everyone who wanted one, and a springboard to a robust peace. The GI Bill of Rights, an inspiring act of faith and gratitude, allowed for a middle-class lifestyle for millions who, in 1940, figured they would lead the desperate lives of their parents. Pearl Harbor energized a dormant economy, creating a military/industrial complex. Iraq created no such economic bump. Rather, the Afghanistan and Iraq Wars helped wreck the economy, bloated the bureaucracy, and failed to inspire Americans to create something better from the tragedy and conflict.

Perhaps most emphatically, Americans understood that the fight must subdue the enemy, resulting in a formal surrender. Martin Dyckman was a young boy living in Clearwater in 1941, a journalist in 2001: "On that ancient day of infamy, there wasn't a moment's doubt as to who was to blame or what we would do about it." Confessed ninety-four-year-old Virginia Lewis: "I didn't have the same apprehensions with Pearl Harbor. Here, I don't know what might happen next. I think the results of this are more far-reaching than we can see at this time. That has me very alarmed."[72]

But if 9/11 was not our Pearl Harbor, how exactly should we understand the events? What are the lessons to be learned from 2001? Did 9/11 signify the fall of America as a great power? In comparison to other shattering events in American history, what were the consequences? When coupled with the 2000 political fiasco, was 9/11 a sign that Florida stood on the threshold of humility and failure?[73]

American historians have aggressively argued for over a decade that 9/11, however frightful and spectacular, should not be characterized as one of the nation's watershed events. The fates of the American Revolution, Civil War, and World War II challenged the very existence of a United States and resulted in the flowering of some of the greatest leaders in the republic: Washington, Jefferson, and Hamilton; Lincoln and Grant; Roosevelt, Marshall, and Eisenhower. Americans never questioned the viability of the republic after 9/11, even if we did question the quality of our leaders. "Sept. 11," argues historian Joseph Ellis, "while it places lives and lifestyles at risk, it does not threaten the survival of the American republic, even though terrorists would like us to believe so."[74]

The contours of 9/11 have pushed and pulled scholars to study American history in a global context. Topics new and old such as American colonialism, the history of violence, the origins of terror, the fragility and strength of civil liberties, and a study of Muslims in America, have been explored. But profound disagreements have accompanied the debates. Others argue that 9/11 provoked the opposite reaction—a study of American exceptionalism, the idea that American story has unfolded in profoundly different ways from other nations' experiences.[75]

David Rothkopf argues persuasively that 9/11 was not even the most momentous event of the decade 2000–2009. He contends that the revolution in social media, the Great Recession, the failure to address global warming, and the rise of China and Russia were more substantive and more profound than 9/11: "We cannot allow single isolated events to warp our view of all around them, like historical black holes twisting the fabric of adjacent time and events."[76]

Few scholars doubt that American confidence, or the confidence of Americans in the nation's future, has taken a beating in the first decades of the twenty-first century. A searing recession certainly contributed to the ebb of optimism. But perhaps most strikingly, Floridians and Americans lack confidence in our leaders and their responses to military, economic, and environmental crises. Historian Michael Ruse identifies what he terms the "Doom Boom," a rising number of books addressing Apocalypse Now. "Perhaps expectedly," he writes, "periods of great social stress have tended to be times when apocalyptic thinking goes into overdrive."[77]

The threats of ISIS, global warming, hemorrhaging national debt, and face-eating zombies notwithstanding, America remains a remarkably safe and prosperous place. In part, the incessant media drumbeat and Americans' echo chambers amplify the omnipresence of doom and gloom. We need perspective. "Decline," writes Adam Gopnik, "has the same fascination for historians that love has for lyric poets." Cities, states, and nations have shown a resiliency in the face of disaster and crisis.[78]

Brushed by conspirators, Florida was never physically attacked on 9/11, but the state's geographic location and prominence cemented the role of Florida in

9/11. The events of 2001 accelerated a culture of fear. Increasing numbers of gun owners were merely one of the ramifications. But this national calamity, unlike Pearl Harbor, never transformed Florida. Other historic catastrophes incited fear but resulted in social and economic upheaval: the global warming of 10,000 years ago, terrible epidemics and pandemics that scoured native Americans in the sixteenth and seventeenth centuries, the shock of Civil War and emancipation, the real estate crash of the 1920s followed by the Great Depression of the 1930s.

In the past, some societies shattered by war, plague, or environmental cataclysm have simply collapsed. The natives of Easter Island slashed and burned the woodlands, resulting in what Jared Diamond called "ecocide." The society never recovered from the deforestation. In other cases, societies have rebounded in luminous advancements. Europe's Renaissance followed the Black Death. In the United States, the disillusionment of the Great War, and the painful episodes of the influenza epidemic, race riots, and the Red Scare, gave way to a blossoming of cultural creativity. Few scholars or commentators have yet identified a burst of inventiveness and imagination resulting from the ashes and fears of 2001.[79]

Writing from the vantage point of 2010, *Time* magazine columnist David Von Drehle argues that once the new century's tripwire was disturbed, America staggered and lurched in a state of disequilibrium. He argues the cascade began the evening of 3 November 2000, in Florida. "But while that surreal night did not alter the path of history," he maintains, "in retrospect it looks less like an ending than an omen of official dysfunction and institutional failure." Von Drehle, who worked for the *Miami Herald* in the 1980s, continues:

> We learned the hard way that the ballot box is not necessarily a reliable means of measuring votes, and this proved to be the first of many similar lessons: That law enforcement is not a very effective way to stop hijackers. That spy agencies don't really know what's going on inside hostile regimes. That one crafty old zealot can outwit a whole army sent to hunt him down. That engineers don't always build sound levees, nor bankers issue sound loans.
>
> Again, and again, the system was tested and the system failed. . . . Time has shown that the Florida recount was the drum major of naked emperors.[80]

The singular problem with analyzing 9//11 is that we lack the advantage of perspective. We simply do not know how the conflict will end. Students who wish to discover the quick and easy facts of 9/11 are enabled by a new tool that was born 15 January 2001: Wikipedia. If Wikipedia provides instant analysis that can be revised by every-student-a-historian, the protean meanings of 9/11 will change according to the new times and old facts. Questions persist. Will America exhaust itself in a long struggle with terrorism, or were the events of 2000–2003 a mere blip in a long era of stability? Did 9/11 expose a fatal flaw in the American dream or regenerate new tenets? Perhaps Florida native Tom Petty put it best in his 1989 hit: "You can stand me up at the gates of hell/But I won't back down."

Despite political mayhem and terrorist fears, Florida resumed its steady population march. Americans may have been traumatized, but they remained in love with Florida. Daily, more than 1,000 new residents arrived. In Florida, the years 2000–2003 tested the mettle of 17 million Floridians. But the hurricane winds of 2004 would test the state's metal awnings and truss beams. The year 2004 would also test Florida's ability to count presidential votes. In the stirring words of Shakespeare's King Henry V, "Once more unto the breach!"

The Colony Beach and Tennis Resort, where President Bush spent the evening of 10 September 2001, is gone, replaced by the St. Regis Hotel and Residences. In 2018, the Town of Longboat Key issued an emergency demolition order, the consequences of a decade of dilapidation and a legal quagmire. In his eulogy of the hands-on founder of the iconic resort, journalist Bob Greene wrote that "'Murf' Klauber died at age 91 this past Thanksgiving—the day after the demolition of his beloved resort was completed." Another tribute came from good friend and journalist Matt Walsh. "There will never be another Colony—like the one that made Longboat Key and brought so many people here." St. Regis Hotel and Residences will succeed, not replace the Colony Beach and Tennis Resort.[81]

3

The Year of Four Hurricanes

Red States and Blue Tarps, Old Demons and New Saints

As the calendar flipped from 2003 to 2004, Florida pulsated with a renewed frenzy and intensity. Daily, a rush of cars, planes, rubber and wooden rafts brought tourists, Canadian snowbirds, Cuban and Haitian refugees. Florida had rebounded from the whiplashing of 9/11.

A profile of Florida in 2004 revealed a state that was defying Father Time and infuriating Mother Nature. Notably, the 2004 population of 17.5 million inhabitants and 80 million tourists was largely confident of the future and disinterested in environmental concerns. Without a serious direct hit since 1992, hurricanes seemed distant and irrelevant to the lives of Floridians.

While events in Baghdad, Kabul, and Washington may have been depressing, some semblance of domestic optimism had been restored. A September 2004 poll asked the question, "In general, how satisfied are you with the way things are going in Florida today?" Fully 64 percent of Floridians answered, "very satisfied" or "somewhat satisfied." Florida real estate prices soared ever higher. A median-price, single-family home sold for $186,700. Florida may have been hot and muggy, but millions of residents and snowbirds addressed that uncomfortable truth by spending summers in Highlands and Cashiers, North Carolina; Woodstock and Montpelier, Vermont; and in old family cabins ranging from the Adirondacks, Catskills, and Poconos to Door County and the lakes of Minnesota. Many more simply returned to their seasonal homes scattered across the Heartlands, New England, and Canada. They typically returned in late October when temperatures began cooling and hurricane threats diminished.

A Hurricane Colony and State

To the state's oldest residents, many who had spent most of their adult lives in Ohio or New York, hurricane warnings must have harkened back to diphtheria and polio alerts—something that had once frightened Americans but now seemed quaint if not anachronistic. Old-timers recalled the wreckage wrought by Hurricane Donna in 1960, but in the three decades between Donna and Andrew, a time when Florida's population exploded, almost every wizened cracker and seasoned snowbird could only recall the hurricane warnings that faded along with the hurricanes that veered away. Meteorologists crying, "Wolf!" made Floridians complacent and overconfident. But Marjory Stoneman Douglas, who may have lived through more tropical storms than any living Floridian, expressed her sentiments on the topic with characteristic simplicity: "There is no hurricane but the hurricane one has lived through."[1]

For millennia, tropical storms shaped and reshaped the place we call Florida. Powerful winds and currents pushed and pulled flora and fauna from distant lands and islands to Florida. The now-extinct Taino Indians of the Caribbean called the destructive storms *el huracán*. Spanish navigators learned the demonic meaning of the native word. In the Caribbean, Spanish officials typically named hurricanes Santa María, San José, and Santa Ana, aligning the storms with saints' days. When compared to the most severe Mediterranean storms, *el huracán* combined a fury and power rarely seen by mariners. On the last voyage of Christopher Columbus, the mariner encountered a hurricane near Santo Domingo. According to the Spanish chronicler Bartolomé de las Casas, "After thirty or forty hours, there came such a rare tempest and so violent, that in many years sailing on the seas of Spain and in other areas had not seen one equal, nor so sorrowful had they experienced . . . it seemed as if all the army of demons had escaped from Hades."[2]

Natives and Creoles learned to read signs of an approaching storm: aching bones, severe headaches, premature births; insects, fishes, and birds behaving strangely, the saw grass blooming—all the result of plunging barometric pressure. The hurricane that swept the Florida Keys in 1935 plunged barometers to their lowest modern reading, tormenting survivors with the feeling that their heads were about to explode.

Despite technological wizardry, modern science offered little help in warning Floridians of an approaching storm until recently. Every town boasted an elderly resident or two who swore they could smell a hurricane advancing or feel it in their bones. When the 1921 hurricane approached St. Petersburg, city officials hoisted storm-warning flags a few hours before landfall. The weather bureau announced in August 1935 that twelve southern cities were now linked by teletypewriters capable of transmitting storm conditions. The technological leap offered little comfort to the many families who lost members during the terrible Labor Day hurricane of that year.[3]

The earliest occupants would be bemused, perhaps even amused, at the hubris shown by modern residents who build their homes snug close to the sand dunes. Native Floridians understood the need to adapt. In 2012, archaeologists uncovered a site that could offer succeeding generations a lesson in living: an ancient Indian burial ground near Cedar Key. While unearthing and relocating the bones of 1,200 inhabitants, the archaeologists discovered that the skeletons had been moved once before! Thousands of years earlier, Native Americans faced the challenge of climate change. Their homes and burial sites that once stood on peninsular soil were threatened by rising Gulf waters. Florida's earliest inhabitants also understood that hurricanes must be respected, and villages and homes be built and situated accordingly.[4]

Hurricanes dashed the dreams of Spanish kings, Old South planters, and New South merchants, altering the arc of Florida and the transnational history of the Caribbean. When "master mariner" Christopher Columbus set sail in 1492 into the Caribbean, he had no knowledge that on the average, eight hurricanes a year cross the Caribbean. "If a hurricane had swamped his three little ships," wondered a historian, "the history of the Americas, and the world, would be a bit different." The hurricane of 1561 brought ruin to the Tristán de Luna colony on Pensacola Bay, thus allowing the upstart settlement of St. Augustine to claim the title of America's oldest permanent European city. San Juan, Puerto Rico, remains the oldest city under the American flag, founded in 1521. Four decades later a hurricane scattered a French fleet dispatched to relieve Fort Caroline, built along the St. Johns River. The Spanish raided the French colony, and then put to the sword the storm-tossed Huguenots. Hurricanes in the 1840s snuffed out the promising antebellum towns of St. Joseph, Magnolia, and Port Leon. A wall of water obliterated Cedar Key's prosperity and promise in 1896. "Cedar Keys is a place of desolation and death," eulogized a newspaper.[5]

Some hurricanes pack such a wallop that they urge political action. In September 1926, a seething storm smashed Miami Beach and Miami, leaving in its wake one of the costliest hurricanes in American history. The storm killed 372 inhabitants and left nearly a third of Dade County's residents homeless. The hurricane helped prick the real estate bubble. In 1928, a storm so powerful that locals swore it "blowed a crooked road straight," killed thousands on the southern shore of Lake Okeechobee. "Corpses were not just found in wrecked houses," wrote the famed author Zora Neale Hurston, "they were under houses, tangled in shrubbery, floating in water, hanging in trees, drifting under wreckage." Congress was so appalled at the disaster that it passed an appropriation to build a huge earthen berm to encircle the lake. The 143-mile Herbert Hoover Dike, erected in the 1930s, now surrounds the lake. It would not be the last effort to engineer the Everglades.[6]

Two hurricanes struck Broward County in 1947, part of a deluge that saw Dania officially register 103 inches of rain for the year. From the lakes of Central Florida to Florida Bay, a sheet of water glistened on the surface. The timing was propitious, as the year also witnessed the publication of Marjory Stoneman Douglass's *Everglades: River of Grass,* and the dedication of Everglades National Park. Floridians cheered that the Glades had been saved and preserved. But less noticed, officials representing agricultural interests fought for congressional authorization to drain new portions of the Everglades. In 1949, Congress authorized the Central and Southern Flood Control District, a powerful body that opened vast acreage for development and agriculture.[7]

In 1953, the Weather Bureau, following naval tradition, began assigning women's names to hurricanes. The debut of Hurricane Alice in May 1953 coincided perfectly with television. The weather map indicating the path of the hurricane fit perfectly inside the small screens. Predictably, TV weathermen exploited the opportunity to feminize nature. "Temperamental" hurricanes "flirted" with Caribbean islands, "teased" the mainland, and "undulated" across the stage. Roxcy Bolton, a Florida feminist and founder of the Florida chapter of the National Organization for Women (NOW) in 1966, confronted the male establishment at the National Hurricane Center in Dade County over the naming of storms. Maine's U.S. Senator Margaret Chase Smith supported Bolton's efforts and fantasized a headline reading, "Goldwater Annihilates Florida." She facetiously floated the idea that tropical depressions be called "him-icanes," recommending that maturing storms honor "bloviating" congressmen. In 1970, NOW endorsed her proposal. Initially, officials abruptly dismissed Ms. Bolton, but her argument convinced the organization to begin naming storms after both men and women. In 1979, the season's second storm debuted as Hurricane Bob.[8]

Hurricane Donna crossed Marathon in the Florida Keys before skirting Naples and making landfall at Fort Myers in September 1960. The storm leveled many beach cottages and wooden hotels, paving the way for modern redevelopment. At the time, Southwest Florida had a population of 80,000 inhabitants. Collier County's seat, Everglades City, was hit the hardest, engulfed by 8 feet of water. The city's housing stock was devastated. The county seat was quickly moved to Naples, a city uplifted by Donna's insurance windfall. The history of Southwest Florida remains tightly intertwined with hurricanes.[9]

In *Anna Karenina*, Leo Tolstoy opened with the memorable sentence, "Happy families are alike; every unhappy family is unhappy in its own way." Similarly, hurricanes bring their own signature styles of approach and destruction. Some loop and meander, whereas others follow unswerving paths; some wreak havoc across a tightly formed eye, whereas others spawn massive centers that sprawl across the entire state.

The historical legacy of hurricanes meant little to the millions of South Floridians who resided along the Gold Coast in 1992, the population-rich region comprising Palm Beach, Broward, and Miami-Dade counties. Few could recall the last hurricane that mattered. The 1970s had experienced a record low of three landfall hurricanes in Florida, a trend that continued through the 1980s. In 1992, all that changed. Meteorologists began tracking the season's first storm, later described by the *Miami Herald* as "a Category 5 chain-saw called Andrew [that] cut a swatch of ruin like no storm before it." Considering how the great hurricane of 1926 pricked the Magic City's real estate balloon, the *Herald* was describing an eventful catastrophe. Fortunately for Miami, Andrew swerved slightly southward. Unfortunately for Homestead, the tropical agricultural community was devastated by winds, some measuring 175 mph. In the 150-year history of hurricane records, no other place had been hit more often than Homestead (five times). The 1992 tally remains sobering: more than 28,000 destroyed homes, 107,000 damaged structures, and 350,000 persons forced to evacuate their homes. A decade after Andrew, a veteran reporter acknowledged the grim legacy: "No storm in modern history did more to change the face of South Florida." Until Hurricane Katrina struck Louisiana in 2005, Andrew was the costliest natural catastrophe in American history.[10]

Homestead's fortunes seemed dismal. Before Andrew, Homestead included 1,176 mobile homes. Six survived. The city also lost the Homestead Air Force Base, essentially wiped out by the storm. Adding insult to injury, the Cleveland Indians abandoned its spring-training facility in Homestead.[11]

In the spring of 1993, an unnamed storm with the intensity of a hurricane remained stranded in the Gulf of Mexico, smashing the coastline for days. It is remembered as Florida's "No-Name Storm." In that era, few television stations had live radar. Weather forecasts were spewed out of a fax printer on paper. Most

National Weather Service offices possessed antiquated radar systems. Weather models simply missed the significance of the 1993 storm. "I believe it was the beginning of modern weather forecasting," observed Mike Clay, a Tampa Bay meteorologist.[12]

No single individual did more to professionalize the study and discussion of hurricanes than William R. Gray. A well-known professor of atmospheric science and tropical meteorology, he introduced the idea of the Atlantic hurricane season and annually predicted the number of storms. For his scientific advances and presence, he was called "a hurricane superstar and media darling." In a 2001 address in Florida, he warned, "We will see damage in Florida like we have never known."[13]

Hurricanes teach humility. Thomas Hallock, a scholar of early Florida history, has written about one of the first recorded storms, the tempest that disrupted and dispirited the first armed *entrada* into La Florida in 1528. "Cabeza de Vaca offers a parable of collapse," Hallock observes. "In a storm story, we lose control. We lost power."[14]

Charley

The early summer of 2004 spawned little hurricane activity. In early August, Hurricane Alex teased Jacksonville before speeding to the Northeast. A few days later, a tropical depression strengthened in the Gulf of Mexico, becoming a tropical storm before it landed in Apalachicola with 45 mph winds. Floridians exhaled. A journalist, reflecting upon the events of 2004 a decade later, marveled, "There was no forecast technology in the world that could have given an indication of what was to come in the next six weeks."[15]

Like most hurricanes, Charley originated off the west coast of Africa near the Cape Verde Islands. In early August, the tropical development passed the Lesser Antilles, entering the warm waters of the Caribbean. The wave developed into a tropical depression off Barbados. On 11 August, the depression was upgraded to a tropical storm, strengthening to hurricane intensity south of Jamaica. Emerging into the Straits of Cuba, Charley weakened to a Category 2 as it moved into the Gulf of Mexico headed to Florida. On the evening of 12 August 2004, meteorologists predicted with a degree of confidence that Hurricane Charley would enter the mouth of Tampa Bay.

On 13 August 2004, the National Oceanic and Atmospheric Administration (NOAA) predicted Charley would remain a Category 2 storm, bringing a 12-foot storm surge. Mass evacuations of Pinellas and Hillsborough counties were ordered. More than 1 million Tampa Bay residents participated in the exodus, hoping to find refuge in one of Metro Orlando's motels. Many residents refused to leave, their memories of Hurricane Floyd still fresh. In 1999, experts projected that Floyd and Florida were about to collide. The greatest mass evacuation in American history wrought panic and chaos, resulting in many refugees stranded on what was quickly dubbed "the world's greatest parking lot"—Interstates 4 and 75. Instead, Hurricane Floyd turned northward and missed Florida.[16]

Charley, however, was forming into a storm about to slam into an area that had grown wildly since the last hurricane to strike it in 1921. The perfect storm revealed the imperfections of weather forecasting. Ominously, on Friday the 13th of August, Charley—whose forecast path was dubbed the "cone of death"—abruptly made a right turn. "God doesn't follow the linear directions of computer models," explained Governor Bush at a press conference. "What people don't understand," explained veteran meteorologist Jim Farrell, "is the forecast for Charley was a good one. The turn to the right was very slow." Approaching Charlotte Harbor as a Category 2 hurricane, Charley shocked forecasters once again when it strengthened quickly to a Category 4. When Governor Bush heard the grim news, he asked, plaintively, "What happened to Category 3?"[17]

Gathering energy in the warm waters of the Gulf of Mexico, Charley roared over Cayo Costa, a barrier island and state park that once was a "fishing rancho" for Cubans. Hurricane Charley saluted its namesake Hurricane Bay and the barrier islands of Lee County. The storm left Sanibel and Captiva islands without a working sewage system, electricity, or water. North Captiva Island, a prestigious retreat accessible only by water or plane, was sliced in two by wind-driven surf.

Charlotte County headlines rarely made the front pages. For centuries, the Calusa Indians thrived, developing a sophisticated culture made possible by the natural abundance of Charlotte Harbor. The county flourished briefly in the late nineteenth century when Gilded Age barons flocked to the Punta Gorda Hotel, an elegant wooden structure. They had arrived to participate in one of the strenuous life's most challenging sporting pleasures: the manly art of tarpon fishing. But sport fishing drew few permanent residents. In 1940, Charlotte County counted only 4,013 residents. The creation of Port Charlotte galvanized the region. In 1954, the fabled Mackle brothers paid $2.5 million for the Frizzell ranch, a sprawling, high-and-dry 80,000-acre land tract. Port Charlotte homes started at $6,960 with $210 down. In the late 1950s, the closest hospital was the 34-bed Charlotte Hospital, near Punta Gorda. Throughout the

1970s and 1980s, Charlotte County became a magnet for less affluent retirees and snowbirds, many living in mobile home parks that had been built in the 1950s and '60s. In some of the trailer parks, such as Park Hill, residents owned their lots, promoting a sense of community. By 2000, Charlotte County's population had grown to 140,000.[18]

It was easy to tell when the storm struck the mainland. Punta Gorda's landmark antique clock stopped at 4:27 p.m. Compact, but deadly, Charley's winds reached 150 mph. The storm destroyed every building but one at the Charlotte County Airport. It destroyed the emergency operations center. When Hurricane Charley reached the mainland, Charlotte County's director of emergency services said simply, "We have met our Andrew." The verdict of Punta Gorda's police chief: "Complete devastation." Motorists found Punta Gorda's streets impassable. The storm blew down so many electric lines and power poles that heavily trafficked US 41 was reduced to one lane leading north.[19]

The winds wrecked neighborhoods from Port Charlotte to Arcadia, from Orlando to Ormond Beach. In Port Charlotte, winds knocked down Beachcomber Liquors, depositing a 20-foot U-Haul in the middle of the store. In Orlando, a city not struck by a hurricane since 1960, Charley's winds were clocked at 90 mph. Charley left a dubious punctuation mark, damaging 34,000 structures. Three of four residents lost power and then endured scorching August heat. They were not alone. By the time the storm followed the I-4 Corridor into Volusia County and beyond to Flagler County, cyclonic gusts had knocked down trees and power lines across an area from Deltona to Flagler Beach. Orlando International Airport reported top winds of 100 mph.[20]

Many residents from Tampa Bay and Sarasota, alarmed that their homes sat in the crosshairs, sought refuge in Orlando only to encounter Charley's revenge. Almost half of the affected residents ignored evacuation orders and remained stubbornly in their vulnerable homes. Shockingly, only about one-half of threatened mobile home occupants evacuated. A reporter observed, "The hurricane turned mobile homes into kindling with only pipes and toilets left standing in the rubble." A *New York Times* journalist wrote: "Life was on view in other ways as well: trailers with sheared-off walls faced the road, each room displayed doll-house-style. In some places, trailers lay one atop the other like collapsed towers of blocks." Many residents complained they never heard evacuation orders, news that Max Mayfield, director of the National Hurricane Center (NHC), found incomprehensible. What made Mayfield angrier was the outrage directed at the NHC for misreading Charley's path.[21]

Hurricane Charley followed US 17 into the agricultural heart of Florida.

In downtown Fort Meade, most of the awnings and rooftops were missing. In Arcadia, Charley toppled the water tower, tore off the roofs of the 1906 Old Opera House and the Turner Agri-Civic Center, which held 1,200 evacuees. The terror-stricken evacuees had to be led, arm in arm, to nearby schools. The winds struck Wauchula with a fury that moved and bent 5,000 aluminum seat stands at the local football stadium. Emergency workers also dealt with isolated farmers in need of help, attempting to navigate country roads littered with fallen trees and debris. Stephen Anderson, who operated an assisted-living facility in Deltona, recalled the sounds of trees snapping and the overwhelming scent of pine.[22]

President George W. Bush and Governor Jeb Bush visited beleaguered Charlotte County. The governor, after touring the area by helicopter, admitted, "Our worst fears have come true." When chronicling hurricanes, the qualitative word "worst" has a short shelf life. One year later, Katrina claimed the title, only to yield the infamous distinction to Hurricanes Maria and Michael in 2017 and 2018.[23]

One of the lasting memories, and for many bedraggled residents far too lasting, was the "FEMA City," or "FEMA-ville," experiment. Temporary home to thousands of homeless residents, the new dwellings consisted of 551 double-wide mobile homes. Located between a Charlotte County cow pasture and a county jail, "FEMA City" had few amenities and many aggravations. In two years, police responded to more than 3,400 calls, including 204 domestic disturbances. Two years after Charley's winds sheared Charlotte Harbor, 165 trailers remained "temporarily" occupied. The last refugees left, appropriately, on Halloween night 2006. Hurricanes provided painful lessons in crisis management: avoid encampments of stressed victims forced to live in a makeshift trailer park in the middle of nowhere.[24]

Another enduring memory was the standoff between armed deputies and desperate evacuees who demanded to see what had happened to their property. On the mainland in Lee County, a melodrama unfolded when police turned away residents who wished to return to their island homes. In a scene more fitting on *Miami Vice*, some Fort Myers Beach habitués tried to swim around the roadblock, only to be intercepted by the Coast Guard.[25]

Charley lives on in memories but not in name. The name is now retired out of disrespect. In recorded history, Charley ranks as one of the twenty most powerful hurricanes. Charley killed ten people, nine in Florida. The tenth person died in faraway Rhode Island, victim of a rip current. Had Charley stayed on its predicted course and struck Tampa Bay, the disaster would easily have surpassed the notoriety of Hurricane Katrina in 2005. Hillsborough and Pinellas counties, originally expected to be in the crosshairs of Charley, escaped largely unscathed. The heavily populated counties were not even declared federal disaster areas.

Frances

Floridians had little time to prepare for a second round. In mid-August, climatologists detected a storm threat gathering strength off the coast of Africa and headed toward the Lesser Antilles. By 30 August, James Franklin of the Hurricane Center made a chilling prediction: "We could have the threat of a significant hurricane in five days here." By the beginning of September, Hurricane Frances was passing north of Puerto Rico, and models projected an east coast Florida landing, likely at Melbourne. By 3 September, 2.5 million Floridians ranging from the edge of the Everglades to Volusia County were ordered to evacuate. As an indication of the power and breadth of Frances, 14.6 million Floridians—out of a population of 17 million—were included under a hurricane watch or warning.

On Labor Day weekend, Hurricane Frances smashed into Sewall's Point (Martin County) at midnight and headed on a west-by-northwest passage, exiting at Pasco County on the Gulf coast. The small community of Lake Wales became a historical footnote as the exact place Hurricanes Charley and Frances crisscrossed. Hurricane Frances left behind extensive beach erosion and flooding. A slow-moving Category 2 storm, dumping as much as 13 inches of rain along the way, Frances traveled all the way to Quebec.[26]

A *Sun-Sentinel* journalist described Hurricane Frances as "a sluggish and super-sized storm, that may leave as its legacy a singular image: A large swatch of Florida, over six-hundred miles from Tallahassee to Key West, enveloped in rain and wind." The storm left a quarter-million Floridians without electricity and collapsed a portion of I-95.[27]

The *Bradenton Herald*'s headline on 6 September 2004 became a collector's item: "Are We Done Yet?" Two hurricanes had exhausted Floridians. But as the witches in Shakespeare's *Macbeth* chanted, "When shall we three meet again? In thunder, lightning, and in rain. When the hurly burly's done . . ." The hurly burly was named Ivan, a name that conjured up images of menacing Soviets in the 1950s.

Ivan

The story is told of forty-two-year-old Ted Williams's last game as a Boston Red Sox. Fenway Park faithful arrived to bid farewell to arguably the greatest hitter there ever was. In his last bat, "the Splendid Splinter" hit a trademark home run. "Like a feather caught in a vortex," wrote John Updike, "Williams . . . ran as he always ran out home runs—hurriedly, unsmiling, head down, as if our praise were a storm of rain to get out of." The cheering fans begged Williams to come out of the dugout, or at least tip his hat for a final encore. Updike explained the madcap finale: "The papers said that the other players, and even the umpires on the field, begged him to come out and acknowledge us in some way, but he never did and did not now. Gods do not answer letters." Nor do hurricanes acknowledge human prayers.[28]

Weary of two powerful hurricanes within weeks, Floridians battened down the hatches and shuttered windows as Hurricane Ivan gathered strength in the warm September waters of the Gulf of Mexico. Meanwhile, meteorologists classified the storm as a Category 5. A downgraded Ivan hit Pensacola Bay squarely and savagely with 135 mph winds and 50-foot sea swells, causing a 13-foot tidal surge. "I know it's the worst thing I've ever seen," sighed Bruce Smith. His Avalon Beach home north of the Escambia Bay Bridge suffered $280,000 in damage. A reporter wrote that Ivan had simply left Pensacola Bay "a graveyard of yachts." Ivan deposited 6 feet of debris at the Grand Lagoon neighborhood. Another reporter thought Pensacola Bay looked like "downtown Beirut." Ivan's winds and waters blasted so many windows from Pensacola's Grand Hotel Crowne Plaza that the downtown establishment closed for over a year.[29]

West Florida's most heavily trafficked roads took a beating from Ivan. US 98—the Panhandle's historic east-west coastal route—became impassable, underwater hours before the worst flooding. Exacerbating the loss of electricity and vital shortages were the logistical difficulties of delivering supplies. If the situation was dire on US 98, the collapse of the westbound lanes of Interstate 10 over Pensacola's Escambia Bay was catastrophic. Ivan knocked 58 spans off the I-10 Escambia Bay Bridge. An iconic photograph depicted a truck dangling over a missing span. Divers found the body of Roberto Alvarado in the bay. He had been driving a truckload of fruits and vegetables from Texas to Miami. Interstate 10 remained closed for three weeks. Symbolically, Ivan overwhelmed a wastewater treatment plant, creating a mini–sewage surge that flowed into downtown businesses and streets.[30]

Ivan wrought terrible death and destruction, killing 20 persons in Florida, but claiming more than 100 lives elsewhere. Pensacola and Escambia Counties had no fresh water, relying upon the kindness and timeliness of emergency deliveries.

Ivan left Florida to pound the American Southeast. Weirdly, Ivan made a wide loop eastward toward the Atlantic Ocean, returning to Florida to haunt the peninsula before it crossed into the Gulf of Mexico destined for Texas.

Some built environments fared better than others. In Walton County, Ivan uncovered and damaged septic tanks that served the county's most isolated and poor residents. The county is also home to one of the state's most celebrated and wealthy communities. Few places in Florida captivated urban critics and upwardly mobile consumers more than Seaside, a community envisioned by Robert Davis and his innovative "New Urbanism" architects Andres Duany and Elizabeth Plater-Zyberk. Designed as an environmentally friendly alternative development in the early 1980s, Seaside introduced some daring concepts. All homes and businesses must stand behind the sand dunes. Homes ("Think new money Norman Rockwell," wrote one journalist) must conform to strict design and zoning guidelines: no fast-food chains, strip malls, and asphalt parking driveways. Seaside became a commercial success. Hurricane Ivan tested New Urbanism's environmental mettle. Seaside's 480 houses, built to some of the state's most demanding codes, suffered minimal damage. Ivan gouged the beaches and covered the wooden staircases with sand, but trial by wind and water rewarded Seaside's old-school look and new-school planning. Critics have caricatured Seaside's coerced conformity, but Rosemary Beach, WaterColor, and Alys Beach, neighboring developments along Highway 30A, pay Seaside the ultimate compliment: imitation.[31]

Jeanne

Groggy, hurricane-weary Floridians could scarcely believe the mid-September news upon hearing that a fourth storm, Hurricane Jeanne, threatened the Sunshine State. Weather maps of the Caribbean and Atlantic resembled a pinball machine as competing storms seemed to be colliding and bouncing off one another. Meteorologist Max Mayfield joked to viewers that on his day off he took down his shutters at his home in Miami. He quickly implored his audience to put the shutters back on! Hurricane Jeanne drifted impatiently. Experts predicted Jeanne would land somewhere between Fort Pierce and Vero Beach. Following Frances's path, Jeanne's first stop was Hutchinson Island, where underwater demolition teams had trained at Fort Pierce during World War II. The Vero Beach city manager summarized 2004 as "the hurricane season from hell." Jeanne raked a 30-mile stretch of coastal homes in St. Lucie County and exited at Weeki Wachee on the Gulf coast.[32]

Jeanne only seemed a child of a lesser storm. Had Hurricanes Charley, Frances, and Ivan never occurred, Jeanne would have become America's third-costliest storm. Jeanne's insurance payouts amounted to $3.66 billion. Jeanne was also the deadliest storm of 2004. While causing only three deaths in Florida, the hurricane claimed thousands of lives in the Caribbean. Inconvenience and material destruction should not be equated with tragedy.[33]

The Reach and Risk of Hurricanes

Almost no part of the state escaped the hurricane-driven winds of 2004. Every single school in Florida closed at least once during this season of displacement and destruction. Millions of Americans and Floridians suddenly became aware of Sewall's Point, Barefoot Bay, Jensen Beach, Perdido Key, and Santa Rosa Island, as well as the Ocean Breeze Trailer Park, the Grande Lagoon subdivision, and the Cracker Trails R.V. Park. In touching gestures of civic communion, strangers assisted one another, while the young reached out to the old, as national guardsmen, first responders, and volunteers assisted the young and old, rich and poor.

Some places became notorious for their geographic misfortunes. Thrice struck, Volusia County's DeBary and Deltona, and Polk County's Babson Park, Lake Wales, and Fort Meade became hurricane capitals, despite their interior locations. Between Lake Wales and Fort Meade—connected by Highway 60, aka "Hurricane Highway"—the eye of three hurricanes passed over tiny Lake Buffum. In tribute to Jeanne's terror and Winter Haven's eerily dangerous location, Cypress Gardens anointed its new roller coaster "Triple Hurricane." Polk County, which had not experienced a hurricane in forty-four years, experienced three hurricanes in forty-four days. The county suffered $1.2 billion in damages. Fort Meade residents still recall the kindness of town and country folk bringing grills to cook for their bruised neighbors.[34]

To paraphrase Branch Rickey, luck may not be the residue of design, but simply lucky residue. In *The Wizard of Oz*, a Kansas cyclone deposited Dorothy Gale atop the Wicked Witch of the East. Floridians also understand the fortunes of wind. The year 2004 had been a brutal one for James Abney. The retired U.S. Air Force veteran was divorced, survived a cancer scare, and then faced a tornado spawned by Hurricane Ivan. Distraught, he was living in a mobile home in Marianna when a tornado—"It sounded like a thousand freight trains"—blew his trailer off the foundation, shredding the airborne structure, taking everything except Abney's life—and a single kitchen faucet, which was left standing. A photograph of the faucet went viral. Delta Faucet Company officials searched for the man behind the faucet, eventually locating him in Jackson County. Company officials handed Abney a check for $10,000. In Punta Gorda's Crystal Lake mobile home subdivision, the storm killed an elderly couple but tossed their grown son across several trailer lots until he crashed through a mobile home. Rescue crews found him embedded, face-first, in a closet. He survived. David Sallisky, his wife, and two cats (one pregnant) chose to ride out Charley inside his Bokeelia Park trailer. He heard chaos all around him—a banyan tree fell on a neighbor's trailer, hurling debris that broke one door and a cabinet. "At one point, I got serious," deadpanned Sallisky, a veteran. He wanted to know what would happen if he opened the other door. As the door was opened, his clothes dryer flew by, breaking off the trailer door hinges. A construction worker, he fixed the trailer himself. His cat gave birth to six kittens two days later.[35]

The hurricanes battered and bent, leveled and disheveled some of Florida's ritziest addresses and poorest zip codes. Twin outposts of glamour and prestige, Sanibel and Captiva, and Jupiter and Hutchinson Islands, faced the wrath of Charley, Frances, and Jeanne. The irresistibly named Easy Street in Port Charlotte could not deflect bad-luck winds. Punta Gorda's Wind Mill Village, home to a yacht basin, a $2 million clubhouse, and recreational vehicles costing $250,000, was flattened, along with 90 percent of its mobile homes. Hurricane Charley also obliterated thirty-one mobile home parks in Charlotte County, including the modest Park Hill mobile home park along Alligator Creek. When the storms veered inland and exposed the migrant labor camps of Zolfo Springs, Bowling Green, and Arcadia, the plight of some of Florida's poorest agricultural workers became painfully visible. The Small Business Administration offered low-interest loans, but to be eligible, Florida's poor and uninsured must demonstrate they can repay the loan. And they must own property. One reporter noticed, "Hurricane Ivan is forcing a second wave of people from their homes six months after it struck." A new wave of homelessness, the result of storm-damaged homes closed because of mold, health hazards, and rising rents, had taken hold across the Panhandle. Charley, Frances, Ivan, and Jeanne had unleashed the explosive energy of what Mike Davis called "natural hazards and social contradictions."[36]

These hurricanes laid bare what Florida leaders and the image-makers of the Sunshine State preferred to sweep under the sand: too many Floridians live on the edge. Poverty had always scarred the Deep South, but Florida leaders preferred to focus upon growth, ignoring intractable problems of poverty and poor health, social justice and housing. Tropical winds blow across political affiliation, class, and geographic boundaries. Million-dollar beach houses and double-wide mobile homes disintegrated under a 16-foot storm surge and 120 mph winds. But class matters. From storm prep to evacuation routes to insurance claims, it helps to be rich. The poorest Floridians do not drive SUVs to haul plywood to shutter homes, do not own generators, and have little disposable income for motels. Along the Gold Coast, some families escaped danger by leasing private jets ($17,000 a flight). Privilege can also isolate Floridians. The residents of Florida's gated communities discovered that the very amenities that attracted them to such locales—private roads, lush landscaping, and restricted access—also kept out emergency crews. Moreover, the question of whether national and state funds should provide aid to private homeowners' associations was hotly debated. FEMA spokespersons clearly stated, "We don't go on private property," yet the agency removed and hauled away four hundred trees at the Gleneagle Country Club near Delray Beach.[37]

The storms exacerbated the difficulties faced by migrant and agricultural laborers. With the agricultural crops in shambles, there was little fieldwork. Even before the storms, migrant workers averaged less than $10,000 a year. By October 2004, American grocery shelves were missing Florida-grown tomatoes, victims of washed-out fields. Consumers paid dearly—three dollars a pound for hothouse tomatoes. Wendy's introduced a new chicken sandwich, absent a slice of Florida tomato. But many migrants feared accepting government assistance lest they be uncovered as illegal immigrants. Many took temporary work in the immense challenge of clearing debris and construction. In Pensacola, so many former restaurant workers found better-paying jobs in the recovery efforts that fast-food establishments suffered a labor shortage.[38]

Pahokee represents a lost and invisible world to most Floridians. Located on the southeastern edge of Lake Okeechobee in Palm Beach County, a place where lives revolve around the cycle of crops ranging from sugarcane to tomatoes, Pahokee is one of the poorest towns in America, made poorer after two hurricanes. How poor? A *Sun-Sentinel* journalist described the scene: "With its downtown all but deserted, the hospital closed, unemployment sky high, and the supply of rental homes exhausted, this rural town . . . looked battered even before hurricanes Frances and Jeanne." The hurricanes also destroyed the city marina, one of Pahokee's economic lifelines. Months after the last hurricane had petered out, the residents of the King Mobile Home Park struggled. Their trailer park was tossed, turned, and condemned. The families, chiefly Hispanic, had been offered new trailers on the bank of Lake Okeechobee, but they refused to leave. They may have been poor, and their trailers may have been tossed like tin cans, but they loved their neighbors and the community they had built with sweat and toil. They continued to pay monthly rent for their lots, fearing eviction. Landlords, more so than renters, understood the maze of FEMA regulations.[39]

Daniel P. Aldrich studies how communities are ripped apart or come together after natural disasters. He concludes that the density and strength of social networks are the most important variables—*not* wealth, education, or culture—in determining resilience in the face of catastrophe.[40]

Pahokee, an isolated and impoverished town in one of America's wealthiest counties, has few of the luxuries or nonprofit foundations of Boca Raton or Palm Beach. But Pahokee has spirit and spunk, and rallies around one institution of communal life that everyone supports: football. Pahokee's teams are legendary in the annals of Florida football. December 2004 might have been a time of gloom and sorrow, but Pahokee celebrated, as 6,000 residents rented buses or drove to Gainesville to watch the Pahokee Blue Devils win their third straight state football championship.

The archipelago of the Florida Keys, long a refuge for smugglers and Conchs, became temporary home to hundreds of expensive craft, whose owners hoped to save the yachts. Loren "Totch" Brown surely was smiling in his grave upon hearing the news. His father had taught him the ways of sea and land and how to ride out hurricanes by tethering boats to the mangroves of the Ten Thousand Islands. In Totch's days, most of the residents of Chokoloskee Island were poor. The stakes are higher today.[41]

The Seminoles had weathered Gulf coast and Atlantic hurricanes for centuries. The image of Seminoles instinctively anticipating hurricanes has served as a backdrop for films (*Key Largo* and *Category 7: The End of the World*) and novelists (Patrick Smith and John D. MacDonald). The hurricanes of 2004 served as real-life threats to old and new traditions. When Hurricane Jeanne sheared Hutchinson Island, the winds and surf exposed the ancient graves of three Native Americans from the Ais tribe. A shaman honored the Ais with a Seminole burial ceremony. The hurricanes also threatened the museums of Collier County. A director ordered historic artifacts, including a cypress dugout canoe carved by Seminoles, removed to safer premises. "We brought the canoe back," quipped the director, "because depending on the storm surge, we may need it!" When Hurricane Frances sped toward South Florida in September, members of the Seminole Tribe evacuated. The Seminole Tribe conveniently owned their shelter, the Hard Rock Hotel & Casino in Hollywood. The cost, which included 164 rooms, meals, movies, and bar tab, came to $123,130. FEMA protested the amount, but ultimately paid the tab in full (minus $13,800 for mini-bar expenses).[42]

Great storms harbor little respect for the built environment's age or rank. Hurricane Charley ripped away sections from an ancient Calusa mound on Pine Island, while destroying day-care centers in the next gust. Author Randy Wayne White emailed friends from his battered home on Pine Island: "Pine Island has been devastated. But these ancient Indian mounds endure as they have for several thousand years."[43]

Hurricane Ivan damaged forty-three historic structures in Pensacola, including twenty buildings at the Pensacola Naval Air Station. Seven of the eight homes on "Admirals' Row" were severely damaged. The homes had been constructed in the 1870s for officers at the Navy Yard. The navy announced it would demolish many of the buildings. A battered ship carpenters' workshop, built in 1868 so well that it survived many storms, could not survive Ivan and the navy's defense that its charge is not historic preservation.[44]

Steeples, Synagogues, and the Tempest

Forty-five miles away from the muck fields of Belle Glade and Pahokee, Palm Beach's Worth Avenue radiated old money and the newest fashions and tastes. But neither King Canute nor Palm Beach dowagers can command the winds, tides, and rains to retreat. Donald Trump's holiday displays, along with 10 feet of debris, decorated Mar-a-Lago. What a remarkable contrast to Pahokee. Pahokee's modest churches paled in contrast to the stately stone cathedrals and temples of Palm Beach. Yet Rev. John Mericantante preached a message of hope and promise at St. Mary's Catholic Church, where he was the only paid staff member.[45]

Hurricane Jeanne's arrival in South Florida eerily coincided with Yom Kippur, the Day of Judgment for Jews. In Palm Beach, Moshe Tutnauer was the newly arrived interim rabbi at Temple Emanu-El. The temple's ten Torahs had been safely put away in a bank vault, but the prized library, the third-largest Jewish library in the state, suffered from a leaky roof, mold, and mildew. In his Rosh Hashanah sermon, the Israeli-born rabbi emphasized that a hurricane is an inconvenience, not a tragedy, maintaining, "One has to put these kinds of things in perspective." In Pompano Beach, the Irish-born Rabbi Ivan Wachmann of Temple Sholom, reflected, "We realize these storms are like those in the Bible—that God is telling us how to live, that we should be a more caring society."[46]

David Clothier, who worked for the Episcopal Diocese in Pensacola, wrote that Ivan "cut through the heart of the Central Gulf Coast . . . touching everyone's lives in one way or the other." Clothier noted that damage included the offices of the Duval Diocesan Center as well as the homes of most of the staff. The storm respected neither the cloth nor the sanctuary. Christ Church in Pensacola was damaged as a bronze bell unloosed from its tower, fell through the roof, landing in the undercroft. Ivan pushed St. Simon's-on-the-Sound Church in Fort Walton Beach from its moorings on the shore to become an island sanctuary, now seemingly floating like Mont Saint-Michel. Before Ivan finally exhausted himself, the hurricane spawned a total of 110 tornadoes across the American Southeast. The Rt. Rev. Philip M. Duncan II urged parishioners to consider Psalm 46:2–3: "Therefore we will not be afraid, though the waters thereof rage and foam and though the mountains be toppled into the midst of the sea."[47]

Charles Chamblee, a pastor at the First Baptist Church in Pensacola, will always associate Hurricane Ivan with "the most terrifying night of my life." He explained, "I just got a praise-and-chorus book and laid down with a flashlight and sang praise choruses—tried to bring some peace."[48]

Jay Johnson, a resident of St. James City on Pine Island, remembered how, during the aftermath of Hurricane Charley's destruction, "All the island churches banded together. St. John's Episcopal Church opened its doors offering shelter and two hot meals a day for more than 80 families. . . . Our Lady of the Miraculous Medal Catholic Church did the same, serving 500–600 meals a day." Rev. "Father Tom" Pohto opened the church doors even though the building had neither electricity nor telephone service.[49]

Few religious sects in America offered more to hurricane victims than the Mennonites. Persecuted in Europe and America, the Mennonites eventually prospered in Canada and the Great Plains. While the Mennonite Church boasted only about 325,000 members in 2004, the Mennonite Disaster Service contributed mightily to ease suffering in Florida. The Mennonites and Amish already had a footprint on the Florida west coast, building the village of Pinecraft on the outskirts of Sarasota. Each winter, about 5,000 Amish and Mennonites flock to Pinecraft, defined as a "melting pot" for these strict religious members. But the hurricanes came in August and September, not January.[50]

Mennonite volunteers immediately rushed to the devastated interior city and rolled out a kitchen on wheels. The Pine Creek Chapel in Pinecraft became a beehive of activities, offering facilities for bathing and showering, as well as RV hookups. The Mennonites either built or rebuilt 160 homes for Arcadians. A spokesperson said simply, "The church is people, not a building." During Hurricane Jeanne, the chapel hosted an ice-cream party, made more memorable by the sounds of 75 mph winds outside. A tone-perfect handwritten cardboard sign read, "Love Thy Neighbor, Don't Hog the Volunteers." When work was finished in Arcadia, a team of Mennonite volunteers headed to hard-hit Wauchula.[51]

When Hurricane Frances hit land, its winds sheared off the steeple of the First Baptist Church in Cocoa Beach. More than one hundred Baptist disaster-relief teams—the largest Baptist relief mobilization in history—spread across the state. Churches served as targets and refuge. The storm blew off a roof of a Pentecostal Church in Ormond Beach, while in Melbourne, parishioners of the First Baptist Church survived Frances's wrath huddled inside the sanctuary. When the fury passed, the congregation participated in a "catacomb service," in honor of the New Testament practices.[52]

The unluckiest—or luckiest—church in Florida was the Lake Buffum Baptist Church in Polk County. The tiny church with a small congregation survived three hurricanes. After each storm, they patiently piled debris behind the church. By September, the 15-foot pile almost dwarfed the church. Pastor Derrick Hensley had moved his family to Central Florida only two weeks before Hurricane Charley began a trio of eventful episodes. "I knew God called me here," Hensley declared. In November, the pastor called the congregation together for a "Thank God Hurricane Season Is Over" party.[53]

Typically, Florida hurricane stories focus upon the deprived, the depraved, and the weird. But the catastrophes also brought out the very best values in the human spirit: compassion and mercy. Red Cross and Salvation Army volunteers worked long and hard, often under desperate conditions. Florida's school principals turned their buildings into emergency shelters. Students learned life lessons not taught in the classroom. Tiffany Logan, a sixteen-year-old volunteer, managed the Christian Heritage Church of God relief center in Zolfo Springs. Inside the church's gymnasium, Tiffany coordinated the work of six volunteers and sixteen prison inmates, ordering them to load cartons of infant formula and boxes of groceries. "You don't want to mess with her," confessed Rev. Bob Blazier.[54]

Teenagers, a much-maligned group, learned firsthand the lesson of compassion. Peggy Hackett recalled how young men and women from Fort Lauderdale volunteered to clean up a ravaged mobile home park in Punta Gorda. Among the tasks they tackled, the teens cleared the debris from several swimming pools. "Just so these old people could cool off. . . . I get goose bumps thinking about it." Students and administrators from the Baptist College of Florida in Graceville headed to Pensacola following Ivan's path. Ironically, they cleared the yard of eighty-eight-year-old Ivan Taylor. Spring Breakers, who typically trekked to Panama City, sweated in unglamorous settings. Rebuild Northwest Florida assured unskilled students that they could always demolish condemned homes.[55]

Hurricane Charley barreled across US 17, slamming Hardee County. For several days, the Pioneer Restaurant was the only business open in Zolfo Springs, a small town of about 1,700 residents. The winds destroyed the police and fire station, as well as three-quarters of the community's homes. New heroes emerged: utility workers. Bubba Bass—he, of the eponymous name in a region that takes bass fishing seriously—operated the sewage treatment plant through trying times. A dozen inmates from the Hardee Correctional Institution volunteered to help in the recovery. "We never got assistance from FEMA when we needed it," declared Andrew Maddox, the public-works superintendent of Wauchula, the Hardee County seat. In Fort Myers, cheers and honks of glee, not scorn, greeted Bob Ramey when he pulled his gasoline tanker into a filling station. "Most of the time, people hate us," he quipped.[56]

One business has been lauded for performing extraordinary service during perilous times. How shall we honor adverse dedication? A reporter explains: "When a hurricane makes landfall, the head of the Federal Emergency Management Agency relies on a couple of metrics to assess its destructive power. First, there is the well-known Saffir-Simpson Wind Scale. Then there is what is called the 'Waffle House Index.'" It seems that Waffle House serves as a capitalist, cultural, and culinary barometer. When the barometer plummets and a hurricane roars across the coastal plain, explains FEMA administrator Craig Fugate, "If you get there and the Waffle House is closed? That's really bad. That's when you go to work." Officially, Code Green means the local Waffle House is serving a full menu; Code Yellow refers to a partial menu; and Code Red means there may not be a Waffle House even standing. The Waffle House chain ranges from the mid-Atlantic to Florida, or in other words, the Hurricane Belt. Explains reporter Valerie Bauerlein, Waffle House "spends almost nothing on advertising, [but] has built a marketing strategy around the goodwill gained from being open when customers are most desperate." Waffle House cash register receipts double or triple in a storm's aftermath.[57]

Strangers in a storm also performed deeds of mercy. Hurricane Charley destroyed much of the Suncoast Estates trailer court in North Fort Myers. A survivor recalled, "One man drove up to the home of a single mother with six children and handed her $2,000. There were four or five like that."[58]

Few brides plan a wedding during a hurricane. "Nowhere on Russhelle Lee's guest list was a wedding crasher named Jeanne," quipped a reporter. The teacher's wedding reception was to be held in the most beautiful building in Hendry

County, the Clewiston Inn. Built in 1938 by and for the U.S. Sugar Company, the august structure had begun to decline, but, in September 2004, it still whispered elegance. Ms. Lee had prepared for this special moment for months, crafting hundreds of jars of guava jelly for guests. A Glades dune buggy awaited the new bride and groom, as did Hurricane Jeanne.

Alas, Hurricane Jeanne was speeding toward Lake Okeechobee and Clewiston. Undaunted but bowed, Ms. Lee turned her carefully planned wedding reception into a party for hundreds of residents in the town's sturdiest evacuation center. "Basically, we partied all night," she beamed, adding, "We're pretty tough out here. We survive." Hurricanes teach lessons of humility and community.[59]

Political Storm

In a state where leaders too rarely summon democratic and republican ideals of shared sacrifice and compassionate conservatism, the hurricanes of '04 brought Floridians together in ways that geography and politics cast asunder. Hurricanes may be natural disasters, but they also are political events, crises addressed or neglected by sheriffs and county commissioners, state legislators and governors. Historically, hurricanes were local events. Victims relied not upon the generosity of strangers or faraway governments but, rather, upon neighbors and local charities.

"Hurricanes come in two waves," observed commentator David Brooks. "First come the rainstorms." Then comes "the human storm." He adds, "We'd like to think that the stories of hurricanes and floods are always stories of people rallying together to give aid and comfort," writes Brooks. "But floods are also civic examinations." Hurricanes also wash away the material surface, exposing inequalities and political power. The turning point was the Labor Day hurricane of 1935. Hundreds of World War I veterans were working on a new highway in the Florida Keys. Many were living on railway cars at labor camps between Marathon and Islamorada. When one of the century's most ferocious storms savaged the Keys, hundreds of hapless workers were killed when the railcars washed out to sea. Many of the victims were sandblasted to death. "Who murdered the vets?," asked Ernest Hemingway, who arrived to write an article for *New Masses*. Hemingway added sardonically, "The writer of this article lives a long way from Washington and would not have the answers to these questions." He added that it was common sense "that wealthy people, Yachtsmen, fishermen, such as Presidents Hoover and Roosevelt do not come to the Florida keys in hurricane months." Fortunately for President Roosevelt, his reelection was more than a year away, and he had banked a great deal of political capital. Other presidents would not be as lucky or politically adept.[60]

Presidents and governors have become more responsive to natural disasters, while citizens now expect and demand prompt federal disaster assistance. The same impulses that empowered the modern presidency also created powerful federal agencies, such as the Weather Bureau and the Federal Emergency Management Administration (FEMA). LBJ's Great Society began the practice of marshaling federal assistance to hard-hit communities. President Carter created FEMA in 1979, cobbling together agencies to streamline disaster efforts. Today, the chief executive and governor also must play the roles of national griever, healer, and provider. The case study for modern leadership occurred when Hurricane Andrew struck South Florida in 1992. Overwhelmed, Miami-Dade County's emergency operations director appealed to Washington on national television, crying out: "We're doing everything we can! Where in the hell is the cavalry on this one?" President George H. W. Bush paid dearly for his hesitation. Critics lacerated the chief executive for lacking sensitivity for the victims of Hurricane Andrew and not visiting Homestead. To be fair, Governor Lawton Chiles waited three days to ask for federal assistance.[61]

President George H. W. Bush's son, President George W. Bush, understood the urgency of the crisis when Hurricane Charley approached in August 2004. Hit by four hurricanes in two months, it helped that President Bush's brother also happened to be the governor of Florida, and for emphasis, 2004 was a presidential election year. "Overall," concluded *Salon,* "FEMA, and more importantly, Bush, scored high ratings for their handling of the election-year hurricanes. No expense was spared bringing relief to storm victims who just happened to live in the most important swing state in the country." President Bush signed a $7.1 billion hurricane-aid package. Still, Black Caucus Democrats criticized the president for not providing enough relief effort for hurricane-ravaged Haiti. In Miami-Dade County, critics accused Miami officials of gorging on public funds intended for more deserving areas. A "foreign policy debate" erupted when Fidel Castro pointed out that Communist Cuba suffered no human losses during the hurricanes. President Bush visited the soggy Sunshine State on five separate occasions in August and September. Democratic challenger John Kerry, not wishing to be a distraction, deferred from campaigning in Florida; instead, he asked his campaign workers to assist the recovery efforts.[62]

Jeb Bush earned the title "Hurricane Governor." Jeb, who had arrived in Miami in the 1980s, attended a cram-session in Hurricanes 101, taught by Andrew. While the storm pelted Miami-Dade County, Jeb, Columba, the Bushes' three children, his mother-in-law, and two Secret Service agents spent a terrifying evening at the Kendall home of a business associate. It was a memorable if scary introduction to the nine hurricanes he encountered as governor of Florida.

The *Miami Herald*'s Patricia Mazzei wrote a moving portrayal of Governor Bush: "He stands in a bunker, wearing no jacket and no tie, warning Floridians to board up their homes, heed evacuation orders and stock 72 hours' worth of food and water. Above him, a radar screen shows a menacing mess of winds and clouds swirling offshore." Hurricane Charley loomed. The governor insisted on visiting Punta Gorda the day after the storm. "There was not even a question that he shouldn't go," remembered the governor's chief of staff, Deirdre Finn. "When he came back he was changed. . . . He told people it shook him." Remarkably, Jeb Bush confronted eight hurricanes during a fourteen-month span, 2004–5. While running for president in 2015, he asked voters, "How would you like to have been governor of a state that had eight hurricanes and four tropical storms, $100 billion of insured losses and billions of uninsured losses over just 17 months? For me it was the greatest joy of service that I could ever imagine." Bush, a policy wonk who could appear cold and analytical, received high marks from the press for his hands-on efforts during these demanding times. A whirling chief executive, he seemed genuinely concerned, passing out bottles of water, holding bilingual press conferences, and comforting migrant laborers who had just lost their mobile homes. In one such touching moment, Governor Bush visited students whose Charlotte Harbor school had been destroyed by Hurricane Charley. He hugged Kaitlyn Greenstone, whose family lost their home in the storm. She managed a perfect score on her FCAT exam! "That's amazing," Bush exclaimed. "You made me cry. I'm so proud of you." Years later, Jeb believed, "These hurricanes kind of etched my soul in many ways."[63]

President George W. Bush, who so adeptly responded to Florida's storm-tossed needs in 2004, failed miserably in 2005, when Hurricane Katrina devastated New Orleans. NBC correspondent Chuck Todd commented, "The initial response from federal officials leaves the impression that they can't walk and chew gum at the same time." Perhaps it was because 2004 was a presidential election year, perhaps it was because the president's brother was governor of Florida, and perhaps it was because most of the victims were Black, but Katrina was both an environmental and a political disaster. President Bush never regained the confidence of the American people following the debacle of New Orleans.

Washington, D.C., once remote, is now inextricably linked to Floridians' lives. Whether Democrat, Republican, or independent, Floridians living in barrier islands communities, retirement villages, or rural hamlets all look to Washington for Social Security, beach renourishment funds, or farm subsidies. One searches in vain for solitary voices complaining of federal interference in state matters regarding hurricane-relief funds. Governments could, of course, prohibit home construction along barrier islands and coastal communities, but powerful interests demand the freedom to build, along with federally subsidized insurance as a hedge against catastrophes.

Debates over costs, blame, and responsibilities rage long after the hurricanes depart. But there is only one thing more certain than future hurricanes striking Florida, and that is that clout and influence will ultimately triumph. Bigger will replace smaller, and new will supplant old. The 22,000 mostly underinsured mobile homes of Charlotte County that lined rivers, lakes, and canals will likely be replaced by expensive condominiums and commercial development. Where will the displaced residents go? Laws of physics do not help with such questions.

Whatever meanings politicians and poets divine from 2004, one point is undeniable: the hurricanes' price tag ($29 billion in insured losses; 25,000 homes destroyed; 270,000 homes damaged) added up to the most expensive and disruptive "natural" disaster in American history. Until, of course, one year later, when Hurricane Katrina rewrote the record book ($45 billion in losses). The hurricanes remind us of our losses. Vero Beach's legendary Driftwood Inn had survived depressions, wars, and deaths, but hurricanes finally forced the historic structure designed by Waldo Emerson Sexton to close. Not far away, McKee Botanical Gardens suffered severe wind damage to its grounds, which toppled its famed toog tree. Miami's Fairchild Gardens, Lake Wales's Bok Tower, and Orlando's Lew Gardens also bore scars. But a sense of perspective is needed. Florida suffered 127 deaths. Contrast that with Haiti's losses of more than 2,000 people, while the December 2004 Pacific tsunami claimed 228,000 lives. "What the rich world suffers as hardships," pointed out Jeffrey D. Sachs, "the poor world often suffers as mass death."[64]

Prime-Time Weather

Assessing the physical damage is the work of insurance agents. Measuring the consequences of disasters is the challenge of the historian. Newspapers offer the first draft of history, and a review of America's so-called Fourth Estate suggests high praise. Once the reader gets past the inevitable "roofs peeled back like sardine cans" and "tall trees snapped like twigs," the reportage is substantive, even inspiring.

Newspapers still mattered in 2004. The medium was reaping handsome profits, but it also took seriously the responsibility of covering important events. One expected the state's major urban papers to excel during such times, but journalists at the *Floridan*, covering Jackson County, the *Bradenton Herald, Fort Myers News-Press,* the *Pensacola News-Journal,* and the *Fort Pierce Tribune* covered the events with courage, élan, and style. Associated Press reporters provided steadfast and informative accounts. Cristina Ledra recalls receiving a call from her editor at the *Charlotte Sun.* "Get into the office," he implored. "And bring a sleeping bag and pillow." Banner headlines became collectors' items: "DEVASTATED," "RAMPAGE," "DEATH AND DESTRUCTION," and "REELING."[65]

News journalists resemble stuntmen riding out hurricanes. "We're like emergency responders," explained the *Pensacola News-Journal*'s Kimberly Blair. "We don't evacuate, we work and dive into the middle of disasters." A harrowing story is sometimes better read than seen. While covering Hurricane Ivan, Ms. Blair "disappeared": the battery in her cell phone died. But she nearly did disappear. The *News-Journal* reporter sought sanctuary in her home at Gulf Breeze, Alabama. As the waters rose, her family hunkered down, only to be forced out by gasoline fumes. She and her husband waded in waist-deep waters to a neighbor's home, but her friends could not open the door because of the high water. Returning home, they spent "the night of terror with terrible Ivan," insecure in the attic.[66]

A blockbuster state story, the hurricanes of 2004 ironically sped the demise of Florida's newspapers, the medium that had delivered such stories for more than a century. Just as 9/11 exposed the inability of print to report and distribute newspapers during fast-changing events, watching a hurricane's catastrophic fury appealed to Americans more than reading about it the next day. Indeed, hurricanes' destructive powers often impose conditions that make it impossible to publish and deliver newspapers. Nevy Kaminski, a *Bradenton Herald* reporter, warned readers as Hurricane Charley approached, "By the time this newspaper hits your doorstep it might be too late to head for a hurricane shelter." Today, television stations, especially the Weather Channel, serve as the primary source of hurricane information.[67]

Hurricanes made the Weather Channel the must-see station for disaster junkies and casual viewers alike. Founded in the 1980s, the fledgling station soared to the top of the cable ratings in 2004, the year of the hurricane. The company's broadcaster Jim Cantore became an unlikely media star. His face is so familiar that a journalist quipped, "Look to your left. Now look to your right. If the person on either side of you is The Weather Channel's Jim Cantore, prepare for a storm of biblical proportions." Jim Cantore sightings have become a popular blog feature. Individuals have been known to brave cosmic winds for a chance encounter with the storm star.[68]

In 2004, the reporting of hurricanes became the domestic equivalent of covering wars. Just as the 1990 Gulf War made war correspondents Wolf Blitzer and Peter Arnett household names, the hurricanes of 2004 boosted the profiles of Jim Cantore and Max Mayfield. Each new storm threat unveils a now-familiar cast and program: vibrant, dynamic weather maps and sophisticated technology (VIPIR and Doppler Radar, NOAA's GOES-R Geostationary Satellite Server), and Hurricanespeak (spaghetti models, storm surge, the cone of uncertainty, and the cone of death), that predict and chart the storm's path; a marathon hurricane watch by TV meteorologists (Tampa's Steve Jerve, Fort Myers's Jim Farrell, the Panhandle's Jason Kelley and Sam Lane) who have become media celebrities; network reporters bent backward by the force of Category 3 winds and blinded by sheets of rain; mandatory close-ups of uprooted live oaks and tidal surges hammering seawalls; and live camera shots from emergency shelters. Jerve, who works for NBC's affiliate in the Tampa Bay area, recalled: "It's all people could talk about and the reaction was very favorable. Some even credited me with saving their lives. They would stop and talk about the event and how you helped them through it—it was emotional for folks." Critics have questioned whether the Weather Channel is in the entertainment or information business. Others call the program "weather porn." Wayne Sallade, the director of Charlotte County's emergency operation center, credits Max Mayfield with saving his life. When Sallade told Mayfield that he was remaining at the center, the latter deadpanned, "I guess this will be the last time we will speak." Sallade moved shortly before the center lost its roof.[69]

Weather drama is profitable. Why would cable viewers in Kansas care about a hurricane in Florida? Or how to explain the story on National Public Radio, "Why Did I Watch Fourteen Hours of the Weather Channel?" Because as the Weather Channel's Stephanie Abrams pointed out on the start of the 2013 hurricane season, "It only takes one—one Sandy or Katrina in order for the entire U.S. or the entire world to feel that hurt and pain." In 2013, the Weather Channel began naming winter storms. Whereas once weather reports represented a small segment of television's morning and evening news, today, climate forecasting represents an arms race to bring obsessive viewers the most technologically sophisticated computer models. The question might be raised why one even needs a meteorologist in Florida's long, hot summer, when the weather forecast is predictably hot, muggy, with a good chance of an afternoon shower.[70]

Our modern obsession with weather is lamentable, writes longtime Florida writer Jeff Klinkenberg: "Hurricane season was different when I was a boy growing up in Miami. We had just as many storms as now, but we seemed to worry about them less." In retrospect, he mused: "In the 1950s, there were no space satellites spying on the clouds as they slipped continuously off the coast of Africa. . . . We heard about hurricanes only when they were a few days from Florida. Ignorance was bliss."[71]

The Environment

Hurricanes leave more than physical damage. Natural disasters shear the social and cultural, economic, and ecological landscape. Tempests inspire and challenge novelists, meteorologists, and historians to put events in perspective and understand what happened. A popular bumper sticker in late 2004 summed up the feelings of many Floridians: "Nature Bats Last."

Should we view hurricanes as evil? Modern societies—and unreconstructed Yellow Dog Democrats who judged hurricanes as divine retribution for the stolen election of 2000—depict the disruptive quadruplets Charley, Frances, Ivan, and Jeanne as evil and aberrational. But a hurricane is a natural, as well as a moral phenomenon. And while it may seem contradictory, a hurricane is not always a natural disaster. There is nothing natural about millions of Floridians building condominiums, seawalls, and paved roads on barrier islands and coastal lands. What has changed is not unloosed nature, but the fact that 22 million people now reside in Florida, most of them living at or near the coasts. Four landfalling hurricanes in a year is highly unusual. The last time that four hurricanes struck a single state in one season was Texas in 1886. At that time, the entire population of Florida numbered about 340,000 inhabitants. As with alligators devouring pet dogs and sharks biting exposed limbs, there is nothing unusual about such cyclonic natural behavior.

Environmentalists and writers will be sorting out the meaning of 2004 for decades. First, the good news. The storms replenished beaches with shells, recharged springs and aquifers, and added color to the coral reefs that are not destroyed. The rising waters also allowed alligators and cottonmouths to roam, which was good for the critters but bad for two- and four-legged creatures. The state's tourism agency, Visit Florida, when asked about the impact hurricanes had upon the Sunshine State, instructed staff to answer with a "positive, proactive" message. A Visit Florida script put new meaning on the phrase positive spin: "Mother Nature knows best and now Florida is benefiting from her knowledge." Charlotte County's public relations director spun the "renewal" theme.

The director asked, "We wondered if it could be called land management?" Hurricanes also disperse red tide.[72]

Overwhelmed emergency rooms kept busy treating a wide-ranging array of ailments and injuries resulting from hurricane-related and environmental issues. The roster of maladies included residents drinking contaminated tap water to heat stroke, electrocution to carbon monoxide poisoning. Hospital administrators added to the long list a rash of broken and punctured limbs, chain saw injuries and electrical burns. Mental health issues also multiplied in the tense poststorm environment. Many elderly Floridians were simply overwhelmed by sleep deprivation, stress, and post-traumatic stress disorder, while others lost their psychotropic medicines. In a survey, a high proportion of seniors said they felt less safe after the storms. Invasive fire ants, swept far away from their homes by rising waters, wreaked havoc among hapless victims. An email proclaimed, "Things we learned: Fire ants can swim!"[73]

Hurricanes rearrange the landscape. When Hurricane Donna passed over South Florida in 1960, the storm knocked down most of the bird nests in Everglades National Park, killing 40 percent of the white heron population. The winds also blew down bald eagles' nests and toppled pine trees inhabited by the red-cockaded woodpecker. State biologists calculated that half of the state's bald eagles' nests were destroyed or damaged. The hurricanes' high winds scythed many of the old-growth trees that eagles favor for their nests. But two years later, state biologists reported that eagles were unruffled and resilient, their numbers returning to pre-Charley days, 2004. Some environmentalists argue that hurricanes bring a positive dimension to the forest, pruning the canopy, allowing sunlight to penetrate the ground, and fostering biodiversity.[74]

Sanibel and Captiva were home to a fierce debate over the future and past. The islands have attracted passionate defenders of the environment, most notably J. N. "Ding" Darling, Rachel Carson, and Anne Morrow Lindbergh. Early settlers planted exotic Australian pines—which are not technically pines—on the islands for shade and lumber. Hurricane Donna in 1960 destroyed much of the native old-growth forest, allowing Australian pine seedlings to form a monoculture. Many grew to more than 100 feet high, but the trees notorious for their shallow roots had not evolved in a tropical, coastal setting. Hurricane Charley sent most of the Australian pines airborne "like a dart," leaving roads covered in 15 feet of debris. In the aftermath, residents debated what their picturesque islands should look like. Some islanders—called "ambience defenders"—expressed affection for the Australian pines and their shady canopy. Sanibel's city manager explained that when residents and tourists returned, "It was very common to see people in the side of the road, their first time, pull off and be literally in tears." A visitor approaching from San Carlos Bay observed: "Slick, leafless, and dead, hundreds of Australian pines lay along North Captiva Island's beach . . . looking as if a petulant giant had slapped them down with a sweeping backhand." In Sanibel's "Back to Natives" movement, the restoration and replanting of Australian pines was condemned, replaced by 50,000 hardwood, native species, including sabal palmettos, gumbo-limbos, and mahogany. Bald eagles, brown pelicans, and ospreys lost nests but rebounded.[75]

Roger Hammer, the senior naturalist for Miami-Dade County's parks, had long theorized "that plants and animals evolved to deal with hurricanes." A photograph of two cacti poking from a ruined air-conditioner unit signaled the triumph of nature and saluted the power of adaptability. Yet even Hammer was crushed when Hurricane Andrew tore into the county's many hammocks, destroying a quarter of the beloved Dade County pines. Hurricane Andrew had felled the largest wild tamarind tree in North America. Rangers feared an explosion of invasive species in the aftermath.[76]

Buzz-sawing Florida's landscape, the storms' winds toppled tree canopies and stands of ancient live oaks, southern magnolias, and bald cypresses that defined the landscape of many Florida communities. Arcadia, Gainesville, Lake Wales, and Vero Beach suffered major losses. Reflecting upon the tenth anniversary of Ivan, retired U.S. Army Brig. Gen. Michael Ferguson, a fifth-generation Pensacolian, swore he would never again take his city's beloved trees for granted. In some places, the wholesale destruction of trees signified a hopeful replanting. "It may be the oaks," suggested the *New York Times*, "best reflect the tensions between how parts of the state once looked, and the way new development continues to alter its appearance with grand royal and date palms." In other communities, the storms confirmed what arborists had been long preaching: laurel and water oaks and Australian pines are vulnerable and dangerous.[77]

Hurricane Ivan brought ruin to mice and men. The fewer than 1,000 beach mice living on Perdido Key became fewer still following the wrath of Ivan along the Florida-Alabama border. Environmental officials "evacuated" 52 mice to the Santa Fe College Zoo, where the survivors remain. Two years later, none of the key's 500 rental units that had been battered had reopened, nor had the two-lane road running the length of the key been rebuilt. A popular beach myth circulated that a frustrated developer released dozens of cats to eliminate the federally protected mice. Regardless, regulations prohibited residents from installing sprinkler systems and deck lights. Moreover, new residents had to sign a "no cat" clause, a.k.a. "beach mouse permit!" In 2015, ground was broken on a $60 million condo project.[78]

Lois C. Jones was living in Marianna in West Florida during Hurricane Ivan. She frequently emailed friends a commentary on life in a region Gloria Jahoda described as "the other Florida." Many of her friends found her musings comforting and inspiring:

> At first eastern light through trees this Friday morning, I heard the chirps of squirrels in their nests! They have a sweet high chirp upon waking. Comforted me to know that God's little creatures were safe in the nest he taught them to build! Soon thereafter, I began to hear a bird calling its kind . . . somewhere in the woods . . . and then the kin reply! Precious sounds of the natural world who kept safe throughout Ivan.[79]

The Panhandle's endangered red-cockaded woodpeckers and the remnants of the once mighty longleaf yellow pine forests also took a beating. These woodpeckers nest only in tall longleaf pine trees, and it takes the birds one to three years to peck away the cavity. Ivan snapped 150 occupied pine trees on the Eglin Air Force Base grounds. The storm also destroyed all the unhatched green sea turtle nests, and biologists feared for the fates of young hatchlings in a turbulent Gulf.[80]

If migrating bald eagles found few nests, at last Florida's chickens came home to roost. For decades, Cassandras had warned that the phosphate mines and the industry's derelict practices were a ticking time bomb. The hurricanes tested critics and defenders. Hurricane Frances overwhelmed a 180-foot-tall gypsum stack in Riverview, unleashing 56 million gallons of acidic wastewater and toxic sludge into the Alafia River and Hillsborough and Tampa bays. Gypsum is the by-product of processing phosphate into a fertilizer. An official with Cargill Crop Nutrition, the fertilizer company responsible for the disaster, admitted that the spill was "a 10 on a 10 scale." A massive fish kill occurred. In the short run, the hurricanes brought little change; rather, the most significant change occurred in the consolidations and mergers within the industry. Quickly, the powerful corporate conglomerate Mosaic became the last phosphate company standing.[81]

Stormy weather and the Everglades enjoyed a long, symbiotic relationship. The torrential rains flushed out sediment from Florida Bay, providing gators, snakes, and birds additional watery terrain. But the 2004 hurricanes, and especially Hurricane Wilma in 2005, simply overwhelmed the ecosystem. Rick Cook, an Everglades Park spokesman, said, "I've never seen the trees bare like this." Cleanup crews paused when they spotted a 9-foot python slithering across the glade.[82]

The 729,000-acre Big Cypress National Preserve occupies a huge swath of the northeastern Everglades. The five hurricanes planted a time bomb. "These woods," wrote Gretchen Parker, "look like a wind-whipped, chaotic tangle of limbs, vines, and teetering trunks." Invasive exotics took advantage of the sunlight to sprout Brazilian pepper trees, melaleuca, and the Old World climbing fern.[83]

Journalist Michael Grunwald offered a different take regarding the storms' impact upon the Everglades. "This time, man defeated nature," asserted the acclaimed author of *The Swamp*. Grunwald contended that "the most remarkable feature of Hurricane Frances was its flooding—or, more precisely, its lack of flooding." In 1947, for example, much of the Everglades and the East Coast of Florida flooded. For decades, environmentalists had warned against tampering with the Everglades' natural flow. "Hurricanes," observed Grunwald, "are inevitably portrayed as object lessons in man's helplessness in the face of Mother Nature's power, and Frances's 105-mph winds certainly reflected that power." He concluded, "But thanks to the world's most extensive and expansive water-control system, featuring thousands of miles of canals and levees as well as hundreds of powerful pumps, most of the flood plains did not flood."[84]

Four hurricanes flooded the channelized Kissimmee River, leaving the river basin's only outlet, Lake Okeechobee, with an abundance of fresh water. But the storm acted like eggbeaters, churning up decades-old polluted muck from the lake's bottom. "The hurricanes were an act of God, but the gunk they stirred up in the lake is the result of our own mismanagement," stated a biologist for Audubon of Florida. "The water is so muddy and so high that sunlight cannot penetrate," reported the *New York Times*. The rising waters killed much of the vital plant life. The bulrush, hydrilla, and eelgrass died, which had been making an encouraging comeback. The air reeked of rotting vegetation. The prized largemouth bass that once attracted large numbers of fishermen were already in steep decline. The Army Corps of Engineers, panicked that the lake crested at more than 18 feet, began dumping water through the eastern and western outlets. The mayor of Pahokee predicted, "What you're going to see is this lake turn just as green and slimy as anything you've seen in a science fiction movie." His vision proved accurate. A two-year drought followed, and the coastal estuaries were awash in algae blooms because of the polluted nitrogen and phosphorous-rich waters. By 2006, the droughts plunged the depth of Lake Okeechobee to an all-time low.[85]

Florida's seashore took a beating as the winds and surf gouged out huge chunks of coastline. However, in some places, the storms left large deposits of new sand. In *The Tempest,* Shakespeare understands that storms transform the natural and political environment. Ferdinand pays tribute to his father's drowning, when he speaks of "pearls that were his eyes . . . But doth suffer a sea change, Into something rich and strange." Pensacola Beach resembled a giant sand dune. Never considered a premium place to collect seashells, Pensacola Beach glittered with angel wings, crown conchs, and moon snails. But, reported NBC correspondent Kerry Sanders from Pensacola Beach the day following the storm, "like so many of the homes here, the shells were broken and crushed by the hurricane." From coast to coast, beachcombers encountered scoured sand dunes. "This is our beautiful beach," lamented Carolyn Terrell of Cocoa Beach, "and it's ugly right now." In readiness, treasure hunters wait for such moments. Equipped with metal detectors, a Pensacola Beach prospector found old class rings lost by spring breakers. On a Brevard County beach, Joel Ruth found 180 near-mint Spanish pieces o' eight.[86]

Florida's citrus industry appeared healthy in 2004. Fully 750,000 acres were still dedicated to the cultivation of citrus. But the industry was struggling with a litany of short- and long-term problems: changing tastes and concerns over the sugary drink; and competition from Brazil, which had already doubled Florida's citrus acreage. The hurricanes of '04 damaged 280,000 acres of grove land. Most of the green citrus crop wound up on the ground. Losses amounted to $3 billion, one-third of the state's agricultural economy. The 2004–5 citrus crop yielded the smallest harvest in thirteen years. The Florida grapefruit harvest was the worst since 1936. Hurricane Wilma (2005) struck the citrus belt the following year, adding additional woe, destroying about 15 percent of the state's crop. Frozen orange juice futures spiked. Like vultures, Brazilian citrus multiconglomerates undercut Florida grove owners by freezing prices to prehurricane levels and dumping cheap oranges into the markets.[87]

Piling misery upon an already troubled industry, the winds that hurled green Valencias and Hamlins to the ground also spread citrus canker, a dreaded bacterial disease. Quickly, grove owners in St. Lucie and Indian River counties detected the brown, corky lesions on the fruit. The disease spread. By February 2005, agricultural officials had destroyed 600,000 citrus trees. The state reimbursed commercial growers $55 for each destroyed tree, while homeowners received $100 for the first tree and $55 for each replacement tree at Walmart. Workers destroyed infected trees as well as all trees within a 1,900-foot radius. Citrus greening was also first detected in Florida in 2004.[88]

Oranges represented only the most visible sign of agricultural wreckage inflicted by Mother Nature. In fact, the nursery industry had already surpassed citrus as the state's most important agricultural sector, a point made every day as newcomers purchased more sod and palm trees and old consumers drank less OJ. The hurricanes inflicted more than $2 billion in damage to the agricultural infrastructure and crops ranging from oranges to tropical fish to cucumbers. From José Luis Avalos's crew of orange pickers in Wauchula to fourth-generation grove owners in Fort Pierce, to Pierson, the ornamental fern capital of America, the losses were calculated in human, as well as economic terms.[89]

"Life isn't about waiting for the storm," a proverb reminds us, "It's about dancing in the rain." In that spirit, the hurricanes helped curb the dreaded West Nile virus. But the torrential rains and standing water fed a mosquito frenzy. In Nalcrest, Polk County, one trap captured 32,000 mosquitoes in September, a dramatic increase in typical yields. Apopka FDA officials were stunned to discover 2.2 million mosquitoes in one trap. Curiously, the number of the mosquito-borne West Nile virus cases declined in the months following hurricane season.[90]

Hurricanes provide instruction in chaos theory, the science of the unexpected. Canals, rivers, lakes, springs, and bays were strewn with many of the state's 1 million registered skiffs, sailboats, cabin cruisers, and yachts. The National Boat Owners Association estimated close to $1 billion in losses and damages resulting from the 2004–5 storms. Marinas absorbed terrible damage. Also strewn along the waterways was an exotic collection of palm fronds, roof tiles, screen doors, spiral staircases, soggy clothing, ruined appliances, and unmentionable disposables. Enterprising Floridians took advantage of opportunities. In Cape Coral, fishermen trolling the canals that interlace the Lee County community began catching unusual trophies. The hurricane blew hundreds of porta-potties and plastic privies, some 7 feet in length and weighing 200 pounds. Cape Coral's many construction sites stocked the canals with an endless supply of porta-potties. When asked what kind of bait toilet-fishermen used, Capt. Ron Davis responded, "Greenbacks!" The comic drama provided an intriguing lawsuit whereby a homeowner sued the Suncoast Portable Toilet Co. for a privy that had blown into a swimming pool. Suncoast pleaded it was not responsible for portable toilets propelled by "an act of God."[91]

Mountains of debris also remained on the land. Rebuilding homes, neighborhoods, and cities is stressful. Environmental concern is not a high priority. In Charlotte County alone, workers hauled away 53,784 truckloads of debris, amounting to 454,521 tons. Inland Alachua County collected 19,000 tons of biomass, so much waste and wood that it would cover UF's Florida Field with 60 feet of trash. Statewide, Charley left behind 18 million cubic yards of debris.[92]

Not all the damage inflicted by hurricanes was visible. The question has lingered for years: What happens to fish during hurricanes? Scientists at the Mote Marine Laboratory in Sarasota tracked the behavior of fish as Hurricane Charley roared into Charlotte Harbor. Researchers concluded that fish and humans shared similar behavioral traits. Six of eight tagged sharks in the lower Pine Island Sound sought refuge in deeper waters while two stayed put. Sharks sense falling water pressure and instinctively move to deeper areas. Other researchers concluded that some fish species did not roam far, finding that fish noises increased in the days following the hurricane.[93]

The Amoral Economics of Hurricanes

Craig Pittman has written about Florida for decades as a *Tampa Bay Times* reporter. "I've covered all kinds of disasters—floods, wildfires, the Legislature, you name it." He recalls that after Hurricane Andrew flattened Homestead, "it took less than a day before the first grinning vendors appeared along the highway selling T-shirts that said, 'I survived Hurricane Andrew.'" Such was not the case for eleven insurance companies that declared bankruptcy. Hurricane Andrew, argued Gray Rohrer, "left Florida's property insurance market in shambles."[94]

Hurricanes generate ample opportunities to gamble in the futures market. The Federal Emergency Management Agency (FEMA) declared 2004 "the most destructive hurricane season in Florida history, as well as the greatest disaster-relief effort in American history, exceeding even 9/11, but not Hurricane Katrina.[95]

The 2004 hurricane season discombobulated Florida's insurance industry. The ripples continue. The four hurricanes cost collectively $29 billion in insured losses. Individuals and families cared little about the corporate bottom line but simply wanted their insurance companies to make good on coverage they loyally paid for. A nightmare of claims and liability fights ensued, complicated by shortages of building material and skilled laborers, and an abundance of con artists. The insurance companies struggled to deal with an avalanche of cases, stemming from 700,000 damaged dwellings and 1.6 million claims. Citizens expressed their wrath at Citizens Property Insurance because it inexplicably had hired so few adjusters. Hurricanes spawned a growth litigation industry. Volusia County filed a $40 million claim with FEMA. The settlement took eight years.[96]

In the 1974 classic *Young Frankenstein,* Marty Feldman, playing Igor, says famously, "It could be worse. It could be raining." The year 2004 could have been worse if Hurricane Charley had not made a sudden turn into Charlotte County and instead headed into Tampa Bay. Experts estimate Charley might have destroyed 50,000 mobile homes. Pinellas County alone counted nearly 50,000 units, while Hillsborough, Pasco, and Manatee amassed over 90,000 trailers.[97]

The Associated Press profiled Chuck Johnson, a fifty-six-year-old film technician who lost his Pensacola home six months earlier. A photograph depicts Johnson; his golden retriever, Molly; and his temporary residence, a camper trailer. "It's like a tennis ball, just back and forth," complained Johnson. "Sometimes I stay awake in bed." By February 2005, the insurance companies had settled 90 percent of the claims, but almost 150,000 persons, including Johnson, still waited. Johnson's predicament was a common point of contention in the Panhandle. Johnson's wind insurer rejected his claim, arguing that Ivan's storm surge, not wind gusts, destroyed his home. Locals waited seven months to find roofers to fix their homes; contractors complained of chronic shortages of roofing shingles and cement. Pensacola resembled the mythical city of Azure, with so many blue tarps flapping from roofs. Blue tarps do not last forever, and papers reported that much of the plastic covering atop 40,000 structures was cracking and deteriorating.[98]

The storms bankrupted insurance companies. National insurance carriers recalculated the risks of offering insurance in Florida. Most of the national insurance firms pulled out en masse. Others, such as State Farm and Allstate, decided to spin off Florida from the megacarriers and create Florida-only policies. This allowed them to drop policies, raise rates, and, in the event of the next costly hurricane, declare bankruptcy, leaving little skin in the game. Some economists believe that Florida is one Ivan or Charley away from collapse. "Florida could go bankrupt," insists Eli Lehrer of the Competitive Enterprise Institute. In the financial chaos, Citizens Property Insurance (CPI), a government-owned, not-for-profit company, became, in the vernacular, "the insurer of last resort." *Miami Herald* columnist Fred Grimm contends that CPI is "a giant casino of an operation that has bet $3 billion in assets to offset $450 billion of exposure." What will happen when the next Category 5 hurricane slams Florida? Lehrer explains, "State taxpayers pony up while Citizens, the state's largest insurer, walks away."[99]

Miami Herald columnist Rick Hirsch reflected upon the profound changes affecting South Floridians and their insurance predicament. In 1992, he explained, he owned a 1,600-square-foot home west of MetroZoo in Miami-Dade County. The home, worth $96,000, was covered by Allstate insurance at a cost of $475 a year. Hurricane Andrew destroyed his home and neighborhood. "Andrew is the pivot point in my life, and if you were here then, probably yours, too," he reflected twenty years later. Hirsch discovered his home had been secured with staples, not nails, "and my home was built with a roof design that enabled strong winds to act as a can opener, ripping the top of the house open to the storm. Neither roofing staples nor gable roofs are allowed today." Allstate paid the family $80,000, but the insurance company "is long gone from the South Florida insurance market." Hirsch calculated that to insure an equivalent 2012 home would cost $3,500 a year—with a $10,000 deductible.[100]

A *Palm Beach Post* study contends that private-sector insurance companies lost $28.8 billion due to the hurricanes of 2004 and 2005. However, they have collected more than $40 billion through 2010 in hurricane-free years. Yet consumers continue to pay higher premiums and accept contracted coverage. In 2012, following seven hurricane-free years, Citizens had amassed a war chest of $6.2 billion, but it still floated the idea of a "hurricane tax" to survive the next storm. Insurance companies raised rates as fast as they dropped policies for Florida's 532,000 licensed mobile homes. Nationwide Insurance proposed doubling the rates for mobile homeowners. The *Miami Herald* asked a question many Floridians wonder: "Can Citizens Property Handle Andrew-Like Storm?"[101]

Floridians bombarded state representatives, county commissioners, and Congress, venting their anger over construction practices, indifferent inspection standards, and weak building codes. Following Hurricane Andrew's devastation in 1992, Miami-Dade County strengthened building codes. "From roof decking to re-bar, the bones of the little box going up in Northwest Miami are thicker, stronger, and far superior to flimsy homes" in the pre-Andrew era. Another wave of reforms followed the storms of 2004. But legislators also listen closely to Florida's building industry and development interests. In the years since Charley and Ivan, lowering standards such as wind loads in certain areas of Florida has gained leverage.[102]

When the hurricane of 1896 wiped away Cedar Key, no FEMA officials, Red Cross workers, or hand-wringing politicians handing out federal aid comforted the survivors. "Though the people support the government," President Grover Cleveland famously proclaimed when vetoing a relief bill for Texas farmers, "the government should never support the people." Americans no longer expect a disaster in Key West to be solely the responsibility of Monroe County charities, friends, and families. National disasters today require massive financial commitments to help the uninsured and underinsured, principles most citizens accept. But the details matter.[103]

The mother of all reconstruction booms began in the fall of 2004. An old proverb, "It's an ill wind that blows nobody any good," may have been true in 1604, but not 2004. These ill winds came with a silver lining, postmarked Washington, D.C. But the winds could be fickle and irrational.

Hurricane Charley essentially wiped away the old Punta Gorda. "No single event may have had a greater impact on Charlotte County," concluded a journalist. The community hit harder than any other Florida city became a blank canvas. A fiercely conservative city, many residents distrusted the federal government but welcomed federal relief. A group of citizens hired a University of Miami urban design professor who spearheaded the great redesign. By August 2014, it seemed as if every newspaper in Florida dispatched a reporter to write a before-and-after story. When asked, Punta Gorda's director of growth-management spoke honestly. "In some ways, Charley was a blessing in disguise. It did urban renewal in one fell swoop." Another official suggested that Charlotte County had become "a poster child for resiliency." A new phrase described what happened here and many places: "Urban renewal by disaster." Half of the city's largest buildings had taken a direct hit. Today, a new riverfront marina and park, a new conference center, new hotels and restaurants dot the downtown. Ten years after an "apocalyptic" storm, a reporter assessed, "Many Charlotte County residents even look on Charley with a certain sense of nostalgia and fondness." Ten years after Charley, about half of Punta Gorda's residents were not even living there in 2004. One of the new restaurants is Hurricane Charley's. Specialty drinks include the Generator, and Looters Will Be Shot. Not every Punta Gordan shares the civic zeal or optimism. Residents of East Punta Gorda, the city's poorest Black neighborhood, feel left out. Three years following Charley, a reporter observed that the neighborhood "has fallen into substantially greater disrepair since the storm."[104]

Neighboring communities grumbled about the reconstruction efforts. In Arcadia and Fort Meade, interior cities east of Charlotte County, a *New York Times* reporter wrote, "there is a general sense that DeSoto County played the part of a stepchild to the more prosperous neighbors in the rush of federal rebuilding money that came to Florida after the storm." Federal money did help rebuild the Turner Agri-Civic Center and renovate DeSoto Memorial Hospital.[105]

Elsewhere in Charlotte County, many residents hoped the insurance windfall might miraculously beautify and redo US 41, the busy thoroughfare that cuts through the county north to south. Like so many roads that were originally two-lane highways, the Tamiami Trail became a commercial artery hopelessly cluttered with fast-food franchises, office complexes, strip malls, and car dealerships. "Big-box stores are next to funeral homes," wrote journalist Tamara Lush.

"Bicyclists and walkers proceed with fear. Despite good intentions, Hurricane Charley and its financial windfall brought little change to US 41, except more traffic and commercial sprawl."[106]

The islands of Sanibel and Captiva rebounded as gracefully and energetically as one might expect. South Seas Island Resort had taken the worst hit, suffering $100 million in damages. For years, the sounds of hammering and chain saws could be heard. The 600-unit, four-star resort reopened in 2007 with a West Indian décor. Ospreys and eagles returned, along with 1,400 newly planted trees and affluent tourists. Millions of dollars from local, state, and federal sources poured in to renourish Lee County beaches.[107]

"It shouldn't take an act of God for Pensacola to make progress," reminisced writer Shannon Nickinson a decade after Ivan roared through the Panhandle, "but sometimes it feels like it does." She noted that three of the most important projects in modern Pensacola occurred because of Ivan: relocating the sewage plant, construction of the Community Maritime Park, and the push for Rebuild Northwest Florida: "Ivan brought us an opening for change that we had lacked the political and social will to embrace otherwise." When pondering Ivan's legacy, Nickinson reflected, "When bad things happen, the government can give us money to fund change, but only we—private business and focused citizens—have the power to make that change last."[108]

Insurance companies paid $4.6 billion for claims involving Hurricane Frances's damages. "Never let a crisis go to waste," became the gospel in South Florida. No one cheered Frances more lustily than lawyers and enterprising individuals who suffered relatively little damage. While the storm track never came within 100 miles of Miami-Dade County, such details did not deter 20,000 Miami-Dade residents from filing damage claims. Upon hearing the news, a dumbfounded American Red Cross official asked, "Where are these people?" The official noted the agency received about one hundred calls. Yet FEMA awarded Miami-Dade claimants $31 million for a storm that a *Sun-Sentinel* reporter suggested packed "the punch of a bad thunderstorm." The federal agency eventually reimbursed 12,382 Miami-Dade claimants. Checks paid for 5,260 television sets, 1,440 air conditioners, two dental invoices, and a funeral for a person who did not die of storm-related causes. The manager of a Liberty City liquor store in Miami estimated his store cashed a half-million dollars' worth of FEMA checks. Three Gannett newspapers in Florida sued the U.S. Department of Homeland Security and FEMA to force the agencies to release information related to the distribution of emergency aid following the storms.[109]

During the 2016 presidential election, reporters discovered that in 2005, Donald Trump received $17 million in an insurance settlement for Wilma-inflicted damages to his Palm Beach mansion Mar-a-Lago. When asked, he could not recall specific repairs, nor could any staff comprehend that amount of damage. "That house has never been seriously damaged," observed Mar-a-Lago's longtime butler. The Palm Beach building department could find no permits filed for reconstruction. Two weeks following the hurricane's damage, Donald Trump Jr. held his wedding reception at the mansion.[110]

Olympic-sized swimming pools could not hold the amounts of antacid required as the result of indifferent insurance adjusters, officious bureaucrats, and endless lines and forms to fill out. Volusia County, thrice struck by hurricanes, received $40 million from FEMA, but it took eight years of pleading and cajoling. And "a lot of perseverance," admitted a county official.[111]

But critics contend that federally subsidized hurricane insurance and beach nourishment simply reward bad behavior. "For sheer arrogance toward the weather," writes Carl Hiaasen, "no place beats Florida." He adds, "And then rebuilding in the same dumb place, if a hurricane knocks down what was there." Why should New Englanders and Heartlanders subsidize beach follies? Researchers characterized such behavior as "our lemming-like march to the sea." The *New York Times* asked in 2005, "Is it time to reconsider retreat from the coast?" Curiously, in the eleven years following Hurricane Wilma in 2005, Florida experienced not a single hurricane. That span marks the longest time between hurricanes in Florida in modern history.[112]

Fighting Past and Future Hurricanes

For centuries, humans have imagined mad scientists stealing the black arts of harnessing nature. The Aztecs sacrificed captives to the gods in hope of bringing rain, while Dust Bowl rainmakers promised Great Plains farmers crop relief for a price. America waged a battle for technological supremacy in World War II. The introduction of terrifying new weapons, as well as lifesaving procedures, created an aura of confidence that America knew no limits. If the United States could fight a two-front war and advance the standard of living on the home front, surely we could tame hurricanes. In 1943, Army Air Corps Lt. Col. Joseph Duckworth took a daring step into the next frontier by piloting a small AT-6 Texan trainer into the eye of a hurricane. He flew the dangerous, unauthorized mission on a bet! Navigator Lt. Ralph O'Hair described the flight as "being tossed about like a stick in a dog's mouth." In mid-August 1945, pilots duplicated the feat, flying into a tropical storm approaching the Florida coast. The information was relayed to the Miami Hurricane Warning Center. The science of hurricane hunting had begun.[113]

At the dawn of the nuclear age, technology seemed both liberating and terrifying. Just hours after the *Enola Gay*—piloted by Miami resident Paul Tibbets—dropped the first atomic bomb, Miami Beach mayor Herbert Frink urged President Truman to hurl the weapon against nature itself to deflect an approaching hurricane. The president demurred. Days later, the Lee County Commission offered the U.S. government a 7,500-acre tract to be used as a base for the "atomic bombing of hurricanes." In 1953, Grady Norton, chief of the U.S. Weather Bureau in Miami, recommended exploding a "baby"-size atomic bomb in the eye of a hurricane to see if the explosion would break up the storm. "It might be worth a try sometime," Norton urged. "Over water, of course."[114]

Researchers have labored for decades on weather modification. In the postwar era, U.S. Navy aircraft attempted to seed hurricanes with silver iodine crystals. Gone are the days of the rainmakers crisscrossing the parched Dust Bowl. Between the 1960s and 1980s, Project Stormfury funded research on storm modification, directed by the Hurricane Research Labs in Miami. A former Stormfury scientist realizes now that the hurricane research was "the alien abductions of meteorology," and he remains skeptical that *homo sapiens* can change the nature of a Category 5 hurricane packing the energy of "a big nuclear warhead going off every half hour."[115]

In 2006, after a flurry of some of America's most terrifying weather, an MIT research scientist proposed dispatching a tugboat into the eye of a hurricane, with twenty jet engines bolted to the vessel. "The B-movie-like script calls for these little engines-that-could fire up and blow away the storm—or at least weaken it," writes a journalist describing the plot. Peter Cordani, a Jupiter businessman with no science degree, has spent millions of dollars to corral hurricanes. The head of Dyn-O-Mat, Cordani has patented Dyn-O-Storm. He claims his water-absorbent product, when sprayed into hurricanes, will "suck the moisture out." He insists scientists at the National Oceanic and Atmospheric Administration are trying to crush him, but researchers tested the product and reported disappointing results.[116]

How does one explain why some places in Florida have been miraculously hurricane-free for more than a century? Sarasota, so the legend goes, was blessed because Native Americans settled along Sarasota Bay. They knew that an Indian force field deflected hurricane. Tampa and St. Petersburg have somehow avoided a direct hit since a 1921 hurricane struck with such force that it separated Hog Island into Honeymoon and Caladesi islands.[117]

The Future

The Weather Channel recently announced that meteorologists have determined that Tampa is the "most vulnerable and overdue" city destined to be hit by a hurricane. Naples, Jacksonville, and Key West also rank in the dubious top ten. Like an avenging angel, Hurricane Irma in 2017 fulfilled the prediction. The cable station has also introduced viewers to new programs with the names *Forecasting the End* and *Deadliest Space Weather.* The Florida zip code with the most to lose was Ponte Vedra, a tony coastal community south of Jacksonville. A major hurricane striking Tampa Bay terrifies authorities. Millions of residents from Sarasota to Cedar Key might be forced to evacuate. "You could see in Tampa Bay," a nervous emergency management spokesman warned, "storm surge totals that would be incredible, 28 to 29 feet." A 2015 estimate suggested that a storm of the century could wreak $175 billion in losses to the Tampa Bay region. Because the continental shelf on the west coast of Florida is shallow, the cyclonic effect of a hurricane would result in a massive tidal surge.[118]

Floridians living "far" from the Gulf coast or Atlantic Ocean should not feel safe. Direct Relief, a California nonprofit organization, compiled a list of the most dangerous rural counties in the Deep South. Outcomes factor not only hurricane risk but the intersection of intense hurricanes and socioeconomic factors such as poverty, the availability of social services, numbers of aging seniors, and mobility. In effect, the study asks, Will residents be overwhelmed by a catastrophe? Three of America's top ten most vulnerable counties are located in Florida, among them DeSoto County (first), followed by Highlands County (fifth), and Glades County (ninth).[119]

In 2008, the Home and Garden channel (HGTV) offered its viewers the opportunity to register for the Dream House sweepstakes. Peter N. Spotts, a reporter for the *Christian Science Monitor,* thought it odd that the home was in Islamorada, the bull's eye for the 1935 hurricane and Tropical Storm Faye in 2008. "The prize was a tidy two-story house that faces the ocean—with landscaping that just dares a hurricane storm surge to come roaring up to the patio."[120]

Surveying the social and material damage resulting from Hurricanes Charley, Ivan, and Katrina, critics asked a pertinent question: Why can't engineers and architects design and build an attractive, inexpensive, hurricane-proof (or safer) home? New Urbanists tackled the question and produced the "Katrina Cottage." The design team paid homage to a 1910 Florida cracker farmhouse and coastal cottages. A stylish, environmentally friendly, 680-square-foot craftsman model designed by Andrés Duany came with wind-resistant panels. Critics loved the homes; consumers ignored them. Why? Americans like things the way they are. We like the freedom to build big homes on beaches without governmental interference and with the expectation the government will rescue us when hurricanes destroy our beachfront mansions.[121]

Weather forecasting has always been on the threshold of new breakthroughs. Experts at the National Hurricane Center believe six-day and seven-day advance forecasts will soon be possible. Pinpointing landfall is one challenge; predicting a storm's intensity is another target.[122]

Today's technology always seems obsolete when measured by the tools of tomorrow. In hindsight, 2004 seemed more like the dawn rather than the crest of a new age. Consider the events of 2004 from the perspective of David Fleshler: "Twitter did not exist, neither did the iPhone. A new web site called Facebook had just been created in a Harvard dorm room." A cell phone was no longer a luxury, but fast becoming a necessity. But cell communication was paralyzed when hurricanes disrupted the power grids. Alas, the few remaining pay phones worked. Young persons, however, had no clue how the old analog technology functioned and had to ask old-timers how to negotiate the low-tech phone booth.[123]

Never in human history have places like Sunny Isles, Manasota Key, and Boca Grande been so seductive and bewitching. Yet demons lurking deep in our collective pasts and the specter of future catastrophes haunt the beach. Will global warming breed new and more powerful hurricanes? Such apocalyptic visions are not new.

In *Condominium*, Florida's John D. MacDonald conveyed the pandemonium of what might happen when the "big one" hits. *Condominium* was MacDonald's sixty-sixth book, but many aficionados believe it best exemplifies the author's code of ethics and best captures his adopted state's shortcomings. The 1985 novel connects all the dots: sleazy county commissioners eager to approve Golden Sands, a doomed, eight-story "geriatric ghetto" on fictitious Fiddler Key; shady contractors performing shoddy work; and fast-talking salesmen. Critics continue to debate whether Hurricane Ella is the protagonist, antagonist, or avenging angel.[124]

John D. MacDonald was not the only doomsday prophet. "Picture Hurricane Andrew churning with devastating power," declared the *Sun Sentinel*, conjuring up a doomsday scenario, "only this time it is aiming right down [Fort Lauderdale's] Broward Boulevard. With ferocious gusts up to 180 mph, it pounds Port Everglades. . . . By the time this compact system departs this area, it has cut a 30-mile swath of destruction . . . causing $70 billion in damage." Max Mayfield interjected: "When I fly over the coast, I just shake my head. Too many people are crammed into coastal communities with too few evacuation routes."

In retrospect, the six weeks Floridians endured in 2004 was wilder than the scariest roller-coaster ride. Journalists at the *Palm Beach Post* may have best summarized the events. "Charley: 145 mph; Frances: 105 mph; Ivan: 130 mph; Jeanne: 120 mph. These were the wind speeds at landfall in Florida from four astonishing hurricanes. . . . The storms moved like slow trains on strange, self-chosen rails, obeying some terrible schedule, making all stops in between unknown destinations."[125]

In the eye of the hurricanes' destruction, Floridians still manage a sense of humor. A popular, if cruel, joke trolled among Florida State and University of Florida alumni. The name of the school in the punch line is interchangeable: "What do FSU alums and hurricanes have in common? They both end up in trailer parks!" The bumper sticker industry and cartoonists had a field day caricaturing Florida. The Sunshine State was lampooned as the Plywood State, a State of Fatigue, and the National Disaster State.

A popular list circulated during the 2004–5 hurricane seasons, "You know you're a Floridian when . . ." Among the favorites:

> You have FEMA's number on speed dial.
>
> When you moved to the coast, you couldn't hang a shower curtain without reading directions; today you can assemble a portable generator by candlelight.
>
> You can recite from memory whole portions of your homeowner's insurance policy.
>
> You can rattle off the names of three or more meteorologists who work at the Weather Channel.
>
> Someone comes to your door to tell you they found your roof.
>
> Relocating to Cleveland, Ohio, doesn't seem like such a crazy idea.

Novelists love the setting: howling winds, late-summer heat and humidity, T-shirt drenched in sweat, and a battery-operated tape recorder playing "Theme from a Summer Place." Add some emergency rations: moldy cheese, soggy crackers, and a warm bottle of wine. More than a few new Floridians owe their very lives to the matchmakers Charley, Frances, Ivan, and Jeanne. "Take away our TV," remembered Robin Kelley of DeLand, "and we found out that really increases our intimacy." The fruit of such intimacy, Zoe Katharine Schneider, was born 9 June 2005. Susan Benson, an English professor in St. Petersburg, recalled: "We made hurricane shutters and hung them, then spent the rest of those two days cooking dinner, drinking wine, and watching old movies. It was the first time we had spent two whole days together in a long, long time." Wells Benson was born 18 May 2005. For Paola Botero of Delray Beach, "We had been without electricity for almost three weeks. It was, well, romantic." Nahia Megats was born 19 May 2005. As the book of Ecclesiastes reminds us, "There is nothing new under the sun." Or hurricane winds. While reporting on the Hurricane Emma's 1947 Category 4 "mowing" of Florida, *Time* magazine noted, "Still, by major hurricane standards," Florida's damage was limited to a few million dollars. But the magazine announced some good news: "Several babies were born safely while things were at their worst, and some got souvenir names—e.g., Glory Be and Mary Gale."[126]

In Shakespeare's *The Tempest,* a hurricane-tossed sea in an exotic land inspired the play that enchanted Elizabethan audiences. On this magical island and refuge, Miranda marvels, "O, brave new world that has such people in it." Miranda's father, the sorcerer Prospero, proclaims, "We are such stuff as dreams are made on." So, too, Florida seemed the stuff of dreams, a dream state that survived the hurricanes of 2004. The fact that the hurricanes coincided with a presidential election wrought extra drama and meaning to voters who hated Washington but demanded increasing amounts of federal relief aid, Social Security benefits, and national security.

4

Election Season

2004

What does Florida do? Florida grows! Despite Elián, hurricanes, the War on Terror, and more melodrama than a soap opera, Florida added more than 1 million new residents between 2000 and 2004. Only two other states grew faster than Florida (Nevada and Arizona), and no state attracted more new residents during this era. Governor Jeb Bush, who won reelection in 2002, explained the essential elements of the Sunshine State more clearly than demographers: "This may be the most dynamic state in all the fifty." And Professor Sean Snaith explained it more succinctly than Governor Scott after Hurricane Irma in 2017: "Irma doesn't change the fact that there is no income tax."[1]

What else does Florida do? It entertains Americans who need sunshine in February and melodrama in November. Whiplashed by four hurricanes in the summer of 2004, Florida evoked elements of spectacle and theater. By October, invasions of gypsy roofers and insurance adjusters collided with battalions of news crews and political operatives. As paint peeled from wind-blasted homes, visits by presidential aspirants dominated the front pages and evening news. Political staffs visited Florida so often they began pronouncing Miami as "My-am-uh," recommending the best Cuban *cortadito* to the press corps. Journalists struggled with the spellings and pronunciations of Kissimmee, Alachua, and Thonotosassa, Boca Raton, Oviedo, and Ybor City. Florida's 9,753,819 registered voters buckled up for a very bumpy ride. He who extracted Excalibur, the sacred sword, claimed the prize of 27 electoral votes. Gallantry was neither required nor expected.

Florida Democrats did not need long memories to understand how long they had dominated the Sunshine State. Between 1877 and 1965 not a single Republican governor was elected. The era between the 1960s and 1980s marked an era that historians have described as a "Golden Age," an era dominated by a new generation of urban Democrats, the result of legal and demographic trends. Court-ordered reapportionment, the urgency of civil rights and environmental issues, and an extraordinary outpouring of talented legislators made their mark in Tallahassee: Bob Graham, Reubin Askew, Sandy D'Alemberte, Betty Castor, Mary Grizzle, Elaine Gordon, Phil Lewis, Terrell Sessums, Louis de la Parte Jr., Lee Moffitt, Buddy MacKay, Jack Gordon, Richard Pettigrew, and Ralph Turlington. Republicans seized control of the Florida House and Senate in the 1990s, but Democrats felt confident that restoration was destiny. After all, in 2004, 3.95 million Republicans were registered to vote. While 4.3 million Democrats were registered, 2.2 million Floridians chose no party affiliation.[2]

Energized Democrats, bum-rushed in 2000, sought vindication four years later. In 2003, rumors circulated that Senator Hillary Clinton was contemplating a run for the presidency. When she appeared at South Florida bookstores to sign her new book, *Living History,* a Miami Beach activist exclaimed, "How can she be doing five events in Florida and not running for president?" Websites for the faithful soon appeared: votehillary.org and hillarynow.com. In a review of her book, Maureen Dowd opined, "'Living History' is neither living nor history. But like Hillary Rodham Clinton, the book is ruthless, a phenomenon that's impossible to ignore and impossible to explain." Ultimately, Hillary chose not to run, in part because of front-runner Howard Dean. Dean's commanding position in the early polls prompted Al Gore and Senators Bill Bradley and Tom Harkin to endorse the former governor of Vermont. Dean's campaign ended disastrously when the candidate was captured exhorting an Iowa crowd with an awkward, "cult-like" primal scream.[3]

In late July 2004, the Democratic National Convention met in Boston to nominate U.S. Senators John Kerry and John Edwards to head the presidential ticket. President Bush, sensing that Kerry would be the nominee, ridiculed him in a February reelection kickoff speech. The Democratic field "is for tax cuts and against them . . . in favor of liberating Iraq and opposed to it. And that's just the Senator from Massachusetts."[4]

George W. Bush and John Kerry projected contrasting personalities and images. In his Texas accent, the president introduced his trademark warnings, "Don't mess with Texas" and "Bring it on!" With the faith of a reborn Christian, the Republican nominee confessed to a wild and wooly youth, drinking and behaving in excess. As an undergraduate at Yale, he was largely indifferent to the Elis' hallowed traditions. He joined the Texas Air National Guard as an alternative to being drafted and fighting in Vietnam. The American people liked his plainspoken style and adored his wife, Laura, a school librarian. But Americans were also becoming restless. Commentators resurrected the Vietnam-era word "quagmire" to measure military progress in Iraq and Afghanistan. On the home front, while Americans continued to express confidence, the economy had stalled in a "jobless recovery."[5]

Senator Kerry came across as a blue-blooded Boston Brahmin, an Ivy Leaguer who earned his bona fide liberal credentials as an attorney general and U.S. senator. His French was pitch-perfect, the result of a youth spent in Swiss boarding schools and a family estate in Saint-Briac, France. Republicans and comedians smirked that "Monsieur Kerry looks French!" Stubbornly and refreshingly, he resisted being manipulated by handlers, and if he enjoyed windsurfing, he would be photographed with tousled hair and body-hugging suit. The photograph prompted the *New York Times* to gibe, "Who among us does not love windsurfing?" An eloquent speaker, his theatrical style seemed more suited to the Victorian stage than the modern stump. Ted Kennedy warned him about "too much Senatese." Kerry may have come across as a lace-curtain, Irish American elitist, but to the surprise of the public—and Kerry—his newly discovered ancestor included a grandfather who was a Czech Jewish brewer who fled to America, changed the family name from Kohn to Kerry, converted to Catholicism, and committed suicide in a Boston hotel room in 1921. Kerry's father was a U.S. diplomat. His mother, Rosemary Forbes, traced her genealogy to John Winthrop. The Forbes family had status and wealth. John was raised as a Roman Catholic. He was also a maverick, enlisting in the U.S. Navy after Yale and becoming a war hero. Lieutenant Kerry first emerged as a public figure when he participated in antiwar rallies, on one occasion throwing combat medals from the steps of the U.S. Capitol. He testified on behalf of Vietnam Vets Against the War in a congressional hearing.[6]

In 1995, Kerry, a divorcé, married the fabulously wealthy, Mozambique-born Teresa Simões-Ferreira Heinz, the widow of U.S. Senator H. John Heinz. Outspoken, progressive, and a Republican until 2003, Teresa contrasted sharply with the soft-spoken Laura Bush. She eventually changed her name to Teresa Heinz Kerry. Many reporters thought Teresa would have been a memorable First Lady and was underutilized during the campaign. Others thought she was a disruptive force, her bluntness more vitriolic than refreshing.[7]

But the two candidates bore remarkable similarities. For all of Bush's Texan mannerisms and malapropisms, he, too, traced his lineage back to America's first families, attended elite New England prep schools, and graduated from

Yale. While George appeared less intellectual than his counterpart, the two men earned almost identical grades at Yale. Bush was not as dumb as he pretended; Kerry was not as brilliant as he imagined. Both men loved baseball, the difference being that John Kerry only adored the Boston Red Sox while George Bush owned the Texas Rangers. Both men had held prestigious political offices.[8]

In one of history's cruel turn of events, Washington and Texas insiders always thought if any of the sons succeeded George H. W. Bush as president, it would be Jeb. After all, he was the more serious and studious son, fluent in Spanish, and a rising star in Florida. When asked about this theory, President George H. W. Bush offered his opinion: "That's all bullshit." And when asked, Jeb replied: "If I were 'The One,' no one told me about it. I didn't get the memo."[9]

But the stars seemed aligned in 1994 for Republicans, as President Clinton had stumbled in his first two years, especially with the ham-fisted rollout of his national health insurance plan. Jeb announced his candidacy for the governorship of Florida, challenging sitting Governor Lawton Chiles, who had left the U.S. Senate in 1988 determined to stem the Republican tide in his beloved Florida. In Texas, George W. challenged the iconic, incumbent Texas governor Ann Richards. For the Bush family, it was personal, when then state treasurer Richards ridiculed presidential candidate George H. W. Bush at the 1988 Democratic Convention. "Poor George," she mocked, "He can't help it—he was born with a silver foot in his mouth." She dismissed George W. as "Shrub," not a bush even, but a little bush. When the political fog lifted, George W. triumphed and Jeb lost. When asked about his two sons both running for state governors in 1994, President Bush recalled: "I thought Jeb had a better chance to win than George when up against Ann Richards. Nobody thought he would win." But Jeb rebounded in 1998, whipping Democrat Buddy MacKay to secure Florida's governorship. Like Horatius at the Sublician Bridge, Jeb helped repulse the Democrats in 2000 and stood resolute, determined to defend Florida for his big brother in 2004.[10]

But for all the FEMA checks and reminders that America had not been attacked since 9/11, President Bush was a lackluster candidate and president. He lacked the oratorical gifts to inspire and struggled to jump-start the economy. Polls indicated that Bush was skating on ice that was becoming perilously thin. Following a spike in approval ratings after 9/11, Americans were becoming more critical of the president's actions. On New Year's Day 2004, 60 percent of those polled indicated approval of the president's job performance, a rating that fell below 50 percent for the month of July. Even the president's father fretted at the sinking poll numbers. "This, of course, caused my aching duodenum to throb, to pulsate, to hurt," the former president wrote Hugh Sidey, the White House correspondent for *Time* magazine. On Halloween, days before the election, the numbers had settled in at 48 percent, not a safe position. Could the challenger seize the opportunities?[11]

Kerry, Bush, and the Ghosts of Vietnam

John Kerry emerged unscathed from the Democratic primaries. He defeated Howard Dean, governor of Vermont; Joseph Lieberman, a U.S. senator from Connecticut and running mate with Al Gore in 2000; and John Edwards, a U.S. senator from North Carolina. On Super Tuesday, 2004, he swept nine of ten states, essentially wrapping up the nomination in March. He chose Orlando as the setting for a kickoff speech in early March. Flanked by fellow Democratic U.S. Senators Bob Graham and Bill Nelson, he proclaimed them "living testimony as to what happens in Florida when you count the votes!" He promised the crowd, "I'll be back here a lot."[12]

John Kerry appeared the perfect Democratic candidate for 2004. He was handsome, intelligent, and athletic. Military service and patriotism had been the Democratic Party's Achilles' heel since Vietnam. Kerry walked the walk. He volunteered for military service and saw combat as a naval officer. Memorably, he began his convention acceptance speech, "I'm John Kerry and I'm reporting for duty!"

Beginning with George Washington, Americans' respect for military service and exaltation of battlefield valor have ushered a succession of war heroes to the White House: Andrew Jackson, William Henry Harrison, Zachary Taylor, Ulysses S. Grant, Theodore Roosevelt, and Dwight Eisenhower. Every Gilded Age Republican president but the youthful William McKinley had earned the general's chevrons in the Civil War, and when the war ended, the twenty-two-year-old Ohioan had been promoted to brevet major. A World War I or World War II veteran distinguished the top of every ticket in every presidential campaign between 1948 and 1996. Of course, war heroes were not invincible. In 1996, the so-labeled draft-dodger President Clinton defeated World War II veteran Bob Dole in the presidential race.

Yale University has proudly sent its sons of Eli to fight our nation's wars. Nathan Hale was a Yale man; 10,000 alumni served during World War II, 514 dying in the conflict. Vietnam roiled the waters and challenged the meaning of Americans' closely held concepts such as patriotism and manhood, duty and sacrifice. Yale faculty voted to sever the ties between the school and the U.S. Navy and Army ROTC programs.[13]

Since 1992, Americans confronted the uncomfortable reality of embracing presidential candidates who not only did not serve in the military but had expressed opposition to the war in Vietnam. Few presidential candidates measured up to Bill Clinton's survival skills in shirking duty and skirting disaster. As memories of Korea and World War II faded, perhaps the military-political calculus no longer mattered. In 2000, Americans preferred George W. Bush to Vietnam veteran Al Gore. But John Kerry seemed the perfect Democratic talisman to exorcise the dovish demons that had haunted the Democratic Party. He was not only a veteran but also a military hero. In contrast, Republican vice-presidential candidate Dick Cheney had received five student and marriage deferments.

Kerry enlisted in the navy, volunteering for duty aboard a fast patrol craft, aka "Swift Boat." These vessels, like the PT 109 that naval officer John F. Kennedy had commanded in the South Pacific, patrolled the rivers of Vietnam. In little over four months of service in 1968 and '69, Lieutenant Kerry was awarded three Purple Hearts, a Bronze Star, and a Silver Star. He demonstrated valor, rescuing a Green Beret, engaging and killing the enemy, and saving a comrade's life.

Defining the opponent before he/she has an opportunity to introduce oneself to the American people has become a political axiom. "The goal," several campaign aides said, "is to first strip Mr. Kerry of the positive image that he carried away from the Democratic primary contests and then to define him issue by issue in their own terms before summer vacation season." Republican strategists had adroitly revealed the effectiveness of this ploy in 1988 when they tar-brushed a Michael Dukakis known to few Americans. Few Washington insiders could have imagined that Kerry's soft spot was his unvarnished status as a military hero. In the spring of 2004, a group of Vietnam veterans staged a press conference to expose what they claimed was John Kerry's shameful military record. A feeding frenzy ensued, followed by talk radio shows, cable news, and books. Texas billionaires T. Boone Pickens and Bob J. Perry helped finance a series of television spots that became known as "Swift Boat ads." Americans listened to and watched Swift Boat veterans attack Kerry's character, discrediting his Purple Hearts, defaming his actions, and doubting his fabricated events and dubious medals. "Swiftboating" entered the lexicon as a verb and synonym for betrayal. A long list of veterans came forth to support Kerry's courage in battle. A *New York Times'* columnist evaluated his record and concluded, "Mr. Kerry stretched the truth here and there, but earned his decorations."[14]

President Clinton, always willing to provide advice, suggested that Kerry "start talking less about Vietnam and more about health care." Why did an unpopular war that had ended thirty years earlier matter in 2004? In a perceptive analysis, an editorial writer speculated that Vietnam "keeps popping out of America's darkest closet not just because John Kerry conspicuously served there, and Mr. Bush did not, but because of what's happening half a world away in real time, a televised war."[15]

Nor was Bush immune to the Vietnam syndrome. The question as to why and how a powerful politician's son avoided the Vietnam-era draft had been raised in 2000. Al Gore was a senator's son, but he volunteered and served in Vietnam. Clearly, the issue gathered little traction in 2000. But America was once again at war, a conflict fast becoming unpopular in an election year. In polls taken during the period June 29–October 7, 2004, fully 49 percent of likely voters in Florida thought the war in Iraq was "the wrong thing to do." More than 1,100 Americans had already died there by October, and while those numbers paled in comparison with the death counts in Vietnam, the new 24-hour media magnified the casualties.[16]

The election's October surprise occurred on 8 September 2004, when *Sixty Minutes II* aired a bombshell broadcast in which CBS anchor and icon Dan Rather accused George Bush of shirking his military obligation. In a series of actions so bizarre that the event became a movie starring Robert Redford reprising his role as Bob Woodward (*Truth*, 2015), the story originated at an obscure website. In 2004 "The AWOL Project" website first appeared. A veteran pilot who had served in the same National Guard unit as Bush came across the website before it went viral. The site included incriminating copies of Air National Guard documents implicating Bush. The pilot described the site as "a bloviated screed against President George W. Bush and his ANG service." The blogger who assembled the website was Paul Lukasiak, a Democratic activist.[17]

CBS News producer Mary Mapes obtained copies from Lt. Col. Bill Burkett, who claimed to have destroyed the original documents after faxing them. The Kerry campaign was aware of the revelations. *For the Record* presented documents, among them a notification that First Lieutenant Bush had been grounded for "failure to perform to USAF/TexANG standards." A second document claimed to "sugarcoat" a "CYA" (Cover Your Ass) note warning officers who might be pressured to cover for Bush.

Critics immediately pounced upon the CBS News conclusions, pointing out inconsistencies in typography, nomenclature, and authenticity, charging that the documents had been falsified. Pundits also questioned the political motivation of CBS News and Dan Rather. Within a week, the CBS defense seemed untenable, and the *Washington Post, New York Times,* and *USA Today* were demanding retractions. CBS News and Rather ultimately conceded, firing Mapes for "myopic zeal" and forcing Rather to apologize. Humiliated, he left CBS in March 2005.[18]

The Campaign for Florida

John Kerry needed a running mate to help win the election. Rumors swirled that Kerry had discreetly asked John McCain to join the ticket. Instead, Kerry chose a former rival, John Edwards, a youthful North Carolinian who appealed to voters as a hero of the working classes, as someone who had escaped the poverty of the mill towns and succeeded wildly. The fact that his father worked as a middle-class mill supervisor most of his career seemed immaterial to the drumbeat–story line. Introduced by John Mellencamp's throbbing elegy "Small Town," Edwards had carefully crafted a speech known as "The Two Americas." Wealthy by dint of his success as a trial lawyer, he reminded audiences that he was always on the side of the factory worker, or those wronged by big corporations, or those who lived on the wrong side of the tracks. He touted the blessings of a happy marriage to Elizabeth Anania, whom he met at UNC law school. The couple returned to Wendy's annually for their anniversary dinner! Elizabeth Edwards could flaunt her Florida credentials: Her parents were married in Pensacola and retired to Sarasota. She was born at the Jacksonville Naval Hospital. A sister lived in Bradenton, and aunts and uncles settled across the peninsula.[19]

Strategists pointed to Edward's energy, accent, and roots as the answer to the question whether the Democratic Party had written off the South in November. "Apart from the fact that Edwards is someone incredibly energetic and charismatic, Kerry's selection of Edwards is much more of a socio-economic play," argued political analyst Charlie Cook. "It is a concerted effort to reach downscale white voters, who may or may not live in small towns and rural America, who might be more open to a message delivered by Edwards than Kerry, and who might better identify with Edwards's roots than Kerry's." The establishment also pointed to Edwards's youthfulness—he was fifty-one—as a counterweight to Vice President Cheney's age and health (he was sixty-three and had already suffered four heart attacks). During the primaries, John Kerry had quipped, "When I came back from Vietnam in 1969, I don't know if John Edwards was out of diapers." Polls indicated that Americans reacted favorably to Edwards's selection.[20]

Almost before the convention confetti was swept away, the Kerry-Edwards ticket headed to Florida. The pair's first stop was the pink-stucco Coliseum in St. Petersburg, a place where many grandparents and great-aunts had danced. The birthplace of Florida's modern Republican Party in the 1940s, St. Petersburg was now drifting Democratic. "Thank you, Florida, where this time not only does every vote count, but every vote will be counted," roared John Kerry to an enthusiastic crowd of three thousand. The audience cheered loudest for Teresa Heinz Kerry. Kerry then introduced his running mate, jesting, "He's a lawyer; I'm a lawyer. His name is John; my name is John. He was named People magazine's sexiest politician of the year; I read People magazine!" From St. Petersburg, the team headed to Broward County, a mother lode of voters and donors. Mitchel Berger, a Broward County attorney and fundraising chair for the Democratic National Committee, gushed, "It's full campaign-boogie in July!"[21]

Presidents draw upon a rich reservoir of tools and resources in a reelection battle. During catastrophes, the public expects its president to possess the compassion and eloquence of Abraham Lincoln and the resolution and confidence of Franklin Roosevelt. Perceptions can be graded harshly or generously, as President Bush would learn during Hurricanes Charley and Katrina. Modern presidents have a powerful weapon, the power granted to declare a national disaster and provide generous federal dollars.[22]

As the 2004 hurricane season melded and melted into the political season, the advantages of incumbency crystallized. President Bush and Governor Bush blanketed Florida with FEMA workers. Michael Brown, the director of FEMA who in 2005 would stumble so badly during Hurricane Katrina, received high marks for his efforts in Florida. With a heaping measure of snark, *Rolling Stone* observed that "teams of federal housing inspectors were deployed to help residents file claims on the spot," although such actions seem more compassionate than cynical. *Government Executive* magazine marveled, "Seldom has a federal agency had the opportunity to so directly and uniquely alter the course of a presidential election, and seldom has any agency delivered for a president as FEMA did for Florida this fall."[23]

While President Bush played the role of Griever in Chief in Punta Gorda, John Kerry took the high road and ceased campaigning in Florida, asking his staff to help with the recovery. One "cannot overestimate the effect of these hurricanes," said the director of the liberal voter-mobilization group America Coming Together. The storms essentially "blew August for us." In campaign terms, observed the *Orlando Sentinel,* "Kerry's nearly two-month hiatus may seem like a lifetime in a state long baptized as a linchpin in this fall's presidential race." Yet unable to campaign in Florida during August and September, his favorability ratings climbed among likely Florida voters. In August, 39 percent of Floridians had a favorable opinion of Kerry, a 1 percent improvement over the president.[24]

By Labor Day, polls indicated a dead heat in the must-win state of Florida.

Significantly, only 4 percent of the voters were undecided. In March, Kerry was leading Bush by 6 points. Two issues dominated voters' minds: the economy and the war against terrorism. Floridians endorsed Kerry as better equipped to handle the economy, while voters trusted Bush with the challenges in Iraq and abroad. The electorate was polarized. Three of four Republicans felt the nation was heading in the right direction, while three in four Democrats swore we were headed south. Konnie Rea of Flagler County illustrated the polarization: "I would vote for a diseased baboon before I would vote for George Bush." In contrast, Cinda Dietrich of Collier County asserted, "Nothing's going to change my mind. I think Bush is very honest; I think he cares deeply about the American people."[25]

Florida's political reality belied the numbers. In 2004, the Democratic Party claimed an advantage over the Republicans in registered voters: 4,066,068 to 3,705,081, giving the Party of Jefferson and Jackson an edge of 360,987 votes (4 percent of the registered voters). Precisely half of Floridians had a favorable opinion of President Bush in October 2008.[26]

Both candidates made overtures to the growing number of independent/no-party voters. In 2004, 1.73 million of Florida's 9.75 million registered voters, fully 18 percent of the total, chose no party affiliation when asked. In March, independent voters preferred Kerry by a two to one margin. But by late August, the cohort was evenly divided between Bush and Kerry.[27]

In September and October, Kerry and Bush blitzed the Sunshine State with rallies and fundraisers. Kerry and Edwards concentrated their energies along the Democratic-rich Gold Coast counties: Palm Beach, Broward, and Miami-Dade.

Jews

Kerry and Bush visited South Florida repeatedly, in part, to plead their cases to one of the state's most powerful voting groups, a half-million Jews, still bitterly disappointed over the 2000 election and the haunted butterfly ballot. John Kerry need not have reminded this group that the Eleventh Commandment expects, "Thou shalt vote Democratic." President Bush was not the first Republican to plea to traditional Jewish voters to reconsider the Republican message. In 2000, he may have won as few as one in ten Jewish votes cast in Florida. He needed to improve on those numbers. Ronald Reagan captured 40 percent of the Jewish vote in 1980. Democratic Congressman Robert Wexler, who represented a predominantly Jewish district in Palm Beach County, warned in an editorial that Bush was a "fair-weather friend" for Israel. John Kerry boasted of his impeccable pro-Israel voting record. In Pembroke Pines, Kerry urged the large crowd to vote early, reminding the many seniors that President Bush had promised wealthy donors that he would "come out strong" to privatize Social Security.[28]

A cavalcade of prominent Jews and Gentiles toured the condominium towers and temples of South Florida in pursuit of a Kerry victory in November. Bill Clinton galvanized Jewish voters in Palm Beach County. Eight Jewish members of Congress reminded voters of Kerry's dedication to Israel. Alan Dershowitz, the Harvard law professor, warned voters of foul play at the polls. Henny Youngman and Milton Berle would have appreciated the event. The yarmulke-donned comedian Larry David pleaded with the audience to vote, lamenting that the first Bush-Kerry debate had so depressed his wife that she no longer wanted sex. New York congressman Gary Ackerman joked, "Can you imagine so many big Jews packed into one bus? It's like a bunch of Hasidim going to the Catskills." In Miami, Cameron Kerry warmed up the crowd for the headliner, Bill Clinton. A reporter noted that unlike his brother, John, Cam did not speak in flourishes. "He does do synagogues, And delicatessens. And any other place where Jewish voters gather, especially in swing states." Kerry told members of the B'nai Torah Congregation in Boca Raton that in 1983 he converted to Judaism. "There are audible gasps in the audience. John Kerry's brother is Jewish? Who knew?" Cameron dreamt of an inauguration day when his daughters would read from the Torah. To counter the 1990s "nostalgia tour," former New York City mayor Ed Koch told a Palm Beach County crowd that for the first time in his life he was pulling the lever for a Republican running for president.[29]

Seniors

To win the election, elderly voters represented a must-win bloc of voters. In a state where large numbers of rich and poor, liberal and conservative, Jewish and Gentile, were over age sixty-five, seniors were also the most likely to vote. The influence of elderly voters in 2004 Florida was scarcely a new phenomenon. "Thousands of old folks, many of them seeking sunshine and longer lives in Florida's cities, towns, and rural spots," observed a reporter in 1940, "are dominating the state's 1940 elections."[30]

In this era, Democrats laid claim to the elderly vote. Just as Ronald Reagan would be remembered for his "It's morning in America" declaration, Franklin Roosevelt and Lyndon Johnson redeemed senior citizens with the creation of Social Security and Medicare. But in Florida, the elderly vote was dynamic and complicated. The "scare seniors" card, warning them of a scorched-earth Republican administration, had worked in the past. But as a journalist observed in 2004, "Today's older voters are typically more educated and affluent than their parents, and they are increasingly willing to align themselves with Republicans." In his 2002 gubernatorial reelection campaign against Bill McBride, Jeb Bush won most votes cast by Floridians aged sixty and older. But the political season would be incomplete without robocalls and innuendo: Democrats charged that heartless Republicans were prepared to gut Social Security, while Republicans hinted that illegal Mexicans had been promised priority housing in assisted living facilities.[31]

One of the hot-button issues of the 2004 race was President Bush's unpopular Medicare prescription drug law. Attempting to seize the high ground with the critical issue of senior medical care, the president managed to secure Senator Ted Kennedy's endorsement, and the landmark $400 billion Medicare prescription bill passed in January 2003. Triumphant, Bush held a rally at Constitution Hall, hailing the measure as "the greatest advance in health care coverage for America's seniors since the founding of Medicare." But the measure was hopelessly complicated, and seniors were confused by the myriad options and angry over "gap coverage and "donut holes." The Alliance for Retired Americans, an organization that claimed 3 million retired trade union members, endorsed Senator Kerry for president. When John Kerry was visiting a senior center in Pembroke Pines, he took advantage of another issue that was aggravating the elderly: the shortage of flu vaccine. "Seniors deserve prescription drugs that are affordable," the candidate thundered. Peppered with questions about public prayer and flu shots, the senator gibed, "I'll tell you that was appropriate because you don't have a prayer of getting a flu shot."[32]

Florida had long established itself as the undisputed capital of senior living. Just how old was Florida? Almost 900,000 residents were eighty years old or older! No ethnic, racial, or demographic group frightened politicians more than the elderly, for the simple reason that they voted with conviction and consistency. Woe to the politician who betrayed seniors. Jeb Bush knew this all too well. In 1994, he seemed to have an insurmountable lead over Governor Lawton Chiles when, the night before the election, 700,000 "mystery" phone messages scared seniors, warning them that Jeb was no friend because he opposed Medicare and wanted to abolish Social Security. Taking cue, the Kerry campaign unveiled a devastating commercial in October. An ominous voice announced, "The truth is coming out. . . . The real Bush agenda? Cutting Social Security."[33]

A new tradition was born in October 2004: President Bush visited The Villages. "I am proud to be the first sitting President ever to have visited The Villages. (Applause). The other ones missed out on a lot." The Villages was earning a reputation as a must-stop for any Republican candidate. What was unusual about the president's visit was that it occurred a few weeks before the election. Typically, candidates kicked off their election at this conservative bastion.[34]

Race

African Americans represented the Democratic Party's most loyal constituency. In August 2004, 56,937 African Americans had registered as Republicans, in contrast to 3.71 million registered Democrats. Bill Clinton may have been the "first Black president," but John Kerry worked assiduously to reach and motivate African Americans. Members of the Congressional Black Caucus joined Kerry and Edwards at rallies. "At the Miami church," a reporter observed, "the congregants leapt to their feet and burst into applause Sunday when Kerry, [Jesse] Jackson, and [Al] Sharpton entered from behind the pulpit as a swaying and clapping gospel choir sang, "I will praise him." The Kerry campaign hoped the "souls to polls" outreach would be successful. Pastor John F. White of Fort Lauderdale's Mount Hermon AME Church declared 31 October, "Early Voting Sunday" for his congregation. Pastor White, with John Kerry at his side, compared John Kerry to a modern Moses leading the children of Israel to the Promised Land. "For the past four years we've been living in the wilderness," he preached, "There is one who can divide the Red Sea for us and we can cross over on dry ground. You've got a vote in your hand . . . use it and be liberated and be set free."[35]

Recruiting young and old African Americans to vote remained a core goal of the Democratic Party. J. B. Taylor registered for the first time in his life. The eighty-seven-year-old African American from Micanopy criticized President Bush over the skyrocketing cost of his medicine. "I always wanted to vote," he said regrettably, "I just didn't go." For many decades he worked at the Franklin Crate Mill, where, he explained, his employer forbade Black workers from voting.[36]

Running the gauntlet of voter registration was one challenge for minorities; ensuring your vote counted was quite another. Gadsden County was the new poster child of election dysfunction. Florida's only Black-majority county held the dubious distinction of having 12 percent of its ballots disqualified in 2000. A dashing Andrew D. Gillum emerged as someone to watch. In 2004, he worked as an organizer with People for the American Way, an empowering get-out-the-Black-votes organization. Gillum, who was elected city commissioner of Tallahassee at age twenty-three, explained, "It's no longer as simple as saying, 'You're of age, you're a citizen, you're eligible to vote.'"[37]

Like Banquo's ghost, the specter of race hung over the 2004 election, as it had four years earlier. Florida, like other southern states in the Reconstruction era, banned convicted felons from voting, even after their debts to society had been paid. The assumption then, of course, was that most convicted felons were Black. In 2004, an astonishing 600,000 ex-felons in Florida could not vote. Whereas most other states accepted ex-felons as citizens with voting privileges, Florida remained obstinate on this issue. African Americans were disproportionately numbered. In a controversial move, Florida's election officials prepared an additional ex-felons list numbering 48,000. Critics screamed that the list was flawed. For instance, the list included relatively few Hispanic names, a group more likely to vote Republican.[38]

Hispanics

Karl Rove, the "evil genius" in the Bush cockpit, put it simply: Florida was "ground zero" for victory. If so, the Cuban vote was "indispensable," wrote William Finnegan, a longtime contributor to the *New Yorker.* Navigating Florida in quest of the Hispanic vote could be treacherous and confusing. From the 1960s through the 1990s, the steadfast Cuban commitment to the Republican Party was the closest thing to an ethnic bloc vote in Florida. "There are some eight hundred and fifty thousand Cubans in Florida, more than half of them registered to vote," explained Finnegan, "not such a large number in a state of seventeen million, except that when they turn out in force and vote en masse, they are huge." In the 2000 election, Cubans provided Bush a quarter-million-vote margin over Gore.[39]

But Florida's 3.2 million Hispanics had become so large, diverse, and far-flung a group that the word "Hispanic" seemed unsatisfactory and imprecise. They constituted 12 percent of the electorate, not counting other non-Spanish-speaking ethnic groups, Haitians, Jamaicans, Brazilians, and Filipinos. Courting the Hispanic vote on a state level required knowledge of a dizzying population of Cubans, Puerto Ricans, Mexicans, Dominicans, Venezuelans, Colombians, Argentineans, Guatemalans, Nicaraguans, Salvadorans, and Hondurans. Political passage through Little Havana required a trip to Café Versailles and a discerning ability to order *café Cubano.* Cubans remained the largest Hispanic group, but increasing numbers of young Cubans, no longer fixated on rolling back Fidel's communism on their grandfather's island, leaned to the Democratic Party. Florida's fastest-growing Spanish-speaking group was Puerto Rican. They had settled, not in Miami-Dade County, but in Central Florida. Many pundits pointed to this constituency as the critical Hispanic swing vote in 2004. The *New York Times*' Abby Goodnough, in an article aptly titled, "Hispanic Vote in Florida: Neither a Bloc nor a Lock," reported, "Colombians, Puerto Ricans, and Dominicans are leaning toward Senator John Kerry, polls suggest, though many have registered as independents and the Democrats do not consider their vote a sure thing. Nicaraguans embrace President Bush, and Cubans, while still overwhelmingly Republican, may throw some support to the Democrats for a change." The fact that so many Hispanics were first-time voters complicated forecasting. Competing polls revealed wildly different forecasts.[40]

Cuban-born hard-liners still dominated the political dialogue and held the most powerful positions in Miami-Dade County. Miami's Al Cardenas, the former GOP chair, served as co-chair of the Bush campaign. U.S. Representative Ileana Ros-Lehtinen fled Cuba with her family, who settled in Miami's Little Havana. Her maternal grandparents were Sephardic Jews. Following graduation from Florida International University, she taught public school and became a principal. Elected to the Florida House in 1982, she broke a panel of glass ceilings, becoming the first Hispanic woman to serve in that body and, later, the Florida Senate. When Congressman Claude Pepper died in 1989, she ran for his seat, becoming the first Hispanic woman to serve in the U.S. Congress.[41] In 2004, Congresswoman Ros-Lehtinen spearheaded an attack on Teresa Heinz Kerry's family foundation for supporting an organization that provided Internet assistance to the Cuban Interests Section.[42]

On 5 June 2004, amid the political hurly-burly, Ronald Reagan died. While Republicans bid farewell to the modern savior of the party, Fidel doused his funeral pyre with gasoline, remarking that Reagan "should never have been born." He added gratuitously, "He forgot to take his worst works to the grave."[43]

No place better illustrates the rise of Puerto Ricans than Buenaventura Lakes, a sprawling complex of 25,000 in Osceola County, located west of Orange County. Many of the residents were transplanted "Nuyoricans," where they had long been loyal to the Democratic Party since Spanish Harlem succeeded Italian Harlem in the 1940s. On the eve of the 2004 election, a massive rally was held at Buenaventura Lakes, located in the Puerto Rican heart of Central Florida. Democratic Party *prominenti* included Caroline Kennedy Schlossberg, Chelsea Clinton, Karina Gore Schiff, Cate Edwards, and Vanessa Kerry. Kerry-Edwards signs urged "*Luchando por Nosotros*—(Fighting for Us), and *Una Nueva Esperanza*—(A New Hope).[44]

The overarching theme of the 2004 campaign could be reduced simply: the battle for the swing vote. If only the Democrats could pick off a sliver of the

Cuban vote, if only the GOP could pry away more Jewish and senior votes, and if either party could arouse students and young workers to the polling place, victory was possible.

Youth

If the Hispanic vote was up for grabs, the youth vote "was blowin' in the wind." In election after election, the Democratic Party invested time, energy, and resources to capture young voters, to little avail. The Kerry-Edwards team appeared a dream ticket, bringing together youth, idealism, and promise. "The sleeping giant of the American electorate, millions of younger people who traditionally do not vote," predicted the *Sun-Sentinel*, "has roused itself this year." In Tallahassee, voter registration of students soared. The opinion polls predicted a much greater turnout in 2004 among voters aged eighteen to thirty than in 2000. An enterprising student organized votergasm.com on Florida campuses and elsewhere. Votergasm, explained a spokesperson, was defined as "the intense rush that a person gets when he or she votes." Confusing T-shirt messages included "Vote for Kerry, Get Screwed."[45]

The Democratic Party organized a variety of events on college campuses. University of Florida student Johnny Yanchunis came away from a rally favorably impressed with John Kerry. Shaking the candidate's hand, Yanchunis exclaimed, "It wasn't sweaty. . . . And he was tall—that's always important." On the eve of the election, Ruben Navarrette Jr. blended hope with confidence, "If young voters vote, Bush is a goner." John Edwards drew a crowd of 9,000 at Florida A&M University. A reporter described Edwards's appearance at Miami Dade College in Kendall as having "the feverish quality of a pep rally, complete with brass band and students doing the wave."[46]

Republicans staged fewer events on college campuses, preferring to lure conservative students to large rallies at civic centers and arenas. In March, President Bush came to the Orlando Convention Center. "I'm young and this is my first president to get involved with and get active with," gushed Ashlee Black. The chair of the College Republicans at the University of Florida articulated, "When the president entered the room, it was about as loud as The Swamp on game day!"

Gays

In what was likely a first in Florida politics, Barney Frank, a Massachusetts congressman, rallied gay voters at Stranahan Park in Fort Lauderdale. It was the first wave of get-out-the-gay-vote in Florida, a movement originating along the Gold Coast and, in most ways, following time-honed methods. "From volunteers going door to door in Wilton Manors to Rosie O'Donnell hosting a rally on South Beach," noted a perceptive reporter, "an unprecedented campaign is under way across South Florida to urge gay and lesbian residents to vote in the closely contested presidential election." The Kerry campaign opened an office in Wilton Manors. Leaders, angered by President Bush's opposition to a constitutional amendment supporting gay marriage, anticipated 350,000 energized voters. The National Board of the Log Cabin Republicans, composed of gays and lesbians, voted 22–2 against supporting President Bush's reelection. The group had supported the candidate in 2000, and pollsters believed that 45,000 gay voters cast ballots for Bush in the 2000 election in Florida.[47]

The Ground Game

A presidential election in a battleground state is sweet news for political consultants, advertising agencies, motel owners, private detectives, newspapers, and television and radio stations. A hundred years earlier, the Democratic nominee for the presidency hardly left his home state, let alone campaigned. In 1904, journalists, politicos, and glad-handers visited Alton B. Parker at his home at Esopus on the Hudson in New York. Like William McKinley in 1896, Parker conducted a "front porch campaign." Until the late twentieth century, the cost of running a national campaign was relatively modest. The costs had skyrocketed by the twenty-first century. In Florida, a statewide campaign requires radio and TV time in ten separate media markets. By late July, John Kerry's deep-pocketed campaign was running short of funds. Senator Kerry sold his $7 million Beacon Hill mansion in Boston to save "his now high-flying presidential campaign from bankruptcy."[48]

In 2004, an army of campaign workers, factotums, canvassers, consultants, activists, volunteers, caterers, drivers, media talking heads and crews, pollsters, journalists, documentarians, lawyers, clairvoyants and fortune-tellers swarmed upon the Sunshine State. The evening news featured obligatory scenes filmed at Domino Park in Miami's Little Havana, Spanish-language newspaper publisher Patrick Manteiga's private table at La Tropicana Café in Tampa, the tricked-out golf carts at The Villages, and the all-too-familiar Florida Supreme Court Building.

The Republican Party enjoyed an early start because of the results of the 2000 election. Brett Doster had served as political director of Florida for George

Bush's 2000 campaign, the second-highest post. By 2004, this fifth-generation Floridian headed the reelection drive in the Sunshine State. Jeb and Brett had first worked together in Florida as baggage handlers and drivers in a 1993 Republican race. A Citadel graduate, Doster also served as an assistant in Jeb's first run for governor in 1994. Doster helped ensure that by the spring of 2004, more than 200 key leaders had been identified as part of the George Bush campaign. On Election Day, the Bush team counted on more than 100,000 volunteers. And vital to any modern campaign, a finance operation was in place. In contrast, the Kerry campaign's first field operations occurred in May 2004, and the state headquarters' office in Fort Lauderdale did not open until late June. Kerry tapped Tom Shea, whose political experience had been largely tested in New Jersey. When asked whether Kerry faced a disadvantage considering that the Bush team had been organizing and mobilizing Florida voters for months, Shea responded, "Bring it on!" Nick Baldick, Kerry's senior advisor in Florida, understood the big picture. "Florida has a registration majority of Democrats, but it is not a presidential voting majority of Democrats," he outlined. Marcus Jadotte also joined the Kerry team as Florida deputy campaign manager. The Opa-Locka native, and the only high-ranking African American in the operation, had directed Al Gore's Florida campaign.[49]

Big money is the oxygen of American politics, and in this election cycle, commentators shook their heads over the escalating costs. In 2002, Congress seemingly addressed the issue with the passage of the McCain-Feingold campaign finance reform law. The legislation banned "soft money" contributions, gifts to political parties for any purpose other than supporting a candidate for federal office. The McCain-Feingold Act allowed contributions to so-called 527s, U.S. tax-exempt organizations created for the purpose of raising unlimited funds for political purposes. In 2004, the 527 loopholes funded the now familiar Swift Boat Veterans for Truth, MoveOn.org, and America Coming Together. Democratic donor George Soros donated $10 million to America Coming Together. The Democrats proved more adept with the new technologies and utilized 527s to register and mobilize voters. The GOP spent massive sums in the final weeks of the election. Later, the Federal Election Commission fined and reprimanded America Coming Together for funneling soft, unregulated money to boost Kerry.[50]

George Bush and Dick Cheney, John Kerry and John Edwards, became intimately familiar with Florida. Their choices of venues and regions tell a great deal about their expectations. The Bush team dedicated more time in Florida than the Kerry ticket. The president toured the Panhandle by bus, a region essentially written off by Democrats. Senators Kerry and Edwards and their wives visited the Gold Coast, the counties of Broward and Palm Beach, as well as Hillsborough and Orange counties frequently. The president's and/or First Lady's travel itineraries in October 2004 included stops in Sunrise, West Palm Beach, Daytona Beach, Boca Raton, St. Petersburg, New Port Richey, The Villages, Sarasota, Fort Myers, Lakeland, Melbourne, Port St. Lucie, St. Augustine, Jacksonville, Orlando, and Gainesville. The official 19 October itinerary failed to include unannounced stops, such as a visit to Enver's Paradise Restaurant in Safety Harbor. Paradise customers generally loved the food, but one partisan diner left a harsh review, "The only down side is having to see the picture of George Bush, who makes me sick to my stomach."[51]

Surrogates and celebrities championed their candidates. Reverends Al Sharpton and Jesse Jackson urged young and old African Americans to vote for Kerry. A reporter described Al Gore sprinting "across six pulpits Sunday morning to exhort African Americans to avenge his 2000 defeat." Michael Moore, the director of *Fahrenheit 9/11*, an inflammatory documentary condemning the president, held an impromptu rally in Tampa, while Roseanne Barr headlined a protest gathering in Gainesville. Under signs proclaiming, "Osama Loves Moore," protestors screamed that Moore was a "moron." Florida-born baseball stars Tino Martínez and Alex Rodríguez wrote checks to the Bush campaign while tennis luminaries Martina Navratilova and Andre Agassi supported Kerry. Outspoken Miami Dolphins fullback Rob Konrad pledged that if he were president, he would "make it illegal to become a Democrat." Florida State University coach Bobby Bowden and Miami Dolphins NFL star Dan Marino pledged support to the Bush campaign. A glittering lineup of musicians agreed to tour in October to raise funds for America Coming Together, a get-out-the-vote 527. One journalist described the musical extravaganza as "benefit concerts doubling as unofficial Kerry rallies." Audiences heard Bonnie Raitt and Sheryl Crow in Jacksonville, Death Cab for Cutie, Neil Young, and Pearl Jam in Kissimmee, James Taylor and the Dixie Chicks in Clearwater, John Mellencamp in Miami Beach, and the Dave Matthews Band in Gainesville. While Pearl Jam played Bob Dylan's "Masters of War," the lead singer's T-shirt was emblazoned with the inscription "Expired," above President Bush's portrait and "Nov. 04" below.[52]

The War on Terror and Political Opponents

President Bush realized a truth: reelection and his place in history depended upon how the public evaluated his handling of the War on Terror and the wars abroad.

By 2004, 100,000 U.S. troops had settled in Iraq. As Americans expressed anxiety about the carnage abroad and missteps at home, George W. Bush needed to assure voters that the ship of state was in the steady hands of a man they trusted. If victory meant stereotyping his opponent as an effete, weak senator who voted for the war in Iraq before he opposed it, the end justified the means.

Senator Kerry also realized the challenge and truth: victory meant convincing the public that President Bush was an ineffective leader who bankrupted opportunities at home to fight the wrong war in the wrong place. Either candidate could point to polls justifying their policies. In a July 2004 Gallup poll, fully three-quarters of Americans, when asked whether the invasion of Afghanistan was a mistake, supported the president's decision to send U.S. troops. But when asked if they were satisfied with "with the way things are going for the U.S. in the war on terrorism," 54 percent of Americans thought they were "very satisfied" or "somewhat satisfied," while 41 percent felt "not too satisfied" or "not at all satisfied." The Iraq War had bogged down, resulting in a polarized, cynical nation. A majority approved the war, but two-thirds of the public believed we entered the war based on incorrect assumptions. Most Americans thought removing Saddam Hussein was a good thing, but many had grave doubts as to whether the war was worth the terrible cost. In a late-September speech in Orlando, Senator Kerry mocked the president's inability to explain the prospects in Iraq. "Ladies and gentlemen," asked the senator in stentorian voice, "Does that make you feel safer? Does that give you confidence that this president knows what he's talking about?"[53]

In one of the most effective political ads ever crafted, "The Wolves" cut to the chase. Viewers first see a dense forest and then shadows moving as ominous music sets the theme. From the hilltop, a pack of snarling wolves advance. A stern voice narrates, pointing out how liberals had slashed the intelligence budget, mindful of the consequences of those actions. As if viewers needed help to understand the message, a voice reminds listeners, "Weakness attracts those who are waiting to do America harm." The Democratic Party countered with a scene depicting a magnificent eagle in flight and an ostrich with its head in the sand. The narrator asks, "Given the choice in these challenging times, shouldn't we be the eagle again?" In these political allegories, voters were asked to choose between strength and appeasement, wisdom and folly.[54]

Michael Moore toured the state with his documentary *Fahrenheit 9/11*. When the film was shown at Century Village, a retirement condominium enclave in Boca Raton, some Republican residents—a minority in deep-blue Palm Beach County—expressed outrage that this "anti-Bush propaganda film, financed by maintenance fees," was shown. The Century Village complex in Pembroke Pines canceled the film showing.[55]

In Miami, Spanish-language viewers viewed a thirty-second commercial depicting images of John Kerry and Fidel Castro. The narrator informs the viewers of the senator's vote against the 1996 Helms-Burton Act, which tightened economic sanctions against the Communist government. "Kerry and the liberals in Congress," the voice intones, "don't understand what a dictator is."[56]

"Some people thought the October surprise would be the president producing Osama," speculated Maureen Dowd. "Instead, it was Osama producing yet another video taunting the president and lecturing America." Rush Limbaugh pounced upon the bizarre moment to ask viewers, "Haven't you noticed that bin Laden is using *Democratic talking points?*"[57]

Senator Kerry continued to hammer the president's weaknesses, pointing out the vulnerability of senior citizens in the Age of Terror. His most effective line came in Daytona Beach. He asked the crowd, "If you can't get flu shots sent out to the American people, how are you going to protect them against bioterrorism?" In a gesture designed to boost Kerry's masculinity, the senator talked to the media after shooting game in a midwestern corn field. "Four dead geese," mocked Maureen Dowd, "are not too high a price to pay for a few rural, blue-collar votes in a swing state." She added, "As long as Kerry doesn't slip and ask Teresa to puree the carcasses into foie gras."[58]

If the political season could be reduced to one event crystallizing the election, the moment seemed awkward, perhaps unseemly. In late October President Bush held a rally in front of 17,000 supporters at Tinker Field in Orlando. Shawn Michaels, the professional wrestling superstar, introduced the president. The crowd's colors resembled a moving American flag. Signs reading "America: Safer Stronger" were everywhere. Michaels, whose *nom de guerre* was "The Main Event," compressed his introductory remarks and the election into a simple sentence with a question: "If your babies were all left alone in the dead of night, who would you rather have setting there on the porch—John Kerry and his snowboard or George W. with his shotgun?" The president followed and riffed on Michael's themes, beginning: "Sometimes I'm a little too blunt—I get that from my mother. [Huge cheers] Sometimes I mangle the English language—I get that from my dad. [Laughter and cheers] But you always know where I stand."[59]

President Bush employed the stagecraft of the presidency to burnish his image as a resolute leader. On 23 October, the president appeared at rallies in Fort Myers, Lakeland, Melbourne, and Jacksonville. A reporter described the atmosphere: "The president's white-top Marine One helicopter landed in the outfield of a baseball stadium in Fort Myers to a swelling soundtrack—themes from the films Top Gun and Air Force One—against a backdrop that read 'Soaring to Victory.'" The president reminded the crowd: "This will be the first presidential election since Sept. 11, 2001. Americans will go to the polls in a time of war and ongoing threats unlike any we have faced before. The terrorists who killed thousands of innocent people are still dangerous and determined to strike us again. The outcome of this election will set the direction of the war against terrorism."[60]

Election Eve

Reporters scanned history books to find out when a sitting president had last visited Alachua County. When President Grover Cleveland arrived by train in 1888, Alachua was the state's second-largest county, an agricultural powerhouse and a leader in citrus grove land. When President George W. Bush flew into Gainesville, the county seat, to speak at an airport rally, Alachua was no longer a Sea Island cotton or citrus power. Nor were its African Americans stalwart Republicans. Home to the University of Florida and its Shands Hospital, Alachua may have been a smugly staunch Democratic bastion, but it was also an isolated, liberal blue island surrounded by conservative, red-leaning Levy, Gilchrist, Columbia, Putnam, Marion, Bradford, Lake, and Union counties. Jeb Bush, who recognized the detours and backroads of Florida, urged his brother to visit a place earlier Republicans had chosen to ignore. More than 16,000 "sign-waving supporters" greeted the Bushes at the airport.[61]

Florida's newspapers, as they had since the nineteenth century, proudly endorsed candidates running for offices ranging from city council to president. John Kerry won endorsements from the *Miami Herald, Bradenton Herald, St. Petersburg Times, Daytona Beach News-Journal, Florida Today, Palm Beach Post, South Florida Sun-Sentinel,* and *Orlando Sentinel.* President Bush's endorsements came from the Jacksonville *Florida Times-Union,* the *Lakeland Ledger,* and the *Ocala Star-Banner.* The *Tampa Tribune* chose not to endorse either candidate. Newspapers still mattered in the early years of the twenty-first century, although endorsements, as well as the papers themselves, had lost the significance they had enjoyed in earlier times. The state's leading newspapers continued to publish a quality product. But the reality was that newspaper endorsements mattered more in the twentieth century, not in 2004. Floridians, like most Americans, were choosing news from a wide variety of sites that reflected and reinforced their social and political opinions. Fox News was to conservatives what MSNBC was to liberals.

The last days of the electioneering witnessed President Bush and Senator Kerry stumping Tampa for last-minute votes. Halloween signs promised, "Spook Kerry" and "Spook Bush." It was Kerry's twenty-seventh visit in Florida since March and his fourth appearance in the last week.[62]

"Getting out the vote" once meant party loyalists driving senior citizens to the polls on Election Day. "Early voting" gained credence and popularity because of and in response to the 2000 election. While this alternative had its own problems and miscues, both parties saw the opportunity of an advantage. Almost one in five ballots requested in the 2004 election were from so-called absentee voters.[63]

A brutal, expensive, and exhausting election was ending. As is often the case, outsiders look past the massive confusion of details and understand the essential nature of the subject. Few figures could bring Elie Wiesel's sense of perspective. A Holocaust survivor, Nobel Prize recipient, and a longtime visitor to South Florida, Wiesel wrote a searing assessment of the 2004 election for the *Miami Herald* that began: "This clamorous and alarming election campaign, which should inspire and mobilize—on both sides—all that America has to offer in the way of political courage, open-mindedness, and vision for a bright future . . . I must sadly admit that it disappoints and depresses me."[64]

Race for the U.S. Senate

Normally, a down-ballot race would not be a critical factor in a presidential election year. But the presidential contest may not have been the year's most fascinating or interesting contest. Two likable, intriguing candidates pummeled one another for Bob Graham's Senate seat.

Betty Castor brought a dazzling resume to the fight. A trailblazer, she had taught school in Uganda, Africa, led a climb atop Mount Kilimanjaro with an all-female crew, raised a family, and earned a master's degree in education at the University of Miami. She taught at Holmes Elementary School in Liberty City. "I had a wonderful experience there," she recalled. "Again, I felt like I could make a contribution." In 1972, running as a reformer, she became the first woman to be elected to the Hillsborough County Commission. She supported and campaigned for the Equal Rights Amendment. In 1974, Castor was asked to leave a luncheon meeting at the all-male University Club in Tampa. "The only women allowed inside the private dining club for lunch were waitresses," remembered Tampa lawyer and power broker John Germany. "I didn't know whether to cry or get mad," Castor remembered. "I decided I ought to get mad." The snub drew the attention of author Calvin Trillin, who wrote about her efforts in the *New Yorker.* Revenge is best served with a glass of cold champagne, and once elected to the Florida Senate, she proposed a bill to prohibit public meetings in places that discriminate. The *Tampa Tribune* endorsed Castor for the state senate, arguing, "Mrs. Castor is not a strident feminist—as indicated by the fact that she is quite willing to be commission chairman rather than chairperson." She won the race.[65]

Castor shattered more glass ceilings when, in the 1978 race for governor, Jim Williams named her as his running mate. The Williams-Castor ticket lost the primary, but she became the director of the state Division of Elections in 1979. In 1986, she became the state's first female commissioner of education. During the era that a journalist has described as the "golden age of Florida politics," Castor had played a prominent role in what many commentators depict as the high-water mark of Democratic progressivism in Florida. In 1994, Castor left the political arena to lead the University of South Florida. Castor understood that the university functioned as a weather vane and lightning rod but had not expected her presidency to ensnare her in a political death trap.[66]

Castor's opponent had also traveled an unconventional path to Florida and the race for the U.S. Senate. Born Melquíades Rafael Martínez Ruiz in Cuba, in 1962 Mel Martínez was one of 14,000 Cuban children to escape Castro's regime as part of the Catholic Church's Pedro Pan (Peter Pan) program. The fifteen-year-old boy was sent alone to Orlando, where he lived with an American family. He thrived in his new setting and was eventually reunited with his parents. After law school, he returned to Orlando, where he was elected to the Orange County Commission. He co-chaired the Bush campaign in Florida in 2000 and was awarded a cabinet position at Housing and Urban Development.[67]

The White House support for Martínez never wavered. In a November 2003 GOP fundraiser in Orlando, President Bush championed Martínez, telling the crowd, "I love his story—it's the story of America." He ignored Katherine Harris, who also attended the banquet. Clearly the president and key Republicans had concluded she was unprepared to hold the office and could do little to help the president to win Florida. Harris was "encouraged" to run for a U.S. House seat. The largely unknown Martínez faced a challenging opponent in a bruising primary: former congressman Bill McCollum, who had lost the 2000 U.S. Senate race to Bill Nelson. McCollum upbraided his little-known opponent for having supported Democratic candidates in the past. The Martínez camp lacerated McCollum, charging him as "the darling of homosexual extremists." Congressman McCollum had favored a federal hate-crimes bill that would have protected victims, among them gays and homosexuals. McCollum demanded an apology from his opponent before he endorsed him in the general election. Stubbornly but reluctantly, Martínez apologized. Howard Troxler, one of the state's most respected journalists, and certainly one of the fairest, lamented, "Hope I'm wrong. I have rarely been more disappointed in a candidate than Mel Martínez in his tactics. . . . Nice guy, slimy candidate."[68]

The race hinged upon one issue: terror. An obscure professor became the face that launched a thousand commercials. In 1986, the son of Palestinian refugees, Sami Amin Al-Arian accepted a position as professor of computer engineering at USF. Betty Castor would not arrive at USF until later, but the circumstances and the questions surrounding them defined the election. The FBI had been suspicious of Al-Arian's activities, especially his involvement with Islamic Jihad, a Palestinian organization identified by the State Department as a terrorist organization. He was accused of bringing Islamic radicals to the campus to speak at a think tank he had founded. Arrested in 2003—four years after Castor stepped down from the presidency—his cause and her predicament became causes célèbre. Martínez demanded to know why she had not fired a professor tainted and tinctured by terrorism. Her defense of academic freedom, as well as the fact that the FBI refused to share relevant information about his furtive doings, satisfied few. She suspended the professor, with pay, an act the public never approved or understood. The university general counsel advised her that insufficient evidence existed to fire him, and if she did, she should expect a faculty revolt. In Shakespeare's *Julius Caesar*, Cassius asks, "Now in the names of all the gods, Upon what meat doth our Caesar feast?" In 2004, the answer was red meat. Howard Troxler wrote, half-joking, half-serious, "I am surprised they haven't as yet claimed that Castor donned a burqa and chanted 'Death to America' on Sept. 11."[69]

The War on Terror's collateral damage included critics of U.S. foreign policy. In the GOP-friendly Panhandle, retired U.S. Army Gen. Tommy Franks campaigned alongside Martínez. Franks had commanded U.S. forces in Iraq. "My opponent called America the bully of the world and that's not right," hectored Martínez. "She doesn't believe America should defend itself."[70]

The race would be the most expensive Senate contest ever waged in Florida. By October, Castor and Martínez had raised more than $11 million. The war chest financed an arsenal of opposition ads. To deflect criticism, a Castor ad pointed out that Al-Arian not only attended a Bush rally at the Strawberry Festival in 2000 but that co-chairman Martínez allowed the terrorist to be photographed with George W. Bush. The Martínez camp answered a volley with deadly fusillades. In one newspaper ad, the sinister face of Osama bin Laden peers at readers. "Who do you think Osama bin Laden would prefer?," asks the headline. Photographs of Betty Castor and John Kerry provide the answer. Other commercials reinforce the themes. "Incredibly," the narrator reminds listeners, "under Betty Castor's weak leadership, Islamic Jihad used her university as a cover. It wasn't one terrorist; it was a cell." The ad ends: "Betty Castor . . . defended them under academic freedom. Freedom to plot terrorism?"[71]

To finance the race, Castor received contributions from groups such as Emily's List and women's rights organizations, lawyers, retirees, and educators. Martínez's support came largely from attorneys and lobbyists, real estate, and the health industries. Signaling change, political parties donated relatively little; rather, individuals constituted more than 90 percent of the contributions. Unanswered questions remained: Would Mel Martínez help or hurt George Bush in November? Would Miami Cubans vote for a Cuban interloper from Orlando? When asked to call the race, political pundit Larry Sabato recoiled, "Oh my god, what a toss-up." On the eve of the election, polls predicted a dead heat in the presidential and U.S. Senate races.[72]

The Vote

What Elie Wiesel heard as "clamor and alarm" mutated into hope and promise on Election Day, 2 November 2004. "I hope to have God on my side," Abraham Lincoln prayed at the onset of the Civil War, "but I must have Kentucky." So, too, Kerry and Bush prayed that an omnipotent and merciful God deliver Florida on Election Day.

It may have been too late for prayer, but it was not too late to run one more infomercial, mail one last insert, or purchase a dozen more yard signs. "A sight that should have made any supporter of George Bush queasy," a reporter described on election eve, "more than 40 vans aligned off Cypress Street in Tampa. These are Hillsborough County vehicles for America Coming Together, the Democratic group that will have by Tuesday at least 10,000 canvassers spread across Florida mobilizing voters." The Democratic Party clearly had spent more lavishly than the GOP to bring in hordes of out-of-state volunteers, but Republican enthusiasts were eager to rally the faithful. "The Republicans had neighbors calling each other," reported Susan MacManus, a longtime political analyst. These two scenes represented a blip on a much wider stage where more than 100,000 "Republican ground troops" aimed to knock on more than 1 million Florida doors on election eve and day. Democrats held early-voting rallies, with fleets of buses shuttling true believers to the polling sites. An opponent sneered at the spectacle, remonstrating that "most of our people have cars!"[73]

Even more striking than the armies of volunteers was the intensity and confidence of the activists. "Whether it's Christian conservatives pounding the pavement in New Port Richey," observed political columnist Adam Smith, "Unitarians from Washington D.C. knocking on doors of farmworkers in rural Hillsborough County, or stay-at-home moms phoning voters in Brandon, the state is brimming with first-time political activists who passionately believe the future of the country depends upon what happens on Tuesday." In Key West, as Halloween coincided with the end of the election cycle, revelers took part in Fantasy Fest. City commissioners in pink tutus roamed Duval Street with Conchs wearing George Bush masks. Passion can be creative but also destructive. In Orlando, protestors ransacked the Republican headquarters, drawing horns and mustaches on Bush and Cheney posters. In Gainesville, a Santa Fe college professor was strolling along the street when he passed the GOP headquarters. "I don't like old brother George," he admitted, and when he saw a life-sized cardboard cutout of President Bush, he punched it. The head of the Alachua County Republican Party rushed to the defense of the flattened victim, and the two men scuffled. The teacher lost his job when an investigation discovered that the professor had been arrested in 1968 for ripping down a George Wallace poster.[74]

State and national polls reflected an evenly divided populace. Zogby and CNN/USA Today/Gallup pollsters rated the election as a tie. Pew Research, Newsweek, and CBS News/New York Times forecast a narrow Bush victory, while Fox News boldly predicted a Kerry win. The Associated Press exit poll found that President Bush and Senator Kerry held on to their political bases, "with whites, the rich and conservatives supporting the Republican president, and blacks, the poor and liberals backing the Democratic challenger." By midday on Tuesday, exit polls indicated that Kerry was leading Bush; one source claimed the challenger had mounted a nine-point lead. Upon hearing the dismal news, Governor Bush telephoned his brother, the president, insisting, "I don't believe it." As the results poured in, Bush began to edge ahead and then widened his lead. "No question now," Dan Rather reminded his viewers with a Texas aphorism, "Kerry's rapidly approaching the point where he's got his back to the wall, his shirttails on fire, and the bill collectors at the door!"[75]

One headline announced hopeful words for Floridians who had been bludgeoned by political overkill: "A Sight to Behold: Problems Down, Turnout Soars." Floridians may have had to wait in long lines, but the 2004 election resulted with fewer computer glitches and scandals. "I am tired of Florida being the laughingstock of America," a relieved Senator Bob Graham told reporters at the end of Election Day. Seventy-two percent of Florida's registered voters turned out, significantly higher than in 2000, but not matching the 83 percent who participated in Clinton's victory in 1992. For the first time in a presidential election in Florida, early voting took place. Early voting appealed especially to seniors. When asked why she turned out early, senior citizen Alicia Balseiro told a reporter, "I don't know if I'll die tomorrow!" In Hialeah, the most Cuban place outside Havana, GOP strategists were surely gladdened to hear reports of long lines.[76]

When the dust cleared and electrodes pulsed the numbers, an embattled Bush won the national vote, 62 million to 59 million. The race was razor close. The early exit polls looked so promising for the Democrats that the chief speechwriter for John Kerry, Bob Shrum, saluted his client as "Mr. President." Had 66,000 Ohioans shifted their vote, John Kerry would have been elected president.[77]

In Florida, Bush received 3.96 million votes, and Kerry netted 3.58 million votes. Ralph Nader, who had caused so much tumult in 2000, drew a scant 32,971 votes. Kerry won the Gold Coast decisively, with Miami-Dade, Broward, and Palm Beach counties providing him a margin of almost 375,000 votes. Moreover, Kerry won Alachua and Leon counties with their college constituencies. The Panhandle and North Florida rejected the Massachusetts candidate. For instance, Baker and Holmes counties punished Kerry, giving him only 21.9 and 21.8 percent of the vote. But Bush kept to the script, winning fifty-six of the state's sixty-seven counties. Escambia County recorded the highest voter turnout in the state, as 84.9 percent of its voters cast ballots. President Bush won Flagler, Osceola, Lake, Wakulla, Walton, Collier, Santa Rosa, and Pasco counties, which happen to have been included in the one hundred fastest-growing counties in America.[78]

If Wellington's victory at Waterloo was won on the playing fields of Eton, Bush's triumph was won at Port St. Lucie, Spring Hill, and Englewood, not Orlando, Miami, or Tampa. More dramatically, President Bush won ninety-seven of America's one hundred fastest-growing counties, the so-called exurban communities. Vast stretches of newly built Florida qualified as "exurban," fast-growing areas populated by young families and commuters in search of the American dream. Specifically, Bush triumphed handsomely in nine such counties: Collier, Flagler, Lake, Osceola, Pasco, Santa Rosa, St. Johns, Walton, and Wakulla.[79]

"Pasco County," began an insightful analysis by *New York Times* journalists, "may be unheard of outside Florida, but that did not stop President Bush, Rudolph Giuliani, and other Republican luminaries from visiting as Election Day approached." Pasco County had been considered reliably Democratic, supporting Bill Clinton and Al Gore. "But since Mr. Gore's defeat, thousands of middle-class families, many of them Republican and independent, have joined the many Democratic retirees who used to dominate here, making it a prime target for Gov. Jeb Bush and his brother." The reporters noted that the ground game worked. They also observed that whereas Gore and Kerry concentrated their energies in Florida's urban centers, "the Bush campaign concentrated on the new face of Florida, winning a margin of nearly 20,000 votes in Pasco and racking up many thousands more in counties like it." On the eve of Pearl Harbor, Pasco County's population had not yet crested 14,000; in 2004, the county had soared to 400,000 inhabitants.[80]

For decades, the I-4 Corridor glowed as the lodestar for journalists, pollsters, and politicians. The thoroughfare composed of seven contiguous counties (some count fourteen counties) earned its trustworthiness as "the hinge on the Swing state of Florida." Republican and Democratic registered voters are evenly divided. Bush flipped five I-4 counties Gore captured in 2000 (Flagler, Hernando, Hillsborough, Pasco, and Pinellas). In Hillsborough County, Democrats enjoyed a registration advantage over the GOP (45 percent to 35 percent), but Bush won the county by more than 30,000 votes. Kerry captured Pinellas County by a thin 316 votes. Political scientist Susan MacManus concluded, "The polls really stunk." In Polk County, the president won by nearly 18 percent, doubling his victory margin in 2000.[81]

FishHawk Ranch typified the newest developments along the I-4 Corridor. Formerly a cattle ranch bordering the Alafia River and unincorporated community of Brandon, the affluent FishHawk Ranch's 2,000 homes and 5,000 largely white voters typified the hard-charging GOP in Florida.[82]

Interstate 4 spans the Heartlands of Florida, the midsection running from NASCAR-Daytona Beach (Volusia County) on the east coast to Tampa (Hillsborough County) and St. Petersburg (Pinellas County) on the Gulf coast. Four in ten Florida voters live along Interstate 4. The I-4 Corridor represents a mirror of Florida, encompassing Disney World, college students, retirement communities, citrus groves, cattle ranches, blue- and white-collar workers, alligator farms, and old and new Hispanic enclaves.[83]

While Kerry secured the state's major urban counties, Bush solidified the rural vote. Suwannee, Lafayette, and Union counties represent what used to be the Solid South; indeed, old customs die hard. Although registered Democrats still heavily outnumber Republicans in these North Florida counties, they helped ensure George Bush's victory. Voters in these counties, where Democrats constitute on the average 74 percent of the registered voters, delivered a nearly three-to-one advantage to the Republican candidate. David Beattie, a talented Democratic Party pollster, got the message. In defeat, he offered a parable. "A lesson America learned from Vietnam is you cannot win the cities and lose the countryside and expect to win the war."[84]

The election occurred in the aftermath of a Florida still scarred and shaken by four hurricanes. Bush scored heavily in rural Florida. How did hurricane-scoured small towns, coastal communities, and cities reward the yeoman efforts of the brothers Bush? The logistical challenge of preparing for an election paled when compared to cleaning up after hurricanes. Hurricane Ivan destroyed ten polling sites in Escambia County. Moreover, the hurricanes displaced many voters. Had the trauma of Charley, Frances, Ivan, and Jeanne so exhausted these Floridians that they would not even bother to vote? Indeed, six of the seven most hurricane-scoured counties recorded a greater percentage of voters (average 75 percent) in 2004 than in 2000. Rudy Wheeler answered the question. Hurricane Ivan had destroyed his family's home. They resettled in Foley, Alabama, 40 miles away. "I have to vote, no matter how far out of the way it is," the forty-seven-year-old repairman insisted. "It might cost me half a day's work. It's just one of these things I've got to do."[85]

No constituency had been more discussed and debated than the critical Hispanic vote. George W. Bush won the Hispanic vote, 56 percent to 44 percent, but he had routed Gore four years earlier with 65 percent of that vote. Cuban-born voters remained loyal to the GOP, but American-born Cubans and Puerto Ricans were embarking on a new political journey in Florida, one that threatened the GOP. Still, critics savaged Kerry, expecting him to perform much better among Hispanics. They pointed out that he had virtually no Hispanic staff. Patrick Manteiga, publisher of *La Gaceta* in Tampa, recounted: "When Kerry visits Florida you don't see any focus on Hispanic voters. This is Party Building 101." The Democratic Party, opined political scientist Richard E. Foglesong, "had no Hispanic messenger. Where the Republicans had Jeb Bush as a spokesman and Mel as a candidate, both speaking in Spanish, the Democrats ran commercials with actors and slogans and music." Here, as elsewhere, Kerry needed greater margins of victory from his core supporters.[86]

Florida Jews smothered Kerry with support, but with less enthusiasm than in 2000. In 2000, Bush received 19 percent of the Jewish vote, improving his record to 24 percent in 2004. "The loss of Jewish support happened with all Democrats in the state," explained Sergio Bendixen, a pollster. Fred Drath, owner of The Deli in Broward County, thought Bush's support for Israel appealed to many

Jewish voters. Dianne Glasser, a Democratic Party vice chair, lamented: "I guess we needed a greater plurality. Normally, South Florida can carry the state, but we didn't do well enough." At a Delray Beach deli, Mac Simon summarized the election hangover: "It's horrible. The whole country's going to hell."[87]

In the halcyon days of 2000, Florida's small but growing Arab community, Muslims and Arab Christians, enthusiastically supported George Bush. In the aftershock of 9/11, Florida's estimated 100,000 Arab voters turned 180 degrees in favor of Kerry.[88]

Buoyed by signs that young Floridians might put Democrats on top, the Kerry camp was elated. The good news was that young Floridians aged eighteen to twenty-nine turned out in greater numbers than anyone had forecast. The bad news is that young voters supported the Democratic candidate, but not at the levels the party needed or expected. Kerry received 54 percent of the youth vote as opposed to Bush's 46 percent. Critics assailed Kerry's advisors for wasting an opportunity. Kerry's commercials ran on MTV, but media consultant Neil Howe complained, "Millennials don't watch [TV] anymore." He added, "You are not going to attract young people with Springsteen and Bon Jovi, who, last I checked, are not young."[89]

Imbued with a democratic spirit, or simply to express rage, Floridians surged to libraries, churches, and city halls to vote. In Ocoee, voters waited two hours to cast ballots. When Mel Martínez showed up to vote at the Herndon branch of the Orange County library, voters stood in line for an hour. The biggest winner on election night in Florida was Mel Martínez, who eked out a narrow victory over Betty Castor. "Out of nearly 7.5 million votes cast, the margin of victory was a mere 82,663 votes. For years," declared the *Chicago Tribune*, "political analysts have called the Latino vote a sleeping giant, huge in potential, but something less on election day. On Tuesday, the giant awoke." Mel Martínez, for instance, won Miami-Dade County by 2,400 votes while John Kerry received 42,000 more votes there than President Bush. Nationally, voters elected two Latinos to the U.S. Senate, Ken Salazar of Colorado and Martínez of Florida. A remark dismissed as political hyperbole in October had become gospel: "If there are any coattails in Florida, they may be Mel's coattails."[90]

In the election aftermath, columnist Steve Bousquet teased readers: "The future of Florida politics has arrived. He is 6-foot-2 with brown eyes and a ready smile. He's from Cuba. He's bilingual. He is a churchgoing Catholic and a socially conservative Republican with a pragmatic side that most Floridians have never seen, other than in his zeal to do whatever it takes to win." Symbolically, a Peter Pan refugee from Cuba was replacing Bob Graham, a pillar in the modern Democratic Party. But Martínez never loved the rough-and-tumble, mean-spirited side of national politics. The future's name was Marco Rubio, *not* Mel Martínez. Rubio, a rising star in the Florida House of Representatives, would become the darling of Florida's GOP.[91]

How had Martínez defeated a formidable opponent, who won every major urban county except Orange and who had not lost an election since 1978? A Democratic spin master explained: "Betty ran against the White House candidate. He was hand-picked by Karl Rove and they put everything they could in it." But the Republicans also worked harder to secure votes in a region virtually ignored by the Democrats, the Panhandle. Martínez's wife, Kitty, born in Mobile, Alabama, was an asset. In Pensacola, she joked, "It just feels really good to come back up where people understand when you order tea what it is you're asking." He joked about his late-found affection for collards and grits. In the Panhandle, Castor received only 30 percent of the votes. Think about this, wrote an analyst: "In the most conservative region of Florida, voters preferred a conservative, up-from-the-bootstraps Cuban immigrant over an opponent who seemed the face of moderation, a woman from Tampa who had spent a career in education."[92]

Ultimately, no pin picked the lock shackling Betty Castor to Sami Al-Arian. She called the race the nastiest in Florida history, but in a state nervous over terrorism, images of radicalized Muslims teaching innocent students trumped Castor's passion for education, veterans, and health care. This was the wrong race in which to be perceived as a Bob Graham moderate, although, as a columnist pointed out, "Lost in the noise of nasty 30-second ads is the fact that Castor and Martinez have track records as moderate, pragmatic politicians." Castor confronted the same challenge as John Kerry: in an Age of Terror, how to convince Floridians that you can best be trusted with issues of war and security, when your opponent (who flies to campaign rallies on *Air Force One*) projects a strong image of masculinity and toughness? Many "Security Moms," who traditionally voted Democratic, felt that America was safer with Bush and Martínez than Kerry and Castor. She ran a better campaign and received more votes than Kerry, but his coattails turned into sackcloth.[93]

In one of the year's best "unscripted" moments, Mel met Michael. On election eve in the Orlando Executive Airport, Michael Moore ran into Mel Martínez. The brutal campaign revealed how polarized America had become. And yet Moore reached out and said, "Even though we're on opposite sides, good luck tomorrow." Martínez replied, "I understand. We're all Americans." Such gracious gestures were becoming rare in the rough-and-tumble world of Florida politics. [94]

A Moral Debate

Confessing to being blindsided by the defeat, Democratic Party leaders also realized their message missed core voters. The wreckage exposed Democrats as ignoring or not engaging churchgoing and rural constituents. "The Democratic Party and allied groups waged an expensive and largely effective effort to increase turnout of urban and minority voters," wrote columnist David Broder, "but Republicans trumped them by finding even more support among white voters outside the cities and inner-ring suburbs—many of them people for whom religion is a central element of their life." Leon Panetta bemoaned that "The party of FDR has become the party of Michael Moore and *Fahrenheit 9/11*, and it does not help us in big parts of the country." Evangelical Christians had turned out in greater numbers in 2004 than in previous elections. A letter to the editor exemplified the party's predicament. "I am a working man," wrote Jesse Joynes from Bradenton: "I would personally benefit from an affordable government-backed health care policy. . . . However, I cannot vote the straight Democratic ticket anymore because above all, I am a Christian. The new 'Ivy League' dominated Democratic Party no longer represents my interests because the Democrats have chosen to adopt 'fringe' social policies that run counter to the most basic tenets of the Christian religion."[95]

The 2004 election was as much a morality debate as political conflict. The culture war persisted, with new battlefronts and warriors. Burdened by the economy and tormented by the war in Iraq, Americans who voted for President Bush said that what mattered most to them was "moral values." Eighty percent of Americans who checked moral values on the list of the most important issues of the election voted for George W. Bush. In contrast, 80 percent of the voters who believed the economy was the driving issue of the election chose John Kerry. Running against a Roman Catholic, Bush captured more than half of the Catholic vote. Once the Democratic Party united generations of Irish, Slavic, and Italian Catholics. The coiled issues of morality and values drove a stake in the heart of the Kerry campaign.[96]

A compelling moment of the campaign occurred at the Missionary Baptist Church in Miami. The Rev. Jesse Jackson asked the congregation to consider some questions. Many hands were held high as Jackson inquired if any family members had cancer or if they knew a relative in jail or probation, or if they had witnessed racial discrimination. But he then startled the congregation by asking who had a family member "marry someone of the same sex." Not a single hand went up. He continued, "If your issues are cancer and Medicare and education and jobs and Social Security and decent housing, then how did someone else put their agenda in the front of the line?"[97]

Homosexuality may have not been on the ballot in Florida, but it was a hot-button issue that pervaded the campaigns. Buoyed and determined by the showdown of the gay rights debate, supporters and opponents drew lines in the sand. It was a bridge not only too far, but too threatening to Americans. Nationally, ten states banned same-sex marriage measures in 2004. John Kerry supported same-sex marriage, citing the equal protection clause. Massachusetts stood in the vanguard of same-sex marriages. A *Boston Globe* columnist wrote that some Democrats blamed the Massachusetts Supreme Court "for creating the perfect storm: unleashing a highly divisive issue that turned out a passionate Republican voter base in critical states just in time for the 2004 presidential election." Garry Wills, a national critic, wrote: "This election confirms the brilliance of Karl Rove as a political strategist. He calculated that the religious conservatives, if they could be turned out, would be the deciding factor." A Miami Herald–St. Petersburg Times poll among Floridians in 2004 found 24 percent of the participants endorsing same-sex marriage while 65 percent opposed the practice. *Time* magazine's Joe Klein wrote: "The Democrats do have a problem. It was partly illuminated by the exit polling, in which 22 percent of respondents said they voted, primarily, on 'moral values,' and reinforced by a subsequent Pew Research poll in which the number rose to 27 percent." Optimistically or pessimistically, depending upon morality and culture, several polls indicated that young Americans were not as agitated over same-sex marriage as their parents and grandparents. Clearly, this contentious issue had energized both sides. A newspaper headline prophesied the future: "Same-Sex Marriage Battle Won't End."[98]

Down Ballot, Down Party

On 18 April, John Kerry made his third campaign trip to Florida. In a speech at the University of Miami, he discussed his "national service" program to help students trim the cost of college and tuition. Scanning the crowd, he quipped, "There must be 3,000 people out there—and that is not a Katherine Harris count." Since her role in the 2000 election recount, Ms. Harris had been tormented by comedians and thwarted by her party. She ran successfully for Congress in 2002, but desperately wished to run for the U.S. Senate. The White House was nervous that she would become a lightning rod in a critical election. Vengeful Democrats brought in a consultant, Joe "The Dragon Slayer" Trippi. A week before the election, a man was arrested in Sarasota for aiming his automobile at Representative Harris and a group of supporters. He admitted to police that he wished to "intimidate them." But on Election Day, as votes were counted at the local, state, and national level, Congresswoman Harris felt redeemed. Victorious, she now eyed the coveted seat of U.S. Senator Bill Nelson, the last statewide-elected Democrat.[99]

The names Katherine Harris and Gadsden County became inextricably linked in 2000. Gadsden County typified what used to be called Florida's Black Belt. The name referred, not to the soil, which is red, but rather to the large numbers of African slaves brought to plant and pick cotton. As late as the twentieth century, Black-majority populations characterized many North Florida counties. One Black-majority county, Gadsden, remained in 2004. For the first time since Reconstruction, Gadsden County voters elected a Black man, Morris Young, as sheriff. Young ran as an independent candidate, and his victory required a recount.[100]

Compared to Bush's narrow triumph in 2004, the Democratic Party had been bludgeoned in 1980 and 1988, but this defeat felt worse. Democrats had been beaten by a candidate they considered a lightweight and worse, a failure. Aubrey Jewett, a student of Florida politics, opined: "There is no silver lining anywhere in this election for Democrats. I just can't be negative enough." The headlines convey the "old ennui" that would depress the bluest blues singer: "Those Poor Florida Democrats," "Bewildered Party Soul-Searches," and "State Democrats Struggle for Relevancy." In his postelection eulogy, Wes Alison spun the unvarnished truth: "They ran a Vietnam war hero on a moderate platform of deficit reduction and reuniting a divided America, against a president facing middling approval ratings, the most job losses in 70 years, and a bloody, uncertain war in Iraq." An editorial began: "Usually, the down elevator doesn't drop any lower than the basement, but don't tell that to the Democratic Party. . . . They dropped what was once a solid seat for them in the U.S. Senate, shrank even smaller in the state House."[101]

A savage backlash and postmortem continued within the state and national Democratic Party following the election debacle. In Florida, only one Democrat, U.S. Senator Bill Nelson, held a statewide office. A journalist posed a painful, but honest question: "Can Democrats win statewide Florida races anymore?" State Representative Dick Gelber of Miami sighed: "This is now the third election in a row where we mistakenly think we've hit rock bottom. Democrats have no clout in Tallahassee." Borrowing a sport metaphor, the Democratic Party has no bench and few future stars on the rise.[102]

Nationally, Democrats turned upon one another. In the annals of presidential campaigns, only Harry Truman had rallied to political victory after a worse presidential approval rating in July (39 percent) than Bush (47 percent). A senior member of the Kerry team admitted, "I don't know that we ever knew what it was we were saying about George W. Bush." Another confessed, "We never gave voters a positive reason to vote for Kerry." In hindsight, the choice of John Edwards as a running mate seemed all style and little substance. To be fair, few vice-presidential choices have made much difference in an election—think Dan Quayle and Dick Cheney—but Edwards was a self-absorbed hypocrite. Democratic guru Bob Shrum related that Kerry told him "that he wished he'd never picked Edwards [and] that he should have gone with his gut [and chosen Dick Gephardt]." In hindsight, Florida's Bob Graham, overlooked in 2000, had been jilted once again.[103]

Adding financial insult to electoral injury, the Kerry camp had raised $220 million and lost the election. To Dan Rather, the effort reminded him of an old Will Rogers line, "It takes a lot of money just to get beaten." The 2004 campaign doubled the amount raised in the previous presidential race. Political parties, candidates, and independent groups spent a total of $1.6 billion on television ads alone![104]

Looking back at the 2004 election, it represented an era described by commentator Michael Barone as "a period of unusual stability in American voting behavior. . . . In other words, almost all voters in 2004 were firmly committed to one party or the other. . . . In 2004, President Bush's Republican base was pretty much united on issues." In a nation where civic duty was increasingly relegated to standing at attention during the National Anthem, 1.64 million more Floridians voted in the 2004 contest than in 2000, the so-called election of the century.[105]

The future seemed starlit for the GOP. On a national map, from Virginia to Florida and across the Gulf Coast uninterrupted to Texas, red had become the old blue. The GOP long ago planted its seal and signature upon the region from the Great Plains to the Rocky Mountains to New Mexico and Arizona. The Sunbelt largely belonged to the Republican Party.

In an astonishingly short time, barely a quarter century, the Democratic Party in Florida had cratered. In 1978, the word "domination" aptly described Democrats' control of Florida. Just when it seemed the upstart GOP might seriously challenge the Party of Jefferson, Jackson, and Roosevelt, the Democrats throttled the Republicans. Bob Graham, "unknown just six months ago," dashed Republicans' dreams when he crushed gubernatorial hopeful and drugstore namesake

Jack Eckerd. The future seemed to belong to the Democrats, whose scorecard listed icons such as Lawton Chiles and Reubin Askew. Victorious, Democrats once again controlled the governor's office, all six cabinet members, eight of twelve congressmen, and both U.S. senators.[106]

The Sunshine State's future seemed lockset. Growth had become the equivalent of crack cocaine, as leaders drove hell-bent to lure even more retirees and build more shopping malls and gated subdivisions. President George W. Bush and Governor Jeb Bush had earned election dividends, while Republican leaders prepared to lead Florida to these new heights. Easily reelected, Marco Rubio, the majority whip, prepared with youthful confidence to become Speaker of the House in the Florida Legislature. Charlie Crist, who had already served as state education commissioner, cakewalked in his reelection as Florida's attorney general. Everyone fully expected the unflappable Crist to be the next Republican governor of Florida in 2006.

In the aftermath of the 2004 election, a fascinating Associated Press story appeared in the state's newspapers. The headline announced, "Charmed Path Carries Chicago Lawyer to Senate." But this was no mere boilerplate, nor was this an ordinary man. The article introduced an individual and name few Floridians could pronounce or likely recognize. The article began, "For a man whose first name means blessed, Barack Obama has truly had a blessed year." Obama, who benefited from Republican scandals in Illinois, had just won election to the U.S. Senate.[107]

Basked in the glow of 2004, few Republicans realized how fleeting was victory. The young man with the funny name and Muslim father would soon campaign in Florida for the office of president of the United States.

A journalist had described Mel Martínez as the future of the GOP. But the future is neither static nor predictable. Another Cuban American, however, seized the future. Marco Rubio was thirty-three years old in 2004 but looked younger. He won his first election, a runoff contest, in 1999 for the Florida House of Representatives. Astonishingly, he was selected as a majority whip in the 2000 Legislature—as much a result of time limits as talent. Less than a year after the 2004 election, Rubio secured enough votes to clinch the position of speakership of the Florida House of Representatives. At the ceremony honoring Florida's first Cuban American House Speaker, a visibly moved Governor Jeb Bush told the crowd, "I can't think back on a time when I've been prouder to be a Republican." Bush then presented Rubio the sword of the mythical and mystical leader Chang, who, Bush explained, "is somebody who believes in conservative principles, believes in entrepreneurial capitalism, believes in moral values that underpin a free society." Bush swore by the sword of Chang, channeling its powers when confronted by a crisis, vowing, "I'm going to unleash Chang." The sword of Chang adorned Rubio's office.[108]

The issues and passions and personalities of 2004 would not die. In September 2007, Senator John Kerry returned to Florida. He had been invited to speak at a Constitution Day forum at the University of Florida. A student approached a microphone to ask a question. Andrew Meyer, an undergraduate mass communications major, handed his camera to a student and asked her to film the episode. Suddenly agitated because he was told that no more questions would be taken, Meyer began to harangue Kerry. He screamed: "Why don't you answer my questions? You will take my question because I have been listening to your crap for two hours." He continued to ramble and rumble, sprinkling his performance with vulgarities. He was so agitated that six university police forcibly restrained him, but he would not be silenced. "Don't tase me, bro!," he yelled as an officer stunned him with a Taser. "Don't tase me, bro!" went viral and became an Internet sensation—along with Soulja Boy, Keyboard Cat, and The Cinnamon Challenge—making Meyer a political martyr and T-shirt entrepreneurs wealthy. His grandmother in Pembroke Pines speculated, "Maybe the passion took over." As the police escorted Mr. Meyer from the auditorium, Senator Kerry rhetorically shot the wounded, jesting, "Unfortunately, he is not available to come up here and swear me in as President." Meyer became a lawyer.[109]

5

The Natural, the Professor, Queen Esther, and the Astronaut

Florida, 2006

The year 2006 marked an important moment in Florida history. Housing prices peaked, creating an illusion of prosperity and optimism. The Republican Party radiated confidence, as two-term popular governor Jeb Bush spent his final year in office. Few Florida governors had exuded more cocksureness and exerted more control than this son and brother of two American presidents. Adding to the confidence of the outgoing governor was the conventional wisdom that Republicans were more motivated to turn out than Democrats. A big question loomed over 2006: Could the GOP triumph in three consecutive elections, a feat Florida's Republican Party had not accomplished since Reconstruction, 1873–77? Few schoolchildren and even fewer party faithful could recite the hoary roll call of Harrison Reed, Ossian Bingley Hart, and Marcellus Lovejoy Stearns.

The historical record, however, indicated that rival parties triumphed in off-year elections. Florida Democrats, moreover, had reasons to be optimistic, considering the Bush presidency and family brand had been tarnished, the result of a lackluster economy, a president in search of a message, increasingly unpopular wars in Iraq and Afghanistan, and the faint whiff of recession. In April 2006, the president's approval ratings slid to a new low, with only one-third of Americans approving Bush's job performance. When asked whether the term "strong and decisive" described President Bush, only 46 percent of Americans said yes, as contrasted to 62 percent in July 2005. The *New York Times* speculated that Florida was one of five states "that could flip to the Democratic column" in the gubernatorial races. "From a math standpoint," explained Massachusetts governor Mitt Romney, "we've got a tough row to hoe this year." More than a few cynics wondered exactly how many rows the blue-blooded Mitt Romney had hoed! Feeling the headwinds, Romney announced that he would not run for a second term.[1]

The Republican Primary

Vying to succeed Governor Bush, two strong candidates emerged: Tom Gallagher and Charlie Crist. Could they convince voters they were Jeb Bush conservatives? Could they deflect Democratic efforts to make this state election a national referendum on the Bush presidency?

Tom Gallagher's resume spilled over with political and financial accomplishments but also personal disappointments. A handsome, youthful-looking sixty-two, he had grown up in a gregarious Irish-Catholic family in Delaware. His father once headed the state Republican Party, while his mother governed the family of eight children with a strict sense of discipline and ritual. An all-state swimmer, Tom won a scholarship to attend the University of Miami.[2]

First gaining notice when, as a thirty-year-old unknown, he ran for a Florida state House seat representing Coconut Grove, a Democratic-leaning district, Gallagher lost amid the Watergate fallout. Undeterred, the determined young candidate was elected in 1974, and reelected for three consecutive terms to the Florida House of Representatives. Although subsequently elected in statewide races to the positions of state treasurer, state commissioner of education, and state comptroller, he failed in three previous bids for governor, as well as a 2000 attempt for the U.S. Senate. Politics had also been very rewarding. When Chief Financial Officer Gallagher became a gubernatorial candidate, he had amassed a fortune worth $2 million. He enjoyed the advantage of statewide recognition but also was known as a playboy. In an awkward media conference call, he admitted to marital infidelity and marijuana use.[3]

Gallagher's principal opponent was Charlie Crist, as natural a politician as ever worked the crowds after Sunday mass or a Rotarian luncheon. Imbued with personal charm and tone-perfect instincts, he was all things to all people. He was the grandson of an immigrant who followed the American dream and shortened his name to Crist. His Greek-Cypriote grandfather Adam Christodoulou immigrated at age fourteen to Altoona, Pennsylvania, where he shined shoes and opened a café. Charles Joseph Crist Jr. was born in Altoona in 1956, but he grew up in St. Petersburg, Florida, where his father was a beloved family physician. Charlie's introduction to politics occurred at age ten, when he passed out leaflets promoting his father's candidacy for the school board. He played quarterback for the St. Petersburg High Green Devils, enrolling at Wake Forest University, where he was a walk-on quarterback, later transferring to Florida State University. Elected homecoming king and student body vice president, Crist early on demonstrated his talent for seeking office and approval.[4]

Crist enrolled at Cumberland School of Law in Birmingham. While a law student, he married Amanda Morrow, but the marriage quickly dissolved. Upon passing the Florida bar exam—on his third attempt—Charlie returned home to St. Petersburg, where he became general counsel to Minor League Baseball. Suntanned and handsome, his prematurely silver-white hair only added to his charm. Senior citizens thought he was a young man who understood the importance of manners and morals. Young voters admired his good looks and energy. Women swooned at the longtime bachelor who, when strangers met for the first time, became instantly your best friend.

His first foray into politics occurred in 1986. The thirty-year-old Crist ran for a state Senate seat. After losing the Republican primary, he sent congratulatory flowers to his opponent. In 1992, he won election to the Florida Senate, defeating popular Tampa state senator Helen Gordon Davis. As a legislator, he compiled a respectable record. In 1994, after the FBI released a report announcing that Florida had the highest crime rates in America, Crist began plotting his campaign to run for state attorney general. The National Rifle Association (NRA) awarded Crist respectable pro-gun grades, and he earned extra credit when, as attorney general, he nominated Marion Hammer to the Florida Women's Hall of Fame. The NRA endorsed Crist over Gallagher for governor.[5]

He burnished his reputation as a tough-on-crime legislator when he held iron shackles on the Senate floor, earning the sobriquet "Chain Gang Charlie." Never mind that only a few Florida inmates wore leg irons, and none were chained together. Such an antic might have smeared the careers of others, but it only added to Crist's luster. Not even when Bob Graham crushed the forty-two-year-old challenger in the 1998 U.S. Senate race did Crist blink or falter. Such ambition might have ruined a less talented politician. Defeated but unbowed, the name Crist acquired a statewide identity. Graham's media advisor observed that Crist "had a quality on television that was very reassuring to people." Not everyone appreciated Crist's ambition or image. Some Republicans questioned whether he was an authentic conservative, while others wondered why he was still single.[6]

In 2000, the Teflon-coated Crist won election as commissioner of education. "Chain Gang Charlie became Chalkboard Charlie," quipped a reporter. Endorsed and boosted by John Walsh, the popular host of Fox's hit television show *America's Most Wanted,* he ran successfully for attorney general 2002. Walsh's son Adam had been murdered in Hollywood, Florida. The father lobbied for the Adam Walsh Act to impose a national leg chain around convicted sex offenders. John Walsh stood by his friend in 2007 when Governor Crist signed his top crime-fighting priority: his antimurder act.[7]

Candidates Crist and Gallagher had certainly filled out impressive political dossiers in their run for governor. Crist remains the only person who has occupied the cabinet positions of attorney general and commissioner of education. When Tom Gallagher announced his intention to run for governor, yet again in 2006, he held the distinction of having held a state office longer than anyone in Florida history.[8]

In 2006, he was regarded as the front-runner in the race for governor. The only question seemed to be whether Crist could convince Republican voters that he was a mainstream conservative, a rightful heir to Jeb's throne. His politics had always been moderate. For instance, he was one of the few Republicans to discuss the harshness of banning convicted felons who had served their time from voting. He reopened the murder case of civil rights activist Harry T. Moore. He also fined gas stations for price-gouging during hurricanes.[9]

The primary became a contest as to whom do you trust as the most legitimate conservative? To ensure fidelity to the cause, each candidate echoed a famous scene from the 1960 film *Spartacus,* vowing, "I am a Jeb Bush Republican." To buttress his credentials, a robocall informed voters: "Hi, this is Charlie Crist calling to set the record straight. I'm pro-life, I oppose amnesty for illegal immigrants. I support traditional marriage and I never supported a new tax or big spending program." But in the end, Crist's appeal was not defined by doctrinaire principles or ideology. Everyone liked Charlie.[10]

A journalist writing a profile of the candidate before the 2006 primary added another exclamation mark to his resume: frugality. "Charlie Crist eats one meal a day. . . . He uses a single Visa card and never carries a balance. He rents a one-room St. Petersburg apartment that has a kitchen décor that debuted the same year as Saturday Night Live. Charlie Crist's tax returns are remarkably bland. The 40-year-old bachelor owns no property or corporate stock, has zero debt." An accountant who reviewed the tax returns of the leading gubernatorial contenders, quipped, "This guy [Crist] could go to H&R Block to get his taxes done." Even odder than a high-profile, low-wealth politician running for Florida's most coveted office was the fact that Crist was being supported "by one of the country's best-known libertines, billionaire developer Donald Trump."[11]

Veteran journalists understood that fundraising, or the lack of it, determined success in statewide political races. In July 2005, smart money was betting on Tom Gallagher. His campaign had raised $3.02 million in only 43 days, a record that not even Jeb Bush had recorded. Yet on 7 July 2005, Crist announced that he had raised $3.8 million in just six weeks.[12]

Floridians had elected Catholics, Catholic-baiters, a converted Jew, planters, small-town bankers, and gun-runners for statewide office. But homosexuality was the kryptonite no gubernatorial candidate could survive. The question had long been whispered around office coolers and Tallahassee bars, "Why is Charlie Crist still single?" Crist's ex-wife was discreet, never discussing the matter.

On 14 January 2005, Crist addressed a Tiger Bay luncheon in Tampa. Tiger Bay reveled in its reputation for unbridled give-and-take; indeed, a prize honored the day's best question. The event was proceeding along traditional lines—inquiries about educational policy and tax reform—expected of a gubernatorial candidate. When Lee DeCesare, a retired English professor and Democratic gadfly, spoke, the audience stirred, knowing her reputation for bluntness. She proceeded to ask a question that no Florida gubernatorial candidate had ever faced: "I have heard you were gay, sir, and I wanted to know if that was true?" Following gasps, the room turned silent. Unruffled and unfazed, Crist responded, "I'm not." Floridians accepted his response, even while the Gallagher camp searched for strange bedfellows, spending $75,000 in an unsuccessful effort to identify gay partners. Afterward, Crist, when asked about his lifestyle, responded gallantly, "I have a mistress. Her name is Florida."[13]

Ironically, concerns surrounding Gallagher and his actions as a cabinet member, not Crist's private lifestyle, surfaced. Critics researched Gallagher's coziness with insurance companies, especially his handling of Citizens Property Insurance during the 2004 hurricanes and aftermath. The fact that he made tidy profits day trading with companies the state's CFO was regulating was unseemly if not dishonest.[14]

In 2006, outside Fort Lauderdale and a few other liberal strongholds, an openly gay candidate was rare. But Americans and Floridians were beginning to have honest discussions about the issue. An NBC/Wall Street Journal poll released in 2006 confirmed that more than half of Americans were "very uncomfortable" with or had "reservations" about having a gay or lesbian candidate for president. The ground may have been shifting quickly, but in 2006, Americans drew a line in the sand.[15]

Overall, the Republican primary focused upon one simple question: Whom do you trust to carry on Jeb Bush's legacy? Both candidates proudly wore their "I Like Jeb!" credentials, and if voters questioned Crist's true faith, an August robocall calmed the flock. Crist ended the robocall, "It's sad that in his fourth try for governor my opponent has resorted to distortions and untruths." Crist coasted to primary victory, demolishing Gallagher by a margin of two to one.[16]

The Democratic Primary

U.S. Congressman James Oscar "Jim" Davis represented exactly what the Democratic Party so desperately needed. Handsome, articulate, and a good family man, he was a thoughtful state legislator, a moderate liberal who had succeeded long-serving Democratic stalwart Sam Gibbons. Gibbons was a party patriarch, a World War II hero who parachuted into Normandy on D-Day and served as a congressman from Tampa since 1962. A journalist described Davis as "part of a blue blood, old money South Florida family," noting that he "lives a surprising modest existence." Described as professorial, a subjective adjective, he could have remained a congressman for life in a safe Democratic seat, but the Tampan grew frustrated with the travel commitments and bitter partisanship of the U.S. Congress. In a competitive primary, Davis defeated state Senator Rod Smith. Davis had been endorsed by President Bill Clinton, U.S. Senator Bill Nelson, and other Democratic leaders. Rarely in Florida history would two gubernatorial party nominees maintain such modest lifestyles.[17]

Davis realized he had become an oddity, a symbol of an astounding transformation of the southern Democratic Party. In 2003, he had become a minority in the U.S. House of Representatives—one of two Florida white Christian Democrats (the other was North Florida congressman Allen Boyd). Could Davis salvage and revive the sagging fortunes of Florida's Democratic Party?[18]

The Campaign

Seminole County was a bellwether of the Florida Dream, offering a setting so beautiful that second-chance retirees, fast-buck artists, and starry environmentalists moved there, each wanting to shape it in their image. Interstate 4 sliced through the county in the 1960s, providing an "easy" commute to Orange County or Daytona Beach. Shopping centers and malls quickly appeared in the once bucolic towns of Altamonte Springs and Sanford. In 1960, Seminole County, then best known for its celery fields, natural springs, and the enchanting Wekiva River, had 55,000 inhabitants. One of the county's best-known residents was the environmental writer Bill Belleville. His 2006 book *Losing It All to Sprawl* recounts his deep love for the hinterlands and swamps, and his battles to preserve them. One of the county's new residents was the flamboyant Jeno Paulucci, founder of Chun King and Jeno's Pizza Rolls. In the early 1980s, the fabulously wealthy icon and conservative Republican battled environmentalists and federal regulators as he developed the "master-planned" community Heathrow. On the eve of the 2006 primaries, Seminole County was inching toward the 400,000-population plateau. Politicians seeking votes and contributions followed the crowd. By 2006, Seminole County had solidified its reputation as solidly Republican. It had last voted for a Democrat in the presidential election in 1948.[19]

"Never in history," reported the *St. Petersburg Times,* "have Florida's big businesses invested more heavily in Republican candidates than this year." Davis and Crist prepared for the most expensive gubernatorial campaign in Florida history. "Money is the mother's milk of politics," preached Jesse "Big Daddy" Unruh. Mitchell Berger, a Fort Lauderdale lawyer, explained the dynamics: "Power and money go together, and money tends to follow power." Insurance companies, gambling interests, and development advocates were especially generous to the GOP, as were trial lawyers to Davis. Huge contributions with euphonious names—Partnership for Economic Freedom and Floridians for Truth and Integrity—underwrote the expensive ads. Crist enjoyed a huge financial advantage ($60 million to his opponent's $20 million), reaping handsome contributions from Florida's largest corporations. When asked if he "owed" anything to the large contributors from Big Sugar, Walt Disney World, and the U.S. Chamber of Commerce, Crist, reminding the press of his service as state attorney general, retorted, "You know better, I've sued half of them." Campaign manager George LeMieux pin-pointed Crist's political skill: "Charlie will ask you for five times more than you can afford, and you end up giving two and a half times more than you can afford."[20]

Crist was a natural fundraiser, but he needed an unswerving assistant who was hardworking, loyal, and committed to the consuming task of raising more money. Jim Greer seemed more qualified to be manager of a strip club than a campaign manager. If Crist was the natural, Greer was the worker bee. Born in 1962, Greer spent his youth along Florida's East Coast. Whereas Crist anchored the western end of the I-4 Corridor, Greer was familiar with the eastern gateway. As a student at Brevard Community College, he worked at a variety of jobs, including bouncer. His bosses liked the young man's work ethic. He soon became an investigator for ABC Liquors along Florida's East Coast. In 1984, he went into business for himself, training employees for bars and taverns. One of his clients was Joe Redner, Tampa's king of the adult entertainment business. An *Orlando Sentinel* reporter recalled: "Jim Greer loved to throw big parties at his big, fancy home. . . . Guests arrived in tuxedos. Later, in the backyard, in front of a rock band, Greer would grab a microphone and belt out a few Elvis tunes." As his portfolio grew, so did Greer's ties to the Seminole County GOP. He was elected to the Oviedo City Council and became deputy mayor. In 2005, Crist and Jim and Lisa Greer met at the GOP Inaugural Ball in Washington. Crist told the couple that he was considering a run for the governorship. Crist asked his new friend to organize a Seminole County fundraiser for him. "Charlie was all about contributions," Greer recalled. "He knew that money determines the campaign's success rate." Greer organized a fundraiser that brought in $118,000.[21]

Facing a candidate who held a stunning financial advantage, Jim Davis attacked the system and the opponent. "It's disgusting," uttered Davis, when discussing corporate interests looking "to protect the agenda in Tallahassee." In Miami's Little Havana, Davis insisted, "The special interests have taken control of the state." His message resonated with the audience: "Florida does not belong to the Republican Party, it does not belong to the insurance companies—it belongs to us." The crowd chanted in Spanish, "*Sí, se puede!*" (Yes, you can). Davis's wife, Peggy, maintained the drumbeat while campaigning at a Beef O'Brady's Family Sports Pub in Tavares. "He will be a governor for all Floridians," she promised.[22]

For all the New Age polling and robocalls, old-school fundraisers allowed strangers to meet the candidate face-to-face. In February 2006, Donald Trump, the celebrity face of *The Apprentice*, hosted a fundraiser at his mansion by the sea, Mar-a-Lago. Four hundred guests attended the soiree. The event raised more than $1 million. A $500 contribution bought an admission ticket. Five thousand dollars allowed one a photo op with Trump and Crist; a more generous check presumably bought prestige and face time. Trump explained the evening's success with a conclusion transcending regression analysis and grounded in Politics 101: "I mean, there's no doubt people love the guy." Trump also sponsored a previous fundraiser for Crist in New York City. Gossip columnists speculated that Trump might run for governor of New York.[23]

The Republican ads were financed by $40 million in "soft money," a term dating from the 1980s. Federal election law allowed political parties to spend unlimited and unregulated amounts for party-building activities, such as "get-out-the-vote" efforts. Soft money contributions exploded in the 1990s. To place the costs in context, in 1970 Reubin Askew raised $737,000 to win the Democratic primary and the race against incumbent Governor Claude Kirk. As late as 1986, Republican Bob Martínez spent $7.4 million to defeat Democrat Steve Pajic. Political commentators expressed outrage at the increasing costs of running for office. In 1956, after all, LeRoy Collins spent just $292,000 in his pursuit of the Democratic nomination for governor. His campaign against the Republican opponent in November cost a total of $174![24]

In July 2006, H. Gary Morse donated a half-million dollars to the Republican Party of Florida. It was the biggest contribution Florida's Republican Party had ever received. Morse was the stepson of Harold Schwartz, the legendary founder of The Villages. The notoriously private Morse began selling vacant lots at a trailer park that became one of America's leading retirement centers. His generosity laid the foundation for a controversial $1 million golf-cart bridge over US 27/441 in The Villages.[25]

Democratic-sponsored commercials poked fun at Crist's tan and fan. One memorable ad spoofed: "Charlie Crist's claims carry about as much weight as a late-night infomercial. Sure, he's slick. But perhaps the Super Tan Man should look into jobs hawking the latest weight loss miracle instead of running for governor." The Crist campaign zeroed in on Congressman Davis's alleged "second-worst attendance record in Congress." Ads depicted an empty chair.[26]

To Davis's credit, he insisted on campaigning in the heart of GOP country. The Sunday before the election, he arrived in Cape Coral, as red a neighborhood as one could find in Florida. It was also the home of Crist's running mate, Jeff Kottkamp. He told the crowd of 150 loyal Democrats that they "face the same major challenges" with high insurance premiums, high property taxes, and an education system that has often failed. "Charlie Crist wants to stay the course," Davis argued. "I want Florida to do better." He also pledged to clean up the polluted Caloosahatchee River.[27]

Crist spent the weekend in Southeast Florida campaigning with New York mayor Rudolph Giuliani in Miami and stopping at a Boca Raton synagogue. Giuliani was a familiar face, having bought a Palm Beach condo after renting a home in Lighthouse Point for years. Channeling his inner Ronald Reagan's "Gipper," Crist carried around a football, telling the crowd that he is the quarterback who needs to punch the pigskin across the goal line for victory. The last weekend of the long contest saw Governor Jeb Bush stumping with and for Crist. At Orlando's Mi Viejo San Juan restaurant, Crist took advantage of the popular governor's coattails. When a Hispanic reporter insisted on asking whether Crist was gay, Bush snapped, answering adeptly in Spanish, "Put a smile on your face and don't be such a horse's ass!"[28]

Concerns over immigration, ethnicity, and electoral rules flared in Lee County and elsewhere. Some Lee County residents demanded an "English-only" ballot, despite the 1975 Congressional Voting Rights Act provision that permitted the 26,000 Hispanic voters' bilingual ballots. Lee's election supervisor admitted, "It's not a very popular thing with a lot of Americans. . . . People won't even carry their voter card because it has Spanish on it." In Collier County, the supervisor of elections' office not only provides ballots in English and Spanish but allows interpreters in Seminole and Miccosukee.[29]

If there was an election-eve surprise, it might have been the Republican camp's "revelation" that Jim Davis never voted in the still-simmering 2000 election. Crist's campaign chief of staff, George LeMieux, called the news "staggering," noting that "it seems to be part of a consistent pattern of not showing up to work." Davis called the news a "cheap shot" and a lie.[30]

Another rather unusual event occurred on election eve in Pensacola. President Bush appeared at the Pensacola Civic Center, an event dubbed "the Florida Victory 2006 Rally." He applauded his brother Jeb, "a great Governor of Florida," along with U.S. Senator Mel Martínez. "Tomorrow," he reminded the crowd, "you get to vote for a new governor, and I strongly suggest you vote for Charlie Crist. . . . He's experienced, he's compassionate, and he'll work on behalf of all citizens of this important state." Curiously, the individual who would seemingly most benefit by a presidential visit on the eve of an important election was *not* on the platform standing next to the most powerful man in the world. In 1998, at the nadir of the Monica Lewinsky scandal, Democratic gubernatorial candidate Buddy MacKay cheered and welcomed President Clinton's visit to Florida. But on 6 November 2006, President Bush was considered more of a drag than an asset to Charlie Crist. "The thing is," explained Crist, on why he was snubbing the president and governor, "I need to be where I need to be to win. The Pensacola numbers are pretty good." The *Washington Post* speculated, "To the White House's embarrassment and irritation, Republican Charlie Crist, whom Bush came to help in his bid to succeed the president's brother as governor, decided at the last minute to skip the chance to be by the president's side."[31]

Terri Schiavo and the Politics of Religion and Ethics

In the spring of 2005, Florida once again became a national flash point. The setting was an unlikely place: Pinellas Park in Pinellas County. Pinellas Park rarely made the newsreels touting the Florida dream or winter vacationland. Only a few decades earlier, Pinellas Park was home to acres of citrus groves and truck farms.

From 691 residents on the eve of World War II, Pinellas Park had grown to 45,658 residents by 2000. Pinellas Park had become home to trailer parks and sprawling subdivisions. The locale was perhaps best known for its iconic Wagon Wheel Flea Market founded by Hardy Huntley, a high-school dropout who had hitchhiked to Florida from North Carolina. He opened a drive-in restaurant and owned a used car lot across the street on busy Park Blvd. He could fix anything his wife brought home from garage sales but was running out of room. In 1966, he solved his problem by opening a roadside stand to sell items. Eventually, so many people asked if they could sell their used stuff, he opened the Wagon Wheel, a sprawling flea market that grew to 2,000 stalls across 125 acres.[32]

A former resident, when asked to define Pinellas Park, observed, "Pinellas Park is a city where people passed through but did not live." But Terri and Michael Schiavo lived there early in the twenty-first century. Journalist Abby Goodnough placed the subjects and setting in perspective: "But a familiar sense of surrealism lingered in Pinellas Park and across Florida, the state that seems to surpass any other in terms of strange but important, lurid but poignant events that say as much about America as they do about whatever sun-soaked Florida town they unfold in." David Shribman observed that by 2005, "it may be no coincidence that the Schiavo tragedy, a modern mix of the most incendiary health, religious, political and family issues, was played out here." He added that trends in medical technology and religious politics converged in Pinellas Park, resulting in "a cultural clash unlike any America ever has seen, but that Florida, rather than California, is the place where the future is best viewed."[33]

Before 2005, few Americans had ever heard of Theresa Marie "Terri" Schiavo. Born in 1963 to devoutly Catholic parents, she was named after the mystical Saint Teresa of Ávila, Spain. A childhood friend and bridesmaid revealed that Terri married the first man she ever kissed. Her friend also noted that Terri was quiet. "She didn't like the limelight. How ironic is that?" In 1990, Schiavo suffered cardiac arrest. She was resuscitated but suffered massive brain damage due to oxygen deprivation. Doctors described her condition as a "persistent vegetative state."[34]

Michael Schiavo, wishing to see his wife die with dignity, petitioned the Sixth Circuit Court of Florida to remove the feeding tube. In 1990, the Florida Legislature had passed the "Death with Dignity Law," allowing for the removal of artificial life support from persons in a "persistent vegetative state." But Terri's parents adamantly opposed the move. The Schiavo ordeal was a legal nightmare of appeals and motions in local, state, and federal courts. In Italian, "schiavo" means "slave," which as the *New York Times*' Clyde Haberman calculated, was all too true. "For 15 years, Terry Schiavo was effectively a slave—slave to an atrophied brain that made her a prisoner in her body, slave to seemingly endless rounds of court hearings, slave to politicians who injected themselves into her tragedy and turned her ordeal into a national morality play." A journalist wrote in 2005: "Terri Schiavo is everywhere. There are pictures of her on the front pages of newspapers, on the Internet, on every news network on TV."[35]

Terri Schiavo died 31 March 2005. The Schiavo case crystallized America's clash of values over the meaning of life and death, the role of the church, state, and family. "And just as the case of Karen Ann Quinlan prompted a debate nearly 30 years ago over the 'right to die,'" wrote Abby Goodnough, "the Schiavo case seemed to focus as much on the 'right to live.'" The cause célèbre of the year evoked myriad end-of-life issues. Conservative columnist Cal Thomas asked, "Why does Terri Schiavo matter?" He answered, "She matters not only because she has an endowed, inalienable right to life, but also because she is a symbol—as Rosa Parks was a symbol when she refused to sit in the back of that Montgomery, Ala., bus." Columnist Jim Defede wrote, "Long ago she [Schiavo] stopped being a person and became a cause."[36]

Powerful forces converged in the early years of the new century: leaps in round-the-clock news and talk shows, advances in medical technology, and the hardening positions on religious-cultural-political issues. Florida was the vanguard for the culture wars. The Schiavo controversy, like the Elián case in 2000, saturated cable news with pontificating prelates and politicians. The Schiavo soap opera became a modern American Passion play.

A Vatican official equated the decision to remove Schiavo's feeding tube with "an attack on God" and a "violation of the sacred nature of life." President George W. Bush implored, "The essence of civilization is that the strong have a duty to protect the weak." The Florida Legislature passed a bill—"Terri's Law"—giving Governor Jeb Bush the authority to intervene and prevent the removal of feeding tubes. The governor, a passionate converted Catholic and pro-life conservative, fiercely and obstinately worked to stop her medical-assisted death. He also said that her case was "the toughest issue" in his political career. The judge who ruled that Schiavo's feeding tube could be removed wore a bulletproof vest during the modern crucible. In March 2005, Congress took up the fight, passing legislation in the wee morning hours to keep Schiavo alive. Brett Kavanaugh, the president's staff secretary, awakened President Bush to sign the bill into law. The U.S. Supreme Court ruled the law unconstitutional, giving a victory to Michael Schiavo. Dr. Timothy Quill eloquently summarized the saga of Theresa Schiavo: "How can it be that medicine, ethics, law, and family could work so poorly together in meeting the needs of this woman?" For all the religious, medical, and political arguments, the case boiled down to ancient and simple questions: When does life end? Who gets to decide life and death? Is all life, regardless of condition, intrinsically valuable? The controversy did have one redeeming outcome: many Americans were encouraged to write living wills.[37]

Terri Schiavo almost derailed Charlie Crist's bid to succeed Jeb Bush as governor of Florida. Crist had largely succeeded in convincing party skeptics that he was, indeed, a Jeb Bush conservative. Confronted with the Schiavo melodrama, Attorney General Crist bobbed and weaved like angels dancing on the head of a pin. Early in the controversy, he maintained he had labored to keep Terri alive. In the gubernatorial debate, he also proclaimed that this case was "not the place for government, and that's why I stayed out." Schiavo's parents and their lawyer insisted otherwise; Terri's father proclaimed loudly that Attorney General Crist "let my daughter die," while Terri's husband declared that Jeb Bush "put me through Hell." The controversy was averted when Governor Bush told the press, "He spoke out to me." Head-shaking conservatives sighed that the governor will rue the day he threw a lifeline to Charlie Crist.[38]

Election Day

Davis was the second of four consecutive Democrats representing the Tampa Bay region to run for governor and stumble in attempting to turn out the vote-rich Gold Coast and persuade African-American voters to pull the lever. Nationally, 2006 proved to be a disaster for Republicans running for Congress. President Bush's flagging poll numbers perplexed the Crist campaign so much that Crist (or his advisors) dared not to stand by the president at a rally in Pensacola. Yet Crist coasted to an easy victory in November 2006, winning the election by seven points.[39]

Journalists placed Crist's ascendency into context. Crist's lightning-quick successes, observed reporter Adam Smith, were "all the more remarkable because little else about Crist suggests a logical winner. . . . Detractors have portrayed Crist as a shaker of hands more than a maker of laws, an office-seeker more than an office-holder, not so much a leader as a chaser—a serial campaigner who is seeking not only votes but more elemental affirmation."[40]

Crist's victory marked the first time in modern Florida history that voters elected back-to-back Republican administrations. "Eighteen months ago," Bill Cottrell and Aaron Deslatte wrote, "Republican Charlie Crist began his race for governor with an untested political team, a formidable primary foe, and the image that he lacked substance." By election night, Crist had been "elected Florida's 44th governor, with a blaring rock soundtrack and hundreds of jubilant supporters at a posh downtown hotel a few blocks from where he grew up." The journalists wondered whether the new governor could deliver the tax cuts and pledges made during the campaign. They also speculated, "If Crist serves a full four years, it would mark the longest run of Republican governors in state history, coming after eight years of Jeb Bush." Many readers must have wondered what could possibly alter the trajectory of Crist's rise?[41]

Few Floridians could have identified three of the election's biggest winners. Relatively unknown, Cape Coral legislator Jeff Kottkamp ran and won as Crist's lieutenant governor. He turned forty-six years old the Sunday before the election. He was the first Southwest Florida politician to run for lieutenant governor since Frank Mann ran on the Democratic ticket with Steve Pajic in the 1986 race. The transformation of Southwest Florida from a Democratic-leaning to solid Republican region was personified by the Kottkamp family, who arrived in Cape Coral in 1975. Its population then was around 20,000, adding 10,000 residents per year, most of them bringing their Illinois and Ohio Republican registration cards with them.[42]

George LeMieux was so indispensable to Crist's victory that on election night, Charlie Crist campaign workers appeared in T-shirts that read, "Ask George LeMieux." It was he who boldly insisted that Crist not appear with President Bush at an election-eve rally in Pensacola. Bush officials fumed over such a brassy, disrespectful gesture. When asked why the Republican candidate for governor would not be standing by the president's side, Karl Rove gruffly bellowed, "Ask George LeMieux!" Born in Fort Lauderdale and raised in Coral Springs, Lemieux distinguished himself at Emory University and Georgetown Law School. As Crist's taskmaster, he orchestrated a flawless race, a "How do you like me now!" vindication for the snickering that accompanied Crist's announcement that a relatively unknown George LeMieux would serve as his campaign manager. In contrast, Tom Gallagher had secured the services of Brad Doster, the wizard behind George W. Bush's Florida campaigns. More conservative than the governor-elect, LeMieux had also urged Crist to name Jeff Kottkamp as running mate. Crist placed LeMieux in charge of the transition team in Tallahassee.[43]

In less than a year, Jim Greer had emerged from obscurity to Olympian heights. On election night at the luxurious Vinoy Hotel in St. Petersburg, George LeMieux congratulated Greer, telling him, "Charlie wants you to come to Tallahassee with us." The governor-elect wanted Greer to chair Florida's Republican

Party. When Governor Crist introduced the obscure aide as the chair of the GOP, columnist Adam Smith noted that the reaction among party activists and press "was pretty much universal. Jim, who?" Greer quickly earned a reputation, skirting the murky boundaries between celebrity and notoriety.[44]

U.S. Senate Race

Timing is everything in politics. A generation earlier, Congressman Davis would have best been known as Governor Davis. Just five years earlier, Secretary of State Katherine Harris was the darling of the Republican establishment, a modern Joan of Arc who survived serial burnings on the late-night televised bonfires. Harris boasts an impressive Polk County family tree. Her grandfather was Ben Hill Griffin Jr., a citrus and ranching baron whose name adorns the University of Florida's football stadium. Her cousin J. D. Alexander was a powerful state legislator. When Harris ran for the Florida state Senate in 1994, she accepted large donations from Riscorp, an insurance company whose founder went to jail for illegal campaign contributions. As Florida's secretary of state, she spent large sums traveling to exotic destinations, promoting the Sunshine State. The Longboat Key heroine capitalized upon her notoriety and popularity by winning a seat in the U.S. House of Representatives in 2002. The chattering classes circulated rumors that she preferred running for the prestigious seat of retiring U.S. Senator Bob Graham. Republican elders instead promoted the relatively unknown Orange County administrator Mel Martínez, who defeated Betty Castor in a hard-fought race.[45]

Harris stubbornly announced her candidacy to challenge U.S. Senator Bill Nelson, who was finishing his first term in office. Fatefully, Harris's favorite opera was Verdi's *Force of Destiny.* Twenty years earlier, she accepted a blind date with a Swedish businessman, Anders Ebberson. That couple attended *The Force of Destiny.* Life seemed to intersect with art, as the opera combines passion, politics, and revenge, although in the opera, Leonora, the daughter of the doomed Marquis of Calatrava, seeks refuge in a convent. Her home is a cave. Harris and Ebberson married in 1996. In 2006, the operatic Harris focused on the campaign, calling Nelson "an empty suit," a Washington insider who is "all talk and no action." The former astronaut, an earnest if unspectacular senator, had spent his first term largely under the radar screen. Many pundits considered Nelson vulnerable; some believed he was the most vulnerable Democrat in the Senate. Harris hoped an evangelical wave would sweep her to victory. In 2005, Dr. James C. Dobson, psychologist and founder of the evangelical organization Focus on the Family, warned Democrats of belching brimstone if they blocked President Bush's conservative nominees. A "bull's-eye" that had taken down South Dakota's Tom Daschle was now focused on Senator Bill Nelson.[46]

On paper and celluloid, stump and dais, Clarence William Nelson II possessed, literally and figuratively, the right stuff. A fifth-generation Floridian, the sixty-four-year-old Nelson was an alumnus of Brevard County public schools, the University of Florida, Yale University, and the University of Virginia law school. Following military service in the U.S. Army, where he rose to the rank of captain, Nelson served in the Florida Legislature, the Florida cabinet, and the U.S. Congress. He had held elective office since 1972. His signature feat occurred in 1986, when for six days he orbited the earth as an astronaut aboard the space shuttle *Columbia.* In 2000, Floridians elected Nelson to the U.S. Senate. Nelson confided to a reporter, "They [voters] kind of like the spaceman thing." In his office in the Senate Hart Building hangs the Fort Pierce artist "Bean" Bacchus's evocative painting, a tribute to astronauts, *Heavenward from the Homestead* (1988). But despite an illustrious dossier that was more Horatio Alger than Horatio Hornblower, Senator Nelson was a bland and largely unknown politician. Floridians hesitated when asked to name his singular political accomplishment. "I'm not a shouter," he confessed to a reporter. "Maybe there's something in my makeup that says humility is a virtue."[47]

Religious faith and deep Florida roots connected Harris and Nelson. "Faith is pretty much the essence of mine and Grace's being," he told a reporter in 2017. An avid jogger, he likes to recite biblical scripture while running on Atlantic beaches. American Beach in Nassau County was his favorite. As the election unfolded, one of Harris's closest confidantes was her "spiritual adviser," Dale Burroughs, the founder of the Biblical Heritage Institute in Bradenton. Her staff often described the 2006 election as a "Christian crusade." Speaking to a rally in Orlando, Harris insisted that God never intended for America to be a "nation of secular laws."[48]

Considering that Florida's Democratic Party was imploding in the early twentieth century, Bill Nelson defied the trend, channeling Mark Twain's proverbial Christian with four aces. Had Senator Connie Mack III not retired, it is unlikely Nelson would have challenged the popular incumbent, let alone won the 2000 race for his seat. He defeated the perennial Republican challenger Congressman Bill McCollum. But in 2006, Nelson drew a royal flush when Katherine Harris became his opponent.

Political quicksand was shifting underneath Harris. Scandals in Congress tarnished Republicans, especially the tawdry emails sent by six-term U.S. Congressman Mark Foley to teenage pages. Ironically, Foley was widely touted as a replacement had the Republican Party persuaded Harris to quit the race. From his youth as an altar boy in Lake Worth to his leadership on the House Ways and Means Committee, Foley had been a rising star in the GOP. Foley's behavior had been called out as early as 2003, when an alternative newspaper called the West Palm Beach congressman "the Liberace candidate." U.S. House of Representatives leaders seemed more concerned with tamping down the scandal than with the well-being of the young men. Foley resigned when a Maltese Catholic priest confessed that he had been involved in a two-year relationship with the congressman. A 16 October 2006 *Time* magazine cover depicted a cartoon of an elephant's rear. The words, "What a mess . . ." decorated the cover.[49]

Florida's Republican Party, seemingly invincible, now appeared vulnerable and out of control. In 2001, Joe Scarborough was a young U.S. congressman from Pensacola, destined for the U.S. Senate. But he abruptly resigned, explaining he wished to spend more time with his family. Conspiracy theories—circulated decades later by President Trump—questioned the mysterious death of a Scarborough aide at a Fort Walton Beach office.[50]

Newsweek magazine revealed that on the eve of the November elections, more Americans trusted Democrats than Republicans on the issue of moral values. The public also entrusted Democrats to fight the War on Terror. The GOP had prided itself on winning the debates over the culture wars and real wars. The tawdry sex scandal also tarnished the party and the president. His approval rating plunged to 33 percent; moreover, only 25 percent of Americans thought America was headed in the right direction.[51]

Katherine Harris's candidacy confirmed Governor Bush's worst fears: no other Republican galvanized Florida's angry Democrats like Harris, and the recurring nightmare of the 2000 election. David Colburn notes that "party discipline went into a free fall when Katherine Harris ran for the U.S. Senate seat." A *New York Times* reporter declared that the Republican establishment was treating Harris "with the warmth of an icicle." Governor Bush made little effort to hide his opposition to Harris's nomination for the coveted Senate seat. When asked who might defeat Senator Nelson in November, the governor recommended Florida's Speaker of the House. When he heard the endorsement, or read the polling numbers, Speaker Allan Bense admitted, with rare political candor, "Outside of Panama City and a four-block radius around the Capitol, I'm an unknown person." In declining to run, Bense essentially handed Harris the nomination. The National Republican Senatorial Committee, a critical conduit for doling out campaign funds, provided Harris with scant resources. In hindsight, the White House would have been kinder rewarding Harris an ambassadorship than allowing her humiliating defeat.[52]

Congresswoman Harris already faced withering criticism. In 2005, she dined with a corrupt defense contractor at the posh Citronelle restaurant in Washington, D.C. The tab came to an eye-popping $2,800. Congressional rules forbade members from accepting gifts of more than fifty dollars or accepting favors "that might create the appearance of influencing the performance of official duties."[53]

Harris's campaign, described as a train wreck by insiders and a remake of *Sunset Boulevard* by comedians, was as undistinguished as it was doomed. An unrepentant Harris compared her public humiliations to the biblical Queen Esther, who risked life and limb to save the Jews. Hounded by fundraising problems, high-profile staff resignations, and rumors of Harris's world-class tantrums, the Republican Party finally begged Ed Rollins to save the ship. Rollins, who had advised President Ronald Reagan, remembered his time in Florida as one of his great regrets. "Katherine is probably the worst micromanager I've ever seen," he confessed, adding that "her instincts are 100 percent wrong." Her campaign workers harbored little nostalgia for the race. When asked in 2012 about the 23,000-square-foot waterfront mansion that she and her husband were building on Sarasota Bay, a political junkie snarked, "She treated staff like the hired help, you can only imagine how she treats the actual hired help."[54]

In September, President Bush highlighted a fundraiser at the Ritz, an event that raised $2 million for the GOP. The president entertained the crowd for forty minutes as he shared the stage with his brother and gubernatorial candidate Charlie Crist. Representative Katherine Harris was in attendance, but conspicuously absent from the limelight. Neither the president nor the governor singled her out. Harris gingerly explained the perceived slight: "Primaries are a family fight . . . and afterward, we come together so we can win."[55]

U.S. Senator Nelson may not have electrified Floridians in his first term in Washington, but he impressed many as a man who displayed qualities the electorate respected: integrity, courage, and a deep concern for Floridians and their issues. Strikingly, twenty-two state newspapers endorsed Senator Nelson. Representative Harris did not even receive the endorsement of her hometown paper. Desperately short of campaign funds, she confided to Fox News's Sean Hannity that she was all in and prepared to spend $10 million of her inheritance to win the election. Her accountant approved her reconsideration. Senator Nelson was so confident of victory that he curtailed campaign spending to help other Democratic candidates. J. M. "Mac" Stipanovich, regarded as one of

Florida's shrewdest political strategists, believed that "Katherine Harris moves in ways so mysterious that the designs of the creator seem transparent by comparison." Ed Rollins concluded, simply, "There's no good ending here."[56]

Senator Nelson and Representative Harris squared off in two debates. The second debate was acrimonious and feisty. Nelson called Harris a liar, contending: "Credibility has been a problem for my opponent in this campaign. She is not going to get away with this." Harris charged that Nelson should be held accountable for "$980 billion in tax increases." Moderator Tim Russert asked Harris to defend a statement she made to a Baptist group, remarking that "if you're not electing Christians, then in essence you are legislating sin." She explained, "In addressing that small group, I was trying to draw a difference between Bill Nelson and me."[57]

Election Day 2006 delivered the expected verdict: neither Ed Rollins or modern alchemists could rescue Harris from a devastating defeat. Senator Nelson routed Representative Harris by more than 1 million votes. One reporter described Nelson "gliding toward a nearly effortless re-election."[58]

The Democratic Party was also gladdened by the cabinet election of Alex Sink. Ms. Sink had served as president of the Bank of America's Florida operations. Articulate and poised, she defeated Florida Senate president Tom Lee of Brandon for state chief financial officer. Nationally, Democrats capitalized upon the GOP's woes. The Republican Party had claimed a majority in the U.S. House of Representatives since 1994, but lost control in the 2006 elections, as Democrats picked up thirty-one seats. In Florida, the Democrats picked up two congressional seats.[59]

Inauguration

The misaligning stars first appeared in January 2007. The inaugural ball was a must-attend event for major donors, favor-seekers, and chest-bumping victors. To pay for the night of revelry, kingmaker and lobbyist Brian Ballard had raised millions for the Governor's Ball. But the mirth quickly soured when Governor-elect Crist, uncomfortable with rising unemployment and dire economic forecasts, canceled the festivities! "He decided against it," sneered Greer, "because his whole mantra was, 'Charlie Crist is a man of the people and for the people.'" To be fair, Greer uttered those words at a time when he was finishing his prison sentence.[60]

On inaugural day, January 2007, Charlie Crist became Florida's forty-fourth governor. Not since Park Trammell in 1913 had a cabinet member been elected governor and taken the oath of office. A book of Florida's greatest inaugural addresses would be heavy on braggadocio and promises and light on memorable moments and substance. In 1949, Governor Fuller Warren received thundering applause when he promised to get cattle off Florida roads and highways. Warren also promised that on his watch, Floridians would never face the burden of a sales tax. Warren finessed the legislature to pass "a gross receipts tax." Critics recoiled, "Same damn thing!" In 1956, an embattled LeRoy Collins addressed a civil rights crisis, attempting the near-impossible: "White and colored citizens alike must see wrong on their side as well as right."[61]

Crist's speech began with a Crist-like proclamation: "What a wonderful day to be a Floridian." He promised the overflow crowd, "We will work together to do what is right." The new governor knew who brung him to the dance, and he lavished praise: "For the last eight years this state has been led by a great governor, a man who in my opinion is America's greatest governor."[62]

Crist was the loneliest inhabitant of governor's mansion. The bachelor lived in a fully staffed, Greek Revival, columned, 13,000-square-foot home at the exclusive address of 700 N. Adams Street. Gubernatorial ghosts included Governor Albert Gilchrist, a Punta Gorda land developer who liked to hand out porcelain monkeys. Gilchrist had campaigned in 1908 on the platform of "Hear no evil, See no evil, Speak no evil."[63]

Gossip followed the governor-elect, even at the inaugural prayer breakfast. Mary Ellen Klas, a well-respected journalist, reported, "Crist was mobbed by well-wishers—including Kara Tucker from St. Petersburg." Who was Kara Tucker? Klas explained: "Today, she's 25, a lawyer living in Miami who along with her adoptive family still suspects Crist is her biological father."[64]

A new era dawned. On election eve, the *St. Petersburg Times*' headlines predicted, "Either Way, Expect Change." A columnist added, "Charlie Crist would offer Floridians something different as governor: a middle-of-the-road Republican philosophy that's easy to grasp and as upbeat as an Amway convention." The day following the election, the *Fort Myers News-Press* headline read, "Time for Charlie to Deliver on Bold Campaign Pledges." Many hard-core Republicans expressed anxiety at the prospects of a Crist administration. For years, conservatives had whispered—even shouted—that Crist was a "RINO"—Republican In Name Only. Crist's first weeks in office did little to salve their fears. But Crist owed Florida's African Americans for their support, in much greater numbers than Governor Bush received in 2002. In April 2007, the *New York Times* reported, "Gov. Charlie Crist persuaded Florida's clemency board to let most felons easily regain their voting rights after prison, saying it was time to leave the 'offensive minority' of states that uniformly deny ex-offenders such rights." Many Republicans were simply dumbfounded as to why their governor would want to add new voters, most of whom would almost certainly vote Democrat. One in five of Florida's 950,000 disenfranchised ex-offenders was African American. A *Salon* staff writer penned an essay on the actions, titled, "What Was Charlie Crist Thinking?" A *Sun-Sentinel* headline announced, "That Does It . . . Charlie Crist Is a Democratic Mole." The governor explained his actions as "simple human justice." His attorney general, Bill McCollum, dismissed the effort as "reckless and irresponsible." But the influential *Sun-Sentinel* was convinced that Crist had begun to effect "a sea-change that should impact the vast majority of non-violent felons immediately." By late 2007, a leading Black Representative of the House dubbed Crist, Florida's "first black governor." But in 2007, the efforts were a bridge too far and would await other reformers.[65]

Throughout the spring of 2007, signs indicated that the great Florida land boom was crumbling. Floridians, weary of tribal politics, welcomed romance. The society pages noticed that Governor Crist was frequently accompanied by a divorcée, Ms. Carole Rome, described as "a wealthy and glamorous fixture on the New York and Hamptons social circuit." They became engaged in July 2008. The last Florida bachelor governor to be married while serving in office was Claude Kirk. In 1967, he wed the German-born Erika Mattfeld, who had been introduced to Floridians as "Madame X" at the inaugural ball. Erika explained that since she and her husband had been divorced, they were not allowed to be married in a church service. But this liturgical glass slipper perfectly fit Ms. Rome's foot. She became Mrs. Crist in December 2008. A reporter described the service held at St. Petersburg's First United Methodist: "Not long ago a lot of pomp for a second wedding would have been enough to fan all 749 pages of *Vogue's Book of Etiquette* into an unholy combustion. Today, it's all the fashion." The *New York Daily News* noted Crist's "glam running mate, known for eye-popping, gravity-defying dresses." The reporter concluded cruelly, "Rome ain't no Lynne Cheney." Rome's two daughters served as flower girls. Ms. Rome-Crist was counseled not to wear the official state flower, orange blossoms, symbol of purity and virginity.[66]

6

The Boom at High Tide

2000–2007

I hear the whistle of the locomotive in the woods. . . .

How is real estate here in the swamp and wilderness?

Ralph Waldo Emerson (1842)

In 1942, a New York City journalist motored across America seeking to answer a pressing question: How had the war changed America? Trundling into Florida, he ignored the obvious places—Miami, Jacksonville, and Tampa—preferring to take the pulse beat of Starke. Located in sparsely populated Bradford County (population 1,480 in 1940), Starke had catapulted to importance. The traveler was Ward Morehouse, an extraordinarily gifted journalist, playwright, and critic. His reportage began with a curious declaration: "Starke is gauche." Geographic fortune had strangely blessed Starke, as it happened to be the closest city to Camp Blanding, a mega–U.S. Army basic-training center, suddenly the fourth-largest "city" in Florida. "Starke, an overnight gold-rush town as a result of the national emergency," pronounced Morehouse, "is as fantastic a spot as America now presents."[1]

Fast-forward and imagine Ward Morehouse motoring across Florida in 2006. What place would he declare "as fantastic a spot as America now presents?" Unless one were monitoring a capital punishment countdown at Raiford Prison or speed traps, modern Starke is, well, rather stark, not to be confused with a trending city. As an urbane intellectual, perhaps Morehouse would find comfort among the bohemians in Sarasota and Miami Beach. A journalist who loved colorful characters and compelling story lines, Morehouse would no doubt head to Pensacola, Lake Wales, and Punta Gorda, cities slammed in 2004, the year of four hurricanes. Expecting to find despair and desolation, he would have applauded the citizens' resiliency and optimism. Fascinated by trends, Morehouse would wonder at Port St. Lucie and Cape Coral, Seaside, and The Villages. One suspects the author would be captivated by the sheer variety of urban life that had taken form from the Panhandle across the peninsula and into the Keys. Almost certainly, the time-machine visitor had never seen a condominium, although it probably seemed a lot like the progressive cooperatives that began in New York City. Neither would he approve cities without downtowns. Morehouse had never heard of or seen boomburbs, urban sprawl, or million-dollar trailer parks, though one suspects he would approve the populist spirit of trailer park–dwellers. Morehouse would, no doubt, find a human-interest story on tony Fisher Island.

Every GI Joe that Ward Morehouse encountered in wartime Florida vowed to return one day. Most did. "Old soldiers never die—they just move to Florida," quipped a journalist in 2008. The military and the GI Bill forged a symbiotic relationship with Florida. As early as 1910, the *Kissimmee Gazette* proclaimed, "Florida should have a national soldiers' home." By 2006, 2 million GIs and veterans resided in Florida, where they frequented the state's six military hospitals.[2]

Ironically, some of the teenage GIs Morehouse portrayed in 1942 lived in Florida six decades later. Early twenty-first-century Florida was home to 2 million active-duty soldiers, veterans, and retirees, and six veterans' hospitals. Those figures included 140,000 retired women veterans. For more than fifty years, World War II and Korean War veterans dominated the population, but that generation has been replaced by Vietnam, Gulf War, and post-9/11 veterans. The military footprint in Florida first exploded after Pearl Harbor in 1941. By the end of the war, the Sunshine State was home to nearly 200 military installations. The Crestview–Fort Walton Beach–Destin Metro area counted more veterans as residents (22.3 percent) than any other place in America. Metro Miami ranked last. The Panhandle was home to Eglin Air Force Base in Okaloosa County, Tyndall Air Force Base near Panama City, and the Naval Air Station in Pensacola. Throughout the decade 2000–2010, the Veterans' Administration sought additional national cemetery sites. So many veterans die each day that in some areas, there is a shortage of buglers to play taps at military funerals.[3]

Still, they came, more than 1,000 newcomers every single day, veterans and draft dodgers, by the carload and jet planes, in recreational vehicles and motor coaches, on wet feet and rubber rafts. Nothing—not even five powerful hurricanes between 2004 and 2005—could deflate the Florida boom or diminish the Florida dream's luster. Mere months after Hurricane Ivan sheared Escambia County, Hurricane Charlie walloped Punta Gorda, and Hurricane Jeanne smashed Stuart, property values rose across Pensacola Bay and snowbirds returned to Charlotte Harbor, Lake Wales, and Martin County.

To shrewd developers and investors, hurricanes were not so much evil omens as rare opportunities. Confidence trumps fear, and investors rushed in to seize opportunity. Condominiums replaced quaint, wooden-clad beach cottages and mom-and-pop motels. Bigger always replaces smaller in Florida. Nothing, it seemed, could halt the march of humanity toward the ocean's edge. Realtors remind us: location, location, location. In the first years of the new century, Florida was the fastest-growing state in the United States, while Port St. Lucie, Cape Coral, Miramar, Orlando, Miami, and Fort Lauderdale were among America's fifty fastest-growing cities. Between 2000 and 2006, nineteen Florida counties, the most of any state, ranked among the nation's one hundred fastest-growing counties. Only Monroe County lost population, largely the result of soaring housing costs. Costs can be calculated in other ways: every single day, Florida was losing 20,000 acres of land to the maw of development.[4]

Results of the 2005 census flummoxed the mayors of Chicago, Cleveland, and Detroit but thrilled the chief executives of United Van Lines and U-Haul. Florida's population in 2005 had soared to 17.84 million inhabitants, maintaining its pace to surpass New York as America's third-largest state. Between 2000 and 2004, 183,000 New Yorkers, 72,000 Illinoisans, and a combined 78,000 residents from the Bay State and Buckeye State moved to Florida. Florida led the nation during those years, attracting 191,000 transplants. More than people left the Rust Belt. Misfortunes in one state enriched another. Weathered and highly desirable St. Louis brick, fashioned from the region's rich clay mines and baked in local factories, was routinely looted by thieves and exported to Florida to be used in backsplashes, walkways, and patio arches.[5]

Florida was the beneficiary of an unexpected relocation of African Americans whose parents and grandparents left the South during the Great Migration: 1915–50. Fleeing the North, especially cities with high crime and low hopes, such as St. Louis, Chicago, Detroit, and Cleveland, African-American migrants, especially the young and college educated, chose dynamic cities, such as Atlanta, Charlotte, Miami, Orlando, and Tampa. During the first years of the new century, New York City lost 40,000 Black residents whose trail led not to the outer suburbs but to Sunbelt cities. Even more astonishing, Chicago lost 200,000 African Americans between 2000 and 2020, many of them headed to Florida. The migration included significant numbers of young, college-educated Blacks. In an unimaginable setting, several dozen African-American friends gathered at the home of a friend in Palm Coast (Flagler County), a Florida city younger than most of the revelers. Mike Morton, a retired corrections officer from New York City, explained the moment succinctly: "It's all about a quality of life." Linda Sharpe Haywood, a retired New York City police officer, also moved to Palm Coast. "You're free to live where you can afford to live," she illuminated. By 2010, Florida was tied with New York, Texas, and Georgia as states with the largest Black populations (3.2 million).[6]

No American county lured more Blacks between 2003 and 2004 than Broward. But the vast number of the 17,893 new Black faces largely hailed from the Caribbean and West Indies, not the Rust Belt. New Black residents more likely came from Kingsport, Jamaica, not Jamaica, Queens, in New York! Large numbers of Haitians also immigrated to Broward County. Palm Beach and Miami-Dade counties also ranked high, drawing respectively 9,092 and 3,085 new Black inhabitants in such a pivotal year. For a sense of perspective, in 1970, the city of Lauderhill in Broward County boasted a population of 8,465, a figure that included a single Black resident. The comedian Jackie Gleason promoted the community. By 2000, Blacks constituted 60 percent of the city's population of 57,585. The foreign-born and native Black population was evenly distributed.[7]

Not all regions of Florida and the South benefited from the New Great Migration. Florida's African-American population once inched close to majority status. In 1870, Florida constituted 96,057 whites and 91,691 Blacks. In 1870, fully seven counties tilted to African-American majorities: Alachua, Gadsden, Jackson, Jefferson, Leon, Madison, and Marion. Jefferson County, two-thirds Black in 1870, was two-thirds white in 2000. The Great Migration and the Florida Land Boom of the 1920s and post–World War II, changed the racial composition of these counties, bringing in many more whites while losing substantial numbers of African Americans. In 2000, only one Florida county boasted a Black majority: Gadsden. Once the economic, educational, political, and demographic heart of Florida, the Panhandle and North Florida were fading in importance. But in a sea of red, Gadsden, Leon, and Jefferson counties still glowed blue on Election Day in 2000.[8]

Leon County was home to a powerful and influential African-American community. In 1860, Leon County's African-American population outnumbered whites by three to one. The seat of Florida government, Leon was home to Florida A&M University and many of the state's most powerful preachers and politicians. The growth of Florida as a modern state propelled the population of the region. In 2000, the county's population had expanded to 239,452 residents, a 24 percent increase over the previous decade. Tallahassee grew to more than 150,000 inhabitants. Many state workers lived in neighboring counties. To many Floridians, year-round government and the expansion of the bureaucracy was anathema. Old-timers quoted a favorite bromide: Until the late 1960s, the Florida Legislature met every other year for sixty days. Cynics argued Floridians would be better served if legislators met every sixty years for two days!

Go Home!

For decades, Cassandras and Jeremiahs, joined by an odd assortment of Birkenstock-wearing environmentalists, tweedy academics, and counterculture warriors and angry housewives, warned that Florida had wobbled on the edge of the chasm too long. In 1970, a group called Zero Population Growth sought to discourage Americans from moving to the Sunshine State. In 1973, a Dade County commissioner delivered some tough love. "By 1980, the good news will be that we'll be drinking raw sewage," he announced. "The bad news will be that there won't be enough to go around." When a 23 November 1981 *Time* magazine story highlighted Florida, a single question splashed across the cover: "PARADISE LOST?" In 1987, the Florida League Against Progress (FLAP) published its first "calamity calendar," alerting future tourists and residents that the Sunshine State led the nation in shark attacks and lightning strikes. The date 26 March marked the time when beachcombers found a human brain in a bait bucket on St. Augustine Beach. A disaster calendar circled important oil spills, race riots, and hurricanes, warning suckers who crossed the Georgia and Alabama borders to abandon all hope. Alas, the calendar ceased publication in 1999, on the eve of the Apocalypse. New Age, bad-taste bumper stickers warned: "Welcome to Florida, Now Go Home," "If It's Snowbird Season, Why Can't We Kill Them?," and "Happiness Is 100,000 Canadians Heading Home with a New Yorker under Each Arm."[9]

The making of modern Florida has come with a steep price: orange groves transformed into shopping malls, villages becoming edge cities, and subdivisions named for things they erased—Panther Trace and Eagle Ranch, Clear Lake and Paradise Key. In Florida, explained Carl Hiaasen, "Dredge pits become 'lakes,' and melaleuca infestations become 'glens.'" In a "Wish You Were Here!" state, one story speaks volumes about the price of progress. "Welcome to Orlando!" beamed a 1990s postcard. A resident inspected the card closely, detecting a flaw. The purported Orlando skyline only resembled Orlando. The skyline, after much scrutiny, belonged to Halifax, Nova Scotia! The City Beautiful had become the City Indistinguishable! And what does it mean when Orlando looks a lot like Halifax, Nova Scotia?[10]

Will there be a here, here? Would twenty-first-century Florida become homogenized as more franchise restaurants, big-box stores, and sprawling subdivisions serve more residents coming from someplace else? Will more gated communities allow new generations a slice of the Florida dream or produce gated disunity? Pell-mell growth transformed Miramar, Margate, Pembroke Pines, and Coral Springs, cities that were small towns not that long ago. Everglades City, Cedar Key, Apalachicola, Bartow, St. Augustine, and Mount Dora brace for growth and change. Small-town roots characterized residents who were more likely to be native Floridians than transplants in large cities.[11]

In a state where growth was gospel, one county defied orthodoxy. Martin County leaders were shocked by the population explosion in the 1970s in its southern meganeighbor, Broward County, which added 400,000 new residents. Branded the "Treasure Coast," Martin County's treasure was its small-town vibe and tranquility. A 1984 *New York Times*' article profiled Stuart as a "No-Growth town . . . a tough little town, tough on developers who would make it a big town." Following Hurricane Jeanne, which in 2004 smashed into Sewall's Point, the city banned billboards. Martin County was home to picturesque communities, such as Jupiter Island, Jensen Beach, and Hobe Sound. More importantly, it was also home to the New England Bush family and Nathaniel Pryor Reed. A blue-blood Republican, Reed was also Florida's greatest native-born environmentalist, advisor to Governor Claude Kirk and assistant secretary of the interior in President Nixon's cabinet. Maggy Hurchalla, a longtime resident, environmental champion, and sister of Janet Reno, recalled, "No one ignored Nat!" Reed founded 100 Friends of Florida, an environmental watchdog. But even Martin County could not halt the tide of growth. In 1950, the county had a modest population of 5,111, a number rocketing to 126,731 a half century later.[12]

Detractors of Florida's growth-at-all-costs policies wrote angry editorials and joined the Sierra Club. Some, however, moved to Florida's hinterlands. Bud Jenkins, the mayor of Davie, resigned midterm and moved with his wife to the edge of the Ocala National Forest. They were not alone. Almost 3,000 Gold Coasters who relocated to Marion County between 2001 and 2004 joined them. "For many," noted a reporter, "Ocala reminds them of what South Florida used to be ten or twenty years ago, before the strip malls and tract houses, the traffic and development that had reached the farthest corners of the region." But even Ocala could not escape urban ills. A 2001 study of sprawl ranked Ocala-Marion County among the nation's worst. Flagler County had also become home to Floridians fleeing traffic jams and urban growth. "We call them the 'Hiccup People,'" remarked a local resident. "Lots of them originally came from the North, went down to South Florida and now they've hiccupped and landed back here."[13]

If calendars did not repel tourist invaders with real-life horror stories, novelists imagined a wild and weird state. No one triumphed with more satirical success than *Miami Herald* columnist Carl Hiaasen. A rarity among Floridians, Hiaasen is a native, born in 1953 in Plantation. "There's no question," he confessed in a 2015 interview, "that there's a glorious abundance of weirdness and depravity in Florida." In his 1985 novel *Tourist Season,* the protagonist, Skip Wiley, realizes the only way to save Florida is to kill off tourists. Wiley feeds one tourist to the crocodiles and another is dispatched by stuffing a toy gator down his throat. His recipe for redemption is simple: "Scare away the tourists and pretty soon you scare away the developers. No more developers, no more bankers. No more bankers, no more lawyers. . . . Now tell me I'm crazy."[14]

The Boom's High-Octane Fuel

Calamity calendars and humorous satire notwithstanding, the Florida boom defied gravity, economics, and growth-planning studies. Roaring back, Florida was never down. Three generations of Americans had enjoyed fifty-five years of sustained prosperity across the Florida Panhandle and peninsula. In 2003, Michael Paterniti explained the relationship: "Florida exists by the good graces of our patronage—by those of us who live in the other 49. That is, it's a pure creation of our demand, of our retirees and relocated, cold-weary brethren; it belongs to us as much as it belongs to itself." Most of the middle-aged and elderly Americans who arrived in Florida between the 1950s and 1990s had enjoyed, by the relative standards of their parents, prosperous and healthy lives. The legacy of the New Deal, World War II, the GI Bill, and the Great Society undergirded modern Florida. Generous state-local-federal governments provided and protected pensions and built new universities and superhighways. A vigorous union movement and progressive tax policies, along with Social Security and Medicare, created a postwar equality that in retrospect, seems enlightened. Cape Canaveral and NASA symbolized America's "right stuff." Technology made possible new amenities. Lest we forget, air-conditioning made Florida livable twelve months a year. DDT may have been in Rachel Carson's words, "the elixir of death," but it allowed year-long living on barrier islands and coastlands.[15]

In 2003, a family jewelry store in Bradenton declared bankruptcy. "After 9/11," a family member explained, "luxury spending just stopped." The tragedy of 9/11 spun a web of consequences, but luxury spending, if temporarily interrupted, resumed. Floridians quickly rebounded, spending wildly and freely. A robustness sheathed Florida in the early years of the new century. From coast to coast, from hinterland and scrub grove, Floridians went on a binge.[16]

Across the state, unemployment was low and construction numbers were breaking records. Every sector of the economy seemed to be thriving, but one was especially vigorous. Boosted by a surge of classified sales ads, department store inserts, and demographics that still associated the morning newspaper with a cup of java, Florida was home to a healthy Fourth Estate. Students of the Fourth Estate lauded the *St. Petersburg Times*, the *Miami Herald*, the *Orlando Sentinel*, and the *South Florida Sun-Sentinel*. Newspapers earned handsome profits, even as circulation declined. But industry insiders pondered the fast-changing dynamics and economics of circulation, and the number of newspapers sold each day. Increasing numbers of tech-savvy consumers had begun reading newspapers and magazines online, for free. Alarmed about the dangers of too many chain-owned newspapers, many wondered what the future would be for chains that became publicly traded companies, such as the *Tribune*. Changing demographics also worried industry watchers, as young people were not getting their news reading newspapers.[17]

A new bromide and an old saw, Florida is a state where almost everyone is from someplace else. In 2003, exactly one-third of Florida residents were born in the state. In contrast, almost half of Floridians were born in a different state, while nearly one in five residents was born in a different country. A century earlier, two of every three inhabitants were Florida natives. Perhaps no one living in America's southernmost state seemed more authentically Floridian than Governor Jeb Bush, Bobby Bowden, Steve Spurrier, and Jimmy Buffett. But the governor was born in Texas, the "Dadgummit" coach called Alabama home, Coach Spurrier was a native of Tennessee, and the "Cheeseburger in Paradise" crooner hailed from Mississippi. Eighth-generation Floridian and commentator Diane Roberts observed, "Florida is a place where people have projected their own dreams and agenda onto the state.[18]

Between 2000 and 2006, "frenetic" may have been the best word to define what was happening across Florida. Daily, hundreds and sometimes thousands of newcomers arrived. But an equally important story is the intrastate movement and mobility. Journalists discovered, for instance, that the origins of newcomers to the Tampa Bay area "are not Chicago or New York, but other Florida counties, particularly neighboring counties." For instance, in Pasco County during the years 2000–2005, almost 80,000 new residents came from contiguous counties while 2,018 originated in Suffolk County, New York. The phenomenon was not limited to the Tampa Bay area.[19]

Many of the new arrivals' parents and grandparents had participated in the greatest exodus of humanity in history, the emigration from Europe and Asia to the Americas that a historian has called "one mighty and irresistible tide."

Immigrants typically settled in America's industrial cities, living in massive ethnic communities that outsiders depicted as disorganized and dirty. Little Italys and Hunky Hollows may have been sooty, but they were not unorganized. Indeed, chain migrations had shuttled Sicilians from Santo Stefano, Sicily, to Tampa and from Warsaw, Poland, to Detroit. So, too, migrations to Florida may have appeared individualistic, but in fact, they reflected face-to-face and city-to-city relationships. "Often," observed a *New York Times* journalist in 2007, "a Florida resort has a chillier twin farther north." He explained: "Seventy-five percent of second-home owners on Ponte Vedra Beach are from Atlanta. . . . Palm Beach County has its counterpart in New York's Nassau and Suffolk counties. Even Staten Island has a colony, in the Villages. . . . For years, the high-toned West Coast resort town of Naples has been a domain of suburban Detroit."[20]

The American dream was on resplendent display in the Sunshine State. Machinists' sons and bus drivers' daughters, the grandchildren of Welsh colliers and Polish peasants, trust-fund heirs and Horatio Algers, all found a place in Florida, be it a mobile home park or modest bungalow, new suburbia or gated community. Almost all had lived better lives than their parents and fully expected their children to live longer and more comfortably than they had. With good reasons, Floridians were confident, or at least hopeful of the future. Sixteen-year-olds who had cried the day the music died in 1959 at Clear Lake, Iowa, hoped to become nonagenarians in Lake Worth and Clearwater. Other than a few minor blips, Florida had not suffered a serious recession or depression since the 1920s and '30s. No aging Rust Belt cities darkened the Sunbelt; rather, Florida's immediate fortune depended upon the blessings of 76 million aging baby boomers born between 1946 and 1964. In 2006, that demographic began collecting their first Social Security checks, retiring, and, depending upon their wealth, health, and politics, moving to Century or Century Village, Lauderdale Lakes or Lauderdale-by-the-Sea. Demographics is destiny. The day of the "Near-Olds" was coming. The Stork had seemingly awarded Florida the "stay out of recession" Monopoly card. On

New Year's Day 2011, a *New York Times*' headline announced, "Boomers Hit Another Milestone of Self-Absorption: Turning 65." The Social Security checks the following day were the tip of a massive demographic iceberg, 79 million strong. A "silver tsunami" was headed toward Florida. Retirement, old age, and Del Boca Vista beckoned. Jerry Seinfeld explained simply, "My parents didn't want to move to Florida, but they turned sixty and that's the law."[21]

Generations poured into active adult retirement communities and high-rise condos, confident that the Sunshine State would, in words attributed to both Abraham Lincoln and the developer of an adult retirement complex, "give years to your life and life to your years." And to put more Bada Bing, Bada Boom into aging men's love lives, a new drug promised enhanced lift and virility, all in a single blue pill. Florida provides to many seniors a final dream, a golden honeymoon, a yearning that love can be rediscovered or rekindled. The Food & Drug Administration (FDA) had approved Cialis in 2003. A rather unusual celebrity endorsement spiked interest in a yet-to-be released drug. In 2006, authorities at Palm Beach International Airport detained radio host Rush Limbaugh after discovering an unprescribed bottle of Viagra in his luggage. The FDA finally approved Viagra in 2008.[22]

Nothing is ever static in Florida. Since the 1950s, the Sunshine State had attracted one-quarter of all retirees who moved out of state. But in 2003, the Census Bureau announced that while Florida remained retirees' number-one destination, the percentage of elderly newcomers migrating to Florida had fallen to 19 percent. Other states—notably Virginia, Georgia, North Carolina, and Arizona—were competing successfully for the senior bowl. With its inexpensive housing and plethora of jobs for the fifty-five and older cohort, Nevada captured the AARP prize for hosting America's fastest-growing senior population. Yet the sheer number of current and prospective retirees moving to Florida—almost 400,000 seniors moved to Florida between 1995 and 2000—maintained and sustained their political and cultural influence across the state. The 2000 census indicated that four of America's top ten metropolitan areas having the highest number of residents age sixty-five and older were in Florida: Sarasota-Bradenton, West Palm–Boca Raton, Tampa–St. Petersburg, and Fort Lauderdale. Almost one in three residents of metropolitan Sarasota-Bradenton was a senior citizen.[23]

An old cliché insisted that grandparents do not immigrate. Historically, young people chose to emigrate. But in early twentieth-century Florida, over a half-million residents were *abuelas, bubbes, nonne,* and *grans.* Cubans who fled to Miami as teenagers in 1960 were eligible for Social Security benefits in 2010.[24]

Amid a population explosion in 2004, Florida was not experiencing a baby boom; rather, most of Florida's demographic gains came from immigrants and migrants, not births. Only Duval, among the state's largest counties, gained population as the result of natural increase (births minus deaths). Notably, relatively few immigrants settled in Jacksonville.[25]

If a single word encapsulated the six-decade-old, silver wave of seniors to Florida, the word was "freedom." To be sure, there was nothing new about Americans on the move; indeed, mobility had long been an American right and rite of passage. What differed profoundly about the movement to Florida was simply demographics. Historically, young people gambled that their lives would be improved if they left rock-strewn Vermont for the Illinois prairie, or the Rust Belt for the Sunbelt. In societies where age fifty was considered old, grandparents rarely uprooted. What connects Haitian *balseros* and Cuban refugees with Donald Trump and Betsy DeVos? They made decisions to move to Florida to be free. They also expected their children to have better lives or to protect their trust funds from confiscatory governments.

If a fortune-teller had prophesied in 1940 that millions of northeastern and midwestern grandmothers and fathers would leave their grown children, friends, and neighbors behind at age sixty-five and move to an active adult senior center in Cape Coral or Hallandale, the prophet might have been institutionalized. After spending a lifetime taking care of elders, volunteering at one's church, ethnic, and civic groups, it was now time for sons, daughters, and volunteers to honor elderly parents and neighbors. But against the ethnic and ethical grain of American history, millions of seniors asserted their freedom to move to Florida.[26]

Before Florida captured the affections of senior citizens, there had to be a revolution in the way Americans thought about growing old. In a world steeped in the Protestant work ethic, the notion of "retirement" in the Sunshine State was as socially unimaginable as it was morally abhorrent. But revolutions in medical care, miracle drugs, and Social Security allowed millions of Americans to live longer and test their new freedoms. Living longer defined the American century; between 1900 and 2000, life expectancy increased by more than thirty years. Never had so many persons lived so well and so far from where they had been born. A woman moving to Florida in 2005 at age sixty could reasonably expect to live a third of her life in retirement. No society in history had ever confronted the moral, political, and demographic challenges and frontiers of so many citizens living so long.[27]

How does one explain the extended boom? For all the treatises on trickle-down economics, the multiplier effect of tourism dollars, and faith-based money supply, a home builder explained it most eloquently. One of three brothers born to a British immigrant carpenter, Frank Mackle helped guide the family business to some of Florida's most stupendous developments: Key Biscayne, Port Charlotte, Spring Hill, Port St. Lucie, and Marco Island. In 1959, Mackle was asked by a *Newsweek* reporter his secret. His answer may be the most precise explanation of the rise of modern Florida. "Everything works toward helping us," he gushed. "We've got doctors trying to get people to live longer. We've got the unions trying to get people to retire quicker. We've got a tremendous growth in pension funds; social security is getting stronger. Companies are retiring people younger." No sociologist or astrologer ever explained America's love affair with Florida or California more succinctly. Richard Nixon lived in one of the Mackle's Key Biscayne vacation homes, described as "one of the few middle-class residential areas in Miami that retains a tropical flavor instead of looking like any other suburban community in the country."[28]

The first years of the new century were heady times. Imagine Willy Loman, Tony Montana, and Gordon Gekko settling down as Realtors in North Port, Port St. Lucie, and Palm Coast. The stars were in alignment, even if we later learned astrologers were cooking the books. As had occurred in the 1990s, the Federal Reserve chairman, acting as a maestro, adjusted interest rates, tamping down fears of inflation or a crash. In this brave new world of computers, economic upheavals and panics seemed relegated to the dustbins of history. If the selling of Florida in the decades following World War II belonged to men such as Leonard Ratner and the brothers Mackle and Rosen, the new century belonged to a new generation.

In 1950, Florida's most popular retirement outposts were found in Miami and St. Petersburg. But partly because of brilliant marketing and partly because of changing tastes, Florida's most popular twenty-first-century retirement destinations were Sumter, Charlotte, Citrus, Highlands, and Sarasota counties.

On 11 September 2006, the United States observed the fifth anniversary of 9/11. For all the handwringing and doomsday predictions, the nation had escaped a second major terrorist act. America's unemployment rate had declined from 5 percent in 2001 to 4.5 percent in September 2006. In January 2001, the Congressional Budget Office boldly predicted that within five years, the federal government should have erased its debt. The reality of foreign wars and deficit budgets dashed planners' dreams. In September 2001, the national debt was $5.8 trillion; five years later, it had spiraled to $7.3 trillion.[29]

Sports provided a social safety valve to Floridians wishing to escape the numbness of identity politics and forever wars. The 2001 University of Miami football team may have been one of the greatest gridiron teams of all time. The Hurricanes went undefeated and captured the national championship. The team produced a record thirty-eight draft picks! The autumn of 2006 was a special moment for University of Florida fans as it marked the one-hundredth anniversary of collegiate football in Gainesville. A new coach had arrived in Gainesville in 2004 and accomplished the impossible: making Gator fans forget Steve Spurrier. In his six seasons, Urban Meyer coached the Gators to two national championships. In a single month, September 2006, the University of Florida won five games, including triumphs over Tennessee and Alabama. Even sweeter, rivals FSU and the University of Miami descended to mediocrity if not blandness. Not even Bobby Bowden could win forever. If football was the state's unofficial religion, the University of Florida basketball team had long suffered as one of the Southeast Conference's weakest members. But a new coach, Billy Donovan, brought new energy to the program. Still, between 2000 and 2005, the Gators had been eliminated in the first round for five consecutive seasons. But the 2006 season was special, awakening lost souls when the Gators won the NCAA national championship. They began the season unranked! Then the hoopsters repeated the feat the following year alongside the Gators' number-one ranked football team. Not since the legendary Duke teams fifteen years earlier had a team won back-to-back national championships in basketball. No NCAA Division 1 school had ever won the national championships in football and basketball in the same year. Moreover, the team stayed together, saying no to the big bucks of the NBA. But football was the state religion in Florida, and the prophet was a humble young man from Jacksonville. Tim Tebow, Florida's quarterback and the "Chosen One," starred as the game's most humble yet charismatic figure, receiving the 2007 Heisman Trophy while saving souls as a missionary during the off-season. A journalist characterized Tebow's persona as a "husky amalgam of Bronko Nagurski, Billy Graham, and Brett Favre," adding, "Whereas most legends are shrouded in myth, Tebow's is fortified by facts." Tebow was voted the greatest football player in Florida history. Stars were aligned over the Sunshine State. Tebow returned his senior year to lead a team Coach Urban Meyer called his best team ever. That championship team saw nineteen Gators eventually drafted by the NFL.[30]

If one wanted proof that the planet had slipped off its rotation, in the autumn of 2007, the University of South Florida football team, a program that had only been in existence for eleven years, soared to number one in five of the six computerized national rankings, and second in two human polls, defeating highly regarded Auburn and West Virginia, as well as knocking off North Carolina.

Even if the Bulls stumbled down the stretch, finishing the season with a record of 9–4, the season represented a high-water mark for the state of Florida. The gridiron success attracted the attention of the venerable *New York Times*, which remarked, "South Florida has come so far so fast that it has its doubters." One naysayer was the game's most successful coach, Alabama's Nick Saban, who sneered that USF had dumb-downed its admissions policies.[31]

In Shakespeare's *Henry V*, French noblemen and officers discuss their warhorses, mistresses, and the certainty of victory on the eve of the Battle of Agincourt. A messenger announces, "My lord high constable, the English lie within fifteen hundred paces of your tents." The cynical constable asks, "Who hath measured the ground?"

Measuring the Boom: Snowbirds and Sunbirds

Measuring Florida and Floridians represents a herculean task. Daily, thousands of individuals—migrants, transplants, legal and illegal immigrants, residents, tourists, soldiers, and homeless—arrive and depart. Florida really is a state of flux. To understand the Sunshine State, journalists and demographers have provided new terms and statistics to explain the fluid state of migration within and without Florida. In 2000, the U.S. Census Bureau announced that Florida's population stood at 16.05 million. But those numbers do not include nearly 1 million persons who resided in Florida for at least one month per year. Counting snowbirds is an imprecise exercise; for instance, if your sister-in-law's family from Albany stayed in your spare bedroom for a month, they would not be included in the count.[32]

In February 2007, the *New York Times*' Julia Lawlor reintroduced readers to a new bird species. "Snow-bird" dates from 1923, referring to northerners who migrate South during the winter months in search of work, but by 1979, snowbird meant tourists in search of warmth. Lawlor explained the phenomenon: "It takes a big state to absorb the entire North every winter, but once again Florida is pulling it off. From Miami to Pensacola, the cold-weather escapees have been filtering in, completing the midwinter migration to the Northerners' land of dreams—or at least the land of polo shirts and khaki shorts." Lawlor completed the jigsaw puzzle: "New Englanders settle around Sarasota, and Philadelphians camp out nearby in Clearwater. Minnesotans congregate on Sanibel Island, Ohioans on the Gulf Coast east of Panama City. Carolinians find their own in Daytona."[33]

Almost one in three of these "snowbirds" roosted the rest of the year in the

Northeast. Large numbers also came from the Midwest. The State of Michigan implored its residents who spent up to five months a year in Florida to claim Michigan residency because, "If Michigan's snowbirds had been counted in the right place, Michigan would not have lost a congressional seat after the 2000 Census." Clearly, many snowbirds think of Florida as more than a vacationland. In 2004, the *New York Daily News* conducted a sweep of voter registration records and discovered 46,000 New Yorkers entitled to vote in the Empire State *and* in the Sunshine State.[34]

The snowbird tapestry is rich, colorful, and complex. To an outsider, these temporary communities may seem disordered, a place without purpose or bonds. Snowbirds, much like Italian immigrants or African-American migrants a century earlier, often follow their neighbors, friends, and fellow workers to specific locales. But whereas the Great Migrations and chain migrations centered around work, family, and local connections, the annual return of snowbirds is fixed upon leisure and lifestyle. "Even in the sunny South," writes Lawlor, snowbirds tend "to be among their own—occupying turf in the company of their clans, their neighbors, their gold buddies, and, in general, people who share the cadences of their accents and the colors of their license plates." But explaining Florida in February is not as simple as consulting a map and following the routes of Interstates 95 and 75.[35]

Snowbirds, like the proverbial swallows, winter in Florida. The general arrival date follows Thanksgiving but fluctuates according to the weather. On 9 November 2006, the *Ocala Star-Banner* announced, "Snowbirds Land Early This Year to Escape Cold." Lines at restaurants were longer, tee times at The Villages' golf courses were more difficult to reserve, and the utility companies noted surging numbers of "signups."

The U.S. Census only began collecting data about snowbirds in the 1980s. The Internal Revenue Service also collects data on the mobile band of migrants for tax purposes. Out-of-state domiciles may reside in Florida for more than 183 days and still retain out-of-state residency for legal purposes. States such as Connecticut, Michigan, and Missouri require a certain number of days within the state to maintain residency. Many eventually return as permanent residents to take advantage of Florida's tax sanctuary.

Canadians constitute one of the largest groups of snowbirds. So many Canadians huddle in the strip between Hollywood and Fort Lauderdale that Québécois can easily find newspapers published in French, as well as cafes serving their national dish, poutine. A new term, Floribec, describes their French-Canadian–Floridian status. Together with Canadians from Ontario and other provinces, more than 2 million Canadians visited Florida in 2005. Many spend anywhere from one week to six months in the Sunshine State. In 2017, Canadians bought $7 billion worth of real estate in Florida. Here, they can listen to familiar radio shows, such as *Canada Calling* and *Canada News*, as well as find copies of the *Toronto Star*. Commentators refer to Florida as Canada's eleventh province. The Canadian Snowbirds Association, which in 2005 boasted more than 100,000 members, monitors the concerns of its countrymen and women under the Florida sun. No single issue has been more vexing issue to Canadian snowbirds than navigating health-care coverage in Florida. In his magisterial study *Florida Snowbirds*, Godefroy Desrosiers-Lauzon argues that Canadians have also contributed to the betterment of Florida, noting "their above-average practice of volunteering and their keen political awareness." Florida communities understand the social and economic bonds between host and visitor. Pembroke Park's population doubles in January. The city hall receptionist speaks French, and banners printed with "*Bienvenue*" drape across Hallandale Beach Boulevard.[36]

A linguist, a modern Henry Higgins, might have detected undecipherable accents in the city of Lake Worth. Each winter, thousands of Finns and their children migrate to Palm Beach County to enjoy the weather but also to patronize Finnish bakeries, Suomi singing societies, and birch-wood saunas. Nine of ten Finns who visit America wind up in Lake Worth. At one time, the town supported fifteen Finnish hotels.[37]

New Yorkers and their Jersey neighbors prefer Florida's Gold Coast, encompassing Palm Beach, Broward, and Miami-Dade counties. The relationship between American Jews and Florida is especially intense. Many Jews first encountered exotic locales such as Miami Beach and Boca Raton as young GIs in World War II. In 1949, Miami Beach's anti-Semitic ordinances had been abolished. The "New Yawk" accent became so prevalent that Miami-Dade County was lovingly referred to as the "Sixth Borough." Winter vacations in Florida served as a gateway and handmaiden to permanent homes in Southeast Florida. In sociological language, snowbirding is synonymous with "retirement migration." The Jewish population in Palm Beach and Broward counties increased dramatically in the early twenty-first century. "As much a collective phenomenon as a seasonal one," writes Jenna Weissman Joselit, "the migration of large segments of the population from one region of the country to another has become a defining feature of modern life, especially among America's Jews."[38]

In Boynton Beach, Boca Raton, and Delray Beach, vanishing Yiddish accents still reverberated at Lox Around the Clock and Flakowitz Deli. Former snowbird and 2007 transplant Alan Sandberg called Boynton Beach, "Long Island plopped down with palm trees." The names of the bagel shops remind patrons of their former homes: Family Bagels of Long Island, Broadway Bagels, the Original Brooklyn Water Bagel Co., Brighton Beach Bagel & Bakery, and the New York Bagel Deli. While the setting for *Seinfeld* may have been Manhattan, the ultimate destination is South Florida. In a memorable *Seinfeld* episode, Jerry's parents, having moved to the mythical retirement home in Del Boca Vista, contemplate the iconic early-bird special. Jerry expresses his disdain for the custom: "Four-thirty? Who eats dinner at four-thirty?" His father, Morty explains, "By the time we sit down, it'll be quarter to five." In 2000, a reporter observed, "the real-life Jerry Seinfeld was spotted taking his mother, Betty, out to dinner near her home in Delray Beach, where she migrated after raising her family in Massapequa on Long Island."[39]

In Naples, Venice, and Marco Island, midwesterners seek their comfort foods: Skyline Chili and Wisconsin cheese curds, Italian ices and Chicago deep-dish pizza. In The Villages, the manager of the local Winn-Dixie translated snowbirds' culinary customs: "Northerners buy different items. Snowbirds tend to buy more of a variety of items and seek out specialty products. They eat sauerkraut."[40]

In Central Florida, snowbirds line up on Tuesdays, hours before the doors open at the Honey Pot, a legendary restaurant in Clermont, home of the Citrus Tower and hungry Canadians. On Tuesdays, patrons await fried chicken and the trimmings.[41]

Snowbirds work off caloric overloads by maintaining an active lifestyle in Florida. While their grandparents threw horseshoes at Fort Myers Beach and played the hammer (last puck in the round) at the St. Petersburg Shuffleboard Center (featuring stadium seating), a new sport was emerging in 2006: pickleball. Combining elements of tennis, badminton, and ping-pong, pickleball was becoming the rage for seniors who could no longer play a rigorous game of tennis and did not have the time for golf. In 2005, the USA Pickleball Association was formed.[42]

So many snowbirds had migrated to Naples from Bloomfield Hills and Birmingham, Michigan, that expats organized a women's club for transplanted Wolverines and Spartans. In one of America's most affluent cities, retired General Motors brass organized an exclusive Gulf Shores GM Retired Executives Club. What's good for General Motors is good for Neapolitans. Less affluent but more demonstrative, Naples's Italian-American Club drew upon the thousands of former Cleveland *paesani* who settled in Collier County and attend its annual ethnic festivals.[43]

In the decade 2000–2010, a steady stream of Minnesotans (most notably from Scott County) moved to Southwest Florida, especially Collier County. Demographers also point to the pull of Minnesotans to Southwest Florida traced to 1991, when the Minnesota Twins moved to Fort Myers for spring training at their new CenturyLink Sports Complex.[44]

Lakeland's bond with Michigan's snowbirds is intimately tied to baseball. Since 1934, the city has hosted the Detroit Tigers for spring training. To many, attending a February afternoon baseball game at Joker Marchant Stadium signifies an annual pilgrimage. Many Michiganders have retired to Lakeland to cement their relationship with their beloved baseball team and neighbors. In 2016, Michigan football coach Jim Harbaugh brought his Wolverine football team to practice at IMG Academy in Bradenton, a move that brought condemnation from rival coaches, but huzzahs from 5,000 approving snowbirds who attended practice. The football squad also attended a Tigers' spring training game.[45]

Florida was America's spring training capital in 2005. Snowbirds who followed their hometown teams to Citrus League training sites were rewarded with back-home, ballpark foods: Nathan's hot dogs could be had at the New York Mets' Tradition Field in Port St. Lucie; full-throated Cincinnati Reds' fans found Big Red Smokeys at Ed Smith Stadium in Sarasota; and Philadelphia loyalists could get an authentic Philly cheese steak at Bright House Field in Clearwater.[46]

Spring training also brings to Florida thousands of professional baseball players, who hunger for a cup of coffee in the big leagues. Hope reigns eternal in spring training. The demographics of baseball have changed dramatically, most notably the dramatic rise in Latin American players. In 2005, Dominican-born and former baseball player Luis Merejo opened the Bravo Supermarket Cafeteria in Port St. Lucie. It has become a favorite place for New York Mets' prospects and big-leaguers to enjoy Latin American favorites: stewed oxtail, white rice and red beans, and *gallo pinto.* The owners shower food and sympathy upon the impoverished prospects, who appreciate the Dominican specialty, *morir soñando* (to die dreaming), a cold drink concocted of evaporated milk, vanilla extract, orange juice, blended with crushed ice.[47]

Snowbird peregrinations changed the seasonal economy and skyline of the Florida Panhandle. Historically, summer, not winter, defined high tourist season on the beaches from Panama City to Santa Rosa. Historian Harvey H. Jackson witnessed the seasonal change from his family home at Seagrove. He recalled that Panhandle snowbirds were less affluent than their Gold Coast namesakes, "but for those whose kids were grown and gone, those who just wanted winter a little warmer and a lot cheaper . . . the Florida Panhandle beckoned." Motels that traditionally closed in November opened to accommodate the new visitors.

"Local chambers of commerce turned public buildings into 'Snowbird Welcome Centers,'" wrote Jackson, "where the newly arrived could register by state so they could find folks from 'back home' to hang out with." A reporter explained simply, "It's why Memphis families returning from spring break will be walking around with white sand from their Panhandle city of Destin (not Fort Myers, certainly not Miami) between their toes." Just how appreciative is the Panhandle of snowbirds? In Panama City, the second Friday in January is now known as Winter Resident Appreciation Day. Winter residents also spend time at the Ark, a snowbird center featuring a woodworking shop, as well classes in stained glass and pine needle basket making. DeFuniak Springs was not endowed with beachfront property, but city officials celebrate "Snowbird Day" each January. Wintertime Destin visitors gather each Tuesday at the Roost to renew acquaintances, discuss the *Snowbird News,* and register to receive prizes donated by local merchants. *Gulf Coast Snowbirds,* a magazine, reaches fellow travelers across the Panhandle.[48]

Not all snowbirds prefer the glamour and urbanity of Naples and Palm Beach. Some seek the natural wonderments of the Sunshine State, what journalist Jeff Klinkenberg calls "Real Florida." The popularity of RVs and mobile homes permit some winter residents to reside at Florida State Parks. Speakers invited to the remote Highlands Hammock State Park are pleasantly surprised at the size of the crowds, comprised largely of seasonal visitors. Cedar Key, a Gulf Coast island known for its laid-back style, attracts snowbirds who are as interested in the migratory bird life as the rustic setting. A journalist described Cedar Key as "a small 'Old Florida' fishing community on an island surrounded by mud flats and oyster bars. There are no beaches, no high-rise condos." In Zephyrhills, "The City of Pure Water," the small community of 15,000 year-round residents in Pasco County is transformed into a parking lot for thousands of out-of-state visitors. Many live in the mobile home subdivisions and drive, Floridians swear, at 10 mph. Cable connections, church attendance, and shuffleboard court reservations spike in November. Snowbirds from Midland County, Michigan, have been flocking to Zephyrhills for an annual gathering since 1982.[49]

Snowbirds "keep to their flyways," and often "those flyways can be very narrow," charted a journalist. And many of Palm Beach County's snowbirds trace their fly path to Suffolk and Nassau counties in New York. Staten Islanders, defiantly proud of their working-class ethos, reminisce about borough life at The Villages, near Ocala.[50]

The overall impact of a million snowbirds spending the winter in Florida is stunning, measured in the billions of dollars. Officials at the Palm Beach County

Tourist Development Council argued in 2007 that snowbirds had boosted the local economy by $1.6 billion. Palm Beach officials point to the statistic that between 2000 and 2003, one in four county residents fifty-five and older started out as snowbirds.[51]

The snowbird population included large numbers of military retirees. Some camp and golf on the state's military bases. Overlooking Tampa Bay, MacDill Air Base offers military retirees a marina, beach, two golf courses, and 400 camping spaces. Most of Florida's other bases offer similar amenities.[52]

Not every snowbird is a retiree; rather, some migrate to Florida to work for part of the year. From pharmacists working three months a year to baggers at Publix, snowbirds fill positions of need. In 2005, more than 700 snowbirds worked at Beall's department stores in Florida. Home Depot and CVS, a major pharmacy chain, have instituted programs that accommodate "snowbird workers" who wish to spend their winters in Florida.[53]

In a state that takes pride in and punishes itself for its hedonism and bronze complexions, Florida welcomes snowbirds who arrive for sun *and* piety. One of the most interesting seasonal migrations occurs in Pinecraft, a small settlement on the eastern edge of Sarasota County. The Amish arrived there in the 1920s to farm celery and build an agricultural community. Today, an Amish and Mennonite village retreat has taken hold, with Der Dutchman, Dutch Haus, and Yoder's serving hearty portions of pot roast, along with "Mom's" egg custard and peanut butter cream pies. Each winter, from 3,000 to 5,000 snowbirds arrive, many by bus, and some stay for the season. Fresh arrivals from Lancaster and Arthur are easily identified by their black dresses, Pennsylvania Dutch speech, and familiar foods such as ground cherries and hearty cheese. Fruit pies with vaulted meringues can be found at every benefit supper, and, since this is Florida, brighter-colored dresses than the traditional black. Buses, not horse and buggies, transport the new arrivals to what insiders jocularly call "Amish Las Vegas." In 1986, a reporter noted the popularity of the phrase "What goes on in Florida stays in Florida." On the other hand, the Amish deeply resented the less-than-pious images portrayed in the popular-culture shows *Breaking Amish* and *Amish Mafia.* Pinecraft Park, described by the *New York Times,* "is a melting pot of Amish and Mennonite America. Old order, new order, and nontraditional congregate." In Pinecraft, more traditional churches compete against a New Order church. Congregants do not drive automobiles in Florida, but three-wheeled motorized bikes have appeared. While they enjoy the comforts of air-conditioning and electric appliances, televisions and computers are unacceptable.[54]

Demographers and ornithologists also study sunbirds in Florida. Like their feathery namesakes, sunbirds also migrate according to the seasons. Unlike snowbirds, sunbirds are residents of Florida. They migrate to cooler climes in the summer, returning in the late fall or winter. Anyone who has studied license plates in New England or North Carolina during the summer understands that another seasonal migration is well established: the summer migration of 300,000 elderly Floridians to cooler climes. These disparate Florida residents who spend between one and five months outside the state are called "sunbirds." The trend originated in the nineteenth century, when yellow fever scoured southern coastal communities in hot weather. Floridians who fled to the mountains of North Carolina escaped the disease, and soon a summer network was established. "Every train bound for South Florida," noted a *Tampa Tribune* reporter in September 1904, "is loaded with Floridians who have spent the summer in the mountains or at the seashore." Around Labor Day 1925, the *Orlando Morning Sentinel* reported, "Fletcher Proctor returned Sunday from a three months' stay in North Carolina." When July reminds most Floridians of the smell of burst radiators and sweating pedestrians, University of Florida administrators fly to Linville, Highlands, and Asheville to court the wealthy Gator alumni who populate the mountain retreats. "More Floridians keep second homes in North Carolina than move here full time," observed *Florida Trend*, adding, "in some cases to avoid a state income tax." Not everyone in the bucolic setting thinks the influx of sunbirds is a good thing. "Why would you want to live behind a gate in the mountains?," asked an Asheville city councilwoman. "There's nothing to be afraid of." And then there are the "Floridiots" who prefer more leisurely driving speeds.[55]

North Carolina also offers a sanctuary to Floridians who have fled the Sunshine State permanently for better climes and lifestyles. Modern Florida is not for everyone. North Carolina is the number-one destination for disenchanted "half-backs," because many have returned halfway back home. A wag once suggested that Florida consider a specialty license plate for expats: "Florida: It's Not What I Thought It Would Be!" Decades ago, audiences roared when the comedian Brother Dave Gardner said that he never heard of anyone retiring *to* New Jersey.[56]

The Greatest Housing Boom Ever

From antiquity through the Middle Ages, alchemists sought to find the philosopher's stone, a substance capable of turning mercury and iron into gold. But it was in Florida that developers and swamp salesmen succeeded in that ancient quest, turning wetlands, savannahs, and sand dunes into high-rise condominiums, mobile home parks, active adult senior retirement centers, boomburbs and microburbs. It was one of the wildest rides in American history.

The construction of hundreds of thousands of houses, neighborhoods, and mini-cities was accomplished by a remarkable group of businessmen whose names often adorned the homes: Levitt, Pulte, Rutenberg, Mackle, Rosen, Colen, and many others. Most never attended business school but learned on construction sites how to mass-produce homes by trial and error. William Pulte turned down a college scholarship for the opportunity to build his first house. Arthur Rutenberg was selling appliances in Chicago when his brother bought ten lots in Clearwater. Art became known as the dean of Florida home design. William J. Levitt is most famous for his namesake Long Island housing development, Levittown. He pioneered the practice of applying assembly-line techniques to the construction of homes. He entered the Florida housing market in the 1970s.

Sidney Colen may not have been as well-known as his contemporaries, but he was a pioneer in constructing active adult condo communities. Born in Erie, Pennsylvania, in 1919, he arrived in St. Petersburg with ambition and a dream. He began building homes in St. Petersburg in 1947, then launched a community of homes that became Kenneth City. He named the city for his son, Kenneth, understanding that Colen City was not a pitch-perfect name. In the 1960s, he constructed On Top of the World, 5,000 condominium-style homes built atop bulldozed citrus groves in Clearwater. In 1975, Colen purchased the 13,000-acre Circle Square Ranch near Ocala. A child of the Great Depression and frightened of debt, Colen financed the project himself. By the time of Colen's death in 2009, Marion County's On Top of the World was home to 10,000 senior citizens. Sidney and Ina Colen moved into On Top of the World in the late 1990s. Building upon the principle of an active adult retirement center, Colen constructed a $1 million recreational center at the Ocala complex.[57]

Condo Fever

The condominium has become so commonplace in modern Florida that we imagine the concept originated in colonial St. Augustine. The term "condominium" is even older than the fourth-century CE bishop and theologian Augustine of Hippo, whose name graces Florida's oldest city. The Latin word, meaning joint dominion, can be traced to first-century Babylon and refers to certain property, *condominio,* that is divided into several units and yet are owned separately. Occupants share common use areas. In New York City and among the progressive Latin immigrants in Tampa, "co-operatives" flourished, where one bought a share in a residential building, medical clinic, or grocery store. The first such cooperative apartment building in Florida was the Cloisters at Pompano Beach, completed in 1946. By 1958, the practice had become popular along the Gold Coast as New Yorkers moved to the area.[58]

The concept may have been ancient, but the word "condominium" did not enter the public parlance until the 1960s. *Florida Trend* introduced the term to its readers, explaining, "A new life-style is evolving in Florida and with it, a new habitat, the condominium." The article added that already the state's 1,200 complexes made Florida the "Condominium Capital of the World." Quickly, the words "condo craze" and "condomania" spread across Florida. Golf, tennis, senior, and conversion condos suddenly appeared.[59]

Florida pioneered a new way of living. Condominiums perfectly conformed to the needs and aspirations of aging, affluent, and mobile Americans and Canadians in the late twentieth and early twenty-first centuries. The amenities customers most desired included location (coastal or lakefront), leisure activities (golf and tennis), and cost (Florida was relatively inexpensive compared to California).[60]

Hallandale, a city in Broward County, was ground zero to the first condominium boom in the 1970s. A *New York Times'* headline described the consequences: "Problems of High Rises Straining Florida Resort." The first wave of condominium owners typically were retirees, many of whom were uncomfortable with what was happening to America in the late 1960s. In 1968, Hallandale's city commissioners considered "banning hippies," described by one official as "odd-balls" with "bare feet, odd dress and unkempt appearance crowned by long hair." By 2000, many of the community's new residents were former hippies. Hallandale's love-hate relationship with "a canyon of high-rise condominium and apartment buildings" become commonplace along both coasts. By then, Hallandale had changed its name to the more enticing Hallandale Beach, and the number of condominiums across the state had grown to more than 1 million units.[61]

If a high-rise condo was an astute business calculation, the time-share condo took Florida's real estate market to a new dimension. The idea was simple: timeshares offered tourists an eternal week-or-two slice of the Florida dream by selling room(s) at a hotel, condo, or resort. The promise of two weeks of golf in wintertime Florida was a powerful sales tactic, one that drew the attention of regulators.[62]

Home, Home on the Fairway

Golf is deeply rooted in Florida. The game may be the perfect year-round sport for a largely flat and malleable place, and for a population that is leisure oriented. The golf community and golf course were symbiotic twins. Appropriately, John Sayles's 2002 film *Sunshine State* opens on a Florida golf course. Three duffers, clearly Yankees judging by their accents, serve as the modern equivalent of a Greek chorus philosophizing about their new home. One of them offers some perspective about the Sunshine State. Not long ago, he states, Florida was "nothing but a place of swamps and alligators, populated by white people who ate catfish." But developers transformed the state, bringing progress. What hath prosperity wrought? Alan King, portraying golfer Murray Silver, answers, "Out of the muck and the mangrove, we created this: nature on a leash." Murray adds that golf courses are not about selling green fairways and doglegs, but selling dreams.

A game originating in Scotland appropriately traces its origins to Florida with the coming of the Scots to the Sunshine State. Scottish colonists arrived in Sarasota in 1885 to a wilderness described by a settler as "a wild country." A foundering colony was salvaged by a pious Scot, John Hamilton Gillespie, who became the first mayor of Sarasota. The city seal honors Scottish frugality and practicality: "A mullet with a rising sun over palmettoes with shells at the base." Gillespie got down to business, constructing the first golf course in Florida in 1886. His successors realized the importance of golf to a city on the make, a booster proclaiming, "A resort town without golf is like the play Hamlet without the main character."[63]

New golf courses followed, sometimes on unfamiliar rough. In 1895, Victorian ladies and gentlemen were navigating greens and moats along Fort Marion (El Castillo) in St. Augustine. The Ocala Heights Golf Club opened in 1912. In 1916, a newspaper headline announced, "Golf Making Its Bow as Leading Winter Sport in St. Petersburg." By 1918, the "fashionable" sport had become so popular that a newspaper headline read, "Golf Is Gaining Ground in Cities of Florida."[64]

The city of Temple Terrace, named for the temple orange, traces its origins to the Florida Boom. In 1923, the city opened a picturesque eighteen-hole golf course designed by Scottish-born Tom Bendelow. Developers constructed the first planned golf community in Florida, luring northerners with Mediterranean Revival homes emblazoned with Cuban-tiled roofs and serpentine columns. Investors quickly realized the perils entwined with golf and real estate—the 1926 Bust and Great Depression arrested the development.[65]

By 2006, the popularity of golf spanned the state, buoyed by the harmonic convergence of baby boomers, the prevalence of retirement communities, generations of golf heroes from Sam Snead to Arnold Palmer to Tiger Woods, the Golf Channel, and optimism that prosperity would last forever. Golf communities appealed to Americans who liked well-manicured greens and gated preserves, combining with the Florida dream the promise of rejuvenation and second starts. The fact that Tiger Woods had a home at the Isleworth Country Club near Orlando simply reinforced the masses who aspired to live and play like Tiger or David Duval. New amenities, such as club massage parlors and gourmet dining, smart shoes and graphite shafts, attracted legions of golfers. For good reasons, Jupiter is home to the National Golf Foundation. Bear's Club in Jupiter, the Seminole Beach Club in Juno Beach, and the Bellasera Resort course in Naples serve as markers of class and prestige.

Developers of golf courses did not so much tame nature as redesign it. In sync with the release of Sayles's *Sunshine State*, the Florida Legislature approved a specialty license plate in 2002: "Golf Capital of the World." In this case, legislators were not guilty of ballyhoo and hyperbole. Home to more than 1,500 golfing destinations, Florida leads the nation. But golf has morphed far beyond mere recreation; it has become a home, a way of life, and, in the words of journalist Frank Deford, "perhaps the finest collaborative work between God and man." Golf course communities perfectly encapsulate modern Florida. With names such as Addison Reserve and John's Island Club, "master-planned golf communities" spread like crabgrass in the early years of the twenty-first century.[66]

The hurricanes of 2004 barely dimmed the alluring combination of golf and development. Naples's oldest golf course, the Naples Beach & Golf Club, reopened a week after Hurricane Charley. In 1950, Collier County struggled to support its single golf course. By 2006, Collier claimed the title of America's golf capital, ranked first in the sheer concentration of facilities, on a path to boast 100 courses. Naples bolstered its reputation as having more golf holes per capita than any American city. A promotional guide to golfers on "Florida's Paradise Coast" informs visitors, "Yes, there IS a Reptile Rule!" The brochure reassures golfers that if an alligator interrupts play, one is allowed "a free drop from the nearest point of relief . . . as long as you're no closer to the hole."[67]

Naples and Ponte Vedra Beach share similar profiles belying their sudden growth and reputations as golf centers and wealthy enclaves. In 1942, German strategists selected Ponte Vedra Beach as the site to release saboteurs to wreak havoc upon America, largely because the community south of Jacksonville Beach was so isolated and unsettled. Ponte Vedra may have been small, but it had an impressive golf course attached to the venerable Ponte Vedra Inn & Club.

Ocean Golf Course had been selected as the site for the 1939 Ryder Cup matches. The golf guru Robert Trent Jones redesigned the course in 1947. In the 1970s, developers completed Sawgrass, a world-class golf course that became home to the PGA (Professional Golf Association). The area has evolved to serve as a golf and residential hub for Northeast Florida. Ron DeSantis lived in Ponte Vedra Beach before moving to the Florida governor's mansion.

The golf communities of Palm Beach County rise to the level of the place-name's reputation for luxury and privilege. Consider the Village of Golf, built on a dairy farm in 1956 and incorporated as a municipality one year later to save it from the maws of Delray Beach and Boynton Beach. In 2006, the 542-acre Village of Golf included about 250 inhabitants. The Village of Golf was no ordinary village; it consistently has ranked among the most affluent places in America. In 2000, it was one of a handful of municipalities in Palm Beach County in which all its residents embraced English as the mother tongue.[68]

Top-shelf golf communities in Palm Beach County include BallenIsles, Frenchman's Reserve, Jupiter County Club, Mirasol, and Old Palm Golf Club. Professional golfers Justin Thomas, Jordan Speith, Rickie Fowler, Brooks Koepka, and Smylie Kaufman reside in Jupiter. Jack Nicklaus, Gary Players, Ernie Els, and Tiger Woods also call Jupiter home. Jack Nicklaus lives at North Palm Beach, on Lost Tree, a golf-oceanfront community.[69]

"Donald Trump," writes journalist Alan Shipnuck, "has always been attuned to the status markers of the ruling class. Private golf clubs were and remain a particular obsession with him." As does marrying beautiful women at private golf clubs. In 2005, THE place to host a wedding reception in Florida was Mar-a-Lago Club resort in Palm Beach. Especially if you owned the resort! On 22 January 2005, fifty-eight-year-old Donald Trump and his new bride, thirty-four-year-old Melania Knauss, held their celebrity-list wedding reception at the Mar-a-Lago Club in Palm Beach. Guests included Bill and Hillary Clinton, Billy Joel, Rudy Giuliani, and Tony Bennett. Few understood the importance of a luxury-brand image like Donald Trump. Three of his prize jewels are in Florida: Trump National Doral, an 800-acre luxury resort and golf complex near Miami; Trump National Golf Club in Jupiter; and the Trump International Golf Club Mar-a-Lago, in West Palm Beach.[70]

Those privileged few who have played golf with the star of *The Apprentice*, the face behind Trump Tower, and the future president of the United States all concur that he "doesn't play a round of golf so much as narrate it." When conducting the business of golf, Donald Trump plays hardball. He may lavish praise upon his world-class golf courses, but his lawyers aggressively challenge property tax bills. His personal attorney Michael Cohen confirmed that, among other misdeeds, Trump falsified evidence to devalue the worth of his Jupiter golf club. Trump has quarreled with Scottish officials over a wind farm that he argues spoils the view. When golfing, he likes to take "floating mulligans," a second chance with no penalty.[71]

Trump's love affair with Palm Beach was cemented with the purchase of one of America's most exclusive properties: Mar-a-Lago. Constructed in 1927 by cereal heiress Marjorie Merriweather Post, Mar-a-Lago radiated exclusivity. The 118-room mansion built along an inland waterway that connected waterfront Palm Beach and Lake Worth was one of the wonders of a wondrous decade. In time, it became a white elephant that had few takers. In 1985, Donald Trump purchased the property for $8 million. It became a centerpiece of the Trump empire, gilded by the purchase of the 643-room Doral resort.[72]

Behind the manicured greens and colonnaded clubhouses, developers imposed their will upon the Florida landscape, creating irresistible names—Rookery at Marco and Pelican Marsh, Esplanade Golf and Country Club and Fiddler's Creek, Burnt Store Marina and Tiburon—and irrepressible dreams. No one dreamed bigger—and transformed those dreams into golf communities—than Alfred Hoffman Jr. A Horatio Alger figure, Hoffman grew up in Chicago, where his Austrian immigrant father dressed chickens for housewives of local steelworkers. His pluck and promise earned him entrance into the U.S. Military Academy. "It was hard," he remembered. He rose to the rank of captain, a U.S. Air Force fighter pilot, flying F-100s that carried 28-kiloton atomic bombs. Following military service, he enrolled at Harvard Business School.[73]

Harnessing the discipline and drive that made him a fighter pilot, Hoffman became a home builder. By 1967, he established his own company, targeting Florida. In 1995, he and an old West Point classmate bet boldly on the future. They purchased WCI Communities, a real estate division of Westinghouse Electric Company, for $550 million. The price included 24,000 acres of land, much of it along coastal Lee and Collier counties. Hoffman's vision was shaped by demographics, specifically the waves of affluent seniors who would soon want a slice of the Florida dream. He explained his game plan in 1997: "Couples start out saying, 'Let's buy a place in Florida and we'll go there for vacations.' . . . Then—lo and behold—it becomes a retirement home for them." He was confident that they wanted luxury homes on the water and along golf courses. He doubled down, and WCI purchased all the land from the MacArthur Foundation. The price was $327 million. Wildly successful, in 2004 Hoffman was named "America's Best Builder" for homes priced above a half-million dollars. He also became a passionate fundraiser for Florida's Republican Party, serving as co-chair of George W. Bush's presidential campaign and a big donor to Governor Jeb Bush's causes.[74]

Ebullient over the future of Southwest Florida, Hoffman preached the gospel of development: "You can't stop it. There's no power on earth that can stop it." In 2001, WCI sales in Florida topped the billion-dollar plateau. "The market is so hot," reported Michael Grunwald in the *Washington Post*, "that some builders start moving dirt without permits because fines cost less than brief delays." WCI promoted its developments in the *Wall Street Journal*. One is reminded of the memorable scene from *Godfather II* set atop a Havana hotel: "Here we are," explains Hyman Roth, "protected, free to make our profits without Kefauver. . . . What I am saying is, we have now what we have always needed, real partnership with the government." Florida, not Cuba, made Hyman Roth's dream a reality.[75]

The golf boom in Lee County dated to the late 1970s. The golf community concept germinated with special intensity in Bonita Springs. "Not many years ago Bonita Springs was only a dot on the map," wrote a reporter in 1947. Its tomatoes were renowned. The community was so threadbare during the Great Depression that its citizens voted to surrender the city charter. The population had not yet reached 500 residents. Located along the Imperial River and the Tamiami Trail, and positioned midway between Naples and Fort Myers, Bonita Springs tied its future to tourism and growth. Everglades Wonder Gardens and the famous Shell Factory greeted motorists. By 2005, a dozen golf courses and country clubs, along with myriad subdivisions, marked Bonita Springs as one of the fastest-growing and most affluent cities in America, its population approaching 40,000 residents. Residents and planners were also fearing future developments, described in one headline as a "Sonic Boom."[76]

Whether cloaked in country club exclusivity or plaid-trousers populism, golf matters in Florida. Fittingly, the greatest golfing movie ever made, *Caddy Shack* (1980), was filmed at Rolling Hills Golf Club (now the Grande Oaks Golf Club) in Davie. The film depicted class tensions at the fictional, upper-crust Bushwood Country Club. In real life, Florida golfers display their sense of privilege on and off the fairways. It may be a sport, but this leisure industry relies upon the state, local, and federal political establishment for everything from zoning to tax breaks to environmental regulations.

Golf serves as a cultural weathervane. In the 1950s, civil rights leaders across the South demanded the integration of public-owned golf courses. Civic leaders in Tallahassee, Jacksonville, and other cities advised selling public courses to private interests (often for one dollar) rather than integrate. Even worse, archaeologists discovered a slave cemetery buried beneath the seventh fairway of the Tallahassee Country Club. But in 2005, the issue was green, not black, when environmentalists questioned the profligacy of golf in general, and golf courses especially. "It is worth pausing to consider what a pernicious phenomenon golf truly is," wrote a journalist for *The Guardian.* The author elaborated, "The construction and maintenance of golf courses are harmful to the fragile ecosystems the world over." Sports commentator Frank Deford, while admitting a golf course "is an awfully lovely place to be frustrated," admits "the whole experience, the whole sport, is utterly dependent on one thing: water." Audubon International has calculated that the average golf course uses 312,000 gallons of water per day, although in hot climates, 1 million gallons of water per day is not unusual. "'Environmentally friendly' golf courses are about as common as feminists in a strip joint," quipped Diane Roberts.[77]

Marco Islanders have ample reason to feel blessed and protected. The large barrier island that had sustained Calusa Indians and later fisherfolk and clam dredges leapt into the modern age when the Mackle brothers developed and enlarged the island in the 1960s. Today, former governor and U.S. Senator Rick Scott is a neighbor, and Marco Island boasts three golf courses and thousands of residents who understand a simple rule: water is necessary for Paradise. Lots of water. In 2005, Marco Island City Hall chided 500 residents, all of whom used more than 40,000 gallons of water in a single month. It is not unusual for homeowners to spend $1 million on landscaping.[78]

To paraphrase President Calvin Coolidge, the business of golf is business. Assembling teams of investors, battling nettlesome environmentalists, and currying favor with politicians require planning and lobbying. Al Hoffman and WCI were masters of the task. They built golf course communities across Lee and Collier counties on environmentally sensitive places that panthers and wood storks roamed. WCI rarely lost a wetlands' permit battle. Developers' Florida dream of waterfront golf communities trumped environmentalists' dream of swallow-tailed kites and ghost orchids. Hoffman earned a reputation as a powerful lobbyist and a ferocious fighter. He played polo in the same rugged style he fought regulators and environmentalists, and the ex–fighter pilot felt comfortable schmoozing with the U.S. Army Corps of Engineers. Journalists Craig Pittman and Matthew Waite ask the question: "How could the Corps sign off on all the 404 permits that doomed Bonita Springs to flooding? Simple. The Corps showed developers how to get around its own rules."[79]

The most improbable luxury golf course in Florida may also be the most exclusive. Located between the crosshairs of four Polk County hardscrabble communities—Fort Lonesome, Brewster, Bowling Green, and Fort Green—the Streamsong Golf Resort sits on reclaimed phosphate lands. A monument to the Mosaic Company, Streamsong is also a spectacular example of success and destruction.[80]

Very Conspicuous Consumption

"What is the American dream?" championed a county commissioner. "It's to have a house of your own, the biggest house you can afford."[81]

Forbes claimed that homes located near a Starbucks or Whole Foods store appreciated faster than homes near Dunkin' Donuts. But Whole Foods and Fresh Market seemed blasé to wealthy Floridians, who preferred more trendy stores, such as Sprouts and Trader Joe's.[82]

Wealth was accelerating at warp speed. The Millionaire's Club was once a privileged sanctuary, with very limited seating. A 1950s television show, *The Millionaire,* titillated blue-collar viewers with the fantasy of suddenly becoming fabulously rich. As late as 1999, "only" 7 million American families qualified. A spectacular surge of wealth increased the number of millionaire families to 9 million in 2005. In its 2006 rankings, *Forbes*' list of the 400 richest Americans included *only* billionaires, including twenty-seven Floridians—a sixfold increase in a brief span. Illustrative of the amassed wealth, the *Orlando Sentinel* ran a front-page story in 2005, asking, "What Kind of House Will $1 Million Buy?" The answer—not as much as you'd think! "In this market," explained the *Sentinel,* a dream house "may lack lake and need some fixing up." According to the 2004 report, Palm Beach County ranked first among $1 million homes (9,558), followed by Miami-Dade (7,128), Broward (5,704), and Sarasota (4,441).[83]

Collier County, once one of the state's most isolated and underdeveloped areas, emerged in the 1960s as one of Florida's most exclusive and wealthy places. The U.S. Census of 2010 confirmed what CEOs, Jaguar dealers, and *The duPont Registry* had known for decades: zip codes indicating Naples and Marco Island defined and exuded wealth. Naples trailed only Los Alamos, New Mexico, among cities with the most millionaires. Nearly one in ten Neapolitans was classified as a millionaire. A 2010 report confirmed that Collier County topped the list of places to which wealth was relocating. Naples is home to a Ritz-Carlton Hotel and a Ritz-Carlton Golf Resort. In 2008, this author was delivering a talk at a museum in Naples. A silver-haired attendee asked an earnest question: "Sir, we know that we Naples residents are the healthiest residents in Florida. Some of us think it's the water; others believe it's the pure air. What do you think?" After a pause, I replied: "Well, it's probably because you're rich! You don't need a nutritionist to know that you have better diets and enjoy great medical care." The crowd was not amused by my answer. Only in America would citizens be offended by being called rich! But the residents are correct: the Naples area generally ranks first or second in Florida for healthy living.[84]

New communities emerged as fashionable islands of luxury. The Panhandle's Walton County, home of the New Urban outposts of Rosemary Beach, Seaside, and WaterColor, was voted the fifth-most-popular destination of "rich Americans." Included in that list was Nassau County, located in Northeast Florida and home to the Amelia Island Plantation Resort. In 2010, wealthy Americans ranked Collier County, home to Marco Island and Naples, as their favorite destination to relocate. In a 2006 list of millionaires compiled by the British TNS Financial Services, Sarasota County boasted the greatest percentage of millionaires, as fully 16 percent of its residents qualified as millionaires, as compared to 15 percent of Palm Beach County's residents.[85]

"There are no islands anymore," wrote Edna St. Vincent Millay in the aftermath of the Great War. She was also expressing fears that the world was becoming smaller and places such as her beloved Sanibel would be discovered. Islands once allowed tourists and locals to escape the hurly-burly of daily life.

The power of zoning and regulations help ensure conformity. In 1974, the residents of Sanibel, alarmed at the prospects of overdevelopment, exerted home rule. A city ordinance bans buildings more than two stories high and fast-food franchises. A single Dairy Queen was "grandmothered" in. While sketching the designs that would emerge as Coral Gables, George Merrick famously declared that he wished to create a place "where nothing would be unlovely." Coral Gables has managed to retain Merrick's dream. The affluent residents of the Miami-Dade County community vowed to maintain its sense of scale and charm when Coral Gables banned pickup trucks, pet snakes, and elephants. Homes must be painted "a city-approved hue." In 2007, a homeowner successfully sued the city for the right to park a pickup truck in the driveway. Cross Creek Estates and Coral Springs, among other Florida neighborhood associations, have attempted to outlaw flapping bed sheets on clotheslines, but the Florida Legislature rescued scofflaws with a "right-to-dry" law. A Dunedin man was fined $30,000 for not mowing his lawn. Boca Raton and Palm Beach Gardens ban garage and yard sales. Among the more interesting rebels protesting an obscure Palm Beach County ordinance was Donald Trump. During election week in November 2006, Trump hoisted an American flag atop an 80-foot flagpole outside the Mar-a-Lago clubhouse. County ordinance banned flagpoles taller than 42 feet. "The day you need a permit to put up the American flag," countered Trump, "that will be a sad day for this country." Trump has also quarreled over his desire to build a yacht basin and whether he has the right to declare Mar-a-Lago as his primary residence. "Almost no one," wrote a journalist, "if they have a choice, wants a neighbor like Trump."[86]

Freedom and control may seem contradictory, but not in modern America. Growing numbers of upper- and middle-class Floridians reside in gated communities. Typically, gated communities comprise upper-class, low-density areas, characterized by restricted access. Walls typically surround the community, and visitors must obtain permission at gate-guard houses. Brickell Key in downtown Miami and the Royal Palm Yacht and Country Club in Boca Raton epitomize such lifestyles. Florida's most infamous gated community is the Retreat at Twin Lakes in Seminole County, the site of the Trayvon Martin shooting. Critics contend that gated communities promote paranoia, segregation, and "gated dysunity." Joan Clos, the United Nations habitat chief, labeled gated communities "dystopian," charging, "The ideal city is not one with gated communities, security cameras, a futuristic scene from *Blade Runner*, dark and dramatic with profound unhappiness." A journalist responding to a question about gated communities wrote, "I guess you could say that a gated community is an association with a security gate."[87]

The ultimate illustration of the power of zoning is Florida's Reedy Creek Improvement District. The planning of Walt Disney World involved high-stakes finances, sophisticated technology, state subsidies, secret negotiations, but most of all Walt Disney's zealous pursuit of power, control, and managerial capitalism. Disney's grandest coup may not have been his bold vision but his political shrewdness. A pro-growth Florida Legislature awarded extraordinary powers to the Disney corporation without a public debate. Legislators granted the Reedy Creek Improvement District, a quasi-governmental body controlled by Disney World, sweeping powers to regulate the environment, to tax, police, zone, and seek federally subsidized municipal bonds with immunity from state and local land-use law. Essentially, the corporation was awarded self-rule, becoming, in the words of scholar Richard Foglesong, "a sort of Vatican with Mouse ears: a city-state." State law even allows Disney World the right to build a nuclear power plant on its property.[88]

Vanishing Homes on and off the Road

A perfect metaphor for a mobile state, the mobile home has become such a fixture that Carl Hiaasen's 1987 novel *Double Whammy* introduced a mobile home camp and a trailer park–hating character. He added injury to insult by suggesting that mobile homes "were the reason God had invented hurricanes." Trailer parks and hurricanes may not mix, but in 2000, more than one in twelve residences in Florida was a double-wide serving as "home."

Satirized in pulp fiction and denigrated in real life, the trailer park has provided residents and visitors a slice of the Florida dream for over a century. Tin-can tourist pioneers arrived after the Great War, many of them pulling behind their Model T's homemade "house trailers." Communities along the Gulf coast were so grateful for the visitors that they opened free campgrounds for the motorists. The construction of the Dixie Highway and the Tamiami Trail accelerated the number of snowbirds venturing southward. In 1936, the lowly "house car" acquired an image makeover when Wally Bynam manufactured the first Airstream. World War II so overwhelmed Florida cities with a flood of servicemen and families, along with shipyard workers and migrants, that trailer parks became instant communities to accommodate the newcomers. In 1955, Sydney Adler opened the nation's first mobile-home subdivision in Bradenton. The introduction of the 10-foot-wide mobile home in the 1950s changed the definition of a house on wheels. Too large to be towed behind a Chevrolet Impala, the double-wide was the first trailer to look like a house. By 1965, a journalist observed "a new national housing trend" appearing in the Tampa Bay area. "It's the inevitable offspring of the wedding of two full-grown American housing trends—the boom for the second home and the trek to the trailer park." The fact that so many of the mobile home dwellers were senior citizens made the phenomenon even more striking.[89]

Capitalism constantly reenergizes and reformulates the wants and needs of Americans and their relationship to the Florida dream. From a house trailer to a mobile home to a motor coach, the market has responded with models across the spectrum. Since mobile home parks are typically populated by seniors who vote, politicians listen. In 1965, the Florida Legislature passed a law that taxed mobile homes as vehicles, not residential property.[90]

In a capitalist state, supply and demand determine trends, and by 2000, Florida's love affair waned. In general, mobile home parks were leaving the saltwater-front counties for cheaper venues in the interior. While the overall demand was fading in the decade after 2000, Florida still led the nation in mobile homes and trailers. Reasons for the decline included repossession, the sheer supply of inexpensive housing, insurance problems, fewer trailer communities, hurricanes, and image. Overall, Florida was home to 842,000 trailer-mobile units, a figure that placed the Sunshine State first. Two North Florida cities vied for the honor of America's highest concentration of mobile homes: Palatka and Lake City. In each city, mobile homes constituted over 40 percent of housing units.[91]

A 2002 portrait revealed that Florida's 843,000 mobile homes led the nation, as did its 2,600 trailer parks. Fully one in ten residences in the Sunshine State was a mobile home. For decades, Pinellas County had held the title of mobile home capital. But in Florida's most densely populated county, land was becoming too expensive for mobile homes. Pinellas fell to number two behind Polk County's 84,000 units in 2006. Polk County's agricultural laborers, retirees on fixed incomes, and laboring classes checked all the necessary boxes defining mobile-home culture: warm weather, snowbird migrations, weak credit, little savings, and cheap property.[92]

By 2005, a clear pattern was emerging. For the first time since statistics had been kept, the trailer park was disappearing, threatened by rising land prices, land-hungry developers, and an outburst of hurricanes. Vulnerable tenants grasped to hold on to their units. A state law requires that local governments ensure that comparable housing be available for displaced residents. A law also requires trailer park owners to provide dwellers the opportunity to buy the property before development, but logic, reality, and the laws of economics determine the fate of tenants. Evicted tenants also realize that mobile homes are mobile in name only.[93]

Parsley's by the Gulf perfectly encapsulated a time when mobile home living could be cheap and grand. Opened in 1973 with waterfront views on Redington Shores on the Gulf of Mexico, the complex accommodated 267 mobile homes on 25 acres. But in 2005, Pinellas County's last beachfront mobile home park was purchased for $28 million. In a familiar pattern, expensive developments displace inexpensive mobile homes, whose owners were paying about $500 in monthly rents. Such stories became a daily soap opera. Manatee County was once the epicenter of mobile home life and living, hosting some of America's largest parks. One such place was Bowlees Creek Mobile Court and Marina in Manatee County. In 2005, the owners of the fifty-year-old complex sold the waterfront property for $6.2 million. The new tenants placed down payments for waterfront townhouses. When asked by a reporter about the fate of the doomed trailer park, a lawyer snapped, "The highest and best use of this property is not as a mobile home park."[94]

If holding on to a waterfront trailer park was becoming difficult on the Gulf coast, the obstacles were even steeper along the east coast and Florida Keys. Future generations will not believe that trailer parks where residents paid $425 in rent per month once flourished in the Florida Keys. But the Gulfstream Trailer Park in Marathon was as real as the 2003 rent quote. In the Keys, trailer parks were not simply a refuge for the underclass but rather a vital lifeline for the islands' workforce, especially teachers, waiters, and public workers. The owners sold the property to developers who planned 83 apartments priced from $300,000 to $1 million each. Residents of the Davie Anchorage and the Ponderosa mobile home parks in Broward County received eviction notices in 2005, when owners of the 2.8-acre complex sold the property for $1.3 million.[95]

In 2007, Frank Bates uplifted trailer culture. To some, his creational masterpiece was an homage to an art deco classic; to others, it was simply tacky and a public nuisance. Near Bates's RV dealership on I-4, he created "Airstream Ranch." Employing a backhoe and large crane, he maneuvered eight Airstream trailers upright at a 20-degree angle in the ground. Admirers called it "Florida's Stonehenge," but the Hillsborough County Code Enforcement declared that the display violated zoning and sign restrictions.[96]

In Florida, life often imitates art. Where else would trailer park news make front-page and literary headlines? Middle River was Wilton Manors' last mobile home park. In 1995, filmmakers selected the Broward County complex, defined by a journalist as a "low-rent, funky trailer park," as a setting for filming Carl Hiaasen's novel *Strip Tease.* The park richly earned its notorious reputation. On one occasion, police were called to stop a fight between two men brandishing samurai swords! In the novel, the Demi Moore character arrives at the park to visit her former sister-in-law, who breeds hybrid wolves. A gay resort developer offered $2.5 million for the property in 2010, but the deal collapsed.[97]

The most famous trailer park in Florida will always be known for what might have been. Briny Breezes is a tale of humble beginnings amid a dreamy setting and a reality-show ending. In 1919, Ward Beecher Miller, a retired Michigan lumber dealer, and his wife, Agnes, bought 43 acres in Palm Beach County. The property lay between the Intracoastal Waterway and the Atlantic Ocean. He built a home on the barrier island, naming it Shore Acres. But the Protestant work ethic gnawed at his idleness, and he opened the Shore Acres Dairy. Occasional tin-can tourists camped on his field, and he sold them milk, turkeys, and strawberries. In 1925, he changed the name of his dairy farm to Briny Breezes, subdivided the land into lots, and sold the estate for $2 million. The Miller family reclaimed the property after the real estate bust in the 1920s. By the late 1930s, about forty campers paid three dollars per week rent for waterfront views and breezes. When the war ended, the seasonal residents purchased Quonset huts to be used as an art studio and hobby club.[98]

By the 1950s, the trailer park faithful decided to purchase the property from the Millers. Residents decided to incorporate the tract, and, in 1963, the municipality of Briny Breezes was born. For the next half century, Briny Breezes was largely unchanged, as mobile homes and lots stayed in the same families. A community loudspeaker announced if dolphins were frolicking in the waters; a clubhouse hosting chess and knitting clubs overlooked the beach. Meanwhile, as Palm Beach County became populous and wealthy, high-rise condos in Delray Beach and Boynton Beach flanked the trailer park like ornamental temples. In 2003, a resident died while participating in a fashion show at the park's auditorium. Her husband recalled the outpouring of sympathy from friends and strangers.[99]

In 2006, as Palm Beach County's population approached 1.3 million, developers coveted Briny Breezes' tiny lots owned by the 419 residents. A Boca Raton developer offered $510 million for 43 acres of real estate envisioned for 900 multimillion-dollar condos and a 300-room luxury hotel. Donald Trump, owner of Mar-a-Lago, expressed interest in the property.

But Briny Breezes was no mere Baltic Avenue trailer park; rather, its progressive citizens had created a corporation whose stockholders and voters bound its residents. Each trailer lot was worth almost a million dollars. One is tempted to recall President Lyndon Johnson blustering about converting the Mekong River into a modern Tennessee Valley Authority—if only North Vietnam would sit down at a peace table. As LBJ was departing, he slapped press secretary Bill Moyer's leg, cackling, "Old Ho can't turn me down, Old Ho can't turn me down!" Ho Chi Minh turned the offer down. But North Vietnam was a Communist dictatorship; Briny Breezes was a democracy. A fierce debate covered by seemingly every newspaper in America occurred among residents over quality-of-life issues. "My thoughts are that this is like winning the lottery," insisted resident John Taylor, "but you have to give up your home." He sighed, "I don't want to give up the ocean." Marguerite Sanford, age ninety-six, would not divulge how she voted. She first came to Briny Breezes in 1954 with her mother, who bought property for $2,500 for her single share. She expected to receive $750,000 from the Ocean Land Investment Co. Unbowed, Mikey Rulli voted to turn down a million dollars. "Means nothing to me. Just plain nothing," she sneered, explaining that she spends six months in Pennsylvania and six months in Florida. "I exist up North. I come alive in Briny." In the end, Briny Breezers voted to sell their beloved slice of paradise to developers for $510 million. But a looming recession scuttled the project.[100]

If clusters of trailer parks were fast fading along Florida's coasts, one would be mistaken to assume that investors and big business had lost faith in betting on the future of double-wides. Unlike Jurassic Park, in Florida, life *can* be contained. For many retirees, snowbirds, and poor people, the mobile home is the last and least resort. In real life, while mobile home parks were disappearing in Hillsborough and Pinellas, Broward and Palm Beach counties, new generations sought a place in the mobile home universe in Lee, Pasco, Hernando, Citrus, Gilchrist, Glades, Marion, Dixie, Putnam, and Columbia counties. Typically, such residents are poorer and live on fixed incomes. Journalist Drew Harwell explained why such demographics are so appealing: "A new wave of investors is spending millions to profit off their business, amid a growing market of retirees and working poor who can't live anywhere else. It is a bet on an older, poorer America, to whom mobile homes are a last resort." The double-wide Rubicon was crossed in 2003, when Warren Buffett, the oracle of Omaha, paid $2.7 billion for Clayton Homes, a mobile home conglomerate. Investors know that 10,000 Americans are retiring every day, and that a new generation of double- and triple-wide mobile homes were safer and homier than previous models.[101]

Popular culture still lampoons mobile home denizens as "trailer trash." Not all mobile homes are alike, however, with wealthy Americans also riding the roads in their fancy house trailers. In the luxury division of mobile homes, credentials and mobility are required. Camps catering to upscale motor coaches offer sanctuary for mansions on wheels that cost up to $2 million. In the rarefied air of luxury, Airstreams and Winnebagos are déclassé. Custom-made Liberty Coaches, Marathon Coaches, and Canadian-made Prevosts and Newells compete in a very exclusive market. A single 55' × 100' lot at the Pelican Lake Motor Coach resort in Naples sold for $500,000. Six Lakes Country Club at North Fort Myers offers 600 motor coach lots surrounded by an eighteen-hole golf course.[102]

If a Geiger counter or divining rod were able to indicate cultural creativity, Florida was aglow in the years 2000–2006. One person's creativity and imagination are another's weirdness. To wit, three separate books titled *Weird Florida* were released in 2005. Among the weird sightings: a lady who concealed a stolen parrot in her bra, a Key West man who robbed a bank using a pitchfork, and a motor home in Tampa converted to a strip club. Florida Man was flourishing.[103]

Alligator Wrestling, Bingo Halls, and Casino Gambling

Decimated by Old World diseases and New World alliances, most of Florida's original Natives perished. In the eighteenth century, dissident members of the

Upper and Lower Creek Confederation in Alabama migrated into Spanish and British Florida. They identified themselves as Seminoles. Three Seminole Wars reduced the population of Natives to a few hundred by 1860. Seminoles and Miccosukee—the two groups spoke different languages—found sanctuary in the harsh but isolated Everglades. Until the 1920s and the construction of the Tamiami Trail, relatively few Americans ever encountered the elusive Seminoles and Miccosukee. Buffalo Tiger, who later became a Miccosukee chief, hauled water to the construction crew along the highway. By the 1930s, tourism provided opportunities to sell trinkets and perform "traditional" customs, such as alligator wrestling.[104]

Desperately poor in 1800, 1900, and 1950, Seminoles and Miccosukee endured poverty and discrimination. Popular culture and capitalism first demonized, then romanticized, and finally enriched Florida's Indians. Capitalism connected the most remote parts of the Everglades with cordwainers and milliners in New York and Paris. Indians bolstered their subsistence economy by trading pelts, plumes and hides in Miami, Fort Lauderdale, and Fort Myers. When the first Model T's appeared along the Tamiami Trail, the Natives quickly understood their value as exotic commodities. A journalist writing a 1917 column about the Great Green Corn Dance held at Josie Billy's camp 70 miles southeast of Fort Myers, observed, "The days of the Seminole canoe are numbered and with it comes a change in his mode of living." One year later, a visitor noted "helpless Seminoles" reeling from the influenza epidemic.[105]

The New Deal extended a helping hand to America's most ignored and downtrodden inhabitants. In 1934, Congress enacted the Indian Reorganization Act, seeking to conserve and develop tribal lands and culture. In the 1920s and '30s, three federal reservations opened in South Florida: the Brighton Indian Reservation in Glades County, the Indian Prairie or Big Cypress Reservation in Hendry County, and the enclave in Dania. Others followed, including the Immokalee Reservation in Collier County, the Fort Pierce Reservation, and Tampa Reservation. What had once been cattle pastures, tomato fields, and scrublands in the 1930s evolved into fabulously desirable property amid dense metropolitan populations in the 1970s. In the 1950s, the Miccosukee received federal recognition following a bruising fight. Revolutionary Fidel Castro invited tribal leaders to Cuba, where he recognized the sovereignty of the Miccosukee.[106]

Federal aid can provide relief and recovery but rarely leadership and imagination. Tecumseh was anointed for greatness at an early age, but the same could not be said of the two greatest leaders in Seminole history. Ironically, neither boasted pure Seminole lineage. Osceola, née Billy Powell, was born in 1804 in

Tallassee, Alabama, the mixed-race son of a Creek mother and William Powell, a Scottish trader. A fierce warrior, Osceola was never a Seminole chief. James Edward Billie was a bigger-than-life character: a Vietnam veteran, talented musician, intrepid hunter, but most of all a charismatic leader. A student of the culture argued that he deserves the title "the most powerful American Indian leader of the past century."[107]

Born on a chimpanzee farm in Dania in 1944, Billie lost his mother, Agnes, at age nine and never knew his father, an American soldier. Infanticide was the penalty for bringing a "half-breed" into the culture. Seminole elders seized her baby and took him to the Dania Canal. Betty Mae Jumper rescued the drowning baby. "It wasn't the baby's fault," she told Peter Gallagher. Raised in the traditional Seminole ways, James showed great empathy for the suffering of his people. But James followed his own drummer, enlisting in the U.S. Army at age nineteen, serving two tours as a commando in the Twenty-Third and 101st Infantry in Vietnam. Billie later lost his right ring finger wrestling an alligator. In a case shrouded in myth and legend, Billie infamously killed a Florida panther and then, more famously, was acquitted by a Hendry County jury. A master craftsman at constructing the traditional thatch *chickee*, he returned to the trade after going bust. A talented singer who resembled a cross between Elvis and Johnny Cash, he appeared at White Springs' Florida Folk Festival in 1978.[108]

Billie's worldview, as well as the Seminoles' standing in the world, was about to change dramatically. White Springs appeared in his rearview mirror, while Wall Street lay straight ahead. In 1979, twenty-five-year-old Jim Billie was elected chair of the Seminole tribe. At the time, Seminole income was a half-million dollars; today, Seminole Inc. is a multibillion-dollar enterprise. In a delicious reversal of fortune, James Billie challenged, vanquished, and then co-opted the white power structure. "History will credit Billie as the Indian chief who finally outsmarted the white man," wrote Peter Gallagher, "using white law and white courts to introduce the great new buffalo—casino gambling—to American Indian country." The *Sun-Sentinel* concluded, "The electronic jingle of slot machines, the spirited din of card games, and the loud chattering of gamblers at the Hard Rock Hotel & Casino in Hollywood would hardly have been possible without James E. Billie."[109]

The story of how the Seminoles ventured into bingo halls and casino gambling casino is pure James Billie and Americana. Earning and enduring scars and stripes navigating the competing worlds of American and Seminole life, he recalled: "At home, I was the white boy. At school and in local schools, I was the

Indian." He added, "I learned to fight." As leader, he aimed to improve the material lives of the Seminoles, trapped in generations of poverty. A 1946 headline reported, "Florida Indians Still Live in Their Primitive Fashion." The story noted that only three schools served all of Florida's Seminoles.[110]

An accountant suggested that the Seminoles sponsor bingo games. "What the hell do I want to mess around with bingo? I just imagine it making money," he recalled in a documentary. The accountant then promised that in six months, gambling could yield $3 million in revenues. Tribal attorneys in Washington explained that a bingo hall in South Florida constituted a "gray area" in legal circles. Billie doubled down, bringing aboard a Miami Beach money man, a former associate of Jewish mobster Meyer Lansky. Efforts to expand and enhance the gambling experience were met with a welter of local and state legal challenges. Ultimately, the courts ruled in a landmark case asserting the sovereign status of Indian nations. The opening sentence of Jessica R. Cattelino's book *High Stakes* begins, "At 5 p.m. on December 14, 1979, the Seminole Tribe of Florida opened Hollywood Seminole Bingo on the Hollywood reservation, which is located just a few sprawling suburban miles west of Interstate 95 between Miami and Fort Lauderdale." She adds, "The modest operation was the first tribally operated high-stakes gaming venture in North America."[111]

In 1988, Congress passed the Gaming Regulatory Act, empowering Natives with the "exclusive right" to regulate and operate high-stakes gambling. Perfectly timed, Florida's Native American leadership seized the opportunity. A law professor concluded, "The Seminole Tribe of Florida . . . has played, perhaps, the most important role in the origins and development of Indian gaming in the United States of any single tribe." Today, more than two hundred Native American tribes sponsor gambling enterprises.[112]

In 1980, city officials and businesses launched an ambitious effort to revitalize downtown Tampa. Archaeologists discovered the graves of several Seminoles. Most likely, they died at Fort Brooke while awaiting resettlement in the West. James Billie pleaded that the Seminole ancestors deserved a sacred burial and demanded the city donate land on which the Tribe would erect a cultural center. The city complied. James Billie quickly swapped the land for a site near Interstate 4. A tax-free smoke shop opened, quickly replaced by a gambling casino. Today, a four-star Seminole Hard Rock Café & Casino lords over that once sacred space. A 90,000-square-foot, music-themed casino features five restaurants and three bars. The Seminole Tribe purchased Hard Rock International for $695 million, beating out seventy-two other bidders. The brand stretches cross four continents. James Billie and aides even built a Hard Rock Café in Managua, Nicaragua. The Seminole brand was on a roll, courted by the likes of Donald Trump, who gave James Billie his private phone number, urging, "I want to build your casino." Journalist and former employee Peter Gallagher recalled, "He [Trump] and his associates visited with James Billie for hours and everyone got hungry for lunch. So we cooked up a big plate of wild game, rattlesnake, squirrel and venison, and everybody ate it."[113]

The Seminoles drew a royal flush. But one brass ring eluded Native Americans in their pursuit to acquire more revenue: Class III games, such as blackjack and slot machines. The Indian Gaming Regulatory Act granted tribes sovereignty to build and operate casinos on their property *as long as* their leaders negotiated and signed compacts with state governments to return some of the casino revenue to their respective states. But the legislation also dictated that casinos could not offer patrons blackjack, baccarat, or slot machines unless the state granted permission. Florida had a love-hate relationship with gambling; the state lottery did not begin until 1988. Throughout much of the twentieth century, Florida governors denounced games of chance. Suddenly, the Seminole Tribe became a major player in the Florida Legislature. The Seminoles keenly understood the importance of political friendship; the Tribe consistently ranks among the state's top ten lobbyists. In 2018, the Seminole Tribe contributed $23.4 million to help defeat Amendment 3, a measure that would expand gambling venues in Florida. The Seminole Tribe would soon become the Tribe.[114]

The Seminoles hired James Francis Allen, a casino genius who had once worked for Donald Trump. Allen managed to circumvent state regulations by adopting a new type of slot machine that seemed like the Vegas models but passed the test as Class II slots. Revenues and profits zoomed. In 2017, the Seminoles settled a dispute with Florida over casino blackjack tables. Under the agreement, the tribe will continue to operate its casinos and blackjack tables until 2030. Meanwhile, the Seminoles paid the State of Florida $300 million in 2018. Capitalism creates winners and losers. While the Hard Rock Hotel & Casino triumphed, Florida's racetracks (greyhound and horse) languished, unable to offer slots.[115]

In October 2019, the Seminoles dedicated a $1.5 billion resort in the form of a gilded guitar that soared one-and-a-half football fields high. It sits on land that was once a trailer park. The Hard Rock Live in Hollywood has already booked a who's who of entertainment celebrities to appear at its 7,000-seat auditorium. Hard Rock Live is the centerpiece of an empire that stretches across twenty-eight countries and four continents. Hard Rock now represents a universal brand. In 2007, the Seminoles purchased Hard Rock from a British gaming and leisure company for nearly $1 billion, an investment that shocked many tribes. Under the agile leadership of Max Osceola Jr., the Tribe's investment expanded, and today the Tribe operates Hard Rock franchises in seventy-four countries. Osceola characterized the era of poverty and alligator wrestling before the 1980s as "B.C.—before casinos!"[116]

Casino gambling catapulted the Seminoles and Miccosukee into one of the wealthiest groups in the world. In 2016, *Forbes* estimated the Seminole Tribe's net worth at $12 billion. As of 2019, every Seminole man, woman, and child share an annual fortune that exceeds $130,000 per year. Such largesse is taxable. For a sense of perspective: in 1994, each Seminole received a check for $1,000 per month "just three or four years ago [1991]," recalled a tribal official, "We were only getting $50 a month." Parents may not touch their children's trust, meaning that eighteen-year-old Seminoles share a place in one of Florida's most exclusive societies: millionaires. The process and product have been called everything from sinful dividends to enlightened capitalism. Jessica Cattelino offers another perspective: "Why do outsiders want to know how much each Seminole receives, rather than, for example, how much the Tribe spends on its school, museum, or citrus enterprise?"[117]

Becoming a Seminole was suddenly as fashionable as it was profitable. To be eligible for tribal membership, one first had to prove that one grandparent was a full-blooded Seminole. Tribal membership had doubled between the 1970s and the twenty-first century. On the surface, the "unconquered" Seminoles seemed to be flourishing, even prospering. Even Donald Trump considered building a casino in the Everglades. The Florida State University Seminoles—the school employs the nickname and mascot with the blessing of the Tribe—have excelled as an extraordinarily successful collegiate football program. Since 1978, a student dressed as Osceola and riding the great horse named Renegade throws a flaming spear onto the field before delirious crowds. Gambling proved to be almost recession-proof. Prosperity brought material comforts—Range Rovers and swamp buggies, along with the ubiquitous *chickee*—to people and places that had never known luxury. Pedigrees once scorned suddenly became coveted. "Luxury," warned the Roman poet Juvenal, "is more ruthless than war." Indeed, staggering sums of new money has created a new order of problems: obesity and diabetes, drugs and alcoholism. James Billie has experienced the roller-coaster ride of fame and infamy: twice ousted from his position as chairman of the Tribe, he has faced an investigation by the FBI, lawsuits, and domestic and health difficulties.

On paper, the early years of the new century seemed ideal: the economy was booming, the state tax coffers were filled, and 1,000 newcomers arrived daily. But for many Floridians, the hurly-burly of growth, new highways already crowded, and sprawl without a sense of purpose made less and less sense. Along the Gold Coast, the *South Florida Sun-Sentinel* began asking some tough questions about Florida's present and future. The newspaper launched an ambitious and timely series, "A Vision for the Future." Urban affairs journalists Neal Peirce and Curtis Johnson surveyed what decades of urban growth had wrought. They challenged readers and leaders, "With population booming and gridlock looming, the region needs a better answer than sprawl." The journalists added a personal and regional reckoning. Returning home after a day's work, driving along the Palmetto Expressway, "sandwiched between 18-wheelers, saturated by a day of interviews about sprawl, land scandals, political shenanigans, and a torturously stretched environment, we began to wonder whether the South Florida doomsayers might not be right." But, appreciative of the "dramatic scenes that keep drawing the world here: the glistening glass towers of Brickell, the breathtaking opulence of Palm Beach Island, Fort Lauderdale's revived Las Olas Boulevard and the region's streams of azure waters and broad beaches, they ask, Focus on such sights, and how can anyone think of crisis, or failure?[118]

7

Instant Cities, Boomburbs, and Little Havanas

If a cultural divining rod could detect social and economic creativity in the 1960s, it would have pointed observers of American popular culture and counterculture to California. In the 1980s, Japan became the epicenter for a new creative wave. A decade later, Red China became a capitalist superpower. In the aftershocks of 9/11 and a new world order, Washington, D.C., unleashed the War on Terror, becoming a citadel and fortress. Meanwhile, Florida radiated new forms of dynamism in creative forms of living. In 2004, Michael Paterniti observed, "Right now the tuning fork points to Florida." The Sunshine State functioned as a social and cultural petri dish. Daily, citrus groves and wetlands were transmogrified into places with strange, new names: boomburbs, exurbs, and microburbs. Port St. Lucie and Wesley Chapel, Palm Coast and Palm Bay, emerged as some of the fastest-growing communities in early twenty-first-century America. Entangled in this extraordinary growth spurt was an inescapable conclusion: old age was being redefined in Florida.[1]

Most Americans recognize the familiar names of Orlando, Miami, Palm Beach, and Tampa. Baseball fans have heard the resonant names Clearwater, Winter Haven, and Sarasota from spring training. The relentless promotion of Florida imprinted identities in Americans' minds. Miami became synonymous with *Miami Vice* and Cubans; Orlando was inseparable from Walt Disney World and Mickey, SeaWorld and Shamu; and St. Petersburg signified great-aunts and elderly relatives who moved to "the world's largest above ground cemetery." But recent land booms created new Florida places, many of them among the fastest-growing communities in the new century. Consider the following questions, and how few Americans (including Floridians) know the answers to the game of demographic, but definitely not trivial, pursuit.

The instant cities of Florida's great land boom.

In 2007, what was the largest city in Florida along the Gulf coast south of Tampa and St. Petersburg? Citizens with some knowledge of geography and demography might choose Bradenton, Sarasota, Fort Myers, or Naples as the correct answer. But those answers are incorrect; indeed, Sarasota was not even the biggest city in Sarasota County. Rather, North Port was the county's largest city/municipality. The largest city on the Gulf coast south of Tampa is Cape Coral, with a 2007 population of almost 155,000. Remarkably, Cape Coral's population almost equaled the combined populations of Fort Myers, Sarasota, and Bradenton!

What was the largest city on the east coast of Florida, which stretches 326 miles between Jacksonville and Fort Lauderdale? The answer was *not* West Palm Beach, Daytona Beach, or Stuart; rather, the distinction belongs to Port St. Lucie.

Astounding advances occurred in unlikely places, such as Lee, Collier, Sumter, St. Lucie, and Flagler counties. In 2005, the U.S. Census Bureau named Port St. Lucie (population 118,000) as the fastest-growing large city in the country, a title it had coveted for several years. For much of its youthful history, critics had savaged the St. Lucie County community first platted by General Development Corp. in 1958 on 80 square miles and 80,000 lots. Journalists cruelly lampooned the place "Port St. Lousy," "an ugly town on a numbing stretch of faceless highway lined with shopping centers and honky-tonk bars," and "nowheresville." A local Realtor confessed that in the 1970s, "we were trying to give away lots for $3,000."[2]

Port St. Lucie is more complicated than the caricatures. In 1987, the New York Mets announced they were leaving St. Petersburg for a lavish facility in Port St. Lucie. The team played its first game in Thomas J. White Stadium, named after the entrepreneur who developed St. Lucie West. To add insult to loss, the St. Louis Cardinals then moved their spring training facilities from St. Petersburg to Jupiter. St. Petersburg had also once served as a longtime spring home of the New York Yankees, and as early as 1914 to Branch Rickey's St. Louis Browns.[3]

Port St. Lucie's success mirrored successes elsewhere with the construction of upscale planned communities offering golf courses, security, refined shopping opportunities and low taxes. "It's also a city without much in the way of cultural amenities," carped the *New York Times* in 2007, even though officials planned an ambitious civic center. History offered buyers a jolt of confidence. In 2001, a model home typically sold for $145,000, a price that climbed to $285,000 by 2006. If urban critics would not praise Port St. Lucie, the thousands of new residents added annually embraced the place. The fastest-growing city in 2005, Port St. Lucie was the third-most-robust in 2006, adding 10,000 more new residents. "I used to live in Miami-Dade County," said Mary Clayton, one such new resident, explaining, "Sometimes I like to drive around and look at all the new development."[4]

Palm Coast's surge was as unlikely as it was sensational. Situated between St. Augustine and Daytona Beach, Flagler County had arguably been the state's most lethargic county since its creation in 1917. Despite scenic seashore, Flagler's first census count in 1920 yielded only 2,442 inhabitants, ranking fifty-third-largest of fifty-four counties. A decade later, it ranked last; its largest city was Bunnell.[5]

Flagler County burst upon the front page in the early twenty-first century when demographers identified it as America's fastest-growing county. "Before it became a people magnet," observed the *Miami Herald*, "its biggest claim to fame was Exit 284—where I-95 runs closer to the Atlantic Ocean than at any other exit from Maine to Florida." Increasingly, the press focused upon a little-known place called Palm Coast. In 1969, International Telephone and Telegraph Corporation (ITT) decided to diversify and test its myriad talents in the field of city building. To fortify its efforts, ITT purchased Levitt & Sons, one of America's best-known home builders. Mr. Levitt was famous for Levittown and his quote, "No man who owns his own house and lot can be a Communist. He has too much to do." ITT Community Development Corporation (Levitt) unleashed a bold plan, paying $10 million for 91,000 acres of pinelands and swamps, a swath of land constituting one-third of Flagler County. Interstate 95 passed through the eastern edge of the development. "Bulldozers are already busy at work," a reporter observed in 1977, "clearing the trees that don't conform to ITT's platted plans for a beautiful city." City planners pointed to the 30 miles of canals that would define waterfront lots. Five hundred Levitt salesmen began selling lots and dream houses. This was no five-dollars-down and five-dollars-per-month operation; rather, ITT demanded $500 down for an 80' × 120' lot. Many properties required drainage. The environmentally sensitive Graham Swamp did not survive the developer's wand. The community's first golf course opened in 1971, followed by a second course two years later.[6]

Only two decades after emerging from swamp and scrub, Palm Coast became a municipality as residents voted to transform the unincorporated development into a city. The population at the beginning of the new millennium approached 30,000; five years later the population had doubled. Strikingly, eight in ten residents of Flagler County lived in Palm Coast, designated by the census as a microburb. No county in America claimed a greater proportion of new housing. In 2005, almost 40 percent of the area's homes had been constructed after 1999. Old-time Flagler County residents have dubbed Palm Coast "Palm Jersey" because of all the retired firefighters and police transplants.[7]

Cape Coral epitomized Florida's post–World War II instant cities and buccaneer approach to land sales and environmental regulations. A rustic outpost on the Caloosahatchee River, Harney Point, Henry Land, and Redfish Point served as refuge for cow herders, fishermen, and hunters. Everything changed in 1957, when the Rosen brothers arrived from Baltimore and purchased 107 square miles of land for $678,000, changing the name to Cape Coral and launching the Gulf American Land Corporation. From four homes in 1958 to a population of 32,000 in 1980, Cape Coral prospered. In 2000, the city topped the 100,000-population plateau. Etched into the DNA of future developers, Cape Coral's lessons were clear: relentless salesmanship, blanket advertising and high-volume traffic, a disregard for environmental regulations, and most importantly, location. Developers created a "waterfront wonderland" and a "Little Venice" by constructing 400 miles of canals and waterways. Cape Coral claimed more canals than Venice! Sales brochures offered forty-dollars-down and forty-dollars-per-month "waterfront" and twenty-dollars-down and twenty-dollars-per-month "waterview" lots.[8]

Critics may have satirized the popular destination as "Cape Coma," but Cape Coral officials pointed to the monthly sales figures. Buyers weren't buying a home; they were purchasing a slice of Paradise. During a one-year period ending in 2006, a total of 11,403 new residents made Cape Coral the fourth-fastest-growing city in the United States. If cynics wanted proof of the Florida dream, boosters pointed to the alignment of the stars in 2007: Cape Coral celebrated its fiftieth anniversary, AND its first resident was still living! Home prices matched the confidence: In the spring of 2006, Lee County's median home price rose to $281,000.[9]

Beyond Suburbia to the Edge

Not everyone can afford the comforts of Sanibel and Captiva, Fisher and Jupiter islands. After all, grandparents reminded us that God ain't making any more beachfront. Demand and price tag have exceeded supply and affordability along Florida's archipelagos. But a world of options awaited Floridians in the early twenty-first century. Never had residents enjoyed so many residential choices. Identifying where we lived seemed easy in the 1960s, when one lived on farms, in cities, or in suburbs. But as suburban rings encircled older cities, dynamic growth occurred in suburbs and towns along the fringes. Urban boundaries seemed boundless. Sociologists found new terms to describe new lifestyles and patterns: exurbs, boomburbs, baby boomburbs, and edge cities. General characteristics include sprawl, low population density, urban-size places with a suburban feel.

Modern Florida was built on sprawl. Gadflies have suggested that the Broward County slogan should be, "Sprawl is good." A buzzword for critics of urban gridlock, civic fragmentation, and progressives' angst, "Sprawl," according to a 2000

Pew Center Poll, "has muscled aside education and jobs as Americans' greatest local concern." In the 2000 election, Al Gore's "livability agenda" indicted sprawl as one of the factors eviscerating American society. Lauding Robert Putnam's book *Bowling Alone,* Al Gore became the "anti-sprawl candidate" in the 2000 presidential election. He cited rampant, unplanned growth as a major reason for the decline in social capital. Because parents spent so much time commuting to and from work, and no longer volunteering as much, a sense of anomie and detachment resulted. "Parents want to spend more time with their kids and less time stuck behind a steering wheel," pleaded the unsuccessful Democratic candidate. The Sierra Club defines sprawl as "low-density development that separates where people live from where they shop, work, recreate, and educate—thus requiring cars to move between zones." But to Floridians who battle traffic jams and confront endless blocks of outdated strip malls, fast-food chains, and big-box stores, uncontrolled growth may be likened to pornography: they'll know it when they see it. A 2001 *USA Today* article must have surprised everyone but Marion County commuters when it ranked 271 metropolitan areas and indicted Ocala as the worst example of urban sprawl in America. The Sierra Club selected Orlando as the American metro area with a population between a half million and 1 million that was most threatened by sprawl, with West Palm Beach ranking fourth.[10]

The use of words "suburbia" and "sprawl" cannot accurately explain residential lifestyles during the years 2000–2007. Critics charged that there was no there, there. In a state that once boasted so many distinctive regions, ecosystems, and downtowns, Florida suddenly lacked a sense of place. Journalists at the *Orlando Sentinel* offered this apt description: "It's the office park that suddenly appears where a cypress swamp used to be and the walled-off neighborhood rising in the middle of orange groves. It's the quickie marts and strip malls that follow the new rooftops."[11]

Authors and critics have described boomburbs as "accidental cities," "suburbs on steroids," and "suburbia with permanent sunshine." Fueled by the movements of middle-class families, the boomburbs boomed. Defined as large and rapidly growing places that look suburban but lack traditional downtowns, these have grown dramatically since 1970. Clearwater, Coral Springs, Wesley Chapel, Pembroke Pines, Palm Bay, Viera, Port St. Lucie, Hialeah, and North Port comprise Florida's boomburbs. In Boomburbia, the automobile is as familiar as drive-through fast food and shopping centers.[12]

Hialeah and Clearwater serve as outliers among Florida's boomburbs. Hialeah is desperately poor, unsuburban, and hyperethnic—over 95 percent of residents are Hispanic. On the lip of a quarter-million inhabitants in 2005, Hialeah was the sixth-largest city in the state. But Hialeah could not escape Miami's enormous shadow. Clearwater is the second-largest city in Florida's most densely populated county, Pinellas. Clearwater's inhabitants are much older than those in Florida boomburbs. Downtown Clearwater is the headquarters of the Church of Scientology, creating a difficult, tense relationship.[13]

The exurbs describe rings of prosperous communities that serve as homes for commuters who work in corporate parks or nearby cities. Exurbs explain the growth beyond suburbia to the fringes. They appeal to growing numbers of "executive gypsies." Florida's exurbs lie at the intersection of the American dream and the Florida dream. Automobiles and sunshine, but also aspirations for a better life, define these places so familiar to Floridians. Young families prefer these places because the schools are typically better, and the homes are easy to sell when the inevitable corporate transfer takes place. Sociologists call this class of mobile Americans "relos," aka "executive gypsies." During the boom times in the 1990s and early 2000s, large numbers of Americans fled the cities to seek sanctuary in the reinvented suburbs. Peter T. Kilborn has described the new world of relos' lives, "segregated . . . less by the old barriers of race, religion and national origin than by age, family status, education and, especially income."[14]

One of the consequences of the furious pace of suburbia/boomburbia/exurbia is the rapid decentralization of Florida's population. Commentator David Brooks writes, "People in the suburbs are moving out to the vast sprawling exurbs that have broken free of the gravitational pull of the cities and now exist in their own world far beyond."[15]

Two developments, the Acreage and New River, illustrate exurbia. The Acreage represents one of many new developments in Palm Beach County. Situated near Royal Palm Beach and Loxahatchee Groves, the Acreage sprawls across 30 square miles and three different zip codes. The typical commute time is thirty-five minutes. The Acreage was ranked dead last in "walkability among all Florida communities." In 2012, the community lacked a single park-and-ride lot. The forested community featured large lots (1.15 acres) and single-family homes and boasted a population of about 30,000 by 2005. The Acreage embodied the American dream and included upwardly mobile immigrant Vietnamese and Caribbean families. Similar to the Acreage, New River—an unincorporated development in an unincorporated exurb, Wesley Chapel—also symbolizes a new way of living in a new America.[16]

New River lay in the heart of one of Florida's fastest-growing counties, Pasco. Once a place of cattle ranches, orange groves, and moonshine stills, Wesley Chapel, located near I-75, had grown so rapidly that its population of 37,000 in 2005 exceeded that of the entire county a half century earlier. In 2005, Pasco County recorded 7,252 single-family home permits, or about the number of residents who called the county home a century earlier. Almost one in three Pasco County residents in 2006 arrived after 2000. A 2005 *New York Times* story, titled, "Living Large, by Design, in Middle of Nowhere," described New River as "a square mile of tightly packed houses . . . four miles from the nearest grocery store and 30 minutes from the nearest major mall." Briargrove, the Edge, and New River residents repeated the Florida mantra that growth is good, and that free enterprise will soon fill their social-retail needs. Or, as a local chamber of commerce put it more eloquently, "Retail follows rooftops." Like the way that the opening of a McDonald's franchise in Loxahatchee near the Acreage made the news, residents of New River and other Florida exurbs celebrated the opening of nearby megamalls, Sam's Clubs, and Home Depots. In 2007, Wesley Chapel dedicated its public park, followed a year later by the opening of the Shops at Wiregrass Mall, "an open-air lifestyle center," and still later by the debut of Tampa Premium Outlets and the 7-acre "Crystal Lagoon," a giant aquatic playground. Commuters also had access to Trinity Town Center, a shopping center that opened in 2006. Increasing numbers of Floridians living the two-car, five-bedroom home, and pool lifestyle accepted the tradeoff of long commutes on clogged roads for the promise of upward mobility and family values. Defenders argue that such choices underscore freedom, independence, and the American dream.[17]

Questions persist. What are the limits of gridlock, sprawl, and patience? Is there a tipping point when Americans will say "no" to Florida because of clogged roads, exhausting and expensive commutes, and polluted springs and lakes? Is the end game simply an endless rerun of strip malls, edge cities, and exhaust fumes? Are smart growth or limited growth realistic answers to a democracy where private big-box corner property is sacred? Should choices to live on the edge be liberating or confining? What lies beyond the edge, on the other side of the brink? Former Florida governor and U.S. senator Bob Graham expressed his sadness at the increasing polarization of Floridians, in part the result of massive population influx, sprawl, and sense of dislocation and disorientation: "They went to school somewhere else, they got married somewhere else . . . they spent most of their lives somewhere else. How to get new arrivals to feel a sense of participation in Florida is a challenge." Diane Roberts is less diplomatic, predicting in 2002, "Florida is rapidly becoming one big, green, chemically fed golf course with space reserved for McMansions, fast food alleys and eight-lane expressways so you never have to get behind some Cracker's old raggedy truck on your way to the beach."[18]

Boomburbs have been characterized as "accidental cities." But the once small communities of Coral Springs, Pembroke Pines, and Hialeah have spiraled beyond the 100,000-population plateau. Boomburbs are defined as much by their lifestyles as by their size. "Boomburbs," write two scholars, are "driving cities" and "are much more horizontally built and less pedestrian friendly than most older suburbs."[19]

Baby boomburbs might be thought of as aspirational suburbs. Officially, a baby boomburb "is defined as a suburban city with a population of 50,000 to 100,000 that is not the core city of the region and has a double-digit population growth in each census since 1970." In Florida, they include Boynton Beach, Davie, Deerfield Beach, Delray Beach, Lauderhill, Margate, Miramar, North Miami, Plantation, Sunrise, and Tamarac—all located along the Gold Coast. In 1960, few urban planners would have imagined that these communities would grow as they did; indeed, in 1960, only North Miami had reached a population greater than 11,000 inhabitants. The year 1960 also marked the moment Cuban refugees first touched and then transformed Miami and then South Florida. A half century later, internationalization of South Florida advanced relentlessly, fueling the growth of boomburbs and their babies.[20]

Few places in Florida encapsulate the furious growth more than Broward County. Founded in 1915, a massive landmass larger than Rhode Island, it was a modest entity on the eve of Pearl Harbor, with a population of fewer than 40,000 residents. Broward's reputation as one of America's richest agriculture counties was well deserved, considering no small amount had been reclaimed from the Everglades. Cities such as Deerfield Beach, Dania, and Hallandale once prided themselves upon their agricultural bounty. Pompano Beach High School's nickname was the Bean Pickers! Broward County's population quadrupled during the 1950s, nearly doubled in the 1960s, reaching 1 million in 1980. By 2000, more people lived west of I-95 than east. By 2005, Broward flexed its urban muscles, registering 1.77 million inhabitants.[21]

Broward's influence can be measured in many ways, including its place in American culture. From space, astronauts claim they can identify two human-made objects: the Great Wall of China and the Broward County line! From space, it occupies the glowing center of a megalopolis stretching 100 miles from Palm Beach to Miami. The term "Browardization" has multiple meanings: "New term, old refrain." A website, The Price of Sprawl, defines Browardization as "a term frequently used to describe a place that is overwhelmed with the consequences of over-development." A 2007 *South Florida Sun-Sentinel* editorial defended the county's name, arguing, "Through proper planning, serendipity, and the willingness of voters to expend tax dollars, Broward County has turned into a great place to live, vacation, work and conduct business."[22]

Governor Lawton Chiles once compared Broward County and its twenty-nine incorporated communities to the Balkans. Commentators have called the area everything from "suburbs without cities" to "the posterchild of growth management" to a "Blob." In 2001, the *Miami Herald* offered readers an ambitious, well-researched series titled "Lure of the Burbs: Beyond Broward's Boom." The editors asked for readers' comments, and South Floridians shared their strong opinions about how their lives had been affected by growth and sprawl. The *Herald* published many of the responses, aptly summarized in an article, " . . . Any New Growth Is Bad Growth." Among the opinions:

> "If allowed, they would completely pave over all of South Florida from Naples to the Turnpike without much regard for anything except the bottom line." Chris S. Fennell, Pompano Beach
>
> "Broward has had enough." Coleen Werner, Weston
>
> "To maintain quality of life in Broward County, we must come to the realization that any growth is bad growth." Craig Steinberg, Miami
>
> "I love my hometown, and it saddens me to see all our beautiful nature slowly being reduced to cookie-cutter burbs." James Somers, Fort Lauderdale
>
> "It's time to stop the growth: The concreting and asphalting over everything green. . . . If the developers, the lobbyists and the politicians have their way, everything will be paved over." Ray McCleery, Pembroke Pines.[23]

If Florida were a Frank Capra movie, its citizens would march upon Tallahassee, torches and feelings aflame, throw the rascals out, ban lobbyists, require every Floridian to read Marjorie Kinnan Rawlings's *The Yearling,* and live in harmony. But despite exposé and outrage, the Sunshine State and Broward County experienced even more development, adding 100,000 new residents between 2001 and 2005.

In the last three decades, Broward has become one of America's most diverse places. A 2010 *Miami Herald* headline proclaimed, "Broward Looking More Like Dade." Spanish, of course, is heard frequently, but how many Americans would guess that Hallandale Beach features video stores selling Russian film classics or a Chabad center beckoning Russian Jews? Or that vibrant communities of Colombians, Jamaicans, and Haitians have taken root in Sunrise, Tamarac, Margate, Miramar, and Lauderhill? Many of these families first settled in Miami-Dade County and then moved to a more middle-class lifestyle in Broward.[24]

Central Florida held one incalculable geographic fact over the Panhandle and coasts: no ocean, gulf, or sand dunes could halt the sprawl. In 1950, Orlando was a modest city in the heart of rich agricultural fields and grove lands. No one would have characterized Orlando as "metropolitan." But Metro Orlando, comprising Orange, Lake, Seminole, and Osceola counties, roared after 1971, with the combination of tourism, aerospace industries, construction, higher education, and immigration. By 2005, Metro Orlando's population had reached 2 million, only behind that of Miami–Fort Lauderdale (5 million) and Tampa Bay (2.4 million). By 2006, Metro Orlando had added 53,376 new residents, more than half of them transplants from other states, and nearly one in five from other countries.[25]

T. D. Allman is a trenchant but observant critic of life in modern Florida. In a 2007 essay in *National Geographic*, he described the crazy-quilt patterns of Metro Orlando:

> Everything happening to America today is happening here, and it's far removed from the cookie-cutter suburbanization of life a generation ago. The Orlando region has become Exhibit A for the ascendant power of our cities' exurbs: blobby coalescences of look-alike, overnight, amoeba-like concentrations of population far from the city centers. These huge, sprawling communities are where more and more Americans choose to be, where job growth is fastest, home building is briskest, and malls and megachurches are multiplying as newcomers keep on coming.[26]

The Villages

The 2000 U.S. Census linked Orlando with an unlikely metropolitan partner: The Villages. Questions arise: Since when did The Villages become "metropolitan"? What place is a MUST stop for Republican candidates, sociologists looking to find "Middletown 2005," and retirees who love pickleball and two-for-a-dollar microbrewed draft beers? The Villages, along with Domino Park and the Versailles Café in Little Havana, has become a destination place for journalists, office seekers, and sociologists. The fact that Gary Morse, the heir to The Villages fortune, contributed $500,000 to the Florida Republican Party in 2006 also burnished the images of The Villages with the GOP.[27]

Sprawling across Marion, Sumter, and Lake counties is one of the most fascinating experiments in senior living, but also one of the great success stories in real estate. It is The Villages, a place, or series of places, that defy urban defini-

Table 1. Florida urban growth, 2000–2010

Cities	2000	2010
Boca Raton	74,764	84,392
Boynton Beach	60,389	68,217
Clearwater	108,789	107,685
Coral Springs	117,549	121,096
Daytona Beach	64,112	61,005
Delray Beach	60,020	60,522
Fort Lauderdale	152,397	165,521
Fort Myers	48,208	62,298
Gainesville	95,447	124,354
Hialeah	226,419	224,669
Hollywood	139,368	140,768
Jacksonville	735,617	821,784
Lakeland	78,452	97,422
Largo	69,371	77,648
Melbourne	71,382	76,068
Miami	362,470	399,457
Miami Gardens	—	107,167
Miramar	72,739	122,041
Ocala	45,943	56,315
Orlando	185,951	238,300
Palm Coast	32,732	75,180
Pembroke Pines	137,427	154,750
Pensacola	51,923	56,255
Port St. Lucie	88,769	164,403
Sarasota	52,715	51,197
St. Petersburg	248,232	244,769
Tallahassee	150,624	181,376
Tampa	303,477	335,709
West Palm Beach	82,103	99,919

Source: *Census Population Counts by County and City, 2000–2010 Florida Population: Census Summary 2010,* April 2011 (Bureau of Economic and Business Research, University of Florida, 2011), table 1.

tion. Few could have imagined the future, when, in the early 1970s, Michigander Harold Schwartz purchased Orange Blossom Gardens, a run-down trailer park sitting along US 27/441 in a cow pasture in northwest Lake County. It was as if Schwartz's life had prepared him for this moment in the sunshine: He had sold swampland out of Chicago boiler rooms and helped launch the career of DJ Wolfman Jack at a pirate radio station in Mexico. A decade later, Schwartz's dream amounted to only 400 mobile homes, so he asked his stepson, H. Gary Morse, to convert a trailer park into The Villages, a massive collection of retirement communities. Schwartz's statue greets visitors to Lady Lake Villages' town square. When he died in 2003, fabulously wealthy, he was residing in a manufactured home on the grounds of the original trailer park. His ashes rest inside the statue of his likeness in the fountain of the Spanish Springs Town Square.[28]

The population of The Villages tripled between 2000 and 2007, when 64,000 residents called the communities south of Ocala home. H. Gary Morse proved to be a very adept successor to his stepfather. In 2012, *Bloomberg* summarized Morse's accomplishments: "On 33-square mile parcel 15 miles south of Ocala . . . he's built and sold more than 44,000 homes since 1983." The Villages has been the subject of several books. Professor Stephen Golant argues its success can be understood in one word: control. At least one resident of every living unit must be fifty-five years old or older. Grandchildren may visit *up to* thirty days a year. The Villages even publishes its own newspaper, the *Daily Sun*. "The land uses are under control," Golant writes. "The people in the neighborhoods are under control." While downtowns never evolved over time, developers have built town centers, such as Spanish Lakes and Lake Sumter Landing. Politically, The Villages, like Walt Disney World, certainly has imposed its will upon neighbors. The Villagers take pride in their reputations as some of the most conservative voters in Florida, a standing that brings many state and national leaders to Lady Lake Villages town square to launch their political campaigns. Richard Cole, a local Republican leader, explained the phenomenon: "It's safe to say that the road to the White House is through Florida, and the road to Florida is through The Villages." He added, for emphasis, "We're a substantial political force." President Bush became the first sitting president to visit The Villages in 2004.[29]

Perhaps the only real-world issue uniting Villagers is a burnished, candy-apple red 1966 Mustang golf cart! A perfect vehicle for a place called "Disney World for Old People," an estimated 40,000 golf carts roam the communities' 26,000 acres, its two zip codes, its streets, its driveways, and even the thirty-one golf courses. Illustrative of the senior citizen lobby, the National Highway Safety Administration established a new category in 1998 called low-speed vehicles.

The new law allowed golf carts to motor along on public roads with speed limits up to 35 mph. Pimping and tricking out one's golf cart represents a competitive sport: one commentator compared the practice of installing Rolls-Royce grills onto golf carts to World War II fighter pilots emblazoning their girlfriends' names on P-38 Lightnings and P-51 Hellcats. "Others have carts painted with patriotic eagles or American flags or the symbol of a beloved sports team," wrote a journalist. "These folks go to church in their golf carts," swore a local. In 2005, The Villages became famous for setting a *Guinness Book* world record by forming a line 3,391 golf carts long.[30]

Tampa Bay

On the West Coast, Hillsborough County also experienced explosive growth. By 2006, it ranked thirty-second among the nation's most populous counties. But whereas Miramar and Pembroke Pines expanded within the boundaries of incorporated cities, Hillsborough County typified the dynamics of growth largely outside municipal boundaries. While Tampa is the county's most significant city, its most significant "noncity" is Brandon. Named after a Mississippi Civil War veteran who farmed the area in the nineteenth century, Brandon remained a rural hamlet until the 1960s. Once famous for its high-quality strawberries, it is now infamous for its unbridled growth. In 1960, census takers counted only 1,655 inhabitants; by 2000, the unincorporated community of 80,000 sprawled over 35 square miles. Brandon had become the nineteenth-largest "city" in the state, a place city planners come to study unplanned sprawl. A journalist volunteered that Brandon "looks as if it were created to make idealistic city planners cringe. It has it all: bad traffic and random sprawl, cul-de-sac subdivisions with nowhere safe to walk or bike. No downtown. No central gathering spot for concerts or socializing." In other words, Brandon is a suburb without a city. The heart of Brandon lies about 13 miles east of downtown Tampa. An interstate highway and an expressway connect Brandon with downtown Tampa.[31]

The 1990 census validated Brandon's arc: More Floridians resided in unincorporated areas than incorporated municipalities. Suburbia verified that more and more Floridians wanted what unincorporated communities offered residents: a feeling of security, affordable homes on big lots, schools without inner-city problems, and most importantly, a refuge from high crime, dysfunctional schools, high taxes, and urban planners telling them how to live.

Hernando County was once one of Florida's most underdeveloped areas. As late as 1950, its population was fewer than 6,700 residents. By 2005, Hernando had rocketed to about 150,000 inhabitants, but boasted only two incorporated communities. Brooksville, the county seat, was a sleepy town of 7,844 people. Weeki Wachee, with a population of 19 souls and some of the world's greatest natural springs, had the distinction of being one of Florida's smallest cities. But the village of Weeki Wachee functioned as a tax haven. The largest community in Hernando County was Spring Hill, an unincorporated enclave (no mayor or police department) of 75,000 residents in 2005. Developed by the famous team of the Mackle brothers and Deltona Corp., Spring Hill is a retirement "city."[32]

New Cities on Everglades Muck, Sand, and Tomato Fields

No region of Florida had developed more slowly and unevenly than Southwest Florida. For most of Florida's history, Collier County belonged to the frontier, raw and uninhabited. In the early 1920s, a hydroplane crashed in the Everglades. Yet, no telephone equipment connected Everglades City and Fort Myers. Since 2000, the region has witnessed some of the state's most rampant growth. As late as 1950, Collier County, with a landmass of 2,000 square miles, claimed only 6,448 residents, and as late as 1970 had not cracked the 40,000 mark. Collier County seemed too isolated to participate in the land stampede, but the 1980s opened the floodgates. Vital transportation links came together in the 1980s: Interstate 75 finally reached Collier County, while Fort Myers completed the modern Southwest Florida Regional Airport, soon to become Southwest Florida International Airport. In 1992, Alligator Alley was widened to four lanes, allowing a speedy connection to the East Coast. Developers had long understood the importance of transportation. Barron Gift Collier owned vast tracts of beachfront and wetlands that became Collier County in 1923. His timely investment and intervention ensured that the Tamiami Trail, US 41, swerved into his domain.[33]

Everglades City may have been Collier's company town, and nearby Goodland may have been an authentic fishing village, but they never exuded luxury and certainly not privilege. Nature revealed Everglades City's limitations; humans improved upon nature in shaping Naples into a dreamscape. In 1960, Hurricane Donna punished Everglades City so severely that officials soon moved the county seat to upstart and upscale Naples. A 1959 *Newsweek* magazine headline announced, "See Naples . . . And Live Lushly." In 1950, Naples was a modest town of 1,465 inhabitants. Founded in the 1880s, Naples-by-the-Sea catered to Kentucky colonels and northern invalids. As late as 1949, the city did not boast a single bank. A half century later, banks seemingly appeared on every corner of the bustling city. The business publication *Florida Trend* reported in 1959 that

Naples claimed, "more important industrialists per capita . . . than any American city." Glenn Sample, an advertising guru, envisioned Naples as a destination place for millionaires. He helped transform the community with the first luxurious development, Port Royal, in the 1950s. In 1950, the first homes in Port Royal were sold for $22,000. "The same lot that sold for $12,000 in 1960 had a selling price of $3.5 million in the early 2000s," wrote a local reporter. By the 1970s, Naples was the fastest-growing city in the fastest-growing county in the fastest-growing state in America. The seemingly impossible occurred in 1982, when Collier County topped the 100,000-population milestone, only to reach 200,000 fourteen years later.[34]

By the early twenty-first century, the Neapolitan metropolitan area ranked first in per-capita income even though fewer than half of its residents worked for weekly wages. What was once seen as an impossibility had become reality, thanks to Social Security and Medicare, statin drugs and improved medical care, prosperity and generous American tax laws. Naples is home to Ann and U.S. Senator Rick Scott; Shahid Kahn, the owner of the NFL Jacksonville Jaguars; and Tom Golisano, founder of Paychex and former owner of the NHL Buffalo Sabers.[35]

The crown jewel of Florida's Southwest frontier was Marco Island, located 12 miles south of Naples. The largest of the Ten Thousand Islands, Marco Island boasted a storied past as a Calusa stronghold, a fishing mecca, a clam factory at Caxambas, a modest Marco Inn and Lodge, and a missile tracking station. Perhaps most dramatically, in 1896, archaeologist Frank Cushing plucked out of a muck pond carved and painted wooden masks and the renowned Key Marco cat. Time seemingly had stood still, but everything changed in 1964. Local and national investors invited the Miami-based Deltona Corporation to develop Marco Island. Headed by three talented brothers, the Mackles had already succeeded in a few Florida projects, but nothing as dramatic as Marco Island. The blueprints revealed almost 11,000 homesites. To ensure that most residents had waterfront or water-view homes, developers moved 35 million cubic yards of earth to create thousands of lawns and waterways, interlacing the island with 91 miles of canals, dredged and diked for mosquito control. The mangrove coast was so obliterated that a 1975 newspaper article titled "Development vs. Destruction" began, "Yes, Virginia, you can still find mangroves growing on Marco Island." Parts of Marco Island that had been dredged and filled into finger islands resembled a zipper. Environmentalists be damned! The Mackle development benefited handsomely from the relatively few toothless environmental laws that would confront future projects. Sales began in 1965, as did the island's first condominium, Emerald

Beach. Prices ranged from $19,900 to $49,500. By 2010, Marco Island claimed a population of 16,500 year-round and part-time residents.[36]

The land rush was on. Golf courses, condominiums, and finger canals left their imprint on Collier County. Not every visionary succeeded. The Rosen brothers, following their fabulous Cape Coral success story, followed the crowd to Collier County. Their Gulf American Corporation eyed the fabled and precious Fakahatchee Strand, purchasing a swath of cypress and Everglades the size of Manhattan. The presence of standing water might have spooked other investors, but the Rosens pushed forward with the marketing and design of Golden Gate Estates. Gold deposits turned out to be quicksand. Today, the remnants of a sprawling city that never was lies abandoned and neglected, a Machu Pichu with roads but no people.[37]

By 2010, Collier County's population had risen to 322,601 people. When describing the county's dramatic growth, commentators typically referenced the concentration of wealth and power in a place that had little of either until recently. But Collier County is also home to concentrated poverty. Observers note the evening rush hour transporting large numbers of maintenance and service workers to their modest homes outside Naples. While Naples ranked second nationally in its proportion of millionaires, the inequality in Naples–Marco Island also ranks second nationally. Fifty miles separates Naples and Immokalee, but socially and economically the gap is much greater. The home to tomato fields and Hispanic farmworkers, Immokalee struggles. One in four residents of Collier County is Hispanic; seven in ten residents of Immokalee are Hispanic, and 20 percent African-American.[38]

New Urban Perfection and Real-World Imperfection

Every man/woman, young and old, Black and ethnic, gay and straight, Democrat and Republican, Cuban and Yankee, New Urbanist and old-school developer, found a niche in Florida. On the edge of the Everglades and in some of Florida's seediest quarters, another group of Floridians coalesced but coerced. Once home to workers in the sugarcane fields, Miracle Village near Pahokee became a refuge for America's most unwanted, stigmatized humans—sex offenders. Organized by Matthew 25 Ministries, Miracle Village is home to about one hundred registered sex offenders. Florida state law prohibits such individuals from living within 1,000 feet of a school, park, or playground. Florida has struggled to find a home for such individuals. Another such refuge of registered sex offenders is Palace Mobile Home Park in Pinellas County, a place once called "Pervert Park." In 2007, half of the trailer park's residents were convicted sex offenders.[39]

Among the state's 73,000 registered sex offenders are 10,000 senior citizens, challenged by both the infirmities of age and the stigma of their past. "Nobody wants a sex offender," explained the ex-wife of one such resident. A journalist asked, "How and where do we allow the most-reviled class of citizens to survive their senior years—especially those with serious age-related medical problems—after they have served their prison terms, while striving to protect children who may be living nearby?" The State of Florida imposes some of the nation's most restrictive challenges to sex offenders. All convicted felons must possess a driver's license or state ID, even if homeless. In Miami-Dade County, restrictions force many of the homeless sex offenders to live under overpasses.[40]

Perhaps the only group envious of Miracle Villagers were the 100,000 Floridians incarcerated in Florida prisons. A growth industry, prison-building was recession-proof in a state where the number of inmates was growing faster than the population. Only Texas incarcerated more persons at a higher rate than Florida. Paralleling developments in education, increasing numbers of Florida prisoners were being outsourced to private facilities.[41]

Florida may have been prosperous, but urban planners and the national press generally lampooned the Sunshine State as sliding swiftly down a slope to Nowheresville. Unrelenting growth was eroding its distinctive identity. Floridians once took great pride in the originality and vitality of small towns and big-city neighborhoods. Rebelling against the uninspired uniformity sweeping across America, the New Urban movement rose to re-create a sense of place.

Walton County Road 30-A seemed an unlikely spot to unveil daring new architectural designs. Its dense tracks of yellow pine had been plundered in what locals called, "cut out and get out logging." After World War II, it was part of what was proudly and derisively called the "Redneck Riviera," the sparsely populated cape of land between Destin and Panama City with summer beach cottages and sawmills, oyster bars and fish camps. High season along the Panhandle occurred in summer, not winter. By 1980, Walton County's population had grown to 21,300, up from 14,576 a half century earlier. If one had a crystal ball in 1980, few soothsayers would have predicted significant experiments along Highway 30A affecting the way we lived and played. The die had seemingly been cast. Destin and Panama City, noted local historian Harvey Jackson III, were battling as to see who could be the tackiest. Panama City may have been the first city to outlaw "drunk walking." "Concrete condominiums," wrote journalist Rick Bragg in 2000, "as imposing as anything in Miami or Fort Lauderdale line the beachfront on both ends of the paradise, blocking views of the Gulf." From the vantage point of Destin, writes historian Jack E. Davis, "high-rise complexes multiplied eastward down the beach, as if the wind had disseminated the seeds of that original invasive species. Mile after mile they popped up, until the Walton County line."[42]

Although history is shaped by powerful social and economic forces, individuals also alter its course. Such was the case with Robert Smolian Davis. The son of successful Jewish merchants in Birmingham, Alabama, Davis nostalgically recalled joyous and unhurried summers spent on Walton County beaches. The Davis family had built a modest wooden home at Grayton Beach. The nineteenth-century Washaway Hotel, built of legendary West Florida yellow pine, stood nearby. In 1946, Davis's grandfather, Joseph Smolian, purchased 80 acres of land between Grayton Beach and Seagrove Beach, undisturbed land that included a half mile of beachfront. He dreamed of developing the property as a weekend retreat, "a summer camp for the employees" at his Pizitz Department Store in Birmingham.[43]

Enjoying the luxury of a humanist education at elite northeastern schools and an MBA from Harvard, Davis moved to Miami in the early 1970s, becoming a successful builder of "tropical-modern" townhouses in Coconut Grove. Never abandoning his ideals, Davis, whom Jack Davis described as possessing "an unassuming dignity," celebrated 1978 by getting married and inheriting his family's undeveloped beach. Together with his wife, Daryl Rose, he toured the coastal towns of Italy and France. Enchanted by the lively village markets and urban architecture, they returned to a Florida that was increasingly becoming tasteless. The couple shared a vision: they wanted to restore a sense of community and re-create Old Florida. They named their dreamscape Seaside. Cooperating with two young, talented architects, Andrés Duany and Elizabeth Plater-Zyberk, their vision included some daring concepts. No buildings would be constructed upon the beach or dunes; all structures would be built of wood frame. Second, they dictated strict design and zoning guidelines. Every home must include a front porch, screen doors, and picket fences. Codes banished fast-food restaurants, strip malls, and asphalt parking lots. Streets were paved with oyster shells. The ideal of "New Urbanism" was the retro concept that Seaside would become a community where home, work, and shopping came together, as American neighborhoods once functioned.[44]

In planning Seaside, the 80-acre site turned out to be the perfect size for a small town. Urban designer Leon Krier maintained that a quarter-mile radius happened to be the distance citizens would comfortably walk to a favorite shop or work. Krier was awarded a Seaside lot for his efforts. Every shop, home, and café in Seaside lies no more than a quarter mile from Seaside's town center. A model design was Baron Hausmann's nineteenth-century renovation of Paris. With the stress on pedestrianism and social cohesion, Seaside embodied "smart growth" principles. Its founders sincerely believed meaningful architecture and sound urban planning had the power to modify human behavior. Perhaps most dramatically, Seaside envisioned the Gulf beaches, not as the exclusive domain of seaside dwellers but as a communal treasure for all to enjoy. The founders erected the Palladian-inspired Seaside Arch, a beach pavilion painted eggshell blue, to serve as a communal gateway to the sea. Locals scoffed at the notion of paying premium prices for lots not even on the beach. The first lot was purchased by an auto dealer from Anniston, Alabama, for $7,500. The early homes and shops were so modest and reminiscent of beach architecture that Davis admired—the Seaside Grill was a recycled sharecropper's home—that critics called them "shack-vernac." Harvey Jackson III contends that Robert Davis was a romantic. He dreamed of re-creating the Florida he had known when he came to the beach as a child.[45]

In 1981, the Davises kickstarted Seaside by building a modest cottage for themselves. But principles and prophets can be thwarted by principals and profits. Seaside was becoming a wildly popular resort town with relatively few year-round residents and year-round traffic headaches. Designed for the middle classes, the original homes cost $100,000 in the 1980s; some of the early lots sold for as low as $15,000. Seaside's cachet has resulted in skyrocketing prices. By late 2001, 430 Seaside "cottages" comprised the housing market. The average cottage and small lot sold for $850,000. In the fall of 2005, the most affordable property was a one-bedroom, 825-square-foot condo named "Cork the Whine," listing for $825,000. Harvey Jackson III observed the transition from his family home in Seagrove. By the late 1980s, commented Jackson, the typical new owners "were very different buyers from those who came first, for they had no intention of becoming residents, not soon, not ever." Most homeowners use their Victorian vernaculars as second homes and rent them out the rest of the year. Seaside's legendary beaches took a beating in 2005 when Hurricane Dennis washed away 10 feet of sand dunes.[46]

In 1990, *Time* magazine surveyed Seaside, concluding, "The heterogeneity is real; the harmony is deep. Seaside could be the most astounding design achievement of the era." Robert Stern, dean of the Yale School of Architecture, argued, "More than anywhere else in America, development in Florida proves that architecture and urbanism can transform the whole image, the value of the place."

Seaside's greatest compliment was imitation; a journalist insisted that Seaside "is America's most imitated town." Developers counted the news clippings and auto traffic surrounding Seaside, and CR 30A quickly became a colorful collection of New Urbanist communities. On the western edge of Seaside sprang WaterColor, a 500-acre emulation of its neighbor. To the east, Rosemary Beach, a Dutch-West Indian–Caribbean-themed community, replaced quaint wooden cottages. The speed limit in Rosemary Beach is 17 mph.[47]

Seaside's mythic place in American culture arrived in 1998, when filmmakers arrived to shoot a movie about a white-picketed fence and pastel-painted place where everything seems perfect. *The Truman Show* and Seaside blurred art and life. Seaside's image has suffered because of its association with a Hollywood movie parodying an imagined perfect place and free market forces that drove away the middle class and Seaside's middle-class dreams. Defenders rightly point out that Seaside's residents allowed *The Truman Show* to be shot on location, to help fund a charter school. Ironically, the film depicts Truman's home manicured with a perfect suburban lawn. The grass was a stage prop since Seaside encourages xeriscaping and indigenous plants.[48]

The driving force behind WaterColor and WaterSound was the St. Joe Company. The corporation sprang from the vision of one man, the irascible Ed Ball, quite possibly the most powerful man in Florida history. While Ed Ball never held political office, he had the good fortune of becoming the brother-in-law to one of America's wealthiest men: Alfred I. du Pont. Upon the Du Pont–Ball marriage in 1921, Ed began managing some of his brother-in-law's sprawling business interests. Fiercely conservative, Ball rejected the glitter of Florida's Gold Coast, preferring to invest in North and West Florida. When Du Pont died in 1935, Ball became the chief trustee of the business holdings. Ultimately, the Du Pont estate became the state's biggest banker and railroader, but also the state's largest private landholder. Ball was most comfortable managing the St. Joseph Paper Company. Located in the company and factory town of Port St. Joe in Gulf County, Ball quietly gobbled up hundreds of thousands of acres of Panhandle timberland. In 1925, Ball negotiated with the Santa Rosa Plantation Company, purchasing 34,000 acres of cutover timberland in Bay and Walton counties. The purchase included 40 miles of snowy-white, undeveloped beachfront. The sales price was twelve dollars per acre. Ball's legacy also included a modern highway system that crisscrossed Florida's poorest region. Ferocious and blunt, Ball helped create the Gulf Coast Highway Association to pave roads so trucks carrying lumber and cars bringing tourists could improve the Panhandle and enhance his bottom line.[49]

Ball's sole passion was making money and protecting his investments; he cared little for the region's unique dune lakes or the distinctive biodiversity. He stayed at modest hotels and conducted business across cast-iron stoves and kitchen tables. Providentially, Ball's land empire abutted the Davis "postage stamp" of land in Walton County. A future playwright will no doubt dramatize what Ball, who controlled more than 1 million acres of Florida timberlands might have said to or thought of his neighbor Robert Davis and his teeny 80-acre bit of land. Or what he would have thought of Davis's work at a Black college, his founding role of the Congress for the New Urbanism, his creation of a Seaside Institute modeled after Aristotle's Greek academy, or his townhouse designs in Coconut Grove?

The new St. Joe Company was not your grandfather's St. Joseph Paper Company; indeed, in 2003, the paper mill was literally blown up. Ed Ball died in 1981, ironically the same year Robert and Daryl Rose Davis built their first home in Seaside. New leadership realized the future was land, not woods. In 1997, the St. Joe Paper Company morphed into the St. Joe Company. The significance of the name changes quickly became apparent: the announcement of an ambitious project: WaterColor. The New Urbanist community may have bordered Seaside, but it entertained none of the populist modesty of the Mother of New Urbanism. "Starting at $1 million, WaterColor's were manor-born, not cracker-style homes," observed Jack Davis. Yet in a move that must have made Ed Ball reel in his grave, WaterColor's first hire was a horticulturist![50]

In 1997, the St. Joe Company introduced its dynamic new CEO, Peter Rummell, a former Disney executive. Land, not timber, was the oxygen of the St. Joe Co. The corporation owned 1 million acres of Florida real estate, and to create a new brand, the Panhandle became "Florida's Great Northwest." To bring tourists and prospective buyers into the area, lobbyists and politicians envisaged the Northwest Florida Beaches International Airport in Panama City. It should be added that the St. Joe Co. has been a sensitive steward of the environment. To design WaterColor, St. Joe hired Robert Stern, the heralded dean of the School of Architecture at Yale.[51]

Alys Beach, unveiled in 2003, represented the boldest architectural statement of the four archetypes of New Urbanism on CR 30-A. To some, the dazzling white buildings remind them of Moorish Morocco; to others, they harken to Greece or Bermuda. Designed by Andrés Duany and architects Erik Vogt and Marieanne Khoury-Vogt on 158 acres a half mile west of Rosemary Beach, Alys Beach featured private walled courtyards instead of front porches.[52]

The most controversial, anticipated, and ambitious experiment in New Urbanism began in Osceola County in the middle of a cypress swamp on the farthest edge of Walt Disney World. Celebration was not simply another artsy subdivision, but a $100 million, 11-square-mile Walt Disney World–branded enclave, the brainchild of wunderkind Peter Rummell. Americans held Disney in such esteem and trust that nearly 5,000 persons waited in line to make a deposit in the hope of being among the first wave to move into Celebration. A lottery selected the 350 "winners." More than just a new house, Celebration seemed to offer residents a social covenant, an opportunity to find a sense of place and community amid like-minded communitarians. If Walt Disney World had the brains and skills to design the "Happiest Place on Earth," just imagine what it could accomplish in real-world neighborhoods and schools. The Disney name promised homesteaders a handsome dividend when they sold their Fantasy Land property, even if they had overpaid to be first in line.[53]

Celebration imposed mandatory guidelines that seemed odd to some, such as curtains facing the street had to be neutral-colored and specified plant varieties for front yards. Homes must conform to pre-1940s southeastern vernacular architecture. The only chain store remains the compulsory Starbucks. Douglas Frantz, Catherine Collins, and their two children joined the first wave of newcomers in 1997. Residents loved that Frantz and Collins were also writing a book about their experience. They later wrote that despite some oddities, "there was a spirit of camaraderie that everyone embraced, even we skeptics." Andrew Ross, a New York University professor, also became a Celebration resident while writing a book about his experiences and observations. He concluded, darkly, that Celebration instilled "a hunger for civic order at all costs."[54]

Celebration attracted its fair and unfair share of critics and boosters. One journalist observed that the "town represents an ambitious, real-life attempt by Disney to employ architecture and urban design to revive the sense of community and place that Americans tell pollsters are missing in the traditional suburbs." "But Disney's expertise is in building theme parks for paying guests," argued social commentator Michael Pollan, "not towns for citizens." By almost any standard applied to urban living—the quality of the homes, schools, and neighborhoods—Celebration deserved scant celebration. Cultural critic Mark Greif unloaded, calling the experiment a "Potemkin Village." He argued: "The pioneers who took out crippling loans . . . to become the first residents of Celebration did so for some admirable reasons. Many wanted a more neighborly community. Some wanted their children to grow up with open space and sidewalks and a sense of place. . . . There was a water tower that dispensed no water," he wrote. He might have added that there was a handsome French bakery constructed of irregular stones that baked no pastries or bread. Some residents sued, pointing out leaking roofs and poorly installed balconies. But developers delivered a charming retro, two-screen movie theater designed by César Pelli. The theater closed in 2010. But it was the profound disappointment with the public schools that hurt the most. Disney's efforts to create small-town values smacked against reality. Celebration was not immune to violent crime, disappointing schools, and urban woes. Frantz and Collins moved away in 1999, reminiscing: "The pixie dust had begun to fade for some of the diehard believers. There had been a spate of divorces, a couple of domestic abuse cases, a handful of stolen bikes and even an armed robbery." Residents also discovered that houses had been shoddily constructed. In 2010, the first murder shocked residents.[55]

The early twenty-first century's New Urbanism footprint spanned Florida from the Panhandle to Central Florida to Miami. Projects included Avalon and Baldwin Park in Orlando, Southwood in Tallahassee, Longleaf (Pasco County), Abacoa, Astor, Latitude, and Cannery Row (Palm Beach and Volusia counties), and Mizner Park in Boca Raton. Critics unloaded, none with more wrath and credibility than Diane Roberts, whose ancestors arrived with General Jackson's invasion in 1818. She grieves for her beloved West Florida, the so-called Other Florida. In a barrage that Old Hickory would admire, she editorialized in 2002: "St. Joe will redraw the map with bulldozers, the promise of 'maximizing economic opportunity' in hardscrabble Panhandle counties, and taxpayer money." She added: "St. Joe claims they want to preserve the 'character' of the places it bulldozes. But obviously all these little red-neck towns would be so much nicer with more Range Rover dealerships, faux Seaside houses, sushi places and marinas where regular citizens like you and me can park our yachts."[56]

A PBS documentary, *Imagining a New Florida,* brought together an assortment of academics and urban planners to exalt the glories of New Urbanism. Ray Oldenberg, a University of West Florida sociologist who famously coined the term "Third Place," opined, "I can't imagine as a child growing up in a subdivision. To me, it seems just terrible." Another academic postulated that sprawl and suburbanization of America have "created a profound disconnection between community and place." The *Miami Herald*'s Glenn Garvin characterized the documentary as "public broadcasting at its aristocratic worst, using your tax dollars to tell you what unmitigated crap you are. You live in the wrong houses in the wrong neighborhoods . . . you might even wrongly believe you are happy." He added, "Yet tens of millions of baby boomers did grow up in the suburbs that flourished in post-World War II America."[57]

New Urbanism has also been attacked by British critics. "Andres Duany, the Billy Graham of American architecture," begins a 2008 essay in *The Guardian:*

"has descended upon Little Britain with his 64-point list of errors to persuade us sinners away from the evils of modern architecture and urban planning of the past 50 years."[58]

For all the flaws and pretensions of New Urbanism's efforts in Florida, one cannot deny that developers and architects have accomplished something significant, creative, and dramatic. "If Seaside is one reality removed from the flotsam of overdevelopment jostling for your attention on [US] 98," concluded the *New York Times* in 2002, "well, that's the whole point." The persistent slam against New Urbanist communities in Seaside and Celebration involves their elitism and the fact they became too expensive for the middle classes. Capitalism produces winners and losers. Michael Pollan concludes, "It may be Disney's boldest innovation at Celebration to have established a rather novel form of democracy, one that is based on consumerist principles."[59]

If New Urbanism failed in its efforts to remain middle-class, Seaside and Celebration never really had a chance to attract and sustain integrated societies. Census takers in 2000 counted 2,376 Celebration residents, of whom 88 percent were white and 7 percent Hispanic. Osceola County, home to Celebration, was correspondingly 59 percent white and 29 percent Hispanic. "In many respects," explained the *New York Times*, "Disney went to extraordinary lengths to foster diversity in Celebration. . . . But fostering diversity in a real town has proved much harder than socially engineering a theme park designed by Walt Disney Imagineers."[60]

In January 2007, this author was a resident of the Seaside Institute, a glorious, one-month gathering. Walking along the WaterColor beach, scanning the Gulf coastline westward, one could see dozens of concrete and steel-clad high-rise condos towering over the sand dunes and coast of Destin and Sandestin. Spanning eastward, Panama City's skyline rises from the dunes. Seaside and WaterColor, Seagrove and Rosemary Beach sparkled, surrounded by the haunting dune lakes, boutiques selling Niçoise olives and artisanal goat cheeses. Strollers and bicyclists passed bird-themed, wrought-iron silhouetted streetlamps. CR 30-A offers stunning visions of scale and harmony. An oasis and refuge, CR 30-A was also a time warp and illusion. But the real world got real, intruding upon the dreamscape. Realtors, waitresses, and oyster shuckers were grumbling over the dramatic slowdown in sales and traffic. Not even the magical words "high price point" could save Florida's trendiest places from the kryptonite called fear. Economists had another name: recession.

8

The Dream and the Nightmare

Immigration, 2000–2010

In America, the bread is soft, but life is hard.

Rosolino Mormino (1906)

A palpable anxiety could be felt as an estimated 3 million immigrants clamored for entrance into the United States. A *Tampa Tribune* reporter described the scene: "Immigration inspectors and special boards of inquiry are working day and night to relieve the unprecedented conditions." Relatives waited nervously. The setting was not the Port of Miami in 1960 but Ellis Island in 1919. Immigrants from Italy, Poland, and Hungary had good reasons to be nervous: the U.S. Congress was preparing legislation that would shut off emigration from Italy, Poland, and Hungary. Italians nicknamed Ellis Island "Isola di Lacrime" (The Island of Tears). The date was December 1919.[1]

The world has been on the move for hundreds of years, but even more so in 2010. The newest immigrants to Florida were not Italians, Hungarians, or Poles; rather, the newcomers were Haitians, Colombians, and Indians.

The United Nations estimated that 214 million migrants had moved or were moving across the globe. Residents of Palm Beach, Broward, and Miami-Dade counties must have thought every immigrant and alien possessed a map of Florida's Gold Coast. But new gateways beckoned the rootless and sometimes stateless: Orlando and Osceola County, Doral and Weston, Palm Coast and Palmetto.

The world seemed turned upside down. Nations that had once hemorrhaged emigrants—Ireland, Spain, and Italy—had become nightly news as ever-more desperate refugees were landing on their shores. "There's more mobility at this moment than any time in world history," maintained Gary Freedman, of the University of Texas. Indeed, the foreign-born population of the United States had not reached such proportions since 1910.[2]

The America dream is a paradox. Lauded for its polyglot masses and its boundless opportunities, America and Americans have waged constant war with immigrants. So, too, the paradox defines Florida. Newly settled transplants and snowbirds often embrace a curious dialectic, declaring that growth must be halted to preserve Florida's quality of life. Sunshine State residents whose family tree can be traced to Europe often argue that today's immigration policies are far too lenient, especially when compared to their ancestors' travails.

Florida's historical trajectory is complete. How fitting and symmetrical that a place called La Florida in 1513—a colony, territory, and state shaped by *floridanos*—has become a lodestar for a dazzling diversity of Hispanics, Asians, and dreamers.

To understand the remarkable transformation of Florida, consider that a century earlier, 1910, New York was the nation's largest state with a population of 4.77 million, including 2 million foreign-born. In 1911, a commission led by U.S. Senator John Dillingham of Vermont assembled data and reports totaling forty-one volumes, concluding that swelling and unassimilable numbers of Jews and of southern and eastern Europeans were straining American resources and threatening an America ruled by WASPs.[3]

In 1910, Florida's population totaled just 752,619 inhabitants, 33,482 foreign-born. To comprehend Florida's Big Bang in the first decade of the twenty-first century, consider that every single day between 2000 and 2010, 2,745 new immigrants arrived in the Sunshine State. During that extraordinary decade, the state added 1,001,830 immigrants. By 2010, the Sunshine State had achieved astonishing gains, lapping at the door of the Empire State. Census takers counted 19.4 million New Yorkers in 2010. Florida registered 18.8 million inhabitants. Each day, Florida edged closer as retirees and disenchanted retirees and dreamers left Yonkers and Buffalo for Fort Lauderdale and The Villages. By 2010, Florida's under-seventy population had already become majority-minority.[4]

No demographic cohort was driving Florida's relentless surge with more intensity than Hispanics. If a single revelation sprang from the 2000 census, it was that Florida's Hispanics now outnumbered African Americans. One million new Hispanics arrived during the 1990s. Consider that in 1870, Florida's white residents outnumbered Blacks by only 5,000. As late as 1910, the state's white residents outnumbered Blacks by only 135,000.[5]

While it is dangerous and specious to explain how millions of Hispanics would end up in Florida, the short answer is Fidel Castro. The man who defied ten American presidents and CIA assassins loved Florida. As a young student and lawyer, he joined thousands of middle-class Cubans who flocked to Miami during low tourist season, the summer months. In 1948, Fidel brought his bride, Mirta Díaz-Balart, to a Miami Beach hotel for a ten-day honeymoon.[6]

No place in America could match Miami-Dade County's dynamism. In 2000, census officials announced that Miami-Dade was the only county in America where 51.4 percent of the residents were foreign-born, a figure outpacing Los Angeles and New York City. Miami-Dade County was a critical factor in Florida's population, adding 1 million immigrants during the decade of the 1990s. During the dynamic era between April 2000 and July 2006, the Miami–Fort Lauderdale Metro area grew by 456,000 persons. A *Miami Herald* headline summarized the growth: "Region Remains Magnet for People: Fueled Almost Entirely by Immigration." If any county challenged Miami-Dade's extraordinary change, it was its neighbor to the north, Broward. A 2010 headline explained what had happened since 2000: "Census: Broward Becoming More Hispanic, Black." While counties such as Orange and Hillsborough also added tens of thousands of new immigrants, the surge also spilled over to counties whose residents historically were largely native-born. Pinellas, Pasco, and Flagler counties also served as receptors, adding thousands of immigrants.[7]

A profound paradox characterized the stereotypes and reality of immigrants as un-American and unassimilable. In 2005, the U.S. Census Bureau announced that if you were an adult female living in South Florida, you were most likely living alone. In Palm Beach, Broward, and Miami-Dade counties, around 57 percent of women were not living with a husband. But immigrant families tended to be much more traditional than "American" families. The high percentage of women living alone was the result of demographics (women live longer than men) and transplants (Florida's unusually high percentage of senior citizens).[8]

The Census Bureau confirmed the tipping point that nativists had long feared and demographers had long predicted: For the year ending in July 20011, Hispanic, Black, Asian, and mixed races outnumbered white births. America's inflection point had arrived. "While overall," observed the *New York Times*, "whites will remain a majority for some time, the fact that a younger generation is being born in which minorities are the majority has broad implications for the country's economy, its political life, and its identity." In Hillsborough County, a 2006 headline announced the new normal: "White Children Now in Minority in County." The U.S. Census Bureau released figures that augured the future: between 2000 and 2005, the percentage of non-Hispanic white children in Florida under age five dropped from 55 percent to 47 percent. Few issues rankled the political Right as much as the notion that immigrants were not only taking Americans' jobs but were also challenging WASP supremacy in America at warp speed. Immigration fueled debates over education and the question of whether older Floridians will be willing to pay more to educate children who do not look like them.[9]

The growth of Florida between 2000 and 2010 was driven in significant ways by Hispanic and Latino immigrants and their children. In 2000, their numbers totaled 2,682,715 persons, 16.8 percent of the population. A decade later, the 2010 census revealed the numbers of Latino-Hispanic immigrants and children had grown to 4,223,806, a figure climbing to 22.5 percent of the state's population. Cubans obviously dominated Florida's statistics. By 2010, 1.23 million Cubans called Florida home. The second-highest concentration of Cubans was in California, with 88,550. Finally, in 2010 Florida boasted the second-highest Puerto Rican population, with 847,092, and the third-highest number of Dominicans: 172,451.[10]

Jews

Sol Silverman symbolized and personified the dynamics of immigration to Florida. Two generations earlier, the names Silverman, Rabinowitz, and Cohen signaled a new Florida, or at least a new South Florida. While many were immigrants, many were also migrants, moving from New York and the Northeast to Miami and Miami Beach in the decades after the 1920s. Jews encountered a virulent nativism and anti-Semitism in Miami. Before the 1950s, hotels often displayed the signs "Restricted Clientele," or "Always a View, never a Jew." On Miami Beach, Jews were forbidden to live north of Fifth Street. In 1939, the German liner SS *St. Louis,* carrying more than 900 Jewish refugees, was denied entry into Cuba and then sought sanctuary in Miami. President Roosevelt turned the desperate passengers away, and the vessel returned to Germany and the Holocaust. But despite lingering slurs and attitudes, postwar Miami became, in Deborah Dash Moore's words, "The Golden City." From 8,000 Jews in 1940 to 55,000 in 1950 to 230,000 in 1970, Miami became one of America's most significant Jewish centers. But nothing is forever in Florida.[11]

By 2010, Miami-Dade County was no longer the epicenter of Jewish life in Florida. Palm Beach and Broward County became the favorite destinations of the first generation's children and grandchildren. "There's been a real shift in the Jewish population of South Florida," explained Ira Sheskin of the University of Miami. "In the 1970s, Jewish meant Miami." In 2007 he pointed out that Boynton Beach was the fastest-growing Jewish community in America. Boynton Beach, Palm Beach Gardens, Boca Raton, and North Palm Beach served as magnets for young and old American Jews. In 2006, Judy Kuritz, who worked as an educator at the Boynton Beach Jewish Community Center, observed, "Twenty-five years ago, I don't think there were even any Jews in Boynton Beach, let alone young Jewish families." In 2006, scholar Ira Sheskin announced, "There's more Jews in Boynton Beach than St. Louis." When Bill Gralnick arrived in Miami in the 1980s, Palm Beach County offered few amenities for New York transplants: "You couldn't even get a decent bagel there." By 2005, a study indicated that one in five Palm Beach County residents was Jewish. Put another way, Palm Beach County was proportionally more Jewish than New York City. Palm Beach County's Jewish population had grown to a quarter-million inhabitants. Daily, obituaries salute a lost world of Jewish culture. Irving Cohen, a Boca Raton resident, died at age ninety-five following a career as a celebrated Catskills maître d'hôtel, where he also served as matchmaker for hundreds of marriages. Or Joan Geller of Sunrise, who was a mother to two Democratic power brokers and a companion to a legendary "condo commando." Or Fred Naftalie, a resident of Hallandale, a German refugee who served as a World War II veteran in the British army's All-Jewish Brigade.[12]

Cubans

The year 2009 celebrated a sacred anniversary: fifty years earlier, Fidel Castro and his *barbudos* had marched into Havana to topple the brutal dictatorship of Fulgencio Batista. While Batista and his priceless collection of Cuban art fled to Daytona Beach, the first steps of one of the great migrations in American history began. Day by day, throughout the next fifty years, groups of Cubans landed in Miami, defiantly asserting they were exiles, not immigrants. A million dreams later, sociologists, anthropologists, and historians claim that the Cuban experience in South Florida constitutes one of the greatest immigrant success stories in American history. In the process, Cubans transformed Florida as much as Florida changed them. By 2020, an astonishing 60 percent of Miami-Dade residents were born abroad, a majority Cuban.

Miami, Los Angeles, and New York are not only great cities; they are also great immigrant cities. Miami, even more than New York or Los Angeles, has the highest proportion of Caribbean and Latino residents (around 60 percent between 2000 and 2018). More than half of the population of Miami-Dade County speak a language other than English at home. In 2002, a *Miami Herald* reporter offered demographers and scholars wishing to understand the shifting ethnic currents a simple clue: Listen to the accents of the waitresses! For Anglos, the simple request, "*Un cafecito, por favor,*" qualified as Miami's gateway sentence. In no other American city does one hear Spanish spoken so often and so passionately. When South Florida bankers, mayors, and engineers speak Spanish or Haitian, the foreign words can seem threatening to Anglos. When Cubans worked as dishwashers and janitors, few Anglos cared if the "help" spoke Spanish. Today, South Florida politicians and businesspeople often say, "*¡Tenemos un trato!* We have a deal!"[13]

In South Florida, language has meaning and power. What was unusual about Spanish in Florida," reflected Joan Didion, "was not that it was so often spoken, but it was so often heard." Put another way, Professor Guillermo Grenier explained, "For Americans coming here is like going to another country without a passport." Strangers express relief when entering a McDonald's in Little Havana to read a sign on the window, "English spoken here." The 2000 census verified the obvious: six in ten Miami-Dade County residents spoke Spanish at home. Most, however, speak English, when necessary. In 1980, Miami-Dade approved a referendum requiring that county business be conducted exclusively in English. The measure passed, marking the bonfires of the vanities of an Anglo majority that was vanishing. Latino voters proceeded to light their own bonfires of cultural resistance, seizing power at the ballot box. Political power also counts. In 1970, a mere 800 Cubans were registered to vote in Miami. In 1985, Miami voters elected their first Cuban mayor. Born in Cuba in 1949, Harvard-educated Xavier Suarez replaced Miami's first Hispanic mayor, Puerto Rican–born Maurice Ferré.[14]

Few American cities matched the ethnic solidarity of Hialeah, Florida. Gritty, working-class, and sprawling, it was also the most Cuban enclave in North America. By 2010, its population had grown to almost one-quarter million residents, the sixth-largest city in the state. Hialeah was 95 percent Hispanic, mostly Cuban. The *New York Times* described Hialeah as "a Hispanic blue-collar enclave outside Miami where households are packed, incomes are tight, and work is essential."[15]

Mexicans

Not until 1960 did Florida's foreign-born population match the U.S. rate. As late as the 1980s, when demographers discussed Hispanics in Florida, they naturally referenced Cubans. But by the early twenty-first century, Florida had become a pan-Hispanic state, with a dizzying array of immigrants ranging from Argentinian to Venezuelan, Bolivian to Uruguayan. In the agricultural interior, Mexican American communities had taken root in Arcadia, Bowling Green, La Belle, Wauchula, and Zolfo Springs, but also in coastal areas like Collier, Gadsden, Manatee, Hillsborough, and Pinellas counties. Mexicans and Mayans also settled in the Panhandle, most notably Gadsden County. Once known for its signature crop of shade tobacco, tomato fields now employ significant numbers of Hispanic farmworkers. Mexican immigrants have also transitioned to the service industries.[16]

Since the 1970s, the source of the greatest number of refugees seeking new lives in America was not Cuba, but Mexico. "In a single generation between 1980 and 2007," writes commentator Michael Barone, "more than 10 million people migrated, legally or illegally, from Mexico to the U.S." Interestingly, in the decade after the Great Recession in 2008, more Mexicans have actually abandoned America and returned home than have arrived. Mexicans in America's early twenty-first century bear great similarities with Italians in the early twentieth century. Wave after wave of Italian and Mexican immigrants reinforced their status as America's largest immigrant groups. Both drew criticism from labor unions and editorial writers decrying their work habits—that they worked too hard, they took jobs from Americans and sent their earnings back to the Old Country. Italians and Mexicans perfected the art of the chain migration. Typically, young men arrive, find work, establish a beachhead, and soon an echo effect occurs, as they begin bringing their relatives. When motorists drive through Belle Glade or Clewiston, they observe a sea of foreign faces and exotic establishments. But behind the sheer numbers lie organization and order. Mexicans and Mayans do not simply wander in search of employment; rather, established immigrants send for their families, for their in-laws, and paisanos from the local village or neighborhood. The most controversial and significant section of the 1965 Immigration Act dealt with family reunification and chain migration.[17]

Not since the waves of Slavs, Italians, Greeks, and Jews spilled upon our shores from 1880 to 1915 had the United States experienced numbers to match the era 2000–2020. One in five Americans—or 12 million—was an immigrant or a child of immigrants. More remarkably or alarmingly, one in three of the nation's foreign-born is an illegal. "Never before," observed the *New York Times* in 2009, "have so many of America's immigrants come here unlawfully." The *Times* continued, nervously noting, "The integration of the new immigrants is all the more uncharted, because for the first time in at least a century, one country and one language have dominated the influx since the early 1990s." Mexico dominated the staggering numbers, while Spanish commanded the conversations—over half of the immigrants comprise Spanish speakers.[18]

Small numbers of Mexicans had been coming to Florida since the late 1940s, working as migrant laborers. The pace quickened in the 1980s and 1990s, with many of the immigrants becoming year-round workers and residents. In 2000, census takers in Florida counted 364,000 Mexicans out of a total of 2.7 million Florida Hispanics. The pace of migration almost doubled in the following decade, the numbers of Mexicans increasing to 634,000.[19]

Mexican immigrants pursued agricultural work in Florida. The 2010 census identified the Florida places, largely located in the central and southwest regions, holding the highest proportion of Mexicans: Fellsmere, Wimauma, Immokalee, Pierson, LaBelle, and Zolfo Springs. Mexicans planted and picked tomatoes, green beans, and ornamental ferns but also harvested citrus. Along Florida's citrus belt, observed National Public Radio, "you see lots of converted school buses on the road; these are company buses, carrying the workers who will harvest oranges and grapefruit." They are predominantly Mexicans. In Okeechobee, Collier, Lee, Hardee, DeSoto, and Hendry counties, Mexicans comprise the largest immigrant constituency. Mexican laborers, roofers, carpenters, and plumbers work at many construction sites across the state. In a region in Florida that not long ago was largely WASP and African-American, not everyone welcomed these foreign laborers. In 2006, the mayor of Avon Park (Polk County) urged the city council to punish landlords who rented to illegal immigrants, chiefly Mexicans, Haitians, and Jamaicans.[20]

Pierson is famous as America's leatherneck fern capital. Located between Crescent City and DeLand, rural Pierson's population fluctuates between 1,800 and 5,000, depending upon work. The percentage of Mexican illegals is high, as are the numbers of Hispanic kindergarten and elementary school students. Many workers migrate across the state to harvest crops by season. In 2001, Monica Boyd, the director of the Center for the Study of Population at Florida State University, astutely predicted, "In Florida, we think of three groups: white, black, and Cuban. But I've been telling people that I think the new census will show a substantial increase in Mexicans. There may be a significant undercount, but it will show up."[21]

Mexicans are resourceful and persistent, and found in places one might not expect, such as Clearwater. A city more famous for the headquarters of the Church of Scientology and senior citizens than for Mexicans, Clearwater represents a classic case of a handful of immigrants building a community and helping relatives and neighbors seeking the American dream. The 2010 census indicated a 56 percent surge in Hispanics, chiefly Mexican, settled in the affluent Pinellas County city. A growing number of Mexican establishments—bakeries, cafes, and groceries—dot the city and county. Beginning in the 1970s, Mexican immigrants from Ixmiquilpan, in Hidalgo, began a colony in Clearwater. The province is comprised largely of Otomí Indians, a region that also has large populations of *hidalguenses* in Atlanta and Orlando.[22]

Few Americans could have imagined fifty years ago that *taquerias,* Cuervas beer, and agave tequila would become wildly popular. A book title summarizes the phenomenon: *Taco USA: How Mexican Food Conquered America.* Cinco de Mayo now rivals St. Patrick's Day in popularity, and according to David Von Drehle, "Cinco de Mayo matters more in the United States" than Mexico!" The fact that Americans misunderstand the meaning of the holiday seems immaterial.[23]

Central Americans

Central Americans began showing up on Florida's radar in the 1970s as the whirlwinds of revolution, poverty, violence, repression, and opportunity took a fearful toll. In the early 1980s, the Sandinista Revolution roiled Nicaragua, sending thousands into exile. The number of Nicaraguans living in 1980 South Florida was estimated at 20,000. A decade later, with the revolutionary fires extinguished but the economy in ruins, an estimated 125,000 Nicaraguans had settled in the region. Streams of Salvadorans, Guatemalans, and Hondurans followed. By 2015, almost a quarter-million Central Americans lived in Metro Miami, making it the fourth-largest concentration in the nation. Central Americans are particularly vulnerable to U.S. deportation policies.[24]

Proud of past Maya civilizations but fearful of the impoverished and strife-riven present, Guatemalans began migrating to Indiantown in South Florida in the early 1980s. Many of the early arrivals were Mayan speakers, emphasized by a refugee who declared, "I am Maya, not Guatemalan nor Hispanic." Antonio Silvestre, a schoolteacher, added: "The Americans didn't know where we came from. We are short, with dark skin, dark hair, and we speak a language they never heard before." In late September, the Guatemalan Mayas celebrate the Fiesta of San Miguel Acatán. Other Mayan communities took hold in Jupiter and Lake Worth, where many of the refugees worked in the landscaping business. The 2000 census documented 28,650 Guatemalans in Florida. Many more were believed to be living here illegally.[25]

Jupiter, one of Florida's most affluent cities, shares a sister-city relationship with one of Central America's poorest cities: Jacaltenango, Guatemala. Immigration makes for strange bedfellows—or, more accurately, strange maids and day laborers. El Sol functions as a combination social and education center, offering job training, language classes, and health services. The name El Sol perfectly fits the symbiotic origins of the center: The name means "the Sun" in Spanish, but the center's father and namesake was a local resident, Sol Silverman.[26]

Puerto Ricans

When Maurice Ferré arrived in Miami in 1953, he was one of only 4,500 Puerto Ricans residing in Florida. By 2000, their numbers had risen to 80,337, ranking the group second only to Cubans. A decade later, a stunning 847,550 Puerto Ricans had flocked to the state, as islanders were fleeing their impoverished homeland. Florida replaced New Jersey as home of America's second-highest concentration of Puerto Ricans, trailing only New York. Shockingly, by 2010, demographers were predicting within the next decade, more Puerto Ricans would call America home than Puerto Rico. Resettlement has hollowed the fabled island.[27]

Wordsmiths coined terms to describe the extraordinary relationship between Puerto Ricans and America. First, Puerto Ricans are *not* immigrants since they are U.S. citizens, and have been so since 1917. Many prefer to call themselves *boricuas,* out of respect to the indigenous people living there before conquest. Ironically, Ponce de León, who in his voyage of exploration sighted and named La Florida in 1513, also served as a brutal governor of Puerto Rico. The island is technically a commonwealth, and natives are prohibited from voting in presidential elections until they have established residency in the United States. Considering that so many Puerto Ricans moved to New York and later to Florida, "Nuyorican" and "Floriricans" seemed pitch-perfect. And finally, because Central Florida became the favorite destination of the newcomers, clever writers suggested "Orlando Ricans" and "Mickey Ricans." Historian Jorge Duany raised a debate question distinguishing native Puerto Ricans and those born on the mainland: "Who are the true Puerto Ricans?[28]

The 2010 Census revealed that Puerto Ricans had concentrated in three major areas in the Sunshine State: Metro-Miami, Tampa Bay, and Central Florida. The presence of more than a quarter-million Puerto Ricans in Orange and Osceola counties shocked demographers and longtime residents. When one thought of Orlando and its surrounding counties, one thought of tourist attractions, urban sprawl, and citrus groves. Orlando's Azalea Park, a celebrated Puerto Rican neighborhood, is known as "Little San Juan."[29]

Osceola County in Central Florida seemed one of the state's least likely places to become an ethnic hothouse. For more than a century, census takers counted more cows than people. A 1943 reporter called Kissimmee, the county's only incorporated city, "the cow capital of the state." In 1980, only 1,000 Hispanics resided in Osceola, a place that had not yet reached a population of 50,000. The Hispanic population of Osceola multiplied twelvefold in the 1980s. A land once renowned for cattle ranches and saddle makers became the fastest-growing Hispanic county in America, suddenly famous for Puerto Rican botánicas, cafés, and panaderías. Latino barbacoa and southern barbecue became common ground and grill. "La fiesta de quinceañera" has replaced the Kissimmee Rodeo as the area's most popular celebration. Symbolically, the struggling Osceola Square Mall morphed into Plaza del Sol in 2014, becoming one of more than 50,000 Hispanic-owned businesses in Central Florida. In one of the more improbable consequences in history, Kissimmee has become a suburb of Puerto Rico. "Puerto Rico has 78 municipalities," boasted Art Otero, a San Juan native and a Kissimmee city commissioner. "Now they will say we will be the 79th." Another way of measuring the footprint of the Caribbean upon Kissimmee was described by journalist Lizette Álvarez: "Restaurants dishing out mofongo are no longer hard to find in this once low-key city."[30]

If there was one place to understand the Florida dream, it was Buenaventura Lakes, or "BVL" as the locals call it. A booming suburb in Osceola County, it was a 1970s inspiration of Mexican millionaire developers. Landstar Homes decided to market the development directly to residents of Puerto Rico. Buenaventura Lakes offered Puerto Ricans the essentials of the American dream: upward mobility, affordable living, and the comforts of suburbia. In 2006, an *Orlando Sentinel* reporter depicted Buenaventura Lakes "as a slice of the new Orlando." Scholar Jorge Duany explained one of the major distinctions between Latino lives in Florida and New York: "They [neighborhoods] look very different from the so-called 'barrios' in the Northern cities. These are primarily suburban housing, subdivisions." By 2010, Buenaventura Lakes had attracted nearly 12,000 Puerto Ricans, in additional to 5,000 other Hispanics. It ranked as Central Florida's largest Puerto Rican community. Orange County's Meadow Woods claimed the title of the region's second-largest Puerto Rican community. Advertisements in New York newspapers, especially the *New York Post*, persuaded many islanders to move to Buenaventura Lakes. As American citizens, they faced none of the bureaucratic hassles confronting other Caribbean immigrants. Many discovered Osceola County in a fashion few Jewish, Polish, or Italian immigrants had experienced: with a visit to Disney World![31]

Since 2000, Central Florida's population exploded due to two disparate groups: New York/New Jersey retirees seeking balmy weather, lower cost of living, and fewer Nuyoricans; and Puerto Ricans seeking escape from the turmoil and oppression of their homeland. For the latter, Walt Disney World and the other tourist attractions have also functioned as engines of economic opportunity. The region's economy has a virtually unlimited demand for service industry workers—hotel domestics, cooks, janitors, gardeners, ticket takers, Goofy impersonators, and laundry workers. The tourist industry also values bilingual employees to cater to the international crowds. "Puerto Ricans land at the Orlando airport and think they're going to meet Mickey Mouse, who will scoop them up in his arms, take them to Cinderella's castle, and the princesses will fix everything for them," reminisced Carlos Merced, an actor in Puerto Rico who moved to Orlando in 2007. He added, ruefully, "But the problem is, those princesses aren't Hispanic, and Mickey doesn't speak Spanish." One study found that Puerto Ricans were more likely blue-collar workers. College-educated and skilled professionals easily find white-collar positions; indeed, many work for Puerto Rican retailers and establishments that followed their customers to Florida. An advertisement in *El Nuevo Día*, the largest daily newspaper in San Juan, touted Central Florida: "You don't have to be a millionaire to live like one."[32]

In 1985, Germán Colón recalled browsing a newspaper while on break. The New York resident came upon an advertisement featuring new homes cradled by palm trees, encouraging readers to "experience the life" in a place called Poinciana, Florida. By 1990, the Colóns were two of Poinciana's 796 residents living in the sprawling community straddling Osceola and Polk counties. A decade later, 14,000 of its residents were Puerto Ricans. State legislator Tony Suarez placed the relationship in perspective: "What Miami is to Cubans; Orlando will be to Puerto Ricans."[33]

Frustrated by their island's failing economy and bleak prospects, many Puerto Ricans see Florida as a salvation, offering an attainable future. Central Florida's Latinos are much younger than their Anglo neighbors. "They came here because of the education system," explained José Hoyos, an Orlando real estate consultant. "They don't mind working here for $10 an hour because their children are getting a good education." The road has been hard, as many new arrivals struggle to escape poverty. In Kissimmee, a city official observed that some Puerto Ricans find housing so expensive that they are forced to live week to week in tawdry motels. Disillusioned, some return to the island.[34]

Hispanic corporations, stores, and teachers have followed the markets and demographics to Florida. Banco Popular is now a fixture in the region. Casa Febus, a furniture business founded on the island, now has stores in Pembroke Pines and Altamonte Springs. Other island businesses, including El Meson (a sandwich chain) and Valija (a clothing boutique), have also moved to Florida. Corporate giant Goya Foods located its Central Florida distribution center near Meadow Woods. Publix has opened several Sabor stores in the area. To appreciate the sweeping demographic changes, consider a 1 January 2007 column in the *Orlando Sentinel* with a curious question: "Ever Wonder Why ATMs in Central Florida Speak Spanish?"[35]

Jamaicans and Haitians

Haitians and Jamaicans represent a rapidly changing segment of non-Spanish-speaking Caribbean immigrants. For centuries, white and Black Bahamians contributed to the economies and culture of South Florida and the Florida Keys. Miami's history is inseparable from the Caribbean. Jamaicans now represent the largest West Indian population in Miami. Several South Florida communities radiate the influence of a large proportion of their populations, most notably in Miramar and Lauderhill Lakes, Melrose Park and Pembroke Park, El Portal and Pembroke Pines. By 2003, Jamaicans commanded a majority of Miramar's city commission; by 2010, a quarter-million Jamaicans called the state home. Florida is on a fast pace to replace New York as home of America's largest Jamaican population.[36]

Wayne Messam has lived the Jamaican American dream. The son of Jamaican immigrants whose father cut sugarcane in Palm Beach County, Messam graduated from Glades Central High in Belle Glade, where he starred on and off the athletic field. He went on to win accolades as a wide receiver at Florida State University. His life off the field has been star-lit, owning a construction company, becoming mayor of Miramar and winning nearly 90 percent of the vote. "The stronger Jamaicans are in the US," he asserted, "the more they can give back to Jamaica."[37]

The distinction of having the largest Black foreign population in Florida, as well as the poorest and most vulnerable immigrant group, goes to the Haitians, now also the largest immigrant group in Broward and Palm Beach counties. By 2010, 425,000 Haitians resided in Florida. Denied entrance into the United States by politics and policies, Haitians have braved the watery passage to Florida, often in dangerously small boats. Neither nautical nor political tides blessed Haitians' efforts to flee their homeland. Headlines like "65 Fleeing Haiti Wash Ashore at Pompano Beach" and "'Good U.S. Life' Lures Another 103 Haitians" underscored the experience. The details were chilling: "For most of the 103 Haitian refugees crowded into a rotting, 50-foot sailing junk they had pooled their money to buy, a jump into the sandy surf was their first step onto American soil." A hand-painted sign proclaimed, "God is Good." Courage and faith notwithstanding, the Haitians were paroled as illegal aliens. U.S. Representative E. Clay Shaw of Fort Lauderdale railed against Haitians in 1991, "If these people are allowed to stay, we're going to see a mass migration from Haiti to the U.S. as we've never seen before. . . . [The ocean will become] a blood bath for sharks."[38]

For Haitians, the journey to Florida has been littered with legal land mines, political and geological earthquakes, a vigilant U.S. Coast Guard, and a lush but punishing native land. Between 1977 and 1982, at least 50,000 Haitians arrived in South Florida, many of them stigmatized as "boat people." Whereas the very presence of Cubans requesting political asylum was prima facie evidence of their legal status, Haitians faced the worst odds of any asylum seekers. Haitian immigrants settled into Miami's African-American neighborhoods, such as Opa-Locka and Miami Gardens. Chariclaire Simon typified the struggle. She labored two years picking tomatoes in Hillsborough County, saving enough to bring her seven children to Pompano Beach. She found work in Broward County at a laundry. Throughout the presidencies of Obama and Trump, critics and supporters have urged the chief executive and directors of Homeland Security to affirm their status as legal immigrants or deport them as diseased, illegal, and undesirable immigrants. South Florida may seem like a fragile asylum, but the Haitian communities are vital to the economy and security of Haiti—fully one-quarter of the country's gross domestic economy comes from remittances of Haitian immigrants.[39]

The Miami–Fort Lauderdale–Pompano Beach Metropolitan area boasts the largest number of Haitians in the United States, with more than 300,000 in 2010. More than a quarter of the populations of Golden Glades, Pinewoods, and North Miami are Haitian. The impact of Haitians in the region is striking. They are the second-largest immigrant group in Broward County. The range of employment is varied, from agricultural to the food industry to small businesses.[40]

One of Miami's most famous neighborhoods is Petite Haïti, Little Haiti, located in a place once known as Lemon City, north of the Miami River. Critics argued that the decision denigrated the Bahamians who helped build Lemon City before Miami emerged as a city. Unofficially, Little Haiti's southern boundary is NW Fifty-Fourth Street, west of Interstate 95 and north of Overtown along NW Eighty-Second Street. In 2016, the neighborhood was younger and poorer than the rest of Miami. The average household size for Miami is 2.6 persons; for Little Haiti, it is 8.1. The colorful murals and loud Konpa music soften the hard lives.[41]

Farther north in Broward County, a *Miami Herald* reporter began her story in the aisles of the Haiti Supermarket on Sunrise Boulevard where men talked politics. "The problem," wrote the journalist, "is that Haitian participation in Broward politics barely exists." Slowly but promisingly, Haitians have translated their numbers into political clout. Priorities matter, in this case Haitians' struggles to avoid deportation, care for their families, and learn a third language, after Creole and French. But Haitians are also becoming citizens, registering to vote, and recruiting candidates, perhaps inspired by their activist heritage that includes a successful slave insurrection against French planters in 1804. In 2010, Haitian-born doctor and lawyer Rudy Moises ran unsuccessfully for Congress.[42]

In 2000, Phillip J. Brutus, a Haitian immigrant, was elected to the Florida House of Representatives. Irish power brokers would admire the political skills a *Miami Herald* reporter described in 2012: "At Little Haiti's St. Mary's Towers, ballot brokers jockey every election season to see who can get in the doors and collect the most absentee ballots. Brokers tout their skills on Creole-language radio, pitch their services to candidates running for office in cities that boast a sizeable Haitian electorate and even brag about their vote-getting prowess on business cards emblazoned with slogans like 'Queen of the absentee ballots.'"[43]

In 2010, a devastating earthquake rocked Port-au-Prince. A cholera epidemic, a drought, and a monster Hurricane Matthew deepened the island's misery. The Obama administration offered a rarely used lifeline of temporary protected status (TPS) to the 58,000 Haitian immigrants, most of them residing in South Florida. Olita Inera, a Haitian living in Lauderhill but fearful of deportation, rejoiced after Obama's announcement: "I feel like I have an identity now!" The government program permits thousands of Haitians living here illegally to remain in the United States until conditions improve. Years after the earthquake and hurricane, Haiti struggles to recover, and the blame game continues over what happened to $10 billion raised for relief.[44]

How does one measure the contribution of an immigrant group to a city?

Today, Delray Beach may be one of the most desirable places in Florida. It was not always so. In the decades after 1960, the impact of Interstate 95, the lure of suburbia, and a drug epidemic threatened the oceanfront city. Urban planners and preservationists certainly played an important role in the transformation of this Palm Beach County city. So did Haitians who moved into the most undesirable sections of Delray Beach, gentrifying the district, while creating "Little Haiti." A journalist called Delray Beach as "close to ideal as it gets."[45]

While Miami-Dade remains one of the most celebrated immigrant centers in America, Broward County has quickly emerged as an immigrant-ethnic-racial refuge and redoubt. In January 2000, state leaders reflected as to what the previous decades hath wrought. As dramatic as the post-1960 era had been, the headline of the state's leading newspaper divined the future: "Ethnic Make-Over of S. Florida Likely to Intensify." Florida's racial and ethnic epicenter was shifting. Many of Broward's newest transplants moved from Broward County, 2000–2010. During this decade, Miami-Dade's population of young Blacks and Hispanics dwindled while Broward County's minority population was becoming its majority. For years, Broward served as an oasis of white flight and later as a springboard to aspiring Miami-Dade immigrants who moved upward and northward. Buttressed by surging numbers of Jamaicans and Haitians, and buffered by declining numbers of non-Hispanic whites, Broward's Black immigrant population surged. In 2010, *Sun-Sentinel* journalists placed these events into context: "Nearly one in three Broward County residents comes from a foreign country, as the county continues its transition from a tourist and retirement haven to a magnet for immigrants." Colombians, Cubans, and Peruvians followed Haitians and Jamaicans as the next-largest foreign-born groups in Broward County.[46]

Race and the Census

As if interpreting and classifying race and identity among Jamaicans weren't challenging enough, how and what census boxes should their fellow nationals, Chinese Jamaicans, check? Originally brought to Jamaica as indentured servants, their descendants speak Hakka, a southern Chinese language, in addition to English and patois. Jamaicans dominate Miami's Chinese Cultural Association.[47]

A 2000 *Miami Herald* headline neatly summarized the impact of intermarriage upon immigrants and their children: "Intermarriage Fuzzes Latin Identity." Love trumps race and ethnicity: Cubans married Haitians, and Brazilians fell in love with Venezuelans. The *Herald* added, "Even the seeming truism that Latins all speak the same language isn't really correct." Second- and third-generation Latins have the highest intermarriage rate of any ethnic group. Two-thirds of Hispanics, according to a Pew Research study, have a parent or grandparent who is NOT Hispanic or Latino.[48]

From its origins as a Spanish outpost and colony, Florida was, in the words of Zora Neale Hurston, "a place that draws people." The Spanish language codified and described an extraordinary collection of races and ethnic groups in La Florida. Between contact and extinction, new multitiered societies evolved that required a new racial and ethnic lexicon: *mestizos* and *mestizaje* (offspring of a European and Native Indian), *criollos* (children of Spanish immigrants born in the New World), *ladinos* (Spanish-speaking Catholic slaves), *conversos* (converted Jews), *moriscos* (converted Moors), and mulattos, quadroons, and octoroons.

Central Florida's West Indian community illustrates the complexities of race, ethnicity, and identity. In 2006, statistics indicated that about 75,000 West Indians had settled in Central Florida. Consider Amrita and Harry Harriram, who had emigrated from Guyana. They opened a Shop and Save West Indian Bakery and Restaurant in 2002.[49]

For many Americans, immigration is a byzantine world, difficult to understand or decipher. A significant story behind the headlines of "boat people" and "reggae festivals" is how new residents are redefining the meaning and accounting of race and ethnicity. Precisely at the point Hispanics edged ahead of African Americans in Florida in terms of population, more and more Floridians wished to redefine the terms and parameters of race. Mayan newcomers challenge the meaning of Hispanic. The Caribbean has been the source of large numbers of Afro-Cubans and other Black immigrants. Historically, the Caribbean and the United States looked upon multiracial identity through very different lenses. In 2010, Hispanics had the option of checking boxes listing white, Black, or Asian. Some Americans wrote in "Latino" or "some other race." More than 1 million Americans who checked "Hispanic" in 2000 labeled themselves "white" in 2010. And of course, some Americans reversed the boxes from white in 2000 to Hispanic in 2010. We live in an age of fluidity, when, if one feels that they have been a woman trapped in a man's body, they are, indeed, a woman. Ethnicity and race are also fluid barriers and frontiers. Of course, the very act of recording a nation's identities can be threatening—consider the volatility over the question of citizenship and immigrants.[50]

Race and ethnicity enrich and complicate lives for citizens and the U.S.

Census Bureau. In 2015, one-third of Metro Miami's Black population came from abroad, a greater proportion than in New York City. Haiti and Jamaica, not Cuba, constitute the greatest numbers of Metro Miami's Black immigrants. The number of Black immigrants in Florida has expanded dramatically since 2000. As late as the early 1970s, only 5,000 Afro-Cubans resided in Miami. Mark Lopez of the Pew Research Center explained the state's special character, "It's a place that is diverse in its immigrant stock in a way that other parts of the country aren't necessarily diverse." The study concluded, "Miami may be a global city surrounded by immense wealth. The concentration of wealth that characterizes modern global cities does not necessarily trickle down to all its residents." More precisely, for Black households in the Miami area, Afro-Caribbean (predominantly Jamaican and Haitian) family net worth was more than three times African American cohorts but dramatically less than white households.[51]

Obama, Cuba, and the Thaw

The election of Barack Obama inaugurated a great deal of speculation as to the future of Cuban-American relations. But modernity, economics, and technology had already been breaking down traditional walls. Young Cubans on both sides of the Straits were connecting with relatives via email. "The truth is that the driver in policy is not the relationship between the United States and Cuba," explained Joe García, once chair of the Miami Democratic Party, "but the relationship between Cubans." He explained with a simplicity that diplomats and politicians lacked: "When you remove some of the barriers, people do what people do—help their families." Philip Peters, an expert in the field, explained the new diplomacy: "Cuban-Americans are normalizing relations one by one." A 2011 *New York Times* article began: "For two consecutive summers, Stephanie Várcia, 11, has done something that was unimaginable five years ago. She has spent four weeks in Havana playing hide-and-seek with her aunts and uncles. When summer vacation ended, her mother flew out to bring her back to Miami." Anyone who spent time in Miami or its airport during this era witnessed the dynamics of this relationship: endless stores selling tennis shoes, jeans, and appliances, goods to be protected by "Secure Wrap."[52]

Though life for ordinary Cubans had not improved greatly in the first decade of the new century, President Obama was on a roll. By 2015, a "secret" poll in Cuba indicated that the American president was more popular than Fidel or Raúl Castro.[53]

Venezuelans

Few soothsayers predicted that Venezuela would emerge as the sick man of the Americas. For many decades, Venezuela boasted one of South America's earliest and healthiest democracies. The nation's standard of living was the envy of its neighbors and served as a magnet for aspiring migrants and immigrants. In the 1970s, observed scholars, "It has the best infrastructure in South America." In 1970, Venezuela's per-capita GDP was higher than Spain's and barely below that of the United Kingdom.[54]

Fast-forward to 2010. The terms "failed state" and "suicide" began appearing next to Venezuela. Venezuela, argue scholars in *Foreign Affairs*, has committed "suicide," a legacy of a "failed state." Dictators ruled Venezuela for the first half of the twentieth century, replaced by several decades of democratic government; indeed, the country became an asylum for South American political exiles. The presence of vast reserves of oil motivated leaders to invest billions of dollars to modernize "The Great Venezuela." Quickly, the quality of life deteriorated, as basics such as food, running water, and even gasoline became precious.[55]

Born to a working-class family in 1954, Hugo Chávez was serving as a paratrooper in the 1980s when he joined a leftist movement bent on overthrowing Venezuela's democratic government. He was one of the founders of the clandestine Revolutionary Bolivarian Movement. Imprisoned for an unsuccessful coup d'état in 1992, he was pardoned after serving two years. The charismatic rebel founded the Fifth Republic Movement and, in 1998, defeated a rival who promised political and economic reform. Chávez quickly seized political and economic control, centralizing power and utilizing roughly $30 million in annual oil revenues to establish a corrupt, left-wing dictatorship. "Chávez," contend scholars, "was brilliant at mining discontent." He denounced Yankee imperialism and American imperialists while forging a strong alliance with the Castro brothers in Cuba. "To me, Fidel is a father, a companion, a teacher of perfect strategy," he proclaimed.[56]

For a time, Venezuela seemed headed in the right direction. Between 2003 and 2012, Venezuelans living below the poverty line fell from 60 percent to 30 percent, while the nation's gross domestic product quintupled. Chávez died of cancer in 2013, leaving the country in chaos.[57]

Marxist ideology, the cult of personality, and the largest reserves of crude oil in the world bonded Cuba and Venezuela. The relationship between Cuba and Venezuela, Chávez proclaimed, was "a merger of two revolutions." The alliance created a textbook example of political-economic symbiosis: Cuba sent teachers, doctors, and medical specialists to Venezuela, while Venezuela shipped daily 115,000 barrels of refined petroleum to the island. The aid sent to Cuba amounted to billions of dollars annually. Cuba watchers compared the one-sided relationship with the Soviet Union's massive aid packages to prop up Cuba. When the Soviet Union imploded in 1989, the Cuban economy and its people suffered terribly in what was called the "Special Period" of the 1990s.[58]

In a predictable scenario, the humanitarian crises in Venezuela have taken a toll upon the working, middle, and propertied classes, resulting in an exodus of 3 million people. In 2000, the Venezuelan footprint in Florida was still faint. The census indicated only 21,593 Venezuelans resided in Miami-Dade County, fewer than the 23,327 Peruvians. When Miami's real estate bubble burst in 2008, South American investors bet heavily on Brickell Avenue condominiums. Venezuelans soon accounted for almost 20 percent of South Florida real estate purchases. In a familiar pattern, poorer, more desperate refugees followed. By 2010, more than 100,000 Venezuelans lived in Florida, most of them residing in South Florida, a region boasting the highest concentration of Venezuelans in the United States.[59]

Two communities vie for Florida's unofficial capital of Venezuela. Doral, a Miami-Dade city of 65,000 residents, has so many Venezuelan residents that its nickname is "Doralzuela." In Broward County at the westernmost border on the Everglades, Weston had once been famous for cattle ranches and its planner who also designed Walt Disney World. In a 1998 article, Weston was portrayed as a magnet for white flight. The "refugees are mostly native-born and white, young and old." But whereas white flight in Pittsburgh and Chicago is typically motivated by fear of Black inner cities, in South Florida, the movement was a reaction to massive immigration. How ironic that Weston would become, once again, a magnet for another generation of refugees. After Chávez seized power, Venezuelans imagined Weston as home, the "Beverly Hills of Miami," not merely a summer retreat. According to the 2010 census, nearly half of Weston's population of 65,333 was Hispanic, of whom 6,360 were Venezuelan. In 2002, Ariel Dunaeveschi and his family were enjoying a vacation in America as Venezuela reeled from a succession of labor strikes. "I had a business in Venezuela . . . everything was working perfectly," he explained to the *New York Times*. "I left everything." His family resettled to Weston, where he opened a new furniture business. Famous residents include Bárbara Palacios, crowned Miss Universe in 1986. Doral and Weston vie for culinary honors, each city renowned for its arepas (a cornmeal cake-crusted sandwich with meats and cheese) and cachitos (cheese turnovers). One of the most famous is El Arepazo, a cafeteria-style restaurant serving the locals in Doral. The café adjoins a gas station and flies the flag of Venezuela. A statue of the nineteenth-century freedom fighter Simón Bolívar reigns in the parking lot. By 2008, five Venezuelan-American newspapers and magazines kept the expatriates informed with news about their old and new homes.[60]

Asians

Asians have been migrating to Florida for centuries. A Japanese agricultural colony called Yamato took root near Boca Raton. Chinese laundries existed in many cities, but the state never had a large "Chinatown." Asians encountered nativist hostility. In 1926, the Florida Legislature passed the Asian Land Bill, which forbade foreigners barred from citizenship from owning land in Florida. Although never enforced, a bill to repeal the law was on the 2008 ballot but failed. Since Asians in Florida comprised such a small constituency (2.2 percent in 2008), and since the vote came not long after 9/11, Floridians voted against the measure.[61]

Following the fall of Vietnam to the Communist forces in 1974, large numbers of South Vietnamese sought refuge around the military bases in the Florida Panhandle. During the first decade of the twenty-first century, Asians constituted the fastest-growing immigrant group, their population increasing by 71 percent. Asians settled principally in South and Central Florida. Orlando has a thriving Vietnamese community. Some have estimated a half-million Asians had settled in Florida by 2010. Southwest Florida had relatively few Asian immigrants in 2000 but witnessed dramatic gains, from 3,600 Asians residing in Lee County in 2000 to 12,000 a decade later. Symbolic of the changes is the growing number of Asian religious temples, shrines, and churches.[62]

Nativism Unfurled

Few issues past or present stoke the political fires more than immigration. Americans clash over borders, paths to citizenship, sanctuary cities, the impact of immigrants upon the economy, allowing border-crossing caravans, and multiculturalism. In 2005, commentator Robert J. Samuelson observed, "Immigration is crawling its way back onto the national agenda—and not just as a footnote to keeping terrorists out." Immigration has remained a central tenet and lightning rod to the American dream. Dreams differ. Baiting the Potato Famine Irish, Sicilian brigands, or Polish peasants is as American as a Thomas

Nast cartoon. The custom of repelling and welcoming foreigners is an ancient rite of passage. The Old Testament's book of Leviticus reminds us, "The stranger who resides with you shall be to you as one of your citizens; you shall love him as yourself, for you were strangers in the land of Egypt."[63]

In the 1993 film *Jurassic Park*, the scientist Ian Malcolm philosophizes: "If there is one thing the history of evolution has taught us, it's that life will not be contained. Life breaks free, it expands to new territories." For thousands of years, migrants and immigrants, refugees and exiles, have been on the move and would not be denied. People break free. More than once, officials have pleaded to governors and presidents, sheriffs and kings, "The breaking point has arrived." Today, the question seems to be, "Which breaking point?"[64]

Immigration has always been a toxic political issue. "Birthers" insist Barrack Obama is an immigrant, not a native of Hawaii. In 2011, Donald Trump appeared on *The View*, imploring, "Why doesn't he [Obama] show his birth certificate? There's something on that birth certificate he doesn't like." On the *Laura Ingraham Show*, Trump charged, "He doesn't have a birth certificate. . . . Now somebody told me . . . that where it says 'religion,' it might have 'Muslim.' And if you're a Muslim, you don't change your religion!"[65]

Armed with placards and picket lines, Americans disagree over immigrants and immigration policies. In 2008, Congresswoman Ginny Brown-Waite was speaking in Brooksville about the immigration problem. Ranting about a U.S. stimulus bill, she said, "The bill sends millions of dollars to people who do not pay federal income taxes, including residents of Puerto Rico . . . I do not believe American taxpayer funds should be sent to foreign citizens who do not pay taxes." Journalists pointed out that Puerto Ricans were American citizens. Similar debates occurred a century earlier, when the Italian, Polish, and Irish grandparents and great-grandparents of many of today's protestors also wished to close the gates and make America great again. "There's no small irony that the ancestors of some of the most prominent voices in the immigration debate," commented historian Chris Klein, "spoke with an Irish brogue, because few groups proved to be as challenging to assimilate into the fabric of American life as the Irish." If anything, the earlier "conversations" were more impassioned. Many "old stock" Americans truly believed that America's genetic destiny and democratic character were imperiled by unwashed and unassimilable hordes. Theodore Roosevelt, among others, worried that the birth rates of the new immigrants would crowd out old-stock Americans. Demographics is destiny.

For all the invectives and filibustering, immigrants have changed Florida's culture and identity as much as America has changed them. The British statesman

Benjamin Disraeli may have railed against "lies, damned lies, and statistics," but numbers don't lie. In 1960, Florida's immigrant population was negligible, but the demographic Rubicon—the Straits of Florida—had been crossed with the first wave of Cuban exiles. Today, more than one in five Floridians is foreign-born. Immigrants have touched every corner and cafeteria of Florida. Is it progress, Capitalism 4.0, or assimilation when McDonald's introduced dulce de leche McFlurries on its menu? Probably all three! *Un cafecito, por favor?*

Immigration has shaped Florida's urban corridors, expanding to once remote corners of the state. Long underpopulated and largely ignored, Flagler County has boomed as the world has discovered Northeast Florida, especially fast-growing Palm Coast. Today, one in ten county residents is foreign-born and predominantly Hispanic. The population is diverse. In 2007, a reporter wrote: "Flagler residents can shop at one of three Russian markets. They can buy homemade ricotta cheese from an authentic Italian market, get fresh produce from Jamaica or grab a cup of coffee and a fresh bolo de arroz [a traditional rice pastry] from the Portuguese bakery off Old Kings Road."[66]

For centuries, the term "frontier" best described the vast landmass that became Collier County. In the nineteenth and early twentieth centuries, Spanish fishing ranchos, Seminole reservations, and tubercular Yankees populated Southwest Florida. Today, Collier County may be best known for its retirees and the hometown of former governor and U.S. Senator Rick Scott, but almost one in four residents is foreign-born. While Naples and Marco Island radiate affluence and privilege, Immokalee and East Naples are mired in poverty, agricultural work, and domestic service. Mexicans predominate the ranks of agricultural labor and domestic service workers. Naples and Marco Island comprise two of the oldest communities in Florida, their median ages respectively fifty-one and sixty-five. A journalist noted in 2012, "School-age minority children in Lee and Collier counties have outnumbered white children for years."[67]

Naples and Marco Island were scarcely the only cities in Florida to attract elderly ethnics. In Winter Park, Slovak Gardens provided modest cabins for retired Pennsylvania Slavic miners and factory workers. Aside from a vibrant colony in Tampa, Italians largely avoided Florida during the golden age of immigration. A list of Florida cities with the highest concentration of Italians includes Cape Coral, New Port Richey, Marco Island, Spring Hill, and Palm Coast. The cities' commonality is they are known as retirement communities.[68]

"Miami," South Florida officials both boast and cringe, "is the only city in America with a foreign policy." Rim shot! To the dismay of many Florida residents, observed journalist Tom Fiedler, "the American system of government does not give states a formal role in determining foreign policy." But immigrants continue to shape the countries they left. Financial remittances support desperate families left behind. Politically, immigrants influence American foreign policy through lobbying, donations, and moral suasion. Poinciana and Buenaventura Lakes, Doral and Weston, exert enormous influence on the future of Puerto Rico and Venezuela. What happens in Florida rarely stays in Florida. In 2011, Muslims, furious over a mock trial and the burning of a Quran at a church in Gainesville, attacked a UN compound in Afghanistan, killing seven foreigners. Pastor Jones was later arrested in Polk County before he had an opportunity to burn three thousand Qurans on the eve of the twelfth anniversary of 9/11.[69]

In June 2010, the *New York Times* published an article by Jason DeParle with the apt title "A World Ever More on the Move." DeParle described a decade of torque and tension wrought by migration, emigration, and immigration: "Perhaps no force in modern life is as omnipresent yet overlooked as global migration, the vehicle of creative destruction that is reordering ever more of the world." Immigration is the issue of the century, even centuries. It is a political nightmare and opportunity, a defining moment and deflection point for generations. The issue will not go away. Florida's future will likely look a lot like its past when it comes to immigrants. In other words, it will look a lot like Florida and America in 1810, 1910, or 2010.[70]

9

Sunshine amid Shadows

Florida on the Brink

Still, they came, by the carload and jet planes, both the barefoot and the bountiful. Hugging rubber rafts and transferring their retirement portfolios. Nothing—not hanging chads, not the incongruity of a Florida hockey team winning the Stanley Cup, not four major hurricanes in the span of forty-four days, not snarky articles by effete intellectuals, not even the optics of John Kerry hunting gators in the glades—could prick the Florida Balloon or derail the Florida Dream.

Or so it seemed. For decades, Cassandras and Jeremiahs had warned that Florida stood on the eve of destruction. Mere months after Hurricane Ivan sheared Escambia County, property values rose across Pensacola Bay. Indeed, investors have long capitalized on hurricanes' destruction to sweep in and purchase battered beach cottages and mom-and-pop waterfront motels at depressed prices. Bigger replaces smaller: Florida was back, but it was never down. Remarkably, between 1 July 2004 and 30 June 2005, the Sunshine State added 400,000 new residents, the largest increase in any single fiscal year of the decade except for the following year.[1]

Growth has consequences. In October 1999, the journalist Michael Browning wrote a thoughtful essay in the *Palm Beach Post*, beginning lyrically: "Like the lower bulb of an hourglass, South Florida is filling up with people and running out of time, simultaneously. A new poll shows that Floridians are getting sicker of Florida, the longer they live here." In early 2000, journalist Julie Hauserman posed a tough-love question for Floridians to ponder: "Yes, we're growing, but into what? Can any reasonable person argue that Florida isn't looking uglier by the minute? Look around: Strip mall. Chain fern bar. Trailer park. Chain discount store. High-rise condominium. Car lot. Fast-food place. Topless bar." The governor of Florida promptly responded, adding his perspective. "I love the fact that we're having a debate about growth," proclaimed Jeb Bush. "It could be far worse. You could live in North Dakota, where they have no growth pressures on the natural systems, and they have no opportunity. I'd rather be here." In 2002, Professor Louis Rene Beres challenged our national priorities, asking provocatively, "What kind of an economy relies for its buoyancy on the ceaseless consumption of more and more 'things,' a consumption that bypasses progress and crowds out our capacity to do anything significant or important? We are what we buy." He concluded: "Let us be candid. In America, the most bountiful and privileged nation on Earth, there is great anxiety and far-reaching unhappiness."[2]

In August 2004, Richard and Barbara Cole moved from Philadelphia to The Villages. On that August day, they were joined by almost 2,000 other future Floridians. When asked about his journey, Mr. Cole replied candidly, "The roads were crowded." Rim shot![3]

Convincing Floridians less is more, especially in an era of dizzying growth, is intellectually challenging and politically dangerous. If a single word encapsulated the first half of the first decade of twenty-first-century Florida, it was confidence. Florida is the place where dreams are confirmed: old age amid palm trees, a second chance after too much snow and misery in Illinois, a new home that also served as an investment and inheritance, and fresh opportunities to find happiness and rekindle romance.[4]

The Florida Boom, 1945–2008, defied gravity, economics, and common sense. Other than a few blips, Florida had not suffered a serious recession or depression since the 1920s and '30s. The future seemed as sunlit as the present, largely because the early years of the new century awaited the arrival of America's first baby boomers/retirees. More than 72 million babies were born in the United States between 1946 and 1964, a demographic so massive that writers strained to find proper metaphors. The baby boom generation has been called many things (mostly ill-suited for print), but few denied the sheer weight and gravity of a single generation. One demographer called the group a pig in a python, referring to the giant bulge in the snake's torso. But on a practical level, baby boomers retiring and headed south seemed to have awarded the Sunshine State a "stay out of recession" Monopoly card. Boomers who arrived in 2006 were different from the elderly retirees of the 1950s. Most dramatically, they brought more financial resources and lived longer. The average post-fifty Southwest Florida resident earned 24 percent more than their younger cohorts, aged eighteen to fifty. A sixty-two-year-old nurse who retired to Florida in 2006 could now expect to live to their eighties or nineties. Moreover, our vocabulary was changing. "Don't call them retirees," warned a series in the *Fort Myers News-Press* titled "Bracing for the Boom," adding: "The word 'senior' is also a massive turnoff to future older residents of Southwest Florida. Baby boomers are active, and they prefer to label retirement as a relocation or refocusing." As a sign of the new times, in 2006, Fort Myers hosted the nation's first baby boomers' beauty pageant, followed by the Florida Senior Games State Championship. A headline in the series summarized the frenzy: "Everyone's Panning for 'Gray Gold.'"[5]

The dawn of a new century in a new millennium fostered a heady optimism. George Bailey and Bernie Madoff, Wonder Woman and Princess Leia, had settled down in Coral Springs and Marco Island, Northport and Port St. Lucie, and become real estate salespeople, all for the "pursuit of happiness." The stars were in perfect alignment, even if we later learned astrologers were cooking the cosmos's books. The Federal Reserve chairman adjusted rates, tamping down fears of inflation or a crash, as if he were a maestro. How does one measure "happiness"? In 2004, pollsters asked residents a simple question: "In general, how satisfied are you with the way things are going in Florida today? Almost two-thirds of Floridians answered the question "very satisfied" and "somewhat satisfied." Only 12 percent responded, "very dissatisfied."[6]

Seminole casinos and the Florida State Lottery, real estate speculators and hedge fund operators were merely creating new wants and desires. Between 2000 and 2007, Floridians were betting on better futures: senior citizens dreamed of second acts and golden honeymoons; Nicaraguans and Cubans were betting on new lives amid new freedoms. Transplanted Iowans and Pennsylvanians bet that a new American dream could be found in Clearwater or Port St. Lucie. Floridians bet and prayed that the Category 5 hurricane churning in the Caribbean would skirt the Gold Coast or Panhandle. Floridians taking their DNA tests bet that their great-grandmother's tales about Seminole bloodlines were true. African Americans moving to Orlando or Lauderhill were betting that Florida was a harbinger of the New South. Florida has always straddled the line between respectability and outrageousness, between honest toil and an easy buck, between strict adherence to the Protestant work ethic and games of luck and chance. Booms and busts rewarded and punished sinners and saints. To be a Floridian was to gamble on the future. The never-ending boom dealt many gamblers a royal flush.

But the Sunshine State was much more than the butt of jokes or a national lampoon; the Sunshine State was becoming a lodestar for intellectuals, commentators, and students. "This is a different place than it was," wrote journalist David Shribman in 2005. "Any state that grows by about 800 people a day almost has to be. But in some ways Florida is the place the rest of the country is becoming." Journalist Abby Goodnough reflected, "But for Florida, there is a curious psychic toll, a sense of merging from an alternate universe where gripping sagas blot out the beloved sun." Professor Diane Roberts explained: "Nothing bad is supposed to happen to you in Florida. It's where the Magic Kingdom is and where you wish upon a star." When asked the meaning of the 2000 election, Elián, Terri Schiavo, and hurricanes, William McKeen, a professor of journalism at the University of Florida, replied: "It's kind of exciting but it drives you crazy, too. It's time for Wyoming to have its chance." The phrase "the Floridization of America" was gaining credence as Florida was becoming a hologram or augury, an eerie glimpse as to what America would become. Or hope to avoid.[7]

Sunny Optimism

For all the auguries, clues, exposés, revelations, lies, and denials, Floridians refused to take seriously Florida native Jim Morrison's apocalyptic lyrics, "This is the end, beautiful friend." Yet Florida is the Sunshine State *and* the Thunderstorm State. Few Floridians took seriously the House Stark family seal that warned, "Winter is coming."

Not even Hurricanes Cassandra and Jeremiah slowed the one-way traffic bringing newcomers across the Florida state line. Florida pulsated with new arrivals and developments. In April 2006, the *Florida Trend* cover story was titled "1,000 New Floridians Every Day." To place that number into perspective, a 1950 headline announced, "Florida Population Gains 3,464 a Week." Reporters mined mobility and demographic data from 2004, researching paths of interstate vans and immigration stiles to answer a fundamental but elusive question: How many people were really added to Florida's census rolls on a typical day? The conventional wisdom suggested a figure of 1,000, but the real answer is more complicated. The figures included 115 newcomers by subtracting deaths from births. Immigrants constituted one-quarter of the total. In total, almost 2,000 newcomers arrived daily![8]

A sobering statistic both underscored and questioned Florida's optimism: while 1,890 people moved to Florida every day, 946 residents were leaving! Rumors circulated that the inmates at Raiford State Prison stamped out a specialty license plate designed for expats: "Florida: It's Not What I Thought It Would Be!" Few Floridians or public officials ever asked, and even fewer had answers to the question, "So, what happens when 1,000 newcomers stop coming?" Growth begat chamber of commerce slogans: Growth is good. Growth pays for itself. Every new Floridian needs new housing, new landscaping, and their taxes paid for roads, teachers, and prison guards. In Florida, the addition of 1,000 daily newcomers was not only healthy, but recession-proof.[9]

Flipping

Like General Motors and Fanny and Freddy, Florida seemed too big to fail. Tempered by sixty years of prosperity and a steady rate of housing inflation, new and old Floridians understandably felt emboldened to join the great Florida real estate stampede. But not everyone expected to be living in that new home for thirty years. Or not even thirty days. In 2005, *Money Magazine* introduced an unfamiliar term to Americans: flippers. Where once purchasing a home was tantamount to a lifetime commitment and aspiration, now flipping—buying a house one week and reselling it days, weeks, or months later—became something between industrial arts and gambling. Flippers, wrote a financial reporter, "have discovered that a modest down payment and a little patience can net them tens (even hundreds) of thousands of dollars in profits." Flippers were becoming urban legends, some acquiring nicknames such as "the king of the Sarasota flip."[10]

If one county seemed recession-proof, it was Palm Beach, home to the super-rich, a place for new and old money. For five years, home prices in that county had spiked 25 percent per year. Prices in Palm Beach and Broward counties rose 36 percent in 2005, third nationwide in increase. Yet by August 2006, the price of a typical family home in Palm Beach County declined for the first time in the new decade. In August 2005, the median-priced home sold for $411,400, a figure declining to $386,000 a year later. Economists cited such declines across America. Even more concerning, in Florida, homes were on the market twice as long as in previous years. The real estate industry thrives on hope, and one analyst promised that if Florida avoided a major hurricane, normalcy would return. The prices of condominiums, for instance, continued to rise.[11]

Speculative Fever: Selling Florida

In 2007, the New Mexico State Legislature authorized an official state question, "Red, green, or Christmas?" The answer refers to the ritual ordering of chili preferences, a hallowed tradition in the Southwest. New Mexico also dictates an official state spelling of the coveted spice/condiment/entree: chile, not chili or chilli! States have official state birds, flowers, and in Florida, even an official state pie (key lime pie).[12]

If the 2005 Florida Legislature had adopted an official state question, it might have been, "Can you guess how much I paid for this house?" Variations include: "Did you hear how much the condos are selling for on Beach Drive?" and "Can you imagine asking a half-million dollars for a 1925 bungalow that sold for $25,000 in 1980?" In the *Sarasota/Manatee Business* magazine's 2005 Year in Review, the lead topic was obvious: "Real estate dominated every other topic in Sarasota and Manatee in 2005. Prices continued to shoot into the stratosphere, with Sarasota/Manatee among the most expensive areas in the Sunshine State." Harold Bubil, the real estate editor for the *Sarasota Herald-Tribune* during this era, knew Florida was headed for trouble "when the real estate stories moved from the real estate section to page 1-A. Especially when the headlines announced increases in median sales prices of 30 percent." He added that another troubling sign occurred at a party in 2005, when "two 30-ish elementary school teachers from North Port . . . were telling me about the rental houses they were buying." The *Naples Daily News,* looking back from the perspective of 2012, called the era 2007–10 "On the Bubble," with the subtitle "It Was Pedal to the Metal on Growth, but a Red Light Loomed on the Horizon." An astonishing 30 percent of Florida home buyers in 2007 already had two or more mortgages![13]

Journalists at the *Naples Daily News* noted that while new residents had been pouring into Southwest Florida for decades prior to 2007, something strange began happening in the late twentieth and early twenty-first centuries: "They were teachers, security guards, doormen, college students supplementing bartending jobs by buying a house or two preconstruction—with no plans of ever living in them or paying the mortgage. They left their day jobs." Another observer wrote, "Homes sold within days or even hours of hitting the market, their prices marked up tens of thousands of dollars." Shelton Weeks, the director of the Florida Gulf Coast University's Lucas Institute for Real Estate, reflected upon Southwest Florida: "You could not go to a cocktail party or reception or local golf club and not have somebody talking about the next real estate deal they were getting into." Weeks added that local governments were asking why new college graduates were turning down good job offers at $35,000 a year. "Well," he explained, "they turned them down because they got an offer from a construction company for $45,000."[14]

One of the consequences of an overheated market and a record demand was housing inflation. Along the Gold Coast, Tampa Bay, and Metro Miami, Floridians were paying dearly for housing. "Affordable housing" became a buzzword. Spiraling real estate prices meant that more and more Floridians were "priced out" of the home market. By 2005, six in ten renters in Miami-Dade, Broward, and Monroe counties were paying 30 percent of their incomes for rent, a significant increase in less than a decade. "The Miami area is now almost as unaffordable as New York and Los Angeles," reported the *Miami Herald.* To understand what just happened, a single-family home in South Florida cost $150,000 in 2000. Five years later, that same home cost $340,000.[15]

Real estate was making many Floridians very wealthy. The wealth was filtering down to architectural firms, roofing contractors, cement manufacturers, custom-cabinet companies, and carpenters. But the surest and riskiest path to quick money was speculation. Billboards and television advertisements admonished Floridians that they, too, could become millionaires if they understood the fundamentals of real estate. Acquiring a real estate license became a ticket to one of Florida's hottest occupations.[16]

Almost anyone, it seems, could profit from Florida's real estate fever. Hydra Lacy Jr. bought seven homes between 2004 and 2007 in St. Petersburg. His first purchase occurred in 2004. Three years earlier he had been in state prison, sentenced for rape. His mortgage company eventually went bankrupt, and in January 2011, armored vehicles knocked down his home that he had barricaded himself in. He had killed two St. Petersburg police officers.[17]

Robert Trigaux had spent decades studying Tampa Bay's economy. He asked in May 2005: "When Florida can claim four of the top five, and eight of the top ten, metropolitan areas in the nation with the greatest home appreciation in the first quarter of 2005, can talk of speculative investing be far behind? The median price of a single-family home in Florida in April 2005 had soared to $218,660, a breathtaking 26 percent increase in one year's time." The Bradenton and Sarasota markets ranked first and second nationally, followed by West Palm Beach/Boca Raton. In a single year, the price of a home there increased 46 percent. Fort Lauderdale/Hollywood/Pompano Beach ranked fifth.[18]

In a society dazzled by wealth and celebrity, Donald Trump was becoming a popular culture icon. On world-class golf courses, hit television shows, and signs announcing luxury condos, Donald Trump was omnipresent. Donald Trump University opened in Boca Raton in 2004, coinciding with the NBC blockbusters *The Apprentice* and *Celebrity Apprentice.* One promotion lauded Trump as "the most celebrated entrepreneur on earth." Advertisements promised students that they, too, could become wealthy by taking online real estate investment classes from "professors" handpicked by Mr. Trump. Tuition was not cheap, and the "Gold Elite" seminars were pricey, but the master of the deal blustered, "Get off your ass, go out and learn something!"

Trump officials sold a licensing agreement to Mike and Irene Milin of Boca Raton. Essentially, Trump sold his brand-name to the Milins. Trump's staff may or may not have known that the Milins had been charged with deceptive marketing practices in several states, including Florida in 2001. Would-be millionaires paid $1,000 and more to attend "The Donald Trump Way to Wealth Seminar," where they were encouraged to spend more money for a "Gold Elite" mentoring program consisting of expert coaches personally selected by Trump. "At Trump University," wrote reporters, "saying yes didn't stop the pressure. . . . [S]aying yes wasn't the end. It was the beginning." Scores of complaints alleging fraud poured into the Florida attorney general's office. Attorney General Bill McCollum never ever acted. In 2013, Trump's charity donated $25,000 to Florida Attorney General Pam Bondi. Soon thereafter Bondi announced her office would not proceed with an investigation of the complaints against Trump University.[19]

For much of American history, owning a house united a diverse citizenry around a core belief, values Ralph Waldo Emerson described as "industry, order, frugality, reverence, purity, and self-control." But a dream house in a dream state was also a commodity. This attitude was hardly limited to the Sunshine State, but in a place where two-thirds of the residents were born somewhere else, "home" often meant Toledo, Queens, or Detroit. But in the early years of the century, everyone—fast-food managers, retired autoworkers, and paladin flippers—shared a bedrock belief vital to real estate: confidence. Paying $250,000 for a 1924 Craftsman bungalow that had originally cost $4,000 but sold for $69,000 in 1999 was not insane *if* one remained confident that the same house would be worth $500,000 in five years. If bought timely and sold shrewdly, a home was making record numbers of Floridians paper millionaires. The grand illusion, of course, was the hope and confidence that the housing boom would last forever.[20]

For much of Florida's history, property was relatively inexpensive. "In Florida, it's not just that the weather's great," began a 1959 story in *U.S. News & World Report,* "it's that the living is easy and cheap." Florida was an affordable version of California. Few new home buyers used the word "cheap" in the years 2000–2005. Old and new Floridians confronted a harsh reality: rapidly rising home prices. When compared to 1999, average home prices in 2005 Florida rose 70 percent, gas prices had risen 78 percent, and homeowners' insurance increased 50 percent. Meanwhile, wages had risen only 19 percent. Increasingly, cities were challenged with hiring teachers, police officers, and municipal workers. Statistics illuminated the sizzling housing boom across Florida. A typical home in Palm

Beach County in January 2005 cost $361,800. Statewide, average housing prices topped the $200,000 plateau. In contrast, a typical home in Youngstown, Ohio, sold for $82,400. Housing prices peaked in December 2006. A real estate agent cut to the chase, "If you're a first-time homebuyer coming into Broward County looking for a $250,000 home, good luck!"[21]

In 2004, Adam Michaelson worked for Countrywide Financial. He witnessed the "next frontier" of financial services: "the Refi boom," Americans' discovery that as their home values soared, they were able to buy more houses. "Americans were using their homes' increased value as ATM machines," wrote Michaelson. "But 'don't worry' everyone said. Home values would continue to rise, and one could always refinance. Again. And again."[22]

The speculative orgy changed the way Floridians lived, worked, consumed, and dreamed. In a trend that would have horrified our Puritan ancestors, who abhorred self-indulgence and preached frugality, personal debt spiraled. In 1960, the debt carried by Americans amounted to about one-half of our national income. By 2007, our collective debt had soared to 133 percent of Americans' income. Credit-card debt nearly tripled between 1989 and 2001. In Judge Hardy's small-town ways, Americans saved and bought homes they could afford. But many Americans, reading newspaper accounts of housing inflation, became bleary-eyed. In late 2006, buying a median-priced home in the Tampa Bay area cost $198,000 and required an annual salary of almost $70,000, making homeownership difficult if not dangerous for a nurse, teacher, or police officer. Salaries had not kept pace with housing inflation. In a study of Sunbelt housing markets, Tampa ranked last in housing affordability. Too many Floridians reasoned that waiting was tantamount to humiliation and defeat and gambled on the future. Cashing in on the great real estate orgy, record numbers of real estate transactions involved *second* home purchases.[23]

Banks and Credit Unions

Debt, the devil, or credit union be damned, home ownership soared, emboldening the American dream. By 2005, memories of soup lines, Hoovervilles, and the Great Depression had largely vanished. Hollywood had once glamorized the popular image of the local bank and home mortgage, most effectively in Frank Capra's 1946 populist masterpiece *It's a Wonderful Life.* In the film, George Bailey is a small-town banker who sacrifices his dreams of travel and fortune to help his Bedford Falls neighbors buy and hold onto their homes. For generations of immigrants, owning a home rationalized the sacrifices of steerage, hard toil, and loneliness. An Italian proverb promised landless peasants, "He that crosses the ocean buys a house." The proverb validated the crossings.

George Bailey would not recognize Florida's banking and savings & loan industry in the early twenty-first century. Local banks had been largely swallowed up by bigger banks. The reckoning came in the 1980s and 1990s, when regional and national banks swooped in to feast upon the Florida market. By 1990, twelve of Florida's largest fifteen banks had national headquarters out of state. By the late 1990s, Florida had officially become a banking colony for Charlotte, Atlanta, and Birmingham. In 1997, on the day his NationsBank acquired the Florida giant, Jacksonville's Barnett, for $15.5 billion, the North Carolina banking mogul Hugh McColl boasted, "Now, I own Florida." What this meant, among other things, was the loss of local and familial ties that banks and their employees once enjoyed before the wave of mergers.[24]

Florida lenders, hell-bent upon succeeding quotas, made some colossally bad decisions. They permitted too many people who had difficulty in good times paying their mortgages, and when bad times arrived, a cascade of foreclosures occurred. Investigators discovered industry code words and acronyms. A "NINJA" meant, "no income, no job, no assets." A "liar" was a client with "no-verification" of stated income or loans, and an "exploding loan" was a mortgage with manageable payments for two years, and then it exploded. The term "subprime" lending was popular.[25]

Increasing numbers of Americans realized the dream of home ownership. In 1960, 62 percent of Americans owned their own home, a figure that peaked at 74 percent in 2005. Florida mirrored the nation. Within the state, wide variations of ownership could be found, from a high of 80 percent in Martin County to a low of 58 percent in Miami-Dade County. For congressmen and presidents, mortgage deductions and legislation made good politics. President Bill Clinton was especially resourceful in securing home mortgages for first-time buyers. Critics conceded the policy made for good politics but bad economics. In what might be called irrational exuberance, many families bought homes they could not afford, rationalizing they could quickly sell their home for a handsome profit and realize the American dream.[26]

Would Calvinist great-great-grandfathers have been more appalled at the shrinking size of our families or the growing size of our homes? "By and large," wrote economic reporter Robert Samuelson, "the new American home is a residential SUV." In 1950, the American home averaged 983 square feet. By the new century, typical homes had tripled in size. "A home is now a lifestyle," observed Samuelson. Popular specialties included home theaters, entertainment systems, and gyms. Journalists coined new terms to describe these new homes—McMansions, Starter Castles, and Faux Chateau. Journalists recycled old terms to describe a new privileged group distinguished by their lavish expenditures: "conspicuous consumption." Coined by Thorstein Veblen in his 1899 book *Theory of the Leisure Class,* "conspicuous consumption" describes spending that satisfies no need other than prestige and vanity. But unlike the idle rich of the Gilded Age, most of the new wealthy worked, or retired after a lifetime of toil.[27]

Wealth

When asked why he robbed banks, Willie Sutton replied, "Because that's where the money is." Why do so many wealthy people live in Florida? Florida state law is very generous to rich residents. Florida has no income or inheritance tax, actions taken by the Florida State Legislature in the 1920s in order to lure wealthy new residents. For those seeking a sanctuary against creditors, Florida law generously protects the entire value of one's home from bankruptcy courts.

You are what you consume. Thorstein Veblen understood this over a century ago. "Let me tell you about the very rich," wrote F. Scott Fitzgerald. "They are different from you and me." Fitzgerald and Veblen realized that the ranks of the wealthy are identified not only by their mansions, but also by their stylish clothes and expensive jewelry, as well as by where they shop and dine. Veblen would have smiled at the 12 December 2005 front-page headline of the *Sarasota Herald Tribune:* "Starbucks, Make That Sarasota, Has Arrived." A city or urban neighborhood was simply not chic if it had not attracted a Starbucks or Whole Foods.

Wealth was accelerating at such a pace that ranks of Florida's wealthiest residents included billionaires. In its 2006 rankings, *Forbes'* list of the four hundred richest Americans included *only* billionaires, among them twenty-seven Floridians, more than a threefold increase in six years. Indicative of the amassed wealth, the *Orlando Sentinel* ran a story on the front page in 2005, asking, "What Kind of House Will $1 Million Buy?" The answer must have shocked longtime residents: "In this market, it [dream house] may lack lake and need some fixing up." According to the 2004 census, Palm Beach ranked first among Florida counties with the most $1 million homes, with 9,558, followed by Miami-Dade (7,182), Broward (5,704), and Sarasota (4,441). Wealth was also migrating to places in Florida that had not attracted the notoriety. Walton County, home of archetypical New Urban community Seaside, as well as swanky Rosemary Beach and WaterColor, had been voted the fifth-most-popular destination of "rich Americans." The top ten included third-ranked Nassau County, home to the Amelia Island Plantation Resort. In 2010, rich Americans ranked Collier County, home to Naples and Marco Island, as the favorite destination to move.[28]

Technology aided Florida's sales pitch to the uber rich and the middling classes. Wi-Fi, cable TV, air-conditioning, computers, and cell phones made the remotest island or gated compound a modern business and communications center. Writers or computer programmers could now live year-round in places such as Sanibel Island, a place so remote in the late 1940s that one telephone served islanders' needs. Today, almost any commodity can come anywhere "in the guise of a brown UPS truck." By 2005, the Amazon delivery truck had become mainstream.[29]

Technology also revolutionized Americans' ability to search for life's answers. The Internet changed the pace and character of our lives. In 2007, what was the number-one query for news on the Google search engine? Revealingly, Americans "googled" the TV show *American Idol!* The third-most-googled item was Britney Spears, a troubled singer. One would have hoped that newcomers to Florida would have dedicated themselves to making their new communities a better place. But in a pattern that was nationwide, Floridians were not joining voluntary associations with the same enthusiasm as their parents and grandparents. In 2006, the Anna Maria Island Woman's Club disbanded after more than six decades of service. The club's roster had plummeted to only thirty members. While Anna Maria Island was booming, residents preferred to "bowl alone." By 2020, the state of Florida ranked dead last in terms of volunteerism, a statistic that would have shocked museum directors who depend upon seniors to serve as guides, docents, and ticket takers.[30]

Floridians and Americans were also receiving their news in alternative media. In a disturbing trend, they were also becoming more cynical about democracy, a series of trends that produced a confluence of crises. David Brooks pronounced America "a broken society." The following decade would realize the costs of such disillusionment and anger.[31]

The first decade of the new century institutionalized "Florida Man." A steady stream of "Florida Man" and "Weird Florida" stories tickled readers of the *Akron Banner* and *Indianapolis Star.* Dave Barry reminisced how, during this era, interviewers never asked, "'Why do you live in Florida?' Or: 'What do you like about Florida?' No, the tone is always, 'What the hell is *wrong* with Florida?'" If Florida were a character on *Seinfeld,* Barry conjectured, "Florida would be Kramer: Every time it appears, the audience automatically laughs, knowing it's going to do some idiot thing." Among other oddities, 2007 highlighted a Tampa middle school principal who was arrested for buying crack cocaine. "In his office. At *school.*" An expert in the field reflected, "Could that event happen in Fargo, N.D.?" Carl Hiaasen replied, "This is a place where people come, and they're either running away from something or running after something." But technology was making it more difficult to escape from one's past. No man is an island in the World of Internet and Google.[32]

A series of technological revolutions also reordered the lives of working-class and poor Floridians. The falling price of cell phones and computers touched the lives of the working classes and poor. The public libraries also provided computer services for those who could not afford purchases, as increasingly, applications for employment and public services required access to a computer.[33]

The Recession Unfurled

The terms "recession" and "Great Recession" seem inadequate to describe the housing crisis and economic collapse that occurred in Florida and across much of the nation. Moreover, there is lack of agreement on the precise beginning and ending of the economic collapse. Some scholars claim it began in 2007; others insist the announcement of the Lehman Brothers bankruptcy in September 2008 marks its inception.

Unlike Black Thursday, when, on 24 October 1929, the American Stock Market spiraled out of control and announced the Great Depression, the massive housing collapse of the early twenty-first century had no such dramatic single cataclysmic moment or signal commencement. The Great Recession—no one has coined a better term to describe this era—began sometime between 2007 and 2008. The Great Malaise? The Era of Bad Feelings? Florida may not have been responsible for the social and economic upheavals, but the Sunshine State played a major role in the causes and suffered disproportionately in the consequences.

The causes are manifold. Americans had been gorging on debt for decades. Easy credit, the promise of a better life through the consumption of more and more electric appliances, recreational pursuits, bigger automobiles, and a second home in Florida fueled the debt binge. An amenities revolution saw the price of houses zoom in price, add-ons, size, and furnishings. The word "McMansion" came of age to describe ridiculously sized homes that did not belong and had no sense of scale for the surroundings. The subtitle of Michael Lewis's book on the subject is insightful: *Panic! The Story of Modern Financial Insanity.*[34]

Disquieting but not alarming news trickled from newspaper headlines and nightly newscasts. Late August in Florida typically produced news of overcrowded classrooms and a flood of new students. But across Central Florida, the heart of Florida's population boom, superintendents asked, "Where have the new students gone?" Pinellas County school officials announced closing five schools at the end of the school year because of vanishing students. Broward County first encountered the drop in school enrollment in 2005, a trend that extended for the rest of the decade. In Broward County, the district usually hired 2,000 teachers annually, but in 2007, only 200 new teachers were needed. In Volusia County, the decline between the start of the 2007–8 school year and 2006–7 was down by more than 1,000 students. In November 2007, Stan Smith, director of the University of Florida's Bureau of Economic and Business Research, reported that Florida's population growth slowed dramatically the previous year. Economists and politicians, accustomed to an annual rise of 400,000 new residents between 2003 and 2006, expressed concern that the Sunshine State grew by *only* 331,000 between April 2006 and 2007. Leaders rationalized that New York and Illinois would be giddy to announce such figures. And besides, the baby boomers will soon be arriving *en masse.* Even the Gators had a bad year (9–4 record)![35]

In Florida, poets and real estate salesmen have endorsed life on the beach: "An ocean breeze puts a mind at ease" and "saltwater cures all wounds." But the laws of supply and demand and the psychology of panic selling pay little heed to poets. In the late summer of 2006, an unusual headline announced, "Waterfront Homes Flood the Market." The Gulf Harbors Civic Association's newsletter included plaintive pleas: "WHY IS EVERYONE SELLING?" and "MORE HOMES FOR SALE MEAN LOWER PRICES!" Real estate insiders dismissed any idea of panic, pointing to New Port Richey's lack of glamour. But a few months later, another headline appeared, "On Clearwater Beach, Condo Dreams Dry Up." Clearwater Beach was very glamorous. A spokesperson explained that Clearwater Beach will "come back stronger, bigger, better than ever." Few realized that New Port Richey and Clearwater were canaries in the coal mine or, in metaphoric Florida, elegant terns in the phosphate mine. Even William Shakespeare understood the nervousness of an economy on the brink. In *Henry IV,* Falstaff laments, "I can get no remedy against this consumption of the purse: borrowing only lingers and lingers it out, but the disease is incurable."[36]

10

Cloudy Skies over "Foreclosureville"

Florida's Great Recession and Reset

In the late fifteenth century, Tuscany was ablaze. No place on earth stirred the human imagination more than Renaissance Florence. Not everyone approved of such tumultuous change. Savonarola, an austere Dominican friar, questioned Florentine manners and morals, urging the faithful and righteous to renounce their worldly possessions. The bonfires of the vanities consumed Florence, but with it, Savonarola.

For several generations, modern-day Savonarolas have lacerated Florida as too materialistic, too tawdry, and too much. Alas, Florida, a modern Icarus, flew too close to the sun, crashing to the earth by overweening hubris and earthly greed. In his 1988 novel *The Alchemist,* Paulo Coelho wrote, "It's the possibility of having a dream come true that makes life interesting." An equally compelling emotion is the reason we love the lottery and stock-car racing and trapeze artists performing without nets: the possibility of having the spectacle or dream crash and burn. Under the Big Top, Florida is the land of booms and busts, part of the state's narrative and DNA.

At its worst, the causes of Florida's economic upheaval, 2007–12, involved a real estate collapse. The pricking of the Great Florida Real Estate Bubble exploded with a big bang, resulting in a housing collapse, a drastic decline in new residents, and a loss of confidence in, even despair over, the future of Florida.

The Room Where It Happened

On Sunday, 14 September 2008, the presidential election campaign advanced full bore. Reports of suicide car bombers in Iraq and a worsening domestic economy torpedoed President George W. Bush's approval ratings and place in history. The Federal Reserve had already bailed out Bear Stearns and AIG, global financial and investment superpowers. But Republican nominee U.S. Senator John McCain was ecstatic, buoyed by the latest Rasmussen and Gallup polls. The computerized tea leaves revealed that for the first time since the Republican convention, McCain had finally taken the lead over his Democratic rival, U.S. Senator Barack Obama.

The next day, Henry M. Paulson Jr., the secretary of the Treasury, called Obama to relay the stop-the-presses headline: Lehman Brothers, the $639 billion financial behemoth, was filing for bankruptcy. The event marked the biggest bankruptcy in history. In an understatement, Paulson projected, "We can expect a very bad market reaction." In Chicago, as Obama's brain trust huddled at the Democratic campaign headquarters on N. Michigan Avenue, the candidate burst into the meeting and informed his aides, "The world is going to change and whatever you guys are working on is going to be different tomorrow." Rahm Emanuel, the brilliant political orchestrator who had once served on the board of directors of Freddie Mac, put the event into perspective: "You never let a crisis go to waste." Following the stunning announcement of the Lehman Brothers collapse, McCain assured a Jacksonville audience, "There's tremendous turmoil in our financial markets. . . . People are frightened by these events. Our economy, I think, still, the fundamentals of our economy are strong." Thirty-six hours later, realizing his gaffe, McCain described the economic meltdown as a "total crisis." Obama thrust with a question, "Senator, what economy are you talking about?" He was not helped by former senator Phil Gramm of Texas, who maintained that the United States was really the victim of a "mental recession." It was too late. The Obama campaign realized McCain's statements and the cratering economy were game-changers. The election was essentially over. Obama's campaign manager, David Plouffe, explained the impact of the week of September 14–20: "The race changed on a dime." McCain never recovered; indeed, he quickly announced that he was returning to Washington to find solutions to the crisis. President Obama later named Emanuel, whom he described as "the enfant terrible in the Clinton administration," his chief of staff.[1]

From the vantage point of 2020, Secretary Paulson pondered the Lehman Brothers collapse: "In 2008, investors lost confidence in all forms of credit . . . with dire consequences for workers, homeowners and savers." Spiraling out of control without reserve funds, new credit, or optimism, financial institutions across the world panicked. The Dow Jones Industrial Average plunged 4.4 percent three days after Lehman Brothers employees, carrying their computers and files, left their Manhattan headquarters. "This was a modern bank failure," explained Adam Tooze. "Then something worse began to happen. The uncertainty spread from individual weak banks to the entire system." Journalist Andrew Ross Sorkin maintained: "The crisis was a moment that cleaved our country. It broke a social contract between the plutocrats and everyone else. But it also broke a sense of trust, not just in financial institutions and the government that oversaw them, but in the very idea of experts and expertise." America's Great Recession morphed into a worldwide recession. Floridians who had no idea who or what AIG or Bear Stearns were or how Fleet Street and Chinese banks affected their mortgages, quickly understood when faraway and domestic economic crises became local headlines. Thomas Friedman's argument that "the world is flat" was loudly confirmed. In a matter of days, new cities in the sand and sun had lost not only breathtaking amounts of capital but faith.[2]

Wall Street was unraveling as financial firms hemorrhaged losses and bankruptcy filings exploded. Flagships were sinking fast. Within days, Bank of America acquired the reeling Merrill Lynch, while several other iconic firms nearly toppled. Floridians learned the depressing news as corporate giants such as Citigroup and Bank of America reported historic losses. Freddie Mac and Fannie Mae, massive financial institutions created by Congress, backed 90 percent of U.S. mortgages. President Harry S. Truman offered a more down-to-earth determination: "It's a recession when your neighbor loses his job; it's a depression when you lose yours." Monday, 16 September 2008, was a day of infamy. The Congressional Budget Office estimated that more value from the U.S. markets was lost on that single day than all the staggering sum budgeted for Iraq and Afghanistan. President George W. Bush addressed the nation. "Despite corrections in the marketplace and instances of abuse," he pleaded, "democratic capitalism is the best system ever devised." The crosshairs of the Great Recession quickly hovered over Florida. America was in panic mode and a depression mood. No county and few cities or neighborhoods escaped the social and economic scars. If 9/11 unified Americans, 9/16 divided Americans as Florida and the Sunbelt experienced an economic free fall.[3]

Crash: The Moment the Economy Turned

Marc Joseph worked as a real estate agent in Fort Myers. He recalled December 2005, a time when home prices crested in Lee County. But then the phone stopped ringing. "It was as if the car came to a stop and all the air went out of the tires." Journalist George Packer used a cartoon metaphor to describe what happened: "When, at Florida's most dizzying mid-decade heights, speculators lost confidence, the faith that kept the state aloft gave way and the economy plummeted like a Looney Tunes character who, suspended in midair, suddenly looks down."[4]

In November 2007, Levitt and Sons filed for Chapter 11 bankruptcy. If the company did not invent modern suburbia, it built the first mass-manufactured, postwar archetype suburb: Levittown. The firm with the magical name and trusted reputation invested heavily in Florida. Among the projects canceled in midconstruction was Tradition in Port St. Lucie. By 2008, few of the planned 1,200 homes were finished and occupied. Many of the residents trusted the development because they had lived in Levitt developments in the North.[5]

The National Bureau of Economic Research and the Federal Reserve assert that the Great Recession officially began in December 2007 and ended in June 2009. But Floridians did not need an economist in Washington or New York to tell them their jobs, homes, and communities were neither too big nor too small to fail.[6]

The Great Recession Unfurled

In March 2009, the *New York Times* proclaimed that America was officially in the grips of a "Great Recession." Beginning in December 2008, use of the term spiked dramatically as increasing numbers of analysts, economists, reporters, and critics had adopted the imprimatur. No one seemed to know who first coined the moniker.[7]

In January 2009, George Packer made an appointment with the author to discuss Florida's woes. He asked if I had a metaphor to describe modern Florida? "Well," I replied, "Florida resembles a Ponzi State. Everything is fine if a thousand newcomers arrive daily. The problem is, no one ever planned for the question, 'What happens when a thousand people *stop* coming to Florida?' It resembles a modern Ponzi scheme when the new investors stop coming." On 9 February 2009, the *New Yorker* magazine appeared. George Packer's cover story proclaimed, "The Ponzi State." *Time*'s Michael Grunwald put his own spin on the causes of Florida's undoing: "The housing bust has exposed a human pyramid scheme—an economy that relied on a thousand newcomers a day, too many of them construction workers, mortgage bankers, real estate agents and others whose livelihoods depended on importing a thousand more newcomers the next day."[8]

The causes of Florida's Great Recession are manifold. Americans had been gorging on debt for decades. Easy credit, the promise of a better life through the accumulation of "things," recreational pursuits, bigger automobiles, and a second home in Florida fueled the debt binge. An amenities revolution and buyer's markets saw houses zoom in price, size, and furnishings. The word "McMansion" came of age to describe ridiculously sized homes that did not belong and lacked a sense of scale.

"Housing bubble" became a familiar term. Journalists from the *Naples Daily News* recalled, "As money flowed into Southwest Florida, few people thought to ask when the bubble might burst, until suddenly, it did." Robert Trigaux, the business columnist for the *St. Petersburg Times,* wrote a prescient 2005 article, "Florida's Housing Bubble: Is It Ready to Burst?" Soon, headlines and evening news stories confirmed the worst fears.[9]

Floridians learned a Great Recession lexicon: underwater/upside-down/toxic/subprime mortgages, short sales, REITs (real estate investment trusts), robo-signings, rocket dockets, arbitrage, derivative trading, flipping, and zombie homes. Purchasing an underwater lot was not unusual in Florida, but an underwater mortgage meant that the value of one's home has shrunk to less than the original mortgage. Translation: not only does the owner have no equity in his/her home, but the mortgage also has negative worth.[10]

A conspicuous success story in the decades before 2006, Florida fell farther and harder than any state. In the 1992 film *Glengarry Glenn Ross,* Alec Baldwin tongue-lashes a nervous sales crew hawking Florida subdivisions from a Chicago boiler room. He scratches his message on a chalkboard: "ABC—A–Always, B–Be, C–Closing!" By the time the musical chairs of death is over, customers realize their land is overpriced and underwater (literally and figuratively). The saga underscores Joseph A. Schumpeter's idea that at the heart of capitalism is "creative destruction."

Creative Destruction: Repo Florida

"Who are we?" Journalist Peter S. Goodman asked this simple but essential question in 2010. "The question has grown resonant as Americans are trying to secure satisfying answers for themselves, reclaiming identities stripped by the downturn." Scenes across Florida—homeless patrons in public libraries and foreclosure signs dotting lawns offered disquieting answers to the question.[11]

New and old occupations and enterprises supplied the Great Recession's changing demands. Carpenters, roofers, and Realtors were out, trashers, board men, and disability lawyers were in. Workers "trashed out" foreclosed houses after previous clients trashed the interiors. Board men boarded up abandoned homes. Locksmiths were also in demand, as owners or managers changed locks so previous tenants could not enter to retrieve their belongings. Lawyers specializing in Chapter 13 personal bankruptcy and assisting clients obtain SSI (Supplemental Security Income) and disability benefits advertised on television, billboards, and mailers. The *Washington Post* featured a popular column called "Half a Tank." It once offered readers "getaways," but in 2009 the column set out "to find the stories of lives altered by a flattened economy." Florida became a popular stop. Perhaps the most creative but disturbing spinoff emerged from Southwest Florida, where a Realtor offered Cape Coral foreclosure boat tours, allowing snowbirds and visitors an opportunity to purchase Florida Recession dream homes. Florida became such a national story line that Princeton University undergraduates studying the foreclosure crisis spent a spring touring Cape Coral. Some students volunteered at the local food bank.[12]

Repo men worked overtime seizing cars and vans from owners unable to make payments. In *Operation Repo* and *The Repo Man*, reality TV traced their edgy world. In a single year, 2009, almost 2 million cars were repossessed. In Jacksonville and Fort Lauderdale, industry officials complained that the inventory of repossessed cars and boats pushed prices down. An industry insider eloquently summed up why the repo business was booming: "So many people have so many things they can no longer afford. This is an excellent time to be a repo man." If the shark hunters in *Jaws* needed a bigger boat, repo workers needed bigger warehouses to store the fruits of their labor. And better technology: transponders and digital recognition systems. "Ken Cage is racing through a private aviation terminal near Orlando when his BlackBerry buzzes with bad news." Thus began a 2010 *Wall Street Journal* story. "The plane he is about to repossess is scheduled to take off for Mexico in three minutes." Mr. Cage and a pilot manage to pick the lock on the door and fly the plane to a secure location." Repo legend Ken Hill calls Florida a "haven" for illegal planes with troubled owners. "For whatever reason, there are a lot of dishonest people in Florida." The Sunshine State is a favorite setting for the reality show *Airplane Repo*.[13]

In *Hardcore Pawn*, the vanishing world of pawn shops revived interest and attracted viewers. Viewers learned that Florida was home to one in ten American pawnshops. In Florida, pawnshops can legally charge monthly interest rates of 25 percent, as opposed to 4 percent in New York. Pawn shops must adapt, and online pawning became trendy. In one case, a Hollywood resident used the site *Pawngo* to pawn an expensive laptop and gold necklace for a $450 loan.

An *Orlando Sentinel* headline announced, "In Central Florida, Across Nation, Pawnshops Go Gangbusters in Tough Times." The owner of La Familia Pawn in Winter Park reported that the recession and reality shows "opened up to a larger customer segment."[14]

Auctioneers worked overtime to sell homes, land, and machines. In 2009, Ritchie Bros. Auctioneers moved a 200-acre lot crowded with Caterpillar wheel loaders, excavators, dump trucks, back hoes, and concrete mixers. Most of the equipment was headed overseas. "Signs of insolvency abound," wrote a journalist. "A truck labeled Florida Trucking rumbles by. It is owned—or was formerly owned—by a Tampa contractor. . . . His company filed for Chapter 11 bankruptcy this year. The same thing happened to Palm City's Concrete Pumping Co."[15]

Recessions tempt the bold and desperate. Trump University pivoted from boom to bust, profiting from the foreclosure nightmare. Donald Trump had become a brand due to the success of his television show. Blanketing future "students" with emails and letters, one such promotion featured a giant image of Donald Trump proclaiming: "The secret of success in life is for a man to be ready for his opportunity when it comes. Are you ready? . . . This one class, how to profit from foreclosures, will get you started on the clearest, sure-fire, money-making opportunity available in a long, long time." Instructors and staff understood the drill outlined in the Trump University manual: "The room temperature should be 68 degrees. Seats should be arranged in a theater-style curve. And government prosecutors had no right to see any documents without a warrant." When prospects seemed reticent to sign up for expensive classes, the suggested response was written out: "I find it very difficult to believe you'll invest in anything else if you don't believe in yourself and your education." If that failed, the manual instructed: "You know who my boss is, right? Mr. Trump is on a mission to create the next wave of independently wealthy entrepreneurs in America. Is that YOU?"[16]

Shadows Blanket Sunbelt Florida

Foreclosures, upside-down mortgages, and Florida became interlocking words and worlds. Foreclosure, the Great Recession's F-word, "is a legal process in which a lender attempts to recover the balance of a loan from a borrower who has stopped making payments to a lender by forcing the sale of the asset used as the collateral in the loan." Simply put, too many people bought inflated homes with little money down, empowered by subprime interest rates. Many hoped to sell the property at a profit; others purchased homes on speculation, never planning to settle; but real people saw their dream home vanish because of events they could neither understand nor control. The foreclosure crisis metastasized, lingering for years. As late as 2012, one in thirty-two homes in Florida faced a bank filing, double the American average. Florida's foreclosure rate ranked worst in the United States.[17]

Owning a home, once the American dream, became a Florida nightmare. By 2010, nearly half of the homes sold in South Florida resulted in a loss. Aside from better Februarys and no state income tax, one of the major incentives to move to Florida was the expectation that one's home would escalate in value. But a study determined that in nine zip codes in Broward and Palm Beach counties, homes had lower median-prices in 2009 than 1999. The *Washington Post* challenged its Mensa Invitational members to create a new word by adding or subtracting one character, adding a new definition. The winner was: "Cashtration (n.): The act of buying a house, which renders the subject financially impotent for an indefinite period of time." Runner-up was "Crecession," a word combining "credit crisis" and "recession."[18]

A prayer offering took place in 2009. The event occurred not at a church but at a Lee County golf course. Unemployed men who had worked in real estate prayed together. "We need something different," sighed a fifty-four-year-old real estate agent from Lehigh Acres. "This community is all bent out of shape," journalist Damien Cave wrote. He provided painful details: "It is a mess of immense volume. . . . In the first six months of 2009, 268,064 properties in Florida received a foreclosure filing. . . . And for those convinced that recent, positive sales figures signal a brisk recovery, consider this: foreclosures outpaced sales of houses and condos in the same period by a factor of nearly three."[19]

The Sunbelt was rocked, with Arizona and Florida especially hit hard. Retirees and Rust Belt refugees had flocked to Florida for simple reasons: people wanted to live in year-round sunshine and buy low and sell high. In 2006, homes that sold for a loss were rare, but four years later, almost half of South Florida houses were underwater. In Miami, home prices plunged by 45 percent between 2006 and 2009. Even as late as 2014, the Miami–Fort Lauderdale–Pompano Beach Metro area contained 458,329 underwater homes, with mortgages considerably higher than the homes' estimated value. Metro Miami and Metro Tampa Bay were "more financially distressed" than Metro Detroit. In Tampa, home values had declined more than half their 2005 prices.[20]

If any Florida county possessed an antirecession formula, it was the kryptonite perfected in Sarasota. By 2000, a wealthy tax base, a world-class cultivation of the arts, and beachfront communities characterized Sarasota County and its 326,000 citizens. Affluent seniors and a generous federal government infused "a gray in gold pipeline" of investments and benefits to Southwest Florida. In 1998, the county's residents derived more income from investments and entitlements than wages. Sarasota may have had the urbanity, but North Port, despite a 2007 study that blamed a litany of urban and economic ills on "poor planning," was growing at an explosive rate. North Port, a sprawling collection of subdivisions, was becoming the largest city in the county. Notably, Sarasota and Manatee counties suffered earlier than most areas. "Property values fell more steeply and earlier than elsewhere," concluded a study. In a four-year span between 2006 and 2010, the tax base lost billions of dollars, while 1,600 firms and 179 storefronts disappeared in Sarasota and Manatee counties. A quarter of the area's department stories went out of business. Almost 42 percent of the mortgages in the Sarasota–North Port–Bradenton Metropolitan Area were underwater, a rate slightly above the state average. As late as 2011, prestigious canal-front homes built in the 1960s on Country Club Shores were selling at half of their 2005 values.[21]

Home to Fort Myers, Cape Coral, and Bonita Springs, Lee County was the hardest-hit county not just in Florida but in the nation. As late as 1950, the landmass encompassing 785 square miles was sparsely inhabited, home to fewer than 25,000 residents. The next sixty years brought massive changes, along with a population of 618,754 in 2010. One way to look at the spectacular growth spurt: this poster child of boom and bust added more new people in the decade 2000–2010 than lived there in 1970. Lee was not simply expanding; its growth ranked tops in Florida and third in America.[22]

Elected mayor of Cape Coral in 2005, Eric Feichthaler realistically believed his greatest challenge was to manage growth. He looked forward to ribbon cuttings: a new high school, new parks, and a modern sewage system. As early as 2007, dreams melded into nightmares: the elimination of public jobs, abandoned homes, and collapsing home sales and prices. Journalist Peter S. Goodman offered Americans a "foretaste of the economic pain awaiting other parts of the country." He reflected, "The Internet made it possible for people ensconced in snowy Minnesota to type 'cheap waterfront property' into search engines and scroll through hundreds of ads for properties here." Goodman introduced readers to Joe Carey. The Ohioan first encountered Cape Coral in 2002, enticed by undeveloped quarter-acre lots for $10,000. He developed the properties through easy construction loans, flipping the units for $175,000 each. He invested in more lots and homes, eventually becoming a real estate agent, then opening a title company. Then the music stopped. Carey's fledgling empire collapsed, along with countless others. Dreams of new schools were now more quixotic than realistic. The good news: an affordable housing crisis overnight became a buyer's market.[23]

The 27 December 2007 dirge-headline of the *Fort Myers News-Press* announced, "Building Permits Crawl to Near-Stop." The 2010 New Year's Eve headline of the paper compressed the decade into three words: "WE SOARED, CRASHED." Journalists flocked to ground zero of the national recession. President Obama, Senator Bill Nelson, and presidential candidate Mitt Romney visited Southwest Florida. A North Fort Myers Realtor explained what happened: "It was a lot of mania. . . . It was a lot of hot air and just collapsed on itself." Another Realtor, Marc Joseph, became famous or infamous for his green bus tours of the properties "For Sale" with a painted sign reading, "Foreclosure Tours R Us." Fatefully, not even Joseph could escape the foreclosure curse, losing his million-dollar home on Hendry Creek. He kept his video recordings of evictions. In 2005, Lee County home prices peaked at $322,300. Yet two years later, the value plunged to barely $100,000. An astounding one in every nine homes in the county received foreclosure notices. Lee County judges created a "rocket docket" to speed up the sheer number of foreclosures. In 2008–9, the county's Circuit Court struggled to process more than 60,000 foreclosures. In addition to foreclosed homes, the county's commercial real estate—the old and new shopping plazas, fast-food franchises and elegant dining establishments—cratered. *Florida Trend* noted the steep dive in the state's commercial property values. One of the exceptions was the Harry Chapin Food Bank of Southwest Florida. The physical and emotional costs were steeper. Journalist Steve McQuilkin wrote an eloquent conclusion: "It was like an infection: Main Street was pulled into the mess that Wall Street made, and many people who didn't get big bonuses, who didn't take out multiple loans, who didn't do anything extravagant, who played it honestly, ended up losing their jobs and their homes. Many went bankrupt. It wasn't their fault, but it was their problem now, their loss, their pain."[24]

The title of the most besieged and beleaguered city in Florida in 2008 was neither Cape Coral nor Fort Myers, but another community in Lee County. While many national reporters vacationed on or heard about Sanibel, Captiva, or Fort Myers Beach, few recognized Lehigh Acres. Some probably had aunts living in Cape Coral. In the pantheon of Florida developers, Leonard Lee Ratner had less charm than George Merrick or the Rosen brothers, but no one had more ambition. Born in Chicago, he dropped out of college to make his fortune. He was, above all, a salesman, hawking everything from novelties to waterfront lots and rat poison. A World War II veteran, Ratner returned to Chicago. Intrigued by a new patented pesticide called warfarin in 1950, he aggressively advertised the new product known as d-Con rat poison, later selling the product brand for $7 million. Ratner moved to Miami in 1951. He purchased almost 20,000 acres of cattle ranches and farmland in lightly populated eastern Lee County. After a few years of raising crops at Lucky Lee Ranch, Ratner envisioned a real estate diamond amid alfalfa fields and cattle barns. He was one of the pioneers in selling half-acre lots for "$10 down and $10 a month." The owners dedicated the new community Lehigh Acres, a subtle nudge that the property was high and dry, not *under* water. "At first," chuckled veteran Florida Realtor Walter Fuller, Lehigh Acres "was frankly a $10 down and $10 a month lot selling snow job." But Lehigh Acres grew as an aggressive legion of salesmen sold 40,000 lots in person and by media and mail. Optimists predicted the remaining 60,000 lots would soon be sold and developed. Never incorporated, Lehigh Acres was a sprawling, poorly designed community. In 1970, 4,400 residents had settled there, with numbers escalating to 87,000 in 2010. A salesman recalled: "They used to bring 20 busloads a day. We had 300 customers, seven days a week. Optimistic that the boom would last, developers completed an additional 13,000 units between 2004 and 2006." It was not unusual during the buying frenzy for new homes to be sold multiple times in a matter of months.[25]

Whereas Cape Coral and Naples marketed their Florida dreams to the middle and upper classes, Lehigh Acres appealed to a new twentieth-century cohort: young retirees and the aspiring middling classes. By the 1950s, prosperity, war, and a generous federal government elevated the status of relatively young military retirees. Some used the GI Bill to learn how to repair air conditioners and televisions.

In 2009, many Americans first learned about Lehigh Acres in a *New York Times* front-page story by Damien Cave. The introduction was brutal: "Desperation has moved into this once-middle-class exurb of Fort Myers, where hammers used to pound." He added, "Welcome to the American dream in high reverse. . . . Crime is up, school enrollment is down, and one in four residents received food stamps in December, nearly a fourfold increase since 2006." A member of the Lehigh Acres Chamber of Commerce lamented, "We don't want to be the foreclosure capital." Jobs disappeared as fast as home buyers. Lee County lost more jobs than any other county in America between 2007 and 2008. "Thieves stole air conditioner parts for scrap," wrote Cave. "And on distant roads with only a few new homes . . . on Narcissus Boulevard and Prospect Avenue—drug dealers moved in." In the conclusion of his study of the impact of the Great Recession upon Florida, George Packer wrote, "Driving around Florida's ghost subdivisions, you feel not just that their influence is waning but that they are physically hollowing out." Singling out Lehigh Acres, he reflected upon a place where "half the driveways are sprouting weeds, and where garbage piles up in the bushes along the outer streets," a place where "it's already possible to see the slums of the future."[26]

Peter Goodman, a reporter touring Cape Coral, felt like an archaeologist at a site "upended and reconfigured by an epochal real estate fiasco. . . . Yes, it has come to this in Cape Coral, a reluctant symbol for the excesses of the great American real estate bubble: foreclosed homes served up as a tourist attraction." Goodman identified "the dominant pursuit of the moment" as "cleaning up the Mess left behind by the era of easy money." He visited abandoned homes, noting, "This is not work for the squeamish." In summary, Goodman wrote, "THE MESS is the product of The Story, the fable that waterfront living beyond winter's reach exerts such a powerful pull that it justifies almost any price for housing." In 2007, Goodman had interviewed the Lee County superintendent of schools, who had hoped to build seven new schools. In 2010, the superintendent confessed that a quarter of his elementary schools were sending home backpacks of food.[27]

"It was a cycle that repeated often—default, foreclosure, repossession, and eviction," observed the *Fort Myers News-Press*. "Jobs were lost, incomes were reduced, homes became unaffordable. Many of the foreclosed mortgages were designed to qualify as balloon notes, loans without documentation of income and interest only payments." Foreclosure and repossession did not end the misery. Years later, companies that purchased bundled foreclosure mortgages hounded hapless former homeowners with legal action. The term "ghost mortgages" was born. "The ghost," explained a journalist, "was in the form of deficiency judgments, a legal demand that dispossessed homeowners pay money for a home they no longer owned." One firm, Dyck O'Neal Inc. of Dallas, Texas, sued former homeowners for the difference in their mortgage balance and the value of the home at foreclosure. Journalists noted, "The collectors came armed with a Florida statute that allows garnishment of debtors' wages."[28]

For writer Paul Reyes, Lehigh Acres unlocked a personal story. In October 1969, his parents honeymooned at the Seville Hotel in Miami Beach. Their son explained the significance of a fateful phone call. A male voice invited the honeymooners for a free trip across Florida. "All that was required of them was that they sit for a brief presentation at the end, a half-hour at most." They and others headed toward Southwest Florida on a Greyhound charter. "The tour was a gimmick, a trap, a means by which the Lehigh Acres Development Company lured potential buyers into the scrubby lowlands of Lee County, into a community not quite a town." There they toured model homes. The Reyes family purchased a lot, ten dollars down, ten dollars a month. Decades later, Reyes found the lot on Charmed Circle. "Charming" was not the first thing that came to his mind upon finding his inheritance. "In the annals of real estate marketing, Lehigh Acres was an incredible success," Reyes concluded. "In the history of urban planning it was apocalyptic."[29]

In late 2009, the president of the Conservancy of Southwest Florida reflected upon what had happened in the previous decade: "Between Fort Myers and Naples you once had 15 miles of open land between the two. Now, pretty much unbroken growth." To the south, not even Collier County escaped the ravages of foreclosure and despair. From Naples and Marco Island to Immokalee and Goodland, the county escaped the early ravages of the recession, filing only 733 foreclosures in 2006. But the following years punished some of the richest and poorest enclaves in America, peaking with 8,203 foreclosures in 2009. In the *Naples Daily News,* journalist Gina Edwards asked a question few leaders and lenders had pondered during the boom years: "What if the workers leave?" Specifically, "Who will serve the dinners, do the dry cleaning, bag the groceries, fix the pool screens, change the hotel bed sheets, care for the sick, build the homes . . . ?" Poignantly, she asked, "Will paradise be lost?"[30]

Collier County felt the pain early and often. In 2009 alone, the county's property value declined $9 billion. The most identifiable problem was housing—too much of it, too expensive and overinflated. When the bubble burst, options ranged from bad to hopeless. A Neapolitan compared the housing bust to the children's game of musical chairs: "At some point the music stops and everyone looks around like, 'Holy Cow, what do we do now?'" Like the game, the people still standing expected to flip the condo for a profit while homes under construction had no buyers. Many developers cut their losses and simply walked away from the projects. Thousands of unfinished homes symbolized the malaise. The construction industry was devastated. An observer noted, "Some of those folks, the last thing they did was drop the keys for the house off at the bank."[31]

Collier County's shopping centers were mauled by the upheaval. "For builders," a local journalist summarized, "it was like watching a row of dominoes falling—people couldn't pay mortgages, stopped going out to eat, started losing their homes and left town. Construction dried up, offices closed, restaurants couldn't pay rent. . . . By 2007, Publix owned 11 shopping centers in the Naples area, renting out office space and store fronts. . . . The bank forced the sales of the plazas for less than what was owed on the mortgage."[32]

Charlotte County lies between Sarasota and Lee counties. Solidly conservative, citizens preferred low-taxed, unincorporated cities. The county has a single incorporated city: Punta Gorda. In 1950, the county had not yet reached a population of 5,000, but the General Development Corporation's purchase of ranchland that spawned Port Charlotte dramatically changed the county's future. In 1979, the railroad line shipping phosphate to Port Boca Grande on Gasparilla Island ceased operations, opening the door for development. Boca Grande, home to celebrities and the elegant Gasparilla Inn, became even more exotic and a magnet for the wealthy. Three miles of Manasota Key belongs to Charlotte County. The desirability of and home prices on such waterfront communities exploded. The Great Recession whiplashed Charlotte's communities, so much so that by 2010, county property values fell below 2004 levels.[33]

Florida acquired the nickname "Foreclosure State" with good reason. Almost one in twenty Florida homes sank into foreclosure in 2008. Lee County may have been the most notorious, but America's top ten foreclosed metro areas also included Fort Lauderdale (number six), followed by Orlando and Miami as seventh and eighth.[34]

Florida's First Coast was politically, fiscally, and attitudinally conservative. One would expect Duval, Baker, Clay, Nassau, and St. Johns counties to have weathered the Great Recession with less pain and fewer bumps. By 2010, the *Florida Times-Union* pronounced, "Area Home Sales: Half Are Distressed." A Workforce official reminisced in 2013, "It wasn't that long ago every single construction worker on the First Coast was employed." Another spokesman observed that the hit to the region's financial affairs industry effectively "wiped out middle management." Some institutions simply went out of business or relocated.[35]

Few Floridians can locate or name one city in Flagler County. Historically, its population growth resembled Baker and Putnam counties more than Nassau and Duval—except 18 miles of the Atlantic Ocean beachfront grace Flagler, unlike its landlocked neighbors. Located south of Jacksonville and St. Augustine, Flagler County was largely irrelevant and forgotten. As late as 1980, its population was only 10,912. But the county's location, bordering the Atlantic Ocean and straddling US 1 and SR A1A made it irresistible to developers.

In February 2007, *Florida Trend* profiled Flagler County in an optimistic article titled "Leader of the Pack." For the second year in a row, it held the title of "fastest-growing county in the nation." The demographics were telling: a county "with nearly as many golf courses as public schools." Nearly half of the households earned $50,000 and more. "How long Flagler's double-digit growth will last is unclear," observed *Florida Trend*. As things turned out, it didn't last long. Palm Coast changed everything. From scrubland and wetlands, the instant city of Palm Coast emerged and became a commercial success. A journalist described the frenetic housing market as "the real estate equivalent of a Viagra party," a period so heady that Flagler was the fastest-growing county in America and Palm Coast grew faster than any city in the country. "So many homes were being built that, at times, in fast-growing Grand Haven, you could not drive down the streets for the congestion of construction vehicles."[36]

News crews congregated in Palm Coast, where a largely unknown city became "the poster child of the Great Recession." The *Washington Post* dedicated a 2011 front-page story to depicting the ills of Flagler County. The story began, "Tony Tobin's luxurious three-bedroom condominium speaks to an unsustainable vision of the good life that not long-ago lured people in droves, transforming this once sleepy retirement community into a boomtown." Housing developments such as Tobin's Tidelands complex dominate Palm Coast. "Similar developments in distress dot the lush landscape in Palm Coast," the writer maintained. "Once they fueled a virtuous cycle of rising property values, new projects, and new jobs. . . . [N]ow they offer evidence of an economy gone bad in ways that are proving difficult to repair."[37]

Palm Coast's woes may have been grievous, but they were scarcely unique: the boom town's economy was built upon growth and a growing housing market. It had no natural attractions, no landmark beaches, tourist attractions, or industry. Officials confessed they missed the comforting sounds of progress. "From the center of Grand Landings subdivision—a 1,500-acre project carved into the sand and scrub of Flagler County, you can sit all afternoon and never hear the *ka-chunk* of a single nail gun."[38]

Deltona in Volusia County is a short drive from Palm Coast. The Volusia County city is another Mackle Brothers development that zoomed from fewer than 5,000 residents in 1970 to 70,000 in 2000. The Great Recession left many homeowners in the city and county with underwater mortgages. As late as 2013, many Volusia County homeowners owed more on their homes than their residences were worth. "The real-estate bubble that burst in 2006–07," observed a reporter, has "left many local residents with the daunting decision of whether to keep paying on a home worth less than what is owed, or walk away, with all the consequences of foreclosure sure to follow them."[39]

To understand the economic devastation, a business writer recommended a ride down Daytona Beach's fabled Atlantic Avenue, now called "Boulevard of Broken Dreams." In 2004, the beachside strip was home to almost 200 hotels, a number that dropped to 134 by 2009. "A drive in either direction from Ocean Walk reveals a streetscape pock-marked with empty strip centers, shuttered restaurants, 'for rent' signs and rundown stores."[40]

On Florida's East Coast, no city soared so high and fell so hard as Port St. Lucie, a community midpoint between Miami and Orlando that grew to 164,603 residents in 2010. In 1983, a headline trumpeted, "Port St. Lucie Suffers No Pain from Steady Growth." Quickly, the instant city eclipsed the population of Fort Pierce, the seat of St. Lucie County. The fastest-growing city in America in 2005 and the third-fastest in 2006, Port St. Lucie soon became one of the nation's most distressed. The *Miami Herald* introduced the community: "Like all legendary parties, the boom-time bash in Port St. Lucie raged on for too long." In 2005, its growth rate reached the double digits, as did its unemployment ranks by 2010. The community in St. Lucie County benefited from its wholesome image, its affordable housing, and the white flight from South Florida. Where does one begin to document the damage? Was it a county commissioner declaring a state of emergency? Or perhaps the figure of 10,764 properties in foreclosure? Or the 10.5 percent unemployment rate? One sign found on almost every block expressed the pain: "For sale by bank."[41]

"Progress Lane is empty." So began a story on what some considered a sign or symbol of Port St. Lucie's woes. The city's mayor promised the $25 million Port St. Lucie Civic Center, dedicated in 2009, was the "beginning of a new era." Instead, it sat empty a year later, quickly becoming a nightmare. "This unmistakably bleak story," a journalist wrote, "manifests in the subdivisions' vacant houses, in boarded-up businesses, in people out of work and in the struggle of soup kitchens and food pantries to fill growing needs." The story profiled a former car salesman who frequented the St. Lucie Catholic Church's free hot meals. "The bottom fell out," he explained. "I have no work right now. My house is in foreclosure. They repossessed my vehicle already." Another resident, a mother of two young daughters, expected her family to soon be evicted from their home. She confessed: "This is just awful, and I know that we are not the only ones going through this. We used to try to go day by day. Now we are just trying to get to the end of each day."[42]

Tom and Dee Prestopnik purchased a home in Port St. Lucie in 2006, a time when home prices crested. "Soon after that the bottom dropped out . . . and the value of our house was halved. How's that for a kick in the slats! Today [2021] my wife checked on Zillow and found that the value of our house has reached the purchase price of fourteen and half years ago."[43]

Hollywood was born in 1920, conceived by the flamboyant developer Joseph

Young. In southern Broward County he built the "dream city of Florida." By 2009, dreams had turned sour. Journalist Damien Cove used the words "dismal" and "stagnating" to describe downtown Hollywood, a place where "chefs now stand outside with their arms crossed at dinnertime waiting for customers that never come. There are ten shuttered businesses in the two blocks of Hollywood north of Young Circle, the city's main shopping district."[44]

For many decades, Walton County was splendidly isolated between Panama City to the east and Destin to the west. Most residents lived inland on farms and small towns. On the eve of Pearl Harbor, DeFuniak Springs' population was about 2,500 and had not even doubled by 1970. Walton County had reached a population of barely 14,000 in 1940; by 1970, it had grown to 16,000. But the discovery of Walton's incomparable beaches recast the region as the "Emerald Coast" and home to Seaside, the high altar of the "New Urbanism" philosophy and architectural style. The volume of seasonal residents, tourists, and dreamers visiting the beach communities along Highway 30A was impressive. More than a few of the homes in Seaside and WaterColor were purchased by wealthy Fulton County Georgians. Hurricanes Ivan and Dennis, and the Great Recession raked the local real estate and tourist industries. By 2009, a newspaper headline that had not been seen since the Great Depression marked the front page of the *Northwest Florida Daily News:* "Hard Times in South Walton." The article began, "'For Sale' and 'For Lease' signs rise like tombstones from the white sand and tawny sea grass that line Highway 30A, which winds through more than a dozen exclusive resort communities along the Gulf of Mexico."[45]

Not even St. Joe Company, the developers of luxury master-planned communities, the owner of 1 million acres in Florida and 573,00 acres along the northern Gulf coast of Florida, was willing to bet against falling markets. Looking at the bottom line—a single profitable quarter since 2008, a $330 million loss for 2011, and what a journalist described as internal and external "convulsive changes"—St. Joe scaled back development plans. Ironically, the company's founder, the briary Ed Ball, made a fortune buying vast swatches of Panhandle forest and beach at bargain prices during lean times.[46]

Although Walton County's Gulf beach towns weathered the foreclosure storm better than other regions in the state, not the same could be said of Seaside's New Urban sister Celebration. The community had passed the much-coveted "popsicle test." The complimentary term means that a child can bike to a store and buy a popsicle without traversing highway-sized streets or freeway. "Utopia at a Discount" ran a front-page story of the *Washington Post.* Located only a few miles from the "Happiest Place on Earth," Celebration appealed to many Americans for its brand-name relationship with Disney. "But if Disney World is the place where dreams come true," a journalist concluded, "Celebration has been a distant fantasy for many would-be residents, a community where houses often sold for $1 million or more." It was a safe place to live: one sheriff's deputy said that their biggest "crime" problems were parking violations and stolen bikes. In 2004, Disney sold Celebration to a private equity firm, a decision that angered many residents who felt the community was never the same. Lawsuits followed, evidence that not even paradise was immune to market forces, leaky roofs, and moldy ceilings. By July 2009, one could find homes beginning at $270,000, a dramatic decline in value. Residents were shocked when, in 2010, a murder occurred, the first such crime in this Disney town where a bike theft once seemed alarming. "Residents long ago got over the idea that their home was another ride at Magic Kingdom," wrote Frantz and Collins. "They know that not everyone lives happily ever after, even in the town that Disney built."[47]

While Disney World created a paradise for children, developers transformed a city and region that defied even Tomorrow Land's wildest fantasies. But not even Cinderella's Castle or Disney's imprimatur was immune to the Great Recession's reach. Central Florida and Orlando struggled with real-life issues during the downturn. Personal bankruptcies in the region soared to "record levels." In cities built upon nostalgia and dreams, many residents wished upon the stars for 2007. Residents encountered a lower standard of living. Jeff Kunerth measured the losses: "Unemployment, underemployment, part-time work, cutbacks on wages and hours, two-income families reduced to one paycheck. . . . Adjusted for inflation, half of all households in Orange County made more than $53,734 in 2007. By 2010, that median income had dropped to $45,140." Only Las Vegas was ranked ahead of Orlando in a Standard & Poors study of "drowning cities," that is, cities that are, for all purposes, "underwater," with more mortgage debt than overall property value. To add insult to image, *Forbes* magazine ranked Orlando as one of America's "emptiest cities," a conclusion based on rental and homeowner vacancy data. In addition, Orlando's tax base and ambitious leadership underwrote the construction of a new downtown dotted with impressive performing arts and professional sports venues. But with the decline of tourism and property taxes, the city faced disaster. The *Orlando Sentinel*'s Mike Thomas editorialized: "Resort-tax collections have taken a record plunge with no end in sight, meaning no money for the city. There may well be no money 10 years from now, a tough new reality."[48]

"The Orlando and Tampa metropolitan areas," predicted an urban planner, "will merge into one super region by 2020. The combined space will be one of 20

U.S. 'megapolitan areas' which will contain more than 5 million residents." The linchpin was Polk County. With its vast interior of farmland, orange groves, and chain of lakes, Polk County boasted 2,011 square miles of land and water. Polk grew rapidly, gaining almost 100,000 new residents in the first seven years of the new century. Proof that the boom's wand and recession's dagger were as beguiling as they was dangerous was the small town of Dundee. Developers envisioned a city ten times the 2000 census count of 2,912, a burgeoning bedroom community for Lakeland and Winter Haven. Few grove owners could resist the temptation to sell their land to developers; indeed, between 1989 and 2010, Polk County has lost 150,000 acres zoned for agriculture. In 2012 a journalist stumbled upon a sign hidden by weeds announcing, "FOR SALE: 99 lot subdivision."[49]

The Great Recession may have been ignited by the housing crisis, but rising unemployment prevented individuals and families from saving their homes. A 2011 headline announced what most residents already understood: "Miami-Dade May Be New U.S. Recession Poster Child When It Comes to Jobs." The jobless malaise was worse than Detroit's. But the hardest-hit community in Miami-Dade County may have been a city dubbed "Foreclosureville, USA." Devastated by Hurricane Andrew in 1992, Homestead recovered heroically only to be rocked by the Great Recession, suffering one of the nation's highest foreclosure rates, with 44 percent of households in "severe" danger. With Homestead doubling its population between 2000 and 2010, families flocked to the community for lower home prices in exchange for a longer commute on the Turnpike. "That all started crashing down in 2007," observed the *Wall Street Journal.* Higher gas prices simply aggravated the economic malaise. "It's not a good sign when gas prices go up and become an added cost factor for these struggling homeowners," said a county official. In 2008, Homestead's tax base shrank by nearly $1 billion.[50]

The Great Recession cruelly heaped more misery upon Florida's poorest communities. Contrasting wealth and poverty exist most glaringly in Palm Beach County, where Belle Glade and Palm Beach are separated by 44 miles. A perfect storm hit Belle Glade as technology displaced many agricultural jobs and an economy gone south dashed hopes for many immigrant and migrant laborers. The annual ritual of cane burning seemed funereal. The city and county had invested $65 million to construct 338 new homes in CityPlace of Belle Glade. The project, dubbed Abidjan Estates, went under. Eliyahu Weinstein, convicted of operating a Ponzi scheme to purchase the Belle Glades Gardens apartment complex, was sentenced to prison. Short-term memories and political favors forgave some transgressions: as President Donald Trump was leaving office in 2021, he pardoned Weinstein.[51]

A few places in Florida escaped the ravages of the crisis. Gainesville, cushioned by its flagship university and health-care industry, fared well during the state's bad times, whereas Ocala, only 38 miles away, was walloped by the recession. Ocala suffered a major blow when wholesale mortgage giant Taylor Bean filed bankruptcy following a federal raid. More than 1,000 workers lost their jobs. Ocala had built a reputation for its thoroughbred industry, but that market also collapsed. Not far away, The Villages prospered. Lee Arnold, a commercial real estate investor, explained, "The Villages is rather an affluent area in the state." Moreover, the sprawling communities continued to attract newcomers during the economic downturn. Household income rose during the era. The rural Florida Panhandle also weathered the crisis reasonably well. Prisons never closed during the recession, and many parts of West Florida are dependent upon the corrections industry.[52]

Lakewood Ranch also rode out the storm in better shape than other new developments. A businessman, John Schroeder, began a cattle ranch across the sprawling scrub and grasslands of eastern Manatee County in 1905. In 1922, the Uihlein family of Milwaukee, who owned Schlitz Brewery, purchased a 28,000-acre tract of timber as an investment. The family introduced polo to the cracker cowmen. In 1995, the Schroeder-Manatee Ranch (SMR) developed a master plan to develop 8,500 acres into Lakewood Ranch. By 2010, Lakewood Ranch boasted 15,000 residents residing in seven separate villages, 1,200 businesses, three golf courses, and several schools and churches. In 2011, a journalist described the area: "Drive around this master-planned community and you will no longer see the overgrown lawns and unkempt vegetation that marked pockets of the foreclosure crisis and the Great Recession." By 2021, Lakewood Ranch was booming amid a pandemic crisis and controversy. Local politicians managed to set up a vaccination center at Lakewood Ranch, home to one of Manatee County's most exclusive zip codes.[53]

Established in 1868, the Florida Department of Corrections (FDC) touts the bold motto, "Inspiring Success by Transforming One Life at a Time." Headed by the commissioner of agriculture into the early 1900s, a century later the FDC has morphed into the state's largest agency—eclipsing Agriculture, Education, and Environmental Protection—with facilities spreading across the state from FDC's original roots in the Panhandle and North Central Florida. By the mid-2010s, legislative reports described the FDC, the third-largest correctional system in the nation, as a "ticking time bomb" overwhelmed by violence and gang activity, escalating use-of-force incidents, and a burgeoning inmate population with mental health challenges, while struggling with perpetual understaffing. Lawmakers passed increasingly punitive laws, and judges enhanced sentences at a time when the typical corrections officer had less than two years' experience and earned less than most county jail guards or similar staff in other states. Lobbyists from the Florida-based GEO Group continued to grease the hands of politicians in the Capitol who have promoted privatization schemes while creaky doors on cell blocks at many state facilities and work camps went unmaintained. After the Great Recession, legislators cushioned the budget crisis by cutting FDC's funding; a decade later, they grilled the corrections secretary with hopes of saving money by closing prisons and further consolidating inmates in dangerous facilities. Some of those who saw their Florida dreams vanish during the height of the Great Recession certainly passed those white-painted Blue Bird buses crisscrossing the state with their shackled passengers as they, too, felt imprisoned by a real estate market with arrested development.[54]

11

The Ponzi State

Zombie Homes and Ghost Towers, Schemers and Adverse Possessors

Liquidity dried up, prices fell, and spreads widened.

—Ben S. Bernanke, Federal Reserve Chair (October 2007)

Zombie Homes and the Ecology of Foreclosure

Zombies may be the rage in books and reality TV, but Florida and Louisiana have a deep relationship with the other-world creatures. In late 1936, upon mailing her completed book manuscript to Lippincott, the anthropologist Zora Neale Hurston set sail for Haiti. Awarded a prestigious Guggenheim fellowship, Hurston traveled to the Caribbean island to study African traditions and what she described as "magic practices among Negroes of the West Indies." In particular, she wanted to know much more about voodoo and zombies. She found on the Island of La Gonave an ancient and powerful folk religion, *vodou*. She later recalled that the island imbued her with "a peace I have never known anywhere else on earth." She also became acquainted with the *bocors*, priests who inflicted harm, with the power of turning humans into zombies. Zora visited a hospital where she saw the "living dead."[1]

In 1968, film director George Romero resurrected our fascination with zombies and their taste for human flesh in *Night of the Living Dead*. The genre took off faster than zombies could run in the first decade of the twentieth century. Max Brooks's 2006 blockbuster *World War Z*, a zombie apocalyptic novel, spun off popular cable shows. Clearly, our fascination with zombies reflects deeper anxieties related to the economy and fears of not being able to trust leaders, neighbors, and especially politicians.[2]

In 2010, *the South Florida Sun-Sentinel* ran a series on that region's crumbling neighborhoods, the residue of reckless home loans. "Orphaned, dilapidated homes dot the landscape from Kendall to Lake Worth," chronicled Megan O'Matz. The real estate industry called such structures "bank walkaways." The homes are no longer maintained by their legal owners or the lenders. The numbers of such abandoned homes are stunning: in Broward County, 8,000, with 7,100 in Palm Beach County. The Gold Coast was devastated. O'Matz wrote, "In Greenacres in central Palm Beach County, one resident got so fed up with the condition of the duplex attached to hers, and the lack of response from Bank of America . . . that she stuck a sign in the window . . . 'House full of Rats & Bank don't care.'" A new name emerged for such abandoned structures: zombie homes.[3]

A zombie home is a home that should be dead but will not stay dead because the economic downturn resulted in hundreds of thousands of houses existing in a financial limbo—vacant, deserted, and deteriorating, with no real future because the system was overwhelmed in foreclosure. Investopedia explained: "Zombie foreclosure is a situation when a home is left vacant by homeowners who incorrectly believe they have to immediately move out after receiving a foreclosure notice, thinking that the foreclosure lender is responsible for the property. If the lender doesn't complete the foreclosure process and sell the home, no one is occupying or caring for the property, so the vacant property falls into disrepair." Max Brooks offered a more understandable explanation of zombies that also applies to zombie homes: "One of the reasons they scare me so much: They don't have rules."[4]

Once trashed out, many of the foreclosed and abandoned homes were sold at steep discounts. Other homes, lost in the limbo of court hearings and multiple court cases, sat empty. In the early years of the new century, scores of novels, movies, and cable series reintroduced zombies to American consumers. Deserted homes, like the blank, ghoulish stare of the half-dead, half-live zombies, sat empty in legal twilight. Fully one-third of America's 152,000 zombie homes could be found in Florida. The number of vacant homes in South Florida nearly doubled between 2001 and 2010. Owners, hoping for a fresh start, assumed that if they simply left their homes, the bank would foreclose. Except Florida banks were so overwhelmed with foreclosures, they never took legal action. Yet owners were still responsible for taxes and bills. In

Lee County, one-quarter of the homes in foreclosure were vacant. Abandoned homes become favorite targets for thieves who loot air-conditioning units and copper piping. Ironically, some looters included the very workers who built the houses, described "as laid-off construction workers in flannel shirts scavenging through trash bags . . . grabbing wires, CDs, anything that could be sold." In Lehigh Acres, an abandoned home bore the spray-painted manifesto "Kill the rich." Foreclosed homes with swimming pools buzzed with clouds of mosquitoes hatching from the blue-green waters. Many homes needed to be torn down because of tainted drywall that emitted a foul odor and sickened residents. The so-called Chinese drywall became a visible and odiferous crisis at home and abroad.[5]

The foreclosure avalanche overwhelmed code enforcement officers. "It's an epidemic," admitted Bill Langford, part of a five-officer team nicknamed "board men" who clean and board up deserted homes in Hillsborough County. "As fast as we clean them, new ones pop up." An occupational hazard occasionally occurred, admitted Langford: "We have to make sure we're not boarding up anyone!" Ten thousand abandoned homes littered the Tampa Bay area as late as 2013. Overwhelmed, the cleanup crews concentrated on priorities and dangers: evicting squatters, mowing overgrowth, and sealing off swimming pools. Occasionally, live animals and dead bodies are discovered. In one home Langford found bathrooms transformed into litter boxes for fifty cats.[6]

The sheer numbers of abandoned and foreclosed homes posed questions: Who will board up and secure zombie homes if a hurricane approaches? Though the legal owner of abandoned properties is the owner, in practical terms, AP reporter Tamara Lush observed, "communities are struggling to get banks to mow lawns, much less put up hurricane shutters—if they weren't swiped from the foreclosed homes, along with appliances." Some wealthier communities have proposed solutions. Wellington, in Palm Beach County, received legal permission to board up homes. In Cape Coral, owners of foreclosed homes must pay $150 to provide information as to who will take care of the property.[7]

Cratered by a record-breaking number of evictions, Floridians responded to the crisis: foreclosure services. Paul Reyes followed "entrepreneur" Chris Velozik, his T-shirt spelling out his mission: "SPECIALIZING IN FORECLOSURE SERVICES." In one case, six police patrol cars arrived to resolve a confrontation among neighbors, workers, and activists.[8]

Many subdivisions had lost not only residences to foreclosures but entire blocks of homes. Pasco County underwent raging boom times and a deflating bust. There, a journalist took readers for a tour of "ghost subdivisions." George

Packer explained: "We drove into a development called Twin Lakes . . . where property values had dropped by more than a hundred thousand dollars. . . . Farther east on State Road 54, in a subdivision called Country Walk, there were streets whose pavement stopped a few feet from where it began, as if the developer had changed his mind. I saw streets with signs and street lamps but no houses, and streets with houses but no occupants."[9]

In the land of zombies, one Sarasota home stands out. The house at 4224 Escondido Drive in Prestancia, a gated community, may be Florida's most haunted house. Developers often name subdivisions after Italian and Spanish places, in this case, Hidden Excellence. Built in 1994 in the Mediterranean Revival style, the home is spacious (3,750 square feet), with a pool. In 2001, the al-Hiijji family lived there, although the home was owned by Mrs. Al-Hiijji's father, a wealthy interior decorator with intimate ties to the Saudi royal family. Three cars graced the driveway: a Range Rover, a Lexus, and a PT cruiser. Tapes revealed several 9/11 hijackers visited the family. The infamous residents fled the morning of 9/11/2001. No home was safe from the Great Recession, and a succession of owners occupied the residence.[10]

Trashing Out

Paul Reyes coined the term "ecology of foreclosure." The economic woes lasted a decade in which property values plunged nearly 60 percent. Between 2009 and 2011, short sales and foreclosures accounted for more than half of the homes sold in Florida. Reyes walked the walk. He worked for his father "trashing out" homes that had been foreclosed upon and/or abandoned. Often the tenants wrecked and defaced homes as they left. Reyes and his crews worked as kind of first responders to Florida's housing crash. "What's left behind, in the way it falls or is tossed," he writes, "is never just junk but a stroke of sorts—a mark, the chalk line around a body, the tags near the casings." He compiled his experiences in a book, *Life among the Ruins of Florida's Great Recession.* Responding to the crisis, some lenders created "cash for keys," "bribing" homeowners with as much as $2,000 not to go medieval on their properties before leaving.[11]

Cutting "hay-like grass" that had not been mowed in months was challenging enough. Such was the responsibility of Total Lawn Care of Cape Coral. The city paid the firm $70 per lot to manage the yards of 700 foreclosed homes. Work crews also encountered buzzing bees, angry fire ants, and slithering snakes.[12]

"Getting people out of a property is the last official act of a foreclosure," explained the *St. Petersburg Times.* "But then starts the sad, or smelly task of getting everything else out." County sheriffs have a truly unfortunate job. "Eight years of handling evictions at foreclosed homes has taught Pasco Sheriff's Office Cpl. B. J. Wright a crucial lesson: always knock. Not to alert residents, who are usually long gone, but to make the cockroaches scurry from the front door frame so they won't drop down his neck. 'It only has to happen once,' Wright promised."[13]

Tim O'Brien wrote a powerful book about Vietnam veterans titled *The Things They Carried.* Sheriff deputies could write volumes about the things foreclosed homeowners leave behind. After taping the court's "Writ of Possession" order on a home in Port Richey in Pasco County, tenants have twenty-four hours to vacate the premises. In one case, a reporter accompanied a cleanup crew hired by the bank. She described the scene: "The living room looked like the residents left in a rush, with underwear, fast-food wrappers, a footstool, fan, and kid's foot-ball helmet making a minefield of the matted green carpet. . . . Unopened mail, flash cards, pill bottles, and a Dunkin' Donut box were piled precariously on the kitchen counter." A listing agent checking out a foreclosed home in West Palm Beach discovered someone had poured roofing tar in the toilets. Mosquitoes also found toilets a breeding ground. Corporal Wright recalled a poignant scene: During one eviction, he knocked on the door and was surprised to see that a woman answered. He realized the furnishings had not been moved. "Who is it, dear?," her husband asked. The deputy asked, "You haven't told him, have you?" The woman shook her head. On another occasion he arrived at a foreclosed home in Tampa. He discovered inside a homeowner who had killed himself. A dead cat and racoon were nearby. In 2010, Corporal Wright explained that he often served fifteen evictions a day.[14]

Bad times haunted new subdivisions and old neighborhoods. Sulphur Springs is one of Tampa's oldest neighborhoods, home to natural springs that once attracted tourists to sip and bathe in its healing waters. But Sulphur Springs was already depressed when the sinking economy raked some of Tampa's poorest neighborhoods. The trashing-out crews arrived with the sheriff serving evictions. Entering the foreclosed home on Hillsborough Lane, Reyes described the scene: "A damp, warm funk wafted out as we moved through the doorway. . . . The walls, once white, were leopard spotted in black and green. . . . The fleas were incredible. We were being devoured by them."[15]

If the Great Recession was good for trashers and eviction servers, exterminators and movers, it was disastrous for carpenters and roofers, real estate agents and politicians. An economic analyst in Jacksonville reminisced, "It wasn't that long ago that every single construction worker on the First Coast was employed." A story and a portrait illustrate the point.

"It used to be a busy scene on the sidewalks of Miami's 184th Street at dawn," began a 2009 article.

> Armed with lunchboxes and sun hats, day laborers once clustered here in the hundreds, awaiting pickups from building contractors eager for their energy and manual skills. Away in the distance stretches the city skyline they helped build. . . . But now it's different. Miami's condo bubble has burst, new home building in South Florida has virtually ground to a halt, and contractors who once cruised 184th St. looking for labor are left seeking work themselves. . . . In the first quarter of 2009, construction began on just 294 houses in South Florida's six-county area. In 2001, it was 20 times that number. . . . In Miami-Dade County, work was launched on just 43 single family homes.[16]

Squatters and Activists

J. P. Morgan famously boasted that he could hire half the working class to kill the other half. Not since the Great Depression had so many families been evicted from their homes. Wrenching portraits of tearful Floridians, their furniture dumped on lawns, prompted Americans to ask how banks could be so cold, how a legal system could be so harsh. Some chose illegal and extralegal tactics. In John Steinbeck's *Grapes of Wrath*, many "Okies" fled for the California dream while others chose to fight. In one poignant episode, a sharecropping family is told they would have to leave their land and home. Sharecropping was simply no longer profitable, and the bank preferred more reward for its investment. Arguments are futile. When a tractor approaches the home the next day, tenant farmer Muley Graves threatens to shoot the driver, whom he recognizes as "Joe Davis's boy." The driver is a neighbor also struggling to save his family home. Browbeaten and desperate, Muley Graves asks, "Then, who do we shoot?" A bank executive dressed in a suit and tie explains that the land is owned by the Shawnee Land and Cattle Company. Muley demands, "And who's the Shawnee Land and Cattle Company?" The businessman explains, "Man, it ain't nobody! It's a company." Then as now, understanding the economy and solutions to inequality are complicated. Public policy scholars Joseph Stiglitz and Linda Bilmes observed, "The parallels between origins of the Great Depression and that of our Long Slump are strong. . . . Factory workers once employed in cities such as Youngstown and Birmingham and Gary and Detroit are the modern-day equivalent of the Depression's doomed farmers." Many of

those retired factory workers were living in North Port and Lehigh Acres and wondering in 2008, "Who do we shoot?"[17]

In 2008, an AP reporter profiled one of Florida's most celebrated housing agents in Miami. "All tile floor!," he says during a recent showing. "And the living room, wow!" But the journalist explains, "He is unlike any real estate agent you've ever met. He is unshaven, drives a beat-up car, and wears grungy cut-off sweat pants. He also breaks into homes he shows. And his clients don't have a dime for a down payment." Tamara Lush was introducing Max Rameau, founder of Take Back the Land, founded in Miami, an organization with a simple bailout plan: fight evictions and solve homelessness. Its aim is simple: place the homeless in foreclosed homes. Take Back the Land, with its office a storefront in Liberty City, matches homeless people with foreclosed, vacant homes. Rameau, born a son of wealthy parents in Haiti, told *USA Today*: "It's morally indefensible to have vacant homes sitting there . . . while you have human beings on the street." The lean organization worked chiefly in some of Miami-Dade's poorest communities, Little Haiti and Liberty City. When it hears of a pending eviction, Take Back the Land springs into guerrilla mode, cheering volunteers to lock arm in arm in civil disobedience when the police arrive. In some cases, overwhelmed police departments choose not to confront the squatters. In Florida, police need a signed affidavit from the property's owner to evict squatters.[18]

A 2009 *New York Times* article, dateline Miami, began: "When the woman who calls herself Queen Omega moved into a three-bedroom house here last December, she introduced herself to the neighbors, signed contracts for electricity and water and ordered an Internet connection." She apparently did not tell anyone she was squatting. "Ms. Omega, 48, is one of the beneficiaries of the foreclosure crisis," readers learned. And Ms. Omega was not alone.[19]

In a celebrated case, Andre Barbosa, a twenty-three-year-old Brazilian who called himself "Loki Boy" after the Norse god of mischief, moved into an empty mansion on Golden Harbour Drive in Boca Raton that had sold for $3.1 million in 2005. He cited an obscure Florida real estate statute to justify his actions. A *Sun-Sentinel* reporter explained: "The police can't move him. No one saw him breaking into the 5-bedroom house, so it's a civil matter. And the real owner, Bank of America, isn't responding to questions about the home." Barbosa invoked a Florida law called "adverse possession." A Sunrise lawyer explained that the law allows a person to move into a property *and* claim title if they remain there for seven years. Typically, such cases are found in poor neighborhoods. "But hey," exclaimed a real estate lawyer, "if you're going to do this, you might as well go big." In 2013, Barbosa was served with eviction papers. His case attracted worldwide press coverage.[20]

In Sarasota, an enterprising Joel McNair created the company Houses for America. He filed a dozen adverse possession cases in 2010. Police believe his intent was to rent the properties for the required seven years and then file a legal claim for ownership. In South Florida, a squatter claimed an abandoned multimillion-dollar ranch. The law allowing such seemingly brazen conduct dates to nineteenth-century Florida and premodern Britain. In 1869, the Florida Legislature, attempting to rebuild a world turned upside down by war, emancipation, and displacement, enacted a law that awarded abandoned property to petitioners if the owners fail to claim the land within seven years. Adverse possession permits individuals to take over neglected property where owners have not paid taxes. It does not permit simply seizing vacant property. If one improves the land, publicly declare themselves to be paying taxes on the property, and pays taxes for seven consecutive years, a judge may award them the property. Lee County and neighboring Charlotte County encountered hundreds of such cases during the recession. Journalists studying a case in North Lauderdale, Florida, observed, "Though they may cringe at the analogy, as squatters with bank accounts, these adverse possessors are like leeches, and it can be difficult to tell at times whether they are cleaning a wound already there, or making it worse." The writers added, "Either way, Florida is where they thrive."[21]

For buyers looking for a bargain, some foreclosed homes had "good bones," but other structures had been stripped of appliances and air conditioners. In North Port, Sarasota County's largest city, Shannon Moore was a real estate broker investing in foreclosed and abandoned homes. Once branded as hyenas for inflation of home prices, Realtors like Ms. Moore were now performing a needed task by helping potential home buyers navigate the credit and financial hurdles involved. For a once heady market, home prices were sobering. "For instance," observed a journalist, "a two-bedroom house in Port Charlotte, just south of North Port . . . recently sold for $8,000, and listings for $25,000 are not uncommon."[22]

Condos in Crisis

In hindsight, buying a condominium in Florida seemed pitch-perfect during the halcyon years, 2000–2005. Owners faced none of the annoying details of home ownership—cutting the grass, emptying the gutters, and cleaning the swimming pool—while enjoying its benefits of ownership—leisure, sunshine, and rising real estate prices. Condos appealed especially to active seniors, who danced at the community center on Friday nights and played tennis on Saturday mornings. On 2 December 2005, an *Orlando Sentinel* headline read, "CONDO-CRAZY ORLANDO (Translation: Good Luck Finding Apartment)." The article began, "Finding an apartment in Orlando is getting about as tough as catching a snowflake on a Florida beach."

In Miami, a condo perfectly fit the designs of foreign buyers seeking a safe harbor for their investments and a future home when regulators or revolutionaries purge the guilty and the unwise. Buyers included lawyers from Mexico's poorest state and Colombian drug lords. Sebastián Rodríguez Robles purchased 13 condos at the Opera Tower in downtown Miami, sealing the deal with a $1.3 million down payment.[23]

In 2010 Orlando, a journalist accompanied Orange County property appraiser Bill Donegan for a tour of "the worst of the worst." Built as apartments in 2000 on the shore of Turkey Lake, the Hamptons complex near Universal Studios was converted into condo units in 2005. Prices plummeted, and at its nadir, only 81 owners lived among the 776 units. Journalist Timothy Egan described this new-turned-bad as "slumburbia."[24]

Southwest Florida's housing market was described as a "death spiral." An official in 2009 estimated 40 percent of the units were either abandoned or in foreclosure. Residents were simply hanging on, unable to pay mortgages or association fees, which means fewer repairs, low occupancy rates, and a downward spiral. The story line of the Oasis high-rise condo in downtown Fort Myers is illustrative. Opened in January 2005, the first tower was quickly filled. By November 2008, both towers were completed. Many original buyers attempted to cancel the contracts. Soon, the Bank of America filed a $157 million foreclosure lawsuit against Related Realty Group of New York, making it the second-largest foreclosure in Lee County history. A single family resided in the 32-story Oasis I condo tower. A New Jersey family who paid $430,000 for a condo held the distinction of being the loneliest couple in town. The family confessed that living there was a "bit creepy." Birds nested in some of the empty units.[25]

The topic of "loneliest Floridians" was more complicated and debated than one imagined. Joshua Hamann moved into Everglades on the Bay, a 49-story downtown Miami condominium with a handful of residents. He compared himself to the last human in a city overrun by zombies. When asked about the mental health issues involved with being the only person living in a ghost tower, sociologists warned against the dangers of isolation and disconnection.[26]

No region deserved the epithet/compliment "condo canyons" more than

South Florida. "Miami is the poster child for the condo bust," said real estate analyst Jack McCabe in 2008. "There's probably only two cities in the world with more construction: Shanghai and Dubai." In Miami alone, dozens of condominium towers had been built and dozens more neared completion when the Great Recession caused more mayhem than a hurricane. Thousands of units purchased by investors and flippers hoping to make a quick profit sat empty for years. To appreciate the crisis, consider that in 2007, Miami-Dade County expected the completion of 8,000 new condo units and 12,000 more in 2008. Prices fell hard. "I see buyers unleashing all possible means to try and get out of their contracts," a Miami lawyer confessed. More than a few customers forfeited their deposit rather than risk even greater losses. Natalie and David Luongo had successfully flipped several properties in South Florida, and then placed a $117,000 deposit on an expensive condo in ritzy Bal Harbour. A reporter observed, "Now the couple are spending restless nights wrestling with the question that looms like a guillotine: Should they walk away from the $117,000 deposit they plunked down on another investment condo in Bal Harbour?" Condo associations, too, filed Chapter 11 petitions. Florida law recognizes that while a condo association is in bankruptcy, utilities cannot be turned off.[27]

Lisa Rab wrote a haunting essay in 2009 about the "ghost towers" and "artifacts of a gilded age" still standing when the music stopped: "Drive down Federal Highway or Sunrise Boulevard in Fort Lauderdale or Okeechobee in West Palm Beach and the 'For Sale' signs seem inescapable. Every lonely strip-mall storefront and empty condominium pleads to become someone else's problem." She takes readers to "the blinding white driveway of the Tao Sawgrass condos in Sunrise. . . . Not a single resident, in 396 units. . . . [T]he marketing director . . . said she could not confirm or deny the presence of residents. . . . Today the complex is an elaborate monument to the folly of the boom years, when it seemed logical to sell a half-a million-dollar high-rise units on the edge of the Everglades."[28]

The building boom redesigned the Miami skyline as condo canyons girded the waterfront. But far beyond the beach and ocean, in places such as Kendall, Hialeah, and Lauderhill, condominiums altered the skyline and daily rhythms. Investors and developers perfected real estate alchemy: turning apartments into condominiums. The numbers are stunning: between 2003 and 2009, almost 75,000 rental apartments were converted into condos in Broward and Miami-Dade counties. In the economic free fall, these conversion units suffered disproportionally, the result of aging structures, record foreclosures, and underfunded condo associations.[29]

Journalists crowned Jorge Pérez as Florida's "Condo King." He has also been called the most influential figure in modern Miami history since Henry Flagler. A combination of Horatio Alger, Tony Montana, and Carl Fisher, the son of Cuban parents, Pérez was born in 1949 and lived in Cuba, Argentina, and Colombia. He immigrated to America in 1968 and became an urban planner. The bureaucrat-idealist who built affordable housing in the 1980s became famous for developing, building, or managing 80,000 condominiums and 90,000 residences, mostly in South Florida. He and Stephen Ross, the future owner of the Miami Dolphins, cofounded Related Companies and Related Group, qualifying for the Forbes 400 List of wealthiest Americans. In 2005, he shared the cover of *Time* magazine with America's most influential Hispanics. "Some of his luxurious condos command as much as $15 million a unit," *Time* noted, but Pérez insisted that he wished to be remembered as someone who helped revitalize downtown Miami.[30]

Pérez's most auspicious project was the ICON Brickell, described as "a $1 billion glass-and-concrete city within a city that includes three soaring towers, a pool the size of a football field, 1,640 condos, a boutique hotel and five restaurants." Admirers called the ICON Brickell, built near the banks of the Miami River, "his masterpiece"; investors derided it as "his undoing." By the spring of 2009, his company, the Related Group, faced losses of $1 billion in the previous year and confronted future losses of $2 billion. But, as Matthew Haggman wrote, "Betting big—and sometimes losing big—has always been part of the craps game that is South Florida real estate."[31]

Few investors had more to lose than Jorge Pérez. *Forbes* magazine estimated his wealth at $1.3 billion as he peered over the brink. Mustering resolve and having the good fortune of being close friends with and supporters of Presidents Bill Clinton and Barack Obama, the Condo King survived to build and thrive again. He has also the reputation of being one of Florida's most generous philanthropists. But as Toluse Olorunnipa wrote in 2011, "As the boom-and-bust epic has played out across South Florida's condominium market, mega-developer Jorge Perez has played the role of either city-building hero or greed-drive villain, depending on who's telling the story." He continued, "Reeling from the downside of much of that risk-taking, Perez has emerged bloodied but breathing from a two-year battle to save his company after a perfect storm of troubled condo projects, a financial system meltdown and a recession handed it a billion dollars in losses." Selling off hundreds of condos from previous projects, the Related Group managed to shed all debt. Pérez announced his latest gamble: Trump Hollywood. "What goes up must come down," the eternal optimist admits. But he adds, "the opposite is also true."[32]

In 2011, when Miami was still reeling from the recession, developers were already planning the next wave of condo towers. "The demand is coming," noted the *Miami Herald*, "almost exclusively, from outside Miami. Buyers based in Latin America, Canada, Europe and the northeast United States have spent more than $3.8 billion on South Florida real estate this year."[33]

Rental Nation: Living Alone

So, what happened to the hundreds of thousands of foreclosed homes in Florida? To be sure, individuals who bet on Florida's comeback, capitalized upon bargains. But many of the homes were gobbled up by big investment companies. Old and new residents confronted a new reality: Florida, long called California for the middling classes because of its affordable housing, was becoming the rental state. Bad credit, depleted savings, and record foreclosures forced many Floridians to rethink the sacrosanct American dream of owning a home.

Miami, West Palm Beach, and Fort Lauderdale may have enjoyed brand-name identities, but *Forbes* stigmatized them on its list of America's "Most Miserable Cities," citing a crippling housing crisis, political corruption, crime, and high unemployment rates. The residents of Miami-Dade, Broward, and Palm Beach counties paid dearly for housing. During a debate over this critical issue, Miami-Dade officials floated a solution: "build apartments on school property and let faculty live there." Fully 42 percent of the working households along the Gold Coast spent more than half of their income on housing. The 2010 Census confirmed that for the first time in decades, the percentage of renters living in Palm Beach County rose. The word "affordability" reverberated more and more in conversations, city hall meetings, and newspapers.[34]

The headline "Orlando Has Lowest Wages of Any Big City in America," brought smiles to some of the biggest employers in Metro Orlando, fury to service workers, and determination to reformers and activists. To borrow a baseball metaphor, Orlando's median annual wage of $30,000 ranked way below the Mendoza line. As late as 2013, when the recovery had begun, one-quarter of all jobs in the region paid less than $20,000. "The numbers," editorialized the *Orlando Sentinel*, "exposed a dark truth ignored by Orlando's sunny marketing campaigns—that many of the workers who make tourists' dreams come true can't even make ends meet for themselves." Another headline connected the dots: "Homeownership Fades in Central Florida."[35]

Osceola County looms large in explaining the success of Central Florida tourism. Many of the industry's lowest-paid workers reside there. Osceola

County is also the home to the greatest concentration of Puerto Ricans in the state, many of whom migrated here to work in the tourist industry and live in Buenaventura Lakes, Poinciana, and Kissimmee. The *Sentinel* responded to the bleak news of the region's wage woes: "You need a lot of low-income housing when you have a lot of low-income jobs." The editorial writer noted that Orange County collects several hundred million dollars annually in hotel taxes—"almost all of which it uses to encourage more tourism." In late 2010, Osceola County ranked second nationally in underwater mortgages; two of every three homeowners owed more than their homes were worth. Neighboring Orange County ranked eighth.[36]

Many young Floridians, having witnessed the pain afflicted by the Great Recession, no longer see renting as a stigma; rather, renting offers flexibility, freedom, and hassle-free living. "Regardless of age," argues the president of the National Apartment Association, "mobility is one of the top reasons people decide to rent. For millennials just entering the workforce or in the process of building their careers, the ability to relocate is a major factor." *USA Today* featured a front-page story, "Renting Homes: The New American Dream?" A demographer estimated the recession drove 3 million former homeowners to rent single-family homes. The *Sarasota Herald-Tribune* announced the hottest real-estate trend, calling 2011 "the year of the Apartment." Single-family renter households surged across the state. Thomas Sugrue argues for what not long ago would have been considered a radically un-American idea: "It's time to accept that home ownership is not a realistic goal for many people." In the wake of the Great Recession, Orlando emerged as the top choice for real estate firms to invest in apartment buildings. Addressing the affordability challenge of Miami—which was ranked as the second-worst place for renters in America—a developer erected a 49-story high-rise offering renters 400-square-foot apartments and no parking spaces. In St. Petersburg and Tampa, the hottest real estate market was for "pricey, posh, tiny apartments." Most everyone agrees these developments have helped rejuvenate Florida's cities. "Downtown areas are on the rebound . . . unlike anything we've seen in the past 30 years," wrote journalist Camille Lefevre.[37]

To gamblers, great recessions offer risky opportunities. Giant investment firms tripled down. Invitation Homes, Starwood Waypoint Homes, Colony Capital, Lake Success Rentals, Blackstone, and American Homes 4 Rent specialized in home rentals and purchased thousands of foreclosed homes in Florida metro areas during the recession. The firms instituted tough new "landlord" rules and regulations, such as renters' new responsibilities for landscaping, pest control, and repairing broken glass. "The investor gold rush," wrote journalist

Drew Harwell, "is funding armies of local agents, contractors, managers and analysts, who binge on bargains and retool them into 'rent ready' homes." Some blame guru Warren Buffett for firing a starter pistol when he hinted at buying "a couple hundred thousand" homes nationwide. The Blackstone Group spent $10 billion betting on foreclosed homes. Business journalist Amy Keller explained the big investment firms' two-pronged strategy: "First by renting out the homes and then by reselling them in a few years." Many local officials expressed anxiety about consolidation and its consequences. "It's a land grab unlike anything we've ever seen," said Peter Murphy, the CEO of Home Encounter, one of the largest managers of rental homes in the Tampa Bay area. "You're going to drive through parts of town and all of it is going to be institutionally owned." Peter McCabe, a real estate consultant in Deerfield Beach, commented, "They [Blackstone Group] are out to buy as many homes as they can. . . . We're shifting from a market controlled by individuals to one that's controlled by institutions, and that's very dangerous." The plethora of so many people renting small apartments resulted in an additional consequence: the growth of self-storage businesses. An editor compressed the issue into a headline: "More People, More Stuff, More Storage."[38]

In the 1932 film *Grand Hotel,* Greta Garbo said famously, "I want to be alone." Demographers, dating sites, and census takers noticed a significant new trend: more and more Floridians and Americans were living alone. Garbo's words seem prophetic. To compare: In 1950, only 4 million Americans lived alone, comprising a mere 9 percent of households. The 2010 census identified 33 million Americans, more than a quarter of the population, living by themselves. The largest cohort belongs to women living solo. Between 2000 and 2010, the percentage of adult Floridians who never married fell markedly from 54.3 percent to 47.1 percent. In Florida, the vast number of elderly widows and widowers skew the population, but the numbers are up across the demographic spectrum. In 2007, demographers observed an extraordinary shift: for the first time in American history, more American women were living without a husband than with one. "An army of women . . . is discovering new capabilities negotiating life without a spouse," observed a journalist. "They are the new majority—women who find themselves, by choice or not, living spouseless." Sociologists debate the meaning and consequences of these trends. Does it reinforce Robert Putnam's thesis in *Bowling Alone* (2000) that Americans are living atomized lives, disconnected from voluntary associations that had enriched previous generations? Anyone who has spent time on South Beach or downtown St. Petersburg realizes living alone is not the same as being lonely.[39]

Lean Times at City Hall and County Courthouses

City and county planners and state officials quickly connected the dots: bankrupt Floridians pay few if any property and sales taxes, foreclosed homeowners are unlikely or unable to pay property taxes, and fewer tourists and snowbirds mean a drastic decrease in local and state revenue. In Central Florida alone, 25 car dealerships shuttered their doors. In September 2009, the Saturn dealership in Kissimmee sprawled over 15 acres and was valued at almost $4 million. Less than a year later it was appraised for $2 million. Taxes constitute the lifeblood of governments and schools. The *Sun-Sentinel* offered a 2011 case study of the new reality. "When Michelais Josemond bought his two-bedroom condo in Tamarac four years ago, he paid $185,000 and had a property tax bill of about $2,500. Today, his apartment is worth $18,000 and his tax bill is zero." He was not alone; indeed, he was one of 35,000 homeowners in Broward and Palm Beach counties who paid no property tax because the value of their home was less than Florida's $25,000 homestead exemption. Such cases skyrocketed in Florida after 2008.[40]

Since property taxes fuel state and local governments, and since such entities cannot operate on deficit budgets, Florida was running on empty. In Seminole County, 100 jobs were eliminated. Osceola County experienced a 17 percent decline in property values. The City of Altamonte cut 15 jobs. A research report concluded that among the fifty states, Florida's combined state and local funding per student never recovered from the Great Recession. Florida cut education funding from about $10,000 per student to $7,000 in three years. That funding has yet to be restored a decade later.[41]

Wobbling cities searched for answers. By the fall of 2009, the state's auditor general's office listed 77 local governments that met the criteria of "financial emergency" while another 99 faced "deteriorating financial conditions." Leaders appealed to Broward County officials who pleaded to state leaders in Tallahassee who appealed to Washington, D.C., for relief.[42]

The fiscal blues afflicted not simply cities, but metropolitan areas. Tampa Bay and Miami/Fort Lauderdale ranked first and third respectively in the category of "most financially distressed metros." Tampa Bay held the distinction in 2011–12 as America's only metropolitan area classified as "Emergency Crisis." Not even Detroit sank so low. Not since the Great Depression had so many people defaulted on their property tax bills. The counties of Pinellas, Hillsborough, Pasco, and Hernando were rocked by 114,000 properties representing $332 million in unpaid realty taxes. Negligent taxpayers included the venerable Safety Harbor Spa, Tierra Verde Marina, and the Tampa Bay Lightning hockey team. "Long vilified as greedy power brokers," wrote a *Tampa Tribune* journalist, "many of the people in the business of turning open spaces into malls and subdivisions are reeling from liens, foreclosure lawsuits and bankruptcies." Between 2006 and 2011, Sarasota County property values plunged by $33 billion.[43]

The De-Malling of Florida

If young Americans thought the printed newspaper was hopelessly dated, one hip institution of American life radiated modernity and change: the shopping mall. Capitalism is always reinventing itself. One scholar has called the era 1950–77, "the Malling of America." These modern shopping bazaars concentrated three creative forces of American life: affluence, the automobile, and conspicuous consumption.[44]

In the 1990s and early 2000s, megamalls vied for commercial and spatial supremacy, each bringing new elements of space, aesthetics, and function. About 100 shopping malls dotted Florida on the eve of the Great Recession. From Altamonte Mall to the Mall at the Millenia to Ocean Walk Shoppes, shopping centers served tourists and locals while adding to the prestige of a community and the tax base. With the opening of Millenia in 2003, Orlando boasted seven "super-regional" malls within 24 square miles. Consumers judged malls by their most prestigious tenants: department stores, food court attractions. Some, such as the Sawgrass Mills Mall in Sunrise, combined elements of the modern theme park and a designer outlet attraction. The era also witnessed the revival of the urban mall and suddenly relevant downtowns.[45]

The arc of the department store illustrates the rise and fall of an American icon. By the 1920s, Jacksonville, Miami, and Tampa earned their reputations as significant cities, in part because of the elegance exuded by their downtowns, in part because of the presence of family-owned department stores. The Cohen, Burdine, and Maas families had begun such stores in the nineteenth century as Jewish-owned, small businesses. They survived wars and depressions but could not survive the vicissitudes of mergers, buyouts, and changing consumer demands. Once the literal and figurative anchor of downtowns, the department store struggled to rediscover its glamour and purpose at a suburban mall. Technology—online shopping—made big-box stores irrelevant. In the 2010 landscape, the shopping mall was becoming as irrelevant as the department store. If classic mall institutions such as Macy's, Sears, and JCPenney were the great losers during this economic upheaval, the winners included Dollar General, Dollar Tree, Walmart, and Ecommerce. Abandoned or sinking malls have been repurposed as new places of workspace, creativity, and senior walkways. In 2009, Hillsborough County commissioners discussed the need for homeless shelters. A serious discussion ensured about converting Floriland Mall, an aging complex, into a homeless shelter.[46]

The fate of Trinity Town Center silhouetted the new normal's sunset. Amid ceremony and optimism, officials broke ground for a shopping center that promised much to fast-growing Pasco County. Trinity was to be more than a shopping mall—it was designed as a community center amid shops and restaurants. Critics challenged the moniker "Town Center," complaining that true community centers offer more than retail space. Regardless, the recession wrecked dreams, but it also robbed workers and contractors of paychecks when the developer simply walked away. A photograph revealed the stark afterlife of half-built structures meant to be movie theaters, coffee shops, and clock towers.[47]

Abandoned malls often become megachurches. But churches, too, suffered the economic slings of fortune. A 2009 headline confirmed what many deacons and altar boys already knew: "Churches Hit Hard, Too." In 2010, more than 100 churches filed for bankruptcy across America. The migration of parishioners to the suburbs and the decline of downtowns doomed many churches. Demographics and timing are destiny. For much of American history, downtown Jacksonville or Daytona Beach, much like downtown Albany or Jersey City, showcased their cities' most powerful banks, haberdasheries, and department stores. Churches figured prominently, and each Sunday parishioners walked or drove to some of the cities' most architecturally significant structures festooned with majestic steeples and Tiffany-designed stained-glass windows. Northern snowbirds swelled attendance during the high season. But as cities grew and downtowns cratered, residents moved farther away. Year by year, as maintenance costs and bills mounted, the abandoned or underused churches were sold or torn down. Since these historic churches occupied prominent downtown sites, the decision to sell the property was financially rewarding. Across Florida, the echoes of last "amens" reverberated during the Great Recession. In 2009, the Grand Lutheran Church of Fort Lauderdale was razed for townhouses. That same year, Archbishop John Favalora of Miami announced that austere measures would soon result in the closing of struggling churches.[48]

As churches struggled to survive during hard times, real estate agents revived an ancient religious ritual. Across Florida, but especially in Catholic communities across the state, sales of statues of St. Joseph spiked. Devotees then buried the statues. "I get a lot of people every day looking for St. Joseph," confirmed Sylvia Sierra, the owner of St. Anthony's Catholic Gift Shop in Tampa. "Real estate people come here and buy them by the dozen," Sierra told reporter Susan Martin. As the father of Jesus and husband of the Virgin Mary, Joseph idealizes home and family. The legend of Saint Teresa also circulated. Born in 1515, Teresa grew up in a wealthy household. As a child she was fascinated by the martyred saints and entered a convent. She felt the cloistered life was still too comfortable and broke away to found the Discalced Carmelite Order. Teresa of Ávila inspired others to join her new order, but they had no funds for a new monastery. Legend has it that nuns buried medals of Saint Joseph and prayed to him. Teresa of Ávila was beatified in 1614. True believers bury St. Joseph near a home's front steps or under the 'For Sale' sign.[49]

Unemployed in the Sunshine: New Attitudes toward Relief

Theologians, politicians, and activists have long debated the meaning of work and its place in society. Saint Benedict and John Calvin preached that to work is to pray. The Protestant work ethic instilled a discipline and calling that helped drive the industrial revolutions of Great Britain and America. The New Deal introduced a broad array of relief programs to soften the cruelties of unemployment, infirmity, and old age.

The decades of the 1930s and 1960s dramatically altered the delicate balance between workers and management, the rich and poor. The New Deal and Great Society introduced a panoply of government programs that added layers of protection for the country's most vulnerable citizens. The 1960s and '70s awakened Americans to the concentrations of wealth and poverty. "From 1979 to 2011," observed commentator Hedrick Smith, "84 percent of the nation's increase in income has gone to the wealthiest 1 percent." In 2013, President Barack Obama explained the wealth gap: "So the income of the top 1 percent nearly quadrupled from 1979 to 2007, but the typical family's income barely budged."[50]

Florida's Great Recession involved flippers, zombie foreclosures, and treasury secretaries. Real Floridians felt the sting of unemployment. At its nadir, the state's unemployment rate was 10.6 percent, but such statistics disguise the more important point that many more men and women simply surrendered and dropped out. In early 2010, Flagler County, home of Palm Coast, led the nation with a jobless rate of 17 percent. The state average stood at a dismal 12.2 percent, the highest since the Great Depression. The Great Recession may have been ignited by the housing crisis, but rising unemployment prevented individuals and families from saving their homes. A 2011 headline announced what most residents already understood: "Miami-Dade May Be New U.S. Recession Poster Child When It Comes to Jobs." The jobless malaise was worse than Detroit's.[51]

A 1987 book by Alan Binder bore the engaging title *Hard Heads, Soft Hearts.* Commentator Paul Krugman though an appropriate title for politicians' attitudes during the Great Recession should have been *Soft Heads, Hard Hearts.* He argued that America's long-term unemployed "are mainly victims of circumstances—ordinary American workers who had the bad luck to lose their jobs at a time of extraordinary labor market weakness, with three times as many people looking for jobs as there are job openings." As if the economy's sting was insufficient, the jobless found the state unemployment sites impossible to navigate. "Fewer than one in eight unemployed workers in Florida receives jobless benefits," contended the *Sun-Sentinel.* The National Employment Law Project singled out Florida as the worst place for laid-off workers to apply and qualify for unemployment benefits.[52]

The Great Recession served as a reckoning for several generations of Americans. Many simply gave up. Never in American history had so many working-age men been out of the labor loop, unlikely to return. On the eve of the Great Recession, about one-third of the working-age population was not employed. The rate reached a modern high in 2010 when the rate plunged to 58 percent of workers. The largest cohort remained relatively uneducated men in their prime, who have dropped out of the workforce. Myriad causes explain the extraordinary trend: the changing nature of jobs, generational shifts, and the lack of skills necessary for high-tech positions. "A male high school graduate in America has almost nothing an employer is going to value," stated a Georgetown University professor. "Meanwhile," writes historian and economist Neil Howe, "the stigma surrounding a person's (particularly a man's) inability to work has dramatically declined."[53]

To many, a safe and secure landing was spelled SSI. It was Richard Nixon, not Lyndon Johnson, who signed the Social Security Amendments of 1972, creating the SSI (Supplemental Security Income) Program. Administered by the Social Security Administration, SSI grew slowly. To be eligible for SSI disability benefits, one must have a medical condition that prevents one from working or adjusting to another position because of an ailment, in which such conditions have existed for at least a year and may be permanent. Unlike Social Security, SSI is not age-restricted. A needs-based system, SSI limits the income and assets of beneficiaries. Recipients also receive Medicaid coverage. The disability income (DI) available through SSI is funded through general trust funds, not Social Security FICA taxes. Economist Howe explains: "With more workers experiencing a decline in hourly pay, a DI check adjusted to the average wage seems like an attractive alternative to work. DI has thus become . . . a 'de-facto welfare' program for low-skilled workers." The process requires doctors' evaluations and testimonials. Administrative law judges (ALJ) preside over hearings, resolving disputes between Social Security determinations and applicants who challenge the decisions. Denied applicants may dispute the decision. A new breed of lawyers specializing in disability rights has thrived.[54]

The commercials and billboards saturated the Sunshine State: "Injured in a workplace accident? Treated unfairly? Call 1-800-A-LAWYER." Disability claims had been rising for decades but spiked dramatically during the Great Recession. Soon, billboards, newspaper ads, and TV commercials trumpeted the promise of SSI. In 2003, 5 million workers received Social Security disability payments, a figure soaring to 8 million in 2010. Children also became eligible for SSI disability benefits. In Florida, applications for benefits rose by 40 percent between 2007 and 2010. Few adult men who have received SSI benefits ever return to the workforce. Perhaps the greatest factor in the rise of disability benefits is that recipients no longer feel stigmatized. "Exposés on *60 Minutes* and *The Wall Street Journal* in 2011 depicted widespread abuse and fraud as millions signed up for benefits," contended the *New York Times.* CBS depicted families pulling their children from school to ensure SSI benefits. Whether millions of perfectly healthy Americans were gaming the welfare system or simply were unqualified at an increasingly complex workplace, the pain was obvious: one in three adult Americans was either not working or not looking for work by 2009.[55]

Florida's Close-up

The Great Recession may have been horrible for homeowners, but it was great for cable TV and filmmakers. Binge-watching Zombie marathons fit the times. Filmmakers and documentarians found Florida irresistible, with its cast of corporate villains, ghost subdivisions where McMansions turned moldy, and cast of Florida Men. But as a critic noted, "Studios have found it tough to turn dialogue about credit-default swaps into popcorn-friendly features." Unlike previous films set in fraught times, such as *Wall Street* (1987), the Great Recession prompted directors to ignore New York and focus on the subdivisions and victims. The original script of *99 Homes* hit too close to home, forcing writers to change the names of some major financial players. The film premiered in 2015. Writer-director Ramin Bahrani spent time interviewing lawyers and visiting foreclosure court. He confessed, "I was startled to learn that real estate brokers carried guns because they were scared about who would be on the other side of the door when they said, 'I'm coming to take your home away.'" He added, "There were so many scams going on that I decided to make a fast-paced thriller combined with a Faustian version of the housing crash story." The film depicts Orlando during the financial crisis and introduces a fictional cutthroat real-estate broker who makes money by evicting families from their underwater homes. He hires an unemployed construction worker to evict other families. He maliciously strips the homes of their appliances, earning additional profits by sending the bill to Fannie Mae to pay for replacements. Rick Carver, a real estate broker, asks, "You think America in 2010 gives a flying rat's ass about me? America doesn't bail out losers. America was built by bailing out winners, by rigging a nation of the winners, for the winners, by the winners." In one of the more wrenching scenes from *99 Homes,* viewers watch Lee County sheriffs and Realtors confronting homeowners, who are told they no longer were homeowners. "You must leave, now."[56]

The most quoted film depicting Florida's woes was *The Big Short* (2015), a work based on and named for Michael Lewis's 2010 nonfiction best seller. In the film, Ben Rickert, played by Brad Pitt, was in Las Vegas with investors buying collateralized debt obligations (CDOs). In normal times, CDOs meant nonrisky home mortgages. However, the investors were betting that "a hard rain was gonna fall," and that the seemingly safe mortgages would slip into foreclosure, thus making the two men a fortune. Pitt tells his partner, who has begun a celebratory dance, to stop, asking, "Do you have any idea what you just did? You bet against the American economy!" A critic admiringly observed that the director "cast Selena Gomez to explain synthetic collateralized debt obligations at a blackjack table and Anthony Bourdain to craft a metaphor about the origins of those C.D.O.s with fish stew." Critics and comics loved the dialogue and oft-repeated quotes, especially: "Truth is like poetry. And most people f**king hate poetry."[57]

A Rogues' Gallery: Ponzi-Schemers

In the front yard of his soon-to-be repossessed Boca del Vista condo, Karl Marx VII cursed Florida's unalloyed capitalism and running greyhounds of free enterprise. To anyone who would listen, he endlessly repeated his more famous relative's law: "History repeats itself, first as tragedy, second as farce." Marx especially enjoyed reading a yellowed newspaper clipping: "Under the blistering heat of this tropical sun," a journalist wrote, "there are a thousand developments scattered about the State . . . with here and there a half-completed building, a former field office or a lonesome shack, marking the graves of the hopes of armies of investors a year ago . . . but for that one might be traveling through a country of the dead." The site and date were neither 2009 nor Leigh Acres nor Palm Coast; rather, it was anywhere "from Palm Beach to Tampa, 1926."[58]

The Great War left Allies and Central Powers mountains of international, intergenerational debt. In 1920, the *Wall Street Journal* published a curious article, "Give Ponzi a Million." The author maintained that the debt would vanish if nations invested their funds with an Italian immigrant who was becoming as famous as he would soon become infamous.[59]

Born Carlo Ponzi in Parma, Italy, in 1882, Ponzi caught America Fever and immigrated to Boston in 1903. "I landed in this country with $2.50 in cash and $1 million in hopes," he later recounted. Better educated than most of his *paesani*, his trek toward the American dream began as a dishwasher. He spent some time working at a bank in Montreal that catered to Italians, but when Bank Zarossi went bankrupt, he was again left threadbare. He served time in prison for writing a bad check.[60]

Returning to Boston, he engaged in some minor scams before he created the confidence game that would become known as the Ponzi scheme. Promising outrageous returns—a 50 percent gain in 45 days to investors, or 100 percent in 90 days—Ponzi paid last month's sucker with today's deposits. Flush with funds, he bought a mansion in Lexington. A 1920 exposé in the *Boston Globe* set off panic resulting in his arrest. Author Daniel Akst marvels at the long arc of scams based on robbing Peter to pay Paul. "These earlier investments find the returns so compelling that they offer to let their earnings ride, and for a while at least their duplicitous maestro compounds them." Put another way, as a Florida real estate broker explained the collapse of the 1920s Florida Land Boom: "We just ran out of suckers!"[61]

Destiny lured Ponzi to Florida. He arrived in Jacksonville in 1925, still owing $2 million to defrauded investors. He organized the Charpon Land Syndicate, guaranteeing 222 percent profit in 90 days. Alas, he was arrested for violating Florida land laws and the "declaration of trust" principle. Deported in 1926, he never served his Florida sentence or reimbursed swindled investors. He died at a charity hospital ward in Brazil. He claimed as his only assets 1,000 lots in Lake City, Florida! He advertised the lots as "close to Jacksonville," even though Jacksonville was more than 135 miles away![62]

Ponzi lives forever. Newspaper headlines during the Great Recession included "Florida: A Ponzi Schemer's Paradise," "Feds Allege $300-Million Ponzi Scheme at Cay Club Resorts," and "How South Florida Became Synonymous with Ponzi Schemes, Financial Fraud." For many Floridians who experienced financial loss, the reason was neither bad timing nor lack of intelligence; rather, for many the game was fixed. A rogues' gallery of nefarious crooks, swindlers, and confidence men stole millions of dollars from well-meaning investors. Bernie Madoff became the human face of misbegotten gains, but the sheer number of convicted embezzlers, fraudsters, and swindlers comprises a long list of Floridians. A journalist declared: "From Scott Rothstein to Jason Shapiro to even Bernie Madoff, there are so many swindlers with South Florida ties, they deserve their own wing in the Scoundrels Hall of Shame. If pooled, the proceeds could run some small countries."[63]

Why is/was Florida the poster state for financial fraud and outrageousness? The short answer is simple: location and wealth. Gilded Age Florida and California are constantly hitting the get-rich reform/reset buttons. Financial scams and schemes flourish in bubble economies, where get-rich hyperbole seems so near, so real. New York City and Miami have ranked first and second in federal prosecutions of securities and investment fraud. When asked whether Miami and/or Florida is the Ponzi capital of America, Andrew Levi, an ex-prosecutor in Miami, replied evocatively, asserting, "But there's no question it's one of the worst." Others noted Florida's demography: so many residents are newcomers, senior citizens, and wealthy. In Palm Beach, elderly wealthy Jews and Jewish charities were frequent targets of con men. In a *Wall Street Journal* study of the places one is most likely to be defrauded by stock and financial brokers, Fort Lauderdale/Boca Raton, Sarasota, Collier/Lee counties, Treasure Coast, and Miami-Dade County, ranked respectively first, third, fourth, and eleventh nationally.[64]

The legend of Carlo Ponzi survives in Florida by name and crime. Buddy Persaud may have been the most fascinating. "When Buddy Persaud promised his investors the moon and stars, he wasn't kidding," wrote *Miami Herald* investigative journalist Adam H. Beasley. "Persaud, an Orlando-based financial broker, believed that markets were affected by lunar cycles and gravitational pull. When—surprise, surprise—the heavens failed him, Persaud paid out their promised high rates of return (up to 18 percent) by simply recruiting investors and using their funds to pay off the old ones. . . . Put simply, he ran a Ponzi scheme." Beasley cautioned: "In the dirty world of Florida Ponzi schemers, Persaud is a small-timer. His enterprise, which totaled $1 million, was a comparable pittance."[65]

"Palm Beach is a fantasy." Lawrence Leamer, a celebrated author and frequent commentator, elaborated how and why the scandal had devastated his hometown: "There are no hospitals, funeral homes, people don't talk about the negative." But there *was* a Palm Beach Country Club, a largely Jewish club formed in the 1950s because the other clubs excluded Jews. Madoff, who owned a $5 million mansion in Palm Beach, belonged to the ritzy club. "If you invested with Bernie," explained Leamer, "you were the elite within the elite. And that was about half the club members." Members nudged to get close to Madoff so he could make them rich. Madoff's actions were so odious that classics scholars and rabbis have analyzed the fraudster. Mark Pinksy imagined Madoff "in the Ninth (and deepest) Circle of Hell." Rabbi David Wolpe said simply, "You shouldn't steal. And this is on a global scale." The *New York Times* reacted, "Here is a Jew accused of cheating Jewish organizations trying to help other Jews." Madoff is a New Yorker, but many of his clients were Jews who lived in Palm Beach. Madoff's $50 billion empire crumbled on 11 December 2008, bringing down one of the largest Jewish philanthropies in America, the Picower Foundation, headquartered in Palm Beach. Its endowment was valued at $1 billion. Established by Palm Beach resident Jeffry Picower, the foundation awarded generous gifts to local schools and museums.[66]

Time magazine's 9 January 2009 issue coronated "the new capital of Florida corruption." Palm Beach, which had become the center of the political universe in November 2000, was rocked to the core by a succession of scandals. Authorities charged five city and county commissioners with corruption. A local reporter asked readers, "Having trouble mustering pity for the rich who invested with Bernie Madoff?" She asked them to consider the repercussions: "Then pity the hungry, homeless, neglected kids, abused women, homebound elderly, the museums, musicians, actors, artists, and disabled. Those with arthritis, birth defects, Alzheimer's, HIV/AIDS, cancer, autism, diabetes . . . The planet." In addition to the Picower Foundation, the Madoff scandal also impacted other Palm Beach organizations, including the Levin Family Foundation, its $6 million endowment wiped out. The Werner Foundation ($1.4 million) and the Gurwin Family Foundation lost all assets ($36 million). His most notable associate in Palm Beach was Jeffry Picower, who profited more than $5 billion, sometimes receiving returns of 950 percent. In October 2009, Picower was found dead at the bottom of his pool at his mansion, Casa del Sud. The *Manchester Guardian* contended, "An accountant turned wealthy investor, Picower, a friend and accomplice of Madoff, was named in court papers as the biggest beneficiary of returns from Wall Street fraudster's corrupt investment empire." In 2010, Barbara Picower, the widow, agreed in the settlement of the Madoff trustee suit, to pay other victims $7.2 billion. But she changed her mind and fought the settlement for many years. Before he died, Jeffry Picower's personal brokerage accounts at Goldman Sachs exceeded $10 billion. In prison, Madoff implicated Picower.[67]

Madoff's clients included 13,000 names, of whom 2,200 resided in Florida. Only New York was hit harder than Florida. The list included celebrities, such as pitcher and Vero Beach resident Sandy Koufax and Miami Beach automobile mogul Normal Braeman. Ronnie Sue and Dominic Ambrosino of Delray Beach lost $1.66 million. When contacted by a reporter, Ronnie Sue confessed: "We're stuck in Arizona. We can't put fuel in the tank to get back to Florida." Many residents of Palm City in Martin County knew Neil Friedman for the artistic note cards he sold every Sunday at the flea market. Before December 2008, he was a wealthy retiree, but he lost everything in the Madoff bankruptcy. "I've lived totally on Social Security and selling note cards since 2008," the day he lost everything when Madoff went bankrupt. He pondered suicide. Another Florida victim, Faye Albert was still working at age seventy in 2013. Her account with Madoff had grown to $800,000 when she was preparing to retire in 2008. Adele Fox, a widow who lived in Tamarac, sighed, "All my savings are just gone." Steven Sondov of Pompano Beach invested with Madoff, as had his father. They called the notorious financier "Uncle Bernie." The family lost almost $2 million. Madoff was sentenced to prison for 150 years. He died in 2021, hoping for a Trump pardon that never came.[68]

Journalists adore stories involving scandals, sleazebags, and money. The Scott Rothstein saga had it all: a gold toilet, racketeering, money laundering, a $1 billion fraud, and escape to Morocco. For journalists writing for the *Palm Beach Post*, the twenty-first century must have seemed like a running reality show: the death of Anna Nicole Simpson at the Seminole Hard Rock Café, the crazy 2000 ballot, and the Madoff-Picower tragedies. But Scott Rothstein even surpassed the Madoff-Picower melodrama.

"Somewhere during Rothstein's growth from earnest teenager to motivated law student to ambitious attorney," an FBI agent wondered, how did Rothstein turn, masterminding what *Sun-Sentinel* journalists concluded "could be the largest fraud in South Florida history." A classmate and legal colleague offered a simple motive: "He was always looking for more. He wanted to make more money."[69]

Rothstein moved from the Bronx to Lauderhill in 1976, following a trail of Jewish developers and designers from New York to Broward County. His family was working-class. He played in a rock band in high school and enrolled at the University of Florida, where he graduated. He entered law school at Nova Southeastern in Fort Lauderdale. Classmates recall him being a "great talker, a great schmoozer." Graduating from law school in 1988, he moved to Hollywood, joining a law firm. He was ambitious and charismatic, qualities matched by his taste for expensive suits and six-figure timepieces.[70]

Rothstein traveled in a very fast lane. Colleagues and clients remember photographs of the successful lawyer shaking hands with presidents, senators, and movie stars decorating his law office in Fort Lauderdale. He donated lavish amounts—nearly $2 million—to political campaigns. "The problem is," CNN reported, "the money is dirty." Rothstein admitted to having a stash of $1 million in cash so he could keep his enterprise afloat. "We were handing out money like Santa Claus, handing out candy to anybody that needed it for our purposes," he confessed. Arrested in December 2010, Rothstein pleaded guilty to federal charges of racketeering, money laundering, conspiracy, and mail and wire fraud. His Ponzi scheme cost investors $1.2 billion. His assets amounted to $100 million. Desperate, the nefarious thief chartered a Gulfstream V jet to seek refuge in Morocco, along with $16 million. Pleading guilty, Rothstein was sentenced to fifty years in prison.[71]

One of the most flamboyant white-collar criminals gained notoriety for wearing the orange and white football jerseys of the University of Miami. Before he became part of Miami's sport culture, Jason Shapiro spent four years at the University of South Florida in Tampa, 1986–90, where he ironically majored in criminology! USF did not have a football program until 1997, but the 6-foot, 6-inch Shapiro was an enthusiastic devotee of intramural flag football. In 1990, his team, "Public Enemy," suffered a heartbreaking loss, 15–14. Blaming a referee for the loss, Shapiro coldcocked the official, prompting his arrest. While Shapiro never graduated from USF, he developed an infatuation with the University of Miami, lavishing gifts to the Hurricanes' athletic department. Many honorable alumni and friends have donated generously to the University of Miami in Coral Gables. The problem was that Shapiro was involved in a $930 million Ponzi scheme.

Shapiro was born in Brooklyn in 1969, moving to Miami Beach and graduating from Miami Beach High in 1986. A born salesman, he launched Capitol Investments USA, a Ponzi scheme. His expensive gambling habits, love for expensive yachts, celebrity sporting events, and $6 million mansion on Biscayne Bay fueled his appetite to cheat more clients. Arrested in 2010, he was charged with securities fraud and money laundering. His generosity to and obsession with the University of Miami—a lounge honored his contributions—were notorious and corrupting. The NCAA investigated Shapiro's relationship to the university and gifts to players, as well as Miami's lack of institutional control. Shapiro was sentenced to twenty years in prison. *Sports Illustrated* called for the University of Miami to shut down its football team. "This is terribly sad, and sadly familiar," wrote Alexander Wolff to President Donna Shalala.[72]

Not all Ponzi-schemers preferred million-dollar Bugatti designer-cars or South Beach. Rita Crundwell may have stolen $54 million, but she chose a modest neighborhood in Englewood. The former bookkeeper from Dixon, Illinois—Ronald Reagan's childhood home—vacationed in an unassuming home worth $287,000 in 2010. She chose not to live on the more desirable waterfront. She did purchase championship quarter horses. She was sentenced to twenty years in prison.[73]

Madoff became a cottage industry in Florida. A *Sarasota Herald-Tribune* headline proclaimed, "Sarasota Ponzi Schemer Art Nadel: Fear of Becoming Known as a 'Mini-Madoff' in the Madoff Era." A disbarred New York lawyer, piano player in sleazy bars, and hedge-fund manager, Nadel bilked millions from investors, many of them Sarasota friends. He abruptly left town when accountants detected that $168 million was missing. The funds were never recovered. It was the greatest financial swindle in Southwest Florida history. Sarasota was also home to an old-fashioned crime, land fraud. Investigative reports uncovered that New Vista Properties sold more than 5,000 mostly rural vacant lots at greatly inflated prices. And a Sarasota lawyer engaged in a foreclosure rescue scheme, promising struggling homeowners that he could save them from foreclosure. Instead, he simply kept their money. Only attorneys may legally solicit homeowners with promises to help forestall foreclosure. Nadel's case was one of five such Ponzi trials in Sarasota, alone.[74]

Perhaps no individual and corporation soared so high and fell so far than Angelo Mozilo, head of Countrywide Financial Corporation. In 2003, while Countrywide was riding high, *Fortune* gushed at its breadth: $400 billion in home loans. Countrywide was breaking market share and profit records, bringing in $2 billion in profits while the CEO earned $1.9 billion in salary. The Great Recession hammered the corporation and its executives, while a team of prosecutors threw the book at Mozilo. The State of Florida, home to some of the most egregious methods, sued Mozilo. More than a few headlines asked, reminding readers that Mozilo had been the subject of more than 100 lawsuits, including insider trading, "Why Is Angelo Mozilo a Free Man?"[75]

Then there was the fake charity that claimed it was supporting fallen police officers. The Police Protective Fund raised millions of dollars but spent a tiny fraction for those it claimed to help. Even though Florida law bans charities and professional solicitors from employing telemarketers who were convicted of fraud, a lengthy investigation by the *Tampa Bay Times* uncovered troubling trends. It named the Police Protective Fund one of America's worst charities. However, the government cannot limit how much charities can spend fundraising because of First Amendment challenges. The nonprofit company ran telemarketing centers in New Port Richey, Clearwater, and Davie. John Donald Cody, aka Bobby Thompson, committed massive fraud running U.S. Navy Veterans Association, a charity based in Tampa that raised more than $100 million in donations. The charity was a fraud. Thompson was sentenced to twenty-eight years in prison.[76]

Business journalist Robert Trigaux pondered, "If we must choose one Florida icon among the recent scam artists—oh, my—how intense is that competition?—my vote goes to Orlando Ponzi schemer and former band boy creator Lou Pearlman." The notorious Pearlman scammed many Tampa Bay investors before he fled to Bali, only to be recognized by a tourist. Pearlman finally pleaded guilty to stealing $300 million from more than 1,000 investors. Karl Marx VII and Ben Bernanke, along with many distressed Floridians, want to know why so few executives went to jail for causing the Great Recession.[77]

As chair of the Federal Reserve from February 2006 through January 2014, Bernanke witnessed the housing crisis that crippled Florida and much of the nation. On 15 October 2007, he addressed the growing financial turmoil and mounting mortgage losses at the Economic Club of New York when he succinctly summarized the crisis: "Liquidity dried up, prices fell, and spreads widened." As the situation slowly began to improve, he traveled to Orlando in February 2012 to discuss national trends of "Housing Markets in Transition" at the National Association of Home Builders International Builders' Show. In his remarks, he shared that Florida's homeowner vacancy rate remained higher than the national average.[78]

Florida led in yet another real estate quagmire, complaints about time-share condominiums. Those one- and two-week escapes at time-share condos craved during the 1980s and 1990s became an unexpected burden during the new millennium. Frustrations escalated during hard times: weeks became difficult to exchange, maintenance fees soared, and the seldom-cleaned Jacuzzi no longer seemed quite as inviting.

Water into Land: Tierra Verde

Condos overlooking the Gulf of Mexico and Atlantic Ocean seemed a perfect match in a state where demand exceeded supply. Beginning in the 1960s, the rush began to smother the waterfront with condominiums. To create more supply, savvy investors created a new way of selling a slice of paradise: the two-week time-share condominium. No place did this new way of living seem more out of place than the barrier islands of Tampa Bay. Saltwater mosquitoes, inhospitable islands, and transportation challenges ensured that places such as Cabbage Key remained largely untouched until the 1960s. In 1913, a land syndicate purchased

Cabbage Key, a 300-acre island off Pass-a-Grille, a barrier island in Pinellas County. Longtime residents guffawed when they learned the new owners paid $50,000. Engineers converted a "large houseboat" into a dredge, "which will be used for dredging in the vicinity of Coon Key and Cabbage Key. . . . A large amount of sand will be pumped on the islands filling in some low places near the shore." The new town would not appear for a half century.[79]

In 1948, *Life* magazine discovered Cabbage Key. But readers found the lone inhabitant more interesting than the cabbage palms and mangroves. Overnight, the white-bearded Silas Dent became the "Hermit of Cabbage Key." Author Hal Boyle described Silas as "Santa Claus gone to seed." Dent was occasionally joined by the heart-broken and soul-crushed who sought his companionship and solitude. He liked to make Christmas presents from shell and wood and deliver them to poor children. He was also joined by the island's citrus rats. To combat the latter, he imported cats. His legs revealed many rattlesnake bites, the only animal he killed. He never wore shoes. Within a few years, "Old Silas" Dent would be better known as the name of a restaurant. He would not have approved Silas Dent's Steakhouse & Bayside Bar at 5501 Gulf Boulevard, that paid homage to him, nor the epic dredge-and-fill that created a new city lined with condos and vegetation that did not belong. Dent had moved with his family from Valdosta, Georgia, in 1900 to Cabbage Key. The family operated a dairy in Largo until mosquitoes drove them away. Silas returned and remained on the island until his death in 1952.[80]

A modern stampede occurred along the Pinellas Gulf coast in the decades after World War II. Along what was once miles of undeveloped coastline, developers imposed their will, constructing finger islands and seawalls. Developers transformed cheap, submerged lands into waterfront property, commanding the technological wand of massive hydraulic dredges that piled bay muck into real estate. The writer John Rothchild's family moved to a "fresh section" on Boca Ciega Bay in the 1950s. There, "dredges were as routine as seagulls." He explained the alchemy of dredge-and-fill:

> The dredging equipment was floated over from Tampa, on two huge barges. Sections of concrete seawall were lowered into the water with a crane. . . . The seawall defined the territorial boundaries of new the new property. From the other barge, a large pipe was extended into the water, like a hose on a vacuum, to suck up the bay bottom. . . . The silt and muck were drawn through a cutter and into a pipe, then pumped along the full length of the barge and spilled out of a discharge and into the seawall mold.[81]

Tierre Verde may have marked the most dramatic chapter in the high-stakes dredge-and-fill derby. The project was so immense that the *New York Times* announced the audacious plans to build a new city on fifteen uninhabited keys on Boca Ciega Bay. Several prominent St. Petersburg developers purchased Pine and Cabbage keys for $2 million. Texas oilman and NFL owner Clint Murchison became part of a group that purchased 1,800 acres and the rights to their submerged lands for $12 million. Federal, state, and local transportation projects made this ambitious development possible: the proposed construction of the Sunshine Skyway Bridge, a 15-mile structure spanning Lower Tampa Bay connecting Manatee and Pinellas counties. To make the project more "public," the projects allowed motorists access to Fort De Soto Park and Beach.[82]

In 1958, the first dredges began to convert land from water. The syndicate named the new city Tierra Verde (Green Land). The vision included golf courses, shopping centers, schools, yacht marinas, and a helicopter port. In 1959 investors sold the Tierra Verde Corporation to New York building mogul Louis Berlanti for $6 million. Advertisements described the ambitious project as "America's Most Unusual Island City." A local journal described the impact: "A huge concrete batching plant stands silhouetted against the sun. . . . Seawalls are taking shape. . . . What were once the islands of Pine and Cabbage Keys . . ."[83]

Not everyone applauded the ambitious plans to alter the face of bay and beach. Local and state opponents criticized the project for its finances—some argued the project represented a public giveaway of free roads for private gains; others understood the environmental implications of dredge-and-fill that was ruining Boca Ciega Bay. With the opening of the bridges and highways, thousands of cars were arriving in Tierra Verde by the early 1960s.[84]

Developers won the battle. Massive construction transformed and consolidated fifteen isolated islands into Tierra Verde, incorporated in 1961. By 1962, a road and bridge connected Tierra Verde to the mainland.

The Pinellas Bayway connected this island to St. Petersburg and the Gulf beaches as the fanciful Guy Lombardo's Port-o-Call Hotel and Motor Inn opened on the northern portion of this island in 1963. Berlanti persuaded Lombardo to open a nightclub on the island before his mysterious death on a sabotaged aircraft. Guy's orchestra dedicated the opening in January 1963. Guy Lombardo was an acclaimed bandleader known for his touring band, the Royal Canadians. For a half century on radio and television, he hosted a popular New Year's Eve show. A part-investor in the property, Lombardo touted this swank south Pinellas destination while touring. The new digs gained national fame when showcased on a 3 May 1963 episode of the popular *Route 66* television show.[85]

By the early 1980s, Tierra Verde Island Resort enjoyed its reputation as a high-class time-share. Picnics, water volleyball contests, boat rides to nearby Shell Island, and other amenities lured both locals and those far away to buy weeks. But in the early 2000s, a growing number of owners passed away or stopped paying their maintenance assessments. The Great Recession sheared away any confidence for buyers burdened with time-shares. Conditions deteriorated. Soon, owners received notices that their condo association had plans to disband so a new developer could purchase and redevelop the site. At meetings in 2006, some elderly time-share unit owners who flew down for contentious association meetings learned the hard truth of time-shares: investors had quietly purchased many weeks that had lapsed or fell into receivership for pennies on the dollar and held enough votes to disband the association before its official end in 2020. Time-share weeks purchased for a few thousand dollars in the early 1980s were valued at $100 for a few lucky folks; many received nothing. The Tierra Verde Island Resort closed, wrecking crews bulldozed the site, and some former owners continued to receive letters promising to help them unload their zombie time-shares well into the 2020s. Guy Lombardo's Port-o-Call was demolished in 2007. Preservationists saved the mural that featured portraits of Mel Torme, Marlene Dietrich, Frank Sinatra, and others who helped make Tierra Verde even more desirable for residents and time-share tourists. When asked about the future site of Port-o-Call, a longtime Realtor explained: "That's a great location, but development has got to wait for the market. You've got to get the condos off the market."[86]

In 2021, an article began, "The Tierra Verde Grand Canal is filling up with sand." A gated community on the Grand Canal suddenly became owners of private beach. Most beach dwellers would cheer such news, but the new beach has created a set of new problems, such as access to the Gulf. Then there is the question of who is going to pay for the expensive dredging.[87]

Piney Point

Tierra Verde and Piney Point represented the two Floridas. Both straddled Tampa Bay. In 1914, Manatee County's Piney Point was hailed as "the coming tourist rendezvous of Florida." But Piney Point was ultimately a prisoner of geographic and geological destiny. A 1914 advertisement touting its assets predicted Piney Point would become the "Atlantic City of the South": "Its climate, fishing, bathing and deep-water facilities combine with its backing of thousands of rich agricultural lands, its easy accessibility to the large phosphate rock deposits, to give it advantages not possessed by any other location in the State of Florida."[88] The article's key words were "phosphate rock deposits." Piney Point was the closest deepwater port for the export of vast deposits of phosphate mined in Bone Valley and formed thousands of years earlier. Ultimately, an extractive industry trumped tourism. Phosphate richly rewarded a few companies that arrived early. But ultimately, the great loser was Florida's environment. Phosphate mining left moonlike craters. Gypsum stacks, called "gypstacks," that resemble earthen Inca or Aztec temple mounds, dot the phosphate belt. Composed of the remnants of strip-mined phosphate and millions of gallons of highly acidic wastewater, gypsum stacks have become the abandoned stepsisters in a phosphate economy that refuses to take responsibility.

In 1966, the Borden Chemical Company constructed the Piney Point phosphate processing plant on its 676-acre site. One year later, local officials discovered that the company was dumping waste into Bishop Harbor, a marine estuary flowing into Tampa Bay. Over the next fifty-five years, four other owners operated the plant, each adding to the human health and environmental disasters. In 1989, emergency crews rushed to Piney Point when a cloud of toxic fumes prompted an evacuation.[89]

A *Tampa Bay Times* journalist described the history of Piney Point accurately: "On the Edge of Disaster." In 1997, a gypsum stack collapsed when a dam broke atop the mound, leaking 56 million gallons of acidic wastewater into a tributary of the Alafia River. An estimated 1.3 million fish died, and 377 acres of vegetation were damaged. In 2001, the Piney Point fertilizer plant closed after the owner, Mulberry Phosphates, went bankrupt. "But the waste from more than three decades of phosphate mining still sits in massive piles at the site," argued *The Guardian*, "the environmental equivalent of a ticking time bomb." The bomb is composed of 1 billion tons of phosphogypsum, tall stacks of waste products that are still growing. "No community should have to suffer the consequence of this toxic legacy for some corporation's short-term financial gain," said Jaclyn Lopez, director at the Center for Biological Diversity. She added prophetically, "There's a local saying that if you go to a Manatee County Commission meeting 50 years from now, there's two things that'll be on the agenda: sewage spills and Piney Point."[90]

We want to believe that nature is resilient. In 2007, a journalist wrote an optimistic article about the consequences of the spill: "A decade after a dam break . . . the worst environmental disaster in the Alafia River's history, the river appears to have returned to normal."[91]

Piney Point became an abandoned child with owners who accepted little responsibility. In 2021, officials fearing that a breach in a gypsum stack might collapse, released 400 million gallons of wastewater. The toxic brew flowed half a mile into Tampa Bay wreaking damage.

Tierra Verde and Piney Point may seem like stark contrasts: the gritty and toxic world of radioactive wastewater and the glamorous stretch of beaches and islands connected like pearls. But engineering, as much as sunshine, explains our extraordinary ability to make land out of water, and phosphate from rock and pebbles. "Super-populated Florida," writes columnist David Von Drehle, "is an invention of modern manufacture, an intricate machinery pf canals, pumping stations, dredges, reclamations, pilins, piers, landfills and drains."[92]

The BP Oil Spill: 2010

If phosphate has soiled the lands and waters of Southwest Florida, oil, in the words of Jack E. Davis, "hijacked the Gulf's identity." Davis, in his Pulitzer Prize–winning history of the Gulf of Mexico, contends the 2010 oil spill from the *Deepwater Horizon* rig "frames how we—from journalists to policy makers, even scientists and tourists—perceive the American Sea. That eighty-seven-day nightmare, including the loss of eleven lives . . . represents the worst accidental spill in history, and perhaps the most poorly conceived cleanup response. The Gulf, as a result, will be living with fatal and unknown consequences far into the future."[93] "It exploded with a fatal fury on the night of April 20, 2010," wrote a Panhandle journalist, describing the first act of what would come to be called the *Deepwater Horizon* Oil Spill. Or the BP Oil Spill, named for the British Petroleum Company that operated the offshore rig. The blown well belched oil into the Gulf waters for nearly three months until it was capped. The toll was immense: 210 million gallons of oil fouling the Gulf and almost 2 million gallons of chemicals that were sprayed onto the inferno. Sixteen thousand miles of beaches and coasts were coated and spoiled.[94]

Captain Gary Jarvis was a charter fishing boat captain in 2010, piloting the *Backdown 2*. The *Deepwater Horizon* oil rig attracted anglers because prized fish like marlin and tuna found a smorgasbord of smaller fish around gulf derricks. Jarvis witnessed firsthand the terrible explosion. A decade later, Jarvis serves as mayor of Destin.[95]

On 4 June 2010, scientists announced the first tar balls to wash ashore in Florida, along Walton and Okaloosa counties' coastline. Ironically, the spill hit Florida's Emerald Coast the hardest. An unlikely hero emerged, Okaloosa County

Commissioner Wayne Harris, who bellowed in defense of Choctawhatchee Bay: "We made the decision legislatively to break the laws if necessary. We will do whatever it takes to protect our county's waterways, and we're prepared to go to jail to do it." Marsha Dowler was living and working at Seaside at this time and recalls: "I had awakened at pre-dawn and walked to the Odessa Pavilion. As the sun rose, I faced east and caught the first acrid waft of burned oil. It broke my heart and remains seared in memory."[96]

The short- and long-term consequences in Florida were enormous. Although not a drop of oil reached Collier or Lee counties, many Americans canceled vacations to Florida, assuming the Gulf coast was now one vast oil slick. The long-term consequences are still being assessed. In 2013, a headline lamented, "Oil Still Lingers in Gulf." Oil from the *Deepwater Horizon* Spill, observed Craig Pittman, "settled on a shelf 80 miles from the Tampa Bay region."[97]

"Off Florida's Gulf Coast," began an article in the *New York Times* in May 2010, "the seas are calm, and the king mackerel are running." But boat captains' phones were not ringing, or if they were, it was to announce cancellations. Florida fishermen reeled from the fish beds affected by the spill to consumers who shied away from Gulf-caught red snapper and redfish. Federal officials closed 6,800 square miles of fishing areas in the Gulf of Mexico. Authorities also imposed a ten-day ban on recreational and commercial fishing. But the impact was measured in years not days. A decade later, Panhandle anglers and commercial boaters bemoaned the state of the fisheries, especially the steep decline in redfish and golden tilefish. Scientists contend the oil also caused lesions in fish. Perhaps even more damaging, the oil spill resulted in a massive die-off of small creatures that constitute the Gulf of Mexico's food chain. As if the oil spill was not devastating enough, scientists also blame the chemical used by British Petroleum and other crews to disperse the oil for damaging marine life and also Keys coral reefs.[98]

The BP Oil Spill of 2010 morphed into books and films. In one of the most eerie coincidences, Omar Mateen appeared in a 2012 documentary depicting the environmental disaster. *The Big Fix* introduces Mateen, who is working the night shift as a security guard. Filmmaker Rebecca Tickell asks him what is happening. He replies, "No one gives a s—, no one gives a s— here. Like, everybody's just out to get paid. They're like, hoping for more oil to come out and more people to complain so they'll have job." Five years later, Mateen committed the deadliest shooting in American history at the Orlando Pulse nightclub.[99]

The oil spill took a terrible toll of seabirds. The brown pelican became an iconic symbol of the disaster as 12,000 volunteers organized by the Audubon

Society attempted to remove the oil from the large birds. A century earlier, the pelican was at the center of another controversy.[100]

A Pelican Parable

Today's headlines are unsettling: mutilated pelicans; unregulated puppy mills and sadistic owners; dead dolphins riddled with bullets; savage beasts unloosed on innocent children; slithering pythons and urban coyotes lurking in the shadows. We live in a harsh, un-peaceable kingdom. In our Age of Cancel Culture, a question arises: What will Americans in 2122 think of our actions and deeds? Perhaps more than anything else, they will question our relationship and attitude toward animals.

But some perspective is needed before we assume animal cruelty is worse than ever. In fact, Americans' past attitudes toward any animal that could fly, swim, crawl or run was predatory at best, scary at worst. Florida residents held wildly different attitudes toward animals. Before the twentieth century, most inhabitants lived on farms, or had grown up in rural communities where survival depended upon harnessing beasts of burden and the slaughtering of cows, pigs, and chickens. Life was hard with little room for sentimentality. Our modern sensibilities would be shattered at the sights and sounds of horses and mules being flogged and dead animals lying in the street. Working classes had little time or inclination to pamper pets. The upper classes saw no contradiction between hunting big game while pampering their dogs and cats.[101]

Tampa Bay's waters and woods must have seemed inexhaustible to early settlers. In a root-hog-or-die world, few lamented the loss or eradication of the Carolina parakeet, the passenger pigeon, or the Florida panther. By the late nineteenth century, hunters discovered and exploited a lucrative new prize: Florida's luxuriant birdlife.

"Plumers" marauded bird rookeries along Tampa Bay, shooting snowy egrets and roseate spoonbills, herons and curlews, for their plumage. The feathers were sold to New York and Parisian milliners for the fashionable hat trade—a pound of ibis feathers was literally worth its weight in gold. The practice wreaked havoc upon Florida's bird populations because the plunder occurred during nesting season, leaving young birds to die.[102]

One of the most notorious plumers was Alfred LeChevalier, known widely as "Chevalier the Old Frenchman." John Bethell, a pioneer settler on Big Bayou, remembered the Frenchman in his 1915 memoir: "The worst scourge that ever came to Point Pinellas was one Chevalier"; his gang once killed more than 1,000 plume birds on Long Key. Bethell added, "Even the harmless pelicans came in for a share of powder and lead."[103]

The elevation of Spot and Muffin to spoiled indoor pets is a very modern notion. The evolution took thousands of years. Tabby cats and Jack Russell terriers served as mousers, in part because they had been acculturated to hunt, and in part because canned cat and dog food was not introduced until the 1920s. Mules and horses, deemed surplus animals after World War I, supplied the canners with ample supplies of meat.

In a mobile, dislocated society still subject to outbreaks of yellow fever, cholera, and influenza, many animals were simply abandoned—or worse. Cities began to impose restrictions and regulations on animals and their owners. Feral dogs and cats posed serious health problems. The phrase "dog days of summer" refers to the fear of rabies in the hot months. Stray dogs and cats lived precarious lives. Suspicious dogs were hunted down and shot.[104]

"All animals are created equal," wrote George Orwell in *Animal Farm*, "but some animals are more equal than others." Beginning in 1915, St. Petersburg embarked on a "cat elimination crusade." A fascinating headline of the *St. Petersburg Daily Times* warned, "Activity of the Audubon Society Spells Death for Vagrant Cats Slinking about Saint Petersburg." A city ordinance protecting songbirds targeted "all tramp cats." Mayor Al Lang declared war "on stray cats of doubtful lineage and flea-bitten anatomy." In actions that could only weirdly be called symbiosis, misfortunate cats were fed to alligators at a tourist site on Ninth Street N.[105]

What does the macabre cat extermination tell us about early twentieth-century St. Petersburg and Florida? The episode underscores the influence of a small, but influential group of women who genuinely wished to protect songbirds and eliminate the birds' mortal enemy—the feral cat. In St. Petersburg, the debate over social and animal control quickly shifted from scruffy cats to brown pelicans. The concerns had shifted from public health and the protection of songbirds to patriotism and mass starvation. The great pelican massacre occurred during the Great War (World War I). Government officials, fearing food shortages, urged housewives to substitute fish on "Meatless Tuesdays." A popular slogan promised, "Food will win the war." Perhaps because red tide had recently scoured Tampa Bay, fish yields plummeted. Amid the tumult of war, angry fishermen needed a scapegoat. Tampa Bay's brown pelican found itself in the crosshairs of guns and controversy. A fierce debate over the fate of the pelican took place on street corners, church pulpits, and editorial pages. Fishermen dismissed the debate, branded the bird "a pirate," and wreaked vengeance upon the hapless bird. Florida's fish commissioner argued that the fish that pelicans destroyed annually amounted to a precise tab: $3,007,600."[106]

The *Tampa Daily Times* succinctly summarized the issues: "Is the pelican a much abused and maligned bird or is he the predatory pirate he is sometimes pictured, robbing the hardy fishermen of the fruits of their toil, a conscienceless violator of the fish laws, a slaughterer of what we call food fishes, imperiling the nation's future supply of fish food?"[107]

The region's newspapers and citizens took partisan sides. "When it comes to a question of the usefulness of the pelican, it can't be found," editorialized the *Largo Sentinel*. The paper added, "Of course, there are people—fanatics, if you will—who put up a howl if you kill any living thing." The *Manatee River Journal* explained that the pelican "is charged with having an ungodly appetite which causes him to gobble up a lot of fish that our fishermen and tourists ought to get."[108]

Fishermen cited biblical verse, quoting Genesis 1:28: "Be fruitful and multiply and replenish the earth, and subdue it and have dominion over the fish of the sea and over the fowl of the air . . . and over every moving thing that moveth upon the earth." William L. Straub, the iconic editor of the *St. Petersburg Times*, asked readers to consider a simple question: "If pelicans are so destructive, how is it that they [pelicans] didn't have the fish exterminated long ago?"[109]

No one, however, fought harder for the preservation of "the fowl of the air" than Katherine Bell Tippetts. She and her husband had arrived in St. Petersburg in 1902, with hopes of restoring his health. The Tippetts purchased the downtown Lake View Hotel, renaming it the Belmont, in honor of her family's plantation. Born in 1865, Katherine Bell had enjoyed the privileges of private tutors and worldly travel. She was fluent in French, German, Spanish, and Italian. She had written a novel under the pen name Jerome Cable. Her husband died in 1909, and despite the demands of raising four children and running the hotel, she became an ardent activist.[110]

In 1909, Tippetts helped found the St. Petersburg chapter of the Audubon Society in a meeting held at the Belmont Hotel. In January 1917, a headline in the *St. Petersburg Times* announced, "Audubon Club Attendance Is Largest Ever." A reporter observed that the crowd was so large that "a number of visitors had to be turned away . . . a number stood out upon the sidewalk to hear the program."[111]

Tippetts poured her energies into the Audubon Society, serving as local and state president for three decades. She promoted the mockingbird as Florida's state bird. The Audubon Society and women's clubs coalesced into a movement to oppose the senseless slaughter of pelicans. In 1918, members of the St. Petersburg Audubon Society voted unanimously to defend the pelican. The *Times* condensed the debate: "The pelican has able counsel in his fight before the tribunal [the federal food administration] in the St. Petersburg Audubon Society." Tippetts's stance was bolstered by May Mann Jennings, former First Lady of Florida, leader of the state women's clubs, and a champion of the environment.[112]

George Lizotte was a prominent commentator during this era. A Frenchman, he had settled at Pass-a-Grille, where he operated a popular hotel famous for its fish dinners. In one of his many letters to the editor, he asked readers: "Doesn't man eat fish? What does man want—all the fish?"[113]

The great pelican massacre ceased when the war ended and the fish returned. The century-old story seems very modern. So many issues today—vaccinations and the balance between civil liberties and national security, gun laws and the battles between developers and regulators—reflect the tensions between individual freedoms and the needs of the greater community.

The great pelican massacre has deep spiritual roots. Eight hundred years ago, the inhabitants of Gubbio, Italy, felt threatened as a vicious wolf stalked the Umbrian hill town, killing villagers and sheep. Francesco (Francis) Bernardone of Assisi pleaded for the wolf's life. Locals already suspected the young man was addled. Francis had renounced worldly pleasures and formed a band of mendicants. His message was revolutionary: limit your needs, simplify your wants, and give comfort to all creatures great and small.

Francis encountered the snarling beast. "Come, Brother Wolf, I will not hurt you," he softly beckoned. The wolf halted. After a soulful discussion, Francis learned that the wolf had been injured and left behind by his pack. Francis explained to the residents of Gubbio: "The wolf has the same needs as you. He only wants to eat and not go hungry." Francis arranged a truce: the villagers would feed the wolf, and the wolf promised not to harm humans or sheep. Harmony blessed Gubbio.

12

A State in Revision

Refining a Sense of Place and Redefining the Dream

When life gets hard, try to remember: the life you
complain about is only a dream to some people.

–Anonymous

The New Public Library, the Old Daily Newspaper, and the Out-of-State Bank

Florida's public libraries have always been cultural weathervanes. The South in general, and Florida in particular, lagged behind the North in the construction of public libraries. Florida did not have a state archive until 1867. In the 1990s, when public libraries began purchasing VHS films, new patrons obtained cards so they could watch free videos. When property taxes filled city and county coffers in the early years of the era 2000–2006, cities went on a library-building binge. The timing was auspicious, because Floridians discovered when bad times hit, libraries had what desperate citizens need: air-conditioning, comfortable chairs, and, most essential, banks of computers.

In 1975, Pam Gibson worked for the Collier County Public Library System. One might imagine the county's enviable property tax base meant gleaming new libraries across the vast landscape. She recalled that the bookmobile made a weekly stop at the community center in Immokalee. Everglades City had no library, and Marco Island "was just getting a branch library, which was a BIG DEAL."[1]

The public library of 1999 is almost unrecognizable a generation later. Then, libraries focused upon readers and books. Today's libraries resemble a flea market where consumers shop for the newest DVD, tax advice, and guitar loans. Libraries also replaced many bookstores, victims of consolidation and e-books. But even librarians were vulnerable in such grim times. Jim Findlay worked as head of rare books at the Broward County Library and understood his colleagues' anxiety. "It weighs on me," he said, "because there has always been this hope, this expansiveness, this welcome of the unusual and eccentric in Florida." He added, "That seems to come to a halt."[2]

Libraries have become day asylums for the homeless and working classes who cannot afford but need computer access to file for government benefits and feel connected. "From downtown to suburban branches, it's the rare library that has no homeless patrons," contended a journalist in 2007. But public libraries pushed back. Many homeless patrons carry their life's belongings in bags, and to counter this, libraries began adopting airport-like security at entrances. If patrons cannot fit their carry-ons into an airport-style box, they are denied entrance. Libraries enhanced security and instituted new behavior policies, making it illegal to speak loudly, watch pornography, or annoy other patrons. Librarians recall bathroom sinks being used as "birdbaths."[3]

The stereotypes of hushing librarians, monocled archivists, and genteel genealogists shattered shortly after Jeb Bush released his proposed budget for the 2003–4 fiscal year in January 2003. As part of his ongoing pledge to reduce and realign the footprint of state government, Bush put forth an ambitious plan to combine the Department of State and the Department of Community Affairs into a new entity to be known as the Department of State and Community Partnerships, place the state's archival collections under the care of the park service, and shutter the state library while sending nearly 11 linear miles of books to another institution. Bush had tipped his hand during his January 7 inaugural when—two weeks before unveiling his budget—he proclaimed, "There would be no greater tribute to our maturity as a society than if we can make these buildings around us empty of workers, silent monuments to the time when government played a larger role than it deserved or could adequately fill." These words became a rallying cry for those who sought to preserve the state's cultural heritage, encouraging many Floridians as well as librarians, archivists, genealogists, and historians throughout the world to mobilize online petitions, social media campaigns, and protests.[4]

Public outrage over Bush's plan grew even as his original scheme faltered. Before the end of February, Florida State University balked at his desire to transfer the State Library of Florida's collection to that institution after zero-funding the library, eliminating all the staff, and also hitting FSU with a $17.6 million budget cut. Given Florida's sketchy history of protecting natural resources, a loud and growing chorus questioned how park officials in the Department of Environmental Protection would curate and preserve the State Archives. More than a few raised concerns about the fate of ballots from the hotly contested 2000 presidential election, fearing they would find their way to a landfill at a time when their disposition remained in limbo. Outgoing Lieutenant Governor Frank Brogan announced a change in plans as he prepared to step down to assume the presidency of Florida Atlantic University at the beginning of March: after FSU refused the collections, the governor had decided to gift the State Library of Florida's extensive holdings to Nova Southeastern University (NSU) in Broward County, so the materials could occupy a new library facility in Davie. Brogan celebrated Bush's move, one that would place these resources in a private university near FAU's Davie branch campus, proclaiming, "Our goal was to transfer the volumes to a place where they would be much more accessible and better utilized by citizens statewide, and at the same time gain a significant savings to the state." At that time, Nova did not even extend courtesy borrowing privileges to Broward County residents, much less those in the other sixty-six counties. Assiduous librarians soon leaked the proposed agreement signed on 25 February that not only handed over the State Library's circulating collections but also promised to pay NSU millions of dollars to liberate these items from the public's hands.[5]

Ironically, Bush's plan to gut and move the State Library to save $5 million each year occurred while he also secured hopes of funding his "Just Read, Florida!" initiative to the tune of $19 million. Seemingly blind to the criticism as tensions grew, he issued a proclamation touting February 2003 as "Library Appreciation Month" and said promoting reading was a top priority during his second term. Journalists from papers throughout Florida and the nation carried regular stories, noting the many ironies, some of which went beyond books and archives: While complaining about budget shortfalls for agencies occupying the Department of State's R. A. Gray Building, the Bush leadership team cared little about the $50,000 damage done to FSU's intramural fields during January's "Black Tie and Blue Jeans" governor's inaugural ball. When Bush delivered his State of the State speech before a joint session of the legislature on 4 March, lawmakers on both sides of the aisle were lukewarm. The reception outside was even more tepid: Nearly 150 protestors confronted Bush at the Capitol, while that same day, a couple of blocks to the west, hundreds held hands and encircled the R. A. Gray Building in protest as others held signs with slogans such as "Honk for History." Bush lost that battle before libraries finished planning their summer reading programs.[6]

Unsuccessful in his bid to move the State Archives and Library, Bush enlisted a different partnership in November 2003 that attracted international attention. A month earlier, he had convened a special session of the legislature to approve his plan to allocate $310 million into a deal to persuade Scripps Research Institute—a nonprofit based in La Jolla, California—to open labs and research facilities in Palm Beach County. At the time, Bush labeled this agreement as a "seminal moment" like the opening of Walt Disney World in 1971 and optimistically predicted that the Scripps deal would attract upward of 500 companies and 44,000 new jobs. As Bush would later consider his options in the 2016 presidential race, reporters scoured archives and library files to show how his gamble to lure biotechnology firms had failed to meet expectations. Despite local, county, and state investments surpassing $1.32 billion by early 2015, these funds had created fewer than 1,400 new jobs, far from the 44,000 predicted; and, at a cost to the taxpayers of almost $1 million per job, the outcome cast doubt on Bush's ability to establish robust public/private partnerships. One of many challenges faced in the Scripps partnership was a lack of infrastructure. Kelly Smallridge, president of Palm Beach County's Business Development Board, summed up the logistical issues that Scripps and the Max Planck Florida Institute for Neuroscience faced in her county: "When the governor went after these institutes to come to Florida, we didn't realize the amount of infrastructure that needed to be in place. . . . You don't just go and pluck two institutes and put them in a county and expect the industry overall to thrive and for companies to flock here." Perhaps a little research or reading the newspapers in the State Library would have given Bush and his advisors better insight as he crafted these plans![7]

In 1999, sun-seeking Canadian tourists purchased daily copies of the *Globe and Mail* at metal newspaper boxes and drugstores while Floridians, weary of the heat and humidity, purchased the *Miami Herald, Tampa Tribune,* and *Orlando Sentinel* at newsstand kiosks in Cashiers, Waynesville, and Asheville, North Carolina. Buoyed by robust ads, newspapers witnessed record profits in the 1990s. Floridians still relied upon newspapers to find a house, clip a coupon for grocery shopping, and read about weddings and sports. Floridians preferred their news the old-fashioned way, in the morning, over a cup of java. In Tallahassee, a cherished tradition ended in 2007. For as long as the most veteran members of the Florida House and Senate could remember, the morning began with one hand clutching a cup of coffee and pastry while the other hand carried "the clips." Staffers had worked for hours assembling two-inch stacks of clippings gathered from newspapers published far away, such as the *Key West Citizen*, the *Pensacola News-Journal*, and the *Miami Herald*. But the very technology that brought modern printing presses and delivery trucks was displaced by the Web and the Internet. "They," wrote journalist Steve Bousquet, "are altering the political culture and the relationship between the media and government in ways that are encouraging and troubling." As a novelty, most of the large dailies offered free online versions of the paper, but the custom of reading one's daily paper on a tablet at Starbucks was on the near horizon.[8]

Beginning in the 1990s, analysts noted troubled trends in the news industry, cutting jobs and cutting bureaus. The newspaper business in Florida was in a more profitable state, simply because of population growth. Among the major publications, only the *St. Petersburg Times* was locally owned and fiercely independent. "This truly is Florida's best newspaper," wrote journalist Martin Dyckman. "That's thanks to Nelson Poynter's vision that a newspaper should be responsible to its community, not to a remote owner, or worse, Wall Street." Except for the independent *St. Petersburg Times*, most other Florida papers were owned by chains. The landscape of the Fourth Estate was dotted with impressive publications: the *Miami Herald*, *South Florida Sun-Sentinel*, *Orlando Sentinel*, *Palm Beach Post*, and *Tampa Tribune*. However, despite population growth, circulation was slipping; young people were largely indifferent to the traditional newspaper, but the business was making money from real estate, department store, and grocery advertisements. A quaint section, "Want Ads," still existed in most papers. Most of the major newspapers still employed cartoonists and book review editors. In a seeming instant, advertising revenues vanished, and newspapers shrunk, victims of new technologies. Like downtown churches, some newspapers began selling their landmark structures, taking advantage of the rocketing price of real estate. Apartments replaced the *Tampa Tribune*'s building.[9]

The fate of a building at One Herald Plaza perfectly symbolizes newspapers' loss of power and prestige. Under the leadership of publisher David Lawrence, the *Herald* received nine Pulitzers in the 1990s. A Malaysian gaming company purchased the century-old 12-acre headquarters of the *Miami Herald* for $236 million. Built in 1963, the building, wrote journalist Andres Viglucci in 2015, "was the grand dame on Miami's bayfront when they started taking her down, chunk by chunk." He added, "But then she was built to be nearly indestructible, to keep the presses running even after a hit from the strongest of hurricanes, and, not incidentally, to remind everyone in the vicinity—and who could miss its commanding presence and the purplish nighttime glow of its massive neon letters suspended over Biscayne Bay?—of the power of those presses in the affairs of the city."[10]

As a young reporter, David Von Drehle wrote for the *Miami Herald.* In 2012, he returned to Florida to cover the Republican National Convention in Tampa. "In the coolness of the press section of what was then called the Tampa Bay Times Forum," he noted, "I observed something I'd never seen in seven prior conventions. The seats were filled, but hardly anyone glanced at the stage or the delegates. My colleagues had their laptops opened to their TweetDecks. Side by side in the dim glow of their screens, they monitored each bon mot and burp of Twitter's commentary on events." Von Drehle lamented "the crystal meth" that had invaded the newsrooms. Yet newspapers remain relevant and adaptive. Consider the *St. Petersburg Times'* launch of PolitiFact in 2007.[11]

Newspaper circulation figures plunged during the Great Recession. The causes were deeply rooted and mired in the moment. In response, a wave of new mergers occurred. Worse, some newspapers with distinguished credentials ceased publication. A 2006 headline in *The Economist* asked, "Who Killed the Newspaper?" In 1998, the combined circulation of the five leading newspapers in Florida (*Miami Herald/El Nuevo Herald, Tampa Tribune, St. Petersburg Times, South Florida Sun-Sentinel,* and the *Orlando Sentinel*) totaled 2.12 million subscribers. By 2012, circulation had plunged to 1.4 million, and shortly thereafter, the *Tampa Tribune* ceased publication. As late as the 1980s, Hillsborough and Pinellas counties featured five dailies. One survived. The Sunday newspaper, once a near-sacred rite in households and a burden for newspaper boys delivering editions on bicycles, has also withered. Between 1998 and 2012, a period in which Florida gained 3 million new residents, circulation among the state's top twenty newspapers declined over 42 percent. Almost every Florida newspaper shed jobs during the recession. In 2008, the *Palm Beach Post* announced the cutting of 300 jobs, while rival papers issued pink slips to thousands of staffers and reporters. More seriously, beginning in 2010, the Halifax Media Group invested $160 million to purchase 36 newspapers, including 19 in Florida alone. The *Daytona Beach Evening News,* one of the last family-owned papers in Florida, succumbed to the new wave. Several Florida newspapers owned by the *New York Times*—notably the *Sarasota Herald-Tribune* and the *Gainesville Sun*—flipped ownership. Even bigger mergers and dislocations followed, with corporate giants GateHouse and Gannett leveraging and merging their power and influence.[12]

If, by time machine, one were able to return to most Florida cities in the halcyon days of 1950, the financial landscape was largely controlled by locals, family-owned and operated. If one wished to raise funds for a worthy cause, one simply asked the *St. Petersburg Times, Orlando Sentinel,* or *Florida Times-Union.* Friendly stops at the local banks typically ended with handwritten checks by local owners. By 1990, however, twelve of the top fifteen largest banks in Florida had national headquarters out of state. The same phenomenon decimated urban utility companies. Distant executives in cities such as Atlanta, Birmingham, and Charlotte now guided policy at institutions that were "hometown" in name only. The same thing had occurred among Florida newspapers.[13]

Hugh Dailey is the president and CEO of Community Bank & Trust of Florida in Ocala. It is also the only Marion County–based bank. Scores of banks once had offices across the county. From his office, Dailey could point to what had once been South Trust Bank. But in 2004, it merged with Wachovia and later was acquired by Wells Fargo.[14]

The Great Recession intensified the pressure. "For a while," a Naples journalist reflected, "it seemed federal regulators closed a bank every Friday. So many banks fell and for essentially the same reason: bad loans." More than 70 banks folded between 2007 and 2012. By the end of 2008, a remarkable event occurred: Wells Fargo & Co. became Florida's biggest bank. The firm had recently acquired Wachovia Corp. A journalist observed, "With two of Florida's five-largest banks under new ownership, some veteran bankers and analysts are calling it an unprecedented shake-up to the state banking landscape. . . . At stake here is a share of the nearly $400 billion in Florida bank deposits and the thousands of customers who come with them."[15]

Homelessness

Songs and dreams rhapsodized that the Sunshine State was a poor man's paradise. The harsh reality was that Florida, like its southern neighbors, dedicated precious few resources toward public welfare. Floridians, like most Americans, approved charity for the "deserving" poor, those who endured hard times through no fault of their own. Americans sternly disapproved of the lazy, shiftlessness deadbeats, the undeserving poor, the hobos, tramps, and transients. Compassion can be fleeting. During the Great War and World War II, Florida governors demanded that county sheriffs enforce "work or fight" laws, a modern form of impressment. In Florida, a state where tourists filled the tax coffers, it was important that the poor be largely invisible, disposable, or irrelevant.[16]

Many southern communities created "poor farms," where the indigent worked and lived. In 1895, a Tampa newspaper reported that "Capt. Jones of the police force and deputy sheriffs sweeped down on a camp of hobos and succeeded in bagging ten non-commercial tourists." Tampa's Old People's Home housed 79 inhabitants in 1936 at the cost of seventy-five cents each day. During the Great Depression, many communities simply dragooned "hoboes" and sent them elsewhere. The City of St. Petersburg erected billboards warning migrants to move on. "WARNING," the sign read, "DO NOT COME HERE SEEKING WORK." The cautionary sign carried an explanation: "A City's First Duty Is to Employ Its Own Citizens." But the 1930s also revealed a kinder, gentler approach to the homeless. The New Deal created and bankrolled Jacksonville's Camp Foster, described in 1933 as a colony of penniless men reaching 1,000 residents. "Its members are men from all strata of society, from the pedestrian to the professor," the *Jacksonville Journal* observed. Shortly after the end of World War II, Miami revived its infamous "Hobo Express." "Systematically," a journalist explained, "Miami police rounded up the undesirables and transported them north to the Dade-Broward County line."[17]

But critics of the treatment of the homeless need not have read microfilm searching for Florida's inhumanity toward the homeless in 1895. Nine decades later, wrote *Sun-Sentinel* reporter Tonya Alvarez, "city commissioners were dead serious when they suggested hosing them while they slept, dumping them in the swamp and poisoning garbage cans." A commissioner proposed, "We can just put them in a nice hot paddy wagon and let them bake." A future Fort Lauderdale mayor suggested busing the homeless to the Everglades. "It would at least take them a while to get back," she said.[18]

The homeless crisis exploded during the Great Recession, but it did not spring to life fully formed like Venus. Florida's homelessness crisis resulted from decades of economic inequality, racial policies, the underfunding of mental health services, and drug addiction. Florida leapt onto the front pages and evening news as ground zero for the public spectacle.

Ronald McKay (pseudonym) personified the old homeless and the new challenges. In 2010, a journalist profiled his life:

> On the day Ronald M. was released from jail, he put on his old, unwashed clothes and caught a bus to Williams Park in downtown St. Petersburg. Miller, 59, was a free man. For police, firefighters, and business owners, that meant trouble. A disabled alcoholic, Miller is taken to the hospital so often that firefighters know his Social Security number by heart. Jailed 20 times last year, for offenses ranging from panhandling to public urination, Miller represents the most visible and problematic segment of Tampa Bay's growing homeless population: those who prefer the streets to shelters.[19]

Bill Heath, Desiree Emory, and Wallace Emory personified the new homeless and old challenges. Heath boasted a chemistry degree but lost his position at Ace Hardware in 2008 because of severe depression and moved to homeless shelter in Broward County. "I've worked throughout my life," he explained as he learned he would begin receiving disability benefits in 2011. In 2009, the Emorys, their five children, and Desiree's mother lived in a spacious rented home in a gated community in Winter Garden. The two-car family worked in Central Florida's thriving tourist industry. In late 2010, they resided at a downtown homeless shelter. "The story of their financial freefall is not particularly remarkable," an *Orlando Sentinel* article detailed; "it involves the typical culprits of layoffs, continued unemployment and escalating medical bills. What's remarkable is the growing number of Central Florida families who now find themselves in similar straits."[20]

The social and economic cataclysm spawned new homeless Floridians. "In a downturn," explained an Irish social worker, "begging goes on an upswing." In newspapers and Rotarian meetings, everyone noticed how different Broward County felt. A journalist described how so: "Drive through major intersections in Broward County, walk through the downtown area, and you'll see more of them than ever: people without homes." By 2010, conservative estimates as to the number of homeless in Broward placed the figure at more than 3,000. Fort Lauderdale checked all the homeless boxes: parks to find free food, a place to sleep, and computers in the main library. For the first time in history, the homeless were wired.[21]

But if Broward County's densely populated cities received the lion's share of publicity, edge cities, boomburbs, and small towns also struggled with the new and old homeless. "Families live in cars in the parking lot of Port Charlotte's 24-hour Wal-Mart, pretending to be customers to use the bathroom," described a journalist in 2008. The journalist continued her tour of Southwest Florida: "A family of five in North Port squat in their foreclosed-upon house without electricity of water. A pregnant woman and her husband, a former construction worker, spend nights under the Peace River bridge." James L. typified the new homeless. He has resided in Charlotte County for more than three decades and lost his job in 2007. "Now he sleeps on the floor of a house in foreclosure in North Port. . . . He lives alone in secret. Others band together."[22]

Fearless leaders emerged to fight for the homeless. From sisters of charity to brothers of the poor, voices rang out. None were louder than Sean Cononie, who made his national debut as the "Homeless Voice" in a 2006 appearance on *Dr. Phil.* In the chess match between Broward County's homeless community and police force, Cononie outmaneuvered his critics. By 2009, the *New York*

Times profiled the tireless advocate. From his Hollywood Coalition of Service and Charity homeless shelter, the needy find safe lodging, hot meals, and if necessary, the blessings of weddings and funerals.[23]

In 2014, Hollywood seemed to borrow a script from its more famous namesake in California. The enterprising Sean Cononie, in a modern remake of *Meet John Doe*, published a newspaper, the *Homeless Voice*. Residents of his homeless shelter sold the paper on the streets to raise funds and to avoid being charged for panhandling. Hollywood commissioners either so desperately wanted Cononie out of their hair or wanted to buy his two-story building on 1203 N. Federal Highway, that they paid the "pied piper of the homeless" $4.8 million. The fine print of the contract specified that Cononie must stay out of Hollywood for thirty years or return the money. Cononie accepted, the homeless shelters were razed, and neighbors cheered. Cononie used the proceeds to purchase a former 125-room Howard Johnson hotel near Haines City in Polk County for $2.1 million and converted it into a homeless shelter. But he sold the Polk County facility for $2.8 million and urged his guests to return to Broward County.[24]

Communities, individuals, and nonprofits tweaked the old or created new institutions to soften the pain. In 2007, Pinellas Hope, a Catholic Charity, opened its doors following a five-month pilot program. Soon the facilities had grown to 255 tents, 28 huts, and 200 beds, but the charity could help only one in five callers. Experts estimated the daily homeless population in Pinellas County as 4,400 in 2006, a number that had quadrupled since 2000. Eight in ten residents of homeless shelters were white males. "The safety net is gone," explained the executive director of the Pinellas County Coalition for the Homeless, "and there is simply no way for them to survive." For years, large numbers of homeless persons slept on the sidewalks and lawn in front of St. Petersburg City Hall. Each morning, work crews sprayed disinfectants on the area sidewalks to combat the stench of human waste. The homeless complained that the disinfectants resulted in skin irritations and chemical reactions. Between 2004 and 2007, St. Petersburg was one of the most dangerous cities in Florida for the homeless.[25]

Williams Park, St. Petersburg's downtown jewel, became a favorite daytime destination for many homeless. A daily ritual took place. The 4.3-acre park served as a busy transportation hub, especially for bus passengers. When evenings arrived, the police expelled the homeless, who would migrate a few blocks away to churches and city hall. As hard as the city tried to dislodge the homeless, the unwanted seasonal visitors found a way back. A journalist described the park in 2013: "Now, in its 125th year, the park is home to a new community: drug dealers and drug addicts, hell-raisers and drunks, hustlers and philosophers.

The economy here runs on bus passes, cheap beer and hand-rolled synthetic marijuana joints."[26]

The harsh reality of homelessness is that many victims simply want the freedom to be left alone. Many chronically homeless people, haunted by mental illness, drug addiction, and antisocial behavior, found a routine and community at the park, even if their visions of normal did not fit a Norman Rockwell world. Many wanted no part in tent cities or group homes. "Life on the street can be confusing and contradictory, without a clear beginning, with no end," observed a journalist in an article aptly titled "No Roof, No Rules."[27]

Florida communities reacted to the homeless crisis in a variety of manners, as it was no longer simply an issue of poor people loitering/relaxing in someone else's neighborhood, but in your downtown, your favorite park and supermarket. In response to the complaints from condo dwellers in downtown Sarasota, officials removed park benches at Selby Five Points Park. To discourage the homeless at the downtown Sarasota library, the city drafted a "heightened" smoking ban. In one of the wackier ideas, an official suggested piping in opera to disperse the homeless![28]

Hate crimes magnified the crisis. Sadly, during the period 1999–2010, Florida and California ranked first and second nationally in the number of violent attacks against the homeless. The year 2010 witnessed a rash of ugly incidents. In Lakeland and Hudson, Dunnellon and Orlando, homeless men were killed. In St. Petersburg, intruders hurled acid-filled bottles at a homeless encampment. In Jacksonville Beach, a homeless woman was sexually battered. Other violent episodes occurred in Lauderhill, Key West, and Jacksonville. In Fort Lauderdale, a man was accused of frightening itinerants with a chain saw. An Internet sensation depicted "bum fighting" or "bum hunting," videos of young kids beating up homeless men.[29]

Palm Beach County waged a legal war with Westgate Tabernacle Church over the latter's right to minister to the homeless. In 2007, a jury ruled that the county did not violate the church's religious freedom by requiring it to obtain a permit to run a homeless shelter. On some nights, as many as 100 people obtained shelter at the church. Two legal suits followed.[30]

Defenders and opponents of vagrancy agreed upon one point: homelessness was becoming painfully expensive. Rearresting and jailing the chronically homeless in Volusia County busted the budget. Between 1989 and 2012, the county arrested five men a total of 1,516 times! The bill to taxpayers: more than $3 million. One individual, Charles S., was arrested 400 times between 1985 and 2013. "These are conservative numbers," Volusia County Judge Belle Schumann explained. In Gainesville, a journalist profiled Ramine D: "He's been homeless the last 25 years and an alcoholic for 40. From the Gainesville Police Dept. to the public defender's office, city and county officials know him by name and see him several times a month. He's been charged with more than 170 misdemeanors, ordinance violations and the occasional felony since 1982 in Alachua County alone." In Central Florida, chronically homeless persons cost each community $31,000 a year to support.[31]

Generations of Orlando families enjoyed the tranquility of Lake Eola Park. Vagrants also appreciated the park's charms. As in most Florida parks, visitors were asked not to litter or feed the alligators. New-order posters warned pedestrians: "Do not lie or otherwise be in a horizontal position on a park bench . . . Do not sleep or remain in any bushes . . . Bathing and shaving in restroom is prohibited." Another sign banned feeding more than 25 persons. Clearly, the city was targeting the homeless. The controversy became part of a 2007 Jay Leno opening monologue. "It's now illegal to feed the homeless in Orlando, Florida," the *Tonight Show* host deadpanned. "Have you seen the fat people walking around Disney World? We should make it illegal to feed THEM." A war of words erupted on the *Orlando Sentinel* website. "Feeding the homeless only encourages more homelessness," one resident responded. Another resident appreciated the plight of the poor but objected to the site. "It is not unreasonable to want to keep Lake Eola Park from becoming a homeless cafeteria." The *Gainesville Sun* asked readers, "Feeding the Homeless: Act of Charity or a Crime?" Alachua County served as a battleground among town, gown, and visitors. A study identified 1,381 homeless persons living in Gainesville in January 2008, a dramatic increase. Gainesville ultimately passed a law restricting the feeding of the homeless.[32]

A destitute community lived under the Julia Tuttle Causeway in Miami. Almost 70 convicted sex offenders, including one woman, called the patch of sand littered with tents and shacks home. "There have been breakdowns, suicide attempts, heart attacks," a *Miami Herald* reporter wrote in 2009. "All set to the backdrop of gentle Biscayne Bay and the evolving Miami skyline." In 2005, the Miami-Dade County Commission barred convicted sex offenders from living within 2,500 feet of places children congregate.[33]

Miami's behavior toward the destitute was tempered by a legal decision that provided them protections not enjoyed elsewhere. The landmark court decision *Pottinger v. Miami* (1998) barred police from arresting homeless persons for "involuntary, harmless" acts without first being offered shelter and a bed. The homeless could now legally sleep on sidewalks, loiter, and start fires in public parks. In 2018, a judge invalidated the 1998 Homeless-Protection Act.[34]

The unrelenting battles over homelessness resulted in paranoia on both sides. The City of Miami accused its county brethren of "dumping" the unwashed and unwanted in the "Magic City." Miami Commissioner Marc Sarnoff complained, "We've caught Miami Beach dumping people in the city of Miami." He maintained that the Aventura, Surfside, and Coral Gables police used Miami as a "dumping ground" for Miami-Dade's homeless.[35]

Florida's most celebrated homeless community was a collection of shacks in Liberty City called Umoja Village, a name meaning "unity" in Swahili. "With 16 huts cobbled together from plywood, discarded closet doors and cardboard," described a *New York Times* reporter in 2007, "Umoja is a shantytown in the shadow of the biggest construction boom Miami has seen since the 1920s." Residents explained that most had been sleeping on the streets before they moved to Liberty City: "The eyesore has become a warm community, with a resident poet entertaining regularly, and has won over some neighbors, including those who now bring by homemade sweet potato pies, despite previous complaints about trash and noise." Max Rameau, a homeless advocate and head of Take Back the Land, was determined to build low-income housing on the site. Construction was scheduled to begin 23 April 2007. Instead, Umoja Village mysteriously burned to the ground. "By day's end," wrote a columnist, "Miami's leaders had to acknowledge that politics took precedence over safety. The city allowed men, women, even the elderly to live in wood and cardboard shanties—without smoke detectors . . . until a candle led to the destruction of all the structures." Miami police arrested a dozen persons, including organizer Rameau, who refused an order to halt the erection of a tent on the site. Rameau vowed that Take Back the Land would continue to occupy abandoned property. In 2009, journalists covering the Super Bowl were provided a "reality tour" of a 50-resident shantytown in Miami.[36]

The struggle in Miami was duplicated in city after city. In Tampa, Catholic Charities requested a permit to erect an encampment for the homeless. A familiar battle line was drawn. Two hundred citizens showed up at a meeting wearing T-shirts that read, "No Tent City." The Hillsborough County Commission voted 4–3 to reject the proposal aimed to house and feed 250 people for up to 90 days in tents.[37]

Key West acquired a reputation as a haven for the "street people." A drifter assured a journalist in 2010, "If you have to be homeless, Key West is the best place to live." In 2005, a study entitled "Keys for Housing the Homeless" was released. The study included an optimistic subtitle: "10-Year Plan to End Chronic Homelessness." But even Key West had limits. By March 2010, police were arresting far more homeless residents for trespassing. Itinerants accused police of "profiling." A transient lamented to a reporter: "The tourists come here and drink all day long. When we sit here and have one drink, we get arrested." In Key West, the environmental movement collided with homelessness. The Salt Ponds area near Smathers Beach had been a favorite place for the homeless to camp. But in 2004, the Florida Department of Environmental Protection declared the Salt Ponds an environmentally sensitive area. In 2008, authorities raided the area before dawn. The outcasts found a refuge at Bridle Path. The settlement resulted largely because of the *Pottinger* case in Miami, which established that cities cannot evict the homeless from public property unless they were offered an alternative place to be relocated.[38]

Addressing this same problem, the Clearwater City Council passed an ordinance banning sitting in designated places from 7:00 a.m. to 10:00 p.m. Previously, the city closed restrooms in public parks, even welding the doors shut at Crest Lake Park.[39]

The metaphor of a surging sea overwhelming a rowboat manned by a crew armed with teacups depicts the herculean challenges of Broward County officials trying to manage homelessness. Each day, about 150 persons were released from the county jail during the Great Recession. Many of the newly freed lacked friends, family, or good options. "The revolving door between jail and the street is a huge issue," explained the Fort Lauderdale mayor. "We have 31 cities in Broward County . . . when they [prisoners] get released and have nowhere to go, they stay in Fort Lauderdale. So we end up with the homeless population from around the county."[40]

"What's the difference between hanging out and loitering?," asked the *Sun Sentinel*. "In Boca Raton," the paper noted, "the wrong answer could land you in handcuffs." Under Florida law, "loitering" results when one's actions alert a police officer of suspicious activity indicating that a crime may be committed. Relatively few arrests resulted in convictions.[41]

The issue of feeding the homeless aroused passions on both sides. In Broward County, the debate was fierce. Coral Springs erected signs discouraging residents from feeding strangers. But it was an incident in Fort Lauderdale, where crowds gathered to wait for food in Stranahan Park, when an act of compassion became a flashpoint in the debate. "To Arnold Abbot, feeding the homeless in a public park in South Florida was an act of charity." Thus, began a story that seemed positive. But to Fort Lauderdale officials, the ninety-year-old man was committing a crime. Arnold, a World War II veteran, along with two other fellow ministers, were arrested for breaking a new ordinance restricting public feeding of the homeless. The *New York Times* observed that Abbot's act of civil disobedience placed him at the crosshairs of the debates across Florida: "How to feed, help and handle the ever-present homeless population in a state that, with its balmy winter climate, draws an outsize share of the dispossessed." Fabiola Santiago joined the debate, writing: "Some people fight wars. Some people fight hunger. Some people fight City Hall. Arnold Abbott . . . has done all three with passion. In a country where compassion was once a source of strength but is now regarded as political weakness, this man is pure sunshine for the soul." Fort Lauderdale, once famous as the setting *Where the Boys Are*, had become "Fort Haterdale." "While the [Fort Lauderdale] city leaders acted dumbfounded," wrote Miami journalist Fred Grimm, "Facebook and Twitter and Tumblr and a giant avalanche of social media instantly defined the controversy as a war on homelessness. Worse, the city officials cast themselves as jack-booted thugs in the inevitable street theatre."[42]

Tempers erupted at Fort Lauderdale Beach over a law that made it illegal to lie down in the park. A homeless man reported a picnicking family to the police. In Pensacola, officials repealed a law that made it illegal for the homeless to sleep on public property with a blanket.[43]

Angry exchanges of views ping-ponged across neighbors' fences and city hall daises, newspaper op-ed pages, and American Civil Liberties Union meetings, raising more questions than answers: Should citizens have the right to panhandle or ask for aid? Does one have the right to sell items or ask for aid along busy intersections? Do the homeless have the right to sleep where they wish? Do the homeless have a right to reject mental health and drug counseling? Must the homeless use public restrooms? What if no public facilities exist? Should children be punished for their parents' misfortune? Should the homeless be shunted aside for gentrification? Should feeding the homeless be interpreted as an act of charity of a crime? Is food a right or a privilege? In some jurisdictions, a person caught urinating in public faces charges that require them to register as a sex offender.

"So where should the homeless go?," asked columnist Tom Lyons. Rosemary District was near downtown Sarasota, but it could have been Anywhere, Florida. For decades, the word "blight" had been used to describe the charming neighborhood that was being revitalized. "But," interjected Lyons, "there is one big and obviously non-gentrified feature you just can't miss: Dozens of homeless people hang out. . . . They cluster on the sidewalks—on blankets and pieces of cardboard, folding chairs or, in some cases, in wheelchairs." Lyons concluded, "I just wish the city, or someone, could offer them a better place to sleep."[44]

Sarasota and the American Civil Liberties Union (ACLU) grappled with policies to address homelessness. In 2005, following two successful challenges by the ACLU, city commissioners banned outdoor lodging and successfully defended the policy. Undaunted, the number of the homeless tripled by 2011. In response, Sarasota removed the benches from Five Points Park and banned smoking at city parks and property. Some merchants plastered signs in downtown Sarasota that read: "DON'T GIVE IN TO PANHANDLING. 93% OF THE MONEY GOES TO DRUGS & ALCOHOL."[45]

For a state obsessed with "the best of" rankings, Florida acquired a dubious top-ten distinction during the Great Recession. For several straight years, Florida led the list for the "Top 10 Meanest Cities toward Homeless." In 2009, St. Petersburg, Orlando, Gainesville, and Bradenton ranked, respectively, as second, third, fifth, and ninth in the list of the nation's "meanest cities" because of their treatment of the homeless. The organization "Homes Not Handcuffs" began the list in 2006 in an effort to track the criminalization of homelessness. The *Orlando Sentinel* asked, "The City Beautiful? How about 'The City Mean?'" National Public Radio summarized the trend: "Give us your tired, your poor, your huddled masses. Just make sure they don't huddle and mass in public spaces."[46]

For well over a century, Americans migrated to Florida during the winter months. Drifters simply followed the paths of the middle classes and snowbirds in choosing where to spend winters. But whereas the middle and upper classes drive or fly to the Sunshine State, the homeless typically hitchhike or come by bus. What changed during the Great Recession was the sheer volume of "undesirables" arriving in Florida and the political-legal backlash. "Drive through major intersections in Broward County," observed a *Sun-Sentinel* reporter in 2011, pointing out the panhandlers. But new attitudes steeled the resolve of communities to push back against the unwanted snowbirds. Daytona Beach was another such community. "For decades," observed a reporter, "one of the favorite homeless hangout spots has been the shady, breezy area under the pier reaching out into the ocean." Municipal workers erected bright-orange plastic barriers, fencing off these camps. The article explained, "Continuing to allow people with addictions, mental health problems and violent tempers to gather daily on the beach wasn't a good idea for anybody, city officials decided."[47]

Across Florida and America, cities challenged the homeless, enacting a wide range of laws outlawing panhandling, sleeping in vehicles on city streets, and public camping. Between 2010 and 2014, bans on sleeping in cars doubled, while antiloitering laws and antibegging laws rose by a third. A fierce debate ensued as to the morality of begging and mercy. President George W. Bush's "Homeless Czar," Philip Mangano, called giving money to a wino a reckless idea, "a random act of enabling." Some Floridians struck a compromise, giving out items such as toothpaste, apples, and clean socks to street-corner solicitors. In Oakland Park, officials not only made it illegal to ask for anything of value, but the ordinance also targets people who give to beggars! Much has changed since the 1920s, when Florida communities erected free campsites for the so-called Tin Can Tourists.[48]

City after city in Florida struggled with a crisis without consensus. In Hillsborough County, authorities maintained that 10,000 residents were homeless by 2010. More than a few worked in busy intersections, holding signs and asking for donations. The *Tampa Epoch,* a homeless newspaper, sold for a dollar, with vendors earning a quarter. When asked by a journalist, Michael G. responded: "This is what I do to help me exist right now. This is the only thing we can do to survive." Newspapers had discovered a loophole in a local ordinance that allows vendors to collect cash even if they are not allowed to beg for money. In Miami, an evasive tactic consisted of an individual or team approaching one's car and washing the windshields and then extending open palms.[49]

Poverty, long embedded in city and country, worsened, intensifying during the decade, rising to 16.5 percent in 2010. Children suffered disproportionately. In Palm Beach, one of Florida's wealthiest counties, children living in poverty increased dramatically to an estimated 64,000. Officials reported upticks in applications for free lunch and families seeking food assistance and subsidized childcare. Between 2007 and 2009, half the children in the Sarasota-Bradenton Metro Area qualified for free or reduced-price school lunches, one in every ten households qualified for food stamps, and even more took meals at soup kitchens. Lakeland mirrored neighbors on the Gulf Coast in the Tampa Bay area, where pockets of severe poverty intensified. Pockets of "extreme poverty" were found in places such as Thonotosassa and Wimauma. A 2009 article described large numbers of children spilling out of downtown Miami's largest homeless shelter for a ride to elementary school. An authority estimated that almost 2,400 students in Miami-Dade County were homeless. A Brookings Institution report studied rates of inequality and concluded that poverty was growing twice as fast in the suburbs as cities. Every Florida county but one with fewer than 110,000 residents qualified as "economically distressed." Only affluent Monroe County did not make the list.[50]

Surging numbers of homeless children lived in shelters or worse. Central Florida stood out for its disproportionate number of homeless students attending public schools. The numbers tripled between 2007 and 2010. Critics pointed to the low-paying, high-turnover jobs in Orange, Osceola, and Seminole counties and the rent-by-the-week motels. "Sometimes," a reporter lamented, "even the shelters have to turn away women and children who have nowhere else to go." William and Desiree Emory and their five children found refuge at the Orlando Union Rescue Mission. "We never imagined we would wind up here," William confessed.[51]

In 2011, a *60 Minutes* story, "Hard Times Generation," exposed the tragedy of homeless families forced to live in their cars and motels in Central Florida. "The problem is getting worse," admitted an official for the Seminole County schools. "We're seeing more families in our program," explained Beth Davalos, "I have many children living in their cars. . . . Many families have no place to turn." The story was so hard-hitting it prompted fact checking. In Hillsborough County, 1,121 families with children were living without shelter in 2011.[52]

Isabel Bermudez was living the Florida dream until the crash. A six-figure income and a home in Cape Coral vanished. But she and hundreds of thousands of other Floridians who never thought they would be on the dole were helped immensely by food stamps. "It's the one thing I can count on every month," she confessed. "I know the children are going to have food." The number of Floridians accepting food stamps doubled between 2007 and 2009. Florida officials pointed to food stamps as evidence that the safety net was working. Critics pointed to the dearth of programs providing cash support as evidence the system was not working.[53]

Florida is where good intentions go to die. An exposé revealed that Hillsborough County spent millions of dollars to house homeless veterans and families. Yet many of these homes only worsened the problems. Too often, the veterans and their families were sent to dangerous neighborhoods where, a journalist wrote, "they were forced to breathe moldy air, step over unmopped puddles of human waste or sleep on mattresses infested with bedbugs."[54]

In 2016, after more than a decade of merciful and merciless debate in Sarasota over everything from proper manners to the Ten Commandments to allusions to the Good Samaritan and the Gospel of Matthew's ancient advice about loving thy neighbor as thyself, columnist Bill Church of the *Sarasota Herald-Tribune* attempted to make sense of it all. He began, "At the asphalt eruption near Five Points Park, a woman screams all the good curse words. . . . As a late lunch crowd enjoys cocktails outdoors, Sarasota Police SUVs converge . . . where an angry man in a wheelchair is waging his own version of civil disobedience." He explains:

Ten years ago, the National Council for the Homeless labeled Sarasota the meanest city in the nation for adopting the anti-camping ban. It's a given that city and county leaders are struggling with the homelessness issue. The past decade hasn't changed the attention. . . . Yet there has been progress. Those who witnessed the one-man wheelchair war were impressed with how Sarasota police officers and emergency responders handled a tense situation with calm and respect.[55]

Homelessness was one act of a social-economic-political tragedy, offering the very worst and best of humanity. Florida and California served as coastal capitals of the national struggle to combat homelessness, as well as an equally taxing and painful drug crisis.

Opioids and Pill Mills

In 2010, Miami was witnessing a profound cultural shift. Veteran journalists, police officers, and filmmakers had no answers as to what had just happened. Since Sonny Crockett and Ricardo Tubbs drove down Biscayne Boulevard, cocaine was synonymous with Miami. But Miami's drug of choice was no longer cocaine; rather, Miami and the rest of the peninsula were turning to prescription drugs, and oxycodone and OxyContin were the rage. Unromantically middle-class and Yankee, Stamford, Connecticut, replaced Medellin, Colombia, as Miami's drug pipeline. "The City That Works" replaced "the Magic City."[56]

If food stamps provided a lifeline for many Floridians, opioid drugs offered an illusion of hope to increasing numbers. Few adults could identify let alone spell opioid in 2000. The drug is both ancient and modern. In 1898, scientists synthesized a new drug advertised as a nonaddictive cough suppressant. Heroin was touted as an over-the counter miracle drug, an alternative to opium. Opioids, explains a journalist, "are a class of drugs derived from opium, a naturally occurring compound in poppies that produces euphoria, pain relief, and sedation in humans." The pharmaceutical company Purdue Frederick introduced the painkilling drug OxyContin in 1996. Prescriptions and profits rocketed. Between 1996 and 2001, sales of OxyContin topped $2.8 billion. Mallinckrodt Pharmaceuticals manufactured OxyContin's evil twin, oxycodone. More than 500 million, fully two-thirds of Mallinckrodt's oxycodone pills made their way to Florida. OxyContin and heroin share similar molecular traits. Opioids proved highly effective in relieving pain; sadly, they were deadly addictive. Patients in terrible pain need the relief of powerful drugs. The problem, however, had few solutions: how to get patients to stop.[57]

While a debate rages as to the cause and effect of the Great Recession and accelerating drug use, the fact remains that prescription drug use in Florida spiked. Doctors, who were often courted by industry lobbyists and salesmen, began prescribing drugs such as oxycodone, and addictions spiked dramatically and tragically. A largely unregulated industry appeared almost overnight: greedy pharmaceutical corporations, pill mills, clinic staffers, and desperate patients with lingering pain, and a new generation of addicts who could not walk away from the powerful drugs. Illegal knockoffs followed, resulting in further misery and tragedy. One estimate is that 40 percent of the most favored high—oxycodone 30-milligram pills—originated in Florida.[58]

Pill mills served as a jackpot, and Florida became the gateway to "prescription tourists." Some needed the drugs to combat pain; others planned to take home doses of OxyContin to sell in Ohio and New Jersey. An investigative reporter followed vans leaving Huntington, West Virginia, that left twice a month for journeys to the 100 pill mills in Palm Beach and Broward counties. A steady stream of trucks with southern license plates carried "pillbillies" to pill mills along Florida's east coast. Others came aboard the "Oxycodone Express" by buses. The payoffs are profitable. An oxycodone pill that costs $4 resells in Kentucky or West Virginia for $30. Doctors made fortunes selling painkillers. In 2010, an astounding 49 of America's top-50 oxycodone-dispensing clinics, and 90 of the top oxycodone-purchasing physicians were in Florida. Drug dealers often simply sold the drugs outside clinic doors. In perhaps the most numbing statistic, between 2006 and 2012, more than 5.5 billion hydrocodone and oxycodone pills flooded Florida. These pills found their way to pill mill clinics but also to large chain drugstores.[59]

When crack cocaine hollowed out urban centers in the 1980s and '90s, the typical offenders were young Black and white males living in the inner city. A new cast of drug users entered Florida's drug frontier in 2000. White factory workers, unemployed Appalachian coal miners, and especially middle-aged white women fit the profile. But one constituency did not fit the stereotypes. A 2012 *Sun Sentinel* headline announced, "Reefer Tokin' Seniors in South Florida See Pain Go up in Smoke." A seventy-year-old Boca Raton woman exclaimed, "It's like taking a magic pill!" She was recovering from chemotherapy and discovering an ancient therapy. When asked how she obtained the weed, she explained, "My husband might get it on the golf course. I don't know where. I don't ask."[60]

The popular new drugs richly rewarded risk-takers and punished pill-takers. Cristopher George testified that despite his criminal record and inexperience in the health-care industry, he made $40 million from a network of pill mills in Broward and Palm Beach counties. As many as 200 out-of-state patients a day patronized his first shop at Wilton Manors. He hired doctors to prescribe the pills and paid the professionals handsomely—as much as $15,000–20,000 per week.[61]

Florida was home to staggering amounts of profits and pills. At its peak, 2009–10, more than 900 pill mills operated in Florida. A single clinic in Tampa dispensed 2.4 million pain pills over seven months in 2009. In 2010, VIP Pharmacy in Tampa infamously dispensed more oxycodone—760,800 doses—than any other retail pharmacy in America. Between 2006 and 2012, Pinellas County pharmacies stockpiled almost 400 million pain pills. A single pharmacy in New Port Richey, a town of 15,000 residents, ordered almost 3,300 bottles of oxycodone each month. Broward County was named the "epicenter." A sheriff's official explained: "You would see 30 to 40 people lined up at a clinic. People came faster than we could arrest them." One such pill mill, Dollar Medicine, accepted only cash, with furnishings consisting of a single table and a few chairs. The *Tampa Bay Times* editorialized, "At the height of Florida's opioid crisis, 5.6 *billion* prescription pain pills were supplied to Florida."[62]

Opioids ravaged Palm Beach County, home to Donald Trump and some of the state's wealthiest citizens. In 2016, paramedics responded to 5,000 drug overdoses. A county obsessive over its image, Palm Beach had for decades been nicknamed the "recovery capital of America," the result of the proliferation of drug treatment centers.[63]

The consequences of the drug epidemic were enormous. National agencies identified a new and clear divide in American death: accelerating unnatural death rates in small-town and rural America. Not since the AIDS epidemic in the 1990s had the death rate of young white adults, ages 25–34, risen so dramatically, as a result of suicides and drug overdoses. White women represented one of the hardest-hit groups. Drug abuse was a major factor in this demographic decline. In Pinellas County, Judge Dee Anna Farnell created a "Ladies Day" in drug court.[64]

The human costs were unimaginable. In 2010, Florida recorded 1,516 overdose deaths. In 2011, seven people died daily in Florida of drug overdoses. Some casualties, desperate for a more intense hit, crushed the pills and snorted or injected the drug. Only in 2001 did the Federal Drug Administration require Purdue Pharma to add a black box warning about misuse. Only in 2010 did Purdue Pharma reformulate the drug to make the pills more difficult to abuse. Frightening numbers of children who were exposed to dangerous drugs in mothers' wombs were born during the decade. Between 2007 and 2012, 1,630 babies were born with Neonatal Abstinence Syndrome, meaning the infants had to be medically weaned from their mothers' drugs.[65]

In 2008, a journalist observed, "For young members of the Seminole Tribe, this should be the best of times." The stars and harvest moons seemed aligned for Florida's 3,300 Seminole members. Every Seminole shared a swelling flow of money from casinos and businesses that totaled $1.4 billion. Benefits included an income of $120,000 a year, free education, and a guaranteed job. But prosperity guaranteed neither happiness nor health. Alarming rates of drug overdoses, alcoholism, and diabetes—called the "Rez disease" (reservation disease)—plagued young tribal members. In 2019, the Miccosukee Tribe sued Big Pharma (Purdue Pharma, CVS, and Walgreens) for more than $100 million for pushing prescription painkillers. Their complaint charged, "Opioid addiction and overdose killed many tribal members and turned others into shells of their former selves." They were represented by Curtis E. Osceola, the first Miccosukee to graduate from law school.[66]

Disappointingly but not shockingly, Florida's leaders waited too long to crack down on the abusive pain clinics. The *Washington Post* explained, "Florida's lax laws, dishonest doctors and unscrupulous pharmacists had turned the state into ground zero for the nation's prescription opioid crisis." The so-called Oxy Express ran smoothly until 2010–11. In 2010, the state shut down more than 400 clinics. Pain-management clinics declined from 921 in 2009 to 371 in 2013. Even more shocking, federal officials did not confront the powerful drug companies—nicknamed "Pharmageddon"—that manufactured OxyContin and other painkillers. Not surprisingly, Big Pharma and the largest chain stores contribute handsomely to state and federal politicians. As in the popular arcade game Whack-a-Mole, once the pill mills closed, a troubling old and new addiction resurfaced: heroin.[67]

Amy Pavuk of the *Orlando Sentinel* asked the most relevant question about the crisis in 2011: "What about Florida makes access to powerful, addictive prescription drugs so seemingly simple?" Bruce Grant, who had been appointed the state drug czar by Governor Crist in 2009 and served until January 2011, when Governor Scott abolished the position, replied honestly and forthrightly: "We failed to enact proper controls and procedures that would keep this from getting out of hand."[68]

Orange Is the New Blue

As if a housing collapse and a mildewed future were not enough, one of Florida's most iconic trademarks declined in the twenty-first century. A long line of muses had waxed upon the glories of *Citrus × sinensis*. Its journey from China to India, Persia to Spain, and Hispaniola to Florida was as enchanting and romantic as it was a business. More than anything else, Florida's signature agricultural commodity, a dream fruit for a dream state, defined the Sunshine State and its promise as the New Mediterranean. In Florida, an orange is not merely a fruit; it's a legacy, a symbol of health and prosperity, an avatar. Drive across the state and count the signposts: Orange City, Orange County, and Port Orange.

By 2005, reality had wilted the orange blossom, the state flower of Florida. The roadside citrus stand advertising a free glass of liquid sunshine was becoming as rare as small grove owners. Big Orange was being pummeled by a perfect storm of changing consumer tastes, rocketing land prices, Brazilian competitors, and a dreaded disease. Florida grove owners are resilient. They have endured the Mediterranean fruit fly, canker disease, killer freezes, and great depressions. Around 2004, a tiny but deadly insect arrived at the Port of Miami. By 2005, scientists confirmed that citrus greening, *Huanglongbing*, had been detected in Homestead and Florida City. "Yellow dragon disease" spread rapidly across the peninsula. The disease sickened and then killed orange trees, first shriveling and misshaping their fruit. A *Washington Post* headline broadcast the seriousness of the challenge: "The End of Orange Juice? A Lethal Disease Is Devastating the State's Citrus Industry." Industry officials called the disease an "existential threat." By 2006, the consequences of citrus greening and sinking demand were evident in the crop forecast. Officials predicted the smallest orange crop since 1989.[69]

The heart of Florida's citrus industry is ever-shifting. The Great Freeze of 1895 wiped out Alachua County groves and resituated the orange belt with Polk County its buckle. Three freezes in the 1980s killed most of the orange trees north of Interstate 4, and a massive shift southward ensued. Oranges soon became the biggest industry in DeSoto County and its neighbors, but the seeds had been planted earlier. In 1970, a journalist, dateline Arcadia, observed, "They are building 'the world's largest orange grove' near here." The grove, twice the size of the Island of Manhattan, sprawled 26,800 acres along the Joshua Creek Valley. Forty-two wells provided millions of gallons of water. The future of citrus was no longer in the hands of the self-made pioneers profiled by John McPhee.[70]

No community more perfectly encapsulated the uncertain roll of the orange dice than Clermont. The Lake County community's heart had bled orange since the nineteenth century. Oranges were synonymous with prosperity, and US 27 took tourists from the North through Clermont and its kitschy roadside stands into South Florida. In tribute, industry and local leaders erected the 226-foot-tall Citrus Tower in 1956 atop a hill. The tower's apex was the highest point in all of Florida. For decades visitors were awed at the sight of millions of orange trees. Rumors circulated that in February, the sheer intensity and spectacle of orange blossom scents wafting across the hills prompted northern ladies to faint from sheer rapture. The attraction drew more than 100,000 tourists its first few years of operation. By 2004, fewer and fewer tourists took the time to ride up the aging Citrus Tower to 525 feet above sea level. The Florida Turnpike and Interstate 4 allowed tourists to whisk to Orlando, bypassing Old Florida. By 2010, tourists saw fewer trees, more condos, and too many foreclosure signs. Clermont suffered almost 12,000 foreclosures in 2009–10. PBS highlighted the locale in a 2010 story about hard times in small towns.[71]

In 2005, Al Repetto announced that he was selling his orange grove. Such news rarely made the front pages in Polk or DeSoto counties, but Repetto was the "Citrus King of Pinellas County." In its heyday, his Orange Blossom Groves filled 100,000 crates of citrus. In 1946, Pinellas County shipped 3 million boxes of citrus. Repetto's Orange Blossom Groves struggled as the county's last commercial grove. Citrus had long dominated the Pinellas peninsula even before it became a county in 1912. A century after Pinellas gained independence from Hillsborough, Repetto died. A 136-room townhouse replaced his grove. Repetto's sale was not unique. In 2005, John D'Albora sold the last 1,000 acres of St. Lucie County citrus groves that had been in his family for four generations. The buyers were practicing "land banking," holding onto the property until developers arrived.[72]

Palm Beach County dwarfed Pinellas County in landmass and citrus trees. As late as 1992, the county still dedicated more than 10,000 acres to citrus. Pinellas's groves had dwindled to 82 acres. Here, too, grove land was too valuable to support oranges and grapefruit. In 2002, Palm Beach County's citrus had shriveled to 2,281 acres. Pinellas had been eliminated from the roster. By the second decade of the twenty-first century, the annual citrus census excluded Palm Beach. Even Polk County, the state's citrus kingpin, was losing groves in droves. From 150,000 acres in 1976, Polk had lost one-third of its citrus acreage by 2004.[73]

Mims, a small community in Brevard County, was once famous for its quality citrus. But even Mims could not resist the forces of change. In 2005, the *Orlando Sentinel* captured the painful change in an article titled "Subdivisions Slip into

Rural Refuge." Barbara Kittles had lived in the rural refuge for decades. "It's like somebody took a map of Florida and put a big X on Mims," she said.[74]

Citrus greening knocked the keystone from Florida's foundational agricultural crop. Despite feverish research—scientists even altered the orange's DNA—citrus greening resisted cures. One by one the dreaded call came: "It's here." In 2000, the orange harvest climaxed with 200 million boxes picked from 665,000 acres. A decade later, the toll was evident: acreage dedicated to oranges plunged to 483,418. Harvests shrank each succeeding year. The disease had spread to Florida's thirty-two citrus-producing counties. Twenty million orange trees had vanished in ten years. Motorists noticed many groves wasting away without care and shriveled Hamlins, Valencias, and Temples. But abandoned groves and homes were not merely consequences of the recession; rather, the neglected groves and abandoned homes with backyard orange trees served as breeders and spreaders.[75]

The year of four hurricanes, 2004, battered the industry, but the most sobering threat in 2010 was not a bacterium spread by a tiny flying insect but consumer demand. Americans' new concerns about sugary drinks and the myriad options for a morning beverage cast clouds over Florida's iconic glass of OJ. Between 2005 and 2014, the consumption of citrus fell by one-third. Two headlines captured Florida's dilemma: "Orange Juice Searches for Fresher Image," and "How Long Can Florida's Citrus Industry Survive?" The industry hangs on.[76]

In 2017, agricultural experts predicted that soon, California would usurp the title "King of U.S. Oranges." Florida has claimed that title since World War II. By 2021, the annual citrus harvest was approaching figures not seen since the 1940s.[77]

Questions persisted. How many new condos and shopping centers will replace historic groves? In the rush to replace the orange, what new crop—blueberry or peach, hops or olives—would sink deep roots in the hinterlands? Or at least until growth made agricultural land more profitable as condos. A journalist placed citrus groves into context in a 2007 story: "There seem to be more tractors tearing up St. Lucie County's old citrus groves than tending them these days." Florida Southern College in Lakeland has long boasted that it offered the only bachelor's degree in the study of citrus. In 1940, Polk County (home of Lakeland) made citrus history, becoming the nation's number-one citrus county, topping Los Angeles. But when Jason Johnson graduated in 2006, landscaping offered a more promising future than citrus. In a repeat, growing cities in Polk County have swallowed citrus groves. "You see urbanization coming in," Johnson pondered. "You see the houses coming in, and what do you do? You put plants around them." Florida Southern College closed the program in citrus studies because of declining interest.[78]

The Exodus: Demography Is Destiny

What does Florida do? Florida grows! In the heady times of 2002, megadeveloper Al Hoffman preached the gospel to a room of powerful Florida leaders. "You can't stop it!" he insisted. "There's no power on earth that can stop it." He was referencing the sweep of subdivisions and golf courses across Southwest Florida, but he was also encapsulating modern Florida. The Great Recession managed to stop Hoffman's development company, WCI Communities, after his firm filed for bankruptcy in 2008.[79]

But the Great Recession accomplished what Hurricane Andrew and Florida Man failed to achieve: it drove people away from Florida and halted the stampede of transplants to the Sunshine State. If hurricanes did not scare Floridians, rising insurance rates did. Had there been an ex-residential license plate, it might have read, "Sunshine Doesn't Pay the Bills!" Not since 1946 had Florida registered a population loss, and that was a freak statistic, reflecting the end of the war and the decommissioning of so many personnel who had been stationed there. By 2008, the U.S. Census Bureau calculated that Hollywood, Coral Springs, Pembroke Pines, Hialeah, St. Petersburg, Clearwater, and Pompano Beach made the top-twenty-five list of American cities with populations greater than 100,000 or more that *lost* residents. The year 2009 was even worse. "We sensed it before the statistics proved it," reflected business journalist Robert Trigaux in the last days of 2009, "but a lot of Floridians grew unhappy over Florida's rising expenses, lack of decent jobs and flabby leadership. So, they moved away." Statistically, the Sunshine State became the Turnover State as it lost 58,294 residents between April 2008 and April 2009. A 2011 *New York Times* piece announced what landscapers, popcorn vendors at spring training games, and census takers understood: "Economy Alters How Americans Are Moving."[80]

Yard sales defined the New Florida, the sign of crushed dreams and soon-to-be expats. A journalist traced one such yard sale in Thonotosassa. Once the site of coveted flint deposits—the name "Thonotosassa" means lake of flint in Seminole—the community had until the 1980s been home to large citrus groves. But the groves yielded to subdivisions. One couple drawn to the community was Cynthia Jolley and Walter Hause. Ms. Jolley's yard sale featured a half-dozen children's violins. She ran a music studio in nearby Temple Terrace. Declining enrollment forced the couple to sell everything and return to Tennessee. "It seemed like we were losing everybody," Ms. Jolley mused.[81]

Mobility, migration, and growth were deeply ingrained in Florida. "The loss is more than a data point," insisted Damien Cave. "That's right, the Sunshine

State is shrinking." He added, "Growth gave Florida its notorious flip-flop and flower-print swagger." The phenomenon was not isolated to Florida. The flow of migrants into the Sunbelt has slowed to a trickle. The oxygen, the cause and effect of the Florida dream had always been growth. Tourism, an accurate barometer of health because every tourist is a potential Floridian, dropped in 2008–9, the first such decline in seven years. When William Frey, a demographer at the Brookings Foundation, commented that the news was "a real psychological blow," Carl Hiaasen quipped: "With all due respect to Mr. Frye, you don't need a shrink to sort out what's going on in Florida. All you usually need is a grand jury." Upon reading the stark numbers, Damien Cave concluded, "That's right, the Sunshine State is shrinking. . . . Florida, in particular, is not built for emptying."[82]

Patterns emerged to define the out-migrations. Young people, tired of the high rents, income gaps, and dead-end jobs, left South Florida. Wordsmiths created a term to describe their plight—"Duppies"—an acronym for depressed urban professionals. Pinellas County closed eleven schools between 2008 and 2009. Miami ranked fifth on a list of "Top Losers, 2008–2010." The majority of my friends have left," confessed Liana Minassian, a twenty-five-year-old who grew up in Pembroke Pines. Essayist Robert Samuelson, noting the disproportionate economic pain heaped upon young adults, asked, "Is the economy creating a lost generation?" A journalist in Sarasota, observing the rush at a Human Services Center, described them as the "new poor."[83]

The 2010 U.S. Census identified the "outer suburbs," aka the exurbs, as one of the hardest-hit places. "The exurbs were the cutting edge of growth in the United States," said William Frye, a Brookings Institution demographer. "That growth has really come to a standstill."[84]

By 2010, about 12,000 fewer babies were born in Florida than in 2007. The explanation? Young mothers who fled Florida chose to begin a family elsewhere. Many mothers, fearful of the present and future economic prospects, held off childbearing. Across the nation, a "Baby Bust" occurred.[85]

But demographers marveled at another trend: Florida's elderly were heading back north. "For the first time since the Depression," observed the *New York Times* in 2007, "more Americans aged 75 and older have been leaving the South than moving there." The reasons are simple and complex. Medical emergencies often prompt such moves. Many elderly females return "home," for the simple reason that on the average, women outlive men. The typical senior who leaves Florida for the North is a widow. Stanley and Joyce Hall checked all the boxes for "Florida lifers." In 1990, they left Rochester, New York, for South Florida. Even after Hurricane Andrew destroyed their home in 1992, they rebuilt. Joyce chose to remain in Florida after Stanley's death in 1994. But Parkinson's disease, her inability to drive anymore, and a hip replacement convinced Joyce to move to a senior complex outside Rochester.[86]

The year the film *No Country for Old Men* was playing in Naples theaters, Collier County was becoming no country for poor men (and women). A study indicated that slightly more households left Collier than arrived in 2007–8. For those 15,150 who arrived in Collier, the average income was $76,161 per person. Those leaving the county had an income per person of only $26,128.[87]

Monroe County served as Florida's canary in the phosphate mine. It is the answer to the question, What is the only county in Florida to *lose* population between 2000 and 2010? Indeed, Monroe County gained only 1,055 persons in the previous decade. Signs on the beach and emblazoned on T-shirts prophesied, "Key West Conchs Don't Die, They Move Away." Authentic Conchs—descendants of Bahamian spongers and wreckers—are as rare as conch meat inside a Key West conch fritter. The fact that most of Monroe County consists of an archipelago of isolated islands is both a cause and an effect of why residents are leaving and why they arrived. The Florida Keys are irresistible, but the natural allure resulted in strict building codes, driving the cost of living and housing even higher. As several generations of public-school teachers, public workers, and retirees living on pensions can testify: living in a watery paradise is crazy expensive. The Keys have a limited supply of housing, and demand drives prices higher and higher. Monroe County remained ground zero for climate change and an affordability crisis before the Great Recession, but the crisis only intensified the difficulties. Beginning in 2010, tourism bounced back in such numbers that officials nicknamed the Seven Mile Bridge "the Road to Recovery." But the Keys' affordability dilemma persists.[88]

Statistics hide the human dimension involving migration. Frustrated by rising crime and rent in East Tampa, Evelyn and Carlos Torres left Florida for Georgia in 2008. "They weren't alone," wrote a *Tampa Tribune* reporter. He added, "From 2007 to 2008, more than 650,000 households . . . vanished from the tax rolls in Florida." In the Tampa Bay area, the two areas most affected by "vanishing taxpayers" were Pasco County's bookends: Holiday and Hudson on the Gulf of Mexico and Zephyrhills on the eastern county line. Holiday and Hudson were rare middle-class and retiree communities on the salt water, whereas Zephyrhills is one of the state's most popular snowbird and retiree destinations. These three communities lost 20 percent of their taxpayers during this brief but intense period. The *Tampa Tribune*, the newspaper that published the story, also vanished.[89]

Florida's construction industry employed armies of carpenters and roofers, electricians and tile-layers. If one hung around boomtime construction sites, Spanish became the lingua franca of work crews. On such a site in 2009 Miami, Selene Echeverría, the director of WeCount!, an organization that assisted immigrant workers in Miami-Dade County, explained to a journalist what had happened: "Many [immigrant construction laborers] have moved to other states to look for work, many have moved back to their home countries." Sarasota and Manatee counties lost 900 construction-related firms and 20,000 jobs in the recession's three worst years. A 2008 investigation of "the exodus" of Hispanics from Lee County concluded that most immigrants fled Florida when the construction industry collapsed. The impact rippled through the school system and local churches.[90]

One piece of evidence speaks volumes to Florida's alter ego: out-of-state migrants. Florida grows; it does not lose population. To demonstrate the traffic rush to Florida, columnists often stood on freeway overpasses on Thanksgiving weekend to count the traffic imbalance headed south. Florida and United, Atlas, and Allied Van Lines enjoyed a symbiotic relationship, so much so that the firm dubbed Florida the "Magnet State." Yet in 2007, Allied Van Lines and United Van Lines released a shocking report, that for 2006–7, the firm moved 6,700 families *into* Florida and moved 8,000 *out*. Such topsy-turvy numbers had never happened. Moreover, new residents applying for Florida driver's licenses also plummeted. Even the migration of Florida's most reliable friends, senior citizens, was down. Other states—Tennessee, Georgia, and North Carolina—were aggressively competing for the silver-gray pipeline. Even more damaging to state pride, many Floridians became legendary "halfbacks," moving not all the way back to New Jersey or Illinois, but halfway back, to North Carolina or Kentucky. The headline of the 19 March 2009 *Sarasota Herald-Tribune* announced, "Florida Growth Fizzle Is Official." For the fourth consecutive year, retiree-rich Charlotte County lost population. Deaths in the county doubled births.[91]

In the final days of the decade 2000–2010, a perceptive journalist pondered the meaning of the roller-coaster decade. Noting the wild years of growth that halted at the footsteps of the Great Recession, Don Lee critically pondered: "Now as the recovery seems to be gaining speed, a central question is whether the population distortions caused by the massive downturn . . . represent a long-term change or whether previous trends eventually will return as the economy strengthens."[92]

In the Bunker: Golf as a Metaphor

In the decades preceding the Great Recession, hitting a golf ball into a sand trap seemed a perfect way for wealthy sixty-something Floridians to spend their mornings. Or a perfect metaphor. By 2005, the popularity of golf and the investment in golf courses were flourishing. Building golf communities was the rage. Between 1990 and 2003, more than 3,000 new golf courses opened. Then came the Great Recession, the decline of the middle class, and Father Time.

Economics and demographics collided in the twenty-first century: golfers grew older while the game of golf failed to evolve in ways to attract new generations. Golf courses demand vast amounts of land, water, fertilizer, time, and wealthy players. Golfing communities in Florida also lost players, members, and residents, as they aged, died, or went bankrupt. Between 2003 and 2011, the number of golfers in the United States declined by 16 percent. The number of golfers in the demographic aged eighteen to thirty plummeted over 35 percent in the years 2005–15. The popularity of golf had always depended upon the charismatic heroes—Arnold Palmer and Jack Nicklaus. The personal scandals of and physical injuries to Tiger Woods after 2009 also curbed the enthusiasm for golf. No new ambassadors claimed Tiger's mantle. Golf's hierarchs have been slow if not hidebound in welcoming women and minorities to the green.[93]

The story of Wildflower Golf Club in Southwest Florida exemplifies the struggle and resolution in one place. In 2006, the owners of the 80-acre course considered selling the unprofitable course to a developer. After the economy tanked, the Lemon Bay Conservancy saw an opportunity. The nonprofit raised $750,000 and took over the rundown project. Volunteers removed acres of Brazilian-pepper-infested lands and planted native species in an evolving nature preserve.[94]

If country clubs and upscale developments have reconsidered their relationship with golf, public golf courses in Florida are also fading. Sarasota's municipal golf course offers a splendid case study. Once a crown jewel of public facilities, the Bobby Jones Golf Club for years was financially solvent, even generating $1.5 million in profit during the golden years, 2004–6. But declining interest in the game and the expensive renovations required more, not less financial support from the City of Sarasota.[95]

Before 2008, the lure of golf and the economics of real estate caught fire, as hundreds of developments centered around golf communities designed by famous architects appeared. Nowhere was this formula more successful than Southwest Florida. But many of these developments have pivoted and asked for rezoning to build more homes along and on the links. Zoned as a golf community, Naples Reserve, a 688-acre project, changed course when developers concluded that Southwest Florida had plenty of golf courses, and the site became a luxury preserve centered around a 125-acre lake. Pickleball is replacing golf as the sport of the aging masses.[96]

Golf courses may project the image of natural harmony, but they pose environmental challenges. With increasing frequency, warm weather means toxic algae blooms across the state's freshwater lakes and Gulf bays, canals, lagoons, and rivers. Environmentalists point to a lineup of usual suspects: Big Sugar, septic tanks, and overfertilized lawns. But they also indict the state's golf courses and the enormous amounts of phosphorous and nitrogen found in fertilizers to maintain picture-perfect golf courses.[97]

The National Glare

The media have long enjoyed a love-hate relationship with Florida. In 1981, *Time* magazine's cover story focused upon South Florida. "Trouble in Paradise" introduced Marielitos, cocaine cowboys, and polluted waters to American readers: "South Florida—that postcard corner of the Sunshine State, that lush strip of hibiscus and condominiums stretching from Palm Beach south to Key West—is a region in trouble. An epidemic of violent crime, a plague of illicit drugs and a tidal wave of refugees have slammed into South Florida with the destructive power of a hurricane." The cover story informed readers that the Dade County morgue had so many dead bodies stacked that a medical examiner "rented a refrigerator hamburger van to house the overflow."[98]

The Great Recession and Florida's woes created an irresistible target for Florida bashing. In blistering staccato bursts, the national media pulverized the Sunshine State. In part envy, in part sadistic delight, and in part impressive research and writing, journalists, academics, and reality-show film crews covered Florida's plight. Provocative essays and articles asked and exposed, "Is Florida the Sunset State?," "Is Florida Over?," "Florida, Despair and Foreclosures," and "The Ponzi State." The prose cut as deeply as the hyperbolic titles. Upon reading the mass critique, a prominent Floridian shrugged: "That's a lot of crises. Has the state that likes to boast of having a world-class this and a world-class that become a world-class whipping boy?" U.S. Senator Bob Graham admitted, "We have some flashing lights."[99]

The *Washington Post*'s Libby Copeland pounded Florida in a rhetorical knockdown. "Florida, home of sunshine and scams," she wrote, "How it continually betrays us. Florida is the place for dreams . . . And for having your dreams dashed." Florida is tough on residents, she argued. "It may be a dream to visit, but it can be hell to live there."[100]

Michael Grunwald's 2008 cover story in *Time*, a magazine with a circulation of 3 million, began, "Water Crisis, Mortgage Fraud, Political Dysfunction, Algae Polluted Beaches, Declining Crops, Failing Public Schools, Foreclosures. Greetings from Florida where winters are great!" He continued his assault. "We're first in the nation in mortgage fraud, second in foreclosures, last in high school graduation rates." The *Herald*'s Andrés Viglucci responded, comparing the 1981 and 2008 *Time* cover stories: "This time around, crime, drugs, and refugees don't even rate a mention." He added, "Instead, there is a broader, and in many ways more troubling litany of sorrows: too many empty condos and houses . . . mortgage fraud . . . Schools, already an embarrassment . . . Ecosystems are collapsing. We don't have enough water, yet most of the state could soon be under the sea." Architect Andrés Duany commented, "I *would* say, we're the worst-dressed state, though."[101]

In the pushback, some defended the state's honor against carpetbagging journalists. The *Sarasota Herald-Tribune* concluded, "Floridians can debate among themselves whether the article is a cheap shot or right on target." Michael Grunwald resided in Miami Beach. His mother-in-law was a local Realtor! Grunwald concluded his essay with a message and a query for his fellow Floridians: "The question is whether it will grow up. If Florida can reinvent itself, it can be the tip of the American spear, showing the nation how to save water and energy, manage growth, restore ecosystems and retool economies in an era of less." Miami historian Arva Parks added: "We know how to crash and how to recover. We don't seem to know how to learn."[102]

The *Miami Herald*'s Fred Grimm asked why the same crippling problems seem ever-present in Florida. He focused on a rhetorical question raised in the 1981 story by Don Paul, a civic reformer: "'How do you deal with these issues in a political climate that demands instant gratification?' Until Paul's question gets resolved, *Time* magazine will have an endless opportunity to rediscover trouble in paradise."[103]

The *New York Times*' Damien Cave wrote several stories capturing the pain and frustration of Floridians in a free-fall economy. In February 2009 he put Florida's housing crisis into perspective: "If every home in Boston received a foreclosure notice, the total would still be less than Florida's." Cave also interviewed journalist and novelist Carl Hiaasen, arguably the state's most respected citizen, someone who loves the old Florida and cringes at the new Florida. "We need to do something bold; we need to do something radical," he told Cave. "Everything is going to be O.K., but not if we do it the same way."[104]

The Withering Florida Dream

The most distressing question that arose during the Great Recession was as simple as it was deflating: Had the Florida dream run its course? So, too, the American dream? It was not the first time such alarming questions had been raised. During the bleakest months of the Great Depression, the poet Archibald MacLeish, the son of Scottish immigrants, contemplated such a free fall.

> We wonder whether the dream of American liberty
> Was 200 years of pine wood
> And 3 generations of the grass.
> And the generations are up, the years over
> We don't know.

By 1940, the threat of fascism and totalitarianism profoundly changed MacLeish's mood. In *The American Cause,* he rhapsodized in one of the most optimistic sentences ever composed: "The American people were people who had the luck to be born on this continent where the heat was hotter and the cold was colder and the sun was brighter and the nights were blacker and the distances were farther and the faces were nearer and the rain was more like rain and the mornings were more like mornings than anywhere else on earth—sooner or sweeter and lovelier over unused hills."[105]

The realities of unemployment, foreclosures, and homelessness pummeled fantasies of dreaming in the first decade of the new century. In 2011, literary scholar Lauren Berlant articulated the mood of many Americans in her book *Cruel Optimism,* the title referring to the author's theme: "When something you desire is actually an obstacle to your flourishing." In our pursuit of dreams, she argues, we delude ourselves thinking that our lives follow trajectories, "but often what we feel instead is a sense of precariousness—a gut-level suspicion that hard work, thrift, and following the rules won't give us control over the story, much less guarantee a happy ending."[106]

In the late 1930s, MacLeish bundled his poems together and titled his book *America Was Promises.* The promise of a better winter and the opportunity to enjoy crystal-clear springs and beachfront sunsets accompanied the Florida dream. But the Florida dream was not simply about swaying palm trees, sand dunes, and better Februarys—it was the promise of a better life.

Yet by 2010, more and more citizens began to doubt whether Florida could adapt to a new century and new challenges. More red tides and fewer oranges dampened dreams. When headlines scream, "'Guacamole-Thick' Algae Fouls

Swath of Florida," dreams are not the first sensation that comes to mind. The economy, housing, and jobs had tanked, and the conversation was more serious, more pessimistic. Some critics were using the word "existential" alongside Florida, about the inability of state leaders to take seriously the looming crises of climate, the environment, infrastructure, education, gun violence, a drug epidemic, and the loosening bonds of civil society. The questions were tough but honest: "What kind of state do we want to be?" "Are we really all in this together?" "Is the dream over?" "Can Florida figure out a better way to grow?" "Is paradise lost?"

In the 1950s, Jack Swenningsen roamed the state profiling the Florida dream state in photographs: a straw-hatted, bikini-wearing model holding a trophy snook; neon-glowing arcades with convertibles; and photos that spoke to shivering Yankees who must be saying, "If we lived in Florida, we'd reach out the back door and pick oranges for breakfast. We'd catch fish in the canal back of the house. Coconuts, Bea!" By 2007, front-page photographs depicted tenants being evicted, pill mills, slimy green algae spreading across canals and rivers, and invasive Burmese pythons and green iguanas.[107]

Fulfilling the Florida dream was once relatively innocent and sincere. The journalist Jon Wilson described his encounter. In 1956 his family moved from Nebraska to Florida. "Through the wide-open windows of our '53 Ford, a Tampa Bay breeze carried my first, good whiff of Florida," he reminisced. "It smelled like fish stew. It smelled like mystery. It smelled like the ocean. It smelled like a dream." He related that Jack Kerouac also wound up in St. Petersburg. "Kerouac went on a different journey," wrote Wilson, "but his prose expressed a mighty yearning." Like Dorothy yearning for Kansas, the Wilsons yearned for warm winters, purchasing a three-bedroom tract home in a subdivision named Westgate Manor. The 1956 price: $12,500.[108]

Michael Kruse was a young journalist at the *St. Petersburg Times* during the economic tumult. In 2009, he wrote a front-page story titled "Greetings from Florida: Why Aren't You Here?" Such a question had rarely been asked before. With the force of a sledgehammer, his subtitle read, "Once an Affordable Paradise Swelling with New Arrivals, the Sunshine State Is Fading as a Dream Destination." The lengthy essay began: "The Florida dream isn't dead. But it is in trouble." Kruse, who today works for *Politico*, noted diminishing numbers of new residents, concluding: "People aren't coming here like they used to. Because Florida isn't what it used to be." He added: "The Florida dream was the American dream, only in sharp, blue-sky focus. The iconic images of the Sunshine State used to be bountiful boxes of citrus, or a pelican flying through the sunset over the bay, all in pastel-postcard chic. Now they're sad, still photos of forlorn foreclosed homes."[109]

Once, owning a home sealed the American dream. Immigrants poured into America and Florida optimistic that here they could achieve something impossible in the old country: homeownership. The educator George B. Emerson proclaimed in 1871, "The prospect of owning one's house, and that a pleasant one . . . must be a strong motive with any man to regularity, good conduct, and economy." Commentator Alexander von Hoffman asked in 2008: "What would Emerson think today? Global investment banks are failing, and mortgage giants Fannie Mae and Freddie Mac, created over the years to support that unimpeachable moral right of home ownership, are on the brink."[110]

In 2010, a headline in Florida's largest newspaper asked, "Owning a Home: Has the Dream Soured?" Sean Snaith, an economist at the University of Central Florida, responded to the unraveling of the Florida dream. Once, he argued, "Joe Lunch Bucket [could] retire from Jersey and live in a trailer by the sea." In 2009, Smith concurred that Joe might still migrate to Florida and live in his trailer, "but his trailer won't be by the sea. It might be in Lakeland or Ocala."[111]

In what seems like a counterintuitive response to the trauma of and lessons learned from the Great Recession, new homes were *bigger, not smaller,* than prerecession housing. Such a trend had been unfolding since the GI Bill. In 1950, the average new American home measured 983 square feet. By 2004, new homes had expanded to 2,340 square feet. And while our homes were growing larger, American and Florida families were getting smaller.[112]

Debating the Florida dream seemed to become an official state question during the Great Recession. A 2011 Gallup poll asked Americans about current economic conditions. Florida, Rhode Island, and Ohio ranked as some of the most pessimistic states in America. Robert Trigaux served as the *St. Petersburg Times*' business editor. "I'm closing in on 17 years in Florida," he wrote in 2007, "but never before have I heard so much talk from so many about leaving." As in:

> "I'm fed up with insurance and housing costs, property taxes, school, so-so jobs . . ." My wife hears it from fellow public school teachers, whose paychecks still pale, next to those in some nearby states. . . . It's not just wages. A part-time resident from Island Estates condos on Clearwater Beach called me this month to say: Goodbye, Florida. . . . What I hear in anecdotes, pollsters register in bulk. Floridians who say the state is headed down the wrong track outnumber those who say the state is on the right track.[113]

One of the state's most prominent journalists shocked readers and leaders when he announced in 2011 that he was retiring early and leaving Florida for North Carolina. Howard Troxler's farewell column opened by paraphrasing Marjory Stoneman Douglas, "There is no other Florida in the world." But he also asked Floridians to look at ourselves with a mirror: "Florida sold itself eagerly, of course. Florida has *always* sold itself eagerly. . . . Only in the last generation did Floridians begin to question the wisdom of this. We saw our lakes and bays choked to death. We saw the highways jammed, the quality-of-life degrading. And enough Floridians said, maybe this is not the state we want." He asked citizens to realize "the full damage of what has already happened in Tallahassee." He concluded, "Despite all this, lately I have been feeling more and more optimistic, precisely *because* more and more Floridians realize what is happening."[114]

A sense of perspective is always helpful. "Sometimes I think I've figured out some order in the universe," writes Susan Orleans, "but then I find myself in Florida." When Congress debated the Adams-Onís Treaty in 1819, John Randolph famously thundered that he "would not give up an eligible position in hell for all Florida." Critics maintained that the notoriously acerbic Virginian knew a great deal more about Hades than Florida. For all the suffering and trauma inflicted by the Great Recession, it was no Great Depression. "This is not a shocking revelatory trend," replied J. Allison DeFoor, a lawyer, preacher, and the state's "environmental czar" under Governor Bush. "It's still going to be paradise, but it's not going to be a cheap paradise."[115]

Somehow, someway, the Florida dream endures. For all the concerns about future environmental calamities, intergenerational warfare, and ethnic divisions, watching a sunrise or migrating birds on Amelia Island, Daytona Beach, or Hutchinson Island, or a sunset at Sanibel Island, Fort De Soto Park, or Dog Island restores the nerves and revives the soul.[116]

"Allegiance to the land," insisted Marjorie Kinnan Rawlings, "is tenderness." The quality of tenderness seemed a major casualty of the Great Recession. But Floridians sought refuge from the mean-spirited news of Ponzi-schemers and state budget cuts. Increasingly, they sought the tenderness and wonderment of Florida's environment as a balm. No one championed a return to nature more than Jeff Klinkenberg, a journalist for the *St. Petersburg Times.* The titles of his books of bundled columns underscored his philosophy: *Real Florida, Dispatches from the Land of Flowers, Seasons of Real Florida, Pilgrim in the Land of Alligators,* and *Alligators in B-Flat.*

Reacting to the barrage of "paradise lost" literature, Klinkenberg offered a dose of optimism tempered by a genuine "tenderness for the land." He wrote,

"Florida is dead only if we lack eyes, ears, and a sense of adventure to go out and explore." He pleaded for a sense of perspective. "Today, thanks to the elimination of the pesticide DDT from the food chain, Florida has more eagles than any state except Alaska. I see eagles every day as I drive from my hometown, St. Petersburg. As for alligators . . . Florida is home to more than a million." He noted, "Even the rarest of the rare, the American crocodile, has staged a remarkable comeback. . . . You have a better chance of seeing a Florida panther or a black bear now than a half-century ago." He concludes with an admiring glance at environmental author Thomas Barbour: "He called the book *That Vanishing Eden: A Naturalist's Florida.*" Klinkenberg adds, "It came out in 1944." Klinkenberg now lives on a mountaintop in North Carolina.[117]

Between 2005 and 2010, what had been promoted as a paradise characterized by massive numbers of newcomers and the promise of a better future was left battered and bruised, a place mocked as the Foreclosure State, the Sunset State, and the Homeless State. For a brief span, more Floridians were leaving than arriving, a numerical oddity but also a warning. Yet signs of hope appeared as tourists, home buyers, and construction workers returned. Politicians may have wrung their hands, but they never left while tectonic shift was happening across Florida's political plates.

13

A Political Earthquake

Florida Politics, 2008–2010

Prologue

In May 2010, the Republican National Committee debated where to hold the 2012 convention. The finalists mirrored the new heart of the New Grand Old Party (NGOP): Phoenix, Salt Lake City, and Tampa. A half century earlier, the prospects of the GOP convening in Tampa were as unlikely as a cold front in August or Floridians beckoning the party of Barry Goldwater and Everett Dirksen. But the American political map was rocked and rearranged between 1960 and 1980. In 1968, the only Sunbelt state won by Democratic candidate Hubert Humphrey was Texas. He lost the election. The Site Selection Committee tapped Tampa, Florida, over its Sunbelt rivals. The Sunshine State checked all the boxes. Florida boasted a Republican governor who bettors speculated might enhance the 2012 ticket. New York, California, Texas, and Florida formed America's megastates, but only Florida passed the political toss-up test. Florida was also a megastate with a diversity that mirrored America. "It's become a nation-state," commented presidential historian Richard Norton Smith, "just as New York and California were at their peak and Ohio was a century ago."[1]

In the Gilded Age, Ohio earned the nickname "the cradle of presidents." Ohio has mothered eight presidents. In contrast, Florida seems barren, having never had a son or daughter elected president or vice president; indeed, the list extends to Speaker of the House, president of the Senate, majority or minority leader of either body. But in the electrifying 2000 election, political pundits realized that Florida matters.[2]

Politically, Florida had become home to a galaxy of Republican luminaries. Mike Huckabee, the former governor of Arkansas, built a $3 million home in Walton County, not far from Karl Rove. Huckabee proclaimed, "This part of Florida is God, grits and gravy." He also made the front pages when, angry at beachcombers strolling along his Gulf beach home, he sued the county to restrict dune traffic. But Palm Beach County, not the Panhandle, became the Republican South Star, home to Roger Ailes, Rush Limbaugh, Ann Coulter, David Koch, Donald Trump, Roger Stone, Dick Morris, Sean Hannity, Betsy DeVos, Lou Dobbs, Stephen Ross, and Rudy Giuliani. Broward County is home to sports mogul Wayne Huizenga. Former Notre Dame football coach Lou Holtz resides in Lake Nona, in Central Florida.[3]

The governor of Florida was a Republican and a resident of St. Petersburg, on Tampa Bay. "Irony," wrote the French novelist Anatole France, "is the last stage of disappointment." No political novelist and certainly no GOP publicist could have scripted that Charlie Crist would announce that he was not going to run for certain reelection but would run for an open U.S. Senate seat. Slack-jawed party leaders were restless and nervous. A year later, amid a national Republican insurgency, Governor Crist bolted the party and ran as an independent.[4]

Compelling reasons *not* to pick Tampa were climate and vice. August is hurricane season in Florida, and the weather is, in the words of comedian Jon Stewart, "hotter than a gorilla's anus in this town." In defense of gorillas, he quipped, "theirs is a dry heat!" Others warned of the dangers of Tampa's reputation as the lap-dance capital of America. And the center of the adult entertainment business was Dale Mabry Boulevard, appropriately named for a martyred dirigible pilot. "Do you know how hard it is to get money down in Tampa that does not have body glitter on it?," the host of *The Daily Show* asked. The show's John Oliver, pondering why Tampa was chosen as the convention host in mid-August, answered: "Tampa symbolizes what Obama has done to America. In just three-and-a-half years, this once bustling metropolis is now a wind and rain-soaked foreclosed shell of itself." *Daily Show* correspondent Jason Jones, reporting from Tampa's "famous strip club district," suggested that Tampa has become a center of moral depravity because of the "anything goes liberalism of the Obama administration." Correspondent Samantha Bee, suspended in air, clutched by a giant palmetto bug, blamed the mess on "a certain socialist tree-hugging president banning DDT." A concerned Stewart offered Bee condolences and good fortune. "Don't wish me luck," Bee screamed. "I'm the one getting out of this s—hole!" St. Petersburg, Tampa's great rival, did not escape criticism. The Republican National Committee held a reception at Tropicana Field, a domed home to the baseball team. To prevent access by the unwashed, the City of St. Petersburg placed barricades around the stadium, drawing comparisons to Beirut.[5]

Beyond the rim shots and satire, the choice of Tampa as the site of the 2012 convention *was* pitch-perfect. Florida mattered. Florida was a political behemoth, voter-rich with bona fide Republican credentials. Tampa Bay also typified an America not yet out of recession's den. In September 2011, Tampa Bay ranked 98th out of 100 metro areas in economic recovery. Cape Coral–Fort Myers ranked, in the words of Ol' Ball Coach Steve Spurrier, "dead ass last." Sunbelt rival Houston ranked first.[6]

The *real* reason the committee selected Tampa as the site for the 2012 Republican Party Convention was the work of a single individual largely forgotten. Al Austin had worked for decades bolstering and boosting the Grand Old Party in a city best known for its Democratic power brokers. In the 1960s, he invested early in South Tampa, especially along a project locals lampooned as "The Road to Nowhere." West Shore Boulevard symbolized the new growth spurts reshaping Sunbelt Tampa. By the time the GOP was considering Tampa's bid to host a convention, West Shore Boulevard had vaulted so fast and so high that while its population represented a mere 1 percent of Hillsborough County, the "West Shore District" housed 13 percent of the county's population, 39 percent of commercial office space, and 45 percent of the hotel rooms. Austin achieved even more success luring Super Bowls to Tampa.[7]

Governor Crist: Riding the Wave

In January 2007, Charlie Crist succeeded a Republican icon, warrior, and conservative governor. "Jeb Bush transformed Florida state government," concluded his biographer, Matthew T. Corrigan. Charlie Crist was neither a transformational governor nor a Republican ideologue. For instance, he vetoed most of the Medicaid reforms the Bush-Republican legislative alliance had passed. Most Floridians preferred Crist's demeanor over Bush's intensity. If Jeb was a full-throated intellectual conservative, Charlie was pragmatic and not an idea man. Most of all, Floridians loved the new governor's sunny disposition. "He's an optimist, you may have noticed," quipped Senate minority leader Steve Geller. In 2007, politically savvy writers were betting that the popular Crist, in his second term as governor, would greet Republican conventioneers.[8]

When Crist came to office, a supercharged, air-conditioned Florida still hummed, but it had just begun to wheeze. From the Englewood Chamber of Commerce to the Realtors of Palm Bay to the solons at and saloons of the Capitol, growth had become a karmic mantra that would solve all the messy residuals of urban sprawl, overcrowded schools, and polluted springs. And if growth simply begat more growth, boosters always pointed to the prohibition on a state income tax. In 1992, Florida voters approved a constitutional amendment that a political genius named "Save Our Homes" (SOH). Amendment 10 capped increases in annual homestead property valuation tax at 3 percent or the percentage change in the Consumer Price Index, whichever was less. SOH richly benefited wealthy homeowners, helping the middle classes in markets where home prices were rising but hurting cities and counties. In September 2009, Crist took credit for the measure, claiming, "I signed the largest single tax cut in the history of Florida. A $25 billion tax cut, directed at property tax cuts." PolitiFact disputed Crist's claim.[9]

The Crist family personified the American dream: A 1956 native of Altoona, Pennsylvania, young Charles Joseph Crist Jr. spent six diaper-age months in his hometown before his family relocated to Georgia while his father attended medical school at Emory University. The Crist family moved to St. Petersburg in June 1960 where the senior Charles began his internship as a physician. Charlie was a proud graduate of Florida State University. His elevation to governor in 2006 followed a decade and a half of elections to state agencies. Sworn in as Florida's forty-fourth governor, Crist may have been the most optimistic governor in Florida history.[10]

Governor Crist enjoyed an extended honeymoon. In 2007, a California journalist described the unflappable politician whose approval ratings reached a high of 73 percent, including an astounding 71 percent support among Democrats:

> Seventeen hours into a day that included three flights, a dinner speech and time slashing $459 million from the state budget, Gov. Crist breezes into an empty hotel restaurant before a 10 p.m. meeting. There's not a wrinkle in his suit or a snowy white hair out of place. . . . Crist moves among his constituents as if he's still campaigning, missing no opportunity to convey with studied humility and solicitation that he's hard at work for every soul in the state. . . . He is, in a *Miami Herald* columnist's description, "a Republican golden retriever who throws his arms around everyone."[11]

At the end of 2007, the headline of the *Fort Myers News-Press* concluded, "Crist's First Year a Busy, Stormy One." While no hurricane struck Florida in 2007, early signs of downward spiraling real estate sales worried investors and markets. Facing a backlash for having promised that property taxes would "drop like a rock," Crist's very use of the term "climate change" was viewed as heresy by conservative Republicans and enlightening by others. In July, Crist hosted an environmental summit meeting in Miami. He astonished friends and frightened enemies when he vowed to restore felons' voting rights. In 2007, the governor barely succeeded in a split-cabinet vote to restore nonviolent criminals and felons' voting privileges. Indeed, Crist walked the walk on what most Republicans regarded a third-rail issue, as he worked to restore the voting rights of 950,000 disenfranchised ex-felons. *The New York Times* applauded Crist's efforts to reform a practice that originated during Reconstruction. Crist's approval ratings remained high, never dropping below 65 percent. In 2008, Governor Crist and legislators heard angry homeowners, and he signed a bill demanding that local governments cut more than $15 billion in property taxes.[12]

The veteran political observer John Kennedy predicted that Governor Crist faced "rougher sailing." He elaborated: "But as Crist enters his second year in office, he's finding that sincerity may not be enough—and his personal warmth is being met by increasingly icy responses. . . . Even worse, in the sharp-elbowed world of Tallahassee politics, legislators and lobbyists are finding they can ignore him—and not pay a price." The *Orlando Sentinel*'s Tallahassee bureau chief concluded, "He's facing deep challenges—beginning with the state's sagging finances." One increasingly influential group, social conservatives, was becoming agitated over the governor's "live and let live" style; they had hoped Crist would support their proposal to ban same-sex marriage. Almost two-thirds of Republicans—63 percent—thought the governor was doing a good job. When Bush left office in January 2007, his favorability ratings among this same demographic were 89 percent.[13]

More than a few headlines profiling the governor asked, "Who is the real Charlie Crist?" Is he a populist politician who takes on special interests? Or is he the opportunist who took on the moniker "Chain Gang" Charlie? Is he Charlie 2.0, or the same old Charlie? But Governor Crist has always understood that there should be a balance between leading and representing, politics and governing. Journalist Steve Bousquet wrote in 2007, "As Crist struggles with the widespread anger over taxes and insurance, and faces the prospect of another bleak budget year, he is to many simply a nice guy, with a smile and a pleasant outlook that has a way of keeping trouble at bay."[14]

Governor Crist's optimism may be regarded by critics as naïve or self-serving, but historically, Americans prefer sunny to dark candidates. Consider the following presidential contests and the winners: Franklin D. Roosevelt vs. Herbert Hoover, John F. Kennedy vs. Richard M. Nixon, Ronald Reagan vs. Jimmy Carter and Walter Mondale, George H. W. Bush vs. Michael Dukakis, Bill Clinton vs. Bob Dole, and George W. Bush vs. John Kerry. Optimism won. In 2008, optimism was a precious commodity as the economy was tanking. But Barack Obama, with his "Yes, we can!" slogan and disarming smile, certainly cornered the market on a better future.

The Presidential Election of 2008: The GOP

An iron law of politics holds that the incumbent and party in power bear the responsibility of misfortune. Searing recessions and forever wars have consequences. On the national level, George W. Bush may have been term-limited, but the Republican candidate for president in 2008 could not escape the ghosts of recessions and wars past and present. Republicans nominated U.S. Senator John McCain. A Vietnam military hero best known for his stoical conduct as a prisoner of war at the Hỏa Lò Prison, the infamous Saigon Hilton, McCain held leadership roles in the U.S. Senate, in which he served with distinction.

The path to the presidency went through Florida. "Name almost any talking point in Washington—health care, immigration, presidential politics, college football and references to Florida pop up," wrote commentator William Gibson in 2007. "The mega-state is well known in the nation's capital, where everyone has an eye on the next election." Gibson compared the Everglades to Florida: both are "unique and irreplaceable."[15]

The 2008 Florida Democratic Party felt good about its present and future. The Democratic bench, while not deep, was promising. Bob Graham had stepped down in 2004, but while attending the Florida delegation breakfast at the Democratic convention in Denver, he surveyed the room, pointing out rising stars: U.S. Rep. Debbie Wasserman Schultz of Weston; Orlando mayor Buddy Dyer; Alex Sink; Rod Smith of Gainesville; Miami congressman Kendrick Meek; and Democratic legislative leader from Hallandale Dan Gelber. Graham also praised Tampa mayor Pam Iorio, as well as Congresswoman Kathy Castor.[16]

In 2008, no single endorsement mattered more than that of the governor of Florida, a voter-rich state with 27 electoral votes. The fandango involving Crist and Republican presidential candidates began only months after the inauguration. He may have appeared casual on the outside, but the governor was disciplined, and held off his endorsement until weeks before the primary in late January 2008.[17]

Crist flirted with Rudy Giuliani, the hero of 9/11 and former New York City mayor, but ultimately endorsed McCain, calling him "a true hero." Giuliani was crushed, personally and politically. "Leading in crisis is what I do best," proclaimed the former mayor of New York City who at one time led the Florida polls by 20 points. Giuliani bet heavily on winning Super Tuesday and Florida. Primary day turned out so disastrously for Giuliani that he dropped out of the race. "If yesterday was the beginning of the end for Rudy Giuliani," wrote Libby Copeland, "it's fitting that it happened in Florida." In a sarcastic *Washington Post* column, she observed that for all the books with sunshine and dreams in their titles, Florida "continually betrays us."[18]

John McCain was no stranger to Florida. Curiously, his life mirrored that of his younger alter ego, the rock star and free-form poet Jim Morrison. Both descended from Scottish stock and lived as military brats; both of their fathers served as navy rear admirals. George Stephenson Morrison had been a gifted aviator who played a role in the Gulf of Tonkin engagement, the incident that sparked the American involvement in Vietnam. Jim lived in Melbourne and Clearwater, Florida, and attended FSU. In October 1967, Jim was a poet-singer-fronter for the Doors. Two months later he was arrested onstage for inciting a riot. He died of a drug overdose in 1971. Meanwhile, John was flying an A-4E Skyhawk over North Vietnam. Enemy missiles intercepted his jet, and he became a prized enemy captive.[19]

John McCain finished fifth from the bottom at his class at the Naval Academy. In 1959, McCain was stationed at the Pensacola Naval Air Station, where he made his first successful carrier landing. As a carrier pilot, he belonged to a special breed. He and his family had lived in Orange Park.[20]

In March 1973, the POW was released, and he took a fateful plane ride home. "McCain left this small town [Orange Park] in 1967 as the underachieving scion of a great military family," wrote Alex Leary. "He returned on crutches in 1973, a portrait of American resolve at age 36. It was Orange Park, outside Jacksonville, that first witnessed the budding power of the war-hero story line. It was where McCain, however, built the foundation of a political career that could land him the presidency." He had spent the previous five and a half years as the most important prisoner of war in North Vietnam. His wife and family were 9,000 miles away in Florida. His hair now white, McCain landed in Jacksonville, Florida, a place where he would reunite with his family and adjust to new challenges. Here, his wounds healed, he learned to fly new, more powerful planes and acquire new leadership skills. For McCain, home alternated between Cecil Naval Air Field, a home in Orange Park, and a seaside refuge at South Ponte Vedra Beach. He later reflected: "For many years in my life, I lacked a fixed address. Jacksonville came closer to being a hometown for me than any place in the country." Jacksonville also nourished his political aspirations and leadership skills. In 1973, McCain told a journalist, "I had a lot of time to think over there and came to the conclusion that one of the most important things in life—along with a man's family—is to make some contribution to this country." In 1974, Cecil Field was the home base for Attack Squadron 174, the largest squadron in the navy. McCain served as the squadron's executive officer, second in command. He later served as the U.S. Senate's liaison for the navy. In 1981, McCain moved to Arizona. The following year, while his marriage dissolved, he was elected to the U.S. Congress. Military duty, the constant moving from base to base, and wars take terrible tolls on relationships. McCain spent twice as much time in Vietnam as he had been married. In 1986, he replaced U.S. Senator Barry Goldwater in the U.S. Senate.[21]

Richard A. Stratton knew John McCain better than almost anyone. They shared a prison cell in Hanoi. Once, when Stratton asked McCain, "What do you want to be when you grow up?," his cellmate answered, "I am going to be president of the United States." Senator McCain's name had often been floated as a presidential aspirant. He challenged George W. Bush for the Republican nomination in 2000, winning the New Hampshire primary. In February 2007, McCain announced his candidacy on the *Late Show with David Letterman,* reviving his "Straight Talk Express." Voters admired the Arizonan's candor. To reach younger voters, his staff made the candidate accessible on the Internet and Facebook. To some, McCain seemed out-of-date. He asked for permission to play Chuck Berry's rock-and-roll anthem at rallies, "Johnny B Goode" with its iconic lyrics, "Go Johnny Go Go Go." The eighty-one-year-old Berry snubbed the request. The campaign finally settled on Abba's "Take a Chance on Me."[22]

Florida posed a critical challenge for McCain, Giuliani, and Mitt Romney. Unlike in New Hampshire and other states, Democrats and independents could not vote in the Republican primary. During one debate, NBC's Tim Russert introduced a McCain quote: "I know a lot less about economics than I do about military and foreign policy issues. I still need to be educated." Conservative radio personalities questioned McCain's credentials and fitness for office. Laura Ingraham questioned "the mental stability of the McCain campaign." Mark Levin insisted on calling McCain "McLame." Mel Martínez and Charlie Crist delivered timely endorsements. When the votes were counted on 29 January, McCain swept the field, earning 36 percent of the votes and winning Florida's 57 delegates.[23]

McCain faced a formidable challenge: he was essentially seeking a Republican third term while the incumbent, President George W. Bush, was sinking. McCain's great hope was that his inexperienced opponent, U.S. Senator Barack

Obama, would stumble. America learned, however, that Barack Obama was a master of self-restraint, an eloquent candidate who exuded optimism. And Obama was also a Teflon candidate. Nothing—not conspiracy theories that his Hawaiian birth certificate was forged or videos of Obama's Reverend Jeremiah Wright Jr. shouting, "God damn America!"—blocked his path to the White House. The Reverend Wright, maintains author David Maraniss, "had a sizeable ego and the personality of an agitator, hot to Obama's cool."[24]

Florida political scientist Aubrey Jewett contends that the pivotal moment in the campaign came in September, a time when polls indicated McCain was leading Obama by more than 5 points. "The defining moment," insisted Jewett, "was when the president went on TV and said that he, the Treasury secretary and the Fed chairman all agreed that we needed this bailout. Every day for about two weeks after that, McCain lost half a point." He added that Obama was outspending McCain by a significant margin.[25]

Journalist Adam Nagourney wrote a poignant portrait of the McCain campaign in Miami in late October 2008. "For Senator John McCain, it was not supposed to be this way," Nagourney began. "From a commanding lead last spring, in a state where Senator Barack Obama did not campaign in the primaries and only hired a state director in June, Mr. McCain is now locked in a neck-and-neck race for a trove of electoral votes that is vital to his hopes of victory." To insiders and outsiders, McCain's relationship to Governor Crist seemed strained. "Mr. McCain clearly could still win the state's 27 electoral votes," observed Nagourney. "But the battle in Florida is offering on the widest stage . . . an object lesson in the disparities in the resources, aggressiveness and political cunning that Mr. McCain and Mr. Obama are taking to contests across the country." And every day and night, the drumbeat of homelessness and foreclosures made the prospect of voters trusting Republicans for another term less likely.[26]

The race to the White House demanded many visits to Florida. If McCain could not win a battleground state that glowed pinkish-red, the race was over. A whispering campaign hinted that McCain might ask the Florida governor to be his running mate. McCain had endorsed Crist in 2006, stumping the state to rally voters. Crist clearly lobbied for the job, raising funds for the Arizonan's campaign and even compromising one of his most treasured positions: opposition to offshore oil-drilling on Florida beaches, a measure McCain proposed. But state journalists believed what they saw and read. Crist's prospects plummeted. Joe Follick wrote in June 2008, "Not since Richard Nixon chose Spiro T. Agnew in 1968 has a running mate been selected with Crist's limited résumé." An author of a book on the American vice presidency used the word "impossible" to describe Crist's chances, adding, "Unless Gov. Crist is some sort of hidden Abraham Lincoln." Inexplicably, Senator McCain asked Alaska governor Sarah Palin to be his running mate, arguably the worst such choice in American history.[27]

The Democratic Candidates for the Presidency: 2008

Rarely had a presidential candidate bolted upon the scene with a message and personality so fresh, bold, and ambitious. His strange name may have jolted many Americans, but they quickly recognized a rising star. He was Barack Hussein Obama II. In 2006, he was a junior U.S. senator from Illinois. A Chicagoan via Honolulu, he had served eight rather undistinguished years in the Illinois legislature. Obama was a keen observer who learned from his missteps. "It's hard, in retrospect, to understand why you did something stupid," he writes in his autobiography. "I mean dumb choices . . . That was me running for Congress." In 2000, he challenged popular U.S. Congressman and former Black Panther Bobby Rush, an icon in his district: "Almost from the start, the race was a disaster." Yet in 2004, he won a race for the U.S. Senate, largely because Republican candidate Jack Ryan was humiliated when released court documents revealed kinky details in his marriage. In May 2006, a time when most presidential aspirants begin to prepare for a long campaign, only half of Americans, when asked, had ever heard of Barack Obama. Almost every adult voter had strong opinions about Hillary Clinton.[28]

Defying the odds, Obama announced his candidacy for the presidency at the Old State Capitol in Springfield, Illinois, in February 2007. Both Hillary Clinton and Barack Obama were residents of Chicago. Ronald Reagan is the only U.S. president born in Illinois; Lincoln and Grant moved there. Like Florida, Illinois is narrow and long, with its capital lying far from the state's populous power center. But whereas Chicago, located on Lake Michigan, dominates downstate politics, Florida's power radiates from the south northward. In 1940, Chicago boasted a population of 3.4 million residents; the entire state of Florida totaled 1.9 million inhabitants. But in 2008, Florida had hurtled past Illinois in population, and both Hillary and Barack understood that winning the Sunshine State was vital to winning the nomination and the presidency. Two years later, Florida's population of 18.8 million residents left Illinois far behind with its population of 12.9 million persons.

Born in 1947, Hillary Rodham grew up in middle-class Park Ridge, a Chicago suburb. A devoted Methodist and Barry Goldwater Republican, Hillary was a bright, earnest, and ambitious student who graduated from Wellesley College and Yale Law School, where she met William Clinton. She followed Bill to Arkansas, where she taught at the law school. They married in 1975; three years later Bill was elected governor. She became First Lady of the United States when Bill was elected president in 1992. "With a professional career unequalled by any previous presidential candidate's wife, Hillary was heavily scrutinized," writes historian Betty Caroli. Conservatives claimed that she had her own agenda because she had worked for liberal causes. A lightning rod, Hillary was divisive and unifying across party lines.[29]

"Hillary's relationship with Florida," observed journalist Adam C. Smith, "not unlike an enduring but exacting marriage, is long and complex." Blood is thicker and thornier than politics. Hillary had always been sensitive to the plight of poor children. Journalist Bill Maxwell, who had been a migrant laborer in Florida, proclaimed in 1992 that "first lady Hillary Clinton will support efforts to improve the lives of the nation's youngest field hands." As a law student, she first encountered Florida migrant workers while working as an activist. Other Yale classmates and interns with powerful New York law firms came away from Senate hearings on working conditions on Florida farms convinced that agribusiness needed public relations help. Hillary, however, was deeply touched: "I suggested the best way to do that would be to improve the treatment of their farmworkers." Ironically, Alfonso "Alfy" Fanjul Jr., the sugar baron whose vast holdings faced myriad complaints of labor abuse, co-chaired Bill Clinton's 1992 presidential campaign. Fatefully, on President's Day 1996, Bill told Monica Lewinsky that he no longer felt right about their relationship. According to Lewinsky, following a hug, "the president got a telephone call from somebody named 'Fanuli.'" It was the Florida sugar magnate. The episode humiliated Hillary Clinton.[30]

Florida was also home to Hugh and Tony Rodham, Hillary's younger brothers, A lawyer and brother-in-law to President Clinton, Hugh played as backup quarterback at Penn State University, served in the Peace Corps in Colombia, moved to Miami, and married an immigrant Cuban lawyer. In 1989, Rodham became assistant public defender in the Miami Drug Court. In 1994 he rocked the Florida Democratic Party and the inhabitants in the White House by running for the Democratic Party nomination for the U.S. Senate. The seat was held by one of the most popular U.S. senators in modern Florida, Connie Mack. Veteran journalists thought Rodham was one of the worst stateside candidates ever. Mack won the election by 40 points. Tony was equally embarrassing to the First Family. In 1999, the brothers Rodham organized a company to harvest and market hazelnuts from the former Republic of Georgia, but press documents unveiled the relationship as more political than economic.[31]

Following eight years in the White House, the Clintons moved to New York, where Hillary Rodham Clinton was elected and reelected to the U.S. Senate. In 2007, she announced her candidacy for the presidency. She was widely seen as the establishment candidate. In one of the Democratic debates, George Stephanopoulos moderated the event. Few complained that he had served under Bill Clinton.[32]

With roots in Kenya, Kansas, New York, and Chicago, Barack Obama stormed the political establishment, possessing the confidence, good fortune, and timing to run for the presidency in 2008. His toughest opponent was never John McCain; rather, Hillary Clinton dominated the early months of the Democratic primaries. Many argued she "deserved" the nomination. The political gods blessed Illinois. The odds looked good for the Land of Lincoln to claim a native daughter or adopted son as president.

Florida had not voted Democratic in a presidential election since 1996. The state bled more red than blue, but Republicans were blamed for the Great Recession. Still, Florida was considered a toss-up in 2008. The early polls leaned Republican. Obama's greatest challenge was introducing himself to a new audience, convincing Floridians that this son of a Kenyan immigrant with an odd foreign name was as American as apple pie and roasted goat. McCain jumped out to an impressive lead in Florida in what must have seemed like a lock.

Democrats, flush with money, blanketed Florida with ads and personnel. Team Obama directed two savvy campaign aides, Steve Hildebrand and Paul Tewes, to oversee Florida operations. A GOP consultant observed, "The fact that McCain is having to spend time and money here is killing us." Yet polls confirmed a dead heat in October.[33]

Hillary's Race against History and Obama

When she left the White house in January 2001, Hillary Rodham Clinton was regarded as the most powerful and/or influential First Lady since Eleanor Roosevelt and/or the most dangerous First Lady since Eleanor Roosevelt. Her name recognition was sky-high, as were her unfavorable ratings. In a word, Hillary drove Democrats and Republicans crazy, in large part because of the Clintons' successes and in other ways because she figured in so many right-wing conspiracy theories involving corruption, murder, and intrigue.

She launched an exploratory committee to run in January 2007, and many expected her to win the important primary. But Florida's 2008 presidential primary garnered controversy. In the past, Florida's primaries had been held later in the spring than most, and as a result, they lacked drama and relevance. Florida's legislature voted to move the primary to January. If Obama or Clinton expected to add Florida primary arrows to their quivers, they were both disappointed. The Democratic National Committee punished Florida and Michigan for breaking party rules by moving up the primary date. Her rival, Barack Obama, reacted to the news by saying, "No one is more disappointed that Florida Democrats will have no role in selecting delegates for the nomination of the party's standard bearer than Senator Obama."[34]

John Edwards also entered the race for president, announcing his candidacy in late December 2006. Edwards's future looked bright. Many Democrats at the time thought Obama was too young and inexperienced while Clinton was too confrontational. Edwards had earlier served as a U.S. senator and John Kerry's running mate and, according to Obama, "never really stopped campaigning full-time for president." In his memoir, Obama noted that while he did not know Edwards well, he had "never been particularly impressed" with the North Carolinian. Nor apparently were American voters, despite his campaign slogan, "Tomorrow begins today." He was widely criticized for remaining in the race after his wife was diagnosed with cancer. Receiving only 7 percent of the vote in the West Virginia primary, Edwards endorsed Obama. One of his campaign planks, "Providing moral leadership in the world," seems hypocritical considering that his wife was dying of cancer during the primaries and Edwards was engaged in a tawdry affair with a campaign aide. *National Enquirer* broke the story.[35]

Traditionally, opposing parties attempt to define a relatively unknown candidate before he or she can introduce themselves. In 1988 and 2004, early waves of political ads tar-brushed Michael Dukakis and John Kerry. Hillary Rodham Clinton's candidacy unloosed the We Hate Hillary hounds, described as a "Michael Moore–style documentary film, book-length exposes, and websites such as StopHerNow.com and StopHillaryPAC.com. Conservative admirers of the Swift Vets and POWs for Truth media blitz that helped torpedo Sen. Kerry's presidential candidacy in 2004 are now agitating to 'Swift-boat' Clinton."[36]

Obama never underestimated Clinton. He found her more impressive and sympathetic than he first imagined. "Maybe it was because in Hillary's story," wrote Obama, "I saw traces of what my mother and grandmother had gone through: all of them smart, ambitious women who had chafed under the constraints of their times, having to navigate male egos and social expectations." He also understood her "guarded, perhaps overly scripted" demeanor: "Who could blame her, given the attacks she had been subjected to."[37]

Hillary Clinton and Barack Obama dominated the Democratic primaries in 2008. Both candidates were relatively young in 2008: Obama was forty-eight and Hillary was sixty-one. Susan Page, a political observer, summarized the pair simply: "Both are groundbreaking politicians. And Democrats. . . . Their strengths and weaknesses are in some ways opposites." Clinton underestimated the power of social media and the possibilities of technology in tracking voters. Hillary was the establishment front-runner who finished third in the Iowa caucus in January, but she recovered and won the New Hampshire primary. Super Tuesday, held February 5, was critical. Clinton emerged victorious in New York, California, and Massachusetts but only managed to take a small lead over Obama. It was the high-water mark for Clinton; Obama proceeded to win the next eleven primaries. By June, Obama passed the delegate threshold. Clinton suspended her campaign on 7 June. "Well, this isn't exactly the party I'd planned," she told her devastated supporters, "but I sure like the company." She exhorted her supporters, asking them to work "as hard for Barack Obama as you have for me." At the Democratic Convention in Denver, Obama accepted the nomination.[38]

Election Day: 4 November 2008

National Public Radio featured a thoughtful essay on 5 June 2008 on Barack Obama and the possibility, even probability, that a Black man might be elected president of the United States. One person interviewed, Robert Whitit, still believed "that electing a black man as president was impossible" ("Black" was not capitalized in 2008!). Yet Whitit was impressed by the diversity of support: "So many people of non-color have voted for him." He cautioned listeners: "Hey, Florida's been a happening spot over the last three or four elections, eh? Who knows what will happen?"[39]

For all the analyses of why Americans and Floridians embraced Barack Obama, Occam's razor provides a model: Never overanalyze; simplicity is the best guide. Obama was optimistic, likeable, and a proper role model. "We've been watching Barack Obama for two years now," observed conservative columnist David Brooks on the eve of the 2008 election, "and in all that time there hasn't been a moment in which he has publicly lost his self-control. This has been a period of tumult, combat, exhaustion, and crisis. And yet there hasn't been a moment when he displayed rage, resentment, fear, anxiety, bitterness, tears, ecstasy, self-pity or impulsiveness." Occam's razor demands simplicity. The alpha and the omega of the election concerned the economy. As late as September, McCain was ahead in the polls. Wall Street's collapse and the economic reverberations dashed McCain's hopes. The election was decided.[40]

On Election Day, 4 November, Floridians voted for Obama. On election eve, the state was considered a "toss-up" by most of the major pollsters. Fully 75 percent of registered voters turned out, the highest since record-keeping began in 1954. Compared to previous elections, Florida avoided melodrama. "In Palm Beach County," observed the Associated Press, "the epicenter in the 2000 election, voters encountered something they didn't anticipate: tranquility." What shocked many observers was that for the first time since 1996, a Democrat won Florida, and only the second time since Jimmy Carter in 1976. The triumph of a Black man for president was a turning point for America. But what happened, and what did it mean for Floridians?[41]

Barack Obama won 50.9 percent of the votes in Florida. John McCain received 48.1 percent of the vote, while Ralph Nader drew 0.3 percent of support. Obama's victory margin of 2.8 percent signified a confluence of factors. Not surprisingly, he built a firewall by capturing 96 percent of the African-American vote. He also shattered the myth that the Latino vote was indelibly red by claiming 57 percent of Hispanic/Latino voters, and 52 percent of independents. The Gold Coast—Palm Beach, Broward, and Miami-Dade counties—with its Democratic-rich vein of voters—went strongly for Obama. Two of every three voters in Broward, a number approaching a half million, endorsed Obama. Only Gadsden (69.1 percent) and Leon (61.6 percent) counties in the Panhandle voted for Obama with as much vigor. The rest of the Panhandle went solidly for McCain. Eight of every ten voters in the lightly populated counties of Baker and Holmes counties checked the ballot for McCain, while more than seven in ten voters in Dixie, Gilchrist, Lafayette, Suwannee, Union, Walton, and Washington counties endorsed the Arizonan. But McCain won only one large county—Duval—and could not overcome Obama's sweep of the biggest prizes and pieces in Florida.[42]

Obama's success among Latinos and Hispanics buoyed the hopes of many Democrats and analysts who had been pontificating for years that demography is destiny. In 2004, George W. Bush carried Florida, in large part because he won 56 percent of the Hispanic vote. Kevin Baker cautioned, "Demographics is not enough." He points to soothsayers who predicted in 1971 that with the Twenty-Sixth Amendment lowering the voting age to eighteen, the future success of the Democratic Party was ensured. Barack Obama's triumph in 2008 was historic. He provided Florida's Democrats hope, albeit fleetingly.[43]

Obama's strategy of spending relatively little time in the Democratic stronghold of South Florida and concentrating on the swing regions of Central Florida and Jacksonville paid dividends. As expected, Obama won more than two-thirds of the state's Jewish voters. Perhaps the most striking takeaway from Obama's triumph in Florida was his success at capturing voters across income and educational levels. While Obama did not win the state's white vote, he performed better than John Kerry four years earlier. Obama never wavered in his "Yes We Can" focus and demand for "change," a winning message.[44]

On the cultural front, the most controversial ballot measure addressed the definition of a marriage. The Florida Marriage Protection Amendment, also known as Proposition 2, read like it was written in a first-year constitutional law class. It asked voters: "Inasmuch as marriage is the legal union of only one man and one woman as husband and wife, no other legal union that is treated as marriage or the substantial equivalent thereof shall be valid or recognized." Committees raised $10 million to frame the debate. The red-hot measure passed by a vote of 62 percent to 38 percent. California and Arizona voters also banned same-sex marriages. Same-sex civil unions were not an option in Florida. The Reverend Joel Hunter, an evangelist in Florida, contended that religious conservatives in Florida were more energized about this issue than about abortion. Florida governor Charlie Crist zigzagged on the issue. When he was running for governor in 2006, he believed such an amendment was unnecessary because state law already forbade gay marriage. In 2008, candidate Crist explained: "It's not an issue that moves me. I'm just a live and let live kind of guy." When interviewed on Election Day, he told a journalist, "I voted for it. It's what I believe in."[45]

Florida was becoming even more culturally and politically balkanized. The terms "Red States" and "Blue States" seem irrelevant in modern Florida. Blue cities and red counties coexist uneasily in the Sunshine State. Tampa and St. Petersburg glow Democrat whereas Hillsborough and Pinellas counties lean Republican. Almost every large city in Florida tilted Democratic whereas the suburbs and countryside leaned red. Florida's population is in constant flux. Miami-Dade County added 94,000 new voters since January 2008. Liberal cities—Gainesville, Miami Beach, Fort Lauderdale and other cities in Broward County already had domestic partnership registries as a loophole to opponents. "Florida is like Italy in the 15th century," contended Elizabeth Birch, a director of the Human Rights Campaign. As in the time of Dante, defending the wrong candidate, movement, or theological point could mean heresy, banishment, even burning at the stake.[46]

Florida's 18.2 million inhabitants offered politicians premium dividends and colossal headaches. To reach Florida's voters, one had to campaign and advertise in ten media markets. The Obama campaign dispatched 400 staffers to Florida, including five of his most senior operatives. Nearly half of the state's registered Republicans reside in the Tampa Bay–Sarasota and Orlando–Daytona Beach–Melbourne media markets, with 10 percent in Jacksonville and 8 percent in the Fort Myers–Naples markets. The greatest concentration of Republican voters is found along the I-4 Corridor. John McCain won most of the counties along the Corridor, but Obama won the important counties: Pinellas, Hillsborough, Osceola, and Orange. Obama was especially effective improving on the John Kerry vote in every county along I-4. Obama captured the Puerto Rican vote in Osceola County. McCain also won the Panhandle, Florida's most conservative region. The 2008 presidential election was the costliest in American history up to that time, with a price tag of $2.4 billion. The Obama advertising campaign outspent the McCain effort four to one: $2.2 million to $659,000.[47]

But many voters were profoundly dissatisfied with Obama's victory and the prospects of liberal rule. The conservative intellectual David Frum voted for McCain: "I'll do this because I'll be voting as much against Barack Obama—the most liberal Democratic presidential nominee since Walter Mondale—as for John McCain." Indeed, Obama quickly faced an insurgent and resurgent coalition of Republicans, conservative Democrats, and independents.[48]

The 2010 Race for Governor: Rick Scott and the Hostile Takeover of Florida

Florida has elected rags-to-riches governors before as well as Floridians who had barely established residency before becoming governor. Florida has elected governors who despise the Fourth Estate. But Florida had never elected anyone like Rick Scott. Scott's ascendency to the governor's mansion in Tallahassee was nothing short of spectacular. Enduring an impoverished and rootless childhood, Rick Scott lived in public housing for several years. But he succeeded wildly in the world of business and finance. Wealthy candidates have run for office before, but few with deeper pockets who were willing to spend it to be elected like Rick Scott.

When the Scotts moved to Naples in 2003, two-thirds of state residents were born elsewhere. The idea of someone migrating from Florida to Iowa or Indiana and becoming governor in seven years is as unlikely as it is preposterous. In modern Florida, only Sidney Johnston Catts, "the Cracker Messiah," who had lived in Florida a mere five years before running for the state's highest office, had spent less time in the state than Scott before becoming governor.

Born Richard Lynn "Rick" Myers in Bloomington, Illinois, in 1952, Rick Scott was a combination of Horatio Alger, Ragged Dick, and Gordon Gekko. That year, Adlai Stevenson II ran for the presidency. Stevenson was raised in Bloomington's upper-crust neighborhoods. Rick Scott grew up in an environment far different from the local patrician Stevenson, who attended Princeton University and whose family owned a large stake in the local newspaper. Rick never knew his abusive, alcoholic father. In 1954, Rick's mother, Esther Jane, married Orba Scott Jr., a decorated World War II veteran. Orba Scott adopted Rick and his older brother.[49]

As a first-grade student in Texas, Lyndon B. Johnson wrote a poem titled, "I'd Rather Be Mama's Boy." When President Lyndon B. Johnson needed a politician's vote on a crucial bill, he asked his staff a simple question: "Is he a mama's boy or a papa's boy?" If the answer was the former, Lyndon would invite the candidate into the White House West Wing and extend his long arms over the victim's shoulders, congratulating the congressman. "Your mamma will be mighty proud of you when you vote for this new dam." A papa's boy required more jawboning and pork.[50]

Rick Scott was a mama's boy, out of necessity and genuine adoration. He idolized his mother, forever grateful for the pain and suffering she endured to preserve the family. When she died in 2012, he wrote that she "was one of the constants of my life." While a student at North Kansas City High School, Rick Scott fell in love with Frances Annette "Ann" Holland, and they married a few months after his graduation in 1970. The following year, Rick volunteered for the U.S. Navy. His love and respect for the navy and military can be seen when on the campaign trail, as he frequently wears his dark-blue cap emblazoned "NAVY."[51]

A determined, ambitious Scott used the GI Bill to attend the University of Missouri at Kansas City, earning his degree in business. Most undergraduates do not purchase an underperforming donut shop and turn it around and purchase two more shops. His mother managed one of the stores. The profits enabled Rick to attend and graduate from Southern Methodist University's Law School in Dallas. Rick accepted an offer from Johnson & Swanson, a firm called one of "Dallas's fat cat law firms," even though it was established in 1970. A local journalist wrote, "For Johnson & Swanson, that edge lies in being faster, more responsive and more aggressive in seeking out emerging fields of law practice." Scott took special delight opposing lawyers who represented some of the finest families in the Lone Star State.[52]

Scott and his law firm were prepared to take advantage of a revolution that was sweeping America's health-care providers. Texan Lyndon Baines Johnson's

Great Society transformed the way Americans, the elderly, and the poor approached health care. Medicaid and Medicare ensured and insured medical services for the poor and elderly. Law firms realized the myriad opportunities to take advantage of Uncle Sam's deep pockets. Scott worked in his firm's mergers and acquisitions division.[53]

Driven by hard work and soaring ambition, Scott determined that he wanted to own hospitals, not merely represent them. In 1987, Scott and Richard Rainwater each invested $125,000 to form the Columbia Hospital Corporation. Rainwater became a legend in Texas business circles when he managed the wealth of the prominent Bass family into a $5 billion fortune. They first purchased two struggling hospitals in El Paso. Like scenes from the contemporary hit show *Dallas*, these Texas lawyers steered Columbia Hospital Corporation to heady heights. From two hospitals in 1987, the firm merged with the Hospital Corporation of America (HCA) in 1994. Columbia/HCA became the largest hospital chain in the country. By the late 1990s, Columbia/HCA owned 340 hospitals, with earnings soaring to $20 billion. Scott had suddenly become a wizard, named one of *Time* magazine's most influential persons and *Financial World*'s "CEO of the Year." Upon moving to Florida in 2003, Scott struck financial magic once again, creating Solantic, a chain of walk-in clinics.[54]

But Scott's mystique and reputation unraveled on the front pages and business sections in 1997. He was in the vanguard of a movement to turn city/county-owned nonprofit hospitals into private facilities. The FBI raided Columbia/HCA's headquarters, confiscating records, files, and computers. The investigation spread across seven states. Federal officials charged that the company was derelict in its operations, overcharging patients and defrauding the government. Examples included profligate and unneeded lab tests and bribing doctors to send patients to Columbia/HCA's hospitals. Scott was resolute, adamant that he was unaware of such misdeeds. But Scott was so central to the investigation that the corporate board voted to fire the beleaguered CEO. Columbia/HCA paid dearly for the alleged corruption: $1.7 billion in civil and criminal penalties for defrauding Medicare and other government health programs. In a deposition, Scott claimed he did not understand the "exact" definition of "fiduciary duty." Perhaps most damning, Scott pleaded the Fifth Amendment 75 times. To be fair, citing the Fifth Amendment is a constitutional right. To be blunt, the optics of pleading the Fifth 75 times is not a path to leadership. The *Miami Herald*'s Carl Hiaasen was not nearly so polite, writing a column headlined "Scott Is Either Incompetent or a Lying Crook." He added, "The fraud was so massive and institutionalized that this statement can't be taken seriously." The fines imposed upon

CEO Scott were the largest penalty in American history. PolitiFact rated the facts regarding Scott's deposition "mostly true."[55]

Because of its Medicare/senior citizen–rich populace, Southwest Florida attracted Columbia and Rick Scott's interest. In March 1994, Rick Scott's photograph—he still possessed a handsome mane of hair!—appeared on the front page of the *Fort Myers News-Press*. The caption read, "Rick Scott, president and executive officer of Columbia/HCA Healthcare Corp. . . . talks to Cape Coral community leaders during a luncheon at Temple Beth-El. Columbia is one of the three hospital organizations trying to buy Cape Coral Hospital." Scott told the audience, "We have a big commitment to Florida." To many Americans, the community hospital was a precious public resource. *Forbes*, a business magazine, noted that Scott "bought hospitals by the bucketful and promised to squeeze blood from each one." Hospital workers' concerns were summarized: "Chaos, concern, and anxiety." Scott contended that if Columbia purchased the hospital, it would transform the facility and put it on local property tax rolls. A journalist observed, "It's hard to imagine, considering his blue eyes and soft-spoken manner, that this is the same guy magazine readers voted one of the most feared people of Louisville, Ky., where his company is headquartered."[56]

Scott's reputation may have been besmirched by the publicity and fines, but he claimed he walked away proud for having built the corporation and proud for taking responsibility. He also walked away with a fortune: $300 million in stock, a $5.1 million severance, and a $950,000-per-year consulting contract for five years. "What does Scott call that? Taking responsibility?," asked columnist Randy Schultz.[57]

Who was the real Rick Scott? Was he an honest corporate leader caught in the maws of a vindictive government or a scheming, avaricious corporate mogul who stole blood money and walked away with a fortune? In "The Real Rick Scott," *Business Observer* defended Scott, arguing: "Talk to the people who worked by his side, sat on Columbia's board of directors or sat across from him at the negotiating table. The Rick Scott they knew was honest 'as a Boy Scout' and revolutionized health care." When asked how Scott was different from other hospital CEOs in the late 1980s, Josh Nemzoff of Nemzoff & Co. LLC, replied, "He's smarter than all of them." Scott's image to many who worked with him closely was not a Gordon Gekko but a Boy Scout. Scott instituted the "no-jerk" rule at Columbia. Colleagues recalled the worst insult Scott could muster was, "He's not a nice person." Scott never cursed. But the scandal would not go away, hanging around Scott's neck like a cursed albatross.[58]

During the 2010 campaign, the *Miami Herald* quoted Scott's claim that he was unaware of corruption and that he would have cleaned up the mess—if only "somebody told me something was wrong. . . . I take responsibility for what happened on my watch as CEO." But federal investigators did find wrongdoings, such as offering physicians bribes and inflating invoices. The FBI's investigation found nine other types of fraud.[59]

Rick Scott's corporate career was judged according to the political leanings of its analysts. Conservative publications rallied around the successful businessman whereas liberal journalists lacerated the public and private figure. The campaign was brutal. In one commercial, a Scott loyalist addresses the Medicare fraud controversy, claiming: "When Rick Scott's company was fined 20 years ago, he took responsibility, and the company paid every penny. That's what strong leaders do; they take responsibility." Journalist Scott Powers questioned that conclusion. He wrote, "News reports from the time of the scandal say Scott took responsibility only by resigning, and he did that under pressure from corporate board members unhappy with his defiant policy toward an FBI investigation." Moreover, Scott walked away from the $1.7 billion scandal fabulously wealthier.[60]

President Obama's ambitious plan for universal health care was a perfect foil for Rick Scott. Scott may have been involved in the largest Medicare fraud case in history, but he castigated federal efforts to take away individual health-care choice. He invested a fortune in attacking Obama for imposing government control and creating an "innocent-sounding board" to rob Floridians' right to keep their family physician. Obama later countered, in what turned out to be a disastrous claim, "If you like your doctor, you can keep your doctor." Scott vowed that "'Obamacare' is not the law of the land." PolitiFact later named Obama's promise "The Lie of the Year."[61]

In late August 2010, Scott picked up one of his most valuable endorsements on the eve of the primary. Leaders of the Florida TEA (Taxed Enough Already) Party threw their support behind the insurgent gubernatorial candidate. He had only been a candidate for a little more than two months. Scott and his rival Bill McCollum had waged a bitter race. It marked the third time McCollum had waged and lost a statewide race. Marc Ambinder analyzed, "Bill McCollum . . . is as conservative as a Blackberry at an Apple convention. But he has ties to the state's now-discredited Republican establishment . . . and his avuncular, amiable, comfortable-as-a-leather-shoe style just doesn't fit with the times." Scott, the outsider, won by three points. In a headline that would be rewritten in November, the election would be the most expensive primary in state history. Scott declared: "It's sobering news for the special interests today. They know I don't owe them anything." Never had so much money been spent in a primary: more than $70 million. Marc Ambinder, writing for *The Atlantic*, observed presciently: "It is fairly clear that the anti-establishment/anti-Washington/pro-radical revolution plankton are feeding more off Republicans than Democrats. . . . Rick Scott didn't need the money, but the Tea Party Express helped him build a volunteer base."[62]

Alex Sink: The Woman with the Right Stuff at the Wrong Time

Born in 1948 in Mount Airy, North Carolina, the model for Mayberry in *The Andy Griffith Show*, Adelaide Alexander "Alex" Sink had the right stuff but ultimately at the wrong place and time. Upon graduation from Wake Forest University, where she majored in mathematics, she taught school in Sierra Leone and the Congo. One of her role models, Betty Castor, had followed a similar path. Her family tree is so bizarre that *Ripley's Believe It or Not* profiled her great-grandfather in its popular newspaper column. Several novels followed. Sink's great-grandfather was Chang Bunker, a conjoined twin born in Thailand. The brothers Eng and Chang were America's original "Siamese Twins," who settled in Mount Airy. They took the American name of Bunker and married two local Tarheel sisters, daughters of a Baptist minister, and the two couples combined to produce twenty-one children. The twins were still attached! A mere five-inch patch of skin connected the twin brothers at the torso.[63]

Sink took pride in her Asian ancestors, who spent sixty-three years attached at the base of their chests. "I have these memories as a child when we'd go down the street—Main Street, Mount Airy. We'd go into the stores and I remember sometimes the clerks would look at me and say, 'Why you must be one of those Bunkers.' Because I had slanty eyes." She was raised in Chang Bunker's farmhouse. "I would stick my chest out and say, 'Yes, I am.' I was taught to be proud about my heritage and I am." Alex articulated her pride in her family tree: "It's an incredible story about survival, and even thriving, with a disability." Alex was named after Chang's wife, Adelaide. Her "Roots" story reinforces John Finotti's 1999 profile in *Florida Trend:* "She is universally considered a genuinely nice person."[64]

Sink returned to the Tarheel State in the 1970s, having accepted a lowly position as a branch planner with North Carolina National Bank (NCNB). The 1970s and '80s transformed American banking, and North Carolina was a big winner whereas Florida lost local and state control of many of its homegrown financial institutions. "North Carolina banks were amassing size and scale that other out-of-state banks weren't close to approaching," described one economic historian.

He added, "Primed to grow, North Carolina banks were ready when the nationwide barriers to cross-state entry began to fall." A profile of her career noted, "Sink was part of the power structure as Charlotte, N.C.-based NCNB became NationsBank which grew into Bank of America, which became the largest bank in the country." Opponents could not find any banking regulators who criticized Sink.[65]

In the late 1990s, Sink's hard work was recognized: She was named president of Bank of America's Florida operations. She was also rewarded handsomely, earning $2.9 million in 2000, her last year at Bank of America. Sink was also emerging as a political power broker in the Democratic Party, and she and her beloved husband, Bill McBride, were becoming one of the most influential couples in the state. Displaying a populist touch with a southern accent, she was once asked for the secret to her success. She replied earnestly: "I worked harder and had to be smarter. I had to be tough and not take 'no' for an answer."[66]

Bill McBride was one of Tampa's most influential attorneys. He may have been the only English major in America to be elected student body president and play fullback for the University of Florida. He began law school at Gainesville in 1968, but his sense of duty compelled him to quit school and join the U.S. Marine Corps. Volunteering for U.S. Ranger school, he finished first in his class. McBride served as a company commander in Vietnam and received a Bronze Star for valor. The veteran had lots of catching up to do. Returning to law school at the University of Florida, he was inspired by the legendary Chesterfield Smith. After law school, McBride joined Smith's powerful law firm in Tampa, Holland & Knight. McBride and Sink met in Miami, fell in love, got married, and had two children. They invested a great deal of energy in philanthropy and volunteerism, and also became Florida's first husband and wife to run for governor. As early as 1998, Alex's name was mentioned as running mate for Buddy MacKay.[67]

In 2002, McBride narrowly upset the favored Democrat and legend, former U.S. attorney general Janet Reno. McBride took on popular incumbent Jeb Bush for governor. Bush crushed McBride by almost 13 points. Alex Sink knew all too well what it was like to run for governor. She had campaigned for her husband in the 2002 race. "That was a very consuming experience for Alex and our family," admitted Bill. "She's learned a lot of good lessons from it."[68]

In 2002, the press was clearly more interested in Alex Sink's wardrobe and relationship with her husband. One headline read, "Mr. McBride's Bride Proves to Be a Campaign Asset." Alex proved to be a quick study on the campaign trail. In Tampa, the power couple shared a podium. Bill's cell phone rang. "Standing beside him," a journalist observed, "his wife, Adelaide 'Alex' Sink, discreetly felt around his belt to turn off the phone, but the crowd noticed, and people started chuckling. 'Somebody call me again,' shouted McBride."[69]

In a 1999 interview with a business magazine, she discussed her future. "Sink won't rule out anything," the reporter noted. "In 10 years, though, she'll be doing something different." Sink added, "I want to leave a better legacy for Florida." When asked about political aspirations, she said: "I'm interested in seeing more women involved in the political process. Florida hasn't had a woman governor."[70]

Alex Sink seemingly had the wind at her back in her race for governor. Republicans had been at the helm during the Great Recession, and the public wanted to punish someone. She had just finished a term as Florida's chief financial officer, a post she was elected to in 2006. She faced few hurdles in the 2010 primaries. A January 2009 poll provided a bit of optimism but a challenge. While 24 percent of Floridians held a favorable opinion of Alex Sink, only 5 percent held an unfavorable opinion. However, 70 percent of the respondents checked the box: "haven't heard enough." Her opponent was Brian Moore, the 2008 Socialist Party USA nominee for president of the United States. A journalist described Moore as "an independent-turned Socialist-turned Democrat" who challenged Sink, but he ended up as a footnote in the campaign. Moore countered, "She's only run for statewide office once. I've been on the ballot twice in Florida. And she's not exciting."[71]

Ironically, Sink's success as a banker did not guarantee a flood of contributions. Alex Sink had lived a remarkably successful life because of her native intelligence and her instincts. Had she been born a decade or two earlier, she would have faced a much more hostile business environment. She was both a product of the feminist movement and a survivor who proved her worth at the corporate level. Still, she faced an opponent who held two invaluable advantages: timing and money. In 2006, she handed out gold shoe-shaped lapel pins as part of her "Running in Heels" campaign to rally women to vote for her. Neither candidate was well-known statewide. Even though Sink had been elected CFO, that post is the most obscure cabinet position in Tallahassee. Sink had always been at the right place at the right time. In 2010, the unbeatable candidate for governor was Charlie Crist, but she caught a break: he was running for the U.S. Senate. Rick Scott may have been megarich, but he also faced a formidable challenge of explaining his controversial corporate record. If Scott displayed the scars of an embattled CEO, the only occupation that engendered a worse first impression in recession-ravaged 2010 would be a banker, as on Sink's CV. One profile of Sink began: "In a normal election year, Alex Sink's run for governor would play heavily on her successful banking career with Bank of America. But this is no normal election." If Alex Sink was barely known in 2010 Florida, Rick Scott was virtually invisible, outside his neighborhood in Naples and country club. Could he reinvent himself? The battlefield favored the GOP because 2010 was an off-year election, traditionally blessing the party out of power.

The gods of fortune and timing smiled upon Rick Scott. It was the year of the outsider, and Scott, the insider corporate executive, managed to define himself as an outsider. The conservative tide was rising, buoying Scott and other Republicans. In May 2009, the *Charlotte Observer,* the leading newspaper in North Carolina, published an article titled "Former Charlottean Alex Sink May Run for Governor—of Florida." The piece speculated that Governor Crist's decision to run for the U.S. Senate could open the door to the governor's mansion. While the reintroduction of Ms. Sink was positive, "anonymous comments" exemplified the era's toxic environment. One comment announced, "Emily's List, a group that supports women candidates who favor abortion rights, Monday asked supporters to back Sink." Another noted, "Her grandpappy's house is up for sale in Wilkes County—watch out for democrats to renovate it with federal $$$."[72]

Scott caught a huge break in late July 2010. A federal appeals court allowed Scott to spend millions of his own wealth while skirting a Florida law enacted to limit the influence of big money in Florida politics. Prior to the ruling, Scott faced a $24.9 million spending cap as dictated by Florida's public financing law. U.S. District Judge Robert Hinkle ruled that the public finance law infringed upon Scott's freedom of speech. At the time of the ruling, Scott was struggling against Bill McCollum in the Republican primary.[73]

Sink was fighting conservative headwinds, a result of the nascent Tea Party movement and successes the GOP had made at the local level in recruiting candidates and raising funds. The 2010 gubernatorial election was the most expensive in state history. Sink also battled a candidate with no political record, an opponent who focused upon a single theme, which he repeated like a tocsin: "Jobs, Jobs, Jobs!" Such a mantra registered with Floridians facing unemployment and a cratered economy. Sink also stumbled during the 25 October debate. During a break, Sink's makeup artist handed the candidate a two-sentence message on a cell phone that recommended Sink not allow Scott to keep talking about her. Scott noticed Sink looking at cell phone and announced the breach of protocol.[74]

While education was the most volatile issue in the earlier McBride-Bush race, the 2010 flash points concentrated on the economy. Florida remained in the throes of a terrible recession, and voters wanted answers and relief. "I'm going to focus on reinventing our state, about how to further diversify our economy, how to bring good paying jobs into the state," Sink pledged. In June 2009, she boasted of having already raised $1.2 million for reelection to her cabinet position, funds she could transfer to the governor's race. A million dollars may have been eye-popping in twentieth-century races, but the new century, a new media, and a win-at-all-costs philosophy required staggering amounts of campaign spending. Veteran politicos gasped in 1994, when the gubernatorial race between Lawton Chiles and Jeb Bush cost $17.5 million. Just sixteen years later, the 2010 governor's race in Florida cost the candidates and parties more than $100 million. Scott was not joking when he announced at his campaign headquarters on election night, "Florida is open for business." Scott, the maverick outsider, spent $70 million of his own fortune.[75]

Seismic political shifts took place within Florida and across America as voters arrived at the polls in 2010. Sunshine State conservatives—some with tea bags hanging from their hats—recoiled from Barack Obama's early years in office and the harsh-tasting medicine that was supposed to be good for them. Their efforts percolated and filtered across the landscape, as they attempted to retake seats from local school boards and commissions, to their county seats and Tallahassee, and in Congress, the White House, and—indirectly—the U.S. Supreme Court; redraw maps to gerrymander and preserve power; and embrace a new brand of identity politics that had a different taste flavored by the potent brew of the online media surrounding them. Those wanting thick mud or *café cubano* no longer were satisfied with the tepid, moderate platforms of yesteryear's middle-of-the-road Republicans, as Crist and others would soon discover.

14

Florida, 2008–2010

Political "Crist"-enings, "Rubio" Red Harvests, and "Sink"-ing Blue Poll Numbers

Politics Makes Strange Bedfellows: The Hugs That Made History

When the presidential election season ended in November 2008, most politicians recovered and ruminated. One got married! Charlie Crist married Carole Rome in December 2008. Carole Oumano was a New Yorker, growing up on suburban Long Island. Her grandfather had founded the Franco-American Novelty Company in 1910. Born in 1969, Carole was a loyal Republican who graduated from Georgetown University. Carole worked as an accountant and auditor, taking over the family's business in 2000. She famously rebranded her father's company with the slogan, "Where Fashion Meets Halloween." Carole was a *fashionista* in New York City circles. While her business prospered, her first marriage foundered, and she sued for divorce in 2008. She began spending more time in Palm Beach and her home on Fisher Island and Miami Beach.[1]

Carole met Charlie Crist in New York City in 2006. She hosted a major fundraiser for Crist in 2007 at Trump Tower. The dashing couple dropped by John McCain's ranch in Sedona, Arizona. The Fourth Estate speculated that Crist's engagement might help his vice-presidential prospects. The celebrity couple attended a White House dinner in March 2009. His marriage proposal was pure Crist. He purchased the engagement ring at a local St. Petersburg shopping plaza. After a romantic dinner, he planned to propose at his downtown condominium. But as the couple entered Bayfront Tower, a friend invited them to watch the Tampa Bay Rays play the Boston Red Sox in his condo. "The governor," explained local reporters, "did not get his job by disappointing people," so he and his date watched the first seven innings. By then, the timing seemed awkward, so he popped the question the next morning. "With a word—"Yes!"—Carole Rome became Florida's first fiancée, the curiosity of the state," concluded the local journalists. Their wedding in St. Petersburg, Florida, on 12 December 2008 was lovely and historic. Not since Claude Kirk had a governor of Florida married while in office.[2]

In December 2008, Crist's greatest challenge was not surrendering his bachelorhood but lifting the anvil of the Great Recession. For all the misfortune that occurred in the years after 2007, Crist still garnered high approval ratings. Yet in a single moment that seemed operatic—imagine Rodolfo touching Mimi's cold hands and singing "*Che gelida manina!*"—Crist's life turned upside down. If his governorship were compressed into a single frame, *the* event occurred on 10 February 2009. President Obama had only been in office for three weeks, but he realized Florida needed a lifeline.

Obama also had an agenda: atop the president's shopping list was his need to pass a $787 billion American Recovery and Reinvestment bill. The only politician who was more eager than Obama to see the bill passed was the governor of Florida, who hoped desperately needed aid would follow. Fort Myers, a community flattened by the Great Recession, served as a perfect setting. Charlie Crist thrived in such settings. He assured his fellow Floridians: "This is not about partisan politics. This is about rising above that, helping America, and reigniting our economy." Crist recollected "the rest of the story" in a *Time* magazine article:

> Ladies and gentlemen, please give a warm Florida welcome to President Barack Obama.
>
> He walked out toward me.
>
> Both of us smiled.
>
> The applause was just about frantic. We shook hands. The new president leaned forward and gave me a hug.
>
> Reach.
>
> Pull.
>
> Release.
>
> As hugs go, it wasn't anything special. It was over in a second—less than that.
>
> It was the kind of hug that says, "Hey, good to see you, man. Thanks for being here. . . ."

I didn't think a thing about it as it was happening. But it changed the rest of my life.[3]

In his 2020 presidential memoir, Obama put the events in perspective:

> Not every Republican picked up on the rapidly shifting mood within their own party. On the day the Senate was to vote on the Recovery Act, I found myself in Fort Myers, Florida, at a town-hall style meeting meant to drum up public support for the bill and allow me to answer questions about the economy. Joining me was Florida governor Charlie Crist, a moderate Republican with a friendly, polished demeanor and the kind of good looks—tanned, silver-haired, sparkling white teeth—that seemed straight out of central casting. Crist was highly popular at the time. . . . He also knew that his state was in big trouble.[4]

Obama also elaborated on the "bro hug":

> It was out of both temperament and necessity, then, that Crist agreed to introduce me. . . . [T]he crowd was raucous and energized that day . . . still swept up in what Sarah Palin would later call the "hopey, changey stuff." After Crist offered up a reasonable, somewhat cautious explanation of why he supported the Recovery Act . . . I gave the governor what was my standard "bro hug"—a handshake, an arm around the back for a pat, an appreciative look in the eye, a thank-you in the ear.
>
> Poor Charlie. How could I know that my two-second gesture would prove to be a political kiss of death for him? . . . In a matter of months, Crist went from a Republican star to a pariah. . . . [T]he immediate lesson was not lost on a lot of congressional Republicans.[5]

Journalist Chris Cillizza called the moment "the most (in)famous political hug, ever." The public reaction to the event, an innocent hug, reverberated. Obama's election had unleashed a hysterical, toxic brew of racism, xenophobia, and insecurity. Republicans were already nonplussed by Crist's avowed support of his $787 billion economic stimulus package. A mere nine days after the hug, a new movement found its footing. Charlie Crist may have been the first victim of the "Tea Party" before the movement had a name. In January 2010, the *New York Times Magazine*'s lead article was titled "The First Senator from the Tea Party?" Author Mark Leibovich contended that the movement arose not because of Charlie Crist but as a reaction to his "consensus-seeking, deal-making, and bipartisanship—three particularly vulgar notions to a simmering Tea Party movement on the right." Leibovich boldly predicted in early January 2010 that Marco Rubio will become "the first senator from the Tea Party."[6]

To paraphrase Christopher Marlowe, "Was this the photograph that launched a thousand attack ads?" Print defines, photographs amplify. Poets, playwrights, and novelists employ material evidence for blackmail and revenge (*The Purloined Letter, Othello,* and *Advise and Dissent*). Rarely has a simple photograph morphed into a scandal that destroyed, rearranged, and elevated careers. The reality—and when considering the number of political dominoes that fell and the career-altering consequences—is that Crist's decision to *not* run for reelection for governor may be one of the most consequential decisions in Florida political history. He would have won reelection in a landslide. Had Crist been reelected as Florida governor, Marco Rubio might have been remembered as a minor-major Republican state legislator and Rick Scott would have been remembered as a controversial CEO who led health conglomerates to fame and misfortune. But an alternative version of Florida history never occurred because U.S. Senator Mel Martínez, a staunch Catholic, had a Lutheran moment when he decided that here he stood, he could do nothing else.

Mel and Charlie: The Politics of Conscience and Resignation; 2009–2010

Mel Martínez and Charlie Crist were strikingly similar. Immigration had profoundly shaped their experiences. They were both handsome, articulate, and grew up essentially small-town boys whom everyone liked and admired. They both attended Florida State University and became lawyers. Both advanced through the ranks of the Republican Party. They were elected to their dream jobs back-to-back in 2004 and 2006. They were the fresh personalities of the Republican Party.

Senator Martínez was much more willing than the governor to fight for principles, and no issue mattered more to him personally or politically than immigration. In 2006, Karl Rove and President Bush urged Martínez to come to the aid of his party and serve as the head of the Republican National Committee. "What we need is a new face for the party," Bush insisted. Martínez later reminisced: "It was a big mistake, one of the worst I've ever made. But when the president calls, it's hard to say no."[7]

In 2007, the senator's steadfast effort to reform immigration ran into the Scylla and Charybdis of nativism and partisan politics. Threading an immigration bill that would please Democrats and just enough Republicans was challenging at best, risky at worst. To the Cuban émigré, the immigration issue was more personal than political. He knew illegals who worked hard, obeyed the laws, and desperately believed in the American dream. Among the prickly issues: What to do with the 12 million illegal immigrants who lived and worked in America? "It was the moment of truth for legislation that would make the most profound changes in immigration policy in more than 20 years," explained a *New York Times* observer. Mel's indelible photographic moment occurred when "the lion" of immigration reform, U.S. Senator Ted Kennedy, walked across the Senate chamber and put his arm around Martínez. As cameras clicked, Kennedy whispered to his "ally": "I thought your Republican friends might like this picture." Martínez's biographer observed, "When the picture of him standing arm in arm with Ted Kennedy appeared the next day in the *Orlando Sentinel*, the bill's passage was probably doomed." Indeed, the immigration bill collapsed. The Left and Right fringe votes overwhelmed the consensual middle. Senators, such as his friend and fellow Republican Pete Domenici of New Mexico, left him at the altar. He was also furious at Senator Jeff Sessions of Alabama, who proclaimed that supporters of the bill had "declared war on the American people." Rush Limbaugh lampooned the immigration bill as the "Comprehensive Destroy the Republican Party Act."[8]

By the summer of 2008, amid a bruising presidential election in which he realized he had much more in common with the Democratic candidate, Barack Obama, than with his own party's nativist drift, Mel Martínez resigned as head of the Republican National Committee. Mel Martínez had already compressed more into one eventful life than almost anyone imaginable. His brother Ralph told a scholar shortly before Mel's swearing in as a U.S. senator in 2005, "Mel is the luckiest son of a gun I know." Fleeing Fidel Castro and his beloved Cuba, Mel wound up in Central Florida through good fortune and the designs of the Roman Catholic Church, which took thousands of Cuban youth and resettled them in the United States. Mel's ascendancy in Orange County was nothing short of spectacular. In 2004, he defeated educator and college president Betty Castor in a tight race that the winner regretted for its name-calling. Politics and Washington had taken a toll on the sixty-two-year-old senator. He arranged a press conference on 2 December 2008 to make another important announcement. "The inescapable truth for me," he said, "is that the call to public service is strong, but the call to home, family, and lifelong friends is even stronger."[9]

Martínez hated the glare of the Washington press corps, the increasingly bitter political partisanship, the staffing controversies, but most of all, he was a family-first man in a me-first town. The 2008 rout by Barack Obama convinced the senator that he would not seek reelection in 2010. He announced to Floridians at his December press conference that he was not running for reelection. Shockingly, Mel Martínez was leaving a dream job as U.S. senator because he loved his wife and family more than power and glory. In May 2009, Crist dropped a bombshell: The governor declared his interest in running for the open Senate seat.[10]

More drama and still another press conference followed. Upon reflection and soul searching, Martínez announced on 7 August 2009 that he was resigning his position as U.S. senator. He finished his remarks, "No regrets or any complaining or anything." Senator Martínez promised that he would remain in the Senate until Governor Crist named a replacement. The unexpected decision placed Governor Crist in an uncomfortable situation. The press corps was abuzz, but with more questions than answers. Why would Crist not run for an almost certain reelection given his poll numbers and popularity? Would Crist be so bold as to appoint himself as senator nineteen months before his gubernatorial term expired? Was Crist's motivation more personal than political? Gossipers chattered that Mrs. Crist was spending little time in the state's capital, that she preferred Georgetown to Tallahassee. When asked about a future in Washington, D.C., she replied: "I think it would be great. It's a fabulous city."[11]

Who would Crist appoint to the prestigious Senate seat? Governor Crist and George LeMieux had forged a winning team. LeMieux had managed Crist's 2006 campaign to become governor. But he pleaded for Crist to run for reelection and *not* run for the Senate vacancy. Crist appointed LeMieux to fill Martínez's seat in Washington, confident that LeMieux would not become fond of the Washington establishment and run for the position. This may have been Crist's greatest misstep, not listening to his trusted advisor.

The second-biggest blunder? When economist Milton Friedman proclaimed in 1965, "We are all Keynesians now," he could not have envisioned a Black president, social media, or the sheer size of the Obama stimulus plan. If hugging a Democratic president was unwise, supporting a Democratic president's $787 billion stimulus bill was the equivalent of playing Russian roulette. Republican governors were sharply divided over the best strategy to help struggling homeowners, citizens, and businesses. Crist was one of a handful of Republican governors who gladly accepted funds from Washington. Crist was also one of the few who went on television to defend his policy. "I think he [Obama] is on the right track," said Crist on NBC's *Meet the Press*, adding, "We still have declining revenues and have to cut the budget." But many Florida Republicans acted like mid-nineteenth-century "Barnburners," willing to see the barn burn to rid the building of rats. President Obama might have erected a sign for Republicans who considered accepting stimulus funds: "Cooperate with the Obama administration at your peril." In the U.S. House of Representatives, the vote in 2009 was 246–183, with not a single Republican supporting the historic measure. At the time the economy was shedding 800,000 jobs per month. In comparison, most Republicans supported President Roosevelt's Social Security Bill in 1935.[12]

The Recovery Act marked a line in the sand for Republicans. "This was the moment I realized what was at stake," Marco Rubio recollected.[13]

Rubio Rising

Jeb Bush was the 800-pound gorilla *not* in the race. Had Bush thrown his hat into the ring, few would have dared to take on the party's most respected figure. In late 2008, "a close source" said that he was seriously considering a run after "an outpouring of public support." But Bush squashed the rumor in early January 2009, saying that "now is not the right time to return to elected office." The press speculated that former senator Connie Mack IV or U.S. Rep. Vern Buchanan would run. The name Marco Rubio was not on any short list.[14]

One could easily argue that Marco Rubio, not Rick Scott, was the darkest horse and most unlikely candidate to leap from near obscurity to the U.S. Senate in 2010. Rubio vaulted out of South Florida to vindicate Jeb Bush's prediction of greatness. In 1996, Rubio volunteered in Bob Dole's ill-fated presidential campaign. In 1998, the twenty-six-year-old Rubio won his first election, to the West Miami City Commission. Jeb Bush wrote a $50 check to support the young candidate. Rarely has a senatorial candidate begun at such a low rung of elective politics. He served as the City Commission's junior-most member, only two years removed from law school. There he sharpened his communications skills. It was there that he praised the genius of small government, clashing with members over garbage fees and police patrolling on bicycles.[15]

In swift succession, Rubio served as majority whip and Speaker of the Florida House, becoming the first southern Republican since Reconstruction to preside over a Republican-majority legislature. Governor Bush presented Rubio with the mythical sword of Chang in 2005, the unofficial tap on the shoulder as his successor and next conservative champion. "I have a special place in my heart for him [Rubio]," Bush told Charlie Rose. "It's hard to describe the pride I feel for his incredible success."[16]

Rubio reminds audiences of his roots. Journalist Michael Grunwald profiled him in *Time* magazine: "Rubio comes from a family of immigrants and married into another family of immigrants and lives in a neighborhood of immigrants,

West Miami, the bilingual bedroom community where he came of age and began his dazzling ascent." In 2010, he became the Tea Party's answer to Barack Obama. Grunwald points out that he is not only a child of immigrants but a child of the conservative movement. Rubio's greatest role model was his Castro-hating grandfather Pedro Victor García, who had left the island in August 1962. Lacking proper credentials, he was almost deported, a predicament Rubio's critics pointed out many recent refugees face.[17]

No Marco Rubio speech omits that phrase that he is a "son of exiles," the son of parents fleeing tyranny. Researchers detect flaws in his compelling story. In Rubio's telling, they escaped Castro's tyranny. But it turns out that his parents' migration is more conventional. The fact is, Rubio's grandparents left Cuba before Fidel seized power. Rubio insisted, "I'm going off the oral history of my family." Mario Rubio received his Social Security card in Florida in 1956, and his maternal grandfather received his card in 1956–57.[18]

Once Rubio caught traction, his rise was meteoric. As early as January 2009, *Politico* boosted the youthful Cuban: "An acolyte of former GOP Gov. Jeb Bush, Rubio is a telegenic conservative with a Newt Gingrich-like knack for coming up with policy proposals, even writing a book called, '100 Innovative Ideas for Florida's Future.'" Leaders cautioned that Rubio was virtually unknown outside South Florida.[19]

Democrats and Republicans understood the rare opportunity to win one of the most prestigious political seats. Some commentators believed Crist's bold maneuver threatened Republican control in Florida. "It's going to be a complete shakeup from top to bottom of the Florida political landscape," said GOP fundraiser Ana Navarro. "The political season could be more active than our hurricane season." Justin Sayfie, a political analyst and former aide to Jeb Bush, believed Democrats could take advantage of the chaos: "It's the biggest opportunity they've had in decades. This is a golden opportunity for Democrats to regain control of the Florida cabinet." In what seemed like a Hail Mary desperation pass, in early March 2009, Marco Rubio, a state representative from Miami, announced that he was launching an exploratory campaign website. In his video, he rails at Obama's stimulus package, not so slyly calling out Crist: After lacerating Florida's leaders in Washington who supported Obama, he added that unfortunately, "even some Republicans here in Florida have embraced this idea." Rubio quickly specified Charlie Crist as the poster Republican who betrayed party and people.[20]

In March 2009, Marco Rubio called Tom DiMatteo, a Republican leader in Pinellas County, about an important plan. On 6 March, Rubio, DiMatteo, and three other Republicans met at a private booth at Bascom's Chop House in Clearwater. Rubio, who drove from Miami, nearly floored his guests when he asked what they thought of his prospects running for the U.S. Senate. Only five weeks earlier, Rubio had told a *St. Petersburg Times* reporter that Crist was clearly "the best candidate" for the position. But DiMatteo and his guests were becoming increasingly concerned about Governor Crist's conduct. When the infamous Fort Myers Obama hug came up, DiMatteo shrugged, "A picture's worth a thousand words." He agreed to commission straw polls to gauge Republicans' discontent with the governor. The die was cast.[21]

Rubio was little known outside South Florida, but he was a darling of the conservative GOP and a hand-picked favorite of former governor Jeb Bush. In his announcement that he was entering the race for the U.S. Senate, Rubio ridiculed Crist as a fake Republican, proclaiming: "Some believe the path to security and prosperity is a larger government involvement in our economy. The majority of us don't agree with that." Republican Congresswoman Ileana Ros-Lehtinen warned that "diehard Republicans are still mad at Charlie" because of his economic policies. And in what might be the cruelest cut of all, acting Senator George LeMieux joined Marco Rubio at several campaign rallies. LeMieux quoted Charlie Crist when asked by Larry King if the governor was disappointed about the vice-presidential snub. "No," quipped Crist, "I was impressed at Gov. Palin being picked. . . . I think she'll be a great candidate." Attack ads broadcast Charlie Crist speaking at a Christian Family Coalition breakfast in February 2010: "I am pro-life, I'm pro-gun, I'm pro-family and I'm anti-tax. And I have always been." An editorial headline in the *Florida Times-Union* encapsulated the significance of the fight: "U.S. Senate Race May Be a Contest for GOP's Soul."[22]

For months, polls bolstered Crist's unwavering confidence. The assistant director of the Quinnipiac University Polling Institute observed in late January 2009: "It is impressive at this time of national Obamamania that Gov. Crist's favorability rating is slightly higher than that of the new President. . . . Charlie Crist looks like a very strong candidate for re-election." Between June and early August 2010, Crist was leading his opponent by double digits, at one time by 35 points. Labor union leaders endorsed Crist.[23]

Congress's passage of Obama's Recovery Act turbo-charged Rubio's campaign. Rubio denounced Crist for his "horrifying decision" to support the president "He was the only Republican governor to campaign for stimulus money." Republican conservatives coined a new word, "Porkulus," for the many larded projects. In Florida, Rubio derided a $3.4 million "Turtle Tunnel," an environmental effort to keep imperiled animals from being squashed on an Everglades back road. Posters appeared at rallies with signs: "Stimulus: The Audacity of Dopes," and "Hey, Barack, Go Stimulate Yourself."[24]

Crist's timing was pitch-imperfect and off-tune. The Republican Party, intensified by the Tea Party rebellion and the anger at President Obama, had little room, let alone patience, for the moderate wing, as represented by Charlie Crist. The pivot to the right came fast and furious. By late 2009, Rubio was gaining traction and tied with Crist for the lead. One Republican fundraiser underscored Crist's frustration. In November 2009, the Alachua County Republican Party hosted a fundraiser. Crist, Rubio, and conservative diva Laura Ingraham attended. Crist's stump speech was repeatedly interrupted with epithets and jabs, such as, "Why don't you hug Obama again?" In Orlando, George P. Bush, the son of former governor Jeb Bush and grandson of President George H. W. Bush, made headlines when he excoriated Governor Crist for endorsing President Obama's stimulus bill. Addressing a national conference of Young Republicans, Bush broke Ronald Reagan's Eleventh Commandment, arguing: "There's some in our party that want to assure that government is the answer to all of our problems. I'm not going to name any names."[25]

April 2010 was Crist's cauldron and crucible. On April Fool's Day, the path to the U.S. Senate was open; two weeks later, the candidate imploded in a series of missteps. "All in all, it was a Charlie Crist kind of week," wrote Neal B. Freeman in *National Review,* one of many right-leaning publications that had never felt comfortable with Crist's conservative creds but had now declared war. "In the span of five business days, the governor managed to sandbag his legislative allies, embarrass his predecessor, alienate his mentor, rile his campaign staff, solidify his new base in the teachers' union, and win oodles of media attention, much of it glowing with fresh esteem." What hath Crist wrought? "By vetoing the education-reform bill he had promised only weeks earlier to support, he seemed to be growing in office at a pace agreeable even to the *New York Times.*" Freeman continued his verbal assault: "Charlie Crist doesn't do bedrock principle. He is the kind of man who, when he looks you in the eye and announces he 'firmly supports educational reform,' makes you muse to yourself, 'I wonder what he meant by that?' I have described the governor elsewhere as a man of no fixed ideological address." Crist's veto of the GOP-controlled legislature's measure that would make it easier to fire teachers based on student performance, a principled act, was the breaking point. Former senator Connie Mack IV, upset with the candidate's decision-making, quit as chairman for Crist's campaign. A few days later, Mitt Romney spurned Crist, endorsing Marco Rubio. Senate majority leader Mitch McConnell, who had been a fervent Crist supporter, backed away when a journalist asked about the Florida governor. He replied that Floridians must make that choice. A Rubio Republican wave was cresting. Journalist Ken Rudin concluded in April that there was "no longer any suspense" as to who would win the August primary. The only question was Crist's future. Would he dare switch parties or run as an independent?[26]

Since late April 2009, Rubio's poll numbers had surged. A hometown journalist asked the question of the day: "Is there room in the Republican Party for Charlie Crist?" U.S. Senator Arlen Specter had just switched from the Republican Party to Democrat, but such successful cases were rare. By the end of April, Crist announced, in front of a cheering hometown crowd, that he was abandoning the GOP to run as an independent for the U.S. Senate. He became the first elected governor in Florida *not* to run for reelection since Farris Bryant in 1964. Crist joined a long list of prominent Florida politicians who had switched parties and survived. Bob Martínez had been a registered Democrat, a social science public school teacher, head of the Hillsborough County Teachers Union, and mayor of Tampa. In 1981, President Ronald Reagan invited Martínez to the White House. Weeks later, he changed his voter's registration card to Republican. In the 1980s, as part of the Reagan Revolution, dozens of prominent conservative Democrats also switched parties. But campaign trails were littered with the skeletons of candidates who dared to switch parties. U.S. Senator George LeMieux met with Crist and assured the media that the question of Crist bolting the party and running as an independent "didn't even come up." LeMieux's remarks prompted journalist Adam Smith to write: "Really?! You were his campaign manager, chief of staff, close friend, and you didn't mention the topic that the political universe is talking about?"[27]

Even more humbling, a straw poll showed Crist losing to Rubio in Pinellas, his home county. Bad news came in waves. The governor's hand-picked chair of the Republican Party was under investigation for fraud and illegal activities. In 2013, Jim Greer pleaded guilty to four counts of theft and one count of money laundering and was sentenced to 18 months' incarceration. Greer went to prison. Later, Greer confided the circumstances of his rapid rise and downfall to author Peter Golenbock in *The Chairman: The Rise and Betrayal of Jim Greer.* Readers encountered a scheming Crist. A journalist profiled Greer in 2013:

> He once controlled the Republican Party of Florida, flying on chartered jets, drinking top-shelf bourbon and mingling with the rich and powerful. Now Jim Greer lives at Gulf Forestry Camp, a low-security prison in a

remote patch of the Florida Panhandle and a world away from the life he lived as a confidant of former Gov. Charlie Crist. . . . The man who used to answer to "Chairman" has a new title: Inmate No. C07705.[28]

On the campaign trail and on television and radio, Rubio pummeled Crist, telling crowds: "I voted for you [Crist] because I trusted you when you said you would be a Jeb Bush Republican. Your record was something very different. You signed a budget that raised taxes. . . . You appointed liberal supreme court judges . . . There are people who believe the way to be more successful as Republicans is to be more like Democrats." *National Review*, a conservative publication, elevated Rubio to the cover of its publication in 2009. The cover story quoted Jeb Bush: "He's got all the tools. . . . He's charismatic and has the right principles."[29]

Many Floridians simply wanted the governor to govern and confront home-front issues. Others questioned Crist's ambitions. "It's fair for Floridians to ask whether Charlie Crist can be a candidate for Senate and a tireless advocate for the state, as governor, during the next two difficult years," editorialized the *Gainesville Sun*. "There's a lot of time between now [May 2009] and the 2010 Senate elections in Florida. That means Crist will spend a lot of time with the equivalent of two jobs: running for a new office and trying to run the state."[30]

In a manner of mere months, the political landscape of Florida imploded and exploded. In an understatement, journalist Damien Cave wrote that Crist's decision creates "a domino effect." Indeed, the dominoes fell harder and faster than anyone could have imagined.

On 12 May 2010, Crist ended the suspense and announced that he was a candidate for the U.S. Senate. He was not alone.

Morning Joe, Senators Smith and Mack, and Congressman Buchanan

In early 2009, Joe Scarborough was becoming a national celebrity. He had already packed much into his forty-six years, serving as an attorney, a rock musician and composer, a newspaper publisher, a football coach, and Harvard fellow. Since 1994 he had been a Republican U.S. congressman representing Pensacola. His decision to resign his congressional seat in 2001 shocked West Florida and the political establishment. His divorce and the sudden death of a political aide prompted rumors that have never been confirmed. Scarborough, whom many regarded as one of the brightest figures in Washington and Florida, may have left the congressional limelight, but he soon entered the celebrity glare. He hosted a popular MSNBC show called *Morning Joe*. One critic described *Morning Joe* as "the most consistently engaging morning talk show on cable television" and "the Algonquin Round Table on steroids, or at least Vivarin."[31]

In February 2009, the cable news impresario was in Bradenton, addressing the Manatee County Republican Party's annual Lincoln Day dinner. While most politicians no longer literally toss a hat into the ring, even fewer write thoughtful books to announce their presence. In *The Last Best Hope: Restoring Conservatism and America's Promise*, Scarborough was being Scarborough, scolding Republicans for not taking the environmental threat more seriously and expanding the party base. When asked by the *Sarasota Herald-Tribune* about running for Senator Martínez's seat, he confessed, "I haven't closed it off." He added that GOP fundraisers had been pushing him to run. Joe's most significant remarks came when he candidly said that he needed to decide whether he would have more influence as one of 100 senators in Washington or as the host of the *Morning Joe* cable show. The timing and place of his remarks were interesting since Sarasota congressman Vern Buchanan was also considering running for the open seat. Party loyalists had also been urging popular former U.S. senator Connie Mack IV to return to office. But in early April 2009, he announced that he would not be a candidate. "As you contemplate your political future," Mack wrote Charlie Crist, "I will be your strongest supporter and champion—regardless of whether you seek re-election or election to the Senate." Scarborough never officially entered the 2010 race for U.S. Senate. Perhaps he realized the MSNBC stage was more rewarding and more profitable than the U.S. Capitol.[32]

The opportunity to win a Senate seat attracted a crowd. Robert C. Smith had moved to Sarasota after serving as a U.S. senator for New Hampshire from 1991 to 2003. He believed the Republican Party needed a "true conservative." One article began, "Bob Smith is ditching the Granite State for the Grapefruit League." Curiously, Smith endorsed John Kerry in 2004. But Smith dropped out of the race in March 2010, citing fundraising difficulties. Bill McCollum, Florida's attorney general who lost Senate bids in 2000 and 2004, said he was exploring the opportunity. But in early April 2009, he announced that he would not be a candidate. In the end, Scarborough, Connie Mack IV, and Vern Buchanan chose to keep their day jobs and not walk along the senatorial tightrope.[33]

Democratic Candidates for the U.S. Senate

The ideological and personal rupture between Charlie Crist and Marco Rubio should have placed the Democratic candidate for the U.S. Senate in an ideal position to return the seat to the Party of Jackson. Three candidates vied for the nomination. For years, commentators employed the baseball term "weak bench" to describe the woes of the state Democratic Party. Never was that term more apt than in 2010. Rarely had the party recruited such weak candidates to pursue such a coveted job.

The U.S. Senate opportunity was tantalizing. The *Washington Post* speculated that U.S. Rep. Ron Klein, Florida banker and CFO Alex Sink, and Tampa mayor Pam Iorio might be interested. Klein chose to run for reelection and lost the congressional race. Sink ran for chief financial officer and won the election.[34]

Ironically, Kendrick Meek enjoyed one of the smoothest paths to a primary victory for a U.S. senator. The son of Carrie Meek, a courageous and well-known African-American congresswoman and icon in South Florida, Kendrick Brett Meek was born in Miami in 1966. A star football player at Florida A&M University, he later served in the Florida Highway Patrol, making history by becoming the first Black man to be promoted to the rank of captain. He was elected to the Florida House of Representatives in 1994. Joining with others to protest Governor Bush's "One Florida" in 2003, he became the first African American to succeed his mother in the U.S. Congress.[35]

Kendrick Meek had wrapped up the nomination by March 2010, prompting journalist Adam Smith to ask, "It seems an insane question to raise 604 days before Florida elects its next U.S. senator: Is Kendrick Meek already on the verge of walking away with the Democratic nomination?" The Democratic establishment candidate had already picked up endorsements from former president Bill Clinton and several powerful unions.[36]

Democratic icons—Bill and Hillary Clinton and Al Gore—campaigned for Meek. On 30 October, Al Gore spoke to a boisterous crowd at the Tampa Convention Center. "I'm going to choose my words carefully," Gore promised. "It's an old charge in politics when somebody flip flops. It's a little unusual to have somebody flip flop and then flop flip. I like the guy [Crist]. I do not really know where he stands."[37]

Other candidates emerged to run for the Democratic nomination. State Senator Dan Gelber and the mayor of North Miami Beach challenged Meek. A native of Miami Beach, Gelber hired several veterans of the Obama campaign to help his efforts. He reconsidered and chose to run for state attorney general, eventually losing to Pam Bondi. Finally, the mayor of North Miami, Kevin Burns, announced his interest in the seat. Burns was also openly gay, reinforcing the point that the Democratic Party had a very big tent.[38]

The most fascinating candidate to run for the U.S. Senate in 2010—in Florida or anywhere—may have been Jeff Greene. Raised in New England, Jeff's mother, a Hebrew school teacher, drilled in her son "to save his pennies, look for value, and never pay retail." His parents moved to West Palm Beach when Jeff was a teenager. He bussed tables at the Breakers, graduated from Johns Hopkins University, acquired an MBA from Harvard, and prospered in Southern California. Greene first ran for office in California as a Ronald Reagan Republican and lost. A journalist described him in 2008 as a "Beverly Hills real estate mogul who single-handedly shorted subprime. His $50 million investment is up tenfold." He only recently moved "back" to Florida.[39]

Jeff Greene's wealth made him an easy target, but he tenaciously fought back, using his resources to sue or scare critics, especially the *Miami Herald* and *St. Petersburg Times.* Greene sued the newspapers for $500 million in damages. Covering Greene during the 2010 Senate race, journalists reported that Greene welcomed boxer-thug Mike Tyson to serve as best man at his wedding, committed mortgage fraud, threw debauched parties aboard his 145-foot yacht, and left 300 families homeless after one real estate deal. A biographer titled his book about Greene *The Greatest Trader Ever,* but former workers describe him as a "cheapskate jerk."[40]

Boosted by $24 million, much of it spent on TV spots, Greene insisted his wealth meant that he was not beholden to special interests. Greene initially surged in the polls to take a lead in the race, but by August, Meek pulled away with a 26-point advantage. One of Meek's first ads, "Meet the Real Jeff Greene," informed Floridians that Greene "became a billionaire on Wall Street betting middle-class families would lose their homes." Lest Meek be too confident, every poll confirmed that not only was Meek headed for a historic loss by a Democratic candidate, but his presence on the ticket siphoned enough votes to give Marco Rubio an advantage. In late October, the airways lit up with the unconfirmed rumor that former President Bill Clinton had secretly met with Meek to plead for him to drop out of the three-way race and endorse Crist. According to several sources, Meek originally agreed to withdraw for the good of the party but changed his mind. At the time, Rubio led Crist by 7 points and Meek by double digits.[41]

Election Day: 2 November 2010

The ballots may have listed Marco Rubio (R), Kendrick Meek (D), and Charlie Crist (I), but the real candidate of that election was Barack Obama. If voters believed in the polls, insisted columnist Jeff Jacoby, "Obama supplanted George W. Bush as the most polarizing president ever." President Obama regretted the toxic polarization of American politics during his terms. But it also takes two parties to cooperate. If columnist David Brooks shocked Republicans with his 2008 endorsement of Barack Obama, he pleased Republicans by writing just a few years later, "President Obama . . . domestically and politically, things are off the rails."[42]

Marco Rubio's triumph marked one of the greatest political feats in Florida history. On Election Day, he received 45.4 percent of the vote, followed by Crist with 32 percent, and Meek with 21.5 percent. Never had a Democratic candidate for U.S. Senate performed so poorly. A mean-spirited campaign button with Kendrick Meek's photograph read: "The Meek May Inherit the Earth But Not a Seat in the U.S. Senate." Rubio raised $17.3 million, followed by Crist ($12.9 million) and Meek ($8 million). Rubio left $2 million unspent. The Democratic Party had been handed a historic defeat.[43]

The meteoric rise of Marco Rubio was due to the candidate's extraordinary personal and political skills but also to an improbable roll of the dice: the resignation of a popular U.S. senator, a Counter-Reformation by the GOP, and Charlie Crist's pride. Most strikingly, the Democratic candidate, Kendrick Meek, finished a distant third in the voting. The day's victor, unlisted on the ballot, was the Tea Party conservative rebellion that elevated Marco Rubio overnight to become the "Great Right Hope." The Republican Right, observed the *New York Times*, "had an action hero: young, dynamic, serious about policy, with a biography ready-made for inspiration." A young Floridian exclaimed: "He's our Cuban Barack Obama. He gives us hope." Rubio, not yet forty years old, is so youthful looking that when he first appeared in Tallahassee as a legislator in 2000, he was mistaken for an aide! The *Christian Science Monitor* anointed Rubio "the tea party's brightest rising star."[44]

On 2 November 2010, as forecasters had predicted, the stars fell on Charlie Crist. No soothsayer could have foretold the swift rise and hard fall of Charlie Crist, whose political skills and instincts had always been peerless. Reporters had become so familiar with the white-haired candidate oozing confidence during election-night festivities at the Vinoy Renaissance Hotel in St. Petersburg that it seemed out of character for him to have to concede his race to the upstart Marco Rubio. In hindsight, Charlie Crist seems to have fallen faster and more painfully than almost any comparable figure in Florida history. On talk shows, Charlie Crist defended his actions, recycling Ronald Reagan's famous line, "I didn't leave the Republican Party, the party left me." Crist told Fusion's host, "I couldn't be consistent with myself and my core beliefs and stay with a party that was so unfriendly toward the African-American president." *Washington Post* columnist Chris Cillizza reacted, "Um, not exactly." Adam Smith, reporting for Crist's hometown paper, noted that the governor "was happy as a Republican when the polls showed him leading Marco Rubio by 20 points." Cillizza contends "the hug" was overrated, pointing out "the impetus for him [Crist] leaving the Republican [P]arty seemed to be his precipitous decline in his primary fight against Rubio—nothing more, nothing less." Crist took no questions from the press on election night.[45]

Crist's sense of timing had never failed him. Steve Schale, a respected Democratic strategist and Obama's campaign manager for Florida, sympathized with Crist. "More than anything," he explained, "Crist proves the axiom that timing and opportunity are the most important variables. Virtually any other cycle, Crist would be punching his ticket to the Senate." What was even more stunning is that Crist's fall from grace occurred without a scandal. Darryl Paulson, a respected political observer and professor, observed, "This is probably the most unprecedented political collapse in Florida's history."[46]

One reporter analyzed the meaning of 2010: "Gov. Charlie Crist started 2010 as a Republican, and the favorite to be the party's nominee for U.S. Senate. He ended 2010 as an independent, and about to join the 12 percent of Floridians who are unemployed as his four-year term as governor ends." Remarkably, neither Crist's defeat nor Rubio's victory was the most shocking of the evening. One could confidently bet that not one in a quarter-million Floridians could have identified Rick Scott in 2000; indeed, he had not even established a permanent residence in the state. Yet when the cock crowed 12:01 a.m., 4 November 2010, Rick Scott was the new governor-elect of Florida.[47]

Scott vs. Sink: 2010 Governor's Race

For all the complexities and odd actors, the 2010 Florida gubernatorial race can be reduced to four words: Money, Message, Angry Voters. Rick Scott won one of the most improbable races to capture the governorship by understanding the mood of the electorate, his checkbook, and focusing upon the economy through his endless reiteration of "Jobs! Jobs! Jobs!"

By his side during many campaign stops was Esther Scott, Rick's mother. If voters missed seeing her in person at rallies, they heard her in commercials calling her son "a good boy" who "made me proud." She also reminded voters: "You've heard a lot about Rick Scott. But I'm going to tell you a few things you don't know. Rick was raised in public housing." Researchers fact-checked the claim, and the Scotts, indeed, lived in public housing for three years. A sign of the times, a debate ensued whether "three years in public housing" justified Scott's claim.[48]

For much of the Republican campaign for governor, Rick Scott trailed Bill

McCollum. But Scott, the outsider, hammered away, unleashing so many commercials that journalists joked that his candidacy was inseparable from the Rick Scott Network (RSN). Scott tagged his opponent "a career politician." Scott barely won the Republican primary, edging out Bill McCollum by 3 points, whereas Sink triumphed by almost 50 points over little-known Brian Moore. Scott tapped into his considerable fortune, spending an unprecedented $78 million to emblazon his name and message over the airways. To be sure, Scott could not have won the election without saturating the airways with expensive attack ads. But money does not ensure political success. In the 2010 California governor's race, Meg Whitman, an eBay CEO, spent almost $150 million and lost to Democrat Jerry Brown. Scott invested his campaign treasure chest wisely, hiring some of the best political strategists to craft a tight message and script. He sprinkled "Jobs! Jobs! Jobs" in between railing against Obama and big government, always closing with, "Let's get back to work."[49]

In 1970, Jack Eckerd—he of the megadrugstore and college name—spent millions of his own fortune to challenge the Republican incumbent. Claude Kirk, the incumbent and self-described "one tree-shakin' son of a bitch," was not amused. "Jack Eckerd was a precursor of a lot of things," Kirk noted. "He was convinced that if you had enough money, you could buy the governor's office. Some people think anything's for sale." Eckerd may have been the first wealthy candidate to self-fund his campaign. But it was Scott who opened the floodgates of campaign spending at unimaginable levels. In the 1952 race for governor, the Democratic candidates—in that era, winning the primary was tantamount to election—spent $250,000. In the 1978 Democratic primaries, Democratic candidates Bob Graham and Bob Shevin each spent $1 million. Rick Scott reset the campaign spending norms.[50]

Scott beat Sink in a squeaker, taking the election by a margin of fewer than 70,000 votes out of the 5.3 million cast. At a joyous victory party, Scott repeated one of his campaign zingers: "Today is the end of politics as usual in Tallahassee. Starting today, I work for every Floridian. Florida is open for business." The moment was a tribute to one of the most well-orchestrated campaigns and a candidate who was relentlessly on point. Scott's La Playa Resort victory party in Naples reminded veteran observers of Joseph Kennedy's remarks on his son's winning the presidency: "I'm happy to buy a victory but I'll be damned if I'll pay for a landslide."[51]

The Republican Party and conservatism won big in 2010 Florida. Remarkably, the party controlled the legislative and executive branches of government throughout the decade. In retrospect, that era easily qualifies as the most successful for the GOP in state history, 1860–2010. While Charlie Crist may be caricatured as the biggest loser, his political career was not over. As a Democrat, he narrowly missed defeating Rick Scott in the 2014 governor's race and won a congressional seat in 2018 Still, Floridians liked, even loved Charlie Crist. A 2012 poll asked Florida voters, "Who has been Florida's best governor over the past 41 years?" Jeb Bush easily triumphed, with 42 percent of the respondents, but Crist received 12.2 percent, slighter lower than Bob Graham. At a 2014 Republican rally, former governor Jeb Bush led a chant, "Charlie Crist has gotta go." He later confessed, "My mother didn't want me to say that." In 2021, Charlie Crist is campaigning for the governorship as a Democrat.[52]

Scott Hensley and Carl Hiaasen may have uttered the best lines on election night 2010. "For those of us who've covered health care for a while," the National Public Radio reporter observed, "the rebirth of Rick Scott as politician and soon-to-be governor of Florida is quite breathtaking." Hiaasen quipped, "Even by Florida's shaky standards, Rick Scott stands out as one of the most outlandish characters ever to pop out of the woodwork."[53]

What Might Have Been

"For of all the sad words of tongue or pen," wrote John Greenleaf Whittier, "the saddest are these: 'It might have been.'" Written in 1856, Whittier's poetic character Maud Muller might well have pondered what might have happened if James Buchanan had not been elected president or Abraham Lincoln had died of blood poisoning while hewing logs. Counterfactual history—"What if . . ." has become very popular. In Florida, the greatest such question is simple: "What if Governor Charlie Crist had run for a second term as governor?" Journalist Steve Bousquet discussed that fantasy in 2014: "Imagine what the landscape would look like if he had stayed put." Bousquet contends, "It opened the door for 'Rick who?" to run for governor. It allowed Jeff Atwater and Pam Bondi to win statewide office. It changed career paths for Bill McCollum and Alex Sink. . . . It was a game changer."[54]

Almost certainly, Crist would have won reelection as governor. In April 2010, shortly before Crist bolted the GOP, a poll revealed that fully 49 percent of voters approved of his job performance. To put those numbers in perspective, the approval rate was higher than Rick Scott received throughout his first term as governor. Had Crist remained a loyal Republican, he would have occupied the precarious moderate faction in a party careening to the right. Bousquet speculates, "He likely would have cut a ribbon to herald the start of high-speed rail between Tampa and Orlando." In 2010, President Obama came to Tampa to trumpet his ambitious plan to modernize America's rail system. He promised Floridians a federally funded high-speed rail line spanning Orlando to Tampa. The long-awaited dream was part of Obama's $8 billion idea for a new national network of fast-moving trains. Alas, Governor Scott had railed against reckless federal spending. California took advantage of Florida's snub. As of 2021, cost overruns and delays have plagued California's dream.[55]

A New Generation Arises

A Rip Van Winkle awakened in 2010 after a half-century slumber would have barely recognized Florida. From a population of 5 million in 1960, the state mushroomed to 18.7 million in 2010. Politically, Florida reversed script. In the presidential election of 1960, the Democratic Party of Florida, with a massive advantage of registered voters, lost to Richard Nixon and the Republicans. The major issue in 1960 was neither Cuba nor the missile gap; rather, it was an ancient tocsin: Roman Catholicism. The Kennedys may have had a winter home in Palm Beach, but a majority of voters preferred the Quaker Richard Nixon to the Catholic John F. Kennedy. Elderly midwesterners found a haven in Southwest Florida, buoying the future of the GOP. Perhaps even more striking, Palm Beach and Broward counties, Democratic behemoths, voted for Nixon. In 1960, many of the elderly residents in Florida were World War I veterans. In 1962, the *St. Petersburg Times* addressed a statement by newly elected Governor Farris Bryant dismissing as poppycock the possibility of Republicans ever competing statewide. "Just the same," the editorial noted, "the Republicans are in Florida. They're here to stay and they're growing in numbers." By 2010, massive numbers of World War II veterans had retired in Florida. But they, too, were beginning to fade away.[56]

Republicans won individual elections before but failed to take over Tallahassee. From the first stirrings of Republicans in the 1940s in Pinellas and Sarasota counties, the GOP flirted with power on several occasions, but factors within and outside the GOP foiled them. The year 1978 seemed promising. The GOP had a "dream ticket" to win the governorship—drugstore magnate Jack Eckerd and "the Maitland housewife," Paula Hawkins—opposed the Democratic ticket of Bob Graham, a little-known South Florida legislator, and Wayne Mixson. But due to too many distractions and detractors—President Nixon and Watergate, and a focused Democratic campaign—the Party of Jackson and Roosevelt retained power. Graham succeeded widely and wildly, becoming an icon over the next four decades. Florida's GOP finally succeeded in the late 1990s, the result of state, local, and federal factors as well as vast external forces. Graham represented a new generation of urban South Florida and Gulf Coast Democrats, the result of U.S. Supreme Court rulings that reapportioned the Sunshine State, resulting in a transfer of power from old rural to new urban areas. An old generation was passing and a new generation rising.[57]

Succeeded briefly by acting governor Kenneth "Buddy" MacKay, Lawton Chiles was the last Democratic-elected governor a new generation of Floridians would ever know. Like Horatius at the gate holding off the barbarians, the "He-Coon" had schooled the young Republican upstart Jeb Bush in 1994. Ironically, Chiles died in his last weeks in office while Governor-Elect Bush waited in the wings. MacKay often reminisced how Democrats once compromised over such controversial issues as pari-mutuel wagering. While backwoods Baptists and small-town Methodists condemned the sinful ways of big cities, rural legislators kept taxes low and roads paved. The fact that counties shared equally the gambling revenues made the bargain palpable and possible. A young MacKay understood that the justification for such actions was the so-called Eleventh Commandment, "found somewhere in the Old Testament."[58]

When Jeb Bush took the oath of office, it marked a turning point in the history of southern politics. In the history of the twentieth century, no southern state had witnessed the ignominy of its governor and legislature controlled by Republicans. That is, until 5 January 1999, when Jeb Bush was sworn in by a cheering Republican-controlled legislature and partisan crowd.

Jeb Bush, Marco Rubio, Mel Martínez, and Rick Scott symbolized the new wave of Republicans, whereas Lawton Chiles, Buddy MacKay, Bob Graham, and Bill Nelson personified a vanishing generation of Democrats. Author Patsy Palmer called this moment (1999) "the sunset of the 'Long Generation,' . . . mostly white, mostly male, mostly Democrats . . . that has held a remarkably protracted and influential position in state government and politics." They had benefited immensely from U.S. Supreme Court rulings that reapportioned the state more fairly."[59]

The first decades of the new century witnessed extraordinary Republican success in Florida and the South. After a century of competing unsuccessfully against the Democrats and being treated like a beaten mule, the GOP ascended to and consolidated power. In 1992, the Republicans won the Florida Senate, followed in 1996 by success in the State House and in 1998, the governorship. The GOP had won the trifecta. More significantly, the trifecta remained in power through the next decade. The last year the Democratic Party held a trifecta was 1992.

In the first decade of the new century, Florida Republicans outnumbered Democrats in Washington in the U.S. House of Representatives, while Democrats Bill Nelson and Bob Graham held seats in the U.S. Senate most of the decade. But Graham was replaced by Republican Mel Martínez in 2006, and Rick Scott defeated Nelson in 2018. That year marked the high-water mark of the GOP in the new century. "Florida has turned from purple to red," proclaimed the *Tampa Bay Times.* Not since Reconstruction had the GOP held every statewide office. Republican U.S. Senators Marco Rubio and Rick Scott went to Washington, where Donald Trump, a Florida resident, served as president. Republican Ron DeSantis occupied the governor's mansion in Tallahassee. If 2018 Florida had been a nation-state, its $1 trillion economy would rank 17th in the world, larger than Switzerland, Saudi Arabia, Argentina, and the Netherlands.[60]

The GOP is home to some of America's fastest-growing states, a major factor in the rise of the Republican Party in the Sunbelt. The U.S. Constitution demands reapportionment every decade and rewards fast-growing states such as Florida. When the results of the 2000 U.S. Census were tabulated, Florida was awarded two additional congressional seats; New York and Pennsylvania each surrendered two. The 2010 U.S. Census awarded Florida two new congressional seats; New York and Ohio lost two seats. Since state legislatures reapportion and redistrict election boundaries for the state and congressional seats, the future of Florida's Republican Party is dependent upon the message and the massaging of geopolitical boundaries.[61]

Politics of Anger and Change and Status Quo

Unemployed, foreclosed, and hopeless, Floridians were angry. From the left and the right, Floridians expressed their fury, spawning the election of Barack Obama, the rise of the Tea Party, Charlie Crist's agony and ecstasy, and the elevation of two largely unknown and unlikely Republican stars, Rick Scott and Marco Rubio.

Midterm elections typically haunt and frustrate American presidents who misgauge the difficulty of translating a presidential victory into a referendum that bolsters the chief executive's party in the House and Senate. Typically, American presidents lost an average of 30 seats in the House of Representatives and U.S. Senate. Since the 1930s, only Franklin D. Roosevelt in 1934 and George W. Bush in 2002 have gained seats in Congress (the House *and* the Senate) in midterm elections.[62]

If Barack Obama was an exuberant, happy warrior in 2008, he was trounced and humiliated two years later. In 2010, Democrats lost 69 seats—63 in the House and 6 in the Senate. Obama's historic victory, his overhaul of the health-care system, ignited a revolt called the Tea Party movement. A perfect storm formed to deliver what the president called a "shellacking" in 2010. On the national level, talk radio supplied daily doses of anti-Obama rhetoric. Obamacare unleashed what critics feared: "a socialistic, oppressive new order to America." Tea Party activists took the fight to Washington, state capitals, and town halls. Upon reflection, Obama held "grudging respect for how rapidly Tea Party leaders had mobilized a strong following and managed to dominate the news coverage, using some of the same social media we'd deployed during my own campaign."[63]

Across America, Obama's dream of a transactional and transformational administration was under assault. "While Mr. Obama's 2008 election helped usher in a political resurgence for Democrats," observed the *New York Times*, "the president today [2015] presides over a shrinking party whose control of elected offices at the state and local level has declined precipitously." To be more precise, the white male was abandoning the Democratic Party.[64]

As the Great Recession lingered, political anger grew louder. Both political parties faltered. As late as 2013, Florida still led the nation in foreclosures; as late as 2015, fewer than one in eight unemployed Floridians received jobless benefits. The system failed the neediest. A study declared that filing for unemployment benefits was "virtually impossible."[65]

Florida legislators elected during the Great Recession faced a bleak task of balancing a budget with plunging revenues. In retrospect, Florida legislators instituted policies and legislation that encouraged hell-bent growth. The *St. Petersburg Times* conducted a special report in 2009 titled "The Fault for Defaults." Journalists studied thousands of foreclosures in Hillsborough County and concluded that individual homeowners have been blamed too harshly: "The truth is that real estate speculators and revenue-hungry local governments bear just as much of the responsibility—and maybe more—for the collapse of the housing market." Local officials, the report argues, assisted investors and flippers "every step of the way." Examples include massive housing projects in rural areas, "waiving impact fees for developers." Examining nearly 12,000 foreclosure cases, journalists discovered that almost all of the properties lacked a homestead exemption—meaning mortgage holders never intended to live in their home as a primary residence. Taxpayers were stuck paying for infrastructure built in empty developments. The fact that developers contribute handsomely to county commissioners' political campaigns should come as no surprise.[66]

Nor did the 2009 Florida Legislature pass a single bill addressing the wide-scale problems plaguing condominium and homeowner associations. The Great Recession walloped the state's condominiums and their shared community owners and associations. A perfect storm fueled by plummeting housing prices, record high foreclosures, and a rocked mortgage industry hit the most vulnerable state and home to the most unprotected consumers in America: Florida. Dozens of proposals creating a special condo police force to ferret out financial fraud within associations and other measures simply withered under the pressure of the real estate lobby. Efforts to protect condominium owners from megacorporate bullies who wish to turn condos into rental units also failed in 2009. Such reform measures hatched in Lansbrook Village and Grand Oasis died in Tallahassee.[67]

In 2010, the Republican-controlled Florida Legislature passed a bill that repealed a regulation that required condo associations to hire qualified experts (engineers or architects) to submit reports on the health and integrity of high-rise structures. The bill was signed by Governor Charlie Crist in June 2010. By that date, Crist had switched parties and was a registered Democrat. The *Palm Beach Post* reported the governor in Broward and Palm Beach counties "signing the same bill three times in a two-hour period. A journalist wrote, "The Republican-turned Independent is pushing hard for Democratic votes in his race for the U.S. Senate." Condominium associations had been hit hard by the Great Recession and were pleading for relief. The bill also permitted condo boards to reject smoke detectors and expensive fire sprinkler systems.[68]

On 24 June 2021, in a compressive moment of the last half century of Florida's growth, the Champlain Towers South condominium in Surfside collapsed, killing almost one hundred of its residents. Constructed in 1979, the condominium that offered hundreds of inhabitants a slice of the Florida dream only steps from the Atlantic Ocean also was cursed by decisions and developments all too familiar in Florida: a 12-story structure built upon reclaimed wetlands, shoddy construction, a climate that is seductive to snowbirds but brutal upon steel and concrete, design flaws, lax management, bickering condo boards, and Florida's love affair with growth.[69]

Political success can be defined by securing projects for the home district. When it came to securing pork, Florida legislators succeeded spectacularly. No one brought home more earmarks than Republican Bill Young, a congressman and defense hawk from Pinellas County. In 2010, he was ranked the "top earmarker," a tribute to his chairmanship of the powerful House Appropriations Committee from 1999 to 2005.[70]

Builders and developers lobby for influence in Tallahassee. When the housing industry collapsed, many customers felt secure knowing that they had placed their deposit on a condo or home in an escrow account. But in Florida, builders have a legal right to access money in an escrow account if it provides bond. A journalist

interviewed an exasperated victim of such practices. "'The oldest and most trusted builder'—that's their slogan," complained Bill Quattrocchi, who lost $25,000.[71]

The tale of Lansbrook Village typifies the perilous state of condos and consumers when standing in the way of profit. A community of 774 condo units located in northern Palm Harbor, Pinellas County, Lansbrook Village found itself in the crosshairs of a 2007 Florida statute. The 2004 hurricanes leveled many condo communities, creating chaos. The 2007 statute amended condo laws, allowing the approval of 80 percent of unit owners to renovate or terminate condominium associations. Previously, law required 100 percent approval. The climatic and financial storms of 2004–7 brought calamity to thousands of condo owners, causing many to default on their mortgages. The intent of lawmakers was to remove derelict units that had become eyesores. "Canny investors began snapping up units at bargain prices," wrote journalist Susan Martin, "knowing that once they owned 80 percent, they'd be in a position to convert the complex to rentals and force the remaining owners to sell." Such shenanigans occurred across the state.[72]

Record levels of unemployment and homelessness represented the human face of the Great Recession, yet the Florida Legislature reacted with indifference and obstructionism. The great Florida disconnect, contended the *Miami Herald*'s Fred Grimm, manifested as the "attendant indignities that Florida heaps upon the unemployed." "The Florida Legislature, though," editorialized the *Tampa Bay Times*, "continues to undermine these efforts. Lawmakers again this year swept hundreds of millions of dollars from the affordable housing trust fund for other purposes—a practice dating more than a decade at a loss of more than $2 billion for affordable housing." A Floridian earning a minimum wage needed to work 108 hours a week to pay rent.[73]

During this era, Florida took an early but big step toward defunding public schools. In 2001 the Florida Tax Credit Scholarship Program began modestly. But in the next eight years, the program has funneled nearly a half billion dollars to scholarships for low-income students to attend private schools. The Florida Legislature held public schools and especially public-school unions in contempt. The passage of SB 2126 in 2010, a bill signed by Governor Crist, expanded funding and eligibility for the Florida Tax Credit Scholarship Program. Although the program's funding was previously capped at $11 million, the new legislation upped the amount to $140 million. In simple English, Florida schoolchildren could use public vouchers to attend private schools. Prior to 2010, the number of Florida children attending private schools utilizing tax vouchers was relatively small: 29,000. The program exploded. The Florida Tax Credit Scholarship Program allowed students below the federal poverty line to pay for tuition and books. At the very moment Florida's public schools faced cuts, vouchers for private schools, including religious academies, took off. Jacksonville's *Florida Times-Union,* a conservative publication, editorialized, "If the goal of Florida's Corporate Tax Credit Scholarship program is simply to reduce state spending on public education, it's graded an A," adding, "If the goal . . . is to improve education for low-income students, it scores an incomplete. But if the goal is to ensure the same educational accountability Florida politicians demand of public schools, then the program gets an F." For instance, the program does not require scholarship students to take state mandatory tests, such as the FCAT. Moreover, the schools lack accountability.[74]

Criticism mounted because of the inactions or actions of the Florida Legislature and Governor Scott. Perhaps the state's most influential columnist, Howard Troxler, lambasted Tallahassee in his final column in 2011. "I do not think most Floridians fully realize, and will not for some time, the full damage of what has already happened in Tallahassee," wrote Troxler. "Our state's governor and the majority of our state's Legislature believed in exactly one thing: making money off Florida. They have repealed many of the laws that Florida passed trying to make itself a better state."[75]

In an "only in Florida" story, a Lee County man was arrested for dating his goat. While it took the Florida Legislature five years to address the issue, dating goats in Florida is now illegal![76]

Legislators may be indifferent to goats, but they do listen to powerful interests and lobbyists. If money is the mother's milk of politics, Florida is awash in green milk. The mother lode was The Villages, a foundation for GOP cash and a first stop for Republican candidates eager to fill the campaign coffers. "Just about every Republican you can think of has made it to The Villages at least once," insisted Lawrence Shipley, a leader of the local Democratic Club. Five square miles of land in Central Florida, The Villages is a GOP bailiwick where Republicans outnumbered Democrats two to one in 2010. The founder, H. Gary Morse, transformed The Villages into one of the most successful retirement communities. Between 1999 and 2012, Morse contributed $6.3 million to Republican candidates in state and federal races.[77]

Hurricanes are becoming fiercer and more destructive. Insurance companies posted significant losses. State Farm, a major player, announced that it was withdrawing, the result of hurricane debts. But the Florida Legislature permitted State Farm to create a conduit insurance company by the name of DaVinci Renaissance Ltd., an offshore firm with no offices or employees that provided hurricane coverage to large numbers of Floridians. A *Sarasota Herald-Tribune* journalist explained the rationale and advantages to State Farm. "In Florida," explained Paige St. John, "the insurance rates State Farm can charge are regulated by the government. Profits are controlled and taxed. The potential loss from a major hurricane is measured in billions of dollars. DaVinci's premiums, on the other hand, are as high as the market will bear. Based in Bermuda, it avoids U.S. taxes and faces no limits on profits."[78]

Florida's tax policies are grossly and inequitably unfair, undemocratic, and unassailable. For most of Florida history, noted author Gene M. Burnett, Floridians or their corporations paid "no income tax, no state property tax, no corporate income tax, and no severance tax on natural resources." For generations, the Florida Legislature had cobbled together balanced budgets dependent upon a rickety combination of gasoline and sin taxes, summed up in a popular jingle: "Bet, buy, die; Drive, drink, smoke." In the 1940s, banker, Du Pont estate trustee, and power broker Ed Ball shrewdly understood that a growing, dynamic state desperately needed additional revenues to pay for state services. Since taxing corporations represented a popular option, Ball successfully lobbied for a state sales tax, which, of course, was regressive and unpopular with voters.[79]

Progressives had long argued for a state corporate tax, to no avail. Reubin O'Donovan Askew, a former paratrooper and Pensacola resident, won election as governor in 1970. He orchestrated a corporate profits tax amendment, deftly omitting the word "income." Despite furious opposition, Floridians overwhelmingly passed the measure in 1971. Yet corporations found ways to avoid the tax. By 2019, a headline in the *Orlando Sentinel* announced, "In Florida, 99% of Companies Pay No Corporate Income Tax." How is that possible? The paper explained, "All of these moves are made possible by two things: aggressive tax-avoidance tactics by big businesses—and elected leaders who choose not to stop them." A law professor observed: "The Florida corporate income tax leaks like a sieve. Business has it pretty much the way they want it."[80]

"I once referred to the past Legislature [2010] as a festival of whores," quipped Carl Hiaasen, "which in retrospect was a vile insult to the world's oldest profession." Growth and money have long been intertwined in the DNA of Florida politics. In 2006, Provost David Colburn frequently ran into University of Florida alumni in the Capitol hallways. When he asked, "So what are you doing?," the replies were invariably, "I'm doing the Lord's work!" Translation: They were lobbyists. In 2005, 47,000 interest groups hired 38,000 individuals who spent almost $1 billion lobbying at America's fifty state capitals. Florida was one of three states that did *not* require lobbyists to disclose campaign contributions. In 2006, the legislature finally mandated the disclosure of lobbyists' salaries and fees. Florida immediately leapt to third place in lobbyist spending. In 2011 and

2012 combined, corporations and special interests spent almost a half-billion dollars to "influence" legislation. When state legislators or staffers leave their positions, many find rewarding new careers as lobbyists. In Florida, once powerful state legislators and cabinet members also become university presidents, witness the careers of John Thrasher, John Delaney, Betty Castor, and Frank Brogan.[81]

The decade's metaphor might be living on the edge. Commentator Frank Bruni thought society was living on the edge of a steep cliff. As cliff dwellers, he writes, "we deal with nothing until the last possible minute and act in timid, impermanent ways, growing all too accustomed to indecision." The decade was pockmarked by crises, tragedies, and catastrophes. Of course, highly competitive, 24-hour news stations reported the news, where seemingly every new bulletin was highlighted by blaring music and pulsing lights. Simply consider a sampling of the decade's over-the-edge events: the Y2K anxieties and the zany 2000 election, 9/11, the Terri Schiavo melodrama, 2004 and the year of four hurricanes, thousands of gun deaths, the opioid crisis, immigration chaos, the Great Recession, Casey Anthony, and the 2010 Gulf Oil Spill. The list conveniently skips the political standoffs. All the while, the reality of climate change loomed over our lives and the planet.[82]

The future of Florida can be gauged in myriad ways. One can fixate on Florida politics and celebrate wildly or become morose and dispirited. Perhaps we should all spend more time strolling along Fort De Soto Beach or Playalinda Beach at Cape Canaveral and realize what a special place this is. Or you could read Florida novels. In *Pineapple Grenade*, Tim Dorsey writes, "A prosthetic leg with a Willie Nelson bumper sticker washed ashore on the beach, which meant it was Florida." Or one might read Zora Neale Hurston: "Spring time in Florida is not a matter of peeping violets or bursting buds merely. It is a riot of color, in nature—glistening green leaves, pink, blue, purple, yellow blossoms that fairly stagger the visitor from the north." And there is always Marjorie Kinnan Rawlings's dose of optimism: "I do not understand how anyone can live without some small place of enchantment to turn to." In 2002, Michael Paterniti wrote that Florida is and has become "a pure creation of our demand." He called Florida "America in Extremis." Perhaps it is time to reconsider and rethink the future of Florida.[83]

Conclusion: Because We Could

Communities amid the Storms of Change

> So we beat on, boats against the current, borne
> back ceaselessly ceaselessly into the past.
>
> —F. Scott Fitzgerald, *The Great Gatsby*

If modern Florida needed an official slogan, it should be, "Because we could."[1] That simple declarative sentence encapsulates centuries of Floridians' dominion over nature and ethical dilemmas. Why would sensible people build high-rise condominiums on barrier islands? Why would politicians, supposedly acting in the public interest, plunder the Everglades, destroy wetlands and natural habitat, straighten rivers, disfranchise felons, build and rebuild six-lane highways while scorning mass transit, and persist on a hell-bent policy that promised growth would pay its way? How does one explain to future generations that we once welcomed—indeed, subsidized—phosphate mining and corporate sugarcane farming? Florida was once home to some of the purest and largest freshwater springs in the world. How do we explain to future generations that we awarded generous extraction rights to a foreign corporation that pumped millions of gallons of water destined for plastic containers, distant markets, and paltry returns? Because we could.

Modern Florida is a growth machine. Why do officials promote growth as Florida's True Faith, shuttling residents to places that should not have been developed? Because we could. The U.S. Census Bureau has confirmed what demographers, furniture movers, and golf cart companies already knew: In 2019, the Sunshine State added almost 1,000 new residents daily. In 2016, only Utah and Nevada grew at a faster clip, and only Texas added more newcomers. Florida, America's third-largest state, hurtles toward the 22-million mark. New York, Connecticut, Pennsylvania, and Illinois lost population in 2018. A recent poll indicated that half of Illinois residents would move to another state if they could. Florida remains their dream destination. *Kiplinger* ranked Illinois as the most tax-unfriendly state in America. Florida legislators take pride in the state's regressive tax policies; indeed, recent governors made phone calls and visitations to Rust Belt states and Sunbelt rivals, encouraging residents there to move to Florida. Florida's Great Recession blues are in the rearview mirror as the Sunshine State shakes, rattles, and rolls.[2]

New Yorkers have earned the honor of serving as Florida's largest "sender state," an antiseptic term for an orphan state or stopover. Men of Troy and women of Sparta, fourth-generation Long Island Jews and twelfth-generation Hudson River patroons, prison guards from Auburn and jockeys from Saratoga Springs, have all been seduced by Florida's balmy winters, spring training sites, and shrewd tax lawyers. For good reasons, Collier, Charlotte, and Pinellas counties are called "God's Waiting Room." In 2019, the quintessential New Yorker, President Donald Trump, officially became a resident of Florida. A new Florida Man was born. And the Sunbelt gods rested.[3]

A sense of perspective: In the first decades of the twentieth century, the fastest-growing and most important cities in America included Buffalo, Detroit, Cleveland, Youngstown, Pittsburgh, St. Louis, and Chicago. The tide of history is retreating. Many of America's most dynamic cities in 1910 have suffered catastrophic population losses. The twenty-first century has witnessed severe depopulation and industrial decline in the Rust Belt. No prophet could have forecast that meanwhile, places with unrecognizable names—Cape Coral and North Port, Port St. Lucie and Miramar, Palm Coast and Palm Bay—would surge.[4]

State leaders should consider hitting the pause button and asking some uncomfortable questions, among them: What are the implications of Florida booms, accompanied by frenzied development and a population surge? How do we preserve the things that drew so many of us here? In a state of constant change, how do communities resist the ceaseless onslaught of development disguised and rationalized as progress? Considering that Florida is a modern Sisyphus, is it even possible to preserve a sense of place in Florida? Is such an effort equivalent to King Canute demonstrating to his sycophantic couriers that not even a king can halt the tide and control natural forces? Unnatural forces, the tides of Florida—growth and development—threaten some of our most beloved places.

The vexing pattern of imposed growth deserves a public forum and tough questions: Can a state possibly alter a culture of growth that created prosperity and abundance *and* preserve Florida's cultural and natural heritage—the distinctive historical architecture and traditions that provide a sense of identity for our neighborhoods, towns, and cities? What will happen to the once pristine bays and springs, the sugar-white beaches and splendid estuaries?

The making of modern Florida has come at a steep price: orange groves transformed into shopping malls, villages becoming edge cities, and new subdivisions branded with ironic names signaling loss—Pelican Landing, Hammock Bay, and the Esplanade on Palmer Ranch. Author Craig Pittman reminisced about the summer he worked on a land-surveying crew: "We spent weeks working through hip-deep water in a titi swamp, laying out a development that would be called 'Paradise Bay.'"[5]

Florida's cities, once glorified by ornate hotels, landmark department stores, and identifiable skylines, have morphed into glass-paneled skyscrapers, high-rise condos, and parking garages. Florida's small towns, too, struggle. Once distinguished by main streets dotted by family-owned cafés, hardware stores, and barber shops, the impact of Walmart, Dollar Tree, and out-migration has been devastating.

The term "placelessness" describes much of modern Florida. In his book on the 2010 oil spill and its impact upon the Gulf Coast, author Rowan Jacobsen surveys New Orleans and asks: "What makes a place a place? What builds its character? And how does it hold on to that character when everything changes?" Such questions are rarely asked in Florida, where new and bigger signify the coins of the realm.[6]

Amid a stampede toward sterility and boredom, a question arises: Will there be a here, here, or will twenty-first century Florida become homogenized as more franchise restaurants, big-box stores, and sprawling Med-Rev subdivisions move in to serve yet more new residents who are from someplace else?[7]

Novelists, anthropologists, and urban planners have all taken their measure of modern Florida. Downtown Sarasota, 1950, serves as an arbitrary signpost of Before and After. "If you stuck a pin in the map at the center of Five Points," explained Jeff LaHurd, "within a mile of that pin could be found everything to satisfy your religious, recreational, medical, and shopping needs. Then in 1955, the Ringling Shopping Center opened . . . Mass Brothers [department store] opened in 1956 and Southgate Shopping Center opened in 1957." In 2014, the Mall at

University Town Center opened—next to Interstate 75. It was one of thousands of shopping malls still standing in America, *but* the first enclosed mall to open in the United States since 2012. Bradenton's De Soto Square Mall, considered state of the art when opened in 1973, shuttered its doors in 2021. Ringling Plaza was demolished in 2018.[8]

"But as I drive around today's Sarasota, somewhat bewildered by the glut of high-rise buildings, McMansions where once bungalows sufficed for housing, and dramatic increases in traffic (roundabouts notwithstanding)," reflected journalist Jeff LaHurd, "it is very apparent, to me at least, that it is too late—way too late." He adds somberly, "And that is a shame."[9]

Florida cities have invented and reinvented themselves ever since the Spanish destroyed the French Huguenot settlement on the St. Johns River in 1565 and Sir Francis Drake burned St. Augustine in 1586. In the 1880s as well as the 1950s and 2010s, Pensacola, Ocala, and Fernandina underwent urban renewal, attracting new waves of residents, and offered amenities such as dining, lodging, shopping, and people-watching. Florida serves as an incubator for new forms of urban life: edge cities, boomburbs, and microburbs.

The road signs are all too clear: the Florida of today is the America of tomorrow. Or, to paraphrase John Locke, "In the end, all the world will be Florida." On a 1955 visit to Miami, the acerbic architect Frank Lloyd Wright, upon gazing at the new wave of modernist architecture invading Miami, gasped, "Why can't Miami be Miami?" Assessing the new hotels and new structures, he opined: "They have no feeling, no richness, no sense of that region. Why don't you do something that belongs?" Today, Wright might scream, "Why can't Florida be Florida?"[10]

Yet some Florida communities, sensitive to these questions and alarmed by sprawl and conformity, have managed to preserve what makes them special, safeguarding historic areas and their stories for new generations.

Why should Floridians care about material culture—the 1920s craftsman bungalows of Bartow, DeLand's 1922 Athens Theatre, the 1860 Wardlaw-Smith mansion in Madison, and Mount Dora's 1883 Lakeside Inn? Living amid and admiring historic structures enriches our lives and enhances our admiration of the built environment. But it also helps us appreciate how individual homes evolve into neighborhoods and how neighborhoods become communities—and how over time these places and structures stand as sentinels of a different era. We become part of history's arc and imagine elderly grandmothers gossiping on front porches while a Western Union messenger delivers telegrams from distant battlefronts.

When we encounter the elegant brick arcade of Ybor City's El Pasaje, the southern gothic charm of the Clewiston Inn, or the neighborhood surrounding East Stanford Street in Bartow, the bungalows of Miami's E. Little Havana and Tampa's Seminole Heights neighborhoods, we pause to appreciate old-fashioned craftsmanship and harmony of scale and space.

How did these structures, neighborhoods, and towns manage to survive? Above all, dedicated individuals and families chose to invest their energies and futures to ensure a sense of community. Volunteers worked tirelessly to preserve workers' cottages, immigrant clubs, and silent-era movie theaters. Converting old structures takes ingenuity. In Fernandina, volunteers converted the old city jail into a history museum!

Poverty is the preservationist's best friend. Many of Florida's most picturesque communities—Fernandina, Cedar Key, and Key West—suffered periods of neglect and decline. Had these places enjoyed continued growth, most of the historic structures would have been replaced with new and less interesting buildings. These cities shared lean decades of mutual poverty and an exodus of workers, allowing these unloved structures to survive. Put simply, no one wanted to tear them down. Many also faced obliteration, the result of hurricanes and fires. In 1888, Cedar Key rivaled Tampa in fortune and promise, its population climbing to 5,000 persons. But the Great Cedar Key Hurricane of '96 burst any optimism.

Mars, the god of war, has brought prosperity and industry to cities, but also poverty and defeat. Naturalist John Muir, destined for Cedar Key on his 1,000-mile walk from the Heartlands to the Gulf coast in 1867, observed, "The traces of war are not only apparent on the broken fields, mills, and woods, but also on the countenances of the people."[11]

Protecting the heritage of small-town Florida involves more than preserving Queen Anne revivals and New Deal murals. Florida's historic communities are bound together by identities largely shaped by the things they once harvested or produced: Apalachicola and oysters; Fernandina and shrimp; Tarpon Springs and sponges; Clewiston and sugar; Cedar Key and lumber; Madison and cotton; Cortez, Niceville, and Everglades City and mullet; and Bartow, Lake Wales, DeLand, and Mount Dora and oranges. What happens when traditional industries are phased out by new competition, technology, or modernization? Beth Dunlop observed in 1987, "As Cortez disappears it is being replaced by condominiums with nautical names—Mariners Cove and, not without a bit of irony, Smugglers Landing—so its beginning will at least be remembered."[12]

What characteristics unite these communities? A sense of place pervades and characterizes these communities. Kermit the Frog said famously, "It's not easy being green." In Florida, Kermit would revise his simple declarative sentence: "It's not easy being old." In a state where new is better, and growth rates are equated with progress, the past takes a backseat, except as tourist attractions.

Technology has always been both a godsend *and* a curse to communities. The railroad shattered Apalachicola's thriving steamboat and cotton trade in the nineteenth century, but because of ice factories and new canning techniques, the community reinvented itself and thrived by harvesting and shipping canned and fresh oysters. Alas, today's oyster industry has been crippled by the lack of fresh water flowing into Apalachicola Bay, the result of Metro Atlanta's appetite for the precious liquid. A rush of new investors, artists, and transplants have reinvigorated Apalachicola. Attracted by the charm and isolation of the picturesque town, newcomers are reinventing Apalachicola once again. Technology now allows Florida's most isolated residents to think and live locally while being connected globally. In an age of online shopping and Internet, borders have vanished and surrendered to consumers.

For many years, ice plants and sleek schooners enabled Panacea, Destin, and other coastal towns to ship fresh seafood to consumers. But by the late twentieth century, Asian fish farms, air freight, and a state-imposed ban on large-scale net fishing walloped local fishermen. In response, locals learned to farm clams, and Cedar Key emerged as the state's clamming capital.

A national transportation system meant Tarpon Springs sponges could be marketed as household necessities across America. But scientists perfected a synthetic sponge in the 1940s, making the livelihoods of Greek sponge divers obsolete. As large numbers of non-Greek residents moved into the area, cultural tourism has helped preserve and promote Tarpon Springs' distinctive Greek signature.

Indeed, tourism and a service economy have become the economic lifeline of many historic communities. Tourists surf the Internet looking for quaint places to find stimulating new experiences. Some historic Florida communities, like Mount Dora, have also become popular destinations for retirees.

Many of these quaint historic Florida towns and cities share geographic isolation. They don't have interstate highways running through or near them. Indeed, Winter Park and Mount Dora opposed the construction of new highways because of quality-of-life issues. No government agency or social scientist has discovered a formula to invent or salvage heritage along six-lane highways.

Jefferson County was once Florida's richest and blackest county, by dint of cotton and slavery. Appropriately, its county seat is Monticello, and its courthouse resembles the Virginia plantation. Columnists employ the word "quaint" to describe the place. "What Jefferson County does *not* have is noise and traffic," writes journalist Steve Bousquet. "And a lot of people here like it that way," he added. Monticello does not have a single stoplight. But in 2019, the Florida Legislature decided to build three toll roads, one that would extend from Crystal River to Monticello, 150 miles away! The locals are neither happy, grateful, nor amused.[13]

Contrast these cities with Orlando. The Orlando International Airport, the Florida Turnpike, and I-4 intersect with Orlando, bringing 75 million tourists to Central Florida, where they can walk the walk on America's most nostalgic address: Main Street, Walt Disney World, Lake Buena Vista, Florida. Cinderella and her castle are neighbors.

America boasts 8,645 streets named "Main," but only one transcends the boundaries of imagination, running aside a castle and attracting residents named Goofy, Cinderella, and a rodent celebrity. The backstory offers more detours and swerves than Mr. Toad's Wild Ride. A Chicago native, Walter Elias Disney had more in common with Carl Sandburg than Snow White. His parents, however, had genuine Florida roots. On New Year's Day 1888, Elias Charles Disney married Flora Call, becoming the first couple to wed in newly established Lake County. They were married on and homesteaded a farm in Kismet, located about 60 miles from Orlando. Flora worked as a grammar-school teacher. Kismet, a Turkish word meaning destiny, proved prophetic, as freezes and the frontier life bedeviled the young couple.[14]

The Disneys left for Chicago in the early 1890s, where Elias worked as a carpenter on the Columbian Exposition. Walter Elias Disney, one of four brothers, was born in Chicago in 1901. Fearful that Chicago would corrupt their four sons, the Disneys moved once again, to a farmstead in Marceline, Missouri.[15]

Young Walt drank deep from the waters of Heartlands' culture: individualism, community, and populism. His father had flirted with socialist causes. Walt's earliest creative works reflect populist sympathies and nostalgic memories of small-town, rural life. In 1955, he rolled the dice on a $17 million gamble in Anaheim, California. Disneyland was a smash hit, but the opening of Walt Disney World in Florida (1971) redefined modern tourism. Crowds adored Main Street, Disney's shrine to Marceline. Evoking a sense of childlike belonging, Disney designed Main Street buildings at five-eighths scale.[16]

Kismet, home to the Florida Disneys, vanished and is now part of the Ocala National Forest. Florida, the incubator state, is also a graveyard of dreams. Kismet and Magnolia, St. Joseph and Tasmania, were once promising new communities in Florida. They are now ghost towns.

Isolation explains why some places avoided development for so long and still managed to blossom, while others merely lingered. Inhabitants are forced to organize and think outside the box, breeding cohesion and creativity. Ironically, Fernandina, separated from Georgia by the St. Marys River, once stood at the epicenter of Florida. The city proudly notes that since 1562, eight flags have flown over its walls. But the city declined in importance in the early twentieth century, its population ebbing to only 3,000 in 1930. Relatively undeveloped until the 1970s, the spacious beaches of Nassau County beckoned tourists and developers with the opening of Interstate 95 and the construction of Amelia Island Plantation. Developer Charles Fraser hired eleven environmental consultants, who studied the local ecology for nine months while making recommendations. The population of Nassau County on the eve of World War II had just topped the 10,000 plateau. It has soared to almost 90,000 by 2020.[17]

Everglades City and its 400 residents continue to languish in splendid isolation, 90 miles west of Miami along the Tamiami Trail. Visitors adore Everglades City and its dreamlike setting on the Barron River overlooking the Ten Thousand Islands. If a visitor to this island in the Everglades feels cramped, one can travel 4 miles down Copeland Avenue and Smallwood Drive to Chokoloskee Island (population 300). Writers have described the setting as "Florida's Last Frontier." Peter B. Gallagher described the area in 2009: "where more endangered people, plants, and animals exist than any other region of the state. You have hermits, outlaws, old men of the sea, good honest people who want to be left alone, gator wrestlers, poets, poachers, all manner of ne'er-do-wells, scofflaws, and mentals mixed in with millionaires, CEOs, and MIAs—and you can't tell any of them apart."[18] Everglades City is the un-Naples, even though until 1961, the fishing village was the seat of Collier County. No Starbucks, no five-star hotels or spas, no fern bars or billionaires. On the other hand, Naples never experienced a predawn morning quite like 7 July 1983, when one of Florida's greatest drug busts occurred. Agents arrested twenty-eight locals and confiscated half of Everglades City's fishing boats.

By the time John Muir arrived at Cedar Key in 1869, the thriving settlement of Cedar Key boasted a railroad depot, a lumber trade built upon cedar, and a seafood industry. Cedar Key's strategic port also underscored its vulnerability. Hurricanes scoured the city.

Cedar Key never recovered from its loss of railroads and denuded cedar forests. Cedar Key adapted. In the late twentieth century, it reinvented itself as an arts destination. It also reembraced nature, becoming home to citizens who wished to avoid Florida's hustle and bustle. The community is surrounded by wildlife preserves. In 2018, I gave a talk in Cedar Key. Since Cedar Key's current population hovers around 700, I wondered if anyone would show up. The venue was packed—by locals *and* snowbirds—the latter quite insistent that they do not wish to spend their winters in St. Petersburg or Fort Lauderdale. They prefer the solitude and natural setting of a camp- or trailer-site in Cedar Key.

Travelers adore these communities precisely because they are everything so much of modern Florida is not—authentic. Cortez, Everglades City, and Mount Dora do not offer tourists simulated experiences, computerized rides, or lane after lane of franchised establishments. In a state that attracted 82 million visitors in 2010 and 126 million in 2018, some take the roads less traveled. Huge crowds attend annual seafood festivals and art and craft shows because of the settings and the possibilities of discovery.[19]

But can a community be loved to death? Witness the challenges facing St. Augustine and Key West. Boasting a rich history, a Spanish colonial outpost, and the distinction of being the oldest inhabited city in the United States, St. Augustine records a modest population of 14,500 residents. But a place visited by 6 million tourists annually faces new challenges.

St. Augustine has survived fierce hurricanes, fires, marauding pirates, and poverty, but the Ancient City now faces even greater threats: overdevelopment and prosperity wrought by tourism and growth. Former mayor Ramelle Petroglou reminisced that once residents shopped for groceries downtown. The city was compact and small. "You went down the end of King Street, turned left, and within two blocks you were in country."[20]

St. Johns County numbered about 50,000 residents in 1980. The population in 2020 topped a quarter million, and was designated one of the nation's fastest-growing units. On the roads leading from I-95 to the city, motorists encounter endless strip malls and chain stores that could be anywhere. Everyplace is no place.

Not that many decades ago, Tallahassee was considered one of America's smallest state capitals. On the eve of the Civil War, Tallahassee's population of 1,932 did not even qualify it as a modern city. On the eve of Pearl Harbor, the city had only grown to 16,240. But as Florida exploded after World War II, Tallahassee paralleled a state hell-bent on growth. In 2020, Tallahassee topped the 200,000-population plateau.

Old Tallahassee may have been small, but it was also charming, a city of nineteenth-century churches, houses, and trees. Tallahasseans no longer shop downtown, but a resident observed in 2020 that "the intersection of Tennessee and Monroe streets in the city's central hub . . . reveals Tallahassee's greatness, our unique character, our challenges—and speaks to our desperate need for change." He added, "The intersection is the face of poverty among unimaginable riches, homelessness among opulence, incentivized development among blight, and failed public policies among promises for a better day."[21]

In 1940, Key West would have been atop a list of the most exotic places in America. A picturesque community of 13,000 residents on the eve of Pearl Harbor, home-front Key West had become a bustling city of khaki and navy whites by 1943, its population spiraling to more than 40,000. Quaint customs had connected generations of diverse Conchs. One such ritual involved the closing of doors to stores while a funeral cortege passed: "All business along the line of a funeral procession must be suspended as a final tribute to the dead." But profits replaced customs as more and more strangers appeared.[22]

Today's Key West, with the population of fewer than 25,000, retains the charm of a historic walking city but is threatened by the 3 million tourists who arrive annually by car, plane, and cruise ship. Recently, frustrated Conchs spray-painted on manifestos, "Kill the TDC," referring to the Tourist Development Council. Tough questions confront Key West and the Keys: Just how many cruise ships and tourists can a fragile archipelago sustain? Key West already faces alarming problems of homelessness and affordable housing.[23]

Across Florida, examples abound of communities preserving the past while harnessing growth. Floridians take pride in places that have survived for centuries. In Bartow, citizens rallied to save the august 1909 Polk County courthouse, understanding that citizens must accept the responsibility of preserving a community jewel that will speak to new generations.

Coastal communities face special challenges when weighing the benefits of enjoying the quality of life in a small town versus selling out to developers. The weathered wooden fishermen's cottages and widow's walks are much admired by locals and tourists—and can be sold for top dollar. These communities have endured poverty and isolation. Can they survive prosperity and climate change?

Dog Island is ground zero for the greatest challenges to Florida: sea-level rise, the threat of too many tourists and too much growth. Miraculously, Dog Island has managed to avoid the fate of most barrier islands. Situated in the Gulf of Mexico about 3 miles from the Panhandle port of Carrabelle, Dog Island is a 7-mile-long, privately owned slice of paradise. The origin of the name is lost in legend. French explorers in 1536 may have found wild dogs roaming the isolated and undulating place they called Isle des Chiens, or perhaps its name derives from its shape—that of a crouching hound. Its neighboring islands are better known: St. Vincent Island (today a national wildlife refuge), St. George Island (a popular vacation and second-home destination across the sound from Apalachicola), and Little St. George Island (an uninhabited barrier island that was purchased to save it from development).

The Union navy occupied the island during the Civil War blockade of Apalachicola. The island once featured a lighthouse. During World War II, Dog Island served as a landing beach for amphibious troops training for the invasions of Normandy, Saipan, and Okinawa. Peace brought a Tallahassee businessman, Jeff Lewis, to the island hideaway. He purchased the entire island for $12,000. He was very selective about whom he allowed to purchase lots. He died in 1981 but sold 1,300 acres to the nonprofit Nature Conservancy for $2 million. He rejected an offer of $4 million from Miami developers. Lewis stipulated that Nature Conservancy must never advertise the island.[24]

In the late 1940s, LeRoy Collins, a state legislator, began camping on the largely uninhabited island. He adored the solitude and the 60-foot interior sand dunes of the undiscovered barrier island. He served as governor of Florida from 1955 to 1961. In 1968, he built a modest home for weekend excursions. "The island has come to be an important part of my life," he wrote in 1987. "Our little house is comfortable, but it is the sea and the island dunes that give me a feeling of peace 'that passeth all understanding.'" He added, "The sea makes me enjoy aloneness, but I rarely feel alone there."[25]

Compared to its neighbor, St. George Island, or almost any barrier island on the Gulf Coast, Dog Island was an untrammeled paradise, but one misaligned with Florida's booming barrier island development. Residents of St. George Island enjoyed a causeway, convenience stores, restaurants, and modern condominium living. Dog Island did not even have a telephone in 1985. A single commercial structure, the Pelican Inn, dots the sand. But not even Dog Island can halt Americans' love affair with sand and isolated islands. "We're holding back a tide," Governor Collins told a reporter four decades ago, content that islanders did not allow seawalls or a bridge.[26]

A journalist in 1985 observed real estate signs across the island. Ugly disputes were erupting between "the naturalists," who wished to preserve the undeveloped solitude, and the developers, who wanted the world to enjoy the charms of a barrier island, and to make money. Today, Dog Island supports about 100 homes. About three dozen residents live on the island year-round.

The 2018 Category 5 Hurricane Michael walloped Dog Island. The serenity of Dog Island—no bridge or causeway—aggravated the reality of removing three tons of debris, including 60 rusted automobiles. Randy Cannon, the "island manager," pleaded: "Everything you do here is an uphill battle. You've just got to take your time." Volunteers hauled 5,500 cubic yards of debris onto barges.[27]

"We have made Italy," proclaimed novelist and nationalist Massimo d'Azeglio in 1861, as the new nation-state of Italy was created. He added, cautiously, "Now we must make Italians." The same might be said about modern Florida. As immigrants across the globe and Americans from across the latitudes pour into Florida, what does "being a Floridian" even mean? A zip code? A tax haven? A seasonal suntan? Should we encourage new residents to become better citizens? Perhaps we should impose a test upon all newcomers, asking them their favorite Marjorie Kinnan Rawlings book?

Geography divides Floridians as it does Italians. Napoleon famously complained that Italy was too long to be a nation. Perhaps Florida is too long to be a state? Do the residents of Pensacola consider Miamians or Neapolitans fellow citizens in bond? In Italy, northern Italians' historic distaste and disdain for southern Italians from Il Mezzogiorno continues to divide and weaken Italy's and Italians' national pride and identity.

Increasingly, architecture divides Floridians. There was something democratic about neighborhoods lined with craftsman bungalows and front porches. Today, our homes are bigger, but our fears are greater. Architects took note. In 2021, gated compounds grate our nervous temperament. The subject of walls has always fascinated poets, historians, and commentators. We are not alone in our fear of invaders. The traditional wisdom suggests that the Ming dynasty rulers between the fourteenth and seventeenth centuries constructed the Great Wall of China to protect the northern border from the marauding barbarians. The Great Wall proved to be a great failure, conceived and implemented by feckless leaders incapable of seeing the big picture.[28]

In his 1915 poem "Mending Wall," Robert Frost wrote one of the most famous and misunderstood opening sentences: "Something there is that doesn't love a wall." It was inevitable that Frost—who spent many winters in Miami at "Pencil Grove," a place surrounded by Dade County pines and citrus groves—would be quoted in the current uproar over illegal immigrants, sanctuary cities, and border walls. Former Alaska governor and vice-presidential candidate Sarah Palin entered the fray when she announced, "And you know what they say about 'fences making good neighbors'? Well, we'll get started on that tall fence tomorrow." Critic Andrew Sullivan, among others, explained that building a wall to keep people out is contrary to Frost's message. Indeed, Frost urges a neighbor to reconsider a wall that alienates neighbors.[29]

Few words convey power and imagination as well as "wall" does. From ancient

China to Cold War Berlin, from the presidential campaign of 2016 to the Kingdom of the North's Wall in *Game of Thrones*, the word evokes and invokes fear and nostalgia. To a desperate immigrant, walls and gates signify old symbols and new frontiers. Semantics matter in the immigration debate. In literary imagination and legendary deed, the frontier signifies freedom, dreams, and individualism. Of course, the word also connotes violence, racism, and nightmares. The Spanish word for frontier is *frontera*, a term conflated with borders and invaders. In AD 711 the Moors sailed the narrow Strait of Gibraltar to conquer and transform Spain's arid south into a garden and oasis. La Reconquista, the religious wars to wrest Spain from the Moors, lasted eight centuries. Today the crenellated walls of the majestic Alhambra in Granada, Spain, attract day-trippers who listen to tourist guides recite Théophile Gautier's "The Moor's Last Sigh."

Between its cable debut in 2011, through the grand finale in 2019, HBO's *The Game of Thrones* captivated Americans and a worldwide audience. Adapted from George R. R. Martin's novels, the cable series had one step in the politics and conflict of the twentieth and twenty-first centuries and one foot in the world of *Ivanhoe*, *The Twilight Zone*, and Tolkien's Shire. The House Stark's family motto, "Winter is coming," seemed oddly and eerily relevant to an America convulsing in its own climate wars. In the series, no landscape was bleaker, no life prospect more pessimistic, no creatures and inhabitants more menacing than the land beyond the Wall. Standing 700 feet tall and 300 feet thick, and stretching 300 miles, the Wall was defended by the Sworn Brothers of the Night's Watch, men who are pledged to monastic and dangerous lives. The Wall protects the civilized but feuding Kingdom of the North against evil White Walkers, the scourge of mankind. Another enemy is the Wildings, a fiercely independent people considered more savage than human. Wildings prefer to call themselves "free folk." The Wall symbolizes good and evil.

The Wall acquired a superheavy connotation when candidate and then President Donald Trump promised he would build a wall on America's southern border. "Bad hombres" were penetrating our porous borders, threatening to weaken American values, bringing drugs and a gang culture to our country. Ratcheting up the bold promise, Trump ensured Americans that Mexico would pay for the wall. The president announced on his Instagram account, "The Wall Is Coming." The *New York Times*' TV critic observed that President Trump loved the idea of "going medieval on national security," but cautioned that the leader of the Free World may not really understand the Wall's meaning. Jon Snow, the leader of the Night's Watch, defends the Wildings, arguing, "They were born on the wrong side of the wall. That doesn't make them monsters." In the series' conclusion, the

Wildings and their enemies make common cause and triumph over evil. James Poniewozik summarizes: "Nationalism and tribalism are not essential forces for preserving society but an existential threat to survival. The Wall is a mighty symbol of protection but ultimately an ineffective one; the only salvation, if there is one, is people deciding that they have more to gain by working together."[30]

If a single word united and divided the years 2000–2010, it would be "fraught." The word seemed to describe everything from political relationships, award ceremonies, to even the playing of the National Anthem. Perhaps future historians will describe the period as the "Era of Fraught Feelings."[31]

Floridians stand at a crossroads in 2021. Will we remain shackled to the mantra of growth-at-all-costs or learn to pause and appreciate the serenity of small-town Florida? Florida would be a poorer state without our historic communities. More than ever, Floridians need to understand we are part of something bigger than our zip code, growth stats, or political party. Florida's distinctive places touch our deepest roots and rekindle special relationships that connect generations.

Once, many communities in Florida seemed frozen in time. In 1930, Tallahassee was a modest city of 10,700 residents, but also a place graced by majestic live oak canopies and churches that still retained the old pews for the enslaved. One resident was LeRoy Collins, the future governor. His favorite place was Old Pisgah, a country church where his circuit-riding grandfather preached. He described his affection for the church in words that touch us today: "In the raucous, violent world of today that too often disdains virtues and values, Pisgah whispers slowly. Slow down, take time to see the old and beautiful, to remember and to cherish what deserves to be loved and honored from the noble past." Lest we forget.[32]

THE END

Acknowledgments

Having spent four and one-half decades in Florida, I am now in a season of reflection, the autumn of my life. I acknowledge House Stark's motto: "Winter is coming." The troubled, coarsening condition of my beloved Florida saddens me. The realities of life in the twenty-first century—the racial and ethnic divides, the yawning inequalities of income and hope, the environmental indifference, or worse, the wanton destruction of the wetlands and desecration of our beloved natural springs and waterways—should concern every Floridian. Perhaps a new generation of Floridians will embrace our magical land and waters in spasms of healing and discovery? Perhaps a new Florida dream will inspire Floridians to reembrace nature and appreciate its special qualities?

The Sunshine State has been very kind to me. I often think about a young-blood teacher strolling the streets of Ybor City and Calle Ocho in Miami, hiking through the Fakahatchee Strand in search of the elusive ghost orchid, and leading a Florida Humanities Council workshop in Everglades City and the old Cuban club in Key West. The words of Gabriel García Márquez resonate, "The world was so recent, many things lacked names." I felt like Colonel Aureliano Buendía, who, upon facing a firing squad, remembered "when his father took him to discover ice."

As a historian and writer who has spent almost five decades trying to understand Florida, I have accumulated a lifetime of debts. At times I felt as if I were riding a real-life roller coaster. My family's Sicilian heritage haunts and comforts me. A Sicilian proverb instructs, "Never return an empty dish."

I remain an optimist, still crying at Frank Capra movies and rereading Ole Rølvaag's *Giants in the Earth.* I cheer for the underdog. Anyone who teaches undergraduate students must be an optimist, hoping youth will learn to appreciate and respect the places and things that make Florida special: the surging grandeur of a Florida spring, the solitude and dignity of canoeing the Upper Hillsborough River, journeying through Highlands Hammock and Torreya State Parks, gazing upon the architectural perfection of Miami Beach's art deco hotels, and the Hyde Park and Old Northeast neighborhoods of Tampa and St. Petersburg.

One of the loveliest places I have visited is the Hermitage Artist Retreat on Manasota Key. On two occasions I enjoyed the rhythms of the Gulf of Mexico and fellow artists and writers. Several book chapters were first composed there. My cluttered study and retreat in the backyard of our Old Northeast neighborhood in St. Petersburg is a perfect place for contemplation. The myriad birdlife, the monarch butterflies, and even the chirping squirrels greet me each morning.

Arriving at the University of South Florida in 1977 at age thirty, I chuckled the first time I visited Sun City Center and Penny Farms. I now appreciate these places. Like many fellow Floridians, I may be old but still behave as if I am young. Each Sunday I look forward to playing tennis with dear friends. I enjoy the freedom of retirement and would say that I miss my colleagues except for the fact that I see many of them daily.

The University of South Florida St. Petersburg has been home for almost two decades. I have befriended many colleagues who made my life cheerful and meaningful. On a typical day, I walk to the USF St. Petersburg campus, only a fifteen-minute walk from our beloved 1918 craftsman bungalow. Thank you, J. Michael Francis, Thomas Smith, Chris Meindl, Felipe Mantilla, Amy Anderson, Erin Mauldin, Thomas Hallock, and Sudsy Tschiderer for tolerating my presence and understanding my technological insecurities. In 2003, my longtime buddy Ray Arseneault invited me to launch the Florida Studies Program at USF St. Petersburg. The Florida Studies Program and St. Petersburg have meant so much to the Morminos. John Belohlavek, one of the first persons I met at the USF Tampa campus, remains a dear friend who is never too busy to discuss politics, sports, or pierogies. He read every word of this manuscript. He remains a scholar and a gentleman.

My Florida Studies colleague and comrade Chris Meindl read several chapters and offered keen insights into issues related to the environment. Darryl Paulson, a colleague at USF St. Petersburg, was especially helpful and generous in his critical readings of chapters focusing upon Florida elections and politics. The university still allows me to teach a class each semester, for which I am grateful. I have been associated with Florida Humanities when it was known as the Florida Humanities Council. Ann Henderson, Janine Farver, Steve Seibert,

Patricia Putman, and Nashid Madyun have generously encouraged a joint exploration of the Sunshine State. The University of Florida's Steve Noll and Jack Davis are dear friends and provide a valuable sounding board. Connie Lester and James Clark at the University of Central Florida have supported this book and other projects.

Historians' best friends are librarians. David Shedden was one of the first graduate students I met who was interested in Florida history. As director of the Poynter Library's archives, David has been invaluable in helping locate arcane documents. David replaced Jim Schnur, who also took classes in Florida history. Jim worked overtime in proofing this manuscript. Andy Huse has remained a good colleague, critic, and an unvaluable resource at Special Collections at the USF Tampa Library. Andy has become an accomplished author. Thanks to all!

Sandy Rief is a dear friend who has made enormous contributions to the study of Florida history. In the late 1990s, he and the Frank E. Duckwall Foundation created the first professorship in Florida history and kindly tapped me to hold that distinguished position. That I have held and represented the Frank E. Duckwall professorship in Florida history is a great honor. The Duckwall Foundation has generously supported this book.

My wife and I have so many good friends in St. Petersburg. We have walked through the neighborhoods of St. Petersburg and hiked through Basque country and the Cotswolds with Diana and Marshall Craig. Diana is also a magnificent editor, and Marshall is one of the most thoughtful persons I know. I still find inspiration from the old *St. Petersburg Times* columns of Jeff Klinkenberg, one of Florida's great writers. George Stovall brings an intimate knowledge and perspective of St. Petersburg and Florida's environment to every conversation we have. A former colleague and now director of the FSU London Program, Kathleen Paul was a gracious host when my wife and I spent a summer in 2017 London. Donna Parrino, a friend from USF Tampa Library days, is a skilled proof reader, an impassioned writer, and champion of her beloved Ybor City. Bob Kerstein and Robin Jones retired to St. Petersburg after careers at the University of Tampa and University of South Florida. Bob is an adept critic and old ally. Steve and Jeana Seibert have become treasured friends and neighbors.

Millikin University in Decatur, Illinois, holds a special place in my life. As a sophomore student—and teenager!—I fell in love with the ravishing, red-haired Donna Lynne Wheeler. First love, best love. I returned to teach at Millikin between 1974 and 1977, years that resonate decades later. Our daughters, Amy Ellen and Rebecca Lynne were born in the Heartlands. Today, Rebecca works at the University of North Carolina's Kenan Institute of Private Enterprise while Amy teaches religion at the University of Tampa and St. Petersburg College when not answering my questions about computer malfunctions. The book is dedicated to them.

Fatefully, Millikin University was also the alma mater of Roger Lotchin. As an accomplished professor and advisor at the University of North Carolina, Roger shaped my career and provided a perfect role model. He also sharpened my tennis skills. Millikin was also the alma mater of John Adney. A brilliant lawyer, he and his wife, Sue, guided me through the legal briar patch of the 2000 election. Millikin also introduced us to dear friends, Steve and Marjory Dodge, who now live in Florida.

Having taught for almost five decades, I owe so much to the thousands of students who took my classes, among them "The Rise of Modern Europe," "U.S. Survey," "World War II," "Food & History," "Immigration History," and "Florida History." It is one of life's great joys to see former students succeed. Pam Iorio took my class in 2000, an extraordinary time considering she was supervisor of elections for Hillsborough County and soon served with distinction as mayor of Tampa. Pam critiqued my chapter on the 2000 election in Florida. Vicki Weber also provided her legal expertise in critiquing the 2000 election chapter. Tom Ankersen wrote his graduate thesis at USF on Florida's ecology, and now teaches environmental law at the University of Florida. We canoed the Hillsborough River many times, memories I cherish. He read several chapters and provided valuable feedback. Evan Bennett, now a professor at Florida Atlantic University, provided invaluable insights as a reader and friend. Marilyn Polson works as a lawyer in St. Petersburg but also takes classes in the Florida Studies Program. She helped clarify some legal issues and was always cheerful and supportive. Lee Irby was a memorable student in the 1990s, who wrote a prize-winning master's thesis on the history of trailer parks in St. Petersburg. Lee is a successful writer, teacher, and critic. Alison Hardage was one of the first Florida Studies students. She is also an astute critic, financial analyst, and keen observer of St. Petersburg and devotee of Sewanee, University of the South. Hugh Tulloch audited several classes and has become a dear friend who read book several chapters. Rodney Kite-Powell wrote his master's thesis on the history of Davis Islands and turned it into a book. He has become one of the voices and faces of Tampa history through his work at the Tampa Bay History Center. Thanks to everyone!

My role model in retirement is the great Roman orator and wordsmith Marcus Tullius Cicero. He wrote two thousand years ago, "How wonderful it is for the soul when—after so many struggles with lust, ambition, strife, quarrelling and other passions—these battles are at last ended." Cicero understood the beauty of solitude and contemplation that retirement allows. Cicero also wrote, "He who has a garden, and a library has everything you need." Scratch a Sicilian and you will find a peasant. Few things are more rewarding than tending a garden, patiently waiting for the monarch and Gulf fritillary butterflies, cultivating magnificent desert roses, and admiring frangipani blossoms. Cicero was the greatest Roman retiree of them all.

The University Press of Florida is a state treasure. From Ken Scott to Meredith Babb to Romi Gutiérrez, the University Press has served as a refuge and beacon for writers interested in all things Florida. The Press has been very kind to me for many decades. Sian Hunter has been pure delight to work with as my editor. Susan Murray copyedited this book for the Press, no easy task. She is a magnificent editor and wordsmith. Thanks to all.

Notes

Abbreviations

AP	Associated Press
AS	*Anniston Star*
BG	*Boston Globe*
BGN	*Belle Glade News*
BH	*Bradenton Herald*
BN	*Bloomberg News*
CL	*Creative Loafing* (Tampa)
CS	*Clearwater Sun*
CSM	*Christian Science Monitor*
CT	*Chicago Tribune*
DBNJ	*Daytona Beach News-Journal*
DFP	*Detroit Free Press*
FHQ	*Florida Historical Quarterly*
FLDN	*Fort Lauderdale Daily News*
FMNP	*Fort Myers News-Press*
FPT	*Fort Pierce Tribune*
FT	*Florida Trend*
FTU	*Florida Times-Union*
GS	*Gainesville Sun*
HP	*Huffington Post*
KWC	*Key West Citizen*
JCF	*Jackson County Floridian*
JSH	*Journal of Southern History*

LAT	*Los Angeles Times*
LG	*La Gaceta*
LKO	*Longboat Key Observer*
LL	*Lakeland Ledger*
MH	*Miami Herald*
MM	*Money Magazine*
MN	*Miami News*
MNT	*Miami New Times*
MRJ	*Manatee River Journal*
NDN	*Naples Daily News*
NFDN	*Northwest Florida Daily News*
NG	*National Geographic*
NR	*New Republic*
NYDN	*New York Daily News*
NYP	*New York Post*
NYRB	*New York Review of Books*
NYS	*New York Sun*
NYT	*New York Times*
NYTM	*New York Times Magazine*
OS	*Orlando Sentinel*
OSB	*Ocala Star-Banner*
PBP	*Palm Beach Post*
PCNH	*Panama City News-Herald*
PNJ	*Pensacola News-Journal*
PPG	*Pittsburgh Post-Gazette*
RS	*Rolling Stone*
SAR	*St. Augustine Record*
SFSS	*South Florida Sun-Sentinel*
SH	*Sanford Herald*
SHT	*Sarasota Herald-Tribune*
SI	*Sports Illustrated*
SLPD	*St. Louis Post-Dispatch*
SPT	*St. Petersburg Times*
SS	*Sun-Sentinel*
TA	*The Atlantic*
TBBJ	*Tampa Bay Business Journal*
TBH	*Tampa Bay History*
TBT	*Tampa Bay Times*

TCP	*Treasure Coast Palm*
TD	*Tallahassee Democrat*
TDT	*Tampa Daily Times*
TE	*The Economist*
TG	*The Guardian* (Manchester)
TMT	*Tampa Morning Tribune*
TNY	*The New Yorker*
TT	*Tampa Tribune*
USAT	*USA Today*
VDS	*Villages Daily Sun*
VF	*Vanity Fair*
WP	*Washington Post*
WSJ	*Wall Street Journal*

Introduction

1. Kevin Starr, *California on the Edge, 1990–2003* (New York: Oxford University Press, 2004), 1; Starr quoted in *NYT*, 28 October 1991.

2. Jim Hicks, "More History from the Will Durants," *Life*, 18 October 1963, 92.

3. David M. Shribman, "The Future Is Florida," *Pittsburgh Post*-Gazette, 1 April 2005; official quoted in "Florida," *NYT*, 7 August 1996.

4. Shribman, "The Future Is Florida."

5. Luigi Barzini, *The Italians: A Full-Length Portrait Featuring Their Manners and Morals* (New York: Touchstone, 1964), ix.

6. Christopher Beam, "The Uh-Ohs," Slate.com, 18 December 2009.

7. Adam Weinstein, "Five Myths about Florida," *WP*, 14 July 2017.

8. Howard Troxler, "Fixing Florida Will Be Fun to Watch," *TBT*, 13 June 2011.

9. "Half of Residents Say Sunshine State Is Losing Its Luster," *SS*, 14 January 2008.

10. Ross Douthat, "The Age of Individualism," *NYT*, 15 March 2014; "100 Largest Churches: Seven Are in Florida," *SFSS*, 26 September 2010; Robert D. Putnam, *Bowling Alone: The Collapse and Revival of American Community* (New York: Simon and Schuster, 2000).

11. Gary R. Mormino, *Land of Sunshine, State of Dreams: A Social History of Modern Florida* (Gainesville: University Press of Florida, 2005), 125; Robert Pittman, "Florida Is the Mistress State," *SPT*, 10 February 1985.

12. Jeff LaHurd, "The Area Was Long Known as a Healthful Location," *SHT*, 26 October 2020; "2010 Census Shows 65 and Older Population Growing Faster," U.S. Census Bureau, 30 November 2011; *SHT*, 16 June 1991; "Retirement under the Sun," *SPT*, 1 October 1965; Mormino, *Land of Sunshine*, 132; Needham Christopher Hines, *The Truth about Florida* (North Miami: Florida Research Press, 1962), 19.

13. "Almost No One Wants a Neighbor Like Donald Trump," *WP*, 18 December 2020.

14. "Rudy's Faithful Give Him a Place in the Sun," *BN*, 4 December 2007.

15. Darryl Paulson, "Why Florida and Its Politicians Don't Get Any National Respect," *TBT*, 4 September 2017.

16. "Florida Has More Hispanics Than Blacks, Census Shows," *NYT*, 28 March 2001; David Rieff, *Going to Miami: Exiles, Tourists, and Refugees in the New America* (Boston: Little, Brown, 1987), 218.

17. Louis A. Perez, *On Becoming Cuban: Identity, Nationality, and Culture* (Chapel Hill: University of

North Carolina Press, 1999), 432–34; Eliot Kleinberg, "Fulgencio Batista Shares Life in Cuba Pre-Fidel Castro," *PBP,* 20 August 2020.

18. "A Teen, a Teacher, a Gun: 2000 School Shooting Staggered Palm Beach County," *PBP,* 21 May 2000.

19. Strawberry Saroyan, "What a Weird, Wired World It Was," *WSJ,* 23 July 2017.

20. Kurt Andersen, "The Best Decade Ever? The 1990s, Obviously," *NYT,* 6 February 2015.

21. Jon Nordheimer, "Florida, Battling History," *NYT,* 15 July 1986.

Chapter 1. Y2K and Hanging Chads, JEB! and Dubya: Florida and the Election of 2000

1. T. Stanton Dietrich, *The Urbanization of Florida's Population: An Historical Perspective of County Growth, 1830–1970* (Gainesville: Bureau of Economic and Business Research, 1978), 11, 102–3; *United States Census 2000: Florida: 2000,* (Washington, DC: US Government Printing Office, 2003), "Profile of General Demographic Characteristics for Florida: 2000," DP-1.

2. "Florida Has More Hispanics Than Blacks," *NYT,* 28 March 2001.

3. "Leon County," *TD,* 28 March 2001; Dietrich, *The Urbanization of Florida's Population,* 117, 143, 151.

4. Nordheimer, "Sunbelt Region," *NYT,* 8 February 1976; "15,982,378 and Counting," *OS,* 29 December 2000.

5. Kevin Prince Phillips, *The Emerging Republican Majority* (New York: Arlington House, 1969), 437; Kirkpatrick Sale, *Power Shift: The Rise of the Southern Rim and Challenge to the Eastern Establishment* (New York: Random House, 1975), 6, 11; Richard M. Bernard and Bradley R. Rice, eds., *Sunbelt Cities: Politics and Growth since WWII* (Austin: University of Texas Press, 1983), 1–26.

6. "Defining Ourselves," *SFSS,* 13 August 2000; "Snowbirds Flock Together for Winter," and "Florida Luring Jerseyans," *NYT,* 2 February 2007 and 2 May 1982.

7. Edr.state.fl.us; *Twelfth Census of the U.S.: 1900,* II, *Population,* part 2, liii, U.S. Bureau of the Census.

8. Charles Krauthammer, "A Second American Century," *Time* (20 December 1999).

9. Ross Douthat, "The Best Year of Our Lives," *NYT,* 6 April 2019.

10. Stephen Jay Gould, *Questioning the Millennium* (Cambridge, MA: Harvard University Press, 2011); "Is This the Real Millennium?," CNN.com, 1 January 2001; "Is It Really a New Century?" *TT,* 1 January 2000.

11. "Is Complexity Interlinked with Disaster? Ask on Jan. 1," *NYT,* 11 December 1999; "Y2K," NPR, 1 February 1999; "The Y2K Problem Is Now Seen as a Bit of a Joke," *TG,* 31 December 2019; Lily Rothman, "Remember Y2K? How We Prepped for the Non-Disaster," *Time,* 31 December 2014.

12. "It's Party Time, not Panic Time," *GS,* 1 January 2000.

13. "Countdown Lakeland," *LL,* 31 December 1999; "And the Band Plays On," *SFSS,* 31 December 1999; "Good Times Rolled," *MH,* 2 January 2000.

14. "And the Band Plays On"; "Fans, Band Groove in Phish Bowl," *MH,* 1 January 2000.

15. "15,000 Gather Downtown Fort Myers," *FMNP,* 1 January 2000; "Good Times Rolled"; "Minor Glitches Only Sign of Anticipated Y2K Chaos," *TT,* 1 January 2001; AP, "Floridians Pack Parties," *PBP,* 1 January 2000; "Gated Residents Throw Own Party," *FMNP,* 1 January 2000; "Trump," *SFSS,* 1 January 2001.

16. AP, "Floridians Pack Parties"; "The Donald Eyes the White House," *WP,* 7 October 1999; "Ivana: He's Not That Dumb!," *NYP,* 9 October 1999; Steve Kornacki, "When Trump Ran against Trumpism," NBCNews.com, 2 October 2018.

17. *SAR,* 31 December 2000; "100 Years to Right Wrongs," *SPT,* 1 January 2000; Dave Barry, "Safe to Come out Now," *MH,* 2 January 2000; "Y2K Turns out A-OK," *FPT,* 1 January 2000.

18. "Babies, Brides, and Grooms," *MH,* 2 January 2000; *TT,* 1 January 2000; *TD,* 2 January 2000; "102-Year-Old," *MH,* 1 January 2000.

19. "Hendry Clan Rings in Second Century," *FMNP*, 1 January 2000; "Fort Myers and Alva Telephone Line," *FMNP*, 4 January 1900.

20. "U.S. Turns Back Boat with 406 from Haiti," *MH*, 2 January 2000; Gary R. Mormino, *Land of Sunshine, State of Dreams: A Social History of Modern Florida* (Gainesville: University Press of Florida, 2005), 291.

21. Lance Morrow, "In the Elian Story, Let's Talk Happy Endings," *Time*, 24 April 2000.

22. Gabriel García Márquez, "Elián González, Stranded," *NYT*, 29 March 2000.

23. "Elián Documentary Revisits Painful Chapter," *MH*, 30 April 2017.

24. Lizette Alvarez, "400 Years Later, Still Revered in Cuba (and Miami)," *NYT*, 10 September 2012.

25. "Celebrating a 50-Year-Old 'Miracle,'" *MH*, 5 September 2011; Jason Berry, "How the Catholic Church Survived in Cuba," *TA*, 18 September 2015; David Montgomery, "Why the Iconic Virgin of Charity Means So Much to Cubans and Pope Francis," *WP*, 22 September 2015; Michelle A. González, *Afro-Cuban Theology: Religion, Race, Culture, and Identity* (Gainesville: University Press of Florida, 2006), 78–79.

26. "Sister Jeanne O'Laughlin," *NYT*, 21 June 2019; "How the Battle over Elián González Helped Change U.S. Cuba Policy," NPR.org, 28 June 2015.

27. "Elian's Story Became a National Affair," *MH*, 9 June 2013; Rick Bragg, "Legacy of a Cuban Boy," *NYT*, 10 May 2000; "Is Brett Kavanaugh the 'Forrest Gump' of Washington?," *WP*, 12 July 2018; "How Barbara Lagoa's Legal Fight for Elian Shaped Her Legal Career," Politico.com, 25 September 2020.

28. Bill Clinton, *My Life* (New York: Knopf, 2004), 905.

29. "Elián González: My Time in the U.S.," *MH*, 19 November 2013; "Elián González and the Cuban Crisis," *TG*, 20 February 2010; T. D. Allman, *Finding Florida* (New York: Atlantic Monthly Press, 2013), 433–34.

30. "Abduction of Elian," *Baltimore Sun*, 26 April 2000; Martin Dyckman, "Elian Gonzalez, a Painful Chapter in Cuban-American History," floridapolitics.com, 2 May 2017; Gregory B. Craig, "Forever a Poster Child?" *WP*, 28 June 2001.

31. William Schneider, "Elián González Defeated Al Gore," *TA*, 1 May 2001; Hiaasen, "When the Going Gets Weird," *Time*, 20 November 2000, 20; Saladrigas quoted in "How the Battle over Elián González Helped Change U.S. Cuba Policy," NPR.org, 28 June 2015; Abraham quoted in "Florida Republicans Help Jurist Lagoa," *WP*, 21 September 2020.

32. Bill Turque, *Inventing Al Gore: A Biography* (Boston: Houghton Mifflin, 2000), xi; "For Gore, Army Years Mixed Vietnam and Family Politics," *NYT*, 29 June 2010; David Maraniss, "Al Gore, Growing up in Two Worlds," *WP*, 10 October 2010.

33. Turque, *Inventing Al Gore*, xii–xiii, 342–43; "The Life of Al Gore, the Path to Politics," *WP*, 28 June 2010.

34. Turque, *Inventing Al Gore*, xiii, 360–61; "Gore May Forgo Help from Clinton," *WP*, 16 October 2000.

35. Michael Ollove, *LAT*, 7 November 2000.

36. Lieberman and woman quoted in "Gore and Company Make a Serious Play for Florida," *NYT*, 24 August 2000; "Gore Ticket, Jewish Vote," *LAT*, 24 August 2000; "After Sides Are Chosen, Turnout Settles the Game," *NYT*, 4 November 2000.

37. Alan Wolfe, "What Scholarship Reveals about Politics and Religion," *Chronicle of Higher Education*, 8 September 2000.

38. "Condo's Boss Death Signals Decline of Political Machines," "Political Giant Trinchitella Dies," and "Joan Geller, Political Mother," *SS*, 5 February and 12 May 2015.

39. Alex Leary, "A Life in Florida of His Making," *TBT*, 14 June 2015; "Jeb Bush Shaped by Troubled Phillips Academy Years," *Boston Globe*, 1 February 2015; Bush quoted in "Next in Line," *Time*, 16 March 2015, 38.

40. Steve Eder and Michael Barbaro, "As Dynasty's Son, Jeb Bush Used His Connections Freely,"

NYT, 14 February 2015; Patricia Mazzei, "How Miami Made Jeb Bush," *MH*, 12 June 2015; radio host quoted in Mara Liasson, NPR, 15 June 2015; "Jeb Bush Dogged by Decades of Questions about Business Deals," *WP*, 28 June 2015; "Recarey's Arrest Leaves Questions," *SS*, 8 October 2015.

41. Whitehead quoted in Steve Bousquet, "Charles Crist's Party Switch Is Like No Other in Florida History," *TBT*, 12 September 2014.

42. "He Was Born Republican Royalty, but 'Jebcito' Is from Miami," NPR, 15 June 2015; Robert E. Crew Jr., *Jeb Bush: Aggressive Conservatism in Florida* (Lanham, MD: University Press of America, 2010), 1–2; "Recarey's Arrest Leaves Questions," *SS*, 8 October 1993.

43. "Senators Find They Have Republican for Chaplain," *SPT*, 1 June 1951; Colburn and Scher, *Florida's Gubernatorial Politics in the 20th Century* (Gainesville: University Presses of Florida, 1980), 26–27; Gary R. Mormino, *Millard Fillmore Caldwell* (Gainesville: University Press of Florida, 2020), 25–26.

44. William Cramer, interview by the author, 2 August 2003, St. Petersburg; "GOP Pinellas Totals Worry County Dems," *TMT*, 7 November 1946; Darryl Paulson, "Florida Has Been Red, It Has Also Been Blue," *TBT*, 6 November 2016.

45. "The Future Is Florida," *PPG*, 1 April 2005; Colburn and Scher, *Florida's Gubernatorial Politics*, 80–85; Edmund F. Kallina, *Claude Kirk and the Politics of Confrontation* (Gainesville: University Press of Florida, 1993), 26–27; "Paula Hawkins, 82, Florida Ex-Senator Dies," *NYT*, 4 December 2009.

46. "Florida's Deficit of Courage on Taxes," *TBT*, 24 September 2017; "Connie Mack in the Running?" *SS*, 1 August 1996; Godefroy Desrosiers-Lauzon, *Florida's Snowbirds: Spectacle, Mobility, and Community since 1945* (Montreal: McGill-Queen's University Press, 2011), 89–90.

47. "The Destruction of Political Norms Started Decades Ago," *WP*, 18 June 2017; Julian Zelizer, *Burning Down the House: Newt Gingrich, the Fall of a Speaker and the Rise of the New Republican Party* (New York: Penguin, 2020); "Was C. W. Bill Young Ever the Only Republican in the Florida Senate?," politifact, 9 October 2013; "U.S. Rep. C. W. Bill Young Dies at 82," *TBT*, 19 October 2013; Allen Morris, *The Florida Handbook, 1961–1962* (Tallahassee: Peninsular, 1962), 55.

48. "Mary Landrieu Is Defeated," *NYT*, 6 December 2014.

49. John Harwood, "Marion Keith," *SPT*, 3 March 1982.

50. S. V. Dáte, *Quiet Passion: A Biography of Senator Bob Graham* (New York: Penguin, 2004), 183–211.

51. David Colburn, *From Yellow Dog Democrats to Red State Republicans: Florida and Its Politics since 1940* (Gainesville: University Press of Florida, 2007), 136–37, 144–47.

52. "Florida Gov. Lawton Chiles Dies," *WP*, 13 December 1998; "Feeling the Burden of a Name, One Bush Focuses on Florida," *NYT*, 14 July 2000; Martínez quoted in Mazzei, "How Miami Made Jeb Bush"; Karen Tumulty, "A Tough Loss in Fla. Taught Bush What It Takes to Win," *WP*, 15 June 2015; Jeb quoted in "Next in Line," 40; Jean Edward Smith, *Bush* (New York: Simon and Schuster, 2017), 78–79; Minutaglio, *First Son: George W. Bush and the Bush Family Dynasty* (New York: Times Books, 1999), 294.

53. Colburn, *From Yellow Dog Democrats*, 157–75; Martínez quoted in Mazzei, "How Miami Made Jeb Bush"; Buddy MacKay, *How Florida Happened: The Political Education of Buddy MacKay* (Gainesville: University Press of Florida, 2010), 201–24.

54. "As Florida Goes, So Goes the Nation," *Time*, 25 September 2000; "The Florida Governor: Feeling the Burden of a Name," *Time*, 14 July 2000; "Jeb Bush's Emails as Governor of Florida Show His Agenda and Goals," *NYT*, 24 December 2014.

55. Darryl Paulson, "Our Tiny Big State," *TBT*, 3 September 2017.

56. "Big Surge in No-Party Voters Could Reshape Florida Politics," *MH*, 4 July 2014; Florida Division of Elections, Data and Statistics, 1972, 1980, and 2000 Voter Registration; John H. Aldrich, *Why Parties? The Origin and Transformation of Party Politics in America* (Chicago: University of Chicago Press, 1995); Paul Kleppner, *The Cross of Culture: A Social Analysis of Midwestern Politics* (New York: Free Press, 1970).

57. Dana Ste. Claire, *Cracker: Cracker Culture in Florida History* (Gainesville: University Press of Florida, 2006).

58. Ex-Felons," *NYT*, 20 February 2005; "Disenfranchised Florida Felons," *NYT*, 28 March 2004;

"Electors," Florida State Statutes, 101:51; Pipa Holloway, "'A Chicken Stealer Shall Lose His Vote': Disfranchisement for Larceny in the South, 1874–1890," *JSH* 75 (November 2009): 931.

59. Jerrell H. Shofner, *Nor Is It over Yet: Florida in the Era of Reconstruction, 1863–1877* (Gainesville: University Presses of Florida, 1974), 164–65, 300–344; Robert E. Crew Jr., *Aggressive Conservatism in Florida* (Lanham, MD: University Press of America, 2010), 92–93.

60. Ari Berman, *Give Us the Ballot: The Modern Struggle for Voting Rights in America* (New York: Farrar, Straus and Giroux, 2015), 207–9.

61. Crew, *Aggressive Conservatism in Florida*, 92–93; Robert Lantigua, "How the GOP Gamed the System," *Nation*, 20 April 2001, 11–17; "Jeb Bush Blamed for Unfair Florida Election," *TG*, 5 June 2001.

62. David Shribman, "The Future of Florida," *PPG*, 1 April 2005; "As I-4 Corridor Goes, So Goes Florida," *Washington Times*, 28 January 2008; "Florida's Interstate Heavy Campaign Traffic," *NYT*, 25 October 2000.

63. "Florida's Interstate Heavy Campaign Traffic"; Colburn, *From Yellow Dog Democrats*, 58, 73–114; Mormino, "Revisiting the Circus of a Special Session in 1945," *TBT*, 19 June 2015.

64. S. V. Dáte, *Jeb: America's Next Bush* (New York: Tarcher, 2007), 178–79.

65. Ibid., 179; "Kendrick Meek Set to Fulfill a Legacy," *MH*, 9 June 2012; Matthew T. Corrigan, *Conservative Hurricane: How Jeb Bush Remade Florida* (Gainesville: University Press of Florida, 2014), 88–90; Crew, *Aggressive Conservatism in Florida*, 90–91.

66. Jason Guerrasio, "Will Ferrell Thinks His 'SNL' Portrayal of George W. Bush Influenced the 2000 Election," *Business Insider*, 16 April 2015.

67. Colburn, *From Yellow Dog Democrat*, 18; AP, "GOP Group Airing Pro-Nader Ads," 27 October 2000.

68. George W. Bush, *Decision Points* (New York: Crown, 2010), 75–76; AP, "Bush Once Pleaded to DUI," *WP*, 3 November 2000.

69. Lieberman, Gore, and Gutiérrez quoted in Jake Tapper, *Down and Dirty: The Plot to Steal the Presidency* (Boston: Little, Brown, 2001), 4, 13.

70. Colburn, *From Yellow Dog Democrat*, 181; Rather quoted in Bush, *Decision Points*, 77.

71. Dáte, *Quiet Passion*, 242; Dáte, *Jeb*, 12. Polls taken after the election revealed that the network's declaration of a Gore victory depressed the voter turnout in Florida's Central Time Zone by 3 percent. The area voted decisively for Bush. "Panhandle Poll Follow-Up," McLaughlinOnline.com, 6 December 2000.

72. Dáte, *Jeb*, 13; Corrigan, *Conservative Hurricane*, 1–2; "Austin Insiders and Observers Look Back at the 2000 Election," *Austin American-Statesman*, 22 September 2012.

73. David Greenberg, "What Roger Ailes Learned from Richard Nixon," *NYT*, 18 May 2017; "Roger Ailes," *NYT*, 19 May 2017.

74. Gabriel Sherman, *The Loudest Voice in the Room* (New York: Random House, 2017), 137, 244–45; Jane Mayer, "Dept. of Close Calls George W.'s Cousin," *NYT*, 20 November 2006, 36.

75. Sherman, *The Loudest Voice in the Room*, 248–50.

76. Ibid., 250–51; Evans quoted in Bush, *Decision Points*, 78.

77. AP, "Networks Try to Explain Blown Call," *WP*, 8 November 2000.

78. Bush, Gore, Evans quoted in Bush, 78; Colburn, *From Yellow Dog Democrat*, 183–85; Jake Tapper, *Down and Dirty: The Plot to Steal the Presidency* (New York: Little, Brown, 2001), 26–27; Peter Marks, "A Flawed Call Adds to High Drama," *NYT*, 8 November 2000; Dáte, *Jeb*, 135.

79. Katherine Harris, *Center of the Storm: Practicing Principled Leadership in Times of Crisis* (Nashville: WND Books, 2002), 35–46.

80. Dana Millbank, "Florida Secretary of State Harris Hires Lawyers Linked to Jeb Bush," *WP*, 16 November 2000; Robert Weiner, "Jeb Bush's Elephant in the Room," *Des Moines Register*, 16 April 2015.

81. Marks, "A Flawed Call Adds to High Drama"; Dave Wilson, "The Night the Election Wasn't Won," *MH*, 9 June 2003.

82. Colburn, *From Yellow Dog Democrat*, 186–87.

83. Smith, *Bush*, 138.

84. Jeffrey Toobin, *Too Close to Call: The Thirty-Six-Day Battle to Decide the 2000 Election* (New York: Random House, 2001), 65.

85. Lucy Morgan, "Turning Tables," *NYT*, 21 November 2010; Laurence Tribe, "Moving Forward," *NYT*, 21 November 2010.

86. Jeffrey Toobin, "Warren Christopher, 1925–2011," *NYT*, 19 March 2011, 19; deHaven-Smith, *The Battle for Florida*, 25.

87. Baur quoted in "Jeb Bush's Recount Role Examined," *LAT*, 14 July 2001.

88. "2000 Recount Shaped Cruz's Image as Outsider," *NYT*, 26 January 2016; "Supreme Court Nominee Brett Kavanaugh," *SFSS*, 10 July 2018; Tamara Keith, "Brett Kavanaugh Investigated a President," NPR.org, 18 August 2018; "After Investigating a President," *WP*, 3 August 2018; "Jeb Bush's Elephant in the Room," *Des Moines Register*, 16 April 2015; "Amy Coney Barrett Worked on *Bush v. Gore*," *Jacobin Magazine*, 28 September 2020; "What Barrett Would Recuse Herself From," NPR.org, 30 September 2020.

89. Tapper, *Down and Dirty*, 61.

90. "The Age of the Votomatic," and "The Palm Beach Ballot," *NYT*, 4 December and 9 November 2000.

91. "Outrage," *MN*, 16 November 1988.

92. "What Counts," Time magazine, 18 December 2000, 36-37.

93. Colburn, *From Yellow Dog Democrat*, 185–95; Tapper, *Down and Dirty*, 6–10; "Voters Statewide Say They Had Poll Problems," *SPT*, 9 November 2000; "Supervisor of Elections," *PBP*, 15 October 1996.

94. Michael Parenti, "The Stolen Presidential Elections," Michael Parenti Political Archive; "Butterfly Ballot Cost Gore White House," *PBP*, 9 March 2001; commissioner quoted in "Florida Democrats Say Ballot's Design Hurt Gore," *NYT*, 9 November 2000; Datz quoted in "Where Balloting for Buchanan Surged, Outrage among Voters," *LAT*, 10 November 2000.

95. Cowles quoted in "Poll Workers Blew Votes," *OS*, 4 February 2000; "Voters Statewide Say They Had Poll Problems," *TBT*, 9 November 2000; "Disenfranchised Florida Felons," and "Ex-Felons," *NYT*, 28 March 2004 and 20 February 2005; "Where Balloting of Buchanan Surged."

96. Adam C. Smith, "Meet Longtime Trump Ally, Roger Stone," *TBT*, 7 May 2017.

97. John Lantigua, "Miami's Rent-a-Riot," *Slate*, 28 November 2000; "Mob Scene," *Time*, 26 November 2000; Fred Grimm, "The 9/11 Terrorists Lived Here, of Course," *MH*, 4 June 2013; Graham quoted in Dáte, *Jeb*, 243; Jerry Ianelli, "A Brief History of Roger Stone's Weirdest South Florida Antics," *MNT*, 29 May 2017.

98. AP, "Excerpts of Harris' Remarks on Florida Vote Certification," 27 November 2000; Ann Louise Bardach, "Hoodwinked: Why Is Florida's Voting System So Corrupt?," *Slate*, 24 August 2004; Dana Milbank, "E-Mails Show Jeb Bush's Office Keenly Interested," *WP*, 21 November 2000.

99. Libby Copeland, "Campaign Gone South," *WP*, 31 October 2006; Brian Montopoli, "Jilted: The Bush Brothers Kick Katherine Harris to the Curb," *Slate*, 30 June 2005; Tapper, *Down and Dirty*, 150, 156–59, 322; Harris quoted in Diane Roberts, *Dream State* (New York: Free Press, 2004), 24, see also 259–60; Harris quoted in Maureen Eha, "In the Eye of the Storm," *Charisma Magazine*, 30 September 2006.

100. Tapper, *Down and Dirty*, 109–93; Adam Winkler, *We the Corporations: How American Businesses Won Their Civil Rights* (New York: Liveright, 2018), 338–40.

101. James T. Patterson, *Restless Giant: The United States from Watergate to Bush v. Gore* (New York: Oxford University Press, 2007), 416. I would like to thank my hometown friend and fellow alumnus of Millikin University, John T. Adney, for helping me unravel the constitutional knot.

102. John F. Harris, "'Washington Was about to Explode': The Clinton Scandal, 20 Years Later," Politico, 21 January 2018.

103. "Haunted by 2000 and 2016: Don't Take Muslim Vote for Granted," *TBT*, 8 August 2020.

104. David Remnick, "The Wilderness Campaign," *TNY*, 13 September 2004; "Florida Recounts Would Have Favored Bush," *WP*, 12 November 2001; "Study of Disputed Florida Election," *NYT*, 12

November 2001; David Margolick, "The Path to Florida," *VF*, October 2004, 310–22, 355–69; Patterson, *Restless Giant*, 408; Dáte, *Jeb*, 240; Martin Metzer, *The Miami Herald Report: Democracy Held Hostage* (New York: St. Martin's, 2001), 188; Lieberman quoted in "Lieberman Put Democrats in Retreat on Military Vote," *NYT*, 15 July 2001.

105. Nader quoted in "Nader Sees Bright Side to Bush Victory," *NYT*, 1 November 2000; Tapper, *Down and Dirty*, 3; "Ralph Nader Was Indispensable to the Republican Party," *Huffington Post*, 11 November 2003.

106. Grunwald, *The Swamp: The Everglades, Florida, and the Politics of Paradise* (New York: Simon and Schuster, 2006), 346–52; Michael Grunwald, "To the White House, by Way of the Everglades," *WP*, 23 June 2002.

107. "Counting the Vote: The Attorney General; a Staunch Gore Ally Influences Florida Ballot Fight," *NYT*, 16 November 2000.

108. Merzer, *The Miami Herald Report*, 4; "Election Remedies Not Enough, Florida Told," *LAT*, 10 March 2001; "Task Force Urges Florida Officials to Eliminate Punch Cards," *LAT*, 24 February 2001; "Optical Scanners Topped Pregnant Chads as Most Flawed in Florida," *OS*, 28 January 2001; "No Justice in Florida," *The Nation*, 17 June 2002.

109. Lance deHaven-Smith, ed., *The Battle for Florida: An Annotated Compendium of Materials from the 2000 Presidential Election* (Gainesville: University Press of Florida, 2005), 252–53; Margaret Talbot, "Mascaragate 2000," *NYT*, 10 December 2000.

110. "Jeb Bush Hopes New E-Book Can Help Relaunch a Struggling Campaign," *WP*, 2 November 2015; Roberts, *Dream State*, 1; Craig Pittman, *Oh, Florida! How America's Weirdest State Influences the Rest of the Country* (New York: St. Martin's, 2016), 112.

111. Charley Wells, *Inside Bush v. Gore* (Gainesville: University Press of Florida, 2013), 123.

112. Grunwald, *The Swamp*, 2–3; Grunwald, "Jeb in the Wilderness," Politico, March/April 2015; MacManus quoted in "Why So Many Recount Lawsuits? Go Back to 2000," WUSF.org, 15 November 2018.

113. "GOP Sen. Mack to Announce Retirement," *WP*, 6 March 1999; "The 2000 Campaign: A Florida Race," *NYT*, 18 October 2000; "Nelson Falls," *TBT*, 18 November 2018.

114. Patterson, *Restless Giant*, 423–25; "America's Mood, Bush Approval, Satisfaction with the Way Things Are Going," Gallup, 28 January 2003; Fareed Zakaria, "The Heirs of Reagan's Optimism," *Time*, 17 September 2012, 27; Sonja Lyubomirsky, "Will an Optimist or Pessimist Win?," editorial, *LAT*, 5 November 2015.

115. Francis Fukuyama, *The End of History and the Last Man* (New York: Simon and Schuster, 1991); "Hyping a New 'American Century," *PBP*, 1 January 2000.

116. Charles Krauthammer, "A Second American Century," *Time*, 27 December 1999.

117. "Shrinking Surplus, a Challenge," *SPT*, 11 September 2001; "U.S. Budget Surplus Shrinks," CNNMoney," and "CNN Fact Check: The Last President to Balance a Budget," 29 October 2001 and 3 February 2010.

118. Canter T. Brown, *Florida's Black Public Officials, 1867–1924* (Tuscaloosa: University of Alabama Press, 1998); Shofner, *Nor Is It over Yet*, 216, 295.

119. Shofner, *Nor Is It over Yet*, 288, 300–303; *Ninth Census of the United States: 1870*, vol. I, 18–19, 97–99.

120. Shofner, *Nor Is It over Yet*, 238, 268, 294–95; L. Glenn Westfall, *Key West: Cigar City, U.S.A.* (Key West: Historic Florida Keys, 1984).

121. Shofner, *Nor Is It over Yet*, 238, 306–7, 311, 320; "Electors," *Florida State Statutes*, 101.51.

122. Shofner, *Nor Is It over Yet*, 300–384; "The Florida Scene Is 1876 All over Again," *WSJ*, 11 December 2000; Charles Hallock, *A Handbook for Sportsmen and Settlers* (New York: Forest and Stream, 1876), chap. 15.

123. Stearns and Cowgill quoted in Shofner, *Nor Is It over Yet*, 331, 340; Susan Bradford Eppes, *Through Some Eventful Years* (Macon, GA: J. W. Burke, 1926), 112; Charles Nelson, "Tampa's Ring Tournament,"

TBH 26, no. 1 (2012): 28–29; Robert P. Ingalls, *Urban Vigilantes in the New South: Tampa, 1882–1936* (Knoxville: University of Tennessee Press, 1988), 1.

124. Lucy Morgan, "Janet Reno Stood Tall in All Ways," *TBT*, 13 November 2016; "A First as Attorney General," *NYT*, 8 November 2016.

125. "A First as Attorney General"; Amy Driscoll, "Janet Reno's Early Years in Miami," *MH*, 8 November 2016.

126. "Janet Reno Remembered," *MH*, 11 December 2016; Dyckman, "Elian Gonzalez"; "West Wing' President to Stump for Reno in Florida," *MH*, 8 May 2002; "Reno Rocks," *TG*, 11 August 2002.

127. "Militant Suspected of USS Cole Bombing Is Killed," NPR.org, 6 January 2019; Clinton quoted in "'I Could Have Killed' Osama bin Laden in 1998," *LAT*, 1 August 2014.

Chapter 2. "Something Wicked This Way Comes": 9/11, the Age of Fear, and the Tropic of Crazy

1. Jim Brown, "Longboat's Future Is an Enclave for Super-Rich," and "Longboat Key—The Island I Love," *SHT*, 28 November 2005 and 10 October 2011.

2. "Historic Evening," *LKO*, 28 April 2010; Bill Sammon, *Fighting Back: The War on Terrorism—from Inside the Bush White House* (Washington, D.C.: Regnery, 2002), 9, 29–30.

3. Bob Martínez, interviews by author, 2012; Jon Meacham, *Destiny and Power: The American Odyssey of George Herbert Walker Bush* (New York: Random House, 2015), 74–75; Jean Edward Smith, *Bush* (New York: Simon and Schuster, 2016), 54–67; Bush quoted in George W. Bush, *Decision Points* (New York: Crown, 2010), 46.

4. Robert Kerstein, *Politics and Growth in Twentieth-Century Tampa* (Gainesville: University Press of Florida, 2001), 160, 189–205; Mary Jane and Bob Martínez, interviews by author, 2008–14; "Martinez Makes the Switch," *SPT*, 30 July 1983; Jody Baxter Noll, "'We Are Not Hired Help': The 1968 Statewide Florida Teacher Strike and the Formation of Modern Florida," *FHQ* 95 (Winter 2017): 356–82.

5. Mary Jane Martínez, interviews by author, 2012–15; Sammon, *Fighting Back*, 9–26.

6. Sammon, *Fighting Back*, 9–26.

7. "He Told Bush That 'America Is under Attack,'" NBCNews.com, 10 September 2009; Compton quoted in "Florida Students Witnessed the Moment," ABCNews.go.com, 25 June 2013; student quoted in "Sarasota, Florida Students with Bush on 9/11," *Huffington Post Education*, 7 September 2011; "The Interrupted Reading," *Time*, 3 May 2011; Sammon, *Fighting Back*, 83–135.

8. Sammon, *Fighting Back*, 92–94.

9. Pamela Gibson, email to author, 27 November 2020.

10. "Smile My Ass," *Radiolab*, 6 October 2015.

11. "On 9/11, the Orlando Shooter's Classmates Mourned: Some Say He Celebrated," *WP*, 13 June 2016; "Read Omar Mateen's 2006 Name-Change Petition," *PBP*, 13 June 2016; "Omar Mateen's Immigrant Family Lived the American Dream," *MH*, 18 July 2016; "Venice's Part in 9/11," *Venice Gondolier Sun*, 10 September 2020.

12. "Site of Former Home of Osama bin Laden's Brother Eyed for Orange County Apartment Complex," *OS*, 8 March 2019.

13. Shay Sullivan, "Two Hijackers on Longboat?" *LKO*, 21 November 2001.

14. "Florida: Terror's Launching Pad," *TBT*, 1 September 2002; Fred Grimm, "The 9/11 Terrorists Lived Here," *MH*, 4 June 2013; Carl Hiaasen, "The Dumb Deed before the Terror Attack," *MH*, 10 September 2011; "Encounters with 9/11 Hijackers Still Haunt Palm Beach Residents," *PBP*, 13 September 2011; "Suspects' Actions," *SFSS*, 16 September 2001; professor quoted in "South Florida Gave Good Cover to Terrorists," *SFSS*, 14 September 2001; "U.S. Says Hijackers Lived in the Open with Deadly Secret," *NYT*, 14 September 2001.

15. "Complete 9 11 Timeline," Historycommons.org; "Bush and Atta Visit Same Resort Hours before 9–11; Daniel Hopsicker, *Mad Cow Morning News*; "Terrorists," *TT*, 24 June 2002; Brian Ross, "While America Slept: The True Story of 9/11," ABCNews.go.com; "Terror's Launching Pad," *SPT*, 1 September 2002; "FBI Follows Terrorists' Trail to South Florida," *PBP*, 13 September 2001.

16. *The 9/11 Commission Report: Final Report of the National Commission on Terrorist Attacks upon the United States* (Washington, DC: U.S. Government Printing Office, 2004), 1–4; George Will, "A Terrorist Attack," *WP*, in *SPT*, 12 September 2001.

17. Michael Smerconish, "9/11 Hero: Jose Melendez," Huffpost.com, 10 September 2005. Smerconish has written a book on the hero, *Instinct* (2009).

18. "9–11 Terror Victim Honored," *FPT*, 27 November 2003; "Appointment with Fate," *OS*, 29 September 2001; "9/11: Flight Attendants & Passengers Who Made Cell Phone Calls from Planes," Let's Roll: Community Forums, 17 April 2010; "We've Been Hijacked! I Love You," *PBP*, 12 September 2001.

19. "Five Years Later, Memories of a Trying Task," Today.com, 11 September 2006; "9/11: How TV Networks Broke the News," HuffPost.Media, 9 September 2011; "The State of the News Media 2012," Pew Research Center's Project for Excellence in Journalism; Eric Deggans, "On TV, Mayhem Unfolded in Waves," *SPT*, 12 September 2001.

20. "Fla. Flight School May Have Trained Hijackers," CNN.com, 14 September 2001.

21. Catherine Wilson, AP, "Special Editions Rushed Out," *FPT*, 12 September 2012; Eric Alterman, "Out of Print: The Death and Life of the American Newspaper," *TNY*, 31 March 2008; *Onion*, 27 September–3 October 2001.

22. Alterman, "Out of Print"; Eric Deggans, "How 9/11 Changed the News," *TBT*, 3 September 2011; "Evil Acts," *MH*, 12 September 2001; "Today, Our Nation Saw Evil," *OS*, 12 September 2001; "Terrorists Have Ignited American Wrath," *TT*, 12 September 2001; "America under Attack," *SPT*, 12 September 2001; Leonard Pitts Jr., "Sept. 12, 2001: We'll Go Forward from This Moment," *MH*, 12 September 2001; Steve Otto, "The Day That Terror Rained from the Sky," *TT*, 11 September 2011; Greg Giordano, "To Tallahassee and Back: 9/11 Memories," patch.com/florida/newportrichey, 11 September 2012; "Newspapers Fly off Shelves," *FMNP*, 13 September 2001.

23. Franks quoted in "Tampa's MacDill Took Center Stage," *TBT*, 8 September 2021; "MacDill Boosts Security," *TT*, 12 September 2001; Dees quoted in "How the 9/11 Attacks Changed U.S. Central Command," *Off the Base*, 7 September 2011; AP, "Florida Bases Tighten Security," *FPT*, 12 September 2001.

24. "Disbelief, Anger Permeate Area," *SPT*, 12 September 2001; "Florida Bases Tighten Security," *FPT*, 12 September 2001.

25. Schwartz quoted in "Hundreds Crowd Blood Banks," *PBP*, 12 September 2001; "Blood Donors Flock to Local Banks," *FMNP*, 12 September 2001; "Sept. 11, 2001: Snapshots from a Fateful Day," *SHT*, 9 September 2011.

26. "PBIA Closed, Flights Diverted," *PBP*, 12 September 2001.

27. Cardello quoted in "Theme Parks Close," *FPT*, 12 September 2001; "What Was It Like at Walt Disney World on 9/11?," *Huffington Post*, 7 September 2011; Governor Bush quoted in "The 11 Best Email Exchanges from Jeb Bush's New Book," *Politico*, 2 November 2015; "Families Delay Their Sightseeing," *PBP*, 12 September 2001.

28. Hartley quoted in "Educators, Students, Parents Cope," *SPT*, 12 September 2001; "Schools Keep Calm in Darkest Hour," *FPT*, 12 September 2001.

29. Michael Gannon, 9/11 speech, 14 September 2001, in author's possession.

30. Azela S., emails to author, 17 October and 2 November 2017. Ms. S. asked that her last name not be used.

31. "State Capitol Evacuated," *TT*, 12 September 2001; Giordano, "To Tallahassee and Back"; "Attacks Aftershock Felt across Florida," *SPT*, 12 September 2001; Bill Cottrell, "9/11 Changed State in Ways Big and Small," *TD*, 11 September 2016.

32. "Local Reaction," *PBP*, 12 September 2001.

33. "Rural Life Shaken by Shock," *FMNP*, 12 September 2001.

34. "Sarasota Family Had 'Many Connections' to 9/11 Terror Attacks," *SHT*, 16 April 2013; AP, "New Allegations Renew Old Questions about Saudi Arabia," *GS*, 7 February 2015; "Barr: Pensacola Air Station Shooting Was an Act of Terror," *WP*, 14 January 2020.

35. "Florida Ex-Senator Pursues Claims of Saudi Ties to Sept. 11," *NYT*, 13 April 2015; Graham quoted in "How the FBI Is Whitewashing the Saudi Connection to 9/11," *NYP*, 12 April 2015; "Graham's Assertion on al-Qaida Lacks Details," *TBT*, 25 August 2016.

36. "Bush Nominates Rep. Goss to Run CIA," *WP*, 11 August 2004; "Porter Goss," *TG*, 12 August 2004; "Bill Clinton: 'I Could Have Killed' Osama bin Laden in 1998," *LAT*, 1 August 2014.

37. "FBI Is Investigating Pensacola Shooting as Terrorism," NPR.org, 8 December 2019; "Pensacola Attack Probed for Terrorism," *NYT*, 8 December 2019; "Navy Grounds Saudi Flight Students," Politico.com, 10 February 2019; "NAS Pensacola Shooter Had Ties to al-Qaeda," *PNJ*, 18 May 2020.

38. Shay Sullivan, "Possible Longboat Key Terrorist Incident," *LKO*, 26 September 2001; *SPT*, 4 July 2004; "Profile: Carroll Mooneyhan," History Commons.

39. John J. Mearsheimer, "Why We Will Soon Miss the Cold War," TheAtlanticonline, August 1990.

40. "13 Years after 9/11, Terror Threat Undiminished," *USAT*, 6 August 2014.

41. Gallup, "Presidential Approval Ratings of George W. Bush and Bill Clinton."

42. "Telling Us to Go Shopping," *Time*, 19 January 2009; Andrew J. Bacevich, "He Told Us to Go Shopping," *WP*, 5 October 2008; "9/11 in Numbers," *TG*, 17 August 2002; George Packer, *Interesting Times: Writings from a Turbulent Decade* (New York: Farrar, Straus and Giroux, 2009), 4.

43. Jim Stratton, "10 Years after 9–11, Central Florida," *OS*, 10 September 2011; "Economic Cost of 9/11," thefiscaltimes.com, 9 September 2009.

44. "Timeline: How the Anthrax Terror Unfolded," NPR, 15 February 2011; "U.S. to Pay Lantana Widow $2.5 Million for 2001 Anthrax Attack," *PBP*, 29 November 2011.

45. Jeffrey Goldberg, "The Things He Carried," *TA*, November 2008.

46. "13 Ways the U.S. Airline Industry Has Changed since 9/11," *Business Insider*, 8 September 2011; "Security at Airports Evolving," *TT*, 11 September 2011; "Economic Cost of 9/11: Three Industries Still Recovering," thefiscaltimes.com, 9 September 2009; travel quote in "10 Years: How 9/11 Changed Travel," *Travel Weekly*, 31 August 2011; "One 9/11 Tally: $3.3 Trillion," *NYT*, 8 September 2011.

47. Letters, *TT*, 11 September 2011; "Terrorist Attacks Impact Treasure Island Residents," *FPT*, 12 September 2001; "Captured in 9/11 Photo," *PBP*, 3 July 2020.

48. Pam Gibson, email to author, 12 October 2020.

49. Robert Samuelson, "The Right Approach," *SPT*, 12 September 2001; "Miami Mercenaries: International Security Business Is Booming in South Florida, *Miami New Times*, 1 August 2013; "Body Guard Business Is Booming," *LAT*, 18 December 2010; "Armed Guards Lack Training and Oversight," *CNN Investigations*, 10 December 2014; "As Private Security Grows in Florida, So Do Gun Incidents Involving Guards, *OS*, 5 July 2014.

50. Dana Priest and William M. Arken, "Top Secret America," *WP*, 19 July 2010; Genevie Abdo, *Mecca and Main Street: Muslim Life in America after 9/11* (New York: Oxford University Press, 2006), 83; Bush quoted in *Decision Points*, 162.

51. Economist quoted in "An Economist Asks: Who Made Money on 9/11?," *Huff Post Business*, 21 September 2011; "State Nears Gun Milestone," *TBT*, 13 December 2012; "Florida Leads in Weapons Permits," *TBT*, 20 August 2012; Charles Blow, "Has the N.R.A. Won?," *NYT*, 20 April 2015; Carl Hiaasen, "Welcome to Florida Where the NRA Rules," *MH*, 22 February 2014; "Guns and Florida," *TBT*, 7 January 2012.

52. Dr. Susan Turner, email to author, 12 November 2015.

53. "Schools More Secure after 9/11," *OSB*, 5 September 2011; "More Schools Use Cellphones as Learning Tools," *USAT*, 7 August 2013; "Bill to Arm School Guards Advances," *SHT*, 24 March 2015.

54. Cottrell, "9/11 Changed State in Ways Big and Small."

55. Florida Bible College moved to Dunedin, Florida, to become Trinity Bible College. See Lois

Ferm, "Billy Graham in Florida," *FHQ* (1981): 74; "Reaction to 9/11," Historychannel.com, 13 August 2010; "Many Turn to Prayer after Tragedy," *PBP*, 12 September 2001; "Quick Dose of 9–11 Religion Soothes," editorial, *USAT*, 7 January 2002; "9/11 Traced New Spiritual Lines," *USAT*, 7 September 2011; Butterworth and journalist quoted in Stephen Buckley, "Show of Faith Rises amid Fear," *SPT*, 12 September 2001.

56. "Finding Fault: Falwell's Finger-Pointing," *NYT*, 15 September 2001.

57. "Al-Arian's Rise in U.S." *TBT*, 20 October 2012; "Threats and Responses: The Professor," *NYT*, 22 February 2002; "Indictment Ties U.S. Professor to Terror Group," *NYT*, 21 February 2003; Alexander Rose, "How Did Muslims Vote in 2000?," *Middle East Quarterly* 8 (Summer 2001): 13–27.

58. David Tell, "The Times and Sami Al-Arian," *Washington Examiner*, 14 March 2002; Nicholas Kristoff, "Putting Us to Test," *NYT*, 1 March 2002.

59. "Al Arian Arraigned on Contempt Charges," *TT*, 30 June 2008; "Ex-USF Professor Deported to Turkey," *TBT*, 5 February 2015; "Talking out of School," *WP*, 28 July 2002; "Schools More Secure after 9/11," "Allies Cite Her Religion in Al-Arian Case," *SPT*, 6 June and 14 September 2002; Jonathan Turley, "Dr. Sami Al-Arian Leaves the United States," jonathanturley.org.

60. "Trump Doubles down on Claim He Saw Thousands Cheer on 9/11," NPR, 22 November 2015; "Tampa's Muslims Prepare for Backlash," *SPT*, 12 September 2001; "A List of Anti-Muslim Hate Crimes and Bias Incidents," Southern Poverty Law Center, 29 March 2011; "9/11 to Now: Ways We Have Changed," *PBS NewsHour*, 14 September 2011; "Florida City Fights 9/11 Quran Burning," *USAT*, 8 September 2010; "Muslims Fear Attacks," *MH*, 12 September 2001; Florida Senate Oks Bill Banning Use of Foreign Law in Family Court Cases," *PBP*, 28 April 2014; "Hate Crimes against American Muslims Most since Post-9/11 Era," *NYT*, 17 September 2016.

61. Gary R. Mormino, "All Disquiet on the Home Front: World War I and Florida, 1914–1920," *FHQ* 97, no. 3 (Winter 2019): 265–71; Edward Keuchel, "A Purely Business Motive: German-American Lumber Company, 1901–1918," *FHQ* 52, no. 4 (1974): 381–95; Robert Siegel, "During World War I, U.S. Government Erased German Culture," NPR.org, 7 April 2017; Tom Gjelten, Sept. 11 Marked Turning Point," NPR.org, 7 September 2016.

62. Howard Troxler, "A Country Gasps, Waits for Answers," *SPT*, 12 September 2001; Packer, *Interesting Times*, 9; imam quoted in "Muslim Leader," *TBT*, 11 August 2016.

63. Mike Vaccaro, "In the Weeks after 9/11, Sports Became Our Great Escape," *NYP*, 11 September 2011; "Playing It Safe at Home," *TBT*, 15 November 2015; "Pentagon Paid Sports Teams Millions for 'Paid Patriotism' Events," NPR, 5 November 2015; "Black Sunday," *NYT*, 5 October 2015.

64. Deggans, "How 9/11 Changed the News"; Eric Deggans, "Glenn Beck Fans Say He Represents Their American Values," *SPT*, 11 September 2009; "Fox News's Mad, Apocalyptic, Tearful Rising Star," *NYT*, 29 March 2009; David Von Drehle, "2000: A Nation Divided," *Time*, 24 November 2010.

65. "9/11 To Now: Ways We Have Changed," *PBS NewsHour*, 14 September 2011; Paul Pillar, "What Impact Did 9/11 Have on America?" *TG*, 6 September 2011.

66. "How Many U.S. Troops Are Still in Afghanistan?" *CNN News*, 9 January 2014; "In Reversal, Obama Says U.S. Soldiers Will Stay in Afghanistan to 2017," *NYT*, 14 October 2015; "To Start Afghan Withdraw, U.S. Would Pull 5,400 Troops," *NYT*, 2 September 2019; "The U.S. Occupation Is Over, Ending America's Longest War," *NYT*, 13 September 2021; https//dcas.dmdc.osd.mil/dcas/pages/casualties.xhtml.

67. "Iraq," Quinnipiac University Poll, pollingreport.com; "Iraq," Gallup; David Rothkopf, "7 Lessons Not Ever to Forget," *TBT*, 17 March 2013; Peter Van Buren, "Sad to Say, I Told You So," *TBT*, 15 March 2013.

68. "One 9/11 Tally: $3.3 Trillion," *NYT*, 8 September 2011; U.S. Military Expenditures since 2001," www.globalissues.org; and U.S. Dept. of Defense, FY Budget request, April 2013.

69. "What Each State's Veteran Population Looks Like," *WP*, 11 November 2014; Florida Department of Veteran Affairs, Fast Facts; Michiko Kakutani, "Human Costs of the Forever Wars," *NYT*, 25 December 2014; "The other 1 percent," quoted in Michiko Kakutani, "Human Costs of the Forever Wars," *NYT*, 25 December 2014; "Florida's Veteran Impact," *FT*, 30 December 2020.

70. John W. Dower, *Cultures of War: Pearl Harbor/Hiroshima/9–11/Iraq* (New York: Norton, 2010), 34–35.

71. Ibid., 30–31.

72. Lewis quoted in "Memories of Pearl Harbor Rush Back," *SPT*, 12 September 2001; "Memories of Pearl Harbor Rush Back," *OS*, 12 September 2001; Martin Dyckman, "Preservation of the Soul," *SPT*, 12 September 2001.

73. "Public Schools May Be Required to Teach about 9/11," wfsu.org, 5 March 2014.

74. Joseph J. Ellis, "Finding a Place for 9/11 in American History," editorial, *NYT*, 28 January 2006.

75. Janny Scott, "9/11 Leaves Its Mark on History Classes," *NYT*, 6 September 2006.

76. David Rothkopf, "The Black Hole of 9/11," foreignpolicy.org, 29 August 2011.

77. Michael Ruse, "Doom Boom," *Chronicle Review*, 3 December 2010, 4–5; Anne-Marie Slaughter, "Our Waning Confidence," *Democracy: A Journal of Ideas* (Fall 2011): 22; Joel Achenbach, "When All Hell Breaks Loose," *WP*, 11 July 2013.

78. Adam Gopnik, "Decline, Fall, Rinse, Repeat," *TNY*, 12 September 2011; "A City Forever Changed? Maybe Not," *NYT*, 7 October 2001.

79. Jared Diamond, *Guns, Germs, and Steel: The Fates of Human Societies* (New York: Norton, 1999), 6.

80. Von Drehle, "A Nation Divided."

81. Bob Greene, "Dale Carnegie and the Parking Attendant," *WSJ*, 14 January 2019; "Bulldozers Heading to Colony Beach," *SHT*, 31 May 2018; Matt Walsh, "Colony Made Longboat Key," *LKO*, 2 August 2018.

Chapter 3. The Year of Four Hurricanes: Red States and Blue Tarps, Old Demons and New Saints

1. Marjory Stoneman Douglas, *Hurricane* (New York: Rinehart, 1958), 3.

2. William H. MacLeish, *The Gulf Stream: Encounters with the Blue God* (Boston: Houghton Mifflin, 1989), 188.

3. Jon Wilson, "We Weren't Always Hip to Hurricanes," *SPT*, 23 October 2005; "Improved Storm Warning Service Established," *Sun Dial*, August 1935.

4. "Resettling America's First 'Climate Refugees,'" *NYT*, 2 May 2016.

5. J. R. McNeill, "Force Majeure," *WSJ*, 3 April 2015; *Tampa Weekly Tribune*, 8 October 1896.

6. "90 Years Later, the Great Miami Hurricane a Scary, 'What If?,'" *MH*, 29 May 2016; Zora Neale Hurston, *Their Eyes Were Watching God* (New York: Harper and Row, 1936), 162.

7. "Dania Withstands Hurricane," *FLDN*, 18 September 1947; "Three 1947 Storms Produced Record Rainfall," *MH*, 3 September 1978.

8. "Roxcy Bolton, 90, Fighter for Equality, Including in Naming Storms, Is Dead," *NYT*, 24 May 2017; "Alice to Wallis," *Time*, 15 June 1953, 102.

9. "Remembrances of Hurricane Donna," and "Hurricane Donna's Legacy in Collier County," *NDN*, 1 and 2 April 2012.

10. "The Fury of Andrew," *MH*, 19 August 2012; Mike Clary quoted in "Hurricane Andrew Still Reverberates," *SFSS*, 19 August 2012; AP, "Homestead Doubles in Size 20 Years Post-Andrew," *NDN*, 29 May 2012.

11. "Hurricane Andrew's Legacy," NPR, 23 August 2012; "Andrew's Howl Still Echoes," *TBT*, 24 August 2012.

12. Mike Clay, "Modern Forecasting Got Its Start," *SPT*, 10 March 2013.

13. William Gray quoted in Bill Maxwell, "Laugh, but I Won't Fool with Hurricanes," *SPT*, 23 May 2001; "William R. Gray, Hurricane Predictor," *NYT*, 20 April 2016.

14. Thomas Hallock, "Florida's First Storm Story," *Creative Loafing*, 21–27 September 2017.

15. "Ten Years Ago, Hurricanes Charley, Frances, and Jeanne," *DBNJ*, 17 August 2014.

16. "Evacuation of 1 Million Ordered in Florida," *WP*, 13 August 2004; "Charley Could Slam Manatee at 105 mph," and "Charlotte Stunned by Charley," *BH*, 13 and 14 August 2004; "Hurricane Floyd," *NYT*, 16 September 1999.

17. Governor Bush quoted in Patricia Mazzei, "Jeb Bush, Hurricane Governor," *MH*, 24 August 2015; Farrell quoted in "Farrell's Eureka Moment: Hard Lessons," *FMNP*, 13 August 2014.

18. "For Mobile Home Park Residents," *NYT*, 15 August 2004.

19. Abby Goodnough, "Florida Digs out as Mighty Storm Rips Northward," *NYT*, 15 August 2004; AP, "Hurricane Power Outage," *JCF*, 26 December 2004.

20. "Hurricane Charley: Florida Assesses Damage in Wake of Storm," *NYT*, 16 August 2004.

21. "Hurricane Charley: Storm's Aftermath," *NYT*, 15 August 2004; "Many Say They Never Got Word of Hurricane Evacuation," *JCF*, 5 April 2005.

22. Ibid.

23. President Bush quoted in "Charley's Aftermath," *SPT*, 15 August 2004.

24. "Cramped Quarters," *SPT*, 3 June 2006.

25. "Hard Lessons after Charley," *FMNP*, 13 August 2014.

26. "The Meanest Season: Florida's Hurricanes of 2004," *PBP*, June 6, 2014.

27. "2004–Hurricane Frances," *SFSS*, 13 July 2008.

28. John Updike, "Hub Fans Bid Kid Adieu," *New Yorker*, 22 October 1960.

29. Smith quoted in "Hurricane Ivan: The Worst of 2004," *PNJ*, 18 August 2005; "Ivan Spreads Floods, Misery," and "It's 'Downtown Beirut' from the Bay," *BH*, 18 and 20 September 2004; "We Knew Hurricane Ivan Would Be Bad," *PNJ*, 16 September 2014.

30. AP, "I-10 Bridge Severed by Ivan," *SPT*, 5 October 2004.

31. "Seaside's Mystique Mostly Unscathed by Ivan," *SPT*, 24 September 2004.

32. "Jeanne Still a Threat," *BH*, 24 September 2004; "Vero Beach: Hard Hit," *SPT*, 26 September 2004.

33. Ted Steinberg, "A Natural Disaster, and a Human Tragedy," *Chronicle of Higher Education*, 23 September 2005, B11.

34. "Ten Years Later, Memories of Hurricane Trio Remain Sharp," *LL*, 9 August 2014.

35. AP, "Faucet Survives Ivan," 12 October 2004; "Hard Lessons: Hurricane Charley, 10 Years Later," *FMNP*, 13 August 2014; AP, "Dark Holidays in Trailer Park," *JCF*, 26 December 2004; Sallisky quoted in "Hard Lessons: Hurricane Charley," *FMNP*, 14 August 2014.

36. "Hard Times on Easy Street," *SPT*, 7 August 2005; "Hurricanes Deliver More Misery to Some ZIP Codes," *SFSS*, 16 August 2012; "Delayed Reaction to Hurricane Ivan," *JCF*, 15 March 2005; "5 Years Past Cat 4 of Hurricane Charley," *SHT*, 13 August 2009; reporter quoted in AP, "Homeless Increasing from Ivan," *OSB*, 15 March 2005; Mike Davis, *Ecology of Fear: Los Angeles and the Imagination of Disaster* (New York: Vintage, 1998), 54.

37. "Leased Jets Evacuate Moneyed Residents," *MH*, 11 September 2004; "Hurricanes Expose the Downside of Gated Communities," and "Gated Communities Want FEMA Cash," *SFSS*, 3 October and 27 December 2004.

38. AP, "Panhandle Restaurants Booming but Short on Workers," 21 January 2005; AP, "You Say Tomato, We Say Expensive," *SPT*, 28 October 2004; AP, "Storms Create, Demolish Opportunities in Florida," *JCF*, 28 November 2004; "Migrant Workers Face Hardships," *BGN*, 23 December 2004.

39. "Pahokee Sees Hurricanes as Winds of Change," *SFSS*, 11 December 2004; AP, "Months Later, Aftermath of Storms Part of Everyday Life," *JCF*, 1 December 2004.

40. Daniel P. Aldrich, "How to Weather a Hurricane," *NYT*, 29 August 2012; Tamara Lush, AP, "Healing, Not Ready to Go at It Alone," *SPT*, 19 September 2004.

41. Loren G. Brown, *Totch: A Life in the Everglades* (Gainesville: University Press of Florida, 1993), 174.

42. "Ancient Graves Given Shaman's Ritual," *SFSS*, 9 December 2004; "Evacuation on Southwest Coast," *LAT*, 22 October 2005; "FEMA Paid Tribe's Hotel Tab," *SFSS*, 29 November 2007.

43. Randy Wayne White, "Hurricane Charley," democraticunderground.com, 15 August 2004.

44. "Up to 43 Historic Structures May Be Demolished in Pensacola," *JCF,* 8 April 2005; "Pensacola Tragedy," *USAT,* 19 September 2004; "Navy Reopens but May Lose History," *GS,* 28 January 2005.

45. Lush, "Healing"; "Father John Came to Pahokee," *PBP,* 25 September 2013.

46. "Father John Came to Pahokee"; "Hurricane Wreaks Havoc across Florida on Yom Kippur," Forward.com, 1 October 2004.

47. "Hurricane Ivan Hits, Recovery Begins," *Coastline* 34 (October 2004).

48. Lush, "Healing"; "Hurricane Ivan," *ABC News,* 16 September 2004.

49. "Hurricane Charley: A Look Back," Pineislandeagle.com, 13 August 2014.

50. "Amish Paradise: Florida Neighbors a Haven for Snowbird Amish and Mennonites," *NYT,* 28 April 2013; Pastor Cory P. Pariseau and Pastor Jim Mullett, *Standing at the Crossroads: A Mentor's Inspirations* (N.p.: Xulan, 2012), 90; "Long after the Storms," *NYT,* 14 February 2005; "Wauchula, Fla: Hurricanes Charley, Frances, and Jeanne," Mennonite.net/projects/completed/wauchula_fl.

51. "A Season Storms," *Behind the Hammer,* December 2004, 1–7; "MDS Officials Tour Region," *Mennonite World Review,* 30 August 2004.

52. "Historic Hurricane Slashes through Florida, Damaging Churches," *Baptist News,* 5 September 2004.

53. "Parishioners Burn Debris to Move Past Hurricanes," *LL,* 29 November 2004.

54. "In Torn Florida Towns, a Weary Calm after the Storm," *NYT,* 25 August 2004.

55. "College Students Help in Hurricane-Ravaged Areas," *JCF,* 15 October 2004; AP, "Alternative Spring Break Helps Aid Florida Hurricane Victims," *JCF,* 1 April 2005.

56. "In DeSoto County"; Maddox quoted in "Wauchula: A Regional Cooperative Success Story," http://www.distributedenergy.com, 30 April 2005; Ramey quoted in "Florida Assesses Damage," *NYT,* 16 August 2004.

57. "How to Measure a Storm's Fury One Breakfast at a Time," *WSJ,* 1 September 2011.

58. Quoted in "Hard Lessons."

59. "We're Pretty Tough Out Here: We Survive," *PBJ,* 31 August 2014.

60. Ernest Hemingway, "Who Killed the Vets?," *New Masses,* 17 September 1935, 9–11; and *KWC,* 5 September 1935; David Brooks, "The Storm after the Storm," *NYT,* 1 September 2005.

61. Timothy Naftali, *George H. W. Bush* (New York: Henry Holt, 2007), 147; "Unlike Andrew, Aid's Right on Charley's Heels," *SPT,* 17 August 2004; Raymond Arsenault, "The Public Storm: Hurricanes and the State in Twentieth-Century America," in *American Public Life and the Historical Imagination,* ed. Wendy Gambler, Michael Grossberg, and Hendrik Hartog (Notre Dame, IN: University of Notre Dame Press, 2004), 278–79.

62. Eric Boehlert, "The Politics of Hurricane Relief," Salon.com, 5 September 2005; Goodnough, "Florida Digs Out."

63. Patricia Mazzei, "Jeb Bush, Hurricane Governor," *MH,* 24 August 2015; "FCAT," *JCF,* 12 May 2005; Bush quoted in "One Bush Gets Praise for Handling of Hurricanes," *WP*, 25 August 2015; Bush quoted in AP, "Bush 'in Awe' of FCAT Scores," *NFDN,* 12 May 2005.

64. Jeffrey D. Sachs, "The Class System of Catastrophe," *Time,* 10 January 2005, 86; Gary Mormino, *Land of Sunshine, State of Dreams: A Social History of Modern Florida* (Gainesville: University Press of Florida, 2005), 364; "Haiti Buries Storm Victims," *SFSS,* 23 September 2004.

65. Kimberly Blair, "We Knew Hurricane Ivan Would Be Bad," *PNJ,* 16 September 2014; "DEVASTATED," *FMNP,* 13 August 2004; "RAMPAGE," *SHT,* 14 August 2004; "DEATH AND DESTRUCTION," *JCF,* 12 August 2004; "REELING," *PBP,* 26 September 2004.

66. "My Harrowing Night Surviving Hurricane Ivan," *PNJ,* 16 September 2004.

67. Nevy Kaminsky, "It's Late, but Not Too Late," *BH,* 13 August 2004.

68. Lane DeGregory, "The Storm Chaser," *SPT,* 20 September 2004; Mike Gruss, *Virginian-Pilot,* 6 September 2008; "The Weather's Always Fine for the Weather Channel," *LAT,* 5 July 2013.

69. "The Weather's Always Fine for the Weather Channel"; "Improved Forecasts Still Lack Accuracy," and "Storm Forecast Wasn't Off Much," *BH*, 15 and 19 August 2004; "Jason Kelley Passes Away," Flhurricane.com, 21 July 2006; Mayfield quoted in "Hard Lessons," *FMNP*, 13 August 2004.

70. Linda Holmes, "Why Did I Watch Fourteen Hours of the Weather Channel?," NPR.org., 29 August 2011; Abrams quoted in "The Weather's Always Fine for the Weather Channel."

71. Jeff Klinkenberg, "Our Innocence about Hurricanes," *SPT*, 9 September 2005.

72. "State Touts Hurricanes' Silver Linings," *NYT*, 3 November 2005; "A Hurricane May Be the Only Way to Get Rid of Red Tide," *SHT*, 10 August 2018.

73. AP, "Seniors in Aging Study Show Lasting Effects from Charley," and "Post Charley Hazards Numerous, Troublesome," *JCF*, 23 December 2004 and 25 August 2004; "Stress-Trauma of Charley on the Rise," *SHT*, 21 August 2004.

74. "Hurricanes Leave Eagles Homeless," *TT*, 8 November 2004; "Unruffled Feathers," *MH*, 9 January 2006; "Our Trees Define Gainesville," *GS*, 19 January 2007; "Central Florida's Tree Canopy Springs Back," *OS*, 12 August 2014; Bill Kaczor, AP, "Storms Took Toll on Florida's Wildlife, Environment," 30 November 2004; "Remembrances of Hurricane Donna," *NDN*, 1 April 2012.

75. "Sanibel Primed for Return of Its Pines," *FMNP*, 11 July 2007; "Sanibel Island's Trees: 10 Years after Charley," NBC-2, WBBH, Fort Myers, 13 August 2014; "Sanibel and Captiva: Rebuilding Paradise," *NYT*, 10 December 2004; "State to Remove Exotics," *FMNP*, 13 October 2016; "Sanibel Island's Trees," NBC-2, 13 August 2014; "Mighty Australian Pines No Match for Wind," *SFSS*, 11 November 2005.

76. Jeff Klinkenberg, "When Aliens Attack," *SPT*, 13 August 2002.

77. "Reservation Comes into Play as Officials Make Water-Management Decisions," *NYT*, 12 September 2004; Ferguson quoted in "Ivan's Surprising Impact a Decade Later," *PNJ*, 15 September 2014.

78. Kaczor, "Storms Took Toll on Florida's Wildlife, Environment"; "Ivan Damaged Key's Recovery," *SHT*, 5 February 2007; "Mice Love the Beach," *GS*, 4 July 2007; "$60 Million Perdido Key Condo," *PNJ* 20 July 2015; "The Mouse That Roared," *FT*, September 2016, 52.

79. "Ivan," Lois Jones, email to author, 17 September 2004.

80. Kaczor, "Storms Took Toll on Florida's Wildlife, Environment"; "Frances Ruins Turtle Nests," *SPT*, 11 September 2004.

81. "Acidic Spill Tops 41 Million Gallons," *SPT*, 7 September 2004; "Frances Caused Spill That Could Lead to Serious Environmental Damage," *JCF*, 8 September 2004; "Spill Corrodes," *SPT*, 8 September 2004; Craig Pittman, "The Clock Is Ticking on Florida's Mountains of Hazardous Phosphate Waste," *Sarasota Magazine*, 26 April 2017.

82. "High Season Is a Casualty after Storms," *NYT*, 23 November 2005.

83. Gretchen Parker, "Seeds of Trouble," *TT*, 27 February 2006.

84. Michael Grunwald, "This Time, Man Defeated Nature," *WP*, 9 September 2005.

85. "After Hurricane, an Unclear Future for Lake O.," *NYT*, 5 June 2005; AP, "The State's 'Liquid Heart' Is Troubled," *TT*, 27 October 2004; "Lake Okeechobee's Rollercoaster Levels," *MH*, 6 September 2006; Mayor quoted in "2004 Hurricanes Aggravate Lake Okeechobee's Ill Health," *SPT*, 25 April 2005.

86. AP, "Pensacola Beach Opens to Public Again," *SPT*, 2 November, 2004; Sanders quoted in "Eerie Calm on Pensacola Beach after the Storm," NBC.com, 17 September 2004; "Pensacola Beach," *NFDN*, 9 July 2015; "Hobbyists Detect Personal Treasures," *DBNJ*, 22 November 2004; "Beaches Take Beating," *OS*, 3 October 2004; "Unburied Treasure," *OS*, 18 October 2004.

87. "Estimates for Citrus Harvest Plummet," *OS*, 10 October 2005; "More Fruit on Ground, *NYT*, 10 September 2004; "Vultures in the Storm," *Newsweek*, 8 May 2005.

88. "Citrus Greening Continues to Plague Florida Orange Groves," WUFT-FM Gainesville, 15 May 2015; "Migrant Workers Face Hardships," *BGN*, 23 December 2004: "Charley Blamed for Huge Canker Outbreak," *TT*, 11 November 2004; "Citrus Endures Second Assault," *SPT*, 5 February 2005; "Wilma's Citrus Toll," *SPT*, 1 November 2005.

89. AP, "Storms Create, Demolish Opportunities in Florida," *JCF*, 28 November 2004.

90. "Flooding Leads to Abundance of Mosquitoes," *JCF*, 14 September 2004; *Florida Current*, 24 August 2012; "Hurricanes May Have Helped Curb West Nile Virus," *TT*, 12 December 2004.

91. "Marine Cleanup Costly," *SHT*, 4 October 2004; "Hurricanes Leaves Florida's Boats and Marinas Battered and Broken," *NYT*, 7 September 2004; "Salvagers Fish for Privies Lost in Hurricanes," *OS*, 1 November 2004.

92. "Tons of Waste," *GS*, 18 November 2004.

93. AP, "As Storm Closes In, Some Fish Run, Some Don't," *SPT*, 17 October 2004.

94. Craig Pittman, "Florida's Natural Disasters Bring out the Bandits," Slate.com, 3 July 2013; Gray Rohrer, "20 Years Later, Andrew's Wake Still Felt in Florida's Property Insurance Market," *OS*, 2 September 2012.

95. "Ten Years Ago," *PNJ*, 17 August 2014.

96. "Hurricane Charley: The Insurance Toll," *NYT*, 15 August 2004.

97. "One of the True Ticking Time Bombs," *SPT*, 22 July 2007.

98. AP, "Shortages, Insurance Disputes Delay Storm Recovery," *JCF*, 25 February 2005.

99. "Florida's Storm Shelters," editorial, *WSJ*, 17 February 2012; Michael Carlson, "Hurricane Season Passes, but Insurance Storm Brewing," *TT*, 29 November 2014.

100. Rick Hirsch, "When I Was Innocent and Insurance Was Cheap," and "Impact of Hurricane Andrew: Better Homes," *MH*, 12 August and 2 June 2012.

101. "Mobile Homeowners Wary of Insurance Premium Hikes," *JCF*, 13 February 2005; "Can Citizens Property Handle Andrew-Like Storm?," *MH*, 25 August 2012; "Parishioners Burn Debris to Move Past Hurricanes," *LL*, 29 November 2004; "No Storms but Insurers Keep Socking It Away," *PBP*, 25 February 2012; "Can Citizens Property Handle Andrew-Like Storm?" *MH*, 25 August 2012.

102. Carl Hiaasen, "In a Storm We're All Sitting Ducks," *MH*, 5 October 2005.

103. Robert Tracinski, "Hurricane Katrina Exposed the Man-Made Disaster of the Welfare State," Pittsburgh Live.com, 11 September 2011.

104. "The Windfall," *TBT*, 11 August 2014; "Risky Rebuilding," *TT*, 5 November 2006; "Comeback after Charley," *SHT*, 8 August 2014; "5 Years Past Cat 4 Hurricane Charley," *SHT*, 13 August 2009; "Poorer East Punta Gorda Continues to Struggle," *SHT*, 12 August 2007; Sallade quoted in "After Charley, Charlotte County Was Resilient," *FMNP*, 13 August 2014.

105. "In DeSoto County, Charley's Wounds Linger," *NYT*, 8 August 2014.

106. Tamara Lush, AP, "County Sees Opportunity amid Ruins," *SPT*, 14 November 2004; "Comeback after Charley," *SHT*, 8 August 2014.

107. "Lee County Approves $1 Million Increase for Captiva Renourishment," *Island Reporter*, 15 April 2014; "State's Money Reaches Southwest Florida Beaches," *FMNP*, 3 May 2014; "The Calm after the Storm," *TT*, 10 December 2006; "After Charley," *FMNP*, 13 August 2014.

108. Shannon Nickinson, "Ivan Was an Ill Wind," Floridapolitics.com, 15 September 2014.

109. "FEMA Gave $21 Million in Miami-Dade," and "Miami-Dade Told Officials That Losses Were Minor," *SFSS*, 10 October and 12 December 2004; "Storm Missed Miami but FEMA Aid Didn't," *SHT*, 23 November 2004; AP, "Newspapers Sue for Release of Hurricane Records," 10 March 2005.

110. "Trump Took $17 Million Insurance Claim," *BG*, 25 October 2016.

111. "Ten Years Ago, Hurricane Charley, Frances, and Jeanne," *DBNJ*, 17 August 2014.

112. "Some Experts Say It's Time to Evacuate the Coast," *NYT*, 4 October 2005; "Risky Rebuilding"; editorial, "Rethinking Where We Build and Live," *PNJ*, 10 July 2005; Hiaasen, "We're All Sitting Ducks"; "Florida Sets Record with No Hurricane in 10 Years," *MH*, 29 November 2015.

113. "First 'Hurricane Hunter' Flight," *SFSS*, 25 July 2013.

114. "Lee Offers Base to Bomb Storms," *MH*, 9 August 1945; "Use of Atom Bomb to Break up Hurricane Called 'Idea,'" *FLDN*, 1 November 1953.

115. "Project Soundfury Attempted to Weaken Hurricanes in the 1960s and 70s," *USAT*, 18 April 2006; "Weather," *PBP*, 18 June 1975; Arsenault, "The Public Storm," 276–77.

116. "Weather Gurus," *TT*, 26 November 2005; "Is His Head in the Clouds?," *SPT*, 24 August 2003; "Jupiter Inventor's Gel," *PBP*, 3 October 2011.

117. "Legend Names Indians in Storm-Safety Theory, *PBP*, 18 June 2007; "Tampa Bay's Escape from Irma Was More Than Luck," *WP*, 16 September 2017.

118. "Experts: Tampa's Storm Risk No. 1," and Hurricane Horrizon Looks Scary," *TBT*, 5 June 2013 and 21 August 2006; "Weather Channel: Tampa Most Overdue Hurricane City," 4 June 2013; "The Cost of the Big One," *TT*, 10 October 2015; "Storm Surge Dollars," *SPT*, 8 June 2012.

119. "Hurricane Danger Zone: The Top Ten Places Most at Risk, *USAT*, 18 June 2014.

120. "Newly Built Dream Houses and Harm's Way," *CSM*, 22 August 2008.

121. "'Katrina' Cottages Get Touch of Florida," *SPT*, 26 August 2006; Witold Rybczynski, "The Katrina Cottage," www.slate.com, 31 March 2006; "A Katrina Cottage You Can Visit," *SHT*, 12 August 2006.

122. "Future Hurricane Warnings?," *PBP*, 4 April 2015; "20 Years after Andrew: Hurricane Forecasting and Communication Improved," *NDN*, 24 August 2012.

123. David Fleshler, "Taken by Storm," *SFSS*, 8 August 2014; "Where Did All the Payphones Go?," *SHT*, 14 April 2015; "As Payphones Vanish, So Does Lifeline for Many," *USAT*, 17 December 2013.

124. John D. MacDonald, *Condominium* (New York: Ballantine, 1985); Jonathan Yardley, "*Condominium*: MacDonald's Dreadful Lemon Skyline," *MH*, *Tropic Magazine*, 6 March 1977.

125. "The Meanest Season."

126. "20 Years Later: The Fury of Andrew," *MH*, 19 August 2012; "Sex and the Snowed-In Cities," *NPR*, 23 January 2016; "In the Path, and in the Mood," *SPT*, 23 June 2005; "Two-Punch Emma," *Time*, 29 September 1947, 23–24; Jonah Berger, "Hurricanes and Hot Baby Names," *NYT*, 10 November 2012.

Chapter 4. Election Season: 2004

1. U.S. Census Bureau, "State Population Growth, 2000 to 2005," 22 December 2005; Bush quoted in "Florida Has Changed a Lot," *USAT*, 8 June 2004; Snaith quoted in AP, "For Some, Irma Casts Doubt on Florida's Boom," 18 September 2017.

2. Robert W. McKnight, "A Faraway Golden Age," *TBT*, 7 March 2014; Florida Division of Elections, By Party Affiliation Archive, 2004.

3. Maureen Dowd, "The Real Hillary," *NYT*, 29 June 2003; "Campaign Follows Clinton," *MH*, 1 July 2004 and 16 December 2003; "Dean Scream," *USAT*, 21 January 2004.

4. "Campaign Begins as Bush Attacks Kerry," *NYT*, 24 February 2004.

5. "Blunt Political Assessments in Bill Clinton's Transcripts," *NYT*, 7 January 2016.

6. "The Republicans' Barb: 'John Kerry Looks French'"; "Who among Us Does Not Love Windsurfing?"; and "Kerry's Grandfather Left Judaism Behind," *NYT*, 3 April, 5 September, and 16 May 2004.

7. "A Long-Obscured Branch on Kerry's Family Tree," *BG*, 13 October 2013; Judith Thurman, "The Candidate's Wife," *NYT*, 27 September 2004; "Sen. Kerry's Wife Changes Surname," *WP*, 12 February 2003; "Kerry's Troubled Campaign," *WP*, 15 November 2015.

8. "Kerry Grades near Bush's while at Yale," *NYT*, 8 June 2005.

9. George H. W. Bush and Jeb Bush quoted in Jon Meacham, *Destiny and Power: The American Odyssey of George Herbert Walker Bush* (New York: Random House, 2016), 548–49.

10. Ibid., 334–35, 547–49.

11. Ibid., 577–78; George Gallup, Presidential Approval Ratings, George W. Bush, 2001–2004.

12. "Bush vs. Kerry Begins in Earnest," CNN.com, 3 March 2004.

13. Evan Walker-Wells, "For Country, Yale and the Military," *Yale Herald*, 28 October 2011.

14. Nicholas D. Kristof, "A War Hero, or a Phony?," *NYT*, 18 September 2004; "John Kerry's Vietnam Crewmates Still Fighting Swift Boaters," *WP*, 20 June 2008; "Two Wealthy Texans Refuel Swift Boat Attack Ads," *LAT*, 5 October 2004; campaign aides quoted, "90-Day Strategy by Bush's Aides to define Kerry," and "Friendly Fire: The Birth of an Attack on Kerry," *NYT*, 20 March and 20 August 2004.

15. "Coming Soon: 'Apocalypse Now,'" *NYT,* 12 September 2004.

16. "Kerry Closes Gap to Make Florida Too Close to Call," Quinnipiac-university-poll/florida/release-detail?, 21 October 2004; "1,100 Fallen," *SFSS,* 24 October 2004.

17. William Campenni, "The Truth about Dan Rather's Deceptive Reporting on George W. Bush," *Daily Signal,* 30 October 2015.

18. "The X Files of Lt. Bush," *Time,* 13 September 2004; "CBS Stands by Bush-Guard Memos," CBS News, 10 September 2004; "CBS Backs off Guard Story," *USAT,* 21 September 2004; "CBS Ousts 4 for Bush Guard Story," NBC News, 10 January 2005.

19. "Kerry Chooses Edwards," and "McCain Is Said to Tell Kerry He Won't Join Team," *NYT,* 7 July and 12 June 2004; "After Meteoric Rise, Edwards Takes a Fall," *MH,* 3 June 2011; "The Return of the Native," *SHT,* 29 July 2004.

20. "Public Warms to Edwards, *NYT,* 17 July 2004; Charlie Cook, "After the Bounce," *Cook Political Report,* 13 July 2004.

21. "Kerry, Edwards Target Florida," and "Kerry, Edwards Hit the Raid," *SFSS,* 8 July 2004.

22. "At FEMA, Disasters and Politics," *NYT,* 15 September 2015.

23. "Did Brownie Buy Florida?" *RS,* 29 December 2005–12 January 2006, 48.

24. Quinnipiac-university-poll/florida/release-detail; "Kerry Will Blitz State," *OS,* 18 September 2004; Johanson quoted in "Florida 27 Electoral Votes," gwu.edu.

25. "Voters Split on Bush, Kerry," *SPT,* 29 August 2004.

26. "Florida 2004 vs. Florida 2008," *TBT,* 20 October 2008.

27. Ibid.

28. "Bush Zeroes in on Jewish Vote," *SPT,* 22 July 2004.

29. "Kerry's Entrée to Jewish Vote," *LAT,* 29 October 2004; "Clinton Courts Jewish Vote," *SFSS,* 27 October 2004.

30. "Clinton Campaign in Florida," *NYT,* 27 October 2004; "Kerry: Vote Early," *SFSS,* 18 October 2004; "Oldster Vote Big Factor in State," *SPT,* 5 May 1940.

31. "Baby Boomers Transform an Old Bloc," *NYT,* 15 June 2003.

32. "Drug Addled: Why Bush's Prescription Plan Is Such a Fiasco," *Slate,* 18 January 2006; "Kerry: Vote Early," *SFSS,* 18 October 2004; "Democrats Give Republicans a Fight for the Elderly," *NYT,* 11 August 2004.

33. "Lawton Chiles' Camp Admits to 'Mystery' Calls," *SPT,* 4 November 1995; "Campaigning Furiously, with Social Security in Tow," *NYT,* 18 October 2004.

34. "President's Remarks in the Villages, Florida," https://georgewbush-whitehouse.archives.gov/news/releases/2004.

35. Reporter quoted in "Jackson and Sharpton Join Kerry," *LAT,* 11 October 2004; "Kerry, Edwards: Get Vote in Now," *SPT,* 18 October 2004; "Kerry in Broward," *SFSS,* 25 October 2004; pastor quoted in "Gore and Kerry Unite in Search of Black Votes," *NYT,* 25 October 2004; "Black Voter Registration in Florida," *SFSS,* 24 October 2004.

36. "Octogenarian Ready to Cast His First Vote," *GS,* 4 November 2004.

37. Abby Goodnough, "Reassurance for Florida Voters Made Wary by Chaos of 2000," *NYT,* 24 May 2004.

38. "Felony Costs Voting Rights for a Lifetime in 9 States," and "Florida List of Purge of Voters Proves Flawed," *NYT,* 3 November 2000 and 10 July 2004.

39. William Finnegan, "The Cuban Strategy," *TNY,* 15 March 2004.

40. Abby Goodnaugh, "Hispanic Vote in Florida," *NYT,* 17 October 2004.

41. "Kerry: Vote Early," *SFSS,* 18 October 2004.

42. "Kerry Camp Denies Ties to Cuba," *SFSS,* 11 August 2004.

43. "Cuba Has Harsh Words for Reagan," *MH,* 8 June 2004.

44. "Buenaventura Lakes Draws Top Daughters," *OS,* 3 November 2004.

45. "Edwards Chases College Crowd," *SFSS*, 28 October 2004; Yanchunis quoted in "Bush, Kerry Focus of Florida, Students," CNN.com, 30 April 2004; "Campus Vibe Blog," CNN.com, 3 November 2004.

46. "Bush, Kerry Focus of Florida, Students,"; "Campaign 2004 Predictions," democrats.com, 2 November 2004; "Edwards Chases College Crowd," *SFSS*, 28 October 2004.

47. "High-Profile Democrats Visit S. Florida," and "Democrats, Activists Work to Energize Vote," *SFSS*, 24 and 23 October 2004; "Gay GOP Group Won't Endorse Bush," *LAT*, 8 September 2004.

48. "No Southern Comfort for Kerry," *OS*, 1 August 2004; "The Political Geography of Florida," *NYT*, 31 January 2012; "Florida GOP Drafts Army of Lawyers to Review Registrations," *SFSS*, 28 October 2004.

49. "Florida Voice Has Kerry's Ear," "Kerry Tabs Florida Campaign Manager," and "Kerry Offices to Open in Florida," *SPT*, 1, 5, and 25 June 2004; "Jeb Bush's Southern Puppet Master," *USAT*, 12 June 2015.

50. "McCain-Feingold's Devastating Legacy," and "Soros-Backed Group Disbands," *WP*, 11 April 2004 and 3 August 2005; "Soros-Linked Group Hit with Large Fine," *Politico*, 29 August 2007.

51. "The Travels of President George W. Bush—October 2004," 2004 org/bush/bushcal1004a.html.

52. "Gore and Kerry Unite in Search of Black Votes," *NYT*, 25 October 2004; "Jackson and Sharpton Join Kerry on Trail," *LAT*, 11 October 20104; "Getting in the Game," *SFSS*, 29 October 2004; "Musicians Rock for Kerry," CNN.com, 13 October 2004; reporter quoted in "Hip-Hop, R&B Stars, Join for Vote Message," *SFSS*, 18 August 2004; "Musicians Rock for Kerry," CNN.com, 13 October 2004; "Michael Moore Holds Hurried Rally," *SPT*, 2 November 2004.

53. George Gallup, "War on Terrorism"; "Bush Poll Numbers on Iraq at New Low," *WP*, 25 May 2004; "Kerry Returns to Florida, Hammering Bush on Iraq," *NYT*, 22 September 2004.

54. "New Ads Use Animal Themes," *LAT*, 23 October 2004; "Bush Ad," NBCNews.com, 22 October 2004.

55. "Anti-Bush Film Stirs Passions," *SFSS*, 25 October 2004.

56. Ibid.

57. Maureen Dowd, "Will Osama Help W?," *NYT*, 31 October 2004; Limbaugh quoted in Mark Danner, "How Bush Really Won," *NYRB*, 13 January 2005.

58. "Campaigning Furiously, with Social Security in Tow," and Maureen Dowd, "Cooking His Own Goose," *NYT*, 18 and 24 October 2004.

59. Danner, "How Bush Really Won."

60. "Bush Preaches to His Choir at Florida Politics," *LAT*, 24 October 2004.

61. "17,000 Greet President on Brief Stop in Gainesville," *GS*, 1 November 2004.

62. "Double Dose for Tampa in Breathless Final Sunday," *SPT*, 1 November 2004.

63. Paul Gronke, "Early Voting in Florida, 2004," paper prepared at the Annual Meeting of the American Political Science Association, 1 September 2005; "Absentee vs. Election Day Voting in Florida," graph in Peter Schorsch, "Sunburn," Florida Politics, 23 July 2018.

64. "Elie Wiesel's 2004 Column," *MH*, 2 July 2016.

65. "A Woman Trailblazer," *SFSS*, 16 June 2015; "Mrs. Castor Broke Barriers," *Tampa Times*, 11 February 1974; Calvin Trillin, "Four People Who Do Not Lunch at the University Club," *TNY*, 11 April 1977, 101–2; "Castor Wins Vote on University Club," *TT*, 1 June 1977; Martin A. Dyckman, *Reubin O'D. Askew and the Golden Age of Florida Politics* (Gainesville: University Press of Florida, 2011), 215–61.

66. Castor quoted in *FT*, October 2007; "Betty Castor: They Have Heard of Her," *SPT*, 11 September 1978; Dyckman, *Reubin O'D. Askew*, 237–40.

67. "Joining the Team: A Right-Hand Man, a Refugee and Capital Returnee," *NYT*, 21 December 2000; Richard E. Foglesong, *Immigrant Prince: Mel Martínez and the American Dream* (Gainesville: University Press of Florida, 2011), 15–124.

68. "Martinez Will Face Castor," *WP*, 1 September 2004; Howard Troxler, "Think My Predictions Are Wrong?," *SPT*, 3 November 2004; Foglesong, *Immigrant Prince*, 152–53, 163–64.

69. Troxler, "Think My Predictions Are Wrong?"; "Jailed Palestinian Prof. Sami Al-Arian Dominates

Florida Senate Race," *Democracy Now!*, 28 October 2008; "Martinez Ad Steps up Attack on Castor," *SPT*, 15 October 2004; "Martinez Blasts Castor over Alleged Terrorist," *NYT*, 14 October 2004.

70. "Castor, Martinez Swap Barbs," *SFSS*, 29 October 2004.

71. "Bin Laden Ad Criticizes Castor," and "Castor Says New Ad Distorts Her Views," *SPT*, 27 October 2004; "Fired Professor Plays Key Role in Ads," *OS*, 28 October 2004.

72. Sabato quoted in "Florida's Castor Wages Fight," *Women's ENews*, 24 October 2004; "Fired Professor Plays Key Role in Senate Ads," *OS*, 15 October 2004; "Bush, Kerry in a Toss-Up," and "Volatile Senate Contest a 48% Tie," *SFSS*, 25 and 24 October 2004.

73. Adam Smith, "Democracy's Foot Soldiers," *SPT*, 1 November 2004; Republican quoted in "Sharp Increase in Early Voting," and MacManus quoted in "It Was Our Turnout," *NYT*, 29 October and 4 November 2004.

74. Smith, "Democracy's Foot Soldiers"; AP, "Festival Ends on Funny, Pretty Note," *SPT*, 1 November 2004; "Protestors Ransack," Local 6 News, Orlando, 5 October 2016; "Democrat Scuffles with Republican," *GS*, 19 September 2004; Raymond Arsenault, interview by author, 26 November 2020.

75. AP, "Exit Poll," *GS*, 2 November 2004; governor quoted in "It Was Our Turnout, Governor Bush Says," *NYT*, 4 November 2004.

76. Graham quoted in "A Sight to Behold: Problems Down, Turnout Soars," *SPT*, 3 November 2004; Balseiro quoted in "Sharp Increase in Early Voting Alters Campaign," *NYT*, 29 October 2004.

77. Meacham, *Destiny and Power*, 578; Danner, "How Bush Really Won."

78. "Plowing Ahead," *OS*, 23 January 2005; "Democrats in Rural Counties Picked Bush," *SPT*, 29 November 2004; "Escambia Logs Top Turnout," *SPT*, 4 November 2004.

79. Ronald Brownstein and Richard Rainey, "Plowing Ahead," *LAT* in *OS*, 23 January 2005.

80. Abby Goodnough and Don Van Natta, "Bush Secured Victory in Florida by Veering from Beaten Path," *NYT*, 7 November 2004.

81. William March, "I-4 Corridor Cemented Its Swing-Voting Role," *TT*, 4 November 2004; "Candidates Eye Voters on Florida's I-4," CNN.com, 11 October 200; "I-4 Corridor Swerves toward GOP," *OS*, 4 November 2004.

82. "A Right Turn into FishHawk," *SPT*, 29 October 2004.

83. Craig Pittman, "The Road to the White House Runs Past Disney World," *Politico*, 6 September 2016.

84. AP, "Democrats in Rural Counties Picked Bush," and "Rural Vote Gave State to Bush," *SPT*, 29 and 14 November 2004.

85. "Long-Gone Hurricanes Threaten Voter Turnout," and "Escambia Logs Top Turnout," *SPT*, 1 and 4 November 2004.

86. "Republicans Increased Support among S. Florida Jews, Hispanics," *TT*, 4 November 2004; Manteiga quoted in "Parties Court the Ultimate Swing Vote," *SPT*, 3 May 2004; "Hispanic Voters Paint a New Picture," *USAT*, 10 November 2004; Foglesong, *Immigrant Prince*, 168–69.

87. "Republicans Increased Support among S. Florida Jews, Hispanics"; "Who Will Win over Jewish Voters in Florida?," NPR.org, 31 October 2008.

88. "Small Groups Seize a Big Role in Florida," *SPT*, 5 September 2004.

89. "Young Voters Did Not Fit into Preconceived Notions," *TT*, 4 November 2004.

90. Strategist quoted in "Both Parties Pin Hopes on Florida Senate Race," *NYT*, 30 October 2004; "Latino Voices Heard," *CT*, 4 November 2004; "Even Martinez Ends up in a Long Line," *OS*, 3 November 2004; Foglesong, *Immigrant Prince*, 174.

91. Steve Bousquet, "Florida's New Face," *SPT*, 7 November 2004.

92. Ibid.; "Panhandle, President Drive Martinez's Win," *SPT*, 4 and 7 November 2004.

93. "Martinez 'Humbled to Be' U.S. Senator," *TT*, 4 November 2004; Steve Bousquet, "Looking beyond Divisive Campaign," *SPT*, 1 November 2004.

94. Lloyd Dunkelburger, "Castor, Martinez Make Final Push," *GS*, 2 November 2004.

95. David Broder, "Need to Connect with Religious, Rural Voters," *WP*, 4 November 2004.

96. "Moral Values Cited as a Defining Issue of the Election," *NYT,* 4 November 2004.

97. "Jackson and Sharpton Join Kerry on Trail," *LAT,* 11 October 2004.

98. AP, "Ten States Ban Same-Sex Marriage," *SPT,* 3 November 2004; Joan Vennochi, "Was Gay Marriage Kerry's Undoing?," *BG,* November 2004; "Young Voters," *TT,* 4 November 2004; Klein quoted in "Kerry's Troubled Campaign," *WP,* 15 November 2004; Gary Wills, "The Day the Enlightenment Went Out," *NYT,* 4 November 2004; "State Bans on Gay Marriage Galvanize Both Sides," *LAT,* 4 November 2004.

99. *USAT,* 2 November 2004; "Man Charged in Car Assault," *LAT,* 28 October 2004; "Katherine Harris Looks to Put Past Negative Image Behind," and "Harris in a Tussle," *SPT,* 20 and 21 October 2004.

100. "Black Sheriff's Election Is Historic for Gadsden," *SPT,* 6 November 2004.

101. "Those Poor Florida Democrats," editorial, and Wes Allison, "Bewildered Party Soul Searches," *SPT,* 5 November and 4 November 2004; Jewett quoted in "Those Poor Florida Democrats"; "State Democrats Fight Face for Relevancy," *GS,* 4 November 2004.

102. Adam Smith, "Has Florida Become a GOP Stronghold?," *SPT,* 4 November 2004; Gelber quoted in Smith.

103. "Kerry's Regrets about John Edwards," *Time,* 30 May 2007; "Politics Dissect Bush Election Win," *Stanford News,* 17 November 2004.

104. "Election Ad Battle," *USAT,* 25 November 2004.

105. Michael Barone, "2012 Campaign Very Different Than Bush vs. Kerry," *Sunshine State News,* 29 July 2012.

106. "Democrats' Domination," *SPT,* 12 November 1978.

107. AP, "Charmed Path," *SPT,* 4 November 2004.

108. S. V. Dáte, "The Myth of Jeb's Protegé," *Politicomagazine.com,* 15 January 2015.

109. "Whatever Happened to . . . the College Kid," *WP,* 27 April 2011; "All Scores Settled in 'Don't Tase Me, Bro' Affair," *NYT,* 30 October 2007.

Chapter 5. The Natural, the Professor, Queen Esther, and the Astronaut: Florida, 2006

1. "Democrats See Hope of Winning Governors' Seats," *NYT,* 26 February 2006; "Bush's Approval Ratings Slide to New Low," CNN.com, 25 April 2006.

2. "Tom Gallagher," *SPT,* 27 August 2006.

3. "Gallagher," *SPT,* 9 July 2006; John F. Sugg, "The Real Tom Gallagher," *CL,* 22 August 2006; Mary Ellen Klas, "Man with a Plan," *FT,* October 2006, 24; "Tom Gallagher Opens up about Messy '79 Divorce," *GS,* 20 June 2006.

4. "Florida Governor Charlie Crist," Time.com, 14 May 2009; Mary Ellen Klas, "Who Is Charlie Crist?" *MH,* 11 August 2014.

5. "The Crist Files: Charlie Crist and Guns," thefloridasqueeze.com, 1 November 2013.

6. Michael Kruse and Adam Smith, "Who Is Charlie Crist? The Answer Is Complicated," *TBT,* 11 August 2014.

7. Steve Bousquet, "Crist: Dismissed, Even Ridiculed," *TBT,* 31 July 2006; "Adam Walsh Case Is Closed after 27 Years," *LAT,* 26 May 2012; "Crist Signs 'Anti-Murder' Act," *SHT,* 13 March 2007.

8. David Colburn, "Florida's Peculiar Cabinet," *TBT,* 24 February 2015.

9. Ibid.

10. "Days before Primary," *NYT,* 4 September 2006; "GOP Candidates Trade Barbs," *OS,* 29 August 2006; "Voice Is 2006's Charlie Crist," *TBT,* 11 August 2014.

11. Scott Barancik, "Charlie Crist," *SPT,* 9 July 2006.

12. "The $50 Million Question for Charlie Crist," *Crowley Political Report,* 25 October 2013.

13. Kruse and Smith, "Who Is Charlie Crist?"; Sue Carlton, "The Gadfly Who Asked Charlie Crist the Question," *TBT*, 29 January 2019.

14. David R. Colburn, *From Yellow Dog Democrats to Red State Republicans: Florida and Its Politics since 1940* (Gainesville: University Press of Florida, 2007), 212–13.

15. Benjamin Fearnow, "Majority of Americans Comfortable with Gay Presidential Candidate, Marking Massive Shift since 2006," *Newsweek*, 1 April 2019.

16. "Voice on Anti-Charlie Crist Robocall Is 2006's Charlie Crist," *TBT*, 11 August 2014.

17. "Davis Lives Modestly," and "Charlie Crist: GOP Candidates Run the Financial Spectrum," *SPT*, 8 and 9 July 2006.

18. Colburn, *From Yellow Dog Democrats*, 142.

19. Bill Belleville, *Losing It All to Sprawl: How Progress Ate My Cracker Landscape* (Gainesville: University Press of Florida, 2006); Gary R. Mormino, *Italians in Florida* (New York: Bordighera, 2008), 81.

20. Berger quoted in "Big Business Investing in State GOP," *SPT*, 5 November 2006; LeMieux quoted in Kruse and Smith, "Who Is Charlie Crist?"

21. Peter Golenbock, *The Chairman: The Rise and Betrayal of Jim Greer* (Montgomery, AL: NewSouth, 2014), 12–15, 20; "Jim Greer's Rise in Florida GOP Was as Stunning as His Fall," *OS*, 17 April 2010.

22. "Governor's Race Rakes in the Cash," and "Jim Davis's Wife Stumps in Tavares," *OS*, 5 and 1 November 2006. The phrase was popularized by Obama and earlier a rallying manifesto of César Chávez.

23. "Trump Raising Money for Crist," *GS*, 4 February 2006; Justin Curtis, "Demystifying the Donald: Trump, Past and Present," *Harvard Political Review*, 15 February 2016.

24. David R. Colburn, *Florida's Gubernatorial Politics in the Twentieth Century* (Gainesville: University Press of Florida, 1981), 60, 75, 87–89; "Soft Money—A Look at Loopholes," *WP*, 1 June 1998.

25. "State GOP Gets $500,000 Donation," *SFSS*, 12 July 2006; "H. Gary Morse, Who Built Mecca for Retirees Is Dead at 77," *NYT*, 20 November 2010; "Developer Gary Morse Puts The Villages on Political Map," *OS*, 5 October 2008.

26. "Davis Says He Voted in 2000," *FMNP*, 3 November 2006.

27. "Davis Hits Cape," *FMNP*, 6 November 2006.

28. "Jeb Bush Rejoins Stump for Crist," and "Crist Campaigns with Giuliani," *FMNP*, 4 and 6 November 2006.

29. "Bilingual Ballots Cause Stir for Voters," *FMNP*, 6 November 2006.

30. "Davis Disputes Voting Report," *SPT*, 2 November 2006.

31. "Stand by Your Man, Unless Poll Numbers Are Low," *SPT*, 5 November 2006; "Remarks by the President at Florida Victory Rally," Office of the Press Secretary, 6 November 2006; "Bush Wraps up Campaign," *WP*, 6 November 2006.

32. "Landmark Flea Market Shutting Down," *TBT*, 11 June 2020.

33. Abby Goodnough, "Strange Brews Are Created in Melting Pot That Is Florida," *NYT*, 3 April 2005; David Shribman, "My Point," *Pittsburgh Post-Gazette*, 3 April 2005.

34. Friend quoted in Jennifer Frey, "Terri Schiavo's Unstudied Life," *WP*, 25 March 2005; "His Unwavering Fight," *TBT*, 18 January 2015.

35. "From Private Ordeal to National Fight: The Case of Terri Schiavo," *NYT*, 20 April 2014.

36. Abby Goodnough, "Schiavo Dies," *NYT*, 1 April 2005; Cal Thomas, "Her Life Matters in Symbol and Substance," *Baltimore Sun*, 23 March 2005; Jim Defede, "May a Dreamful Peace Be Yours, Terri Schiavo," *MH*, 3 April 2005.

37. President Bush and Vatican official quoted in "Long Legal Battle Over," *WP*, 1 April 2005; "Perspective: Terri Schiavo—A Tragedy Compounded," *New England Journal of Medicine*, 21 April 2005, 1630; "Brett Kavanaugh Florida Ties," *PBP*, 10 July 2018.

38. "Schiavo Issue Haunts Crist," *SPT*, 1 November 2006; Crist quoted in "Far from Staying Out, Crist Played Crucial Role," *SS*, 2 November 2006; father quoted in "Schiavo Case Still Stings," *SPT*, 23 August 2006; Michael Kruse, "Jeb 'Put Me through Hell," *Politico Magazine*, 29 January 2015.

39. "Martinez Calls Crist 'Perfect' for Governor," and "Joke about Crist's Tan," *SPT,* 30 June and 30 July 2006.

40. Adam Smith, "Who Is Charlie Crist? The Answer Is Complicated," *TBT,* 8 August 2014.

41. "Time for Charlie to Deliver on Bold Campaign Pledges," *FMNP,* 8 November 2006.

42. "Kottkamp's Stock Rises with Victory," *FMNP,* 8 November 2006.

43. "In Crist's Camp, He was the 'Maestro,'" *TBT,* 12 November 2006; "Can LeMieux Escape Crist's Orbit?" Politico.com, 15 December 2010.

44. Greer quoted in Golenbock, *The Chairman,* 30; Adam Smith, "An Unknown to Lead Florida's GOP," *TBT,* 26 January 2007.

45. "Drama Ends with Heirs Splitting Citrus Millions," *OS,* 17 August 2003; Brian Montpoli, "Jilted: The Bush Brothers Kick Katherine Harris to the Curb," Slate.com, 30 June 2005; Craig Pittman, *Oh, Florida! How America's Weirdest State Influences the Rest of the Country* (New York: St. Martin's, 2016), 112–15.

46. "Katherine Harris' Most Steadfast Supporter," "Harris Calls Nelson an Empty Suit," *SPT,* 20 October and 20 April 2006; "Evangelical Leader Threatens to Use His Political Muscle Against Some Democrats," *NYT,* 1 January 2005.

47. Alex Leary, "For Health and Politics, Nelson Runs," and "Nelson Has an Identity Crisis," *TBT,* 24 September 2017 and 21 May 2018.

48. "For Health and Politics, Nelson Runs," and "Harris Puts Her Faith in Religion," *TBT,* 24 September 2017 and 25 March 2006; "Rep. Harris Condemns Separation of Church, State," *OS,* 26 August 2006.

49. "Liberace Candidate: Mark Foley's Gay Closet," *New York Press,* 28 May 2003; "Priest Tells of Foley Relationship," *SHT,* 19 October 2006; "Retired Priest Admits Encounters with Foley," *WP,* 20 October 2006; "Campaign Doubts," *NYT,* 14 March 2006.

50. "U.S. Rep. Scarborough to Resign," Jacksonville.com, 25 May 2001; "Trump Suggested the 2001 Death of a Joe Scarborough Aide Is an 'Unsolved Mystery,'" *WP,* 29 November 2017.

51. Daniel Schorr, "Dividing the 'Moral Vote' after New Scandals," NPR.org, 25 October 2006; "Newsweek Poll: GOP in Meltdown," *Newsweek,* 6 October 2006.

52. Bense quoted in Montpoli, "Campaign Doubts Arise for a Divisive Candidate," *NYT,* 14 March 2006; "GOP Can't Elude Harris vs. Nelson," *TBT,* 11 May 2006.

53. "Harris, Davis Dined," *SHT,* 23 May 2006; Colburn, *From Yellow Dog Democrats,* 209.

54. "Katherine Harris Bets $10 Million on Senate Bid," and "Political Consultant Ed Rollins," *SHT,* 16 March 2006 and 22 June 2009; "Harris Staffers Leaving," *LL,* 14 July 2006; Montpoli, "Jilted."

55. "He Came. He Spoke. He Raised $2 Million," *OS,* 22 September 2006; political junkie quoted in "Catching up with Katherine Harris," *WP,* 21 May 2012.

56. "Political Consultant Ed Rollins"; "Harris, Nelson Tout Testimonials," *FTU,* 8 November 2006; "Nelson Goes 22–0," *MH,* 30 October 2006.

57. "Nelson, Harris Feisty in Final Senate Debate," *FMNP,* 2 November 2006; "Nelson, Harris Get Harsh," *SPT,* 2 November 2006.

58. "The Florida Senate Race," *NYT,* 8 November 2006.

59. Colburn, *From Yellow Dog Democrats,* 214–15.

60. Golenbock, *The Chairman,* 45; "Apprentice to Power Brian Ballard," *OS,* 5 August 1990.

61. Bill Cotterell, "My Fellow Floridians . . . ," *FMNP,* 1 January 2007; Gary R. Mormino, *Millard Fillmore Caldwell: Governing on the Wrong Side of History* (Gainesville: University Press of Florida, 2020), 108.

62. "Inaugural Address Governor Charlie Crist," https//votesmart.org/public-statement/236585/inaugural-address-gov, 2 January 2007.

63. Paige St. John, "Furnished Mansion Awaits New Resident," *FMNP,* 1 January 2007.

64. Mary Klas, "Who Is Charlie Crist?" *MH,* 11 August 2014.

65. "Either Way, Expect Change," *SPT,* 5 November 2006; "In a Break from the Past, Florida Will Let Felons Vote," *NYT,* 6 April 2007; Farhad Manjoo, "What Was Charlie Crist Thinking?," Salon.com,

6 April 2007; "That Does It . . . Charlie Crist Is a Democratic Mole," *SS*, 22 February 2007; McCollum quoted in "Felons Rights Restored," *TBT*, 6 April 2007; "Time for Charlie," *FMNP*, 8 November 2006; "Crist Helps Restore Felons' Voting Rights," and "Crist's Agenda Earns Respect from Blacks," *SFSS*, 30 August 2008 and 11 October 2007.

66. "Rome-Crist Wedding Shows How Etiquette Has Changed," *SHT*, 10 December 2008; "Potential Veep Charlie Crist Has Glam Running Mate," *New York Daily News*, 5 June 2008; "Rep. Charlie Crist Is Divorcing His Wife, Carole," *TBT*, 24 February 2017.

Chapter 6. The Boom at High Tide: 2000–2007

1. *NYS*, 16 February 1942.

2. Gary R. Mormino, *Land of Sunshine, State of Dreams: A Social History of Modern Florida* (Gainesville: University Press of Florida, 2005), 143, 151–64; *Kissimmee Gazette* reprinted in *TMT*, 18 December 1910; journalist quoted in "Military Veterans Are Marching to Florida," *OS*, 9 November 2008.

3. "McCain Revisits His Military Roots," *OS*, 4 April 2008; "Where Veterans Live," Forbes.com, 10 November 2014; "City Dedicates Korean War Memorial," *FMNP*, 31 March 2008; "Women in the Military," *USAT*, 23 December 2009; "VA Seeks Land for 2 Fla. National Cemetery Sites," *SHT*, 6 September 2010; "South Florida Short on Buglers," *SFSS*, 3 July 2007; "Veterans Cemetery Approved," *TT*, 14 March 2006; "When It Comes to Joining the Military, Miami Is No Match for Small Towns," *MH*, 30 June 2019.

4. "They Keep Coming for a Life in Florida," *MH*, 21 April 2006; "Taken by Storm," *SS*, 5 September 2017; "Will They Stay or Go?" *SFSS*, 24 October 2004; "Birds Are Back," *SHT*, 4 November 2005; Stanley K. Smith and Scott Cody, "Trends in Florida's Population Growth, 2000–2012," Bureau of Economic and Business Research, University of Florida, 11 March 2013; "Florida Is Fastest-Growing State in U.S." *TT*, 22 December 2005; "Suburban Cities Growing Fast," *SPT*, 21 June 2006; "100 Fastest Growing Counties," http://money.com/2006/03/15real_estate/fastest_growing_counties/index.htm.

5. *Demographia, State Population Growth 2000–2005*, based upon the U.S. Census Data, 22 December 2005; demographer quoted in "State-to-State Migration," *NYT*, 20 April 2006; "More Are Moving out of California Than In," *LAT*, 18 December 2008; "Thieves Cart off St. Louis Bricks," *NYT*, 19 September 2010.

6. "Blacks Leaving Major Cities," *USAT*, 22 March 2011, "More Black Residents Are Leaving Major U.S. Cities," "Many U.S. Blacks Moving to South," and "Black Families Helped Define Chicago: Why Are They Leaving?" *NYT*, 12 September 2007, 24 March 2011, and 17 February 2020; "Census Finds Black Exodus from City," *NYS*, 9 August 2007; Morton quote, "For Blacks, A Return to Southern Roots," *USAT*, 30 June 2011; Haywood quote, "After Nearly 100 Years, Great Migration Is Reversing," *USAT*, 2 February 2015.

7. "A Magnet for Blacks," *MH*, 11 August 2005; "Lauderhill Symbolic of Changing Demographics," *SFSS*, 16 December 2007.

8. "Leon County," *TD*, 28 March 2001; Dietrich, 117, 143, 151.

9. "Florida Group Is Trying to Keep People Away," *NYT*, 14 June 1970; "Calamity Bill and the Sinkhole State," *OS*, 26 August 1990; "Every Day's a Disaster," *SS*, 8 November 1993; Dade County commissioner quoted in "Development Boom in Southeast Florida," *NYT*, 22 April 1973.

10. Carl Hiaasen, "Fanciful Names for Looted Lands," *MH*, 9 September 1999; "Wish You Were Here—But Where Is Here?," *OS*, 14 August 1991; Mormino, *Land of Sunshine*, 8–9.

11. Mormino, "Preserving History as Florida Booms," *Forum: The Magazine of the Florida Humanities Council* 41 (Spring 2017): 10–16.

12. "Nat Reed, Environmental Icon, Dies at 84," *PBP*, 11 July 2018; "A 'No-Growth' Town," *NYT*, 18 November 1981.

13. "The Rush to Utopia," and "An Old Town's New Face," *MH*, 27 September 2005 and 23 May 2007; "Ocala's Sprawl Is Worst," *GS*, 24 February 2001.

14. Mormino, *Land of Sunshine*, 111; Hiaasen quoted in "Florida Icon," *FT*, July 2015; Carl Hiaasen, *Tourist Season* (New York: Warner, 1986), 103–66.

15. John Kenneth Galbraith, *The Affluent Society* (Boston: Houghton and Mifflin, 1958); Michael Paterniti, "America in Extremis," *NYTM*, 21 April 2002.

16. "Haynes' Jewelers," *BH*, 13 November 2003.

17. *The State of the News Media 2007: An Annual Report of American Journalism*; Mormino, *Land of Sunshine*, 174–75.

18. "Quality of Life Index," *SPT*, 21 August 2006; *Twelfth Census of the United States: 1900*, vol. 1, *Population*, Part 1, pp. cxxv, cxlvii; Roberts quoted in "Searching for the Soul of Florida," *OS*, 30 July 2007.

19. "From Near and Far," *SPT*, 10 June 2010.

20. "The United States of Florida," *NYT*, 2 February 2007; Jia Lynn Yang, *One Mighty and Irresistible Tide* (New York: Norton, 2020).

21. "Boomers Hit Another Milestone," *NYT*, 1 December 2011; "Next Wave of Retirees," *SHT*, 18 December 2011; "As the Boomers Turn," *LAT*, 12 September 2011.

22. "Viagra," *MM*, 24 February 2008; "Viagra at 20," *WP*, 3 April 2018; "Rush Limbaugh Detained with Viagra," CBS News.com, 27 June 2006; Mormino, *Land of Sunshine*, 142–43.

23. "Florida Slips, but Still Retirees' No. 1 Choice," *USAT*, 13 August 2003; "Retirement Choices Stretch beyond Fla.," *SHT*, 11 June 2006; "Of Gambling, Grannies, and Good Sense," *TE*, 22 July 2006, 33.

24. "The Abuela Factor," *TBT*, 20 September 2015.

25. "Florida Trend: 20 Million and Counting," *TBT*, 20 September 2015.

26. Mormino, *Land of Sunshine*, 123–27.

27. Ibid., 126.

28. Mackle quoted in "The New Florida Land Rush," *Newsweek*, 5 January 1959, 57; "Key Biscayne: An Island in the Mainstream," *SPT*, 22 December 1968.

29. Pew Charitable Trusts report on budget predictions and other date quoted in "9/11: The Decade," *SPT*, 11 September 2011.

30. "A Legacy Forged: Yes, It's All True," *TBT*, 4 August 2019; "'The Gator Boys' Choose Team over NBA Riches," *MH*, 2 April 2007; "Hoop History," *OSB*, 3 April 2020.

31. Richard Johnson, "Never Forget USF Ranked No. 2 in the BCS," www.sbnation.com; "With Its Roots in a Trailer, Upstart South Florida has Title Dreams," *NYT*, 16 October 2017.

32. AP, "920,000 'Snowbirds,'" 23 November 2004.

33. Julia Lawlor, "Snowbirds Flock Together for Winter," *NYT*, 2 February 2007.

34. "Sunshine State Has 930,000 Snowbirds," *TT*, 25 November 2004; "Snowbirds and the Census," https://michigan.gov/documents/cgi/2010_Census_Snowbirds; "Exposed: Scandal of Double Voters," *NYDN*, 22 August 2004.

35. Lawlor, "Snowbirds."

36. Godefroy Desrosiers-Lauzon, *Florida Snowbirds: Spectacle, Mobility, and Community since 1945* (Montreal: McGill-Queen's University Press, 2011), 3, 189, 242; Mormino, *Land of Sunshine*, 114; "Snowbirds Return to South Florida," *SS*, 13 November 2011; "Oh, Canada Is Big Business," *TBT*, 22 June 2019.

37. "Under the Florida Sun, an Enclave of Finns," *NYT*, 23 September 1982; "Finnish Society," and "Little Finland in the Sun"; *SFSS*, 14 June 2005 and 18 July 1993.

38. Jenna Weissman Joselit, "Going South for the Winter: How Florida Became Home to Jewish Snowbirds," www.tablemag.com/jewish-life-and-religion/, 21 December 2017; Mormino, *Land of Sunshine*, 96–97, 128–30, 137–38.

39. Sandberg quoted in Lawlor, "Snowbirds"; "JewishRoutes," http://www.tablemag.com/jewish; http://www.momentmagazine.com/2014-jewish-routes/.

40. "Snowbirds Are Starting to Leave The Villages," *OSB*, 4 March 2006; "The Sky's the Limit at Skyline Chili," *NDN*, 10 August 2006.

41. "Snowbirds Flock to 'Chicken Night,'" *OS*, 30 March 2018.

42. "Pickleball a Rising Star at Recreation Centers," *TBT*, 14 January 2015.

43. Mormino, *Italians in Florida*, 66; "A Chip off the Italian Ice Block," *NDN*, 11 June 2008; "Cities with the Highest Percentage of Italians in Florida," ZIPAtlas.com; "Michigan Snowbirds' Top Rental Search Is Naples," *DFP*, 15 October 2015.

44. "In the Know: Where Are SWFL's Newest Residents Moving From?" *NDN*, 10 May 2021.

45. "Wolverines Open Practice at IMG," *LL*, 29 February 2016; Gordon L. Olson and Frank N. Schubert, "'It Beats Any Spring Camp I've Ever Seen': The Detroit Tigers Move to Lakeland, Florida, in 1934," *Nine: A Journal of Baseball History and Social Policy Perspectives* 3 (Spring 1995): 432–35.

46. "For Spring Training Locations, Florida Wanes as the Desert Booms," *NYT*, 10 February 2008.

47. "The Supermarket Cafeteria That Major League Baseball Players Love," *NYT*, 20 March 2018.

48. Harvey H. Jackson, "Trying to Reason with the 'Snowbird' Season," *AS*, 2 January 2013; "Appreciation Days," *PCNH*, 13 January 2017; www.destinsnowbirds.org/.

49. "Florida's Cedar Key a Favorite Roost for 'Snow Birds' to Fish," *CT*, 22 February 1987; journalist quoted in "Snowbirds Find Other Snowbirds down South," *River Falls Journal*, 22 January 2014; "Snowbirds Flock to Zephyrhills," *TT*, 1 February 2015; "Churches Feel Seasonal Swing," *FMNP*, 24 March 2004; "Sunshine & Snowbirds: Florida Reunion," *Midland County News*, 5 March 2012.

50. Lawlor, "Snowbirds."

51. "One in Four Snowbirds Finds a Roost in Florida," *SS*, 4 March 2007.

52. Bobbie O'Brien, "Camping, Golfing, Tiki Bars; Military Bases Are Vacation Spots for Some Retirees," WUSF.edu, 16 March 2018.

53. "Snowbirds Work Where It's Warm," *CSM*, 8 February 2006; "Briefcase: Job Slots Follow 'Snowbird' Workers," *NYT*, 3 March 2006.

54. "Florida: An Amish Playground," *TD*, 17 February 1986; "Where Amish Snowbirds Find a Nest," *NYT*, 13 April 2012; "New Sarasota Hotel Has Modern Amenities with Amish Flavor," *SHT*, 13 March 2018; Donald B. Kraybill, Karen M. Johnson-Weiner, and Steven M. Nolt, *The Amish* (Baltimore: Johns Hopkins University Press, 2013), 242–43; "A Growing Backlash Against 'Amish Exploitation' in Pennsylvania," NPR.org, 24 August 2014.

55. "Shifts in Florida's Older Population," *UF News*, 11 December 2006; "Birds Are Back," *SHT*, 4 November 2004; city councilwoman quoted in Cynthia Barnett, "The Carolina Connection," *FT*, October 2007: 52–59; reporter quoted in *TMT*, 10 September 1904; Proctor quoted in "While Others Dream of Beaches, Floridians Seek Higher Ground," *OS*, 6 September 2015.

56. Barnett, "The Carolina Connection," 55; "Retirees Seek Good Life," *WSJ*, 8 August 1994; "States Pan for Gold," *NYT*, 18 March 2003.

57. "On Top of the World Developer Colen Dies," *OSB*, 3 November 2009; "Retirement Community Developer Driven by 'Purpose,'" *TBBJ*, 1 December 1997.

58. Gary R. Mormino and George E. Pozzetta, *The Immigrant World of Ybor City: Italians and Their Latin Neighbors in Tampa, 1885–1985* (Gainesville: University Press of Florida, 2017), 197–203; "Broward in Lead of Co-op Parade," *FLDN*, 29 March 1958.

59. "Condominiums—a New Life-style," *FT*, October 1970, 24; "Happy Birthday Dear Condo," *MH*, 21 November 1982.

60. "Condominiums—a New Life-style,"; *Florida Statistical Abstract, 2002* (Gainesville: Bureau of Economic and Business Research, 2002), 639.

61. "Town Would Ban Hippies," *SPT*, 14 November 1968; "Problems of High-Rises Straining Florida Resort," *NYT*, 22 April 1973; Florida *Statistical Abstract, 2002* (Gainesville: Bureau of Economic and Business Research, 2002), 639.

62. Desrosiers-Lauzon, *Florida Snowbirds*, 107–9.

63. Jeff LaHurd, "Dumped in a Wild Country," and "Golfing Mayor," *SHT*, 29 and 20 July 2017.

64. "Golf Makes Its Bow," *SPT*, 2 January 1916; "Golf Is Gaining Ground in Cities of Florida," *MRJ*,

31 January 1918; Thomas Graham, *Mr. Flagler's St. Augustine* (Gainesville: University Press of Florida, 2014), 318–19.

65. "Troubled Golf Club," *TT*, 29 January 2014; "Billy Graham Found His Calling as a Bible College Student," *TBT*, 21 February 2018.

66. Mormino, *Land of Sunshine*, 72–73; "Doral Resort," *MH*, 20 August 2013; Frank Deford, "Water Thirsty Golf Courses Need to Go Green," NPR.org, 11 June 2008.

67. "Golf Capital of the World," *NDN*, 8 November 2007; "Golf on Florida's Paradise Coast," www.paradisecoast.com.

68. "Village of Golf a Former Dairy Farm," and "Village of Golf Enjoys Its Anonymity," *PBP*, 20 May 2007 and 13 March 2002.

69. "Donald Trump to Buy Ritz-Carlton," *PBP*, 15 November 2012.

70. Alan Shipnuck, "First Golfer," *SI*, 7 August 2017, 50; "The Clintons Really Did Attend Donald Trump's 2005 Wedding," politifact.com/florida, 21 July 2015.

71. Shipnuck, "First Golfer"; "Did Trump Falsify Value of Jupiter Golf Club?," *PBP*, 1 March 2019.

72. Gwenda Blair, *The Trumps: Three Generations That Built an Empire* (New York: Touchstone, 2000), 364–66.

73. "Al Hoffman Is a 'Florida Icon,'" *FT*, December 2017.

74. Susan Burns, "Tales of Hoffman," *Gulfshore Business*, September 2010; Hoffman quoted in "Heading for Higher Ground," *FT*, December 1996.

75. Michael Grunwald, "Growing Pains in Southwest Fla.," *WP*, 25 June 2002.

76. Peter Michaelson, "Explosive Growth at Bonita Springs," *FT*, February 1981, 76–77; "Bonita Faces Sonic Boom," and "Bonita Springs, Fort Myers among Fastest Growing Cities in Country," *FMNP*, 14 October 2007 and 24 May 2017.

77. "Capital City Country Club: Slave Cemetery," *USAT*, 27 December 23019; "The Case Against Golf," *TG*, 14 June 2007; "Will Golf Course Sale Serve the Purpose?" *FTU*, 30 September 1959; Deford, "Water Thirsty Golf Courses Need to Go Green"; Diane Roberts, "How Golf Courses Grow Like Weeds," *SPT*, 14 September 2003.

78. Tamara Lush, "Pricing Paradise by the Gallon," *SPT*, 12 June 2005; "Making Marco," *NDN*, 1 April 2012.

79. Craig Pittman and Matthew Waite, *Paving Paradise: Florida's Vanishing Wetlands* (Gainesville: University Press of Florida, 2009), 59; "People of Influence: Al Hoffman," *FMNP*, 24 October 2014.

80. "Streamsong," *USAT*, 12 April 2018.

81. Robert Samuelson, "Homes as Hummers," *WP*, 13 July 2005; county commissioner quoted in "The Five-Bedroom," *NYT*, 1 June 2005.

82. "Englewood Hopes Starbucks & Whole Foods Create 'Ripple Effect,'" *CT*, 28 September 2016; Svenja Gudell, "Living Near Whole Foods Can Boost Your Home's Value," Forbes.com, 19 June 2017.

83. "Billionaire Club Still Growing in Florida," *SPT*, 25 September 2006; "What Kind of House Will $1 Million Buy?" *OS*, 6 November 2005; "New Rise in Number of Millionaire Families," *NYT*, 28 March 2006.

84. "Cities with Most Millionaires," *USAT*, 7 December 2011; "Naples Nabobs," and "Naples Area Ranks No. 2 in Florida for Healthy Living," *FMNP*, 25 December 2008 and

26 March 2014; "Where America's Money Is Moving," wallstreetpit.com/32346-yankees-seek-tax-refuge-in-the-deep-south, 20 June 2010.

85. "Where America's Money Is Moving," *Forbes Magazine*, June 2010; "New Rise in Number of Millionaire Families," *NYT*, 28 March 2006.

86. "Where America's Money Is Moving," *Forbes Magazine*, June 2010; "New Rise in Number of Millionaire Families," *NYT*, 28 March 2006; "A City Defines Beautiful," *NYT*, 31 August 2007; "Coral Gables Residents," *MH*, 31 October 2012; "Don't Be Arrested in Florida Know Your Laws," https://www.tripadvisor.com; "Florida Clothesline Law," *FMNP*, 5 December 2015; AP, "Palm Beach Cites Trump for Flag,"

FMNP, 1 November 2006; "Lawn Trimming," *TBT*, 9 May 2019; "Boca Raton Is Rolling Out Tougher Restrictions on Yard Sales," and "Signs of Changing Time in Stuart," *PBP*, 18 January 2019 and 16 April 2007; "Almost No One Wants a Neighbor Like Donald Trump," *WP*, 28 December 2020.

87. Edward J. Blakely and Mary Gail Snyder, *Fortress America: Gated Communities in the United States* (Washington, DC: Brookings Institution Press, 1997), 5, 122–23; Benjamin Rich, "The Gated Community," *USAT*, 2002 Joan Clos, "Gated Communities," *TG*, 2 May 2014; "What's a Gated Community?," *OS*, 27 January 2001. Frank Migliore of Tampa coined the term "gated dys-unity."

88. Richard Foglesong, *Married to the Mouse: Walt Disney World and Orlando* (New Haven, CT: Yale University Press, 2003), 34–54; Mormino, *Land of Sunshine*, 103; "Old Florida Law Says Disney Can Build Nuclear Power Plant," *OS*, 14 February 2019.

89. "Motor Gypsies," *SPT*, 27 February 1933; Gary R. Mormino, *Hillsborough County Goes to War* (Tampa: Tampa Bay History Center, 2001), 69–70; "The Two Trailer Family," *STP*, 5 December 1965; Chiori Santiago, "House Trailers," *Smithsonian* 29 (June 1998): 76–85; "Houses on Wheels," *OS*, 6 September 1998.

90. Mormino, *Land of Sunshine*, 266–67; "Voters Will Set Trailers' Status," *SPT*, 1 November 1965.

91. "Florida Tops in Mobile Homes," *SHT*, 26 May 2002; "Two North Florida Cities Boast the Highest Density of Mobile Homes in Any Metro Area," CNNMoney.com, 23 September 2009.

92. "Polk Mobile-Izing," *TT*, 6 May 2002; "Polk County Has the Most Mobile Homes," *LL*, 10 April 2007.

93. "No Parking Zone," *SPT*, 28 July 2003.

94. "Hitting the Trail(ers)," *TT*, 2005; lawyer quoted in "Mobile Home Parks, Once a Retiree Oasis, Vanishing," *SHT*, 5 October 2005.

95. "Trying to Stay Put in Florida Mobile Homes," *NYT*, 22 June 2003; "Trailer Parks' Future Hazy," *MH*, 3 January 2006.

96. "Airstream Ranch's Creator," *LL*, 7 March 2008; "Airstream Ranch," *TBT*, 9 February 2017; "Airstream Ranch Is Not Junk," *TT*, 12 February 2010.

97. "Add Murder, Mayhem to Trailer Park's Credit," and "Gay Resort Builder Ends Bid," *SFSS*, 8 October 1995 and 19 July 2010.

98. Eliot Kleinberg, "Developer Set to Buy Entire Oceanfront Town," *PBP*, 13 December 2006.

99. "Flirtation with Fortune Breaks Hearts in Briny," *PBP*, 29 October 2007.

100. Rulli quoted in "A Price on Paradise," *SPT*, 5 February 2006; "Serene Seaside Sells in Landslide" and "Meet Briny Breezes' Potential Millionaires," *PBP*, 11 January 2007 and 16 December 2006; "In Florida, Upwardly Mobile Homes," *WP*, 7 January 2007.

101. Drew Harwell, "Mobile Home Park Investors Bet on Older, Poorer America" and "It's Not Your Mother's Mobile Home," *TBT*, 18 May 2014 and 17 April 2005; "Most Mobile Homes Are in the South," CNNMoney.com, 23 September 2009.

102. "Where Jobs Ride on a Luxury on Wheels," *NYT*, 30 March 2009; "Custom Made," *FT*, May 2010, 10–11.

103. AP, "How Weird Is Fla?," *FMNP*, 1 January 2006; Craig Pittman, *Oh, Florida! How America's Weirdest State Influences the Rest of the Country* (New York: St. Martin's, 2016).

104. Patsy West, *The Enduring Seminoles: From Alligator Wrestling to Ecotourism* (Gainesville: University Press of Florida, 1998).

105. *FMP*, 25 June 1917; *FTU*, 11 December 1918.

106. Mormino, *Land of Sunshine*, 189–92; Harry A. Kersey Jr., *An Assumption of Sovereignty: Social and Political Transformation among the Florid Seminoles, 1953–1979* (Lincoln: University of Nebraska Press, 1996), 182.

107. Peter B. Gallagher, "The Rise and Fall of Jim Billie," *Sarasota Magazine*, January 2005, 17.

108. Ibid.; Barbara Oeffner, *Chief: Champion of the Everglades* (Palm Beach: Cape Cod Writers Inc., 1995), 59–60, 65, 87–89, 103; Patricia R. Wickman, *Osceola's Legacy* (Tuscaloosa: University of Alabama

Press, 1991), 6; "Sheriff Makes Futile Hunt for 'Doomed' Indian Maid," *MH*, 4 June 1946; Betty Mae Jumper and Patsy West, *A Seminole Legend: The Life of Betty Mae Tiger* (Gainesville: University Press of Florida, 2001), 91.

109. Gallagher, "The Rise and Fall of Jim Billie"; "Documentary Follows the Wild Life," *SS*, 24 March 2017.

110. "Florida Indians Still Live in Their Primitive Fashion," *TMT*, 1 February 1946.

111. "Documentary Follows the Wild Life"; Oeffner, *Chief*, 15; Kersey, *Assumption of Sovereignty*, 121; Jessica R. Cattelino, *High Stakes: Florida Seminole Gambling and Sovereignty* (Durham, NC: Duke University Press, 2008), 1.

112. Matthew L. M. Fletcher, "The Seminole Tribe and the Origins of Indian Gaming," *FIU Law Review* 9 (2014): 255, 264; Charles Wilkinson, *Blood Struggle: The Rise of Modern Indian Nations* (New York: Norton, 2005), 331–36.

113. "Rift," *SPT*, 12 April 2005; Lauren Debter, "An Alligator Wrestler, A Casino Boss and a $12 Billion Tribe," *Forbes*, November 2016; Gallagher quoted in "20 Years Ago, Trump Had Eye on Seminoles," *CDC Gaming Reports Inc.*, 9 March 2016; "Seminoles Invest in Nicaragua," *OS*, 7 April 2001.

114. "Seminole Tribe Puts Another $1 Million behind Amendment 3 Push," floridapolitics.com, 1 November 2018; "Spending Big on Lobbyists in Florida," floridatrend.com, 30 April 2014.

115. "New Deal: Florida and Seminoles Settle," floridapolitics.com, 7 July 2017; "Seminole Tribe," and "Seminole Hard Rock Collects $579 Million," *MH*, 14 May 2019 and 18 February 2018.

116. "The New Hard Rock Live," *SS*, 23 October 2019; "How the Seminole Tribe Came to Rock the Hard Rock Empire," and "Former Seminole Tribe Leader Who Built Hard Rock into Worldwide Brand Dies," *MH*, 22 May 2016 and 9 October 2020; "Max Osceola Jr. 70," Osceola quoted in *NYT*, 21 October 2020.

117. Tribal official quoted in "Seminole Families Reap Jackpot from Gambling," *SFSS*, 21 December 1994; Cattelino, *High Stakes*, 103, 104.

118. Peirce and Johnson, "The Search for a Sustainable Solution," *SFSS*, 10 December 2000.

Chapter 7. Instant Cities, Boomburbs, and Little Havanas

1. Michael Paterniti, "America in Extremis," *TNYTM*, 21 April 2002, 6; Brooks, "Take a Ride to Exurbia," and "The Fallows Question," *NYT*, 9 November 2004 and 7 February 2007.

2. "Florida City Heads Growth-Boom List," NPR.org, 30 June 2005; Eve Samples, "Port St. Lucie Is No 'Tomb,'" *TCP*, 22 December 2013; "Sun, Water, and the Mets Put a 'Nowhere' on the Map," *NYT*, 16 February 2007.

3. Gary R. Mormino, "Spring Training, 1914," *TBT*, 22 February 2014.

4. "Sun, Water, and the Mets"; "Port St. Lucie," *PBP*, 17 February 2008; Clayton quoted in "Growth Steady for Port St. Lucie," *PBP*, 28 June 2007.

5. T. Stanton Dietrich, *The Urbanization of Florida's Population: An Historical Perspective of County Growth, 1830–1970* (Gainesville: University of Florida Bureau of Economics and Business Research, 1978), 22.

6. "ITT's Boom in Palm Coast," *MH*, 1977; "When Flagler County Caught the Development Eye of ITT," *DBNJ*, 8 April 1989.

7. "Counties with the Highest Proportion of Housing Units Built after 1999," *USAT*, 3 October 2006; "An Old Town's New Face," *MH*, 23 May 2007.

8. Gary R. Mormino, *Land of Sunshine, State of Dreams: A Social History of Modern Florida* (Gainesville: University Press of Florida, 2005), 52–53.

9. "First Things First: City History Still Standing," and "Cape Ranks as Fourth Fastest-Growing City," *FMNP*, 3 November and 6 July 2007.

10. PEW Research poll cited in D. J. Waldie, "Do the Voters Really Hate Sprawl?" *NYT*, 3 March

2000; Sierra Club quoted in www.sierraclub.org/sprawl/overview; Robert Putnam, *Bowling Alone: The Collapse and Revival of American Community* (New York: Simon and Schuster, 2000), 407–8; "Ocala's Sprawl Is Worst," *GS*, 24 February 2001; AP, "Sprawl Plagues Florida," 10 September 1999; "The USA TODAY Sprawl Index," *USAT*, 22 February 2001; Richard Lacayo, "Sprawl," *Time*, 22 March 1999, 45–48.

11. Christine Shenot and Jim Stratton, "Pushing Our Growth to the Brink," *OS*, 23 April 2000. The article was part of a series titled "Living with Sprawl."

12. Robert E. Lang and Jennifer B. LeFurgy, *Boomburbs: The Rise of America's Accidental Cities* (Washington, DC: Brookings Institution Press, 2007), 10, 71–72.

13. Ibid., 56–57, 70–71; Mormino, *Land of Sunshine*, 30; "Defectors Say Church of Scientology Hides Abuse," *NYT*, 6 March 2010.

14. Peter T. Kilborn, "The Five Bedroom, Six-Figure Rootless Life," *NYT*, 1 June 2005.

15. David Brooks, "Take a Ride to Exurbia," *NYT*, 9 November 2004.

16. "The Acreage Scores Worst in Florida," *PBP*, 2 January 2012.

17. Kilborn, "The Five Bedroom, Six-Figure Rootless Life"; Wiltz; "'Boomburbs' Mark an Era of Sprawl," *USAT*, 31 October 2003; Robert Steuteville, "Boomburbs: Suburbs on Steroids," *Public Square: A CNU Journal*, 1 September 2001; "Kids Are Stranded in Region's 'Exurbs,'" *OS*, 24 April 2000; William L. Hamilton, "How Suburban Design Is Failing Teen-agers," *NYT*, 6 May 1999; "Clogged Roads Will Get Worse," *OS*, 24 April 2000; chamber official quoted in "Wesley Chapel Growth Continues with Crystal Lagoon," WUSF.edu, 8 February 2018; "Pasco Boomtown Rises," *TBT*, 25 October 2015; "200,000—in Flick of a Switch," *SPT*, 17 January 2006.

18. "For GOP in Florida, It's Boom Burbs or Bust," *WP*, 52–53, 22 January 2012; Diane Roberts, "Old Florida Is Falling to the Developers," *SPT*, 12 August 2002.

19. Lang and LeFurgy, *Boomburbs*, 8, 13, 70.

20. Ibid., 8; "Politically, Broward Is Balkanized," *MH*, 28 May 1997.

21. "Politically, Broward Is Balkanized"; "Where Do We Grow from Here?" *SFSS*, 6 June 1999; Mormino, *Land of Sunshine*, 23–24.

22. Guy Kingsley, "'Browardize' a Good Thing," *SFSS*, 24 January 2007.

23. ". . . Any New Growth Is Bad Growth," *MH*, 30 December 2001.

24. Ibid.; Mormino, *Land of* Sunshine, 24; "Russian-Language Version of Census," and "Miramar Haitians Earn Most in Area," *SFSS*, 6 April 2008 and 9 September 2005; "Broward Looking More Like Dade," *MH*, 19 December 2010.

25. Mormino, *Land of Sunshine*, 116–17; "Metropolitan & Central City Population: 2000–2005, Demographia.com; "Searching for the Soul of Florida," *OS*, 30 July 2007.

26. T. D. Allman, "Beyond Disney," *National Geographic*, March 2007.

27. "State GOP Gets $500,000 Donation," *SS*, 12 July 2006.

28. Mormino, *Land of Sunshine*, 138–39; "Villages' Founder Dies at 93," *OSB*, 24 December 2003.

29. "Billionaire Morse," Bloomberg, 4 June 2012; Golant quoted in "Retiree Dreams Come True," *OS*, 24 November 2002; "The Villagers Set to Play Crucial Role in Primary," *NYT*, 26 November 2007; Coe quoted in "Retirees' Dreamland Is Republican Bastion," *MH*, 16 September 2007; "Company Is Bullish on The Villages," *OS*, 26 March 2007.

30. "A Custom Ride, Legal for the Street or the 18th Tee," *NYT*, 9 April 2007; "The Strange World of Florida's Golf Cart City, The Villages," *The Telegraph*, 11 January 2015; "Drive the Cart, Skip the Golf," *OS*, 20 August 2000.

31. "Brandon Residents," *TT*, 7 August 2011; "Suburbs without Cities," *NYT*, 21 May 1992.

32. Mormino, *Land of Sunshine*, 31, 56.

33. Tebeau, *Florida's Last Frontier* (Coral Gables: University of Miami Press, 1966), 188–91; Mormino, *Land of Sunshine*, 71–72; *FMNP*, 3 March 1920.

34. "Naples," *FT*, June 1959, 27; "Naples Confronts Growth," *TT*, 8 June 1987; "See Naples . . . and Live Lushly," *Newsweek*, 5 January 1959, 57; "They Called It 'Port Royal,'" and "Boom Town," *NDN*, 1 April 2012.

35. "Cities with Most Millionaires," *USAT*, 7 December 2011; "Southwest Florida Still Home to Six of the World's Richest Billionaires," *NDN*, 6 March 2018.

36. "Marco—Year in the Life of an Island," and "Development vs. Destruction," *SPT*, 24 January and 22 December 1965, 23 July 1975; Frank Hamilton Cushing, *The Florida Journals of Frank Hamilton Cushing*, ed. Phyllis E. Kolianos (Gainesville: University Press of Florida, 2005).

37. Mormino, *Land of Sunshine*, 58; David E. Dodrill, *Selling the Dream: The Gulf American Corporation and the Building of Cape Coral, Florida* (Tuscaloosa: University of Alabama Press, 1993).

38. Aisling Swift, "Who We Are: Rich, Poor Divide One of the Most Unequal in U.S.," *NDN*, 22 April 2012; Mormino, *Land of Sunshine*, 209–10, 220–21.

39. "The Miracle of Muck City," "Floridian" sec., *TBT*, 4 August 2013; "Sex Offender Village," *NYT*, 21 May 2013; "Pervert Park," *TBT*, 8 July 2016; "Trailer Park Becomes 'Paradise' for Sex Offenders," CNN.com, 18 October 2007.

40. Meryl Kornfield, "Florida Has 10K Elderly on Sex Offender Registry," *MH*, 20 June 2019.

41. "Florida Prison Population," Florida Department of Corrections; "Summary of Florida State Correctional Facilities: 2006–2007 Annual Report"; Paige M. Harrison and Allen J. Beck, "Prison and Jail Inmates at Midyear 2005," *Bureau of Justice Statistics Bulletin* (May 2006), table 3, "Prisoners Held in Private Facilities," 1–11.

42. Rick Bragg, "Destin Journal," 14 August 2000; Harvey H. Jackson, *The Rise and Decline of the Redneck Riviera: An Insider's History of the Florida-Alabama Coast* (Athens: University of Georgia Press, 2012), 114, 144, 151; Jack E. Davis, *The Gulf: The Making of an American Sea* (New York: Liveright, 2016), 471.

43. Davis, *The Gulf*, 471–73; Robert Smolian Davis, "Visions of Seaside, 1946–2011," seaside.library.nd.edu.

44. Davis, *The Gulf*, 472; "Daryl Davis, Seaside Co-founder," *NFDN*, 10 April 2016; "Utopia-by-the-Sea," *NYT*, 3 May 2000.

45. Davis, *The Gulf*, 474; Jackson, *The Rise and Decline of the Redneck Riviera*, 116, 118–19, 138–40.

46. Jackson, *The Rise and Decline of the Redneck Riviera*, 140; Beth Dunlop, "In Florida, a New Emphasis on Design," and Fred A. Bernstein, "Seaside at 25: Troubles in Paradise," *NYT*, 9 December 2001 and 9 December 2005.

47. Dunlop, "In Florida, a New Emphasis on Design"; "Design: Best of the Decade," *Time*, 1 January 1990; Stearn quoted in Dunlop, "In Florida, a New Emphasis on Design."

48. "Seaside," in *A Guidebook to New Urbanism in Florida 2005* (Hialeah: Dutton, 2005), 30–31; Davis, *The Gulf*, 473; "Seaside," 30.

49. Kathryn Ziewitz and June Wiaz, *Green Empire: The St. Joe Company and the Remaking of Florida's Panhandle* (Gainesville: University Press of Florida, 2004), 5, 13, 42–43, 70–72, 98–99.

50. Ibid., 11; Davis, *The Gulf*, 475.

51. Ziewitz and Wiaz, *Green Empire*, 8, 75, 121, 158, 163.

52. "Alys Beach," *PBP*, 27 January 2018.

53. Michael Pollan, "Town Building Is No Mickey Mouse Operation," *NYTM*, 14 December 1997.

54. Douglas Frantz and Catherine Collins, "It's a Small Town after All," *NYT*, 4 December 2010; Andrew Ross, *The Celebration Chronicles: Life, Liberty, and the Pursuit of Property Value in Disney's New Town* (New York: Ballantine, 2000), 309.

55. Frantz and Collins, "It's a Small Town after All"; "Leaks and Mold Are Ruining the Disney Magic," *WSJ*, 15 November 2016; Frantz and Collins, "It's a Small Town after All"; Douglas Frantz, "Living in a Disney Town," *NYT*, 4 October 1998; Mark Greif, "Potemkin Villages," *American Prospect*, 3 January 2000, 54; Pollan, "Town Building."

56. "The New Look of the Community," *TBT*, 14 August 2006; Diane Roberts, "Old Florida Is Falling to the Developers," *SPT*, 12 August 2002; "A Cure-all for Sprawl," *SFS*, 6 August 2000.

57. "WPBT Is Stuck in the Past with 'Imagining Florida,'" *MH*, 13 May 2010.

58. Jonathan Glancey, "Thou Shalt Not Follow Duany's Architectural Gospel," *TG*, 3 December 2008.

59. Rob Walker, "Making a Pilgrimage to Utopia-by-the-Sea," *NYT*, 2 May 2002; Pollan, "Town Building."

60. "Failed Disney Vision: Integrated City," *NYT*, 23 September 2001.

Chapter 8. The Dream and the Nightmare: Immigration, 2000–2010

1. "Ellis Island Congested with Unprecedented Immigrant Rush," *TMT*, 29 December 1919.

2. Freedman quoted in Jason DeParle, "Global Migration: A World Ever More on the Move," *NYT*, 26 June 2010; "Growing Share of U.S. Is Born on Foreign Soil," *NYT*, 13 September 2018.

3. *Seventeenth Census of the United States*, table 24; "Florida has Passed New York," *OS*, 23 December 2014; "One Hundred Years of Multitude," *NYT*, 26 March 2011.

4. "2010, Foreign-Born Population in the United States Statistical Portrait," table 12, Pew Research Center, Hispanic Trends, 21 February 2012.

5. "Florida Has More Hispanics Than Blacks, Census Shows," *NYT*, 28 March 2001; T. Stanton Dietrich, *The Urbanization of Florida's Population: An Historical Perspective of County Growth, 1830–1970* (Gainesville: University of Florida Bureau of Economics and Business Research, 1978), 11.

6. Louis A. Pérez, *On Becoming Cuban: Identity, Nationality and Culture* (Chapel Hill: University of North Carolina Press, 1999), 432–34.

7. "Region Remains Magnet for People," *MH*, 5 April 2007; "Born in U.S.A.? Not in Miami," *SPT*, 3 September 2003; "Census: Broward Becoming More Hispanic, Black," *SFSS*, 20 December 2010.

8. "The Numbers, from Palm Beach County to Miami-Dade," *SS*, 25 March 2007.

9. "Whites Account for under Half of Births in U.S.," *NYT*, 17 May 2012; "Florida's Under-70 Population Now Majority-Minority," *TBT*, 25 June 2019; "White Children Now in Minority," *TT*, 15 August 2006.

10. *The Hispanic Population: 2010*, tables 2 and 4, U.S. Census Bureau, 2011.

11. Deborah Dash Moore, *To the Golden Cities: Pursuing an American Jewish Dream in Miami and Los Angeles* (New York: Free Press, 1994), 46; Uriel Heilman, "Miami Beach Loves the Jews, but It Wasn't Always This Way," *Jewish Telegraphic Agency*, 23 October 2014.

12. "Once Sleepy Florida Suburbs Center of Jewish Population Boom," *Jewish Telegraphic Agency*, 6 July 2006; Sheskin quoted in Sara Liss, "The Jewish State of Florida," *Hadassah Magazine*, February 2007; "Palm Beach County: More Jewish Than New York," historicpalmbeach.blog.palmbeachpost.com, 23 October 2005; "Joan Geller, Political Mother, Dies at 84," *SFSS*, 12 May 2015; "Irving Cohen," *NYT*, 4 October 2012; "World War II Veteran to Recount Experiences in All-Jewish Brigade," *MH*, 4 February 1999.

13. Gary R. Mormino, *Land of Sunshine, State of Dreams: A Social History of Modern Florida* (Gainesville: University Press of Florida, 2005), 282–95; "Cup of Culture," *MH*, 23 June 2002; "One of the Least Diverse Cities in the US Is Almost All Latino," NBCNews.com, 24 February 2017.

14. Mormino, *Land of Sunshine*, 289–90; *Twenty-Second Census of the United States: 2000*, Profile of Selected Social Characteristics: 2000, Summary File 3; Alejando Portes and Alex Steppick, *City on the Edge: The Transformation of Miami* (Berkeley: University of California Press, 1993), 161; Guillermo quoted in "The Melding Americas," *LAT*, 27 September 1994.

15. "As Virus Wanes in Florida, a City Battles Pandemic Fatigue," *NYT*, 2 September 2020.

16. "Five Months after Michael, Farm Workers Struggle in Gadsden County," *TD*, 17 March 2019; Mike Vogel, "Hispanic Diversity in Florida," *FT*, 1 May 2013.

17. Michael Barone, "A Nation Built for Immigrants," *WSJ*, 21–22 September 2013; "Three Charts That Challenge the Conventional Wisdom of 2015," *WP*, 2 January 2016.

18. "Remade in America," *NYT*, 15 March 2009.

19. Mormino, *Land of Sunshine*, 291; *The Hispanic Population: 2000*, table 2.

20. "Cities with the Highest Percentage of Mexicans in Florida," Zipatlas.com; "A Florida Mayor Turns to an Immigration Curb," *NYT*, 10 July 2006; Dan Charles, "Guest Workers," NPR.org, 28 January 2016.

21. Boyd quoted in "Pierson Fern Cutters," *Leesburg Daily Commercial*, 13 November 2016.

22. "Hispanic Population Is Growing in Clearwater," *Clearwater Beacon*, 27 February 2015; Ella Schmidt and Maria Crummett, "Spheres of Influence and Area Studies: The Hidalgo-Clearwater Connection," paper delivered at the 2003 meeting of the Latin American Studies Association, Dallas, Texas; "Mercado and Festival," *TBT*, 5 September 2017.

23. Gustavo Arellano, *Taco USA: How Mexican Food Conquered America* (New York: Scribner, 2012); David Von Drehle, "Cinco de Mayo," *WP*, 3 May 2019.

24. Migrationpolicy.org, 5 April 2017.

25. "Guatemalan Mayans Settle in South Florida," *WP*, 1 February 2004; Mike Vogel, "Melting Pot," *FT* 46 (August 2003): 41–43; "Guatemalan Mayas to Celebrate Festival," *SS*, 21 September 2012; Patrick Hiller, J. P. Linsroth, and Paloma Ayala Vela, "'I Am Maya, not Guatemalan, nor Hispanic'—the Belongingness of Mayas in Southern Florida," *Forum: Qualitative Social Research* 10 (September 2009); "Modern Maya," *SS*, 3 October 2019.

26. "Jupiter's El Sol," *NYT*, 26 February 2011.

27. Mormino, *Land of Sunshine*, 291; Alfono Chardy, "How Puerto Ricans Are Changing the Face of Florida," *MH*, 22 January 2017.

28. "Puerto Ricans Are Citizens, Not Immigrants," editorial, *NYT*, 17 December 1993; Jorge Duany, "Mickey Ricans? The Recent Puerto Rican Diaspora to Florida," in *La Florida: Five Hundred Years of Hispanic Presence*, ed. Viviana Díaz Balsera and Rachel A. May (Gainesville: University Press of Florida, 2014), 224.

29. Victor Manuel Ramos, "Between Two Worlds," *OS*, 6 February 2006.

30. Mormino, *Land of Sunshine*, 117, 292, 366; Otero quoted in Lizette Álvarez, "Puerto Ricans Seeking New Lives," *NYT*, 24 August 2015.

31. Simone P. Delerme, "The Fractured American Dream: From Country Club to 'Suburban Slum,'" *FHQ* 95 (Winter 2017): 383–426; "How We're Changing," and "Between Two Worlds," *OS*, 20 November and 5 February 2006; Duany quoted in AP, "Emigrating Puerto Ricans," *SPT*, 4 March 2005.

32. "Minorities on the Move," *NYT*, 6 June 1993; Suarez quoted in Duany; Merced quoted in "Flocking to Florida," *USAT*, 26 August 2015; "Poinciana's Growth," *OS*, 29 March 2001.

33. Mormino, *Land of Sunshine*, 292; "Couple Escape New York for Central Florida," *OS*, 5 February 2006.

34. "Puerto Ricans Seeking New Lives," *NYT*, 24 August 2015.

35. "Puerto Rican Firms Follow Their Market," *WSJ*, 20 April 2017; "Florida Beckons Business," *TBT*, 26 December 2015.

36. "National Origin in the Miami Area, #3, "Country by Birth," Statisticalatlas.com.

37. "Who Is Democratic Presidential Candidate Wayne Messam?," *MH*, 25 June 2019; Messam quoted in *Jamaican Observer*, 1 October 2016.

38. "65 Fleeing Haitians," *MH*, 13 December 1972; "Good U.S. Life," *FLDN*, 12 October 1980; "Rep. Shaw Defends Policy of Blocking Haitians," *MH*, 24 November 1991.

39. Lizette Alvarez, "58,000 Haitians in U.S. May Lose Safeguard," *NYT*, 21 May 2017; "Growing Community Putting up a Quiet Struggle," *SS*, 4 October 1990.

40. "Ancestry Map of Haitian Communities," Epodunk.com; "Top 101 Cities with the Most Residents Born in Haiti," City-Data.com; "National Origin in Palm Beach County," #2, Country of Birth," Statisticalatlas.com; "National Origin in Broward County, #3 "Country of Birth."

41. "Little Haiti Neighborhood in Miami," City-Data.com; "'What's in a Name?' Little Haiti," *MH*, 31 May 2016; Jan Nijman, *Miami: Mistress of the Americas* (Philadelphia: University of Pennsylvania Press, 2011).

42. Marjorie Valbrun, "Immigrant Community Struggles for Unity, Power," *MH*, 6 October 1991.

43. "Haitian-Americans: Their Search for Political Identity in South Florida," Aliciapatterson.org, 2001; Nadege Green, "Ballot Brokers Also Target Haitian Vote," *MH*, 23 September 2012.

44. Alvarez, "58,000 Haitians in U.S. May Lose Safeguard"; "Haiti Still Suffering," *USAT*, 12 December 2014; "Bill, Hillary and the Haiti Debacles," and "Five Years Later: Where Did All the Haiti Aid Go?," *WSJ*, 19 May 2014 and 10 January 2015; Inera quoted in "Change Could Increase Haitian Count in Census," *SS*, 4 February 2010.

45. Joel Millman, "Delray Beach, Little Haiti's Little Sister," Aliciapatterson.org, 14 April 2011; Otis White, "The Best-Run Town in Florida," *FT*, February 1995, 36–43.

46. "Ethnic Make-Over of S. Florida," *MH*, 2 January 2000; Ray Downs, "Broward County's Minority Population Is Now the Majority," *Broward New Times*, 15 April 2015; "Broward's Foreign-Born Population Soars," *SS*, 11 May 2012.

47. "Minority Movement," and "Chinese Jamaicans Straddle Multicultural Force," *MH*, 9 August 2007 and 2 July 2012; "South Florida's Chinese-Jamaicans," *SS*, 1 July 2012.

48. "Intermarriage Fuzzes Latin Identity," *MH*, 2 January 2000; Mark Hugo Lopez, "Hispanic Identity Fades across Generations as Immigrant Connections Fall Away," Pewhispanic.org, 20 December 2017.

49. "How We're Changing," *OS*, 20 November 2006.

50. Gene Demby, "Black Like Who?," NPR.org, 15 April 2020; Mormino, *Land of Sunshine*, 295; "Latinos Defy Labels," *TBT*, 14 October 2020.

51. Lopez quoted in "Miami's Black Population Becomes More Foreign," *TT*, 11 April 2005; "Black Cubans Get Brunt of Bias," and "Haitian, Jamaican or American . . . If You're Black in Miami, Odds Are You're Struggling," *MH*, 16 September 1973 and 25 February 2019.

52. Lisette Alvarez, "Pull of Family Reshapes U.S. Cuban Relations," *NYT*, 22 November 2011; "Travelers Pay to Protect Luggage with Plastic Wrap," 2 April 2014, CNBC.com; "Remittances to Cuba in 2016," The Havana Consulting Group & Tech., 20 July 2017; "Sally Jacobs, "Cubans See What's Out There," *WP*, 5 July 2016.

53. "Poll in Cuba: Obama More Popular," *MH*, 9 April 2015.

54. Moisés Naím and Francisco Toro, "Venezuela's Suicide: Lessons from a Failed State," *Foreign Affairs*, November/December 2018, 1.

55. Ibid.; AP, "A Country Running Dry," *TBT*, 1 July 2020.

56. Ibid.

57. Ibid., Jon Lee Anderson, "Slumlord: What Has Hugo Chávez Wrought in Venezuela?," *TNY*, 28 January 2013, 40–51; "Debating Chávez's Legacy," *NYT*, 8 March 2013.

58. "For Cuba, Chávez's Health Is a Vital Statistic," *WSJ*, 23–24 June 2012; "For Venezuela, a Staunch Ally: For Cuba, Lots of Subsidized Oil," *NYT*, 27 January 2019; "Venezuela Is Giving Away Oil to Cuba," and "Venezuela Can't Sell Its Oil," *MH*, 15 and 4 October 2019.

59. "Venezuela's Loss in Miami's Gain," USNews.com, 13 July 2017.

60. "A White Migration North from Miami," *WP*, 11 November 1998; "Rise of Chávez Sends Venezuelans to Florida," *NYT*, 23 January 2008; "Westonzuela," *SS*, 19 March 2013.

61. "In Florida, an Initiative Intended to End Bias, Is Killed," *NYT*, 5 November 2008; "Florida's 'Last Vestige of Discrimination' Alien Land Law, Remains in Constitution," *OS*, 15 August 2017.

62. Stefan Rayer, "Asians in Florida," Bureau of Economic and Business Research, 27 August 2014; "Asians Flock to SW Florida," and "Asian Companies on a Roll," *FMNP*, 3 April 2011 and 22 February 2012; "The Asian Equation," *TBT*, 28 April 2013.

63. John Higham, *Strangers in the Land* (New York: Atheneum, 1960); Robert J. Samuelson, "Candor on Immigration," *WP*, 8 June 2005.

64. "Immigration System at the 'Breaking Point,'" NPR.org, 27 March 2019.

65. "Keeping a Bombastic Relative at Bay," *NYT*, 4 July 2018; Gwenda Blair, *The Trumps: Three Generations That Built an Empire* (New York: Touchstone, 2000), 23–124; "Donald Trump's Grandfather Got Business Start in Seattle," *Seattle Times*, 21 September 2015; "Trump Referred to Haiti and African Countries as 'Shithole' Countries," NBCNews.com, 11 January 2018; "14 of Trump's Most Outrageous 'Birther' Claims," CNN.com, 16 September 2016.

66. "The Global Face of Flagler County," *DBNJ*, 2 September 2010.

67. The U.S. Census Bureau, *Quick Facts: Collier County, Florida* (2017); "Minority Majority Not New to Lee, Collier Counties," *FMNP*, 28 May 2012.

68. Gary R. Mormino, *Italians in Florida* (New York: Bordighera, 2008); "Cities with the Highest Percentage of Italians in Florida," ZIPatlas.com.

69. "Foreign Policy: Florida Has One," *NYT*, 22 May 1994; "Some Haitians Want U.S. to Weigh in on Crisis," *MH*, 30 October 2019; "Pastor Terry Jones Arrested," NPR.org, 11 September 2013; "Quran Burning in Florida Spurs Afghanistan Deaths," *TT*, 2 April 2011.

70. Jason DeParle, "A World Ever More on the Move," *NYT*, 26 June 2010.

Chapter 9. Sunshine amid Shadows: Florida on the Brink

1. "Taken by Storm," *SS*, 5 September 2017; Stanley K. Smith and Scott Cody, "Trends in Florida's Population Growth, 2000–2012," 11 March 2013, Bureau of Economic and Business Research, University of Florida; Art Levy, "Incoming," *FT*, February 2007, 72–73.

2. Browning, "Are We Full Yet?" *PBP*, 20 October 1999; Hauserman, "Yes, We're Growing, but into What?" *SPT*, 27 February 2000; Louis Rene Beres, "Have We Sold Our Souls?," *CT*, 13 October 2002.

3. Cole quoted in Vogel, "Good Migrations," *FT*, April 2006, 26.

4. "Fiscal Facts: The Great Debt Shift," www.pewtrusts.org, 30 April 2011.

5. "Traditional Language Offends Boomers," *FMNP*, 1 January 2006.

6. "4 Years of Florida: The Way We Were and Are," *SPT*, 19 October 2009.

7. David Shribman, "The Future Is Florida," *PPG*, 1 April 2005; "Florida," *NYT*, 7 August 1996; McKeen and Roberts quoted in Abby Goodnough, "Strange Brews Are Created in Melting Pot That Is Florida," *NYT*, 3 April 2005.

8. Mike Vogel, "The Mega-Trends: Good Migration," *FT*, April 2006; "1,000 Residents Each Week Move into Florida," *SPT*, 5 November 1950; "Time Has Come to Dissolve City of Weeki Wachee," *TBT*, 11 December 2014.

9. Mormino, *Land of Sunshine, State of Dreams: A Social History of Modern Florida* (Gainesville: University Press of Florida, 2005), 194–208.

10. "The King of the Sarasota Flip," *SHT*, 21 July 2009; Jon Birger, "They Call Them Flippers," *MM*, 14 March 2005.

11. "Florida's Housing Bubble," and "Top Ten," *SPT*, 25 May 2005; "Prices of Homes Slip from Last Year," *SFSS*, 26 September 2006.

12. "New Mexico Takes Its Chile Very Seriously, Even the Spelling," *NYT*, 26 February 2011.

13. Harold Bubil, email to author, 2 October 2017; "Flippers' Role in Housing Flop Larger Than Thought," *PBP*, 25 December 2011.

14. "On the Bubble," *NDN*, 1 April 2012.

15. "The Price of Paradise" and "Priced Out," *MH*, 3 October and 26 February 2006.

16. "The Wealth Machine," *MH*, 19 February 2006.

17. "Housing Sage Plays out in Lacy's Deals," *TBT*, 27 January 2011.

18. Trigaux, "Florida's Housing Bubble: Is It Ready to Burst?," *SPT*, 25 May 2005.

19. Alex Leary, "In Trump Institute, Donald Trump Had Florida Partners with a Record of Fraud," *TBT*, 30 June 2016; "Trump University Customer," NPR.org, 6 June 2016; "Many in Trump U. Fight," *WP*, 28 July 2020; John Cassidy, "Trump University: The Scandal That Won't Go Away," *NYT*, 7 September 2016.

20. Alexander von Hoffman, "Home Values Are Down, and Not Just at the Bank," *WP*, 20 July 2008.

21. "Big Home-Price Gains," *SHT*, 26 February 2005; Realtor quoted in "South Florida among Leaders in Rising Home Prices," *SS*, 28 April 2015; "Price Tag Escalates on Being Floridian," *SPT*, 19 June 2005.

22. Adam Michaelson, *The Foreclosure of America: The Inside Story of the Rise and Fall of Countrywide Home Loans, the Mortgage Crisis, and the Default of the American Dream* (New York: Berkley, 2009), 1–2.

23. David Brooks, "The Next Cultural War," and "The Great Seduction," *NYT,* 28 September 2009 and 10 June 2008; "Priced out of Affordable Housing," *SPT,* 12 January 2007.

24. Mormino, *Land of Sunshine,* 170–71.

25. "10 Years after the Housing Crisis," NPR.org, 28 April 2018.

26. U.S. Census Bureau, *Homeownership in the United States, 1960–2005; Homeownership for Florida,* Federal Reserve. Fed.stlouisfed.org, FL-HOWN; "Real Estate: American Dream," *FT,* February 2006, 37.

27. Robert J. Samuelson, "Homes as Hummers," *WP,* 13 July 2005.

28. "Billionaire Club Still Growing in Florida," *SPT,* 25 September 2006; "What Kind of House Will $1 Million Buy?," *OS,* 6 November 2005; "Where America's Money Is Moving," *Forbes Magazine,* June 2010.

29. Joel Garreau quoted in Teresa Wiltz, "Returning to the Exurbs," *Stateline: Pew Charitable Trust,* 15 April 2015.

30. "Our Revealing Searches in 2007," *TT,* 29 December 2007; "Anna Maria Island Woman's Club," *SHT,* 12 April 2006; "Study: Florida Is the Second Least Patriotic State in U.S.," *Florida Politics,* 21 June 2021.

31. David Brooks, "The Broken Society," *NYT,* 19 March 2010.

32. "In Media Circus, We're Big Top," *SPT,* 24 February 2007; David Barry, "Florida: The Punchline State," *WSJ,* 3 September 2016; Craig Pittman, *Oh, Florida! How America's Weirdest State Influences the Rest of the Country* (New York: St. Martin's, 2016), 1.

33. "With No Internet at Home, Miami-Dade Kids Crowd Libraries," *MH,* 12 October 2014.

34. Michael Lewis, *Panic! The Story of Modern Financial Insanity* (New York: Norton, 2009).

35. "Florida's Growth Is Slow, but Steady," *GS,* 8 November 2007; "Where Have All the Students Gone?" and "Florida's Population Growth Slows a Bit," *OS,* 20 August 2007 and 8 November 2007; "Broward County's Enrollment Keeps Dropping," *SFSS,* 15 October 2008; "Numbers Reflect the State of Our State," *DBNJ,* 25 January 2009.

36. "Waterfront Homes Flood the Market," *TT,* Pasco ed., 2 September 2006; "On Clearwater Beach, Condo Dreams Dry Up," *SPT,* 12 November 2006.

Chapter 10. Cloudy Skies over "Foreclosureville": Florida's Great Recession and Reset

1. "Campaigning in a Crisis," and "McCain on U.S. Economy: From 'Strong' to 'Total Crisis' in 36 Hours," *NYT,* 26 May 2020 and 17 September 2008; Barack Obama, *A Promised Land* (New York: Crown, 2020), 177–79, 209; Adam Tooze, *Crashed: How a Decade of Financial Crises Changed the World* (New York: Viking, 2018), 83.

2. Henry M. Paulson Jr., "Lessons from the 2008 Economic Crisis," *WP,* 12 March 2020; Andrew Ross Sorkin, "The Echoes of Lehman in Our Time of Distrust," *NYT,* 11 September 2018; Tooze, *Crashed,* 148.

3. "Great Recession Won't Recede for Many," *SHT,* 29 September 2013; Robert Rich, "The Great Recession," federalreservehistory.org, 22 November 2013; "9/11 Was Big: This Is Bigger," *WP,* 5 October 2008.

4. George Packer, "The Ponzi State: Florida's Foreclosure Disaster," *New Yorker,* 9 and 16 February 2009, 82.

5. "Levitt Bankruptcy Leaves Homeowners in the Cold," NPR.org, 27 February 2008.

6. Rich, "The Great Recession."

7. Catherine Rampell, "'Great Recession': Brief Etymology," *NYT,* 11 March 2011.

8. Packer, "The Ponzi State," 82; Michael Grunwald, "Is Florida the Sunset State?" *Time,* 10 July 2008, 82.

9. "Florida Housing Bubble," *SPT,* 21 May 2005; "Bay's Home Boom Suddenly Belly-Up," *SPT,* 18 November 2006.

10. "Great Recession: A Brief Etymology," *NYT,* 11 March 2009.

11. Peter S. Goodman, "The Great Rupture," *NYT,* 3 July 2010.

12. "Utopia at a Discount," *WP*, 21 June 2009; "10 Years after and Tasks Housing Crisis," NPR.org, 28 April 2018; Meghan Lewit, "The Recession Hits Reality TV," *TA*, 6 May 2011; "How Did the Great Recession Affect Social Security Claiming?" www.urban.org, July 2013; "Realtor Uses Boat to Display Foreclosed Homes," *LL*, 27 March 2009; "Princeton University Students Tour Cape Coral Foreclosures," www.winknews.com, 19 March 2012.

13. "Economic Tide Is Rising for Repo Man," and "The Wired Repo Man," *NYT*, 20 May 2008 and 26 February 2010; Cries of "'Hey, That's My Jet!' Don't Deter High-End Repo Men," *WSJ*, 20 March 2012; "Repo Glut," www.tradeonlytoday.com, 30 September 2008; "Car Repo business Joins Economy in Downturn," *FTU*, 5 July 2009; Hill quoted in Zachary Crockett, "The Man Who Repossesses Multimillion-Dollar Planes," *Hustle*, 15 November 2019.

14. Chris Bart, "Lousy Economy Means Pawn Shops Are Cashing In," www.forbes.com, 16 November 2011; "Floridians Turn to Online Pawn Shops," *SFSS*, 7 October 2011; "In Central Florida, Pawnshops Go Gangbusters in Tough Times," *OS*, 11 November 2011.

15. "Behemoths of the Boom Sold Off," *SPT*, 18 October 2009.

16. Lewit, "The Recession Hits Reality TV"; AP, "Trump University Model: Sell Hard," 2 June 2016; "Former Trump University Workers Call the School a 'Lie' and a 'Scheme,'" *NYT*, 31 May 2016.

17. "State's Foreclosure Rare Worst," *TBT*, 17 January 2013.

18. "45 Percent of South Florida Home Sales Are for a Loss," *OS*, 7 July 2010; Nick Timiraos and Alan Zibel, "Reviews Begin for Borrowers Disputing Foreclosures," *WSJ*, 27 December 2014; "Home Values Lower in South Florida Than a Decade Ago," *SFSS*, 18 September 2009.

19. Damien Cave, "On the Mat, Florida Wonders Which Way Is Up," *NYT*, 16 August 2009.

20. "Phoenix Leads the Way Down in Home Prices," *NYT*, 29 April 2009; "45 Percent of South Florida Home Sales Are for a Loss," *OS*, 7 July 2010; "Homeowners Still Mailing Out," and "Tampa Still Suffering," *USAT*, 18 April 2014 and 23 January 2012; "Bay Area's Blues Worst in U.S.," *TBT*, 10 May 2012; "South Florida Still Leads in Distressed Mortgages," *SFSS*, 9 May 2012.

21. "Billions Vanish from Sarasota County Tax Base," and "Almost 42 Percent of Local Mortgages are 'Underwater,'" *SHT*, 24 May and 7 June 2011; Gary R. Mormino, *Land of Sunshine, State of Dreams: A Social History of Modern Florida* (Gainesville: University Press of Florida, 2005), 145; "Census Figures Flesh Out Picture of Recession's Impact," and "Sarasota Property Values Drop Again," *SHT*, 2 September 2012 and 7 June 2011; "North Port Grappling with History of Poor Planning," and "Canal-Front Homes at Half the '05 Price," *SHT*, 15 October 2007 and 20 March 2011.

22. Mormino, *Land of Sunshine*, 52–53, 72.

23. Peter S. Goodman, "This Is the Sound of a Bubble Bursting," *NYT*, 23 December 2007.

24. "Top 10 Fastest-Growing Metro Areas," *MH*, 5 April 2007; Steve McQuilkin, "Economy Bounces Back, but Many Still Recovering from Devastating Downturn," and "Building Bust Hits Shopping Plazas," *FMNP*, 8 February and 21 December 2008; Mike Vogel, "The Other Shoe Dropping," *FT*, October 2009, 61–62; "Foreclosure Crisis Cut Deeply," *FMNP*, 17 February 2018.

25. "Lee Growth Continues," *FMNP*, 20 March 2008; Mormino, *Land of Sunshine*, 48–49; Damien Cave, "In Florida, Despair and Foreclosure," *NYT*, 7 February 2009.

26. Cave, "In Florida, Despair and Foreclosure"; Packer, "The Ponzi State," 93.

27. Peter S. Goodman, "Real Estate in Cape Coral Is Far from a Recovery," *NYT*, 2 January 2010. Warfarin has more recently been marketed as an anticoagulant to prevent blood clots.

28. "Foreclosure Crisis Cut Deeply; The Sting Is Still Felt," *FMNP*, 17 February 2018.

29. Paul Reyes, *Exiles in Eden: Life among the Ruins of Florida's Great Recession* (New York: Henry Holt, 2010), 203–10, 214.

30. "Boom and Bust," *NDN*, 1 April 2012; president quoted in "We Soared, We Crashed," *FMNP*, 31 December 2009.

31. "Boom and Bust"; "Collier's Overall Property Value Declined $9 Billion," *NDN*, 27 May 2010.

32. "Great Recession, 10 Years Later," *NDN*, 19 February 2018.

33. "Charlotte Property Values Fall below 2004 Levels," *SHT*, 28 May 2010.

34. "Fort Myers–Cape Coral No. 1 in 2008 for Foreclosures," *NDN*, 15 January 2009.

35. "Area Home Sales: Half Are Distressed," and "First Coast Job Market Damaged by Recession," *FTU*, 8 August 2010 and 26 January 2013.

36. Tobin, "Palm Coast, Flagler Co.; Villano, "Leader of the Pack," 74–75; "Fastest-Growing Counties, 2000–2006," *USAT*, 22 March 2007.

37. "Swing States Still Struggling after Housing Bust," *WP*, 4 June 2011.

38. "In Flagler, a Fast Fall," *OS*, 28 June 2009.

39. "Area Homeowners Struggle with Underwater Loans," *DBNJ*, 20 October 2013.

40. "Boulevard of Broken Dreams," *DBNJ*, 15 November 2009.

41. "Port St. Lucie Suffers No Pain from Steady Growth," and "Port St. Lucie Hit Hard by Housing Slump," *MH*, 8 July 1983 and 10 March 2008; "Housing 'Bargain' Port St. Lucie," and "The Civic Center Becomes Sign of Port St. Lucie's Woes," *PBP*, 10 July 2008 and 27 February 2010.

42. "Just Trying to Get to the End of Each Day," *MH*, 10 February 2009.

43. Tom Prestopnik, email to the author, 23 January 2021.

44. "After Century of Growth, Tide Turns in Florida," *NYT*, 29 August 2009.

45. "The Almighty Tourist," *Emerald Coast*, 24 September 2007; "Hard Times in South Walton," *NFDN*, 22 February 2009.

46. "St. Joe Pares Back Its Florida Vision," *WSJ*, 28 January 2012; "Panhandle Developer Declares Huge Loss," *TBT*, 28 February 2012; Gary R. Mormino, *Millard Fillmore Caldwell* (Gainesville: University Press of Florida, 2020), 105–7; Kathryn Ziewitz and June Wiaz, *Green Empire: The St. Joe Company and the Remaking of Florida's Panhandle* (Gainesville: University Press of Florida, 2004), 3.

47. "Utopia at a Discount," *WP*, 21 July 2009; "Killing Jolts a Disney Town," *TBT*, 3 December 2010; Tarpley Hitt, "Celebration, Florida," 18 December 2019; "How Disney's Community of Tomorrow Became a Total Nightmare," dailybeast.com, 26 December 2019; Douglas Frantz and Catherine Collins, *Celebration U.S.A.: Living in a Disney's Brave New World* (New York: Henry Holt, 1999); Douglas Frantz, "Living in a Disney Town," *NYT*, 4 October 1998.

48. Jeff Kunerth, "Orlando Area's Income Drops as Poverty Soars," "Orlando Area's Consumer-Bankruptcy Rate Soars to Record," and "Orlando—One of America's Emptiest Cities," *OS*, 22 September 2011, 19 May 2010, and 22 February 2009; Mike Thomas, "Who Cleans up When Venues Bubble Bursts?" *OS*, 10 February 2010; "That Sinking Feeling," editorial, *SPT*, 20 October 2011; "America's Top 15 Emptiest Cities," Forbes.com, 24 October 2008.

49. "Orlando, Tampa: Collision Course?" *OS*, 27 April 2008; "Florida Town Rides Housing Boom, Bust," NPR.Marketplace.org, 28 August 2012; "As Florida's Fastest-Growing Counties Grow, So Grows Polk," *LL*, 20 March 2008.

50. "Rising Gas Prices Hit Home" and "Areas with Troubled Mortgages," *WSJ*, 4 March 2011; "Foreclosureville, USA," *MH*, 19 October 2009.

51. "Belle Glade Housing Dream Gone to Seed," *PBP*, 9 April 2011; "Trump's Pardons Full of Florida Scammers, Rappers," *TBT*, 21 January 2021.

52. "A Lender Closure Shocks Town," *SPT*, 7 August 2009; "Taylor Bean Files for Bankruptcy," *WSJ*, 25 August 2009; "Fla. Horse Industry Thoroughly Hurt by Weak Economy," *OSB*, 6 September 2010; "A Tale of Two Economies: Gainesville and Ocala," *GS*, 18 October 2010; "A Haven of Stability for U.S. Homeowners," *VDS*, 17 October 2018; AP, "Rural Florida Panhandle Avoids Recession's Worst," 5 July 2009.

53. "Lakewood Ranch: How Town Was Born," and "Lakewood Ranch," *SHT*, 10 October 2010 and 14 August 2011; "DeSantis Defends His Choice of Wealthy Senior Community for Pop-Up Vaccination Site," *SHT*, 17 February 2021; Pam Gibson, email to author, 22 October 2020.

54. "How Florida Handles Her State Convicts," *Pensacola Journal*, 18 December 1910; David M. Reutter, "Clock Is Ticking on Understaffing in Florida's Prison System," *Prison Legal News*, 31 Janu-

ary 2018, www.prisonlegalnews.org/news/2018/jan/31/clock-ticking-understaffing-floridas-prison-system/; "GEO Group Still Invests in Florida Politics," *Prison Legal News*, 30 September 2016, www.prisonlegalnews.org/news/2016/sep/30/geo-group-still-invests-florida-politics/; Michael Fortino, "GEO Group, Largest Private Prison Contractor, Cranks up Political Contributions during Trump Years," *Prison Legal News*, 1 April 2020, www.prisonlegalnews.org/news/2020/apr/1/geo-group-largest-private-prison-contractor-cranks-political-contributions-during-trump-years/; Laura Cassels, "FL Legislature 2021: Top Corrections Chief Says State Prison System Is in Crisis and Could Collapse," *Florida Phoenix*, 22 February 2021, www.floridaphoenix.com/2021/02/22/fl-legislature-2021-top-corrections-chief-says-state-prison-system-is-in-crisis-and-could-collapse/.

Chapter 11. The Ponzi State: Zombie Homes and Ghost Towers, Schemers and Adverse Possessors

1. Valerie Boyd, *Wrapped in Rainbows: The Life of Zora Neale Hurston* (New York: Scribner, 2003), 295–98.

2. "Zombies Are Everywhere," *LAT*, 23 February 2021.

3. Megan O'Matz, "Neighborhoods Crumble," and "Vacant Homes in South Florida Double over Past 10 Years," *SFSS*, 29 April 2012 and 28 March 2011.

4. "The Zombie Survival Guide," *WP*, 30 October 2003.

5. "'Zombie' Homes Haunt Florida." www.publicintegrity.org, 15 September 2015; "'Zombie' Homes Creeping into Southwest Florida," *NDN*, 6 October 2013; construction workers described in "In Florida, Despair and Foreclosures," and "Drywall Flaws," *NYT*, 8 February 2008 and 17 September 2017; "Swimming Pools at Foreclosed Homes Become Mosquitoes' Home," *OS*, 22 July 2008.

6. "The Board Men," *TBT*, 25 August 2013.

7. AP, "The Perfect Storm," 2 June 2009.

8. Paul Reyes, *Exiles in Eden: Life among the Ruins of Florida's Great Recession* (New York: Henry Holt, 2010), 181, 186.

9. George Packer, "The Ponzi State," *TNY*, 9 &16 February 2009: 82.

10. "A Look inside the 'Hijacker House,'" *SHT*, 19 July 2016.

11. Reyes, *Exiles in Eden*, 78, 111; "Some Ex-Owners Trashing Their Foreclosed Homes," *SFSS*, 8 April 2008; "Trash Collector," *SPT*, 13 September 2010.

12. "TEAM Labors in Foreclosed Yards," *FMNP*, 7 September 2008.

13. Kris Hundley, "Evict and Erase," *SPT*, 27 March 2011.

14. Ibid.; "Some Ex-Owners Trashing Their Foreclosed Homes," *SFSS*, 8 April 2008.

15. Reyes, *Exiles in Eden*, 60.

16. "First Coast Job Market Damaged by Recession," *FTU*, 26 January 2013; "Only 43 Homes Built in Three Months? Must be Miami," *CSM*, 13 May 2009.

17. Joseph E. Stiglitz and Linda J. Bilmes, "The Book of Jobs," *VF*, 6 December 2011.

18. "Homeless Turn Foreclosures into Shelters," *USAT*, 10 December 2008; Reyes, *Exiles in Eden*, 158–61.

19. "With Advocates' Help, More Squatters Call Foreclosure Home," *NYT*, 10 April 2009.

20. "Loki Boy Gone, but Housing Bubble Fallout Remains," and "Brazilian Squatter Served Eviction Papers," *SS*, 13 February and 31 January 2013.

21. "Squatters Take Advantage of Housing Crisis," *SHT*, 24 March 2013; "Squatters in a Million-Dollar Home?" *MH*, 6 February 2013; Catherine Skipp and Damien Cave, "At Legal Fringe, Empty Houses Go to the Needy," *NYT*, 9 November 2010.

22. "Picking up the Pieces in Florida," *NYT*, 6 April 2011; Roger Williams, "Squatter House," *Fort Myers Florida Weekly*, 16 March 2011.

23. "Politically Connected Lawyer from Mexico's Poorest State Bought 13 Miami Condos," *MH*, 5 June 2016.

24. "Metrowest Condo Complex Is 'Worst of Worst,'" *OS*, 7 November 2010; Timothy Egan, "Slumburbia," *NYT*, 10 February 2010.

25. "Related Group Opens Oasis Tower," *Fort Myers Florida Weekly*, 25 June 2008; "Anybody Home? One Family Lives in 32-Story Condo Tower," *SS*, 30 July 2009; "The Loneliest Condo Dweller in Florida," *WSJ*, 8 March 2010; "Condo Dwellers Finding Empty Buildings," *MH*, 22 June 2009.

26. "Condo Caverns," and "Living in an Empty Condo May Be Mental Health Risk," *MH*, 22 June 2009.

27. "As Condos Rise in South Florida, Nervous Investors Try to Flee," *NYT*, 26 May 2007; "Condos Desperate as Dues Dry Up," *MH*, 14 July 2009.

28. Lisa Rab, "South Florida's Housing Crisis Leaves behind Ghost Towers," *Broward New Times*, 18 June 2009.

29. "South Florida Condo Conversions Collapse," *MH*, 3 August 2009.

30. Chloe Sorvino, "Real Estate Billionaire Jorge Perez's Immigrant Roots Are Helping in a Slowing Miami Market," Forbes.com, 5 October 2016.

31. Matthew Haggman, "A Condo King," *MH*, 1 March 2009; "25 Most Influential Hispanics in America," *Time*, 22 August 2005.

32. "Developer Jorge Perez Has Been at the Center of the Region's Condo Boom and Bust," and "Condo King Jorge Perez Not Finished," *SS*, 17 February and 20 May 2011; Pérez quoted in "Miami Magnate Is Rebuilding," *WSJ*, 11 May 2011.

33. "Condo-Mania 2.0," *MH*, 30 October 2011.

34. "West Palm Beach No. 4," and "South Florida Housing Burden Leads Nation," *PBP*, 4 February 2012 and 26 February 2011; "The Price of Paradise," and "Teachers Can't Afford Miami Rents," *MH*, 3 October 2006 and 26 March 2018; "Bigger Percentage of Palm Beach County Households Renting in 2010," *PBP*, 18 August 2011.

35. "Orlando Has Lowest Wages of Any Big City in America . . . Again!" editorial, *OS*, 5 April 2019; "Homeownership Fades in Central Florida," *OS*, 18 December 2014.

36. "Homeownership Fades in Central Florida"; "Owning a Home: Has the Dream Soured?" *SPT*, 21 September 2010; "In Housing Bust, A 'New Normal,'" *USAT*, 8 February 2011; "Home Prices Unfriendly to Working Families," *SHT*, 17 November 2013.

37. "Forget Owning, Renting Is Becoming the End Game for Many Millennials," *WP*, 8 May 2018; "Renting Homes: The New American Dream?," *USAT*, 6 June 2012; "New Homes Get Built with Renters in Mind," and "The New American Dream: Renting," *WSJ*, 4 November 2013 and 15 August 2009; "Orlando No. 1 for Apartment Building," 13 November 2017; "Miami Is Toughest Place to Rent in U.S.," and "Will Tiny Apartments without Parking Solve Miami's Rent Crunch?" *MH*, 16 December 2015 and 22 July 2016; "In Many Cities, Rent Is Rising out of Reach of Many," *NYT*, 14 April 2014; "Pricey, Posh, Tiny Apartments Rule Tampa Bay's Big-Money Rental Rule," *TBT*, 23 July 2014; "Camille Lefevre, "Influx of Urban Residents Prompts Growth of Amenities in Cities," 3degreesmedia.com, 8 July 2014; "2011 was the Year of the Apartment," *SHT*, 4 October 2012; "Blackstone, Other Investors Snap up Thousands of Tampa Bay Rental Homes," *TBT*, 23 March 2013.

38. "Huge Rental-Home Companies Active in Tampa Bay Agree to Merge," *TBT*, 11 August 2017; Amy Keller, "Landlord Inc.," *FT*, February 2013, 52–53; Peter Murphy quoted in "Blackstone to Buy $1 Billion Worth of Tampa Bay Homes for Rentals," and "More People, More Stuff, More Storage," *TBT*, 20 September 2012 and 13 April 2018; McCabe quoted in "Investment Firms Snap up Southwest Florida Homes," *SHT*, 15 June 2013; "Investment Firms Buying up Foreclosures," *PBP*, 19 February 2012; Buffett quoted in Drew Harwell, "Blackstone, Other Investors Snap up Thousands of Tampa Bay Rental Homes," *TBT*, 24 March 2013.

39. Eric Klinenberg, "Living Alone Is the New Norm," *Time*, 12 March 2012, 60–62; "In USA, More

Choose to Live Alone," *USAT*, 11 October 2012; "Number of Single Women Growing in South Florida," *SS*, 25 March 2007; "Families Changed," *TBT*, 8 January 2012.

40. "Soaring Numbers of Owners Pay No Property Taxes in Broward, Palm Beach," *SFSS*, 1 July 2011; "Car Dealership Closings Dot Central Florida Landscape," *OS*, 28 July 2010.

41. "Property Values Nose Dive," *OS*, 2 June 2009; "Layoffs Hitting Public Workers," NPR.org, 20 June 2012; "Many Public Schools Never Recovered from the Great Recession," *WP*, 2 April 2017.

42. "Lauderdale Lakes Bungled Its Budget, Wants Bailout," *SS*, 19 June 2011.

43. "Bay Area's Blues Worst in U.S.," *TBT*, 10 May 2012; "Unpaid Realty Taxes Skyrocket: $332M," *SPT*, 30 April 2009; "Economic Hammer Pounds Developers," *TT*, 11 October 2011; "Sarasota Property Values Drop Again," and "Billions Vanish from Sarasota County Tax Base," *SHT*, 24 May 2010 and 24 May 2011.

44. Liz Cohen's work brilliantly analyzes the impact of mass consumption and malls upon American society (see Lizabeth Cohen, *A Consumers' Republic: The Politics of Mass Consumption in Postwar America* [New York: Knopf, 2003]); William S. Kowinski, "The Malling of America," *NYTM*, 10 May 1978, 30–55.

45. Gary R. Mormino, *Land of Sunshine, State of Dreams: A Social History of Modern Florida* (Gainesville: University Press of Florida, 2005), 256–64; "Millenia," *OS*, 13 October 2003; "An Enormous Landmark Joins Graveyard of Malls," *NYT*, 24 December 2003; "Dadeland's Formula," *WSJ*, 13 April 1987.

46. "History of Burdines Chronicled in New Book," *SS*, 21 December 2015; Michael Lisicky, *Remembering Maas Brothers* (Charleston, SC: Arcadia, 2015); "Mercantile Magic: Cohen Brothers Department Store," *FTU*, 25 June 2009; "Burdine Macy's," and "Wal-Mart Soars as Mall Crashes," *SPT*, 28–31 January 2004; "What Can Save This Mall?" *PBP*, 27 February 2004; "Divided Decade: How the Financial Crisis Changed Retail," marketplace.org, 20 December 2018; "Floriland Mall as a Homeless Shelter," *TT*, 21 October 2009.

47. "A Center That Didn't Hold," *SPT*, 31 October 2010.

48. "Even Churches Going Bankrupt These Days," *OS*, 30 January 2011; "Churches Hit Hard, Too," *GS*, 22 December 2008; "Even God's House for Sale," and "Struggling Catholic Churches," *MH*, 8 November and 27 May 2009.

49. Susan Martin, "St. Joe Boosts Faith in a Sale," *TBT*, 2 January 2015; "When It Takes a Miracle to Sell Your House, Realtors Bury a Statue of St. Joseph," *WSJ*, 30 October 2007.

50. "Remarks by the President on the Economy—Knox College, Galesburg, Il."; Hedrick Smith, "Mayday for America's Middle Class," *LAT*, 4 August 2013.

51. Palm Coast Registers Worst Jobless Growth," *DBNJ*, 6 January 2010; "Unemployment at Record 12.2%," *SPT*, 27 March 2010.

52. "Good Jobs Are Hard to Find," and "Florida's Unemployment Benefits 'Virtually Inaccessible,'" *SS*, 4 August 2012 and 22 September 2015; Paul Krugman, "Writing off the Unemployed," *NYT*, 9 February 2014.

53. Neil Howe, "The Boom in Disability Benefits," Forbes.com, 30 June 2015.

54. "Social Security's Cost," *WP*, 25 May 2020; "Why Those Working-Age Men Who Left the U.S. Job Market Aren't Coming Back," *LAT*, 4 September 2015; "The Incredible Shrinking Workforce," *WSJ*, 8 December 2017.

55. "Why Those Working-Age Men Who Left the U.S. Job Market Aren't Coming Back," *LAT*, 4 September 2015; "Disability Applications Plunge as the Economy Strengthens," *NYT*, 19 June 2018; "The Tattered Safety Net for the Disabled," *WP*, 12 May 2012; "More Men in Prime Working Ages Don't Have Jobs," *WSJ*; "Disability Claims by the Unemployed Skyrocketing," *SFSS*, 24 September 2011.

56. Housing Bust, as a Thriller," *WSJ*, 28 September 2015; "'99 Homes' Film Mostly on Point Depicting Orlando Foreclosure Crisis," *OS*, 10 October 2015; "The Crisis behind '99 Homes'—and How It Fueled the Film's Script," NPR.org, 25 September 2015.

57. "In 'The Big Short,' Adam McKay Uses Absurdity as His Guide," *NYT*, 30 December 2015.

58. "Stake in the Weeds," *LAT*, 27 July 1926.

59. "Give Ponzi a Million," *WSJ*, 2 August 1920.

60. Daniel Akst, "The Original Ponzi Schemer," *WSJ*, 17 October 2020; "Charles Ponzi Biography," Biography.com.

61. Akst, "The Original Ponzi Schemer."

62. "'Wizard' Ponzi Dead," *Jacksonville Journal*, 19 January 1949; AP, "Death Claims Charles Ponzi, Ace Swindler," 19 January 1949.

63. Adam Beasley, "Men of Steal," *MH*, 8 July 2012.

64. "Florida: A Ponzi Schemer's Paradise," and "Feds $300 Million Ponzi Scheme," *MH*, 8 July 2012 and 16 September 2014; "Fla. 'Fertile Ground' for Ponzis," *TBT*, 19 May 2013; "In Spotting Troubled Brokers, Geography Mattered," *WSJ*, 12 November 2014.

65. Beasley, "Men of Steal."

66. "A Palm Beach Enclave, Stunned by an Inside Job"; "If Bernie Met Dante"; "Foundation That Relied on Madoff Fund Closes"; "Jews Feel an Acute Betrayal," *NYT*, 14 March 2009, 15 December and 20 December 2008, 27 August 2012; "Florida's Palm Beach Rocked by Madoff Scandal," NPR.org, 16 December 2008.

67. Leamer quoted in "Oy! Madoff Scandal Stirs Anti-Semitic Glee in Palm Beach," abcnews.go.com, 19 February 2009; Christine Stapleton, "Madoff Scandal Ripples among Palm Beach County Foundations"; "Madoff's Alleged Victims"; and "Philanthropist Tied to Madoff Found Dead," *PBP*, 6 February 2009 and 25 October 2009; *MG*, 26 October 2009; Nathan Vardi, "Barbara Picower's Crocodile Tears," Forbes.com, 12 April 2011; "A Lasting Shadow," *NYT*, 11 December 2011; "Madoff Says Palm Beach Client Jeffry Picower Knew of Scam," *PBP*, 27 August 2012.

68. Hector Florin, "Palm Beach: The New Capital of Florida Corruption," *Time*, 10 January 2009; "Scars from a Fraud," *WSJ*, 10 December 2013; "South Florida Investors Lost Enormous Amounts of Money," *SFSS*, 6 February 2009; "Floridians Fleeced," *MH*, 6 February 2009.

69. Quotes in "Scott Rothstein's Rise and Fall," *SFSS*, 5 December 2009.

70. "Scott Rothstein's Rise and Gall," *SFSS*, 5 December 2009.

71. Jen Christensen, CNN.com, 18 February 2010; "Scott Rothstein: Scope of Scandal Emerges," *SFSS*, 21 November 2011; "Rothstein Says He Kept $1 Million in Cash Handy for Payoffs," *MH*, 22 December 2011.

72. "Shapiro Found Trouble at USF," *TBT*, 25 August 2011; "Nevin Shapiro: Miami's Caligula," *MNT*, 16 December 2010; "Lawyer, Nevin Shapiro Is Building NCAA's Investigation of Miami," *USAT*, 17 August 2011; Alexander Wolff, "16 Years Later, It's Time to Get Real," *SI*, 25 August 2011, 67.

73. "A Big-Time Embezzler on a Small-Town Street in Englewood," *SHT*, 3 December 2012.

74. "Florida's Wealth a Magnet for Ponzi Schemes," and "Art Nadel, Convicted Ponzi Schemer, Dies in Prison," *SHT*, 16 March 2014 and 17 April 2012; "Selling Hope: Foreclosure Rescue Schemes," and "Englewood Ponzi Case Is Fourth for Sarasota," *SHT*, 7 October 2014 and 3 December 2010; "Fear of Becoming Known as 'Mini-Madoff,'" *SPT*, 25 February 2010; "Familiar Terrain with Their New Vista Venture," and "Land Sharks in Florida," *SHT*, 24 and 26 April 2013.

75. Connie Bruck, "Angelo's Ashes: The Man Who Became the Face of the Financial Crisis," *TNY*, 29 June 2009; "Florida Gets Closer to Putting Mozilo on Trial," *WSJ*, 1 May 2009.

76. "America's Worst Charities," "Felons Found at Charity," and "Bogus Charity," *TBT*, 15 and 16 September 2013 and 17 December 2013.

77. "Pearlman's Pals," *SPT*, 27 February 2011; "Ben Bernanke: More Execs Should Have Gone to Jail," *USAT*, 5 October 2015.

78. Ben S. Bernanke, "The Recent Financial Turmoil and Its Economic and Policy Consequences," speech delivered at the Economic Club of New York, New York City, 15 October 2007, www.federalreserve.gov/newsevents/speech/bernanke20071015a.htm/; Ben S. Bernanke, "Housing Markets in Transition," remarks delivered at the 2012 National Association of Home Builders International Builders' Show, Orlando, Fla., 10 February 2012.

79. "Cabbage Key Is Sold," *TMT*, 31 October 1913; "Houseboat Changed into Large Dredge," *SPT*, 18 May 1913.

80. Hal Boyle, "The Happy Hermit of Cabbage Key," *Life* (1948); "Silas Dent Loved People," and "The 'Happy Hermit' of Cabbage Key," *SPT*, 1 and 3 October 2005.

81. John Rothchild, *Up for Grabs: A Trip through Time and Space in the Sunshine State* (Gainesville: University Press of Florida, 2002), 33–34.

82. Mormino, *Land of Sunshine*, 34.

83. "Berlanti," and "Tierra Verde Development Forges Ahead," *SPT*, 23 June 1963 and 15 August 1960.

84. "County Orders Tierra Verde Fill Rehearing," and "Tierra Verde over the Hump," *SPT*, 10 March 1961 and 15 March 1963; Bruce Stephenson, *Visions of Eden: Environmentalism, Urban Planning, and City Building in St. Petersburg, Florida, 1900–1995* (Columbus: Ohio State University Press, 1997).

85. "Lombardo Toots Tierra Verde," and "Mystery, Tragedy Swirled over Tierra Verde in 1963," *SPT*, 15 March 1963 and 28 August 2005; "From a Dream in 1959—through up & downs a Final Result—Two Fine Communities," Gulf Beaches Historical Museum, https://gulfbeachesmuseum.com/article/dream-1959---through-downs-final-result-two-fine-communities/.

86. "Tierra Verde Resort Changes Hands," *Tampa Bay Business Journal*, 14 January 2011; James A. Schnur, interview by author, 1 May 2021; Nick Hanson, "Shaping the Sand: The Environmental History of Tierra Verde," manuscript, University of South Florida, St. Petersburg, 2006.

87. "Tierra Verde's Grand Canal Needs Major Dredging, *TBT*, 8 July 2021.

88. "Piney Point, Florida: The Atlantic City of the South," Seaboard Railroad advertisement, 1914.

89. "Piney Point from 1966–Present," *TBT*, 6 April 2021.

90. "'No Community Should Suffer This': Florida's Toxic Breach Was Decades in the Making," *TG*, 11 April 2021.

91. "Alafia River Appears to Have Healed after Acid Spill," *LL*, 9 December 2007.

92. David Von Drehle, "Champlain Towers South, in Some Ways, Lost Its Battle with Primal Florida," *WP*, 29 June 2021.

93. Davis, *The Gulf*, 10.

94. Ed Killer, "Deepwater Horizon Oil Fouled the Gulf of Mexico," *PCNH*, 18 April 2020.

95. Julie Wraithmell, "Florida Defends Its Shores Ten Years after the BP Oil Disaster," *Audubon*, 15 July 2020.

96. "10 Years Later: Emerald Coast Remembers Deepwater Horizon Oil Spill of 2010," *PCNH*, 18 April 2020; Marsha Dowler, email to author, 3 July 2021.

97. "Study: Oil Still Lingers in Gulf," *TBT*, 21 August 2013.

98. "Florida Worries about Effect on Tourism," *NYT*, 19 May 2010; "For North Florida Fishermen, Passion and Livelihood at Risk," *MH*, 3 May 2010; "Our Fish," *PCNH*, 18 April 2020; "Big Gulf Die-Off Tied to BP Spill," and "Oil Dispersant Mix Is Toxic to Keys Coral Reefs," *TBT*, 5 April 2013 and 11 January 2012.

99. "Omar Mateen Appeared in a Documentary about BP Oil Spill," *NYDN*, 16 June 2016.

100. Wraithmell, "Florida Defends Its Shores."

101. Gary R. Mormino, "The Great St. Petersburg Pelican Massacre," *TBT*, 13 February 2015.

102. "The Annual Slaughter," *TMT*, 25 November 1915; "Unscrupulous Bird Killings," editorial, *SPT*, 23 June 1920.

103. Jack E. Davis, *An Everglades Providence: Marjory Stoneman Douglas and the American Environmental Century* (Athens: University of Georgia Press, 2009) 172, 174, 182; Harry A. Kersey Jr., *Pelts, Plumes and Hides: White Traders among the Seminole Indians, 1870–1930* (Gainesville: University of Florida Press, 1975), 36–37, 44–45, 130–33; John A. Bethell, *A Brief History of the Lower Point* (St. Petersburg: Independent Press, 1914).

104. Gary R. Mormino, "Dogs of War," *TT*, 1 March 2007.

105. "Gators Make Merry Meal of Eight 'Exterminated' Felines," *SPT*, 11 May 1917; "Rats and Cats . . .

Are Speedily Killing Mocking Birds," and "Stray Tom and Maria Cats May Get in Bad," *TMT*, 9 July 1914 and 15 April 1919.

106. "Fishermen Generally Seem to Hold Pelican a Pirate," *TDT*, 28 February 1918; "Pelican and Others Destroy $3,007,600 Fish Yearly," *TDT*, 19 February 1918.

107. "Say Folks, Whaddye Know about the Old Man Pelican?," *TDT*, 17 February 1918.

108. "The Pelican: He Has His Strong Friends and Foes," and "The Pelican: His Enemies Take a Swing at Him," *MRJ*, 1 and 4 March 1918.

109. "Shall the Pelican Be Outlawed?," editorial, *SPT*, 7 April 1917.

110. "Mrs. Katherine Tippetts, Pioneer Clubwoman Dies," *SPT*, 21 December 1950; Raymond A. Arsenault, *St. Petersburg and the Florida Dream* (Gainesville: University Press of Florida, 1996), 122–23, 156; Leslie Kemp Poole, *Saving Florida: Women's Fight for the Environment in the Twentieth Century* (Gainesville: University Press of Florida, 2015).

111. "Audubon Club Attendance Is Largest Ever," *SPT*, 20 January 1917.

112. "Audubon Society in Defense of Pelican Presents Strong Case," and "Pelican Given Audubon Club's Unanimous Vote," *SPT*, 17 February and 13 March 1918; Jennings quoted in "The Pelican: He Has His Strong Friends and Foes."

113. G. H. Lizotte, "Must the Pelican Go?," *TMT*, 20 February 1918.

Chapter 12. A State in Revision: Refining a Sense of Place and Redefining the Dream

1. Pam Gibson, email to author, 22 October 2020.

2. "School Libraries Take Cues from Bookstores," *BG*, 19 July 2017; Findlay quoted in Cave, "After a Century of Growth," and "Libraries See Openings as Bookstores Close," *NYT*, 30 August 2007 and 27 December 2012.

3. "Jackie's Story," *SPT*, 8 June 2007.

4. Gloria Colvin and Lawrence Webster, "Reprieve for the State Library of Florida: A Case Study in Grassroots Advocacy," *American Libraries* 34 (December 2003): 30–32.

5. Bruce Craig, "History Hit Badly by Proposed Budget Cuts in Florida and New Jersey," *Perspectives on History* (American Historical Association), March 2003; "Despite Protest, State May Transfer Materials to NSU," *South Florida Business Journal*, 28 February 2003; Florida Library Association, *State Library of Florida: Questions and Answers*, flyer, February 2003; Florida Library Association, *State Library of Florida: Just the Facts*, flyer, February 2003; Florida Library Association, *State Library of Florida: A Collection of Great Value*, flyer, February 2003; State of Florida, "Agreement for Transfer of the Circulating Collections of the State Library of Florida by the Department of State, Division of Library and Information Services to Nova Southeastern University, Inc., a Florida Not-for-Profit Corporation," 25 February 2003.

6. Diane Roberts, "Bush Winces at Price Tag on State History," *SPT*, 8 February 2003; John Kennedy, "Bush Wants to Close Book on Library Flap," *OS*, 2 February 2003; Gary Fineout, "State of State Speech Draws Cool Response," *GS*, 5 March 2003.

7. Rex Dalton, "Florida Welcomes Scripps as Critics Predict Big-Money Flop," *Science*, 6 November 2003, 4; Noah Bierman, "How One Big Promise Jeb Bush Made to Florida's Economy Has Yet to Deliver," *LAT*, 24 August 2015; Jason Szep, "How Jeb Bush's Big Bet on Florida's Economy May Come Back to Haunt Him," Reuters, 2 March 2015.

8. "Catching a Buzz at Internet Speed," *SPT*, 26 December 2007; Gary R. Mormino and David Shedden, "Under the Gaze of the Sun," *The Forum: The Magazine of Florida Humanities* (Fall 2021): 33–35.

9. Mormino and Shedden, "Under the Gaze of the Sun," 35–37; Martin Dyckman, "The Times, They Have a-Changed," and "Fine Print," *TBT*, 29 May 2005 and 7 March 2021; "More Newspapers

Are Departing Their Landmark Homes," *CT,* 3 February 2018; "As Herald Relocates Its Operation," *MH,* 17 May 2013.

10. Andres Viglucci, "Miami Herald's Iconic Building Is History," *MH,* 3 March 2015.

11. "Twitter Is the Crystal Meth of Newsrooms," *WP,* 25 January 2019; "More than 13,000 Fact-Checks Later, PolitiFact Celebrates 10 Years," *TBT,* 24 August 2017.

12. Aubrey Jewett, "Florida Newspapers Fight to Survive," Sayfiereview.com, 10 May 2016; "Times Buys Tribune," *TBT,* 4 May 2016; Mark R. Howard, "Flipped," *FT,* March 2015; "2021: Who Killed the Newspaper?" *TE,* 24 August 2006; "The Rise and Fall of South Florida's Newspapers," *PBP,* 19 November 2009; "Gannett, GateHouse Approve Merger," *WP,* 14 November 2019.

13. Gary R. Mormino, *Land of Sunshine, State of Dreams: A Social History of Modern Florida* (Gainesville: University Press of Florida, 2005), 170–73.

14. "Only One Bank Based in Marion County," *OSB,* 29 October 2017.

15. "Florida Banks Suffer Seismic Shake Up," *SHT,* 3 November 2008; "Banks Fell in the Great Recession," *NDN,* 9 February 2018.

16. David Wagner, *The Poor House: America's Forgotten Institution* (Lanham, MD: Rowman and Littlefield, 2005).

17. "Transients," *TMT,* 3 January 1895; Raymond O. Arsenault, *St. Petersburg and the Florida Dream* (Gainesville: University Press of Florida, 1996), 279; "Force Vagrants to Go to Work," and "Old People's Home," *TMT,* 9 February 1919 and 25 January 1936; "Quick Check to Be Kept on Men Quitting Jobs to Loaf," *KWC,* 27 February 1943; "Men at Camp Foster," *Jacksonville Journal,* 18 November 1933; "Miami Revives 'Hobo Express,'" *FTU,* 25 August 1945.

18. Tonya Alvarez, "Homelessness in Fort Lauderdale: A Tortured History," *SS,* 16 November 2014.

19. Emily Nipps, "No Roof, No Rules," *SPT,* 17 January 2010.

20. "Disability Claims by Unemployed Skyrocketing," *SFSS,* 24 September 2011; Kate Santich, "Recession Created 'Epidemic' of Homeless Families," *OS,* 10 January 2011.

21. "Broward County's Homeless Numbers Up," *SFSS,* 24 April 2011.

22. Anna Scott, "New to Need," *SHT,* 23 November 2008.

23. "Marriages at Life's Margins," *NYT,* 26 June 2009.

24. "Hollywood May Pay $4.8 Million for Homeless Shelter," and "Paid $4.8 Million to Leave, Advocate Sean Cononie May Return," *SS,* 11 October 2014 and 15 March 2016.

25. Director quoted in "Priced onto the Street," and "No Roof, No Rules," *SPT,* 18 February 2007 and 17 January 2010; Alex Pickett, "St. Pete Homeless under Attack," *Creative Loafing Tampa Bay,* 26 December 2008; "Glimmers of Hope," *SPT,* 30 November 2008.

26. "Homeless Return to Park," and "St. Petersburg Tries to Deal with Homeless Who Prefer Street to Shelter," *TBT,* 27 December 2015 and 31 October 2012; "A Day in the Park," and "Park Problems Spilling Over," *TBT,* 23 February 2013.

27. Nipps, "No Roof, No Rules."

28. "To Chill Homeless, Sarasota Pulls Park Benches," *SHT,* 17 May 2011; "For Years Homeless Sold Newspapers," wwwlocal10.com, 25 October 2020; "It Is Not an Opera Yet, but This Story Could Be," *SHT,* 6 December 2009.

29. *Hate Crimes against the Homeless: Violence Hidden in Plain View: A Report from National Coalition for the Homeless* (January 2012), 1–48; "St. Petersburg Tries to Deal with Homeless," *TBT,* 27 December 2015; Pickett, "St. Pete Homeless under Attack"; AP, "Florida Leads Nation in Homeless Beatings," *GS,* 9 April 2007; "Florida Led the Nation Last Year in Violence against the Homeless," *OS,* 8 August 2009.

30. "After Losing One Case against County, Westgate Tabernacle Files Another," *PBP,* 9 March 2010.

31. "Arresting, Jailing Homeless Has Cost Volusia Taxpayers Millions," *DBNJ,* 25 November 2013; "Hard-Core Homelessness Proves Costly for Alachua County," *GS,* 5 August 2007; "Cost of Homelessness in Central Florida?," *OS,* 21 May 2014.

32. "Orlando Homeless Laws Stir Heated Debate," *OS*, 3 February 2007; "Feeding the Homeless: Act of Charity or Crime?," *GS*, 7 November 2014; "Far from Home: Gainesville's Continuing Struggle with Homelessness," and "Homeless Center Site Raises Ire," *GS*, 27 April and 2 September 2007.

33. "Life among the Outcasts," *MH*, 3 May 2009.

34. "Homelessness: Miami's Shadow City" and "Miami to Go to Court to Undo Homeless Protection Act," *MH*, 28 May and 11 April 2013; "Judge Invalidates Miami's Landmark Homeless-Protection Order from 1998," *Miami New Times*, 15 February 2019.

35. "Other Miami-Dade Cities Deny 'Dumping' Homeless People in Downtown Miami," *MH*, 1 July 2013.

36. "An Experiment and a Protest in Shantytown for Homeless," *NYT*, 16 January 2007; "Shantytown Fire Renews fears," and "Housing Activists Try Squatter Strategy," *MH*, 8 September and 24 October 2007; "Face-off Looms over Old Shantytown Site," *MH*, 12 July 2007.

37. "'Tent City' of Homeless Is Rejected in Florida," *NYT*, 14 October 2009.

38. "A Heaven for the Homeless Becomes Less So," *NYT*, 31 March 2010; Bob Kerstein, email to author, 22 August 2008.

39. "Clearwater Considers 'Sitting' Ban to Curb Homeless," *TT*, 16 July 2012; "Clearwater Poised to Institute More Laws That Target the Homeless," and "Clearwater Supports Tougher Laws against Homeless," *TBT*, 13 and 19 July 2012.

40. "Downtown Fort Lauderdale Homeless Population Swelled by Jail Releases," *SFSS*, 21 February 2013.

41. "Boca Raton Cracks down on Loitering," *SFSS*, 15 June 2013.

42. "Florida Activists Arrested for Serving Food to Homeless," NPR.org, 6 November 2014; AP, "Feeding the Homeless," *GS*, 7 November 2014; "Florida Finds Tricky Balance over Feeding of the Homeless," *NYT*, 13 November 2014; Fabiola Santiago, "When Did Compassion Become Crime?" *MH*, 13 November 2014; "Coral Springs to Discourage Panhandling," *SFSS*, 23 June 2013; Fred Grimm, "Social Media Takes Broward City by Storm," *MH*, 14 November 2014.

43. "Florida Finds Tricky Balance."

44. Tom Lyons, "So Where Should the Homeless Go?," *SHT*, 6 February 2013.

45. "Sarasota's Sporadic Approach to Homelessness," *SHT*, 26 November 2012; "Homeless Say Booming Cities Have Outlawed Their Right to Sleep, Beg and Even Sit," *WP*, 2 June 2016.

46. "Bradenton in Top 10 'Meanest' Cities," *BH*, 14 July 2009; "The 10 Meanest Cities in America," NPR.org, 15 July 2009; "Orlando 3rd Meanest City for Homeless," *OS*, 14 July 2009.

47. "Daytona Homeless Lose Beach Hangout under Pier," 30 January 2010.

48. "More Cities Passing Laws That Target the Homeless," *USAT*, 17 July 2014; Sue Carlton, "Panhandling Paradox," *TBT*, 7 March 2018; "Florida Ordinance Targets People Who Give to Beggars and Peddlers," *LAT*, 17 April 2010; "Homeless Say Booming Cities Have Outlawed Their Right to Sleep, Beg, and Even Sit," *WP*, 2 June 2016.

49. "Tough Times Keep Panhandlers Busy," *TT*, 28 April 2012.

50. "Recession and Homelessness," *TE*, 27 January 2011; "Rural Florida," *FT*, September 2017, 24; "More Children Living in Poverty in Palm Beach, Broward Counties," *SFSS*, 19 December 2012; "Pockets of Severe Poverty Intensify and Spread around Tampa Bay Area," and "More of Us Live in Poverty," *TBT*, 4 November 2011 and 8 January 2012; "More Leaving Florida Than Moving In," *OS*, 24 December 2009; "Number of South Florida Homeless Students on the Rise," *MH*, 13 February 2009.

51. Emory quoted in "Recession Created 'Epidemic' of Homeless Families," and "Osceola Motel Families," *OS*, 10 January 2011 and 26 May 2012; "Florida Ranks 36th in Child Welfare," *SPT*, 28 August 2011; "Soaring Number of Homeless Students," *OS*, 20 March 2015.

52. "'60 Minutes' Revisits Central Florida Homeless," *OS*, 26 November 2011; "Homeless Stat Goes Viral," *TBT*, 8 December 2011.

53. "Living on Nothing but Food Stamps," *NYT*, 2 January 2010.

54. "Filth Didn't Stop Referrals," *TBT*, 27 October 2013.

55. Bill Church, "Who Is the Meanest in Paradise?," *SHT*, 23 January 2016.

56. "Cocaine No Longer the Drug of Choice," *MH*, 14 September 2011.

57. Grace Niewijk, "Ancient Analgesics: A Brief History of Opioids," *Yale Scientific*, 20 January 2017; Travis Rieder, "The Perilous Blessings of Opioids" and "The Great Opiate Boom," *WSJ*, 15 June 2019 and 6 June 2015; Barry Meier, "In Guilty Plea, OxyContin Makers to Pay $600 Million," *NYT*, 27 October 2017; "The Government's Struggle to Hold Opioid Manufacturers Accountable," *WP*, 2 April 2017.

58. Richard Florida, "The Real Cause of the Opioid Crisis," Bloomberg.com, 14 February 2014; Pat Beall, "How Florida Spread Oxycodone across America," *PBP*, 6 July 2018.

59. Beall, "How Florida Spread Oxycodone across America"; "Florida Joins States Fighting 'Prescription Tourists,'" *SHT*, 9 July 2012; "Pharmageddon: How America Got Hooked on Killer Prescription Drugs," *TG*, 9 June 2011.

60. "Reefer Tokin' Seniors in South Florida See Pain Go up in Smoke," *SS*, 23 July 2012.

61. "Jailed Pill Mill Owner Says He Made Millions," *SFSS*, 25 June 2013.

62. "Tampa Pharmacy," *TT*, 17 January 2011; Beall, "How Florida Spread Oxycodone across America"; "New Front Opens in Florida Pill War," *WSJ*, 8 March 2012; "The Human Cost of 5.6 Billion Pain Pills," editorial, *TBT*, 28 July 2019.

63. Frank Owen, "The Heroin Crisis in Trump's Backyard," *Politico*, 4 July 2017.

64. "A New Divide in American Death," *WP*, 11 April 2016; "Drug Overdoses Propel Rise in Mortality Rates of Young Whites," *NYT*, 16 January 2016; "Pills Killing More Women," *TBT*, 3 July 2013; "Suicides, Drug Overdoses Push down Life Expectancy," *TBT*, 30 November 2018.

65. "Florida Heals from Pill Mill Epidemic," *TBT*, 1 September 2014; Beth Macy, "Failures That Fueled the Opioid Epidemic," *NYT*, 24 February 2021; "As Mills Closed, Drug Deaths Dropped," and "Addicted Mom, Dead Child," *MH*, 21 March 2014.

66. "'Rez Disease' of Alcohol, Drugs Is Deadly among Seminole Youth," *SFSS*, 28 September 2008; Rachel Buxton, "Diabetes No. 1 Problem among Native Americans," *Seminole Tribe Official Newspaper*, 21 February 2012; "Addiction-Hit Miccosukee Tribe Sues Big Pharma," Yahoo.com, 24 February 2019.

67. "Billions of Pills, Millions in Cash," 26 July 2019; "Heroin Taking Oxy's Place for More Addicts," *SFSS*, 19 February 2013; "Florida Shutting down 'Pill Mill' Clinics," *NYT*, 1 September 2011; "The Government's Struggle to Hold Opioid Manufacturers Accountable," *WP*, 2 April 2017.

68. "How Did Florida Become 'Pill-Mill' Hotbed?," *OS*, 12 June 2011.

69. Gary R. Mormino, "The Orange: A Florida Icon Is under Siege," *Forum: The Magazine of the Florida Humanities Council* (Spring 2014): 2–11; "The End of Florida Orange Juice," *WP*, 9 November 2019; Growers Dread Citrus Greening," *SHT*, 2 February 2014; "Florida's Frenzied Fruit Fly Fiasco," *WP*, 19 July 1981; "Squeezed: Smallest Florida Orange Crop in 17 Years," *Futures Magazine*, 13 October 2006.

70. "Orange Groves Changing Face of DeSoto Plain," *SPT*, 6 September 1970; "Growers Dread Citrus Greening," *SHT*, 2 February 2014. See also John McPhee, *Oranges* (New York: Farrar, Straus and Giroux, 1975).

71. "Citrus Tower Is a Reminder of Clermont's Past," *SS*, 14 March 2004; "Florida's Economic Dilemma," pbs.org, 12 April 2010.

72. "Pinellas Fruit Harvest," *SPT*, 10 November 1946; "Squeezed Out," *TBT*, 11 April 2016; "Citrus Industry Challenged," *LL*, 15 November 2005

73. "All Citrus Acreage and Trees, by County and Year of Inventory—Florida, 2016–2019," *USDA Citrus: Commercial Citrus Inventory* (Maitland, FL: USDA, August 2019), 4–5; "Declining Acreage," and "A Grower's Last Pickins," *TT*, 4 November 2005; *Florida Agricultural Statistics, Citrus Summary 2002–03* (Tallahassee: Florida Department of Agricultural and Consumer Services, 2003), 29.

74. "Subdivisions Slip into Rural Refuge," *OS*, 5 December 2005.

75. "Abandoned Groves Spread Scourge of 'Citrus Greening,'" *OS*, 14 February 2011; Thomas H. Spreen, "Fewer Trees = Smaller Citrus Crop," *Florida Grower*, November 2010, 18; "A Race to Save the Orange," *NYT*, 28 July 2013; "Citrus Crop Shrinking at Alarming Rate," *SHT*, 11 December 2015.

76. Adee Braun, "Misunderstanding Orange Juice as a Health Drink," *TA*, 5 February 2014; "Nation's Orange Juice Supply Shrinking," *OS*, 28 October 2016; "Save Our Citrus," *TBT*, 15 February 2005; "Orange Juice Searches for Fresher Image," *WSJ*, 27 September 2014; "How Long Can Florida's Citrus Industry Survive?" NPR.org, 27 November 2015.

77. "With Low Yield, Citrus Growers Feel the Squeeze," *TBT*, 14 July 2021.

78. "'Polk County Tops Los Angeles as Nation's No. 1 Citrus County,'" *TT*, 24 November 2010; "Citrus Groves Fading from State's Landscape," *SPT*, 19 October 2007; "Citrus Industry Challenged," *LL*, 15 November 2005.

79. Hoffman quoted in "Growing Pains in Southwest Fla.," *WP*, 25 June 2002; "A Home Builder Files for Bankruptcy Protection," *NYT*, 5 August 2008.

80. *SHT*, 10 July 2008; "Fewer People Moving to Florida," *SFSS*, 30 January 2011; Trigaux, "A Decade's Worth of Lessons," *SPT*, 27 December 2009; Justin B. Hollander, *Sunburnt Cities: The Great Recession, Depopulation, and Urban Planning in the American Sunbelt* (New York: Routledge, 2011), 40–45; "Economy Alters How Americans Are Moving," *NYT*, 27 October 2011.

81. Dan DeWitt, "Sunshine Doesn't Pay the Bills," *SPT*, 11 June 2007.

82. Cave, "Tide Turning," and "Economy Alters How Americans Are Moving," *NYT*, 30 August 2009 and 27 October 2011; Carl Hiaasen, "Yes, Florida Is Shrinking, but Not Enough," *MH*, 16 September 2009; "Some Fancy Neighborhoods Open Gates to Section 8," *SS*, 13 September 2012.

83. "Many Younger People Leaving South Florida," *MH*, 13 December 2011; "Recession Slang," *CSM*, 8 March 2010; Robert Samuelson, "Is the Economy Creating a Lost Generation?," *WP*, 9 December 2012; "Many Turn to What Was Once Unthinkable: Public Assistance," *SHT*, 12 January 2013; "You are Now Leaving Florida," *TT*, 23 April 2009.

84. "Census Data Offers Look at Effects of Recession," *NYT*, 5 April 2012.

85. "Florida Experiencing a 'Baby Bust,'" *SS*, 21 October 2011.

86. "Making the Return Trip: Elderly Head Back North," *NYT*, 26 February 2007; "Trials of Aging Drive 'Boomerang,'" *USAT*, 22 February 2007.

87. Bill Bonner, "Where America's Money Is Moving," *Wall Street Pit*, 20 June 2010.

88. "Priced out of Key West," *NYT*, 27 December 1982; "Florida Keys Cost of Living: More People Struggle," and "Tourism Lifts Keys' Recovery," *MH*, 6 February 2019 and 23 July 2012; "Cost of Living in Keys Goes Up," *SHT*, 3 August 2019; Bonner, "Where America's Money Is Moving"; Robert Kerstein, *Key West on the Edge: Inventing the Conch Republic* (Gainesville: University Press of Florida, 2012), 232; "Florida Keys' Population Shrinks as Florida Grows," Keysnews.com, 30 March 2011.

89. "A Great Recession of Income, People," *TT*, 28 July 2011; Jeff Kunerth, "Shrinking Florida Faces Tough Choices as Residents Flee," *OS*, 15 November 2009.

90. "Only 43 Homes Built in Three Months? Must Be Miami," *CSM*, 13 May 2009; "In the Data, a Portrait of the Slump," *SHT*, 3 September 2012; "Hispanic Exodus Is Under Way," *FMNP*, 9 March 2008.

91. Dougherty, "Is Florida Over?" *WSJ*, 29 September 2007; "As Florida's Economy Slows," *SHT*, 30 September 2007; "Do Stats Show Florida's Allure Dimming?" *SPT*, 26 January 2007.

92. Don Lee, "Census Shows Ebb, Flow," *LAT*, 29 December 2010.

93. "'Perfect Storm' Wreaking Havoc on Florida Golf Courses," *OS*, 29 November 2014; "Why America Fell out of Love with Golf," *WP*, 5 March 2015; "More Americans Are Giving up Golf," *NYT*, 21 February 2008; "Why Game of Golf Is in Serious Trouble," *USAT*, 14 April 2014.

94. Susan Cosier, "Bye-Bye Golf Courses, Hello Nature Preserves," Audubon.org/magazine, September 2013.

95. "Struggling Bobby Jones Course," *SHT*, 26 July 2018.

96. "Developers Holding Back on Golf Communities," *FMNP*, 26 May 2015; "As Golf Communities Lose Popularity, Real-Estate Developers Change Course," *WSJ*, 23 April 2016; "Country Clubs Changing with Times in Southwest Florida," *NDN*, 2 November 2018.

97. "Following Fertilizer Leads to Farms, Golf Courses, Landscaping," *FMNP*, 19 September 2018.

98. James Kelly, "South Florida: Trouble in Paradise," *Time*, 23 November 1981.

99. Floridaloanspecialist.wordpress.com, 12 September 2018.

100. Libby Copeland, "Beware of the Sunshine State, Where It's East to Get Burned," *WP*, 20 January 2008.

101. Michael Grunwald, "Is Florida the Sunset State?" *Time*, 10 July 2008, 27–32; Andrés Viglucci, "Hard Times Make Paradise an Easy Target," *MH*, 20 July 2008.

102. Parks quoted in Grunwald, "Is Florida the Sunset State?," 31.

103. Fred Grimm, "Blame Political Climate for Our Ailing Paradise," *MH*, 14 July 2008.

104. Hiaasen quoted in "Florida's Soul-Searching after the Real Estate Bust," *NYT*, 15 August 2009.

105. Archibald MacLeish, *Land of the Free* (New York: Harcourt Brace, 1938), 23.

106. "Lauren Berlant, 63, a Critic of the American Dream," *NYT*, 7 July 2021; Hua Hsu, "Affect Theory and the New Age of Anxiety," *TNY*, 18 March 2019.

107. Jeff Klinkenberg, "Bring Back Jack!," *SPT*, 4 April 2007.

108. Jon Wilson, "My Florida Dream," *SPT*, 21 October 2007.

109. Michael Kruse, "Greetings from Florida," *SPT*, 25 November 2007.

110. Alexander von Hoffman, "Home Values Are Down, and Not Just at the Bank," *WP*, 20 July 2008.

111. "Owning a Home: Has the Dream Soured?" *SPT*, 21 September 2010; Sean Snaith quoted in "Greetings from Florida," *SPT*, 25 November 2007; "61 Square Miles of Optimism," *NYT*, 28 August 2011.

112. "Housing Market Then and Now," *TT*, 11 August 2006; "While Families Get Smaller, New Houses Grow Larger," *USAT*, 10 June 2013.

113. Robert Trigaux, "Sunshine Not Enough to Keep Us Smiling," *SPT*, 26 November 2007.

114. Howard Troxler, "Fixing Florida Is Going to Be Fun," *SPT*, 11 June 2011.

115. Philip Coolidge Brooks, *Diplomacy and the Borderlands: The Adams-Onís Treaty of 1819* (Berkeley: University of California Press, 1929), 8; DeFoor quoted in "What's Time Magazine Got Against Florida Anyhow?," *MH*, 14 July 2008.

116. Jim Brown, "It's Tough, but No Great Depression," *SHT*, 31 August 2020.

117. Jeff Klinkenberg, "Open Your Senses to Paradise," *SPT*, 20 July 2008.

Chapter 13. A Political Earthquake: Florida Politics, 2008–2010

1. "Tampa Wins Bid to Host 2012 GOP Convention," *GS*, 13 August 2010; Smith quoted in "Why Here? Size, Diversity, Clout," *TBT*, 26 August 2012.

2. Darryl Paulson, "Why Florida and Its Politicians Don't Get Any National Respect," *TBT*, 3 September 2017. Donald Trump was elected president in 2016 as a resident of New York. He became an official Florida resident in 2019, when he filed a "declaration of domicile" swearing that his property in Palm Beach County would be his permanent home ("Trump, Lifelong New Yorker, Declares Himself a Resident of Florida," *NYT*, 31 October 2019).

3. "GOP Stars at Home Here," and "As Florida Grows, It Still Lacks Corporate Brands with Global Clout," *TBT*, 26 August 2012 and 10 March 2014; "Mike Huckabee's Epic Fight to Keep Beachgoers off His Patch of Florida Sand," *MJ*, 22 May 2019; "Celebrities: South Florida," *FT*, April 2015, 20–21, 25.

4. "Restless in Tallahassee," *NYT*, 12 May 2009.

5. Debra Pangestu, "Stewart Mocks Tampa," www.nbc.com.

6. "At the Bottom," *SPT*, 15 September 2011.

7. Michael Kruse, "His Legacy, City's Chance," *TBT*, 5 August 2012.

8. Matthew Corrigan, *Conservative Hurricane: How Jeb Bush Remade Florida* (Gainesville: University Press of Florida, 2014), 168–69, 172–73; Geller quoted in "For Crist, It's Sunshine," *TT*, 30 December 2007.

9. "Charlie Crist Takes Credit for Florida's Largest-Ever Tax Cut," PolitiFact, 10 November 2009.

10. R. Boyd Murphree, "Charles Joseph 'Charlie' Crist Jr.," in *The Governors of Florida*, ed. Murphree and Robert A. Taylor (Gainesville: University Press of Florida, 2020), 638–39.

11. "In Florida, Liking Crist Is a Breeze," *LAT*, 2 June 2007.

12. "Inaugural Address Governor Charlie Crist," 2 January 2007, votesmart.org; "Crist First Year a Busy, Stormy One" and "Gov. Crist Maintains Popularity," *FMNP*, 30 and 26 December 2007; "In a Break from the Past, Florida Will Let Felons Vote," *NYT*, 6 April 2007.

13. John Kennedy, "Year 2 for Gov. Crist: Rougher Sailing," *OS*, 30 December 2007.

14. William March, "Who Is the Real Charlie Crist?" *TT*, 2 December 2012; Adam Smith, "The Real Charlie Crist," *TBT*, 23 June 2013; Steve Bousquet, "A Tale of 3 Governors Provides a Lesson," *SPT*, 4 December 2007.

15. William Gibson, "Welcome to Juice," *SS*, 22 August 2007.

16. "Florida Democrats Revel in Gained Ground," *SPT*, 26 August 2008.

17. "Finally, Crist Decides: It's McCain," *OS*, 27 January 2008.

18. Copeland, "Beware of the Sunshine State," *WP*, 30 January 2008; "Gov. Crist Could Benefit from McCain Win," *USAT*, 30 January 2008; "Calling McCain a 'True American Hero,' Fla. Governor Endorses Senator," *BG*, 27 January 2008; "Poll Says Giuliani Leads but Faltering," *FMNP*, 21 December 2007.

19. Alex Leary, "After Vietnam, John McCain Returned to Florida," *SPT*, 20 August 2008; "Jim Morrison Is Candidate for Pardon in '69 Arrest," and "Jim Morrison, 25, Lead Singer with Doors Rock Group Dies," *NYT*, 16 November 2010 and 9 July 1971.

20. Alex Leary, "The Pensacola Proving Ground," *SPT*, 5 October 2008.

21. "One Story Ends, Another Begins: John McCain's Homecoming 45 Years Ago in Jacksonville," *FTU*, 16 March 2018; Leary, "After Vietnam, John McCain Returned to Florida."

22. "Chuck Berry Snubs John McCain," *TG*, 11 June 2008; "McCain Dumps Chuck Berry for Abba!," huffpost.com, 19 January 2008.

23. "McCain's Press Secretary Is Proud UF Graduate," *University of Florida News*, 15 April 2008; "Conservative Radio Hosts Stake Their Reputation on a McCain Defeat," msnbc.com, 31 January 2008; "Florida Gov. Crist Endorses McCain," *WP*, 27 January 2008; "McCain Wins Florida," cnn.com, 29 January 2008.

24. David Maraniss, *Barack Obama: The Story* (New York: Simon and Schuster, 2012), 165, 557.

25. Jewett quoted in "Obama Wins Florida en Route to White House," *USAT*, 5 November 2008.

26. Adm Nagourney, "While McCain Looked away, Florida Shifted," *NYT*, 24 October 2008.

27. Joe Follick, "McCain/Crist?" *SHT*, 8 June 2008; "Sunnily Crist Campaigns for McCain," *SPT*, 19 October 2008.

28. Obama, *A Promised Land*, 36–37; Susan Page, "Hillary and Obama: Different Campaigns, Opposite Tasks," *USAT*, 7 July 2014.

29. Betty Boyd Caroli, "Hillary Clinton," britannica.com.

30. Adam Smith, "Hillary Clinton's Connections in the Sunshine State Are about Loyalty and Longevity," *TBT*, 19 October 2016; Bill Maxwell, "Hillary Clinton Seen as Beacon of Hope for Farm Workers and Their Children," *SFSS*, 21 December 1992; Jeffrey Klein, "Sweet Rewards," motherjones.com, November 1998.

31. "Florida Vote Goes to Brother of First Lady," "First Brother-in-Law Has Tobacco Talks Role," and "Siblings Who Often Emerge in an Unflattering Spotlight," *NYT*, 5 October 1994, 23 April 1997 and 23 February 2001.

32. "Florida Vote Goes to Brother of First Lady," "First Brother in-Law Has Tobacco Talks Role," and "Siblings Who Often Emerge in an Unflattering Spotlight."

33. "McCain Needs to Win Left-Leaning Florida," Politico.com, 28 October 2008.

34. "Clinton Wants Florida and Michigan Delegates Seated at Convention," *New York Observer*, 25 January 2008.

35. Obama, *A Promised Land*, 87; "John Edwards Joins Presidential Race," *WP*, 28 December 2006; "Edwards to Endorse Obama," CNN.com, 14 May 2008; "John Edwards and the Mistress: A Breakdown of One of America's Most Sensational Scandals," abcnews.com, 11 November 2013; "Sometimes There's

News in the Gutter," *NYT*, 15 December 2012; "How the National Enquirer Broke the John Edwards Love Child Scandal," *National Enquirer*, 19 June 2014.

36. "To Derail Clinton, Her Foes Take Swift Action," *LAT*, 18 February 2007.

37. Obama, *A Promised Land*, 88.

38. Page, "Hillary and Obama: Different Campaigns, Opposite Tasks"; Caroli, "Hillary Clinton."

39. Whitit quoted in "Obama's Triumph: A Turning Point for America?," NPR.org, 5 June 2008.

40. "Thinking about Obama," *NYT*, 16 October 2008; Jewett quoted in "Obama Wins Florida," *USAT*, 5 November 2008.

41. "Florida Swings Its Votes to Obama," *LL*, 4 November 2008.

42. "Election Results 2008," *NYT*, 5 November 2008.

43. "Among Hispanics in Florida, 2008 Voter Registration Rolls Swing Democratic," Pew Research Center: Hispanic Trends, 29 October 2008; "The Hispanic Vote in the 2008 Election," Pew Research Center, 5 November 2008; Kevin Baker, "Delusions of the Democrats," *NYT*, 15 November 2014.

44. William Gibson, "How Obama Won Florida," *SS*, 6 November 2008; "Obama's Winning 'Change' Strategy," NPR.org, 10 November 2008.

45. "Bans in 3 States on Gay Marriage," *NYT*, 5 November 2008; Crist quoted in "On Support of Gay Marriage," politifact.com, 8 May 2013.

46. Elizabeth Birch quoted in Thomas Chapman, "Sexual Politics and the Sunshine State," 219; Chapman, "Sexual Politics," 226.

47. "The Six Political States of Florida," *WP*, 8 September 2020; "The Political Geography of Florida," fivethirtyeight.com, 31 January 2012; Jeanne Cummings, "2008 Campaign Costliest in U.S. History," politico.com, 5 November 2008; "Big TV Spending in Three Southern Swing States," facingsouth.org, 5 November 2008; "Map: Campaign Ad Spending—Election Center 2008 from CNN.com; "Final Fundraising Figure: Obama's $750M," abcnews.go.com, 4 December 2008; "Obama Bets Big on Florida Turnout," *LAT*, 17 October 2008; "Obama Wins Florida en Route to White House."

48. David Frum, "Here's Why McCain Will Still Get My Vote," nationalreview.com, 16 October 2008.

49. R. Boyd Murphree, "Richard Lynn 'Rick' Scott," in *The Governors of Florida* (Gainesville: University Press of Florida, 2020), 659.

50. "The Mama's Boys Who Became Our Presidents," *WP*, 12 May 1985; Doris Kearns, *Lyndon Johnson and the American Dream* (New York: Harper and Row, 1976), 1922.

51. "Florida's Governor Always Wears This Navy Hat," *USAT*, 13 October 2018; "Gov. Scott's Mother, Esther, Dead at 94," *PBP*, 15 November 2012.

52. Margaret Putnam, "Dallas' Fat Cat Law Firms," *D Magazine*, June 1983.

53. Murphree, "Richard Lynn 'Rick' Scott," 660.

54. Ibid.

55. Ibid., 660–61; "HCA to Pay $95 Million in Fraud Case," *NYT*, 15 December 2000; "Studying Gov. Rick Scott's Style, from Columbia/HCA to Governor," *TBT*, 20 October 2014; "Once Scrutinized by the Government, Rick Scott Will Soon Govern," NPR.org, 3 November 2010; "When Rick Scott Was Deposed in Lawsuits about His Company, He Took the Fifth 75 Times," poltiifact.com, 22 June 2014.

56. "Columbia Promises Cape Hospital Fight," and "Columbia President Makes Presence Known Everywhere," *FMNP*, 24 March 1994; *Forbes* quote from Allman, *Finding Florida*, 445.

57. "Gov. Rick Scott Took Responsibility? No, He Took $300 Million," *SFSS*, 2 October 2018.

58. Matt Walsh, "The Real Rick Scott," *Business Observer*, 5 November 2010.

59. "Rick Scott's Role in Columbia/HCA Scandal," *MH*, 27 June 2010.

60. Scott Powers, "How Much Responsibility Did Rick Scott Really Take in Medicare Fraud Scandal?," floridapolitics.com, 30 September 2018.

61. Michael Grunwald, *The New New Deal: The Hidden Story of Change in the Obama Era* (New York: Simon and Schuster, 2012), 301; "Obama: 'If You Like Your Doctor, You Can Keep Your Doctor,'" *WSJ*,

15 June 2009, "Gov. Rick Scott says 'Obamacare' Is Not the Law of the Land," politifact.com, 1 December 2011; "PolitiFact Lie of the Year," *TBT*, 13 December 2013.

62. "TEA Party Backs Rick Scott," *Sunshine State News*, 31 August 2010; "Rick Scott Beats Bill McCollum to End Nasty GOP Governor's Primary Fight," *OS*, 25 August 2010; Marc Ambinder, "That's a Wrap, Folks," *TA*, 25 August 2010.

63. "Former Charlottean Alex Sink May Run for Governor—of Florida," *Charlotte Observer*, 11 May 2009; Darin Strauss, *Chang and Eng* (New York: Dutton, 2000); "The World's Most Famous Conjoined Twins, Chang and Eng," ripley's.com, 14 July 2017.

64. Adam Smith, "Alex Sink Says Grit and Pride Were Legacy of Famous Ancestors," *SPT*, 26 September 2010; John Finotti, "Alex Sink: A Study in Contrasts," *FT*, 1 June 1999.

65. Doug Campbell, "Branch by Branch: How North Carolina Became a Banking Giant," *Region Focus*, Fall 2006, 53. "Alex Sink Is Player in Her Own Right," *OSB*, 22 September 2002; Rod Thomson, "Shhhhh . . . Sink Was a Banker," *Business Observer*, 8 October 2010.

66. "Alex Sink Mastered Banking, but Political Ease Is a Stretch," *TBT*, 15 October 2010.

67. Michael T. Moore, "A Life Well Lived: Bill McBride of Tampa," floridabar.org, 25 April 2019; "Bill McBride, 67, Former Candidate for Governor, and Husband of Alex Sink, Dies," *TBT*, 23 December 2012.

68. "The 2002 Elections: The Florida Vote," *NYT*, 6 November 2002; "Economy Puts Sink in Different Position Than Her Husband," *OSB*, 7 June 2009.

69. "McBride's Wife Has Clout of Her Own," *SHT*, 22 September 2002.

70. Finotti, "Alex Sink: A Study in Contrasts."

71. Moore quoted in "Low-Profile Alex Sink Faces Even More Obscure Opponent in Democratic Race for Governor," *PBP*, 24 July 2010; "Florida Voters Like Gov. Crist," www.quinnipiac.edu, January 21, 2009.

72. "Former Charlottean Alex Sink May Run for Governor—of Florida."

73. "Ruling Lets Rick Scott Spend All He Wants in Governor's Race," *OS*, 30 July 2010.

74. "Aide Fired over Florida Debate Foul," cnnpolitics.com, 25 October 2010.

75. AP, "Money, Message, and Electorate Make Scott Gov.," 3 November 2010; "Economy Puts Sink in Different Position Than Her Husband."

Chapter 14. Florida, 2008–2010: Political "Crist"-enings, "Rubio" Red Harvests, and "Sink"-ing Blue Poll Numbers

1. "Carole Rome Regains Joint Custody of Girls," *SHT*, 5 April 2013; "Meet Carole Rome," *SPT*, 13 July 2008; "Crist's Wife Sells Fisher Island Condo for $3.5 Million," *SS*, 24 June 2011.

2. "Charlie Crist: A Fuzzy Line Divides Personal and Political Lives," and "Meet Carole Rome, the Governor's Fiancée," *SPT*, 12 October and 13 July 2008; "Crist Engagement Just in Time to Revive That Shot at V.P.," *OS*, 9 July 2008; "Crist's December Wedding to Follow Tradition," *TT*, 13 November 2008.

3. Charlie Crist, "The Hug That Killed My Republican Career," *Time*, 4 February 2014; "GOP Seethes over Charlie Crist's Stimulus-Plan Support," *MH*, 13 February 2009; Obama, *A Promised Land* (New York: Crown, 2020), 262.

4. Obama, *A Promised Land*, 262.

5. Ibid.

6. Mark Leibovich, "The First Senator from the Tea Party?," *NYTM*, 6 January 2010; Chris Cillizza, "The Most (In)Famous Political Hug, Ever," *WP*, 21 January 2016.

7. Richard E. Foglesong, *Immigrant Prince: Mel Martinez and the American Dream* (Gainesville: University Press of Florida, 2011), 195–98.

8. Ibid., 199–204; "Last Gasp of Immigration Bill," *NYT*, 9 June 2007; "Immigration Debate Puts up a Wall in the GOP," *LAT*, 27 May 2007; "Is Rush Limbaugh Right?," Salon.com, 23 May 2007.

9. Foglesong, *Immigrant Prince,* 1; Martínez quoted in "Martinez Wants More Time with Family," "The Buzz on Florida Politics," tampabay.com, 2 December 2008.

10. Foglesong, *Immigrant Prince,* 214–15; "Martinez to Step Aside," *SPT*, 3 December 2008; "Florida's Martinez Announces Resignation from Senate," *NYT*, 7 August 2009.

11. Rome quoted in *SPT*, 20 September 2009.

12. "Governors' Fight over Stimulus May Define GOP," *NYT*, 22 February 2009.

13. Marco Rubio quoted in Michael Grunwald, *The New New Deal: The Hidden Story of Change in the Obama Era* (New York: Simon and Schuster, 2012), 286.

14. "Jeb Is Considering the Senate," *OS*, 2 December 2008; "Jeb Bush Not Running for Senate," CNN.com, 6 January 2006.

15. "The 17-Year Story behind Marco Rubio's Cut-Down of Jeb Bush," *WP*, 30 October 2015.

16. Marco Cogan, "Forgive Me Mentor, For I Will Run," *NR*, 12 March 2013.

17. Michael Grunwald, "Immigrant Son," *Time*, 7 February 2013; "Mario Rubio's Policies Might Shut the Door to People Like His Grandfather," *NYT*, 5 March 2016.

18. "Marco Rubio's Compelling Family Story Embellishes Myths," *WP*, 20 October 2011.

19. "GOP Could Win 3 Key Senate Seats," *Politico*, 14 January 2009.

20. "Is Rubio Criticizing Crist?" politico.com, 20 March 2009; Sayfie and Navarro quoted in "Crist Senate Bid Could Threaten GOP Control in Fla.," TheHill.com, 10 May 2009.

21. Alex Leary, "Rise and Stall: The Political Trajectory of Marco Rubio," *TBT*, 13 March 2016.

22. Rubio and Ros-Lehtinen quoted in "Governor of Florida Plans Bud for Senate," *NYT*, 11 May 2009; "Jeb Bush Picks Rubio," *PBP*, 6 May 2010; Crist quoted in "Charlie Crist," *TBT*, 28 August 2012; Crist quoted in "Charlie Crist was Pro-Life, Pro-Gun and Anti-Tax says George LeMieux," politifact.com, 6 September 2012.

23. "Florida Senate—Rubio vs. Meek vs. Crist," RealClearPolitics.com/epolls/2010/senate/fl; Max Fisher, "Why Crist Now Leads Rubio in Florida Senate Race," *TA*, 21 June 2010; Polling Institute quoted in "January 21, 2009 Florida Voters Like Gov. Crist," Quinnipiac.edu.

24. Grunwald, *The New New Deal,* 300.

25. Boyd Murphree, "Charles Joseph 'Charlie' Crist Jr.," in the *Governors of Florida*, ed. Murphree and Robert A. Taylor (Gainesville: University Press of Florida, 2019), 650–51; "Jeb Bush's Son Chides Gov. Crist," *OS*, 22 February 2009.

26. Ken Rudin, "The Fast Rise and Remarkable Fall of Charlie Crist," and Neal B. Freeman, "National Review: Charlie Crist's Moment in the Sun," NPR.org, 19 and 20 April 2010.

27. "After Specter's Switch, Focus Turns to Crist's Future in GOP," and Steve Bousquet, "Charlie Crist's Party Switch Is Like No Other in Florida," *TBT*, 3 May 2009 and 12 September 2014.

28. "Crist Loses Straw Poll to Rubio in His Home County," *SPT*, 12 January 2010; "Ex-Fla. GOP Chair under Investigation," *GS*, 31 March 2010; "Jim Greer Prison House Interview," and "18 Months for Greer," *TBT*, 7 September and 27 March 2013; Peter Golenbock, *The Chairman: The Rise and Betrayal of Jim Greer* (Montgomery, AL: NewSouth, 2014).

29. "Marco Rubio Says Charlie Crist Worked with ACORN to Restore Voting Rights for Felons," politifact.org, 29 March 2010; "Marco Rubio Is National Review's Cover Boy," *FT*, 21 August 2009.

30. "Crist's Two Jobs," editorial, *GS*, 14 May 2009.

31. "Aide Found Dead," *SPT*, 28 August 2001; Nick Gillespie, "In Reagan's Steps," *NYT*, 10 July 2009.

32. "Question: 'Morning Joe or Sen. Joe'?," *SHT*, 9 February 2009; "Mack Won't Run for Senate," rollcall.com, 2 April 2009.

33. "Smith Drops out of Senate Race Again," *SHT*, 30 March 2010; "Sink, Rubio, McCollum Ponder Senate Race," *SPT*, 2 December 2008; "Snowbird Smith Running in Florida—Again," Politico.com, 9 April 2009.

34. "Pam Iorio for Senate? No Brainer," *CL*, 4 February 2009; "Tampa Mayor May Run for U.S. Senate" *LL*, 21 February 2009; "Iorio, Baker to Skip U.S. Races," *SPT*, 12 May 2009.

35. "The Honorable Kendrick B. Meek," "History, Art, and Archives: United States House of Representatives: Interview," 19 March 2012.

36. Adam Smith, "Florida Democrat Kendrick Meek Builds Support," *SPT*, 7 March 2009.

37. "Meek Still a Factor," *SHT*, 1 October 2010; "Political Intrigue Already Is Starting to Mount," *FTU*, 5 April 2009.

38. AP, "State Sen. Gelber to Run for US Senate," *GS*, 26 January 2009; "Could Florida Have Its First Openly Gay U.S. Senator?," *MH*, 16 February 2009; "Real Estate Mogul Jeff Greene," cnbc.com, 29 February 2008.

39. Jane Wells, "Real Estate Mogul Jeff Greene: The Man Who Shorted Subprime," cnbc.com, 29 February 2008.

40. "Judge Dismisses Libel Suit Filed against Times," "Jeff Greene's Libel Lawsuit," and "Another Round in the Jeff Greene, Tampa Bay Times Feud," *PBP*, 26 May 2016; Nicole Allen, "Billionaire Jeff Greene Is Not Well-Liked by People Who Worked for Him," *TA*, 2 August 2010; Alex Pareene, "Jeff Greene Is a Nightmare Boss," salon.com, 2 August 2010; Andy Kroll, "FL's Jeff Greene 'Not a Partier,'" *Mother Jones*, 26 August 2010.

41. "Meek Launches First TV Ad," *GS*, 26 July 2010; "Bill Clinton Urged Florida Democrat to Quit Bid," *NYT*, 28 October 2010.

42. Jeff Jacoby, "Obama Regrets Polarized Rancor: He Should," *BG*, 24 January 2016; David Brooks, "Obama Doesn't Seem to Be Learning from Failure," *NYT*, 19 November 2014.

43. "In Florida, Senate Seat Looks Like Rubio's," NPR.org, 22 October 2010.

44. "Marco Rubio Defeats Charlie Crist in Florida Senate Race," *LAT*, 2 November 2010; "In Rubio, Some See Rise of 'Great Right Hope,'" *NYT*, 3 November 2010; "Is Marco Rubio Brightest Rising Star of Tea Party?," *CSM*, 3 November 2010.

45. Chris Cillizza, "Charlie Crist Didn't Leave the Republican Party Because of Racism," *WP*, 18 April 2021; "Keith Laing, "Yearly Roundup," *PBP*, 31 December 2010.

46. Paulson quoted in "Crist's Fall," *LL*, 3 November 2010; Schale quoted in "Charlie Crist Sees Career Halted," northescambia.com, 3 November 2010.

47. "Charlie Crist Sees Career Halted on GOP's Night," Northescambia.com, 3 November 2010; "Rubio Rising," and Jim Geraghty, "When Rubio Was the Man of Florida's House," *NR*, 20 August 2009 and 13 April 2015.

48. "Gov. Rick Scott's Mother," *FTU*, 13 November 2012; "Rick Scott Lived in Public Housing 3 Years," *SS*, 16 October 2010.

49. "Money, Message, Mad Electorate Make Scott Fla. Gov," *WP*, 3 November 2010; "Political Spectacle 2010," *Fort Myers Florida Weekly*, 9 June 2010.

50. David Colburn and Richard Scher, *Florida's Gubernatorial Politics in the Twentieth Century* (Tallahassee: University Presses of Florida, 1980), 60, 87–88; Kirk quoted in "The Race for Your Next Governor, Is Still . . . Neck and Neck," fortmyers.floridaweekly.com, 28 October 2010.

51. "Rick Scott Wins Tight Florida Governor Race," CBSNews.com, 4 November 2010.

52. "Charlie Crist's Personal Approval Numbers," politifact.org, 1 September 2010; gubernatorial poll in Matthew T. Corrigan, *Conservative Hurricane: How Jeb Bush Remade Florida* (Gainesville: University Press of Florida, 2014), 178; Bush quoted in "Souls to the Polls," *MH*, 2 November 2014.

53. Scott Hensley, "Once Scrutinized by the Government, Rick Scott Soon Will Govern," NPR.org, 3 November 2010.

54. Steve Bousquet, "Had Crist Stayed," *TBT*, 25 May 2014.

55. Ibid; "Wheels Turn on Rail Plan," *TBT*, 24 May 2021.

56. "1960 United States Presidential Election in Florida," wikipedia.com; David R. Colburn, *From Yellow Dog Democrats to Red State Republicans: Florida and Its Politics since 1940* (Gainesville: University Press of Florida, 2007), 56; "The Moving Finger Writes," editorial, *SPT*, 18 February 1962.

57. Colburn, *From Yellow Dog Democrats*, 100–101; Robert Hooker, "Democrats' Domination," *SPT*, 12 November 1978.

58. Patsy Palmer, "The Sunset of the 'Long Generation,'" *SPT*, 20 December 1998; Buddy MacKay and Rick Edmonds, *How Florida Happened: The Political Education of Buddy MacKay* (Gainesville: University Press of Florida, 2010), 9–10.

59. Palmer, "The Sunset."

60. "Florida Turns Red," editorial, and "Florida's Economy Passes $1 Trillion Mark," *TBT*, 8 November and 13 July 2018.

61. "House Apportionment 2000: States Gaining, Losing," everycrsreport.com, 9 January 2001.

62. "Seats in Congress Gained/Lost by the President's Party," www.presidency.ucsb.edy/statistics.data.

63. Obama, *A Promised Land*, 404.

64. "In Obama Era, G.O.P. Bolsters Grip in the States," *NYT*, 12 November 2015.

65. "Florida First in Foreclosure Woe," *PBP*, 14 February 2013; "Florida's Unemployment Benefits 'Virtually Inaccessible,' Study Finds," *SS*, 22 September 2015.

66. "The Fault for Defaults," *SPT*, 8 November 2009.

67. "Will Florida See Condo and HOA Reforms in 2010?," *SS*, 29 December 2009.

68. Karen Murphy, "Crist Not Only Repealed Law Some Say May Have Prevented Surfside Collapse, He Campaigned on It," *The Capitolist*, 12 July 2021.

69. Patricia Mazzei, "Rethinking Florida Dream after Tower Collapse," *NYT*, 13 July 2021; "Surfside Building Collapse Sparks Scrutiny over Power of Condo Boards," NPR.org, 9 July 2021; "Before Condo Collapse, Rising Seas Have Long Pressured Miami Coastal Properties," *WP*, 25 June 2021.

70. "Struggles in His Past, Burdens in His Present," *NYT*, 5 August 1999; "How Your Representatives Rank on Earmarks," and "U.S. Rep. C. W. Bill Young Dies at 82," *TBT*, 5 December 2010 and 5 January 2014.

71. "Levitt Bankruptcy Leaves Homeowners in the Cold," NPR.org, 27 February 2008.

72. "Condo Owners Feel Bullied," *TBT*, 14 July 2019.

73. "How to Make the Rent? Work 108 Hours a Week," editorial, *TBT*, 24 June 2019; Fred Grimm, "Florida Connect," *MH*, 1 February 2014.

74. "Concerns Raised over Florida's Corporate Income Tax Credit Scholarship Program," *FTU*, 31 October 2010.

75. Howard Troxler, "Fixing Florida Will Be Fun to Watch," *SPT*, 12 June 2011.

76. "Carl Hiaasen," *SHT*, 14 March 2014.

77. "The Villages: Florida's Retirement Community Provides Foundation for GOP Candidates," *TBT*, 13 August 2012; Shipley quoted in "Republican Cash Flows from The Villages," politico.com, 17 August 2012.

78. "How State Farm Crashed in on a Crisis," *SHT*, 5 December 2010.

79. Gary R. Mormino, *Millard Fillmore Caldwell: Governing on the Wrong Side of History* (Gainesville: University Press of Florida, 2020), 107–9; Martin A. Dyckman, *Reubin O' D. Askew and the Golden Age of Florida Politics* (Gainesville: University Press of Florida, 2011), 70–80, 94.

80. "In Florida, 99% of Companies Pay No Corporate Income Tax," *OS*, 13 November 2019.

81. Carl Hiaasen, "The Best Legislature Money Can Buy," *MH*, 2 April 2011; Kevin Bogardus, "Statehouse Revolvers," Sarah Laskow, "State Lobbying Becomes Billion-Dollar Business," and Leah Rush, "Influence: A Booming Business," *Center for Public Integrity*, 12 October and 20 October 2006, and 20 December 2007; "Lobbyists Paid $212 Million Last Year to Lobby Florida Government," *OS*, 15 February 2013.

82. Frank Bruni, "Don't Look Up," *NYT*, 19 June 2012.

83. Michael Paterniti, "America in Extremis," *NYTM*, 21 April 2002.

Conclusion: Because We Could; Communities amid the Storms of Change

1. The author credits Ron Cunningham and his columns in the *Gainesville Sun* for the idea behind "Because we could."

2. "4 Ohio Metros on List of 'Fastest Shrinking' U.S. Cities," *Cincinnati Enquirer*, 21 March 2019; "U.S. States That Lost Population in 2018," *U.S. News & World Report*, 15 January 2019; "Population Growth: The Fastest-Growing and Shrinking States in the U.S." *USAT*, 31 January 2019; Brad Weisenstein, "Illinois Is Shrinking as Taxes Drive a Mass Exodus," *SLPD*, 16 October 2019; "Why Are Residents Leaving Illinois in Droves?," Governing.com, 19 June 2019.

3. Gary R. Mormino, "Preserving History as Florida Booms," *Forum: The Magazine of the Florida Humanities Council* 41 (Spring 2017): 6–10.

4. "Population Migration: These Are the Cities That Americans Are Abandoning the Most," Commercialappeal.com, *USAT*, 5 July 2018; "The States People Really Want to Move To," *WP*, 28 December 2015.

5. Craig Pittman, *Oh, Florida! How America's Weirdest State Influences the Rest of the Country* (New York: St. Martin's, 2016), 26.

6. Rowan Jacobsen, *Shadows on the Gulf: A Journey through Our Last Great Wetland* (New York: Bloomsbury, 2011), 147.

7. "Wish You Were Here!—But Where's Here?," *OS*, 14 August 1994.

8. Jeff LaHurd, *Quintessential Sarasota* (Sarasota: Clubhouse, 1990), 14; Ashley Gurbal Kritzer, "How Much of an Anomaly Is Sarasota's New $315 Million Mall?," *TBBJ*, 21 August 2014; "DeSoto Square Mall in Bradenton to Close Permanently," *SHT*, 30 April 2021; "See Ringling Plaza from Its Construction in 1955 to Its Demolition Today," *SHT*, 10 December 2018.

9. Jeff LaHurd, "STOP! Comes Too Late," *SHT*, 1 June 2017.

10. Wright quoted in *MH*, 3 November 1955.

11. John Muir, *A Thousand-Mile Walk to the Gulf*, ed. William Frederic Badé (Boston: Houghton Mifflin, 1916), 84.

12. Beth Dunlop, *Florida's Vanishing Architecture* (Englewood, FL: Pineapple, 1987), 38.

13. Steve Bousquet, "An Unwelcome Toll Road Shatters the Peace," *SS*, 20 December 2019.

14. Gary R. Mormino, *Land of Sunshine, State of Dreams: A Social History of Modern Florida* (Gainesville: University Press of Florida, 2005), 102–3.

15. Ibid.

16. Stephen Watts, *The Magic Kingdom* (Boston: Houghton Mifflin, 1997), 722–23, 422–24.

17. "Amelia Island, a $200 Million Gamble," *FT*, March 1973, 22.

18. Peter B. Gallagher, "Meet the Outlaws, Poets, and Old Men of the Sea on Florida's Last Frontier," *Forum* 30 (Fall 2009): 8.

19. "Florida Tourist Count," *FT*, 16 February 2021; "COVID-19 Slashes Florida Tourism Numbers," and "Florida Tourism Numbers Lowest since 2010," *TBT*, 16 February 2020 and 16 February 2021.

20. "Changing Face: Longtime Residents Describe Impact of Development, Tourism," *Saint Augustine Record*, 16 February 2019.

21. Bill Shack, "One Street Corner Tells the Story of Two Tallahassees," *TD*, 10 August 2020.

22. *Miami Herald*, 26 July 1943.

23. Robert Kerstein, *Key West on the Edge: Inventing the Conch Republic* (Gainesville: University Press of Florida, 2012).

24. "Pristine or Progressive? Dog Island Can't Agree," *OS*, 29 September 1985.

25. Ibid.; LeRoy Collins, "Finding Refuge and Wisdom in the Peace of an Island's Solitude," *SPT*, 9 February 1987.

26. "Pristine or Progressive?"
27. "A Junkyard Dog Island No More," *TD*, 24 October 2019.
28. Michael Schuman, "China Built a Big, Beautiful Wall, Too: It Failed," *NYT*, 18 January 2019.
29. Eleanor Barkhorn, "Sarah Palin Misinterprets Robert Frost," *TA*, 25 May 2010.
30. James Poniewozik, "Donald Trump Doesn't Get 'Game of Thrones,'" *NYT*, 7 January 2019.
31. Stephen Miller, "The Word 'Fraught' Carries a Heavy Burden," *WSJ*, 26 March 2017.
32. LeRoy Collins, "An Old Church Lives On," *SPT*, 21 March 1988.

Index

GARY R. MORMINO is the Frank E. Duckwall Professor of History Emeritus at the University of South Florida St. Petersburg. He is the winner of the Florida Humanities 2015 Florida Lifetime Achievement Award for Writing and serves as Florida Humanities scholar in residence. His many books include *Land of Sunshine, State of Dreams: A Social History of Modern Florida*.